Let Them Pray

Pray

BY LORI PAGEL

Stonebridge
Publications
Veneta, Oregon

*Dedicated to George Pagel, Darryl Fisher, and Jo Kent.
Thank you Darryl for encouraging me and helping me to get
started. Thank you Jo for your inspiration, encouragement, and
helping me finish. Thank you to my husband, George Pagel, for
always being there for me.*

Acknowledgment

By Jo Kent

When we first chatted about this book, I felt a whisper from the Holy Spirit assuring me to encourage you to go for it! After reading this beautiful book in its entirety, I was not at all disappointed! I felt like I was sitting in the presence of Deity!

You have such an exciting journey ahead of you and I pray our Heavenly Father's presence guides your steps.

Reading this book took me on a living journey through the many prayers in the Bible and God's answers to each of them. I found myself visualizing sitting at Jesus' feet as though He was sharing this beautiful story with me. I could visualize many of my favorite characters in the Bible such as David, Job, or Jeremiah, having these personal conversations with God.

"Let Them Pray" is powerful and contains biblical and practical information on how to build a meaningful prayer life.

This special book would make a lovely coffee table piece as a gracious way to share God's words with your guests! That's what I plan to do with my copy!

Forward

By Kim McDougal

Read Hebrews 11:32-40

Some things I've been praying about for years and I haven't gotten an answer yet. Other times, I had to wait years before a prayer was fulfilled and still other times, I prayed and got an instant answer. Why is God so difficult to understand?

As I read the passage above, it's incredible to think of all the things the early Christians endured all because they believed on Jesus. And verse 39 says, *"And all of these, though they won divine approval by [means of] their faith, did not receive the fulfillment of what was promised..."* But they died still believing that God has not broken His word. WOW! This is something we need to get in our minds today.

So, if my prayer isn't answered in this life... God had a better purpose in mind (verse 40). What's difficult isn't necessarily God; it's more what we think vs. what God knows. The bottom line is that we MUST trust the Lord even when we don't understand the whole picture.

We'll have plenty of times in our Christian walk where we don't understand something about God, or how He answers prayers. But, if we can really come to the place where it doesn't matter if we have the whole blueprint but just place our entire trust in Jesus, we'll have that "perfect peace" He speaks about.

If you don't understand something in your life, why it's allowed to happen, you're in good company with the rest of us. Some things we may learn later on and some things we may have to wait till we're in Heaven but one thing I can say now and that is… we are in good hands with the Lord Jesus. I may not understand it all, but as long as He does, that's all that matters.

A Prayer for our Country

"If my people which are called by my name shall humble themselves and pray, and seek my face, and turn from their wicked ways, then will I hear from Heaven, and will forgive their sin, and will heal their land."
– 2 Chronicles 7:14

You, God have made us all
We were still Yours even after man's fall
We've strayed so far away from You Lord
You tried to love us, but we cut You off with the sword

Forgive us Father, we are down on our knees
We ask now for Your wonderful mercies
Our land so needs Your touch again
We must make You Lord, our friend

I know you see the sadness, the grief, the pain, the tears
so many of us are faced with fears
Our world is in an unknown place
Please God, do not turn Your face

Our people need You Father,
They're looking for You in strange places
Running from one thing to another
So many different faces

We stretch our arms to worship only You
You are Lord over us, You alone are true
We lay all our burdens down at Your feet
And take Your yoke which is ever so sweet

Smile on us O' Lord, cause Your sun to shine
Forgive us our sins, it is us who crossed the line
We see Your grief, the sadness of Your heart
Help us Lord, we no longer want to be apart.
-In Jesus Name, Amen.

By Kim McDougal

Introduction ～ﾆﾞﾛｰ

Except where otherwise indicated, all scripture quotations are taken from the KJV.

Before you begin to read this book I suggest you get a good yellow highlighter and mark your favorite prayers or the part of the prayer you like the best so that you can find the prayers you need quickly by flipping through the pages when you need them.

The disciples said to Jesus,
"Lord, teach us to pray" Lk. 11:1
James, the brother of Jesus said
"Is any among you in trouble, Let them pray" Jms.. 5:13 NIV

This is a book of the prayers in the Bible
There are some who will say that all you need to do is pray,
"Lord, help me!"
And of course God will hear that prayer. Even a child can pray a simple, innocent prayer and God will hear. You can just pray what's in your heart and God hears. The Bible has a lot to say about prayer and there are many prayers in the Bible that we can learn from. We can see how the people in the Bible prayed to get their prayers answered. If you want to see what the Bible has to say about prayer, and how to get God to answer your prayers, then keep reading. The most important thing in prayer is to pray from the heart and be sincere; God will see your heart and hear you if you do that. You can use these prayers in the Bible as your own or incorporate them into your prayers.

I guess the first question we can ask is what is prayer?
It's talking to God, having conversations with God and asking God for whatever it is we need. We can praise Him, and thank Him in our prayers.

Not every prayer in the Bible is all cute, warm, and fuzzy; and maybe not always what we want to hear; sometimes we're going to say, "Why did they say that?" Or "why did they pray that way?" Or "Why did God say,

'I won't listen or hear your prayers anymore?'"

"Therefore pray not thou for this people, neither lift up cry nor prayer for them, neither make intercession to Me: for I will not hear thee." Jer. 7:16

The answer
"But your iniquities have separated between you and your God, and your sins have hid His face from you, that He will not hear" Is. 59:2

He wouldn't listen because they had broken His Commandments and worshiped idols. They had committed fornication, and killed their babies. He had warned them over and over to repent and stop doing these things, but they didn't listen and didn't believe that God would actually let these things happen to them. They didn't listen to God, and God stopped listening to them. We had better take a warning from them. Because if you read Revelation, you can see that God will again let His wrath fall, because we won't do things God's way.

I've written down the prayers just the way they are, even if we don't understand them because maybe we can learn something from them. They are in the Bible after all! Not every prayer is for us; sometimes they were for the ones who prayed them in the past;

sometimes for special circumstances and certain people. We must look at the prayers in their context and in the times in which they were written, but there are prayers we can actually use today. If you have any questions, you can always look up the verse in the Bible and see what the surrounding verses are about. You can research the stories and get the whole picture. You can ask God, "How does this affect me and my life? Is there something here you want me to know?" We can ask for wisdom to understand, and God is always willing to give it to us.

"If any of you lack wisdom, let him ask of God, that giveth to all men liberally, and upbraideth not; and it shall be given him." Jms. 1:5

Note to readers

Biblical prayers are centered on the page. Unitalicized words within a quoted passage are the author's comentary or a different use of wording in a different version of the Bible.

The Lord's Prayer

Let's look at how Jesus taught us to pray
Mt. 6:9-13.
We start with:
"Our Father in heaven"
Identify which Father we are praying to – the One in heaven. Is. 37:15

"Holy is Your name"
Acknowledge that He is God, and He is holy.
"In all your ways acknowledge Him and He will direct your paths."
Prov. 3:5

"Let Your will be done on earth as it is in heaven"
We should want God's will to be done not our own will I Jn. 5:14.
When we have our will done against God's advice, we always end up in trouble. So many people are afraid to pray "God's will be done," but we don't need to be afraid of God's will; He wants what's best for us.
"I wish above all things that thou mayest prosper and be in good health" 3 Jn. 2:1

Hezekiah asked God for healing when he was about to die; God gave him what he asked for, but maybe it wasn't what he should have asked. Because he lived longer, he showed the Babylonian king everything of value that he had, and the king coveted the riches of Israel and eventually took them captive.

We can close our prayers with:

In Jesus' name Jn. 14:13; and we can end our prayers with *"Amen."* Jesus is the *"Amen"* in Rev. 3:14 and when Jesus said, *"Truly, truly"* in Jn. 8:58 and Jn. 5:19, it meant *"Amen, amen"* in the Greek.

#281 *"transliteration, Amen; sometimes translated, verily, of a truth, most assuredly, so let it be"*

Watch and pray

"Watch" is usually connected with *"pray"*; and sometimes the words *"be sober"* are used with *"watch and pray."*

It is high time we awake; the closer we get to the second coming of Jesus, the more we should wake up out of our spiritual slumber.

"And that, knowing the time, that now it is high time to awake out of sleep: for now is our salvation nearer than when we believed. The night is far spent, the day is at hand; let us therefore cast off the works of darkness and let us put on the armour of light. Let us walk honestly, as in the day; not in rioting and drunkenness, not in chambering and wantonness, not in strife and envying. But put ye on the Lord Jesus Christ, and make not provision for the flesh, to fulfill the lusts thereof." Rom. 13:11-14

"Watch ye, stand fast in the faith, quit you like men, be strong. Let all your things be done with charity." I Cor. 16:13

"Watch ye therefore, and pray always, that ye may be accounted worthy to escape all these things that shall come to pass, and to stand before the Son of man." Lk. 21:36

"Praying always with all prayer and supplication in the Spirit, and watching thereunto with all perseverance and supplication for all saints..." Eph. 6:18

"Continue in prayer, and watch in the same with thanksgiving; withal praying also for us, that God would open unto us a door of utterance, to speak the mystery of Christ, for which I am also in bonds..." Col. 4:2-3

Jesus told the disciples,

"... *tarry ye here, and watch with Me.*" Matt. 26:38

"*And He cometh unto the disciples, and findeth them asleep, and saith unto Peter,*

What, could ye not watch with Me one hour? "*Watch and pray, that ye enter not into temptation: the spirit indeed is willing, but the flesh is weak.*" Matt. 26:40-41

"*Watch ye therefore: for ye know not when the master of the house cometh, at even, or at midnight, or at the cockcrowing, or in the morning: lest coming suddenly He find you sleeping. And what I say unto you I say unto all, Watch.*" Mk. 13:35-37

"*Behold, I come as a thief – therefore watch and pray. Blessed are those servants whom the Master, when He comes, will find watching.*" Lk. 12:35-36

"*Be ready... for the Son of man is coming at an hour you do not expect.*" Lk.1 12:40

"*But watch thou in all things...*" II Tim. 4:5

We are told to wake up!
"*Awake to righteousness*" I Cor. 15:34

How do we watch? How do we awake spiritually?

We study the Word.

"Study to shew thyself approved unto God; a workman that needeth not to be ashamed, rightly dividing the word of truth." II Tim. 2:15
"Take heed no one deceives you." Matt. 24:4
If we study God's Word, we won't be deceived!

We fast, we deny ourselves
"And He said to them all,

> *If any man will come after Me, let him deny himself, and take up his cross daily, and follow Me."* Lk. 9:23

The Bible tells us to be sober!
We get up early or in the night to seek God; not that we should go without sleep but be sensitive to the moving of the Holy Spirit.
"Therefore let us not sleep, as do others; but let us watch and be sober. For they that sleep sleep in the night; and they that be drunken are drunken in the night. But let us, who are of the day, be sober..." I Thess. 5:6-8
"Wherefore gird up the loins of your mind, be sober..." I Pet. 1:13
"But the end of all things is at hand: be ye therefore sober, and watch unto prayer." I Pet. 4:7
"Be sober, be vigilant..." I Pet. 5:8

We wait patiently for God's answer.
Ps. 40:1; Mk. 13:33

We ask God to show us any sin in our lives that might be hindering our prayers.
"Behold, the Lord's hand is not shortened, that it cannot save; neither His ear heavy ("dull" NIV) *that it cannot hear but your iniquities have separated between you and your God, and your sins have hid His face*

from you, that He will not hear." Is. 59:1-2

We see in the Bible that we can have many different postures in prayer. All of these scriptures are written out in this book, and you can look them up in Biblical order.

The verses marked with an asterisk are in this book

We can be on our knees, kneel, kneeling:

*Deut.9:25   *Dan.6:10
*Josh.7:6   Lk.22:4
*II Sam.12:16   *Lk.22:40
*I Kings 8:54   *Acts 7:59,60
*II Chron.6:13   Acts 9:36,40; 20:36; 21:5
Ps.95:3,6   Eph. 3:14-20
*Is. 45:23-Someday *"every knee shall bow"*

We can bow down, bow our head, bow our head to the earth, and even fall down or cast ourselves to the ground; be on our face.

Gen. 17:3;17:17
*Gen.18:1-5
*Ex.34:8
*Num.16:4,44
*Deut.9:25,26
*Josh.7:6
*Judges 13:20;16:30
I Sam. 25:29
*I Chron.21:16
*II Chron.20:18;29:29,30
*Ezra 10:1
*Ps.35:13;38:6;44:26;57:6;95:6;1
45:16
*II Chron.20:18

*Num. 16:22-38,44
*Josh.7:6
*Judges 13:20,22
Matt.2:11
*Mk.14:33,38,39
Lk.5:12
Acts 9:4
II Sam.25:39
*I Kings 18:21-39 Abigail fell on her face before David
II Sam.12:16 lay all night on the earth
*Rev.1:17;5:8

We can put our face between our knees like Elijah.
"And he (Elijah) *cast himself down upon the earth, and put his face between his knees..."* I Kings 18:42

We can lift our eyes and hands to Heaven.
Ex.9:23
I Kings 8:54
*I Chron.21:16
II Chron.6:12
*Ps.28:1-6
Ps.63:41
*Ps.86:1-17 (lift up soul);123:1;125:4

Ps. 134:2
Ps.141:1-5
*Ps.143:1-12
Mt.14:1,19
Mk.6:38
Lk.9:16
*Jn. 11:41;17:1;
I Tim.2:8

We can stand.

I Kings 8:14,55

II Chron.6:12;20:18

*Neh.9:5

Mk.11:25

*Lk.18:11-13

Ps. 106:30

They can sit before the Lord.

*I Chron.17:16

*Acts 16:30

When Hezekiah was sick, he turned his face to the wall because he couldn't kneel.

*II Kings 20:1-3

*Is.38:2,3

We can pray in our hearts.

*I Sam. 1:13

*II Sam.7:18

Here are some suggestions of how to have God hear us when we pray:

•   Ask God to send His Holy Spirit to help us pray.

"Likewise the Spirit also helpeth our infirmities: for we know not what we should pray for as we ought: but the Spirit itself maketh intercession for us with groanings which cannot be uttered." Rom. 8:26.

•   Approach God with reverence. *"Holy is Your name"*

•   Love and obey God.

•   Repent & confess our sins. Num.21:5-9; Job 42:6; Jer.39; Acts 8:20-24

•   Forgive those who've wronged us.

•   Make things right with those we have wronged.

•   Be sincere and pray from the heart; God knows everything, He knows our heart and if we're playing games with Him, He'll know; we cannot fool Him.

•   Believe and have faith that God will answer. Mk. 9:11:24;16:27;

Jn. 16:27; 17:1; Acts 4:24; II Thess. 1; 11, 12; I Tim. 4:4,5; Jms. 1:5-8

- Husbands be considerate with your wives (so your prayers won't be hindered I Pet. 3:7).
- Make requests with thanksgiving and praise.

"Be careful for nothing; but in every thing by prayer and supplication with thanksgiving let your requests be made known unto God." Phil. 4:6

- Acknowledge our need and dependence on God.
- Recognize Him as the Creator.
- Come through Jesus.

"Jesus said unto him, I am the way, the truth, and the life; no man cometh unto the Father, but by Me ("except through Me" ISV).*"* Jn. 14:6

- Believe to receive.

"... if thou shalt confess with thy mouth the Lord Jesus, and shalt believe in thy heart that God hath raised Him from the dead, thou shalt be saved." Rom. 10:9

" Believe on the Lord Jesus Christ, and thou shalt be saved." Acts 16:31

- Pray for those who persecute you. Mt. 5:44,45
- Plead the blood of Jesus

What does it mean to "plead the blood?" Satan accuses us day and night; and we are guilty before God because of our sins, but we plead the shed blood of Jesus because He paid for our sins. I am now righteous through the blood of Jesus, and not of myself. I acknowledge that I can never be good enough to receive eternal life but the blood of Jesus gives me the right to eternal life if I believe that Jesus is God come in the flesh and receive His death on the cross for my sins. He did for me, what I couldn't do for myself; that is He lived a perfectly righteous life (which I cannot do) and He died in my place. *"They overcame by the blood of the Lamb."* Rev. 12:11

"To Him who loves us and has freed us from our sins by His blood." Rev. 1:5

Jesus said about the Communion cup,

"And He took the cup, and gave thanks, and gave it to them, saying, Drink ye all of it; For this is My blood of the New Testament, which is shed for many for the remission (removal "forgiveness" ESV) *of sins."* Matt. 26:26-28

"How much more severely do you think someone deserves to be punished who has trampled the Son of God underfoot, who has treated as an unholy thing the blood of the Covenant that sanctified them, and who has insulted the Spirit of grace?" Heb. 12:29

What they did in the Bible to get God to hear them:

They offered thanks & praise with their prayers: We should make our prayers with thanksgiving and give thanks when our prayers are answered.

I Chron. 16:8,9,34,36;29:23	Dan.2:17
II Chron.20:18,21;29:29,30	Mt.2:11
Neh.9:3	Lk.10:21
Ps.9:1,2; 18:3,49; 21:13; 30:12;	Rom.1:8
48:1; 56:4;	I Cor.14:13-17
52:9; 57:9; 61:8; 66:3-7; 71:8; 75:1;	Phil.4:6
76:8; 79:13; 109:1,28; 138:1,2;	I Thess.1:2
139:14; 145:1	I Tim.2:1;4:4
Jer.20;13;31:7,12	

Where two or three gather together and agree in prayer God answers:
Matt. 18:19,20

They humbled themselves; He hears the humble:
God said to Pharaoh, How long do you refuse to humble yourself?

Ex.10:1

Ex.10:3

I Kings 8:30

II Kings 19:1

II Chron. 7:14; 20:3; 32:26; 33:12; 34:27; 30:11;33:12,13,18,19;34:23-

28

Ps.10:1,17;35:13;145:1

Lk.18:14

Acts 10:30;13:3;14:23

Rev.5:13;19:5

They Fasted and prayed:

I Sam.7:6

II Sam.12:16

I Chron. 16:8-11,34-36;20:3-12;29:9-23

II Chron.20:3,21-23;31;29:29,30

II Kings 19:1

Ezra 8:21,23;10:6

Neh.1:4;9:1,4-38

Esther 4:15

Ps.26:2;35:13;65:1;67:1-7; 69:10;75:1,2;29:13:108:1-

12;109:24; Ps.116:16,17; 119;132:12-18;138:1-8

Is.58:6

Jer.14:12;17:13-18

Dan.6:18-23;9:3

Mt.17:21

Mk.9:29

Lk.2:37;5:33-35;18:10-14

Acts 9:9;10:30;13:3;14:23;27

I Cor.7:5

Sometimes they wore sackcloth:

II Kings 19:1

I Chron.21:6

II Chron.33:12,13

Ezra 8:21

Neh.1:4;9:1

Ps.30:11;35:13;69:11

Dan.9:3

Lk.2;36

They put dust & ashes on their head:

Josh.7:6

Job 42:6

Ps.102:9

Dan.9:3

Sometimes they tore their clothes:

II Kings 2:12;19:1	Josh.7:6
II Chron. 34:19	Dan.9:3

Sometimes they sang and played music with their prayers:
Elisha asked for someone to come who could play the harp and
"while the harp was being played the power of" God came upon him.

II Kings 3:15	Acts 16:25
I Chron.16:9	I Cor.14:13-17
II Chron. 20:21;29:30	Jms..5:13-18
Ps.9:2; 13:6; 21:13; 30:12; 51;	Rev.5:8-10
18:49; 57:7,9;59:17;61:8;65:13;	Music and instruments – II
66:2; 71:22,24;101:1;138:5;144:9	Chron.20:25-30;
Jer.20:13;31:12;39	Ps.89:1;108:1-12;144:1-15
Is.38:20	

Sometimes they gave offerings with their prayers:
Acts 10:1,2,4 Cornelius gave offerings to God and prayed and God
heard him

**They repented, confessed their sins, and turned from them. They
asked God to forgive them and cleanse them by the blood of Jesus:**

Ex.9:27;10:16,17	Neh.1:4,5
Num.24:1,2	Job 33:26-30;42:6
Judges 10:10	Ps.32:5-7;51:3;88:9;143:6
I Sam.7:3;12:10;25:39	Is.1:15
I Kings 8:22,38,47	Jer.14:7,19-22;31:19;Jer.31:19
I Chron.6:13-42;21:1-8	Dan.9:3,13,21
II Chron.20:18	Josh.10:10
Ezra 10:1,10,11	

They forgave:
Mk.11:26

They prayed for others:
Lk.22:32
Job prayed for his friends. Job 42:7
When Job prayed for his friends, his own captivity was overturned.
Job 42:7
We are to pray for those who use us and persecute us. Matt. 5:44

They acknowledged that He is God alone and that His name is holy:
Is. 37:15

They prayed corporately as a group:
Acts 1:14; 12:12
Where two or three gather together in My name I will answer.
Matt. 18:19

They kept praying and did not faint; they had persistence and perseverance:

Gen.18

Lk. 18:1,2; 1:36

Eph.6:18

Col.1:3-12; 4:2

I Thess.1:2,3

II Thess.1:11

Acts 6:4-Some gave themselves to prayer and prayed continually
Col. 4:2-Continue in prayer
I Thess. 5:17,25-Pray without ceasing
II Thess. 1:11-Pray always

We are to abide (dwell) in Him and let Him abide (dwell) in us:
If we abide in God and He abides in us, He will hear our prayers,

Jn.15:7-10.
He abides in us through Communion Jn. 6:51.
We abide in Him by keeping His Commandments I Jn. 3:24.

The Bible says to be good to your wife to get your prayers heard:
Husbands should treat their wives the way God wants them to, or their prayers will be hindered. I Pet. 3:7,12.

We are to ask according to His will:
If we ask according to His will, He hears us I Jn. 5:14-16

Don't pray just to consume it on your lusts:
Jms.. 1:9
"Ye ask and receive not, because ye ask amiss, and that ye may consume it upon your lusts." Jms..4:3

We are told to pray without ceasing:
Acts 12:5;Rom. 1:8-10;II Tim.1:3

We can get up during the night to pray or rise early:

Gen.32:26-30
Ex.8:20;9:13
Num.22:9-41
Ps.5:3;88:1-18;57:8;143:8
Prov.1:28 *"...they will seek Me early..."*
Ps.17:3 *"Thou hast visited me in the night"*
Ps.55:17 *"evening, morning, & noon"*
Ps.119:62 *"At midnight I will rise*

to give thanks unto Thee because of Thy righteous judgments."
Jer.29:19
Ps.119:147 NIV *"I stay up all night thinking about Your promises"*
Dan.6:18
Mk.1:34,35 *"(Jesus) and in the morning, rising up a great while before day, He went out, and departed into a solitary place, and there prayed."*

We can Speak out loud or in a loud voice, lifting up our voice, shout (that doesn't mean we scream or yell):

I Kings 8:55
II Chron.20:18
Neh.9:4-38
Ps.35:28;55:17
Jer.31:9
Dan.9:21
Mk.11:24;15:35
Lk.23:34,46

Acts 4:24;7:59;12:12
Lk.23:34,46
Mk.15:35
I Tim.2:8
Rev.12:7;19:1,2 Jesus prayed
with a loud voice
Acts 2:24 They lifted up their
voice in one accord

Sometimes they wept, cried, and had tears with their prayers:

I Sam. 1:10;7:1
II Kings 20;3,5;II Chron.34:27
Ezra10:1
Ps. 6:8; 30:8;39:13;56:8; 69:3,10;
88:13; 102:1;119:136
Neh.1:4 *"mine enemies turn
back: this I know; for God is for
me."*

Jer.3:21;31:9,15,16
Jer.7:16 God told Jeremiah not
to cry for them
Is.38:3,5
Mk.9:
Heb.5:7 *"...put Thou my tears
into Thy bottle: are they not in Thy
book? When I cry unto Thee, then
shall"*

Moses took off his shoes because He was standing on Holy ground, and talked to God in a burning bush that didn't burn up, Ex. 3:5.

God spoke to Samuel as a child and Samuel said, *"Speak Lord, for Thy servant heareth."* I Sam.3:9

Making Vows

A vow is when you say to God "If you do something, then I will do something." Examples of making vows: Ps. 116:14,18;132:2.

We should be very careful when making vows. If you make a vow, you must keep it or you can come under a curse. Job 22:27-28; Ps. 61:1-8; Jonah 2:9 Jephthah made a rash vow and jeopardized his daughter, Judges 11.

"Thou shalt make thy prayer unto Him, and He shall hear thee, and thou shalt pay thy vows." Job 22:27

"… I will pay that that I have vowed…" Jonah 2:9

"… pay thy vows unto the most High…" Ps. 50:14-15

"For Thou, O God, hast heard my vows: Thou hast given me the heritage of those that fear Thy name… So will I sing praise unto Thy name for ever, that I may daily perform my vows." Ps. 61:5-8

"I will go into Thy house with burnt offerings: I will pay Thee my vows, which my lips have uttered, and my mouth hath spoken, when I was in trouble." Ps. 66:13-14

"I will keep my promises to the Lord in the presence of all His People." Ps. 116:14,18

"He took an oath before the Lord. He vowed to the Mighty one of Israel. . . ." Ps. 132:2

In the New Testament, we are not to take oaths.

"But I say unto you, Swear not at all; neither by heaven; for it is God's throne: nor by the earth; for it is His footstool: neither by Jerusalem; for it is the city of the great King. Neither shalt thou swear by thy head, because thou canst not make one hair white or black. But let you communication be, Yea, yea; Nay, nay: for whatsoever is more than these cometh of evil." Matt.5:34-37

"…but most of all, my brothers and sisters, never take an oath, by heaven or earth or anything else. Just say a simple yes or no, so that you will not sin and be condemned for it." Jms..5:12 NLT

Jacob makes a vow in Gen. 28:20-22. 1 Sam. 12:10.

Israel made a vow.

"And Israel vowed a vow unto the Lord, and said,

"If thou wilt indeed deliver this people into my hand, then I will utterly destroy their cities." Num. 21:2-3

Hannah wept and made a vow.

"And she vowed a vow, and said,

> *O Lord of hosts, if Thou wilt indeed look on Thine hand maid,*
> *and remember me, and not forget Thine handmaid, but wilt*
> *give unto Thine handmaid a man child, then I will give him*
> *unto the Lord all the days of his life, and there shall no razor*
> *come upon his head."* I Sam. 1:11

The rules for vows in the Old Testament are found in Numbers 30.

There was a time that God wouldn't hear even when they fasted and prayed because they were worshiping idols and wouldn't get rid of the sins in their life. First, we must stop doing the things that God hates and then our fast will mean something. *"When they fast, I will not hear their cry... I will consume them by the sword, and by the famine, and by the pestilence."* Jer.14:12

"Now the Lord hath brought it, and done according as He hath said; because ye have sinned against the Lord, and have not obeyed His voice, therefore this thing is come upon you." Jer. 40:3

We are not to be hypocrites and make long, pretentious prayers just for everyone to see and think we are righteous but go into a secret place when we need something from God, Matt.6:5;23:14; Mk.12:38; Lk.20:46. It's not the praying in front of people that's wrong, it's the attitude that we have when we are praying.

We are not to be repetitious; God will not hear just because we repeat a phrase over and over. Matt. 6:5

We are to forgive others before we ask God for anything or He will not forgive us. Matt. 7:7

Abbreviations for Bibles in this book:

CEB = Common English Bible
ESV = English Standard Version
GWT = God's Word Translation
HCSB = Holman Christian Standard Bible
KJV = King James Version
LB = Living Bible
MB = Message Bible
NIV = New International Version
NIV fn - New International Version footnote
NIV Reader's Version
NLT = New Living Translation
PB = Peshitta Bible (Peshitta means, "*simple, common, straight*" - sometimes called the "*Syriac Vulgate*" - "*The general, but not universal, consensus is that the Old Testament of the Peshitta was translated into Syriac from the Hebrew, probably in the 2nd century AD, and that the New Testament of the Peshitta was translated from the Greek.*)
RSV = Revised Standard Version
UKJV = Updated King James Version
YLT = Young's Literal Translation

Abbreviations for Books of the Bible

Old Testament

Gen. = Genesis   Ex. = Exodus
Lev. = Leviticus   Num. = Numbers

Deut. = Deuteronomy   Josh. = Joshua
Judges   Ruth
I & II Sam. = I & II Samuel   I & II Kings
I & II Chron. = I & II Chronicles   Ezra
Neh. = Nehemiah   Esther
Job   Ps. = Psalms
Prov. = Proverbs   Eccl. = Ecclesiastes
Song of Solomon   Is. = Isaiah
Jer. = Jeremiah   Lam. = Lamentations
Ez. = Ezekiel   Dan. = Daniel
Hosea   Joel
Amos   Ob. = Obadiah
Jonah   Mic. = Micah
Nahum   Hab. = Habakkuk
Zeph. = Zephaniah   Hag. = Haggai
Zech. = Zechariah   Mal. = Malachi

New Testament

Matt. = Matthew   Mk. = Mark
Lk. = Luke   Jn. = John
Acts   Rom. = Romans
I & II Cor. = I & II Corinthians   Gal. = Galatians
Eph. = Ephesians   Phil. = Philippians
Col. = Colossians   I & II Thess. = I & II Thessalonians
I & II Tim. = I & II Timothy   Titus
Phil. = Philemon   Heb. = Hebrews

New Testament

Jms.. = James

I, II, & III Jn. = I, II, & III John

I & II Pet. = I & II Peter

Rev. = Revelation

12 Hebrew words for prayer
Taken from "Every Prayer in the Bible" by Larry Richards p. 3-8

Original	Translations	Connotations
Hebrew	**To pray, entreat**	**Childlike confidence & reliance on God**
Atar	To pray	Calling on God to evaluate and intervene
Palal	To entreat, intercede	Coming freely and making contact with God
Paga	To hear, listen to	Confident expectation of God's response
Shama	To inquire, beg, ask	Seeking a favor from God
Sha'la	Request, petition	Earnest prayer for something important
Sa'al	To desire, request	To seek from God what one wants or needs
Hanan	To supplicate, beseech	Relying on God's grace and kindness
T'hinna	Supplication	A formal appeal for grace and mercy

Original	Translations	Connotations
Tahanun	Supplication	An emotional appeal for grace and mercy
'ana	To answer, respond	A cry to God for deliverance
Na'	I pray	A particle indicating a phrase is a prayer
Greek		
Proseuchomai	To pray	The basic word for prayer of any kind
Aiteo	To ask for	To seek from God because He cares for us as a Father
Deomai	To request	To ask, confident of God's grace and favor
Erotao	To ask, request	To seek guidance or response from a close Friend
Gonypeteo	To kneel	To urgently request help
Aineo	To praise, thank	To express gratitude to God
Eucharisteo	To praise, thank	To express gratitude to God

Old Testament
Prayers

Genesis

Adam and Eve

In the beginning, Adam and Eve conversed freely with God face-to-face. They spoke to God, and He spoke to them. They saw God face-to-face and knew Him as a friend.

When God first created the world, there was nothing coming between them. Here we see God talking to Adam.

"And they heard the voice of the Lord God walking in the garden in the cool of the day… And the Lord God called unto Adam, and said unto him…" Gen. 3:8

This was a very sad day when Adam and Eve hid from God because they had just committed the first sin. They were afraid to talk to God; instead, they hid.

God had a plan, though, even before the creation of the world to save mankind and now He would only reveal a small part of that plan to Adam and Eve. Only after the cross did man fully realize what God's plan was; to bring a Messiah or Savior that would first suffer and allow Himself to be put on a cross for our sins, and then someday come as King of kings and Lord of lords to rule this earth for eternity.

Enoch

We know that Enoch must have talked to God; because it says

that Enoch walked with God every day; now you usually don't walk with someone without talking to them. In fact, God liked walking and talking to Enoch so much that He took Enoch to be with him. He was one of only two men that went to Heaven without seeing death before the 2nd coming of Jesus.

"And Enoch walked with God: and he was not; for God took him." Gen. 5:22,24

The other person who went to heaven without seeing death was Elijah.

Noah

Noah also walked and talked with God. God gave him the instructions of how to build an ark to save them from the flood. Many people laughed at Noah, and thought he was crazy. In the end, they saw that he really did hear from God but it was too late for them.

"...Noah was a just man and perfect in his generations, and Noah walked with God." Gen. 6:9

Here we see God talking to Noah.

"And the Lord said unto Noah,

> *Come thou and all thy house into the ark; for thee have I seen righteous before Me in this generation.*
> *Of every clean beast thou shalt take to thee by sevens, the male and his female: and of beasts that are not clean by two, the male and his female.*
> *Of fowls also of the air by sevens, the male and the female; to keep seed alive upon the face of all the earth.*

For yet seven days, and I will cause it to rain upon the earth forty days and forty nights; and every living substance that I have made will I destroy from off the face of the earth.

And Noah did according unto all that the Lord commanded him." Gen. 7:1-5

The key here is that Noah did what God told him to do without question.

Abraham and Moses

Abraham and Moses had many conversations with God. But the more sin crept into the world; the less they were able to converse directly with God.

The prophets

We see that God talked with the prophets; sometimes they saw God and sometimes they just heard His voice. For quite a while after sin, they still talked to God face to face but eventually they lost that ability and had to rely more and more on faith. Soon there were only a few who heard from God, like the prophets and the others would have to go to them to seek God's answers. After time, man could no longer see or hear God but they still turned to Him in their need and we see that God still heard and answered their prayers.

"And the Word of the Lord was precious ("rare" NIV) *in those days;*

there was no open visions..." I Sam. 3:1

We can learn a lot from these prayers about how to approach God and how to get the answers to our prayers that we need.

We can use the prayers that we find in the Bible as our own prayers, or incorporate them into our prayers; we can even pray these prayers out loud to God. We can remind God what He said in the Bible by quoting the promises of God. We can start our prayer with, *"Lord, You said in Your Word...,"* and then quote the verse.

Jonah

God hears your every thought and prayer no matter what you say and how you say it. You can pray in the car, you can pray in your mind, you can pray out loud by yourself or with others and God will hear you because God knows everything and sees everything – God even heard Jonah in the belly of a whale.

"Then Jonah prayed unto the Lord his God out of the fish's belly." Jonah 2:1

Asa

Asa's prayer was:
"...Lord,

> *it is nothing with Thee to help, whether with man, or with them that have no power: help us, O Lord our God: for we rest on Thee, and in Thy name we go against this..."*
> II Chron. 14:11-13

"Thou art the help of Thy people; and when Thou dost deliver... then all the inhabitants of the earth shall know that it is good to rely on Thee; help us O Lord our God because in Thy name we have come against this... delay not Thy might from us." II Chron. 14:11,13 PB

Abraham

Abraham pleads for Sodom and Gomorrah

Abraham talked to God face to face and he heard God's voice many times.

The Lord appeared to Abraham in the plains of Mamre as he sat in his tent door in the heat of the day (Gen. 18:1).

Abraham ran to meet Him and bowed himself to the ground and said,

"My Lord,
if now I have found favour in Thy sight, pass not away, I pray
Thee, from Thy servant. Let a little water, I pray You, be
fetched, and wash Your feet, and rest yourselves under the tree:
and I will fetch a morsel of bread, and comfort ye Your hearts;
after that ye shall pass on:
for therefore are ye come to Your servant." Gen. 18:3-5

God speaks

And they answered Abraham and said,

"do as you have said." Gen. 18:5

Because Abraham is a friend of God's, He tells Abraham

what He plans to do to Sodom and Gomorrah

Abraham ends up pleading for Sodom because of his nephew Lot. They have a long conversation about it, and God did save Lot and his two daughters. He tried to save the whole family, but the married daughter and her husband wouldn't leave. Lot's wife turned around, and became a pillar of salt. It says, *"And the Lord went His way, as soon as He had left communing with Abraham: and Abraham returned unto his place."* Gen. 18:33

God saves Lots life because of Abraham but He also calls Lot a "just man" in the New Testament

"And delivered just Lot, vexed with the filthy conversation of the wicked..." II Pet. 2:7-8

Abraham is very persistent with God in his prayer for Sodom; we can see another prayer of persistence in the parable of Lk. 11:5. The judge heard her, because she was persistent.

Abraham prays for king Abimelech

Sarah is so beautiful that Abraham is afraid that king Abimelech will kill him to take his wife. God is not happy with Abraham for telling this lie when Abraham should have trusted in God to take care of him. Even though Abraham makes this mistake, God still tells Abimelech that Abraham will pray for him and his family to be healed, and be able to have babies.

"...for he is a prophet, and he shall pray for thee, and thou shalt live..." Gen. 20:7

The Bible tells us that Abraham did pray for them and they were healed and had babies.

The 1st actual recorded prayer in the Bible

Abraham sent Eliezer, his servant, to find Isaac a wife. Eliezer prays for God to help him find a wife for Isaac and asks God to give him a sign.

Eliezer's prayer

> *"O Lord God of my master Abraham, I pray Thee, send me good speed this day, and shew kindness unto my master Abraham. Behold, I stand here by the well of water; and the daughters of the men of the city come out to draw water: and let it come to pass, that the damsel to whom I shall say, Let down thy pitcher, I pray thee, that I may drink; and she shall say, Drink, and I will give thy camels drink also: let the same be she that Thou hast appointed for Thy servant Isaac; and thereby shall I know that Thou hast shewed kindness unto my master."* Gen. 24:12-14

God answers

> *"And it came to pass, before he had done speaking, that, behold, Rebekah came out, who was born to Bethuel, son of Milcah, the wife of Nahor, Abraham's brother, with her pitcher upon her shoulder. And the damsel was very fair to look upon... And when she had done giving him drink, she said, I will draw water for thy camels also, until they have done drinking."* Gen. 24:15,16,19

I have heard preachers use her as an Illustration of how the Church gives the living water of Jesus to the world.

Isaac prays for Rebeckah to have children

> *"Isaac pleaded with God for his wife because she was barren..."* Gen. 25:21

God answers

> *"...and the Lord answered him."* Gen. 25:22

Rebeckah gives birth to Jacob and Esau.

God speaks

"And the Lord said unto her,
Two nations are in thy womb, and two manner of people shall
be separated from thy bowels:
and the one people shall be stronger than the other people;
and the elder shall serve the younger." Gen. 25:23

Rebeckah convinced Jacob to deceive his father Isaac and get the blessing

Jacob was afraid he would receive a curse instead of a blessing if he lied to his father but Rebeckah said, *"Upon me be thy curse my son: only obey my voice..."* Gen. 27:13

The curse did come upon her because she never saw her favorite son again before she died. He had to leave home because Esau wanted to kill him. Jacob was alone and afraid and God gave him a dream of a ladder reaching to heaven with angels ascending and descending on it. God told Jacob that he would receive all the blessings and promises of Abraham and Jacob set up a stone for a pillar and poured oil on it and called it Bethel. Jacob promised to give God one tenth of everything he had.

"And Jacob vowed a vow, saying, If God will be with me, and will keep me in this way that I go, and will give me bread to eat, and raiment to put on, so that I come again to my father's house in peace; then shall the Lord be my God: and this stone, which I have set for a pillar, shall be God's house; and of all that thou shalt give me I will surely give the tenth unto Thee." Gen. 28:20-22

When Jacob was ready to return home after his mother and father died, he was afraid of Esau

He didn't know if Esau still intended to hurt him and now he had a family to protect as well. Jacob goes to pray to God for protection and ends up wrestling with God (Jesus pre-incarnate).

Jacob wrestles with God

Second actual recorded prayer in the Bible.

Jacob's prayer

Jacob humbled himself by saying, "*I am not worthy of the least of Thy mercies.*"

"*And Jacob said,*

> *O God of my father Abraham, and God of my father Isaac, the Lord which saidest unto me, Return unto thy country, and to thy kindred, and I will deal well with thee: I am not worthy of the least of all the mercies, and of all the truth, which Thou hast shewed unto Thy servant; for with my staff I passed over this Jordan; and now I am become two bands. Deliver me, I pray Thee, from the hand of my brother, from the hand of Esau: for I fear him, lest he will come and smite me, and the mother with the children.*

God speaks

And God said,

> *I will surely do Thee good, and make thy seed as the sand of the sea, which cannot be numbered for multitude.*"
>
> Gen. 32:9-12

Jacob wrestled with God that night and God touched his thigh.

God speaks

"*And He said,*

Let Me go, for the day breaketh. Gen. 32:26

Jacob speaks
And he said,
> *I will not let Thee go, except Thou bless me.* Gen. 32:26

God speaks
"And he said unto him,
> *What is thy name?"* Gen. 32:27

Jacob speaks
"And He said,
> *Jacob."* Gen. 32:27

God speaks
"And He said,
> *Thy name shall be called no more Jacob, but Israel;*
> *for as a prince hast thou power with God and with men, and*
> *hast prevailed."* Gen. 32:28

Jacob speaks
"And Jacob asked Him, and said,
> *Tell me, I pray Thee, Thy name."* Gen. 32:29

God speaks
"And He said,
> *Wherefore is it that thou dost ask after My name?*

And He blessed him there.
*And Jacob called the name of the place Peniel: for I have seen God face
to face, and my life is preserved."* Gen. 32:29-30

God asked the same question of Manoah when he asked what His name was. Manoah thought he had seen God because he said to his wife,

"We shall surely die, because we have seen God." Judges 13:22

Jacob perceived that this was God because he said, "I have seen God face to face." Gen. 32:30

Exodus

Moses

Moses and the burning bush

Moses was raised by an Egyptian princess and went to the best schools; having every advantage, while he saw his brethren being cruelly treated. He might have been the Pharoah one day, but he chose to suffer with the people of God rather than enjoy the riches and fame of Egypt. *"choosing rather to suffer affliction with the people of God, than to enjoy the pleasures of sin for a season."* Heb. 11:25

He knew that God would use him to deliver the Israelites someday, but he tried to do it in his own strength and time. When that didn't work, he ran away to Midian at 40 yrs. old; married Zipporah, and had two children. He lived as a shepherd in the wilderness for 40 years. He probably thought that his ministry and mission were over at 80 yrs. old; but after he'd been there for 40 years, he saw a burning bush at Mt. Sinai and talked with God. God told him to go back to Egypt and deliver His people, but now Moses didn't have the confidence he once had.

Moses speaks

Moses asks God to please send someone else to do the job (Ex. 4:13). God isn't happy with Moses but He reassures him that,

God speaks

"I will be with thy mouth… and will teach you what ye shall do." Ex. 4:15

God speaks

God asks Moses,

"Who made your mouth?" Ex. 4:15

God sends Aaron to be with him and they head back to Egypt to confront the current Pharoah. God says to Moses, you will be like God to Aaron, and Aaron will be like a prophet to Pharoah, Ex. 7:1.

When Moses and Aaron talk to Pharoah and tell him what God wants them to do, he says,

"Who is the Lord, that I should obey His voice to let Israel go? I know not the Lord, neither will I let Israel go." Ex. 5:2

Pharoah didn't know the God he was dealing with. He would soon find out, but then would be too late.

How many people in the world today could say the same thing? They don't know God, and they don't want to obey Him. Pharoah would learn a grave lesson that would end in the death of his son, and ultimately his own death in the Red Sea.

After talking to Moses, Pharoah went out and made their work harder and mistreated them. The people complained to Moses and Moses went to talk with God.

Moses speaks

"Lord, wherefore hast Thou so evil entreated this people? Why is it that Thou hast sent me? For since I came to Pharaoh to speak in Thy name, he hath done evil to this people; neither hast Thou delivered Thy people at all. Ex. 5:22

God speaks

Then the Lord said unto Moses,

Now shalt thou see what I will do to Pharaoh: for with a strong hand shall he let them go, and with a strong hand shall he drive them out of his land. Ex. 6:1

God speaks

And God spake unto Moses, and said unto him,

> *I am the Lord: and I appeared unto Abraham, and unto Isaac, and unto Jacob, by the name of God Almighty, but by My name Jehovah was I not know to them. And I have also established My Covenant with them, to give them the land of Canaan, the land of their pilgrimage, wherein they were strangers. And I have also heard the groaning of the children of Israel, whom the Egyptians keep in bondage; and I have remembered My Covenant. Wherefore say unto the children of Israel, I am the Lord, and I will bring you out from under the burdens of the Egyptians, and I will rid you out of their bondage, and I will redeem you with a stretched out arm, and with great judgments: and I will take you to Me for a people, and I will be to you a God: and ye shall know that I am the Lord your God, which bringeth you out from under the burdens of the Egyptians. And I will bring you in unto the land, concerning the which I did swear to give it to Abraham, to Isaac, and to Jacob; and I will give it you for an heritage: I am the Lord."* Ex. 6:2-8

Moses talks to God when the Israelites won't listen.
God speaks

God came again and spoke to Moses,
"And the Lord spake unto Moses, saying,
> *Go in, speak unto Pharaoh king of Egypt, that he let the children of Israel go out of his land.* Ex. 6:10

Moses speaks

And Moses spake before the Lord, saying,

Behold, the children of Israel have not hearkened unto me;
how then shall Pharaoh hear me, who am of uncircumcised
lips? Ex. 6:12

God answers

And the Lord spake unto Moses, and unto Aaron, and gave them a charge unto the children of Israel, and unto Pharaoh king of Egypt, to bring the children of Israel out of the land of Egypt." Ex. 6:13

Moses speaks to God throughout the plagues of Egypt
God speaks

And again God spoke to Moses and said,

> *"...see, I have made thee ("a god") to Pharaoh: and Aaron thy brother shall be thy prophet.*
> *Thou shalt speak all that I command thee: and Aaron thy brother shall speak unto Pharaoh, that he send the children of Israel out of his land. And I will harden Pharaoh's heart, and multiply My signs and My wonders in the land of Egypt. But Pharaoh shall not hearken unto you, that I may lay My hand upon Egypt, and bring forth Mine armies, and My people the children of Israel, out of the land of Egypt by great judgments. And the Egyptians shall know that I am the Lord, when I stretch forth Mine hand upon Egypt, and bring out the children of Israel from among them."*
> *Ex. 7:1-5*

So Moses told Aaron to throw his rod down and it became a serpent; the magicians threw their rods down and they became serpents but Aaron's' rod ate their rods.

Promise:

"Greater is He that is in you then he that is in the world" I Jn. 4:4

In the morning, Moses and Aaron met Pharaoh as he was going down to the water.

The 10 Plagues of Egypt

Moses talks to God a lot during the plagues.

1. River turned to blood

Moses told Aaron to take his rod and stretch it out over the river, and it became like blood. The people had to dig beside the river to get water to drink, Ex. 7:24. This plague came *"upon the waters... their streams... rivers... ponds... pools of water... in vessels of wood...* (and) *stone..."* Ex. 7:19

After seven days, Moses and Aaron again went before Pharaoh and spoke for God.

God speaks

Let My people go, that they may serve Me." Ex. 8:1

2. Frogs

God speaks.

> *"And if you refuse to let them go,*
> *I will smite all the borders with frogs."* Ex. 8:2

The magicians were able to do the same thing (but why would they want to, I wonder?).

The magicians couldn't eliminate the frogs, so Pharoah:

"called for Moses and Aaron, and said, Intreat the Lord, that He may take away the frogs from me, and from my people; and I will let the people go that they may do sacrifice unto the Lord." Ex. 8:8

And Moses said unto Pharoah,

"... when shall I intreat for thee, and for thy servants, and for thy people, to destroy the frogs from thee and thy houses, that they may remain in the river only?
And he (Pharaoh) said,
"Tomorrow" (and why not today I wonder?)
And he (Moses) said,
Be it according to thy word: that thou mayest know that there is none like unto the Lord our God." Ex. 8:8-10

Moses prays to the Lord about the frogs

"And Moses and Aaron went out from Pharaoh: and Moses cried unto the Lord because of the frogs which he had brought against Pharaoh. Ex. 8:12

God answers

And the Lord did according to the word of Moses; and the frogs died..." Ex. 8:12-13

The frogs died and the land stank! Pharaoh hardened his heart and would not let the children of Israel go after he said he would.

3. Lice

God sent the plague of lice and God wouldn't allow the magicians to do this one and they said, *"...this is the finger of God."* Ex. 8:19 Pharaoh's heart was so hardened at this time; he wouldn't even ask Moses to pray.

4. Flies

In the morning, Moses and Aaron met Pharaoh at the Nile River again. This time God sent flies. The flies only came to the Egyptians, and not to the Israelites, so that they would know that:

"I am the Lord in the midst of the earth. And I will put a division between My people and thy people…" Ex. 8:22-23

Pharaoh again agreed to let them go, and he asked Moses to pray again. *"intreat (God) for Me"* Ex. 8:28

"And Moses said,

Behold, I go out from thee, and I will intreat the Lord that the swarms of flies may depart from Pharoah, from his servants, and from his people, tomorrow… And Moses went out from Pharaoh, and intreated the Lord." Ex 8:29-30

God answers

And the Lord did according to the word of Moses; and he removed the swarms of flies…" Ex. 8:31

Pharaoh again hardened his heart, and wouldn't let them go.

5. Cattle sick

Then God sent a disease on the cattle of the Egyptians and they died. Ex. 9:1-7 The cattle of God's people did not die. Again Pharaoh hardened his heart, and didn't even ask Moses to pray.

6. Boils

God sent boils, but Pharaoh, still hardened his heart and didn't ask Moses to pray.

God speaks

"Let My people go, that they may serve Me. For I will at this time send all My plagues upon thine heart, and upon thy

*servants, and upon thy people; that thou mayest know that
there is none like Me in all the earth. For now I will stretch
out My hand, that I may smite thee and thy people with
pestilence; and thou shalt be cut off from the earth.* (fulfilled in
Ex. 14:28)
*And in very deed for this cause have I raised thee up, for to
shew in thee My power; and that My name may be declared
throughout all the earth. As yet exaltest thou thyself against
My people, that thou wilt not let them go?"* Ex. 9:13-17

7.   Hail, thunder, rain, and fire

The next day God sent hail on the Egyptians, but His
people did not have hail. Pharoah confesses but, still
doesn't completely give in; then he hardens his heart.
*"And Pharaoh sent, and called for Moses and Aaron, and
said unto them, I have sinned this time: the Lord is righteous,
and I and my people are wicked.   Intreat the Lord (for
it is enough) that there be no more mighty thunderings
and hail; and I will let you go, and ye shall stay no longer.
And Moses said unto him, As soon as I am gone out of the city,
I will spread abroad my hands unto the Lord; and the thunder
shall cease, neither shall there be any more hail; that thou mayest
know how that the earth is the Lord's.   But as for thee, and thy
servants, I know that ye will not yet fear the Lord God."* Ex. 9:27-30

*"Pharaoh... sinned yet more, and hardened his heart, he
and his servants... neither would he let the children of
Israel go; as the Lord had spoken by Moses."* Ex. 9:34-35

God speaks

"How long wilt thou refuse to humble thyself before Me?

Let My people go, that they may serve Me." Ex. 10:3

By this time even Pharaoh's servants were saying to him, *"How long shall this man be a snare unto us? Let the men go, that they may serve the Lord their God: knowest thou not yet that Egypt is destroyed?"* Ex. 10:7

8. Locusts

Again Pharoah confesses but is not changed. Pharaoh refused to let them go. God sent the locusts, and the locusts ate up everything that was left from the hail. Pharoah asks Moses to pray for him. *"Pharoah called for Moses and Aaron in haste, and he said, I have sinned against the Lord your God, and against you. Now therefore forgive, I pray thee, my sin only this once, and intreat the Lord your God, that He may take away from me this death only. And he* (**Moses**) *went out from Pharaoh, and intreated the Lord."* Ex. 10:16-18

9. Darkness

God sent thick darkness in all the land of Egypt. They couldn't see each other, and they stayed in their homes for three days. Pharaoh agreed to let them go, but then changed his mind. Pharoah asks Moses to pray for him. *"Pharaoh said unto him, Get thee from me, take heed to thyself, see my face no more; for in that day thou seest my face thou shalt die. And Moses said, Thou hast spoken well, I will see thy face again no more."* Ex. 10:28-29

God speaks

God spoke to Moses and told him,
   "Yet will I bring one plague more upon Pharaoh, and upon

Egypt: afterwards he will let you go hence: when he shall let you go, he shall surely thrust you out hence altogether." Ex. 11:1

God told the people to:

"...borrow jewels of silver, and jewels of gold. And the Lord gave the people favour in the sight of the Egyptians. Moreover the man Moses was very great in the land of Egypt, in the sight of Pharaoh's servants, and in the sight of the people." Ex. 11:2-3

Remember that Joseph gathered grain for seven years to prepare for the seven years of famine. When the famine came, his family got free grain; they were the only ones free in all the land, but somewhere in the next few generations it reversed itself and the Israelites were the only slaves. They never received pay for their hard work, so God compensated them with these jewels for all the misery that they had endured.

10. Death of firstborn

The Israelites were instructed to put the blood of a lamb on the door posts of their homes to keep the Destroying angel out; this was the first Passover and would mark the first month of the year for them. God warned the Egyptians that any firstborn without the blood on the door posts would die. God said all the first born would die at midnight even the animals. Everyone, except those with the blood of the Lamb on the door posts, would die because, *"God doth put a difference between the Egyptians and Israel."* Ex. 11:1-7

God speaks

*"**I** will pass through the land of Egypt this night and **will smite all the firstborn** in the land of Egypt,* (You see here

that God says He will smite them) *both man and beast; and against all the gods of Egypt I will execute judgment; I am the Lord. And the blood shall be to you for a token upon the houses where ye are;* **and when I see the blood, I will pass over you, and the plague shall not be upon you to destroy you,** (Here God says that He will protects them for being destroyed) *when I smite the land of Egypt. And this day shall be unto you for a memorial; and ye shall keep it a feast to the Lord...*" Ex. 12:12-14

"*For the Lord will pass through to smite the Egyptians; and when he seeth the blood upon the lintel, and on the two side posts, the Lord will pass over the door* (to protect)*, and* **will not suffer the Destroyer to come in** (We see here that God doesn't allow the Destroyer to come in and kill the 1st born) *unto your houses to smite you.*" Ex. 12:23

It is God who stands in front of the door, and doesn't let the Destroyer come in. This is a lesson for us today. We need to be covered with the blood of Jesus so that the Destroyer cannot harm us. After the Israelites left, Pharoah again changed his mind, and the Egyptians came after them; God was a cloud to the Israelites and a pillar of fire to the Egyptians.

Moses told the people, "*Fear ye not, stand still, and see the salvation of the Lord, which He will shew to you today; for the Egyptians whom ye have seen to day, ye shall see them again no more for ever. The Lord shall fight for you, and ye shall hold your peace..*" Ex. 14:13-14

The people went through the Red sea, and the Egyptians were drowned when they tried to follow them. God gave them a marvelous victory over their enemies.

God answers

"*For the Lord fighteth for them against the Egyptians.*" Ex. 14:25
"*And there remained not so much as one of them.*" Ex. 14:28

That meant Pharoah died also. All the fighting men died, and there was no one left to protect Egypt and some think that Egypt may have been taken over by another country shortly after that.

When the Israelites got to the desert, they ran out of water and became thirsty. God had a plan and would give them water from a rock.

1st Time water comes from Rock

Moses prays for water in Horeb. After everything they went through, now they have no water and the people cry out, "*Why did you bring us here to die?*" Ex.14:11

Moses speaks

"*And Moses cried unto the Lord, saying,*

What shall I do unto this people? They be almost ready to stone me. Ex. 17:4

God speaks

"*Behold, I will stand before thee, there upon the rock in Horeb; and thou shalt smite the rock and there shall come water out of it; that the people may drink.* Ex. 17:6

And Moses did so in the sight of the elders of Israel. Ex. 17:6

God speaks

And the Lord said unto Moses,

Go on before the people, and take with thee of the elders of Israel; and thy rod, where with thou smotest the river, take in thine hand, and go. Behold, I will stand before thee there upon the rock in Horeb; and thou shalt smite the rock, and there shall come water out of it, that the people may drink.

And Moses did so in the sight of the leaders of Israel. And he called the name of the place Massah, and Meribah, because of the chiding of the children of Israel, and because they tempted the Lord, saying ,Is the Lord among us, or not?" Ex. 17:4-7

God sent Manna to the children of Israel.

God speaks

"Then said the LORD unto Moses
  Behold, I will rain bread from heaven for you; and the people
  shall go out and gather a certain rate every day, that I may
  prove them, whether they will walk in my law, or no." Ex. 16:4

Moses on Mt. Sinai

While Moses was up on Mt. Sinai getting the Ten Commandments, the people were making a golden calf and worshiping it, Ex. 32:19. Moses literally broke the stone Ten Commandments as an illustration that the people had broken their Covenant with God. Moses had to go up on the mountain the second time to get another set of Ten Commandments. Moses cut the stones out of the Rock, but God wrote on the Commandments with His own hand twice, Ex. 31:18; Deut.4:13,19:10.

Moses made a tent to meet with God in; it was called the Tent of Meeting or Tabernacle, with the tablets of the Covenant; and there God would talk to Moses face to face. God said that he would talk to Moses on the Mercy Seat of the Ark of the Covenant.

*"And there I will meet with thee, and I will commune
with thee from above the Mercy Seat from between the two
Cherubims which are upon the Ark of the Testimony..."*
Ex. 25:22

*"And it came to pass, as Moses entered into the Tabernacle, the
cloudy pillar descended, and stood at the door of the Tabernacle,
and the Lord talked with Moses. And all the people saw the cloudy
pillar stand at the Tabernacle door: and all the people rose up
and worshiped, every man in his tent door. And the Lord spake
unto Moses face to face, as a man speaketh unto his friend. And
he turned again into the camp: but his servant Joshua, the son of
Nun, a young man, departed not out of the tabernacle."* Ex. 33:11

Moses speaks

And Moses said unto the Lord,

*See, Thou sayest unto me, Bring up this people: and Thou hast
not let me know whom Thou wilt send with me. Yet Thou hast
said, I know thee by name, and thou hast also found grace in
My sight. Now therefore, I pray Thee, if I have found grace in
Thy sight, shew me now
Thy way, that I may know Thee, that I may find grace in Thy
sight: and consider that this nation is Thy people.* Ex. 33:14

Moses asks for God's presence to go with them: Moses realized
that they will be hated by the whole world and that they would need
God's presence with them, or they were in trouble.

God speaks

"And He (God) *said,*

My presence shall go with thee, and I will give thee rest."
Ex. 33:14

Moses speaks
"And He (Moses) *said unto him,*

> *If Thy presence go not with me, carry us not up hence. For wherein shall it be known here that I and Thy people have found grace in Thy sight? Is it not in that Thou goest with us? So shall we be separated, I and Thy people, from all the people that are upon the face of the earth."* Ex. 33:15-16

God speaks
"And the Lord said unto Moses,
> *I will do this thing also that thou hast spoken:*
> *for thou hast found grace in My sight, and I know thee by name."* Ex. 33:17

Moses asks to see God's glory and speaks.
And he (Moses) *said,*

> *I beseech Thee, shew me Thy glory."* Ex. 33:18

God speaks
And He (God) *said,*

> *I will make all My goodness pass before thee, and I will proclaim the name of the Lord before thee: and will be gracious to whom I will be gracious, and will shew mercy on whom I will shew mercy."* Ex. 33:19

God speaks

"And He (God) said,

Thou canst not see My face: for there shall no man see Me, and live." Ex. 33:20

"And the Lord said,

Behold, there is a place by Me, and thou shalt stand upon a rock: and it shall come to pass, while My glory passeth by, that I will put thee in a clift of the rock, and will cover thee with My hand while I pass by: and I will take away Mine hand, and thou shalt see My back parts: but My face shall not be seen."
Ex. 33:21-23

Moses talks to God face to face

"And the Lord said unto Moses,

Hew thee two tables of stone like unto the first: and I will write upon these tables the words that were in the first tables, which thou brakest, and be ready in the morning, and come up in the morning unto Mount Sinai, and present thyself there to Me in the top of the mount.
And no man shall come up with thee, neither let any man be seen throughout all the mount; neither let the flocks nor herds feed before that mount.
And he hewed two tables of stone like unto the first; and Moses rose up early in the morning, and went up unto Mount Sinai, as the Lord had commanded him, and took in his hand the two tables of stone, And the Lord descended in the cloud, and stood with him there, and proclaimed the name of the Lord.

And the Lord passed by before him, and proclaimed. . ."
Ex. 34:1-6

God speaks
God reveals His glory

"The Lord, The Lord God, merciful and gracious,
longsuffering, and abundant in goodness and truth. Keeping
mercy for thousands, forgiving iniquity and transgression and
sin, and that will by no means clear the guilty;
visiting the iniquity of the fathers upon the children, and
upon the children's children, unto the third and to the fourth
generation." Ex. 34:6-7

Moses speaks
"And Moses made haste, and bowed his head toward the earth, and
worshiped. And he said,

If now I have found grace in Thy sight, O Lord, let my Lord,
I pray Thee, go among us; for it is a stiff-necked people;
and pardon our iniquity and our sin, and take us for Thine
inheritance." Ex. 34:8-9

God speaks
"And He (God) said,

Behold, I make a Covenant: before all thy people I will do
marvels, such as have not been done in all the earth, nor in
any nation: and all the people among which thou art shall
see the work of the Lord: for it is a terrible thing that I will
do with thee. Observe thou that which I command thee
this day: behold, I drive out before thee the Amorite, and

*the Canaanite, and the Hittite, and the Perizzite, and the
Hivite, and the Jebusite. Take heed to thyself, lest thou make a
Covenant with the inhabitants of the land whither thou goest,
lest it be for a snare in the midst of thee: but ye shall destroy
their altars, break their images, and cut down their groves: for
thou shalt worship no other god: for the Lord, whose name
is Jealous, is a jealous God* (not that He's jealous of you
but that He is jealous if you worship other gods): *lest thou
make a covenant with the inhabitants of the land, and they
go a whoring after their gods, and do sacrifice unto their gods,
and one call thee, and thou eat of his sacrifice...Thou shalt
make thee no molten gods....And none shall appear before
Me empty. Six days thou shalt work, but on the seventh day
thou shalt rest: in earing time and in harvest thou shalt rest...
Write thou these words: for after the tenor of these words I
have made a Covenant with thee and with Israel."*
Ex. 34:10-17,20,21,27

Moses' face shines from the glory of the Lord after talking to God.

*"And he was there with the Lord forty days and forty nights; he did
neither eat bread, nor drink water. And He* (God) *wrote upon the tables
the words of the Covenant, the Ten Commandments* (Here we see that
the Covenant is the Ten Commandments). *And it came to pass, when
Moses came down from Mount Sinai with the two tables of Testimony
in Moses' hand, when he came down from the mount, that Moses wist
not that the skin of his face shone while he talked with Him. And when
Aaron and all the children of Israel saw Moses, behold, the skin of his
face shone; and they were afraid to come nigh him... and he gave them
in commandment all that the Lord had spoken with Him in Mount
Sinai. And till Moses had done speaking with them, he put a vail on his*

32

face. But when Moses went in before the Lord to speak with Him, he took the vail off, until he came out. And he came out, and spake unto the children of Israel that which he was commanded. And the children of Israel saw the face of Moses, that the skin of Moses' face shone: and Moses put the vail upon his face again, until he went in to speak with Him **(God)**." Ex. 34:1-35

Numbers

Prayer of Blessing

God gave them a prayer of blessing to give to the people. Moses was to speak this blessing and then they would be blessed.

"And the Lord spake unto Moses saying, Speak unto Aaron and unto his sons, saying, On this wise ye shall bless the children of Israel, Saying unto them,

> *The Lord bless thee, and keep thee: the Lord make His face shine upon thee, and be gracious unto thee: the Lord lift up His countenance upon thee, and give thee peace."*
> Num. 6:23-26

And they shall put My name upon the children of Israel; and I will bless them." Num. 6:27

> *"And it came to pass, when the ark set forward, that Moses said, Rise up, Lord, and let Thine enemies be scattered; and let them that hate Thee flee before Thee.*
> *And when it rested, he said,*
> *Return, O Lord, unto the many thousands of Israel."*
> Num. 10:35-36

The people complain

"And when the people complained, it displeased the Lord: and the Lord heard it; and His anger was kindled; and the fire of the Lord burnt among them, and consumed them that were in the uttermost parts of the camp. And the people cried unto Moses; and when Moses prayed unto the Lord." Num. 11:1-2

God answers

And when Moses prayed unto the Lord

"...the fire was quenched. And he called the name of the place Taberah: because the fire of the Lord burnt among them." Num. 11:1,2,11-16

Quail

The people begged for fresh meat and God sent quail but He wasn't happy with them. Sometimes God gives in to our requests but we suffer the consequences.

"And the mixt multitude that was among them fell a lusting: and the children of Israel also wept again, and said, Who shall give us flesh to eat? We remember the fish, which we did eat in Egypt freely; the cucumbers, and the melons, and the leeks, and the onions, and the garlick: but now our soul is dried away: there is nothing at all, beside this manna, before our eyes ...Then Moses heard the people weep throughout their families, every man in the door of his tent: and the anger of the Lord was kindled greatly; Moses also was displeased..." Num. 11:4-10

2nd Time water comes from Rock

The 1st time water came from the rock was in Ex. 17:6 and the rock was at Horeb. Now Moses is in Kadesh, and they run out of water again. Moses was supposed to hit the rock the 1st time, but this time he is suppose to speak to the Rock. Instead he hits it again. God still gave them water, but Moses messed up the illustration that Jesus was to die only once for our sins.

"And the Lord spake unto Moses, saying,

> *Take the rod, and gather thou the assembly together, thou, and Aaron thy brother, and speak ye unto the rock before their eyes; and it shall give forth his water, and thou shalt bring forth to them water out of the rock: so thou shalt give the*

congregation and their beasts drink.

And Moses took the rod from before the Lord, as he commanded him. And Moses and Aaron gathered the congregation together before the rock, and he said unto them,

Hear now, ye rebels; must we fetch you water out of this rock? And Moses lift up his hand, and with his rod he smote the rock twice: and the water came out abundantly, and the congregation drank, and their beasts also. And the Lord spake unto Moses and Aaron,

> *Because ye believed Me not, to sanctify Me in the eyes of the children of Israel, therefore ye shall not bring this congregation into the land which I have given them. This is the water of meribah; because the children of Israel strove with the Lord, and He was sanctified in them."* Num. 20:7-13

God answers

He gives in to them and gives them what they ask for but He's not happy with them.

"And there went forth a wind from the Lord, and brought quails from the sea, and let them fall by the camp, as it were a day's journey on this side, and as it were a day's journey on the other side, round about the camp, and as it were two cubits high upon the face of the earth. And the people stood up all that day, and all that night, and all the next day, and they gathered the quails; he that gathered least gathered ten homers (about 60 bushels) *and they spread them all abroad for themselves round about the camp. And while the flesh was yet between their teeth, ere it was chewed, the wrath of the Lord was kindled against the people, and the Lord smote the people with a very great plague. And He called the name of that place Kib-roth-hat-ta-a-vah: because there they buried the people that lusted."* Num. 11: 31-34

This was caused mostly by the mixed multitude (Ps.78:25-32). The problem was gluttony and lust and lack of restraint. Could it be that they were so anxious to eat the meat that they didn't cook it properly? Or maybe they ate too much.?They didn't want to trust the Lord and accept what He thought was best for them. Whatever happened, we know that God had a good reason.

Moses speaks to God

"And Moses said unto the Lord,

Wherefore hast Thou afflicted Thy servant? And wherefore have I not found favour in Thy sight, that thou layest the burden of all this people upon me? Have I conceived all this people? Have I begotten them, that Thou shouldest say unto me, Carry them in thy bosom, as a nursing father beareth the suckling child, unto the land which Thou swarest unto their fathers. Whence should I have flesh to give unto all this people? For they weep unto me, saying, Give us flesh, that we may eat. I am not able to bear all this people alone, because it is too heavy for me. And if Thou deal thus with me, kill me, I pray Thee,out of hand, if I have found favour in Thy sight; and let me not see my wretchedness." Num. 11:11-15

We see this same prayer with Elijah and Jonah:
"... and he requested for himself that he might die; and said, It is enough; now, O Lord, take away my life; for I am not better than my fathers." I Kings 19:4

"Therefore now... take, I beseech Thee, my life from me; for it is better for me to die than to live." Jonah 4:3

Sometimes God's ministers get so discouraged and want to give up, but God still cares for them and encourages them and holds them up in His strong arms; He is faithful even when we are not.

70 elders
God speaks
"And the Lord said unto Moses,

Gather unto Me seventy men of the elders of Israel, whom thou knowest to be the elders of the people, and officers over them; and bring them unto the Tabernacle of the Congregation, that they may stand there with thee. And I will come down and talk with thee there: and I will take of the Spirit which is upon thee, and will put it upon them; and they shall bear the burden of the people with thee, that thou bear it not thyself alone. And say thou unto the people,

Sanctify yourselves against to morrow, and ye shall eat flesh: for ye have wept in the ears of the Lord, saying, Who shall give us flesh to eat? For it was well with us in Egypt: therefore the Lord will give you flesh, and ye shall eat. Ye shall not eat one day, nor two days, nor five days, neither ten days, nor twenty days; but even a whole month, until it come out at your nostrils, and it be loathsome unto you: because that ye have despised the Lord which is among you, and have wept before Him, saying, Why came we forth out of Egypt?

And Moses said,

The people, among whom I am, are six hundred thousand

footmen;
and Thou hast said, I will give them flesh, that they may eat a
whole month. Shall the flocks and the herds be slain for them,
to suffice them? Or shall all the fish of the sea be gathered
together for them, to suffice them?

And the Lord said unto Moses,
Is the Lord's hand waxed short? Thou shalt see now whether
My Word shall come to pass unto thee or not.

("With God all things are possible" Matt. 19:26)
And Moses went out, and told the people the words of the Lord, and gathered the seventy men of the elders of the people, and set them round about the Tabernacle." Num. 11:16-24

70 men prophecy
God answers

"And the Lord came down in a cloud, and spake unto him, and took of the Spirit that was upon him, and gave it unto the seventy elders: and it came to pass, that, when the Spirit rested upon them, they prophesied, and did not cease. But there remained two of the men in the camp, the name of the one was Eldad, and the name of the other Medad: and the Spirit rested upon them; and they were of them that were written; but went not out unto the Tabernacle: and they prophesied in the camp. And there ran a young man, and told Moses, and said,

Eldad and Medad do prophesy in the camp. And Joshua the son of Nun, the servant of Moses, one of his young men, answered and said, My lord Moses, forbid them. And Moses said unto him, Enviest thou for my sake? Would God that all the Lord's people were prophets, and that the Lord would put His Spirit upon them!" Num. 11:25-29

The New Testament tells us to desire prophecy.
"Follow after charity, and desire spiritual gifts, but rather that ye may prophesy." I Cor. 14:1

Moses prays for Mirriam

Miriam and Aaron were the older sister and brother of Moses and they begin to question Moses' authority, and think that they have just as much authority as he does.

"And Miriam and Aaron spake against Moses because of the Ethiopian woman whom he had married: for he had married an Ethiopian woman (most likely Zipporah, who was a Midianite, died and Moses married a second wife – taken from NIV fn) *And they said, Hath the Lord indeed spoken only by Moses? Hath He not spoken also by us? And the Lord heard it.* (Now the man Moses was very meek, above all the men which were upon the face of the earth). *And the Lord spake suddenly unto Moses, and unto Aaron, and unto Miriam,*

Come out ye three unto the Tabernacle of the congregation.

And they three came out." Num. 12:1-4

God speaks

God spoke to Moses face to face.
"And the Lord came down in the pillar of the cloud, and stood in the door of the Tabernacle, and called Aaron and Miriam: and they both came forth. And He said,

Hear now My words: If there be a prophet among you, I the Lord will make Myself known unto him in a vision, and will speak unto him in a dream. My servant Moses is not so, who is faithful in all Mine house.

With him will I speak mouth to mouth, even apparently, and not in dark speeches; and the similitude of the Lord shall he behold; wherefore then were ye not afraid to speak against My servant Moses?

And the anger of the Lord was kindled against them; and He departed. And the cloud departed from off the Tabernacle; and, behold, Miriam became leprous, white as snow: and Aaron looked upon Miriam, and, behold, she was leprous. And Aaron said unto Moses, Alas, my Lord, I beseech thee, lay not the sin upon us, wherein we have done foolishly, and wherein we have sinned. Let her not be as one dead..." Num.12:5-12

Moses' prayer

This is a prayer of desperation, God - Heal her now! I beg You! How many times have we prayed similar prayers to this one out of our desperation?

"And Moses cried unto the Lord, saying,

Heal her now, O God, I beseech Thee." Num 12:13

God answers

"And the Lord said unto Moses,

If her father had but spit in her face, should she not be ashamed seven days? Let her be shut out from the camp seven days (according to the Law of Moses), *and after that let her be received in again.*

And Miriam was shut out from the camp seven days: and the people journeyed not till Miriam was brought in again." Num. 12:14

Moses prays for rebellious Israel

God wants the people to go into the Promised Land but the people rebel. God threatened to destroy the people with a plague and make a greater nation through Moses but Moses prays to God.

"And Moses said unto the Lord,

> Then the Egyptians shall hear it, (for Thou broughtest up this
> people in Thy might from among them); and they will tell it
> to the inhabitants of this land: for they have heard that Thou
> Lord art among this people, that Thou, Lord, art seen face to
> face, and that Thy cloud standeth over them, and that Thou
> goest before them, by day time in a pillar of a cloud, and in a
> pillar of fire by night.
> Now if Thou shalt kill all this people as one man, then the
> nations which have heard the fame of Thee will speak, saying,
> Because the Lord was not able to bring this people into the
> land which He sware unto them, therefore He hath slain them
> in the wilderness.
> And now, I beseech Thee, let the power of my Lord be
> great, according as Thou hast spoken, saying, The Lord is
> longsuffering, and of great mercy, forgiving iniquity and
> transgression, and by no means clearing the guilt, visiting the
> iniquity of the fathers upon the children unto the third and
> fourth generation. Pardon, I beseech Thee, the iniquity of this
> people according unto the greatness of Thy mercy,
> and as Thou hast forgiven this people, from Egypt even until
> now." Num. 14:13-19

God answers

"And the Lord said,

> I have pardoned according to thy word: but as truly as I live,

all the earth shall be filled with the glory of the Lord. Because
all those men which have seen My glory, and My miracles,
which I did in Egypt and in the wilderness, and have tempted
Me now these ten times, and have not hearkened to My voice;
surely they shall not see the land which I sware unto their
fathers, neither shall any of them that provoked Me see it: but
My servant, Caleb, because he had another Spirit with him,
and hath followed Me fully, him will I bring into the land
whereunto he went ; and his seed shall possess it. Tomorrow
turn you, and get you into the wilderness by the way of the
Red Sea.
And the Lord spake unto Moses and unto Aaron, saying,
How long shall I bear with this evil congregation, which
murmur against Me? I have heard the murmurings of the
children of Israel, which they murmur against Me.

Say unto them,

As truly as I live,

Saith the Lord,
As ye have spoken in Mine ears, so will I do to you: your
carcases shall fall in this wilderness; and all that were
numbered of you, according to your whole number, from
twenty years old and upward, which have murmured against
Me. Doubless ye shall not come into the land, concerning
which I sware to make you dwell therein, save Caleb the son
of Jephuneh, and Joshua the son of Nun. But your little ones,
which ye said should be a prey, them will I bring in, and they
shall know the land which ye have despised. But as for you,
your carcases, they shall fall in this wilderness. And your
children shall wander in the wilderness forty years, and
bear your whoredoms, until your carcases be wasted in

44

the wilderness. After the number of the days in which ye searched the land, even forty days, each day for a year, shall ye bear your iniquiteies, even forty years, and ye shall know My breach of promise ("know what it is like to have Me against you" NIV). *I the Lord have said, I will surely do it unto all this evil congregation, that are gathered together against Me: in this wilderness they shall be consumed, and there they shall die."* Num. 14:20-35

"Now may the Lord's strength be displayed, just as You have declared: the Lord is slow to anger, abounding in love and forgiving sin and rebellion. Yet He does not leave the guilty unpunished... In accordance with Your great love, forgive the sin of these people..." Num. 14:17-19 NIV

Korah, Dathan, and Abiram

Korah, Dathan, and Abiram led a rebellion of the people against Moses saying that God was just as much with them as with Moses.

"And Moses was very wroth, and said unto the Lord,

Respect not Thou their offering:
I have not taken one (donkey) *from them,*
neither have I hurt one of them." Num. 16:15

Moses and Aaron prayed for the people.

"And they fell upon their faces, and said,

O God the God of the spirits of all flesh,
shall one man sin, and wilt thou be wroth with all the congregation?"
Num. 16:22

45

God answers

"And the Lord spake unto Moses, saying,

> *Speak unto the congregation, saying, Get you up from about the tabernacle of Korah, Dathan, and Abiram.* (a fire consumed them)

… and the Lord spake unto Moses, saying,

> *Speak unto Eleazar the son of Aaron the priest, that he take up the censers out of the burning, and scatter thou the fire yonder; for they are hallowed. The censers of these sinners against their own souls, let them make them broad plates for a covering of the altar: for they offered them before the Lord, therefore they are hallowed: and they shall be a sign unto the children of Israel."* Num. 16:23-38

We see here that God is God over everyone whether they acknowledge it or not; He created them and redeemed them and we all owe God our worship and our very lives.

Even though this seems harsh to us, God was very merciful in that He didn't let the whole congregation die for the sins of one man; He only let this one family die probably because they were in sympathy with the one who sinned. We have to remember that everything God did in the Old Testament with Israel was to preserve a people who would one day give birth to the Messiah. So whatever threatened to wipe out the Israelites, God would have to deal with it.

"And the Lord spake unto Moses, saying.

> *Get you up from among this congregation, that I may consume*

46

them as in a moment. And they fell upon their faces.

And Moses said unto Aaron,

Take a censer, and put fire therein from off the altar, and put on incense, and go quickly unto the congregation, and make an atonement for them: for there is wrath gone out from the Lord; the plague is begun.

And Aaron took as Moses commanded, and ran into the midst of the congregation; and behold, the plague was begun among the people: and he put on incense, and made an atonement for the people And he stood between the dead and the living; and the plague was stayed." Num. 16:44-50

"And Moses sent messengers… unto the king of Edom (descendants of Esau), *Thus saith thy brother Israel,*

Thou knowest all the travail that hath befallen us: how our fathers went down into Egypt, and we have dwelt in Egypt a long time; and the Egyptians vexed us, and our fathers: and when we cried unto the Lord, He heard our voice, and sent an angel, and hath brought us forth out of Egypt: and, behold, we are in Kadesh, a city in the uttermost of thy border: let us pass, I pray thee… (but) *Edom refused"* Num. 20:14-21

To the Edomites would not listen. When the Canaanite king of Arad was going to attack the Israelites and had captured some of them, then Israel made a vow to God if He would deliver them.

Israel prays

"And Israel vowed a vow unto the Lord, and said,

> *If Thou wilt indeed deliver this people into my hand,*
> *then I will utterly destroy their cities."* Num. 21:2

God answers

"And the Lord hearkened to the voice of Israel, and delivered up the Canaanites; and they utterly destroyed them and their cities: and he called the name of the place Hormah." Num. 21:3

Delivered from serpents

"And the people spake against God, and against Moses, Wherefore have ye brought us up out of Egypt to die in the wilderness? For there is no bread, neither is there any water; and our soul loatheth this light bread.

And the Lord sent fiery serpents among the people, and they bit the people; and much people of Israel died.

Therefore the people came to Moses, and said,

(First they confessed their sin – then they asked Moses to pray)

We have sinned, for we have spoken against the Lord, and against thee; pray unto the Lord that He take away the serpents from us. And Moses prayed for the people.

God answers

"And the Lord said unto Moses,

Make thee a fiery serpent, and set it upon a pole: and it shall come to pass, that every one that is bitten, when he looketh upon it, shall live.
(It represented Jesus on the cross)

And Moses made a serpent of brass, and put it upon a pole, and it came to pass, that if a serpent had bitten any man, when he beheld the serpent of brass, he lived." Num. 21:8-9

The people eventually made an idol of the serpent on the pole and prayed to it instead of God; Hezekiah destroyed it.

"Hezekiah... did what was pleasing in the Lord's sight, just as his ancestor David had done." II Kings 18:1-3 NLT

"He removed the high places, and brake the images, and cut down the groves, and brake in pieces the brazen serpent that Moses had made: for unto those days the children of Israel did burn incense to it: and he called it Hehushtan ("that is a piece of brass" KJV fn)." II Kings 18:1-4

"And as Moses lifted up the serpent in the wilderness, even so must the Son of man be lifted up: that whosoever believeth in Him should not perish, but have eternal life. For God so loved the world, that He gave His only begotten Son, that whosoever believeth in Him should not perish, but have everlasting life. For God sent not His Son into the world to condemn the world; but that the world through Him might be saved. He that believeth on Him is not condemned: but he that believeth not is condemned already, because he hath not believed in the name of the only begotten Son of God." Jn. 3:14-18

Balaam

Balak was king of the Moabites; descendants of Moab the son of Lot, Abraham's nephew. He sent some men to ask Balaam to come and curse Israel but as long as Israel obeyed God they were blessed and could not be cursed.

God speaks to Balaam

"He (Balak) *sent messengers therefore unto Balaam, the son of Beor... saying, Behold, they* (Israel) *cover the face of the earth, and they abide over against me: come now therefore, I pray thee, curse me this people; for they are too mighty for me... "* Num. 22:5-6

"And God came unto Balaam, and said,

What men are these with thee?

And Balaam said unto God,

Balak the son of Zippor, king of Moab, hath sent unto me, saying, Behold, there is a people come out of Egypt, which covereth the face of the earth: come now, curse me them; peradventure I shall be able to overcome them, and drive them out.

And God said unto Balaam,

Thou shalt not go with them; thou shalt not curse the people: for they are blessed (and what God has blessed cannot be cursed). Num. 22:9-12

"And Balaam rose up in the morning, and said unto the princes of Balak, Get you into your land: for the Lord refuseth to give me leave to go with you. And the princes of Moab rose up, and they went unto Balak, and said, Balaam refuseth to come with us. And Balak sent yet again princes, more, and more honorable than they. And they came to Balaam, and said to him, Thus saith Balak the son of Zippor, Let nothing, I pray thee, hinder thee from coming unto me: for I wilt promote thee unto very great honour, and I will do whatsoever thou sayest unto me: come therefore, I pray Thee, curse me this people. And Balaam answered and said unto the servants of Balak, If Balak would give me his house full of silver and gold, I cannot go beyond the word of the Lord my God, to do less or more (Balak thought that Balaam could use God for his own means but God is in control and we are His servants to do His bidding). *Now therefore, I pray you, tarry ye also here this night, that I may know what the Lord will say unto me more."* Num. 22:13-19

God's mind didn't change – He let Balaam do what he wanted even though he was told not to because He knew that in Balaam's heart he really wanted to go; ultimately God would use Balaam to bless His people.

"*And God came unto Balaam at night, and said unto him,*

If the men come to call thee, rise up, and go with them;
but yet the word which I shall say unto thee,
that shalt thou do.

And Balaam rose up in the morning, and saddled his (donkey), *and went with the princes of Moab. And God's anger was kindled because he went: and the angel of the Lord stood in the way for an adversary against him. Now he was riding upon his* (donkey), *and his two servants were with him. And the* (donkey) *saw the angel of the Lord standing in the way, and his sword drawn in his hand: and the* (donkey) *turned aside out of the way, and went into the field: and Balaam smote the* (donkey), *to turn her into the way. But the angel of the Lord stood in a path of the vineyards, a wall being on this side, and a wall on that side. And when the* (donkey) *saw the angel of the Lord, she thrust herself unto the wall, and crushed Balaam's foot against the wall: and he smote her again. And the angel of the Lord went further, and stood in a narrow place, where was no way to turn either to the right hand or to the left. And when the* (donkey) *saw the angel of the Lord, she fell down under Balaam: and Balaam's anger was kindled, and he smote the* (donkey) *with a staff. And the Lord opened the mouth of the* (donkey), *and she said unto Balaam* (Why wasn't Balaam surprised that his donkey talked to him I wonder?), *What have I done unto thee, that thou hast smitten me these three times? And Balaam said unto the* (donkey), *Because thou hast mocked me: I would there were a sword in mine hand, for now would I kill thee.*

And the (donkey) *said unto Balaam, Am not I thine* (donkey), *upon which thou hast ridden ever since I was thine unto this day? Was I ever wont to do so unto thee? And he said, Nay. Then the Lord opened the eyes of Balaam, and he saw the angel of the Lord standing in the way, and his sword drawn in his hand: and he bowed down his head, and fell flat on his face.*

And the angel of the Lord said unto him,

> *Wherefore hast thou smitten thine* (donkey) *these three times? behold, I went out to withstand thee, because thy way is perverse* ("reckless" NIV) *before Me: and the* (donkey) *saw me, and turned from Me these three times: unless she had turned from Me, surely now also I had slain thee, and saved her alive.*

And Balaam said unto the angel of the Lord (Balaam confesses), *I have sinned; for I knew not that thou stoodest in the way against me: now therefore, if it displease Thee, I will get me back again.*

And the angel of the Lord said unto Balaam,

> *Go with the men: but only the word that I shall speak unto thee, that thou shalt speak.*

So Balaam went with the princes of Balak. And when Balak heard that Balaam was come, he went out to meet him unto a city of Moab, which is in the border of Arnon, which is in the utmost coast. And Balak said unto Balaam, Did I not earnestly send unto thee to call thee? Wherefore camest thou not unto me? am I not able indeed to promote thee to honour? And Balaam said unto Balak, Lo, I am come unto thee: have I now any power at all to say anything? The word that God putteth in my mouth, that shall I speak. And Balaam went with Balak, and they came unto Ker-jath-hu-zoth. And Balak offered oxen and sheep, and sent to Balaam, and to the princes that were with him. And it came to pass on the morrow, that Balak took Balaam, and brought him up into the high places of Baal, that thence he might see the utmost part of the people." Num. 22:20-41

"And Balaam said unto Balak, Build me here seven altars, and prepare me here seven oxen and seven rams **(Represents the Holy Spirit who is Sevenfold Rev. 1:4;4:5;5:6)**. *And Balak did as Balaam had spoken; and Balak and Balaam offered on every altar a bullock and a ram. And Balaam said unto Balak, Stand by thy burnt offering, and I will go: peradventure the Lord will come to meet me: and whatsoever He sheweth me I will tell thee. And he went to an high place.*

And God met Balaam: and he **(Balaam)** *said unto Him* **(God)**,

> *I have prepared seven altars, and I have offered upon every altar a bullock and a ram.*

And the Lord put a word in Balaam's mouth, and said, Return unto Balak, and thus thou shalt speak. And he returned unto him, and, lo, he stood by his burnt sacrifice, he, and all the princes of Moab. And he took up His parable, and said, Balak the king of Moab hath brought me from Aram, out of the mountains of the east..." Num. 23:1-7

1st Blessing from God

Balaam prophecies over Israel.

". . .Come, curse me Jacob, and come, defy Israel. How shall I curse, whom God hath not cursed? Or how shall I defy, whom the Lord hath

not defied? For from the top of the rocks I see Him, and from the hills I behold Him: lo, the people shall dwell alone, and shall not be reckoned among the nations. Who can count the dust of Jacob, and the number of the fourth part of Israel? Let me die the death of the righteous, and let my last end be like his!

And Balak said unto Balaam, What hast thou done unto me? I took thee to curse mine enemies, and, behold, thou hast blessed them altogether. And he answered and said, Must I not take heed to speak that which the Lord hath put in my mouth? And Balak said unto him, Come, I pray thee, with me unto another place, from whence thou mayest see them: thou shalt see but the utmost part of them, and shalt not see them all: and curse me them from thence. And he brought him into the field of Zophim, to the top of Pisgah, and built seven altars, and offered a bullock and a ram on every altar. And he said unto Balak, Stand here by thy burnt offering, while I meet the Lord yonder. And the Lord met Balaam, and put a word in his mouth, and said, Go again unto Balak, and say thus. And when he came to him, behold, he stood by his burnt offering, and the princes of Moab with him. And Balak said unto him, What hath the Lord spoken? And he took up His parable, and said, Rise up, Balak, and hear; hearken unto Me, thou son of Zippor. . ." Num. 23:7-18

2ⁿᵈ blessing from God
They are blessed because there is no sin in them.

"God is not a man, that He should lie; neither the son of man, that He should repent: hath He said, and shall He not do it? Or hath He spoken, and shall He not make it good? Behold, I have received commandment to bless: and He hath blessed; and I cannot reverse it. He hath not beheld iniquity in Jacob, neither hath He seen perverseness in Israel: the

Lord his God is with him, and the shout of a king is among them. God brought them out of Egypt; He hath as it were the strength of an ("wild ox"). Surely, there is no enchantment against Jacob, neither is there any divination against Israel: according to this time it shall be said of Jacob and of Israel,

What hath God wrought! Behold, the people shall rise up as a great lion, and lift up himself as a young lion: he shall not lie down until he eat of the prey, and drink the blood of the slain.

And Balak said unto Balaam, Neither curse them at all, nor bless them at all. But Balaam answered and said unto Balak, Told not I thee, saying, All that the Lord speaketh, that I must do? And Balak said unto Balaam,

Come, I pray thee, I will bring thee unto another place; peradventure it will please God that thou mayest curse me them from thence. And Balak brought Balaam unto the top of Peor, that looketh toward Je-shi-mon. And Balaam said unto Balak, Build me here seven altars, and prepare me here seven bullocks and seven rams.

And Balak did as Balaam had said, and offered a bullock and a ram on every altar." Num. 23:19-30

"And when Balaam saw that it pleased the Lord to bless Israel, he went not, as at other times, to seek for enchantments, but he set his face toward the wilderness. And Balaam lifted up his eyes, and he saw Israel abiding in his tents according to their tribes; and the Spirit of God came upon him. And he took up his parable, and said, Balaam the son of Beor hath said, and the man whose eyes are open hath said: He hath said, which heard the words of God, which saw the vision of the Almighty, falling into a trance, but having his eyes open. . ." Num. 24:1-4

3rd Blessing from God

"How goodly are thy tents, O Jacob, and thy tabernacles, O Israel! As

the valleys are they spread forth, as gardens by the river's side, as the trees of ...aloes which the Lord hath planted, and as cedar trees beside the waters. He shall pour the water out of His buckets, and His seed shall be in many waters, and His king shall be higher than Agag, and His kingdom shall be exalted. God brought him forth out of Egypt; He hath as it were the strength of an ("**ox**") He shall eat up the nations His enemies, and shall break their bones, and pierce them through with His arrows. He couched, He lay down as a lion, and as a great lion: who shall stir Him up? Blessed is he that blesseth thee, and cursed is he that curseth thee. And Balak's anger was kindled against Balaam, and he smote his hands together: and Balak said unto Balaam, I called thee to curse mine enemies, and, behold, thou hast altogether blessed them these three times. Therefore now flee today to thy place: I thought to promote thee unto great honour; but, lo, the Lord hath kept thee back from honour. And Balaam said unto Balak, Spake I not also to thy messengers which thou sentest unto me, saying, If Balak would give me his house full of silver and gold, I cannot go beyond the commandment of the Lord, to do either good or bad of mine own mind; but what the Lord saith, that will I speak? And now, behold, I go unto My people: come therefore, and I will advertise thee what this people shall do to thy people in the latter days. And he took up his parable, and said,

Balaam the son of Beor hath said, and the man whose eyes are open hath said: He hath said, which heard the words of God, and knew the knowledge of the most High, which saw the vision of the Almighty, falling into a trance, but having his eyes open. . ." Num. 24:5-16

4th Blessing
A prophecy of Jesus – the coming Messiah.

"I shall see Him, but not now: I shall behold Him, but not nigh: there shall come a Star out of Jacob (**Jesus**), and a Sceptre shall rise out of Israel, and shall smite the corners of Moab, and destroy all the children *of Sheth. And Edom shall be a possession, Seir also shall be a possession for his enemies; and Israel shall do valiantly. Out of Jacob shall come He that shall have dominion, and shall destroy him that remaineth of the city. And when he looked on Amalek, he took up his parable, and said, Amalek was the first of the nations; but his latter end shall be that he perish for ever. And he looked on the Kenites, and took up his parable, and said, Strong is thy dwelling place, and thou puttest thy nest in a rock. Nevertheless the Kenite shall be wasted, until Asshur shall carry thee away captive. And he took up his parable, and said, Alas, who shall live when God doeth this! And ships shall come from the coast of Chittim, and shall afflict Asshur, and shall afflict Eber, and he also shall perish for ever.And balaam rose up, and went and returned to his place: and Balak also went his way."* Num.24:17-25

Balaam eventually succeeded in cursing Israel by leading them into fornication, Num. 25:1. Balaam came to a bad end; he died in battle against the Israelites. God told the Israelites to avenge themselves on the Midianites and Balaam was slain with the sword, Num. 31:8.

Bible verses about Balaam

"Bad advice by the counsel of Balaam" Num. 31:16

"All the dedicated things of the house of God did they bestow on Balaam" II Chron. 24:7

"the way of Balaam" II Pet. 2:15

"error of Balaam" Jude 11

"But I have a few things against thee, because thou hast there them that hold the doctrine of Balaam, who taught Balak to cast a stumbling block before the children of Israel to eat things sacrificed unto idols, and to commit fornication." Rev. 2:14

Moab seduces Israel

We see here how much God hates idolatry and the things that go along with it.

"... the people began to commit whoredom with the daughters of Moab... and the people did eat, and bowed down to their gods. And Israel joined himself unto Baalpeor; and the anger of the Lord was kindled against Israel.

And the Lord said unto Moses,

> Take all the heads of the people, and hang them up before the Lord against the sun, that the fierce anger of the Lord may be turned away from Israel.

... And the Lord spake unto Moses, saying,

> Phinehas, the son of Eleazar, the son of Aaron the priest, hath turned My wrath away from the children of Israel, while he was zealous for My sake among them, that I consumed not the children of Israel in My jealousy (Ex. 20:5) Wherefore say, Behold, I give unto him My Covenant of peace: and he shall have it, and his seed after him, even the Covenant of an everlasting priesthood; because he was zealous for his God, and made an atonement for the children of Israel."
> Num. 25:1-14

Deuteronomy

Moses prays to enter the Promised Land

God would not hear that prayer and told Moses not to even pray it anymore.

Because Moses messed up God would not allow him to enter the Promised Land even though Moses prayed earnestly for God to change His mind.

"... I besought the Lord at that time, saying,

> O Lord God, Thou hast begun to shew Thy servant Thy greatness, and Thy mighty hand: for what God is there in heaven or in earth, that can do according to Thy works, and according to Thy might? I pray Thee, let me go over, and see the good land that is beyond Jordan, that goodly mountain, and Lebanon.

But the Lord was wroth with me for your sakes, and would not hear me: and the Lord said unto me,

> Let it suffice thee; speak no more unto Me of this matter. Get thee up into the top of Pisgah, and lift up thine eyes westward, and northward, and southward, and eastward, and behold it with thine eyes: for thou shalt not go over this Jordan. But charge Joshua, and encourage him, and strengthen him: for he shall go over before this people, and he shall cause them to inherit the land which thou shalt see.

So we abode in the valley over against Bethpeor." Deut. 3:23-29

Because of the golden calf, God was angry enough with Aaron enough to destroy him, but Moses. . .*"prayed for Aaron..."* Deut. 9:19-20.

And it came to pass, as he continued:
"Thus I fell down before the Lord forty days and forty nights, as I fell down at the first; because the Lord had said He would destroy you. I prayed therefore unto the Lord, and said,

O Lord God, destroy not Thy people and Thine inheritance, which Thou hast redeemed through Thy greatness, which Thou hast brought forth out of Egypt with a mighty hand." Deut. 9:25-26

Joshua

Joshua

Joshua prays that God will defeat their enemies.

Joshua told the people: it is not because you are righteous, but because the nations were wicked that God is going to drive them out. If you forget God and follow after other gods, you will be destroyed for not obeying God just like they are being destroyed (Deut. 8:19,20;9:4,5). God told them: when you become as ungodly as they are, then I will be against you also.

While they were destroying Jericho, Achan took a Babylonian garment, 200 shekels of silver, and a wedge of gold worth 50 shekels, despite God commanding them not to take anything. God destroyed Achan and his family.

"And Joshua rent his clothes, and fell to the earth upon his face before the ark of the Lord until the eventide, he and the elders of Israel, and put dust upon their heads.

And Joshua said,

Alas, O Lord God, wherefore hast Thou at all brought this people over Jordan, to deliver us into the hand of the Amorites, to destroy us? Would to God we had been content, and dwelt on the other side Jordan? O Lord, what shall I say, when Israel turneth their backs before their enemies!
For the Canaanites and all the inhabitants of the land shall hear of it, and shall environ us round, and cut off our name from the earth: and what wilt Thou do unto Thy great name?"
Josh. 7:6-9

God wouldn't hear their prayers until they removed to the sin in the camp.

And the Lord said unto Joshua,

> *Get thee up; wherefore liest thou thus upon thy face? Israel hath sinned, and they have also transgressed My Covenant which I commanded them:*
> *for they have even taken of the accursed thing, and have also stolen, and dissembled also, and they have put it even among their own stuff.*
> *Therefore the children of Israel could not stand before their enemies, but turned their backs before their enemies, because they were accursed* (remember that Balaam could not curse them because as long as they were in obedience to God and under forgiveness, they were blessed and could not be cursed Num. 22:12): *neither will I be with you any more, except ye destroy the accursed from among you. Up, sanctify the people, and say, Sanctify yourselves against to morrow: for thus saith the Lord God of Israel, There is an accursed thing in the midst of thee, O Israel: thou canst not stand before thine enemies, until ye take away the accursed thing from among ...*"
> Josh. 7:10-15

When there are cursed things in our life, God's presence is withdrawn. We need to ask God what is in our lives that is keeping Him from blessing us and get rid of those things that are cursed.

Gibeonites

When the Gibeonites fooled the Israelites and said they lived a long way away they should have asked for God to help them but they didn't ask God to guide them in their decision. This is a lesson for us today that we should pray about every decision that we make and seek God's help.

"… and asked not counsel at the mouth of the Lord." Josh. 9:14

Joshua commands the sun and moon to stand still!
God speaks
"And the Lord said unto Joshua,

> *Fear them not: for I have delivered them into thine hand; there shall not a man of them stand before thee."* Josh. 10:8

God answers
"The Lord cast down great stones from heaven upon them unto Azekah, and they died: they were more which died with hailstones than they whom the children of Israel slew with the sword." Josh. 10:11

Joshua speaks
"Then spake Joshua to the Lord in the day when the Lord delivered up the Amorites before the children of Israel, and he said in the sight of Israel, Sun, stand thou still, upon Gibeon; and thou, Moon, in the valley of Ajalon." Josh. 10:12

God answers
"And the sun stood still, and the moon stayed, until the people had avenged themselves upon their enemies… and there was no day like that before it or after it, that the Lord hearkened unto the voice of a man: for the Lord fought for Israel." Josh. 10:13-14

Judges

The Israelites' Confession

The Israelites did evil in the eyes of God, and served Baal and Ashtoreth, the gods of the surrounding people. They wanted to be like the people around them. When they would follow other gods, then those people crushed them and oppressed them. That is when the Israelites would cry out to God, and He would deliver them.

First they confessed their sin and then they put away their idols.

"And the children of Israel cried unto the Lord, saying,

> *We have sinned against Thee, both because we have forsaken our God, and also served Baalim.*

And the Lord said unto the children of Israel,

> *Did not I deliver you from* (the surrounding heathen people)… (and they) *did oppress you; and ye cried to Me, and I delivered you out of their hand. Yet ye have forsaken Me, and served other gods: wherefore I will deliver you no more."* Judges 10:10-13

God will not answer us, if we serve other gods.

"Go and cry unto the gods which ye have chosen; let them deliver you in the time of your tribulation.

And the children of Israel said unto the Lord,

> *We have sinned; do Thou unto us whatsoever seemeth good unto Thee; deliver us only, we pray Thee, this day.*

And they put away the strange gods from among them, and served the Lord: and His soul was grieved for the misery of Israel." Judges 10:14-16

"And Jephthah vowed a vow unto the Lord, and said,

> *If Thou shalt without fail deliver the children of Ammon into mine hands, then it shall be, that whatsoever cometh forth of the doors of your house to meet me, when I return in peace from the children of Ammon, shall surely be the Lord's and I will offer it up for a burnt offering.*

> *So Jephthah passed over unto the children of Ammon to fight against them; and the Lord delivered them into his hands."* Judges 11:30-32

Jephthah made a rash vow to God and paid dearly for it. His daughter was the first one to come out of his house and we don't know what happened to her. We should be very careful in making vows, that we don't get ourself into a similar situation.

 Samson

Manoah prays

The angel of the Lord comes to Manoah and his wife.

"And the children of Israel did evil again in the sight of the Lord; and the Lord delivered them into the hand of the Philistines forty years. And there was a certain man …whose name was Manoah; and his wife was barren, and bare not. And the angel of the Lord appeared unto the woman, and said unto her,

> Behold now, thou art barren, and bearest not: but thou shalt conceive, and bear a son. Now therefore beware, I pray thee, and drink not wine nor strong drink, and eat not any unclean thing: for, lo, thou shalt conceive, and bear a son; and no razor shall come on his head: for the child shall be a Nazarite unto God from the womb: and he shall begin to deliver Israel out of the hand of the Philistines.

Then the woman came and told her husband, saying, a man of God came unto me, and His countenance was like the countenance of an angel of God, very terrible: but I asked Him whence He was, neither told He me His name: but He said unto me,

> Behold, thou shalt conceive, and bear a son; and now drink no wine nor strong drink, neither eat any unclean thing: for the child shall be a Nazarite to God from the womb to the day of his death." Judges 13:1-7

Manoah prays to God to teach him

"Then Manoah intreated the Lord, and said, O my Lord,

let the man of God which Thou didst send come again unto us,
and teach us what we shall do unto the child that shall be
born." Judges 13:8

God answers Manoah's prayer.

"And God hearkened to the voice of Manoah; and the angel of God
came again unto the woman as she sat in the field: but Manoah her
husband was not with her. And the woman made haste, and ran, and
shewed her husband, and said unto him, Behold, the man hath appeared
unto me, that came unto me the other day."

And Manoah arose, and went after his wife, and came to the man,
and said unto Him, Art Thou the man that spakest unto the woman?"
"And He said,

I am."

"And Manoah said,

Now let Thy words come to pass.
How shall we order the child, and how shall we do unto him?"

"And the angel of the Lord said unto Manoah,

Of all that I said unto the woman let her beware.
She may not eat of any thing that cometh of the vine,
neither let her drink wine or strong drink, nor eat any unclean
thing: all that I commanded her let her observe."

"And Manoah said unto the angel of the Lord, I pray Thee,

let us detain Thee, until we shall have made ready a kid for Thee."

"And the angel of the Lord said unto Manoah,

Though thou detain Me, I will not eat of thy bread: and if thou wilt offer a burnt offering, thou must offer it unto the Lord."

"For Manoah knew not that He was an angel of the Lord. And Manoah said unto the angel of the Lord,

What is Thy name, that when Thy sayings come to pass we may do Thee honour?"

"And the angel of the Lord said unto him,

Why askest thou thus after My name, seeing it is secret?" ("Wonderful" KJV fn "beyond understanding" NIV fn "glorius" PB #6383 Hebrew "pili or pali = wonderful, incomprehensible")

"So Manoah took a kid with a meat offering, and offered it upon a rock unto the Lord; and the angel did wonderously; and Manoah and his wife looked on. For it came to pass, when the flame went up toward heaven from off the altar, that the angel of the Lord ascended in the flame of the altar. And Manoah and his wife looked on it, and fell on their faces to the ground. But the angel of the Lord did no more appear to Manoah and to his wife. Then Manoah knew that he was an angel of the Lord. And Manoah said unto his wife,

*We shall surely die, **because we have seen God*** (Manoah believed this to be God)." Judges 13:1-22

Samson asks for water

Samson slew 1000 Philistines and is dying of thirst so he asks God to give him water to drink.

"And he was sore athirst and called on the Lord, and said,

> *Thou hast given this great deliverance into the hand of Thy servant: and now shall I die for thirst, and fall into the hand of the uncircumcised?"* Judges 15:18

God answers

"But God clave an hollow place that was in the jaw, and there came water thereout; and when he had drunk, his spirit came again, and he revived..." Judges 15:19

Samson prays to avenge his eyes

Samson was betrayed by Delilah, and because of that betrayal he lost his strength and his eyes. Even though God forgives us where we go wrong, there are still sometimes devastating consequences. I'm sure that Samson wished with all his heart he had never gotten mixed up in that mess.

"And Samson called unto the Lord, and said,

> *O Lord God, remember me, I pray Thee, and strengthen me, I pray Thee, only this once, O God, that I may be at once avenged of the Philistines for my two eyes."* Judges 16:28

God answers

"And Samson took hold of the two middle pillars upon which the

house stood, and on which it was borne up, of the one with his right hand, and of the other with his left.

Samson's last prayer before he died

"And Samson said,

Let me die with the Philistines."

God answers

"And he bowed himself with all his might; and the house fell upon the lords, and upon all the people that were therein. So the dead which he slew at his death were more than they which he slew in his life. Then his brethren and all the house of his father came down, and took him, and brought him up, and buried him between Zorah and Eshtaol in the burying place of Manoah his father, and he judged Israel twenty years."
Judges 16:28-31

1 & 2 Samuel

Samuel

Hannah's prayer for a son is expressed in Samuel. She not only prayed for a child, but for a man child — a baby boy and God heard and answered!

"*So Hannah rose up after they had eaten in Shiloh, and after they had drunk. Now Eli the priest sat upon a seat by a post of the temple of the Lord. And she was in bitterness of soul, and prayed unto the Lord, and wept sore. And she vowed a vow, and said,*

> *O Lord of hosts,*
> *if Thou wilt indeed look on the affliction of Thine handmaid,*
> *and remember me, and not forget Thine handmaid, but wilt*
> *give unto Thine handmaid a man child, then I will give him*
> *unto the Lord all the days of his life, and there shall no razor*
> *come upon his head.*

And it came to pass, as she continued praying before the Lord, that Eli marked her mouth. Now Hannah, she spake in her heart; only her lips moved, but her voice was not heard...

Eli speaks faith to her
Then Eli answered and said, Go in peace: and the God of Israel grant thee thy petition that thou hast asked of Him.

Answer to her prayer
"*... and the Lord remembered her. Wherefore it came to pass, when the time was come about after Hannah had conceived, that she bare a son, and called his name Samuel, saying, Because I have asked him*

of the Lord... For this child I prayed; and the Lord hath given me my petition which I asked of Him: Therefore also I have lent him to the Lord; as long as he liveth he shall be lent to the Lord. And she worshiped the Lord there." I Sam. 1:9-17,20,27,28

Hannah's prayer of thanks

Hannah did not forget to thank God for what He had done. "And Hannah prayed, and said,

My heart rejoiceth in the Lord, mine horn (symbolizes strength) is exalted in the Lord: my mouth is enlarged over mine enemies; because I rejoice in Thy salvation.
There is none holy as the Lord: for there is none beside Thee neither is there any rock like our God.
Talk no more so exceeding proudly; let not arrogancy come out of your mouth: for the Lord is a God of knowledge, and by Him actions are weighed.
The bows of the mighty men are broken, and they that stumbled are girded with strength.
They that were full have hired out themselves for bread; and they that were hungry ceased: so that the barren hath born seven; and she that hath many children is waxed feeble.
The Lord killeth, and maketh alive: He bringeth down to the grave, and bringeth up.
The Lord maketh poor, and maketh rich: He bringeth low, and lifteth up.
He raiseth up the poor out of the dust, and lifteth up the beggar from the dunghill, to set them among princes, and to make them inherit the throne of glory: for the pillars of the earth are the Lord's, and He hath set the world upon them.
He will keep the feet of His saints, and the wicked shall be

silent in darkness; for by strength shall no man prevail. The adversaries of the Lord shall be broken to pieces; out of heaven shall He thunder upon them: the Lord shall judge the ends of the earth; and He shall give strength unto His king, and exalt the horn of His anointed." I Sam. 2:1-10

God answered her prayer

"And the Lord visited Hannah, so that she conceived, and bare three sons and two daughters. And the child Samuel grew before the Lord." I Sam. 2:21

Hannah kept her vow and gave Samuel to the Lord; he became a mighty man of God.

Samuel's prayer for deliverance from Philistines

The Ark was at Kirjathjearim for 20 years and all the house of Israel *"mourned and sought after"* God. And Samuel said to the people,

"If ye do return unto the Lord with all your hearts, then put away the strange gods and Ashtaroth from among you, and prepare your hearts unto the Lord, and serve Him only: and He will deliver you out of the hand of the Philistines. Then the children of Israel did put away Baalim and Ashtaroth, and served the Lord only.

*And Samuel said, Gather all Israel to Mizpeh, and I will pray for you unto the Lord. And they gathered together to Mizpeh, and drew water, and poured it out before the Lord, and fasted on that day and said there, We have sinned against the Lord... And the children of Israel said to Samuel, Cease not to cry unto the Lord our God for us, that He will save us out of the hand of the Philistines. And Samuel took a sucking lamb, and offered it for a burnt offering wholly unto the Lord: and **Samuel cried unto the Lord** for Israel. . ."* I Sam. 8:6

God answers

"...And the Lord heard him. And as Samuel was offering up the burnt offering, the Philistines drew near to battle against Israel: but the Lord thundred with a great thunder on that day upon the Philistines, and discomfited them; and they were smitten before Israel." I Sam. 7:9-10

Israel asks for a king

When Samuel grew up, he did the same thing that Eli had done; which was let his sons go undisciplined. The people loved Samuel and knew that he was honest but they didn't trust his sons because they had, "...turned aside after lucre, and took bribes, and perverted judgment." I Sam. 8:3

They wanted Samuel to give them a king like the nations around them. "But the thing displeased Samuel, when they said, Give us a king to judge us. And Samuel prayed unto the Lord." I Sam. 8:6

God answers Samuel

"And the Lord said unto Samuel,

Hearken unto the voice of the people in all that they say unto thee: for they have not rejected thee, but they have rejected Me, that I should not reign over them.
According to all the works which they have done since the day that I brought them up out of Egypt even unto this day, wherewith they have forsaken Me, and served other gods, so do they also unto thee.
Now therefore hearken unto their voice; howbeit yet protest solemnly unto them, and shew them the manner of the king that shall reign over them.

And Samuel told all the words of the Lord unto the people that asked of him a king." I Sam. 8:7-10

They confessed their sin

Before Samuel died he chastised the people for their sins.
"And they cried unto the Lord, and said,

> *We have sinned, because we have forsaken the Lord,*
> *and have served Baalim and Ashtaroth; but now deliver us out*
> *of the hand of our enemies, and we will serve Thee."*
>
> I Sam. 12:10

God gave the people a king

Samuel told the people:

"If ye will fear the Lord, and serve Him, and obey His voice, and not rebel against the Commandment of the Lord, then shall both ye and also the king that reigneth over you continue following the Lord your God: but if ye will not obey the voice of the Lord, but rebel against the Commandment of the Lord, then shall the hand of the Lord be against you, as it was against your fathers. Now therefore stand and see this great thing, which the Lord will do before your eyes. Is it not wheat harvest to day? I will call unto the Lord, and He shall send thunder and rain; that ye may perceive and see that your wickedness is great, which ye have done in the sight of the Lord, in asking you a king. So Samuel called unto the Lord;

God answers

". . .and the Lord sent thunder and rain that day: and all the people greatly feared the Lord and Samuel. And all the people said unto Samuel, Pray for thy servants unto the Lord thy God, that we die not: for we have added unto all our sins this evil, to ask us a king. And Samuel said unto the people Fear not: ye have done all this wickedness: yet turn not aside from following the Lord, but serve the Lord with all your heart; and turn ye not aside: for then should ye go after vain things,

*which cannot profit nor deliver; for they are vain. For the Lord will not forsake His people for His great name's sake: because it hath pleased the Lord to make you His people. Moreover as for me, God forbid that I should sin against the Lord in **ceasing to pray for you**: but I will teach you the good and the right way. Only fear the Lord, and serve Him in truth with all your heart: for consider how great things He hath done for you. But if ye shall still do wickedly, ye shall be consumed, both ye and your king."* I Sam. 12:18-25

Notice that he considered it a sin to stopping praying for them.

David

There are more prayers of David recorded in the Bible than anyone else.

David's Prayer

"Therefore David inquired of the Lord, saying,

Shall I go and smite these Philistines?" I Sam. 23:2

God answers

And the Lord said unto David,

Go, and smite the Philistines..." I Sam. 23:2

Abigail pleads with David

Abigail can be used as an example of how to approach an angry God. David was going to avenge himself on Nabal because he wouldn't help him by feeding David and his men, after he had protected him. We can learn a lot about how to approach God by the way that Abigail pleaded with David. Abigail hurriedly gathered up a gift of food for David and rode out to meet him.

"Then Abigail made haste, and took two hundred loaves (and other food items) *...and David and his men came down against her; and she met them. Now David had said, Surely in vain have I kept all that this fellow hath in the wilderness, so that nothing was missed of all that pertained unto him: and he hath requited me evil for good. So and more also do God unto the enemies of David, if I leave of all that pertain to him by the morning light any* (male persons)*... And when Abigail saw*

David, she hasted, and lighted off the (donkey) *and fell before David on her face, and bowed herself to the ground, and fell at his feet, and said, Upon me, my lord, upon me let this iniquity be: and let thine handmaid, I pray thee, Speak in thine audience, and hear the words of thine handmaid.*

Let not my lord, I pray thee, regard this man of Belial, even Nabal: for as his name is, so is he; Nabal is his name, and folly is with him: but I thine handmaid saw not the young men of my lord, whom thou didst send. Now therefore, my lord, as the Lord liveth, and as thy soul liveth, seeing the Lord hath withholden thee from coming to shed blood, and from avenging thyself with thine own hand, now let thine enemies, and they that seek evil to my lord, be as Nabal. And now this blessing which thine handmaid hath brought unto my lord, let it even be given unto the young men that follow my lord, I pray thee, Forgive the trespass of thine handmaid: for the Lord will certainly make my lord a sure house; because my lord fighteth the battles of the Lord, and evil hath not been found in thee all thy days. Yet a man is risen to pursue thee, and to seek thy soul: but the soul of my lord shall be bound in the bundle of life with the Lord thy God; and the souls of thine enemies, them shall he sling out, as out of the middle of a sling. And it shall come to pass, when the Lord shall have done to my lord according to all the good that he hath spoken concerning thee, and shall have appointed thee ruler over Israel; that this shall be no grief unto thee, nor offence of heart unto my lord, either that thou hast shed blood causeless, or that my lord hath avenged himself: but when the Lord shall have dealt well with my lord, then remember thine handmaid." I Sam. 25:18-24

Blessing

And David said to Abigail,

Blessed be the Lord God of Israel, which sent thee this day to meet me: and blessed be thy advice, and blessed be thou, which hast kept me this day from coming to shed blood, and from avenging myself with mine own hand. For in very deed, as the Lord God of Israel liveth, which hath kept me back from hurting thee, except thou hadst hasted and come to meet me, surely there had not been left unto Nabal by the morning light any (male person).

So David received of her hand that which she had brought him, and said unto her, Go up in peace to thine house; see, I have hearkened to thy voice, and have accepted thy person... And when David heard that Nabal was dead, he said, Blessed be the Lord, that hath pleaded the cause of my reproach from the hand of Nabal, and hath kept His servant from evil: for the Lord hath returned the wickedness of Nabal upon his own head. And David sent and communed with Abigail, to take her to him to wife." I Sam. 25:39

God blessed Abigail later with a son named Chileab from David (II Sam. 3:3).

David's prayer

"And it came to pass after this, that David inquired of the Lord, saying,

Shall I go up into any of the cities of Judah?

And the Lord said unto him,

Go up,

And David said,

Whither shall I go up?

And He said,

unto Hebron." II Sam. 2:1
David eventually becomes king.

David's prayer

"Then went king David in, and sat before the Lord, and he said,

Who am I, O Lord God?
And what is my house, that Thou hast brought me hitherto?
And this was yet a small thing in Thy sight, O Lord God; but
Thou hast spoken also of Thy servant's house for a great while
to come.
And is this the manner of man, O Lord God?
And what can David say more unto Thee? For Thou, Lord
God, knowest Thy servant. For Thy word's sake, and according
to Thine own heart, hast Thou done all these great things, to
make Thy servant know them. Wherefore Thou art great,
O Lord God: for there is none like Thee, neither is there any
God beside Thee, according to all that we have heard with
our ears. And what one nation in the earth is like Thy people,
even like Israel, whom God went to redeem for a people to
Himself, and to make Him a name, and to do for You great
things and terrible, for Thy land, before Thy people, which
Thou redeemedst to Thee from Egypt, from the nations and
their gods?
For Thou hast confirmed to Thyself Thy people Israel to be a
people unto Thee for ever: and Thou, Lord, art become their
God. And now, O Lord God, the word that Thou hast spoken
concerning Thy servant, and concerning His house, establish
it for ever, and do as Thou hast said. And let Thy name be
magnified for ever, saying,
The Lord of hosts, is the God over Israel: and let the house of

Thy servant David be established before Thee.
For Thou, O Lord of hosts, God of Israel, hast revealed to Thy
servant, saying, I will build Thee an house: therefore hath Thy
servant found in his heart to pray this prayer unto Thee.
And now, O Lord God, Thou art that God, and Thy words be
true, and Thou hast promised this goodness unto Thy servant:
Therefore now let it please Thee to bless the house of Thy
servant, that it may continue for ever before Thee: for Thou,O
Lord God, hast spoken it: and with Thy blessing let the house
of Thy servant be blessed for ever." II Sam. 7:18-29

David's prayer
David prays that God will heal his baby son. David sinned by killing
Uriah and taking Bathsheba; and their baby died as a result of his sin.
"David therefore besought God for the child; and David fasted, and
went in, and lay all night upon the earth." II Sam. 12:16
This was one of the rare times that God did not answer this prayer.

David's prayer
David's son Absalom tried to take the kingdom away from his father
David.
  "And one told David, saying, Ahithophel is among the conspirators
with Absalom, And David said,

O Lord,
I pray thee, turn the counsel of Ahithophel into foolishness."
II Sam. 15:31

1 & 2 Kings

Solomon

God tells Solomon to ask for anything

Solomon is the 2ⁿᵈ son of David and Bathsheba.

"And Solomon loved the Lord, walking in the statutes of David his father, only he sacrificed and burnt incense in high places. And the king went to Gibeon to sacrifice there; for that was the great high place: a thousand burnt offerings did Solomon offer upon that altar. In Gibeon the Lord appeared to Solomon in a dream by night: and God said,

Ask what I shall give thee." I Kings 3:3-5

Solomon's prayer pleases God (3:10)

"And Solomon said,

Thou hast shewed unto Thy servant David my father great mercy, according as he walked before Thee in truth, and in righteousness, and in uprightness of heart with Thee; and Thou hast kept for him this great kindness, that Thou hast given him a son to sit on his throne, as it is this day. And now, O Lord my God, Thou hast made Thy servant king instead of David my father: and I am but a little child: I know not how to go out or come in. And Thy servant is in the midst of Thy people which Thou hast chosen, a great people, that cannot be numbered nor counted for multitude. Give therefore Thy servant an understanding heart to judge Thy people, that I may discern between good and bad: for who is able to judge this Thy so great a people?

And the speech pleased the Lord, that Solomon had asked this thing."
I Kings 3:6-10

God answers

"And God said unto him,

> *Because thou hast asked this thing, and hast not asked for thyself long life; neither hast asked riches for thyself, nor hast asked the life of thine enemies; but hast asked for thyself understanding to discern judgment; behold, I have done according to thy words: lo, I have given thee a wise and an understanding heart; so that there was none like thee before thee, neither after thee shall any arise like unto thee.*
> *And I have also given thee that which thou hast not asked, both riches, and honour: so that there shall not be any among the kings like unto thee all thy days. And if thou wilt walk in My ways, to keep My statutes and My Commandments, as thy father David did walk, then I will lengthen thy days.*

And Solomon awoke; and, behold, it was a dream. And he came to Jerusalem, and stood before the ark of the covenant of the Lord, and offered up burnt offerings, and offered peace offerings, and made a feast to all his servants." I Kings 3:11-15

"Then spake Solomon,

> *the Lord said that he would dwell in the thick darkness. I have surely built Thee an house to dwell in, a settled place for Thee to abide in for ever."* I Kings 8:12-13

"Blessed be the Lord God of Israel, which spake with His

88

mouth unto David my father, and hath with His hand fulfilled
it, saying, since the day that I brought forth My people
Israel out of Egypt, I chose no city out of all the tribes of Israel
to build an house, that My name might be therein; but I chose
David to be over My people Israel." I Kings 8:15-16

Solomon asks God to hear their prayers

In the Old Testament, they prayed facing the temple in Jerusalem; today our prayers are directed toward God in Heaven, the New Jerusalem.

"And he said, Lord God of Israel,

there is no God like Thee, in heaven above, or on earth
beneath,
who keepest Covenant and mercy with Thy servants that walk
before Thee with all their heart:
who hast kept with Thy servant David my father that Thou
promisedst him:
then spakest also with Thy mouth, and hast fulfilled it with
Thine hands, as it is this day. Therefore now, Lord God of
Israel, keep with Thy servant David my father that Thou
promisedst him, saying, There shall not fail Thee a man in
My sight to sit on the throne of Israel; so that Thy children
take heed to their way, that they walk before Me as thou hast
walked before me. And now, O God of Israel, let Thy word, I
pray Thee, be verified, which Thou spakest unto Thy servant
David my father. But will God indeed dwell on the earth?
Behold, the heaven and heaven of heavens cannot contain
Thee;
how much less this house that I have builded? Yet have Thou

respect unto the prayer of Thy servant, and to his supplication,
O Lord my God, to hearken unto the cry and to the prayer,
which Thy servant prayeth before Thee to day: That Thine eyes
may
be open toward this house night and day, even toward the
place of which Thou hast said, My name shall be there: that
Thou mayest hearken unto the prayer which Thy servant
shall make toward this place. And hearken Thou to the
supplication of Thy servant,
and of Thy people Israel, when they shall pray toward this
place: and hear Thou in heaven Thy dwelling place: and when
Thou hearest, forgive (Rom.3:23;I Jn.1:8).
If any man trespass against his neighbour, and an oath be laid
upon him to cause him to swear, and the oath come before
Thine altar in this house: then hear Thou in heaven, and do,
and judge Thy servants, condemning the wicked, to bring his
way upon his head;
and justifying the righteous, to give him according to his
righteousness. When Thy people Israel be smitten down
before the enemy, because they have sinned against Thee, and
shall turn again to Thee, and confess Thy name, and pray,
and make supplication unto Thee in this house: then hear
Thou in heaven, and forgive the sin of Thy people Israel, and
bring them again unto the land which Thou gavest unto their
fathers. When heaven I shut up, and there is no rain, because
they have sinned against Thee; if they pray toward this place,
and confess Thy name, and turn from their sin, when Thou
afflictest them: then hear Thou in heaven, and forgive the sin
of Thy servants,
and of Thy people Israel, that Thou teach them the good way
wherein they should walk, and give rain upon Thy land, which

Thou hast given to Thy people for an inheritance. If there be
in the land famine, if there be pestilence, blasting, mildew,
locust, or if there be caterpillar;
if their enemy besiege them in the land of their cities;
whatsoever plague, whatsoever sickness there be; what prayer
and supplication soever be made by any man, or by all Thy
people Israel,
which shall know every man the plague of his own heart, and
spread forth his hands toward this house: then hear Thou in
heaven Thy dwelling place, and forgive, and do, and give to
every man
according to his ways, whose heart Thou knowest; (for Thou,
even Thou only, knowest the hearts of all the children of men);
that they may fear Thee all the days that they live in the land
which Thou gavest unto our fathers. Moreover concerning
a stranger, that is not of Thy people Israel, but cometh out of
a far country for Thy name's sake; (for they shall hear of Thy
great name,
and of Thy strong hand, and of Thy stretched out arm); when
He shall come and pray toward this house; Hear Thou in
heaven Thy dwelling place, and do according to all that the
stranger calleth to thee for: that all people of the earth may
know Thy name, to fear Thee, as do Thy people Israel; and
that they may know that this house, which I have builded, is
called by Thy name. If Thy people go out to battle against their
enemy, whithersoever Thou shalt send them,
and shall pray unto the Lord toward the city which Thou hast
chosen, and toward the house that I have built for Thy name:
then hear Thou in heaven their prayer and their supplication,
and maintain their cause. If they sin against Thee, (for there is
no man that sinneth not),

and Thou be angry with them, and deliver them to the enemy,
so that they carry them away captives unto the land of the
enemy, far or near; yet if they shall bethink themselves in the
land whither they were carried captives, and repent, and make
supplication unto Thee in the land of them that carried them
captives, saying, We have sinned, and have done perversely,
we have committed wickedness; and so return unto Thee with
all their heart, and with all their soul, in the land of their
enemies, which led them away captive, and pray unto Thee
toward their land, which Thou gavest unto their fathers, the
city which Thou hast chosen, and the house which I have
built for Thy name; then hear Thou their prayer and their
supplication in heaven Thy dwelling place, and maintain their
cause, and forgive Thy people
that have sinned against Thee, and all their transgressions
wherein they have transgressed against Thee, and give them
compassion before them who carried them captive, that they
may have compassion on them: for they be Thy people, and
Thine inheritance, which
Thou broughtest forth out of Egypt, from the midst of the
furnace of iron: that Thine eyes may be open unto the
supplication of Thy servant, and unto the supplication of
Thy people Israel,
to hearken unto them in all that they call for unto Thee.
For Thou didst separate them from among all the people
of the earth, to be Thine inheritance, as Thou spakest by
the hand of Moses Thy servant, when Thou broughtest our
fathers out of Egypt,
O Lord God.

And it was so, that when Solomon had made an end of **praying all
this prayer and supplication** unto the Lord, he arose from before the

altar of the Lord, from kneeling on his knees with his hands spread up to heaven. And he stood, and blessed all the congregation of Israel with a loud voice, saying, Blessed be the Lord, that hath given rest unto His people Israel, according to all that He promised: there hath not failed one word of all His good promise, which He promised by the hand of Moses His servant. The Lord our God be with us, as He was with our fathers: let Him not leave us, nor forsake us: that He may incline our hearts unto Him, to walk in all His ways, and to keep His Commandments, and His statues, and His judgments, which He commanded our fathers. And let these my words, wherewith I have made supplication before the Lord, be nigh unto the Lord our God day and night, that He maintain the cause of His servant, and the cause of His people Israel at all times, as the matter shall require: that all the people of the earth may know that the Lord is God, and that there is none else. Let your heart therefore be perfect with the Lord our God, to walk in His statues, and to keep His Commandments, as at this day." I Kings 8:23-61

2nd time God appeared to Solomon
God speaks
"...the Lord appeared to Solomon the second time, as He had appeared unto him at Gibeon. And the Lord said unto him,

I have heard thy prayer and thy supplication,
that thou hast made before Me: I have hallowed this house,
which thou hast built, to put My name there for ever;
and Mine eyes and Mine heart shall be there perpetually.
And if Thou wilt walk before Me, as David thy father walked,
in integrity of heart, and in uprightness, to do according to all
that I have commanded thee, and wilt keep My statues and
My judgments;
then I will establish the throne of thy kingdom upon Israel for

ever, as I promised to David thy father, saying,
There shall not fail thee a man upon the throne of Israel.
But if ye shall at all turn from following Me, you or your
children, and will not keep My Commandments and My
statues which I have set before you, but go and serve other
gods, and worship them:
then will I cut off Israel out of the land which I have given
them; and this house, which I have hallowed for My name,
will I cast out of My sight; and Israel shall be a proverb and
a byword among all people: and at this house, which is high,
every one that passeth by it shall be astonished, and shall hiss;
and they shall say, Why hath the Lord done thus unto this
land, and to this house?
And they shall answer, Because they forsook the Lord their
God, who brought forth their fathers out of the land of Egypt,
and have taken hold upon other gods, and have worshiped
them, and served them: therefore hath the Lord brought upon
them all this evil." I Kings 9:2-9

Solomon's kingdom became the high point of all the kings of Israel. It was everything it was meant to be – a little taste of what it will be like on the New Earth. But eventually Solomon married heathen wives, which he was told not do. Unfortunately, they did turn his heart away from God, just as he was told they would.

"The Lord had clearly instructed His people not to intermarry with those nations, because the women they married would lead them to worship their gods. Yet Solomon insisted on loving them anyway." I Kings 11:2 LB

Solomon had **700** wives and **300** concubines and they did lead his heart away from the God.

"Thus, Solomon did what was evil in the Lord's sight; he refused to

follow the Lord completely, as his father, David, had done." I Kings 11:6 LB

God was angry with Solomon

"And the Lord was angry with Solomon, because his heart was turned from the Lord God of Israel, which had appeared unto him twice, and had commanded him concerning this thing, that he should not go after other gods: but he kept not that which the Lord commanded. Wherefore the Lord said unto Solomon, Forasmuch as this is done of thee, and thou hast not kept my Covenant and My statutes, which I have commanded thee, I will surely rend the kingdom from thee, and will give it to thy servant." I Kings 11:9-11

God promised to split the kingdom. He did not do it in Solomon's day, but shortly after his son became king. God always kept a descendant of David on the throne in Jerusalem for David's sake; just as He promised He would do.

King Jeroboam

Israel after the split

A prophet prophesied that Josiah would be born and would get rid of the wicked priests. King Jeroboam tried to stop him, and his hand shriveled up. He had to ask the prophet to pray for him.

Prayer to restore Jeroboam's hand

Jeroboam was angry at the prophet and wanted to kill him, but God made his hand turn to leprosy.

"And it came to pass, when king Jeroboam heard the saying of the man of God, which had cried against the altar in Bethel, that he put forth his hand from the altar, saying, Lay hold on him. And his hand, which he put forth against him, dried up, so that he could not pull it in again to him. The altar also was rent, and the ashes poured out from the altar, according to the sign which the man of God had given by the word of the Lord.

And the king answered and said unto the man of God, **Intreat** *now the face of the Lord, thy God, and* **pray** *for me, that my hand may be restored me again.*

And the man of God besought the Lord, I Kings 13:4-6

God Answers

and the king's hand was restored him again, and became as it was before." I Kings 13:4-6

Elijah

Prayer to bring boy back to life

"And he cried unto the Lord, and said,

O Lord my God, hast Thou also brought evil upon the widow with whom I sojourn, by slaying her son?

And he stretched himself upon the child three times, and cried unto the Lord, and said,

O Lord my God, I pray Thee let this child's soul come into him again.

God answers

And the Lord heard the voice of Elijah; and the soul of the child came into him again, and he revived." I Kings 17:20-22

Elijah on Mt. Carmel

Israel was worshiping Baal, and Elijah prayed that there would be no rain for 3 ½ years. At the end of the 3 ½ years, Elijah had them all meet him on Mt. Carmel and see whose God would answer by fire.

At the evening sacrifice Elijah confronts the people:

"You have forsaken the Commandments of God and followed Baal." I Kings 18:18

When we forsake God's Commandments, we forsake God.

"And Elijah came unto all the people, and said, How long halt ye

between two opinions? If the Lord be God, follow Him: but if Baal, then follow him. And the people answered him not a word.

... call on the name of your gods, and I will call on the name of the Lord: and the God that answereth by fire, let Him be God. And all the people answered and said, It is well spoken..." I Kings 18:21, 24

They pray to Baal

"And they took the bullock which was given them, and they dressed it, and called on the name of Baal from morning even until noon, saying

O Baal, hear us, But there was no voice, nor any that answered, and they leaped upon the altar which was made. And it came to pass at noon, that Elijah mocked them, and said, Cry aloud: for he is a god; either he is talking, or he is pursuing, or he is in a journey, or peradventure he sleepeth, and must be awaked. And they cried loud, and cut themselves after their manner with knives and lancets... And it came to pass, when midday was past, and they prophesied until the time of the offering of the evening sacrifice, that there was neither voice, nor any to answer, nor any that regarded. And Elijah said unto all the people, Come near unto me. And all the people came near unto him. And he repaired the altar of the Lord that was broken down. And Elijah took twelve stones, according to the number of the tribes of the sons of Jacob, unto whom the word of the Lord came, saying,

Israel shall be thy name: and with the stones he built an altar in the name of the Lord: and he made a trench about the altar, as great as would contain two measures of seed. And he put the wood in order, and cut the bullock in pieces, and laid him on the wood, and said, Fill four barrels with water, and pour it on the burnt sacrifice, and on the wood. And he said, Do it the second time. And they did it the second time. And he said,

Do it the third time. And they did it the third time. And the water ran round about the altar; and he filled the trench also with water. And *it came to pass at the time of the offering of the evening sacrifice, that Elijah the prophet came near. . ."* I Kings 18:26-36

Elijah's prayer

"... and said,
Lord God of Abraham, Isaac and Israel,
let it be known this day that Thou art God in Israel, and that
I am Thy servant, and that I have done all these things at Thy
word.
Hear me, O Lord, hear me, that this people may know that
Thou art the Lord God, and that Thou hast turned their heart
back again." I Kings 18:36-37

God answers

"Then the fire of the Lord fell, and consumed the burnt sacrifice, and the wood, and the stones, and the dust, and licked up the water that was in the trench. And when all the people saw it, they fell on their faces: and they said, The Lord, He is the God; the Lord, He is the God." I Kings 18:26-39

Elijah told his servant to go and look seven times toward the sea, and the seventh time he saw a small cloud the size of a man's hand.

"And Elijah said unto Ahab, Get thee up, eat and drink; for there is a sound of abundance of rain. So Ahab went up to eat and to drink. And Elijah went up to the top of Carmel; and he cast himself down upon the earth, and put his face between his knees, and said to his servant, Go up now, look toward the sea. And he went up, and looked, and said, There is nothing. And he said, Go again seven times (The number of the seven-fold Holy Spirit). I Kings 18:41-43

God answers

Elijah prayed seven times.

And it came to pass at the seventh time, that he said, Behold, there ariseth a little cloud out of the sea, like a man's hand. And he said, Go up, say unto Ahab, Prepare thy chariot, and get thee down, that the rain stop thee not.

And it came to pass in the mean while, that the heaven was black with clouds and wind, and there was a great rain. And Ahab rode, and went to Jezreel. And the hand of the Lord was on Elijah; and he girded up his loins, and ran before Ahab to the entrance of Jezreel." I Kings 18:44-45

Promise:

Elijah is like us.

"... the effectual fervent prayer of a righteous man availeth much. Elias was a man subject to like passions as we are, and he prayed earnestly that it might not rain: and it rained not on the earth by the space of three years and six months. And he prayed again, and the heaven gave rain, and the earth brought forth her fruit." Jms.. 5:16-17

Even though Elijah wasn't perfect, God still answered his prayers.

Elijah runs from Jezebel

"...he himself went a day's journey into the wilderness, and came and sat down under a juniper tree: and he requested for himself that his might die; and said,

> *It is enough; now, O Lord, take away my life; for I am not better than my fathers.* I Kings 19:4

An angel appears to Elijah

"And as he lay and slept under a Juniper tree, behold, then an angel touched him, and said unto him, Arise and eat. And he looked, and, behold, there was a cake baken on the coals, and a cruse of water at his head. And he did eat and drink, and laid him down again. And the

angel of the Lord came again the second time, and touched him, and said,

Arise and eat; because the journey is too great for thee.

And he arose, and did eat and drink, and went in the strength of that meat forty days and forty nights unto Horeb the mount of God (the same place that God gave the ten Commandments Ex. 3:1;Deut.1:2) *And he came thither unto a cave, and lodged there; and, behold, the word of the Lord came to him, and He said unto him. . ."* I Kings 19:5-9

God speaks
"What doest thou here, Elijah?" I Kings 19:9

Elijah speaks
"And he said,

I have been very jealous for the Lord God of hosts: for the children of Israel have forsaken Thy covenant, thrown down Thine altars, and slain Thy prophets with the sword; and I, even I only, am left: and they seek my life, to take it away." I Kings 19:10

God speaks
"And He said,

Go forth, and stand upon the mount before the Lord."

"And, behold, the Lord passed by, and a great and strong wind rent the mountains, and brake in pieces the rocks before the Lord (We see here that Elijah is actually talking to God); *but the Lord was not in the*

wind: and after the wind an earthquake; but the Lord was not in the earthquake: and after the earthquake a fire; but the Lord was not in the fire: and after the fire a still small voice. And it was so, when Elijah heard it, that he wrapped his face in his mantle, and went out, and stood in the entering in of the cave." I Kings 19:11-13

God speaks
"And, behold, there came a voice unto him, and said,

> *What doest thou here, Elijah?"* I Kings 19:13

Elijah speaks
"and he said,

> *I have been very jealous for the Lord God of hosts: because the children of Israel have forsaken The Covenant, thrown down Thine altars, and slain Thy prophets with the sword; and I, even I only; am left; and they seek my life to take it away."* I Kings 19:13-14

God speaks
"And the Lord said unto him,

> *Go, return on thy way to the wilderness of Damascus: and when thou cometh, anoint Hazael to be king over Syria: and Jehu the son of Nimshi shalt thou anoint to be king over Israel: and Elisha ...shalt thou anoint to be prophet in thy room. And it shall come to pass, that him that escapeth the sword of Hazael shalt Jehu slay: and him that escapeth from the sword of Jehu shall Elisha slay.*
> *Yet I have left Me seven thousand in Israel, all the knees which*

have not bowed unto Baal, and every mouth which hath not
kissed him." I Kings 19:15-18

King Ahaziah

King Ahaziah fails to seek God, fell through a lattice in his upper room, and was very sick. He inquired of Baalzebub the god of Ekron instead of the God of his fathers.

"But the angel of the Lord said to Elijah the Tishbite,

> *Arise, go up to meet the messengers of the king of Samaria, and say unto them, Is it not because there is not a God in Israel, that ye go to inquire of Baalzebub the god of Ekron?*

Now therefore thus saith the Lord,

> *Thou shalt not come down from that bed on which thou art gone up, but shalt surely die.*

And Elijah departed." II Kings 1:1-4

Elisha

Elisha prays for a double portion of the Holy Spirit

Elisha asks Elijah but it is God who must answer this prayer.

"And it came to pass, when they were gone over, that Elijah said unto Elisha, Ask what I shall do for thee, before I be taken away from thee. And Elisha said, I pray thee, let a double portion of thy Spirit be upon me. And he said, Thou hast asked a hard thing: nevertheless, if thou see me when I am taken from thee, it shall be so unto thee **(from God)**; *but if not, it shall not be so. And it came to pass, as they still went on, and talked, that, behold, there appeared a chariot of fire, and horses of fire, and parted them both asunder; and Elijah went up by a whirlwind into heaven. And Elisha saw it, and he cried, My father, my father, the chariot of Israel, and the horsemen thereof. And he saw him no more: and he took hold of his own clothes, and rent them in two pieces."*

II Kings 2:9-12

God Answers

Elisha saw Elijah go to Heaven, the sign that he would receive what he asked for and Elijah's mantle fell down from the chariot and Elisha received the double portion of the Holy Spirit.

"He took up also the mantle of Elijah that fell from him, and went back, and stood by the bank of Jordan; and he took the mantle of Elijah that fell from him, and smote the waters, and said. . ." II Kings 2:13-14

Elisha speaks

"Where is the Lord God of Elijah?

And when he also had smitten the waters, they parted hither and thither: and Elisha went over. And when the sons of the prophets which were to view at Jericho saw him, they said, The Spirit of Elijah doth rest on Elisha." II Kings 2:14-15

Jehoshaphat seeks a miracle from God

"But Jehoshaphat said, Is there not here a prophet of the Lord, that we may inquire of the Lord by him? And one of the king of Israel's servants answered and said, Here is Elisha the son of Shaphat, which poured water on the hands of Elijah. And Jehoshaphat said, The Word of the Lord is with him." II Kings 3:11-12

"And Elisha said…But now bring me a minstrel. And it came to pass, when the minstrel played, that the hand of the Lord came upon him.
And he said, Thus saith the Lord, Make this valley full of ditches.
For thus saith the Lord,
Ye shall not see wind, neither shall ye see rain; yet that valley shall be filled with water, that ye may drink, both ye, and your cattle, and your beasts. And this is but a light thing in the sight of the Lord: He will deliver the Moabites also into your hand. And ye shall smite every fenced city and every choice city, and shall fell every good tree, and stop all wells of water, and mar every good piece of land with stones." II Kings 3:14-19

God Answers

"And it came to pass in the morning, when the meat offering was offered, that, behold, there came water by the way of Edom, and the country was filled with water. " II Kings 3:20

"And they rose up early in the morning, and the sun shone upon the water, and the Moabites saw the water on the other side as red as blood:

and they said, *This is blood: the kings are surely slain, and they have smitten one another: now therefore, Moab, to the spoil. And when they came to the camp of Israel, the Israelites rose up and smote the Moabites. So that they fled before them: but they went forward smiting the Moabites, even in their country."* II Kings 4:22-24

God gave them the victory that day over their enemies like He promised.

Elisha brings a boy back to life

"And when Elisha was come into the house, behold, the child was dead, and laid upon his bed. He went in therefore, and shut the door upon them twain, and prayed unto the Lord." II Kings 4:32-33

God answers

"…and the child sneezed seven times (the number of the seven-fold Holy Spirit Rev.1:4), *and the child opened his eyes."* II Kings 4:35

The Syrians are blinded by God

Elisha prays his eyes be opened. The king of Syria made war against Israel and Elisha answered,

"And when the servant of the man of God was risen early, and gone forth, behold, an host compassed the city both with horses and chariots. And his servant said unto him, Alas, my master! How shall we do? And he answered, Fear not: for they that be with us are more than they that be with them." II Kings 6:15-16

Elisha prays

"And Elisha prayed, and said, Lord,

I pray Thee, Open his eyes, that he may see." II Kings 6:17

God answers

"And the Lord opened the eyes of the young man; and he saw: and, behold, the mountain was full of horses and chariots of fire round about Elisha." II Kings 6:17

Elisha prays

"And when they came down to him, Elisha prayed unto the Lord, and said,

Smite this people, I pray Thee, With blindness." II Kings 6:18

God answers

"And He smote them with blindness according to the word of Elisha. And it came to pass, when they were come into Samaria, that Elisha said,

Lord, Open the eyes of these men, that they may see."
II Kings 6:18-20

God Answers

"And the Lord opened their eyes, and they saw; and, behold, they were in the midst of Samaria." II Kings 6:20

Hezekiah

Sennacherib, king of Assyria, threatens war against Israel and Hezekiah tore his clothes and put on sackcloth and went into the temple to seek God.

"And it came to pass, when king Hezekiah heard it, that he rent his clothes, and covered himself with sackcloth, and went into the house of the Lord." II Kings 19:1

Hezekiah says,

*"This day is a day of trouble, and of rebuke, and blasphemy: for the children are come to the birth, and there is not strength to bring forth. It may be the Lord thy God will hear all the words of Rabshakeh, whom the king of Assyria his master hath sent to reproach the living God; and will reprove the words which the Lord thy God hath heard: wherefore lift up **thy prayer** for the remnant that are left."* II Kings 19:3-4

Hezekiah's Prayer

"And Hezekiah prayed before the Lord, and said,

> *O Lord God of Israel, which dwellest between the cherubim (I Sam.4:4;II Kings 19:15;Ps.80:1;99:1;Is.37:16),*
> *Thou art the God, even Thou alone, of all the kingdoms of the earth; Thou hast made heaven and earth (the Creator).*
> *Lord, bow down Thine ear, and hear: open, Lord, Thine eyes, and see: and hear the words of Sennacherib, which hath sent him to reproach the living God. Of a truth,*
> *Lord, the kings of Assyria have destroyed the nations and their lands, and have cast their gods into the fire: for they were no*

gods, but the work of men's hands, wood and stone: therefore
they have destroyed them.
Now therefore, O Lord our God, I beseech Thee, save Thou us
out of his hand, that all the kingdoms of the earth may know
that Thou art the Lord God, even Thou only."
II Kings 19:15-19

God speaks

"Then Isaiah the son of Amoz sent to Hezekah, saying, Thus saith the
Lord God of Israel,

That which thou hast prayed to Me against Sennacherib king
of Assyria I have heard.
This is the word that the Lord hath spoken concerning him:
the virgin the daughter of Zion hath despised thee, and
laughed thee to scorn; the daughter of Jerusalem hath shaken
her head of thee.
Whom hast thou reproached and blasphemed?
And against whom hast thou exalted thy voice, and lifted up
thine eyes on high?
Even against the Holy One of Israel. By thy messengers thou
hast reproached the Lord, and hast said, With the multitude
of my chariots I am come up to the height of the mountains,
to the sides of Lebanon, and will cut down the tall cedar trees
thereof, and the choice fir trees thereof: and I will enter into
the lodgings of his borders and into the forest of his Carmel.
I have digged and drunk strange waters, and with the sole of
my feet have I dried up all the rivers of besieged places. Hast
thou not heard long ago how I have done it, and of ancient
times that I have formed it?
Now have I brought it to pass, that thou shouldest be to lay

waste fenced cities into ruinous heaps.

Therefore their inhabitants were of small power, they were
dismayed and confounded; they were as the grass of the field,
and as the green herb, as the grass on the housetops, and as
corn blasted before it be grown up. But I know thy abode, and
thy going out, and thy coming in, and thy rage against Me.
Because thy rage against Me and thy tumult is come up into
Mine ears, therefore I will put my hook in thy nose, and My
bridle in thy lips, and I will turn thee back by the way by
which thou camest.

And this shall be a sign unto thee, Ye shall eat this year such
things as grow in themselves, and in the second year that
which springeth of the same; and in the third year sow ye, and
reap, and plant vineyards, and eat the fruits thereof. And
the remnant that is escaped of the house of Judah shall yet
again take root downward, and bear fruit upward. For out of
Jerusalem shall go forth a remnant,
and they that escape out of mount Zion: the zeal of the Lord
of hosts shall do this. Therefore thus saith the Lord concerning
the king of Assyria, He shall not come into this city, nor shoot
an arrow there, nor come before it with shield, nor cast a bank
against it. By the way that he came, by the same shall he
return, and shall not come into this city, saith the Lord. For I
will defend this city, to save it, for Mine own sake, and for my
servant David's sake." II Kings 19:20-34

God answers

Sennacherib is slain by his sons.

"And It came to pass that night, that the angel of the Lord went out,
and smote in the camp of the Assyrians an hundred fourscore and five
thousand (185,000): and when they arose early in the morning, behold,

they were all dead corpses. So Sennacherib king of Assyria departed, and went and returned, and dwelt at Nineveh. And it came to pass, as he was worshiping in the house of... his god, that Adrammelech and Sharezer his sons smote him with the sword: and they escaped into the land of Armenia. And Esarhaddon his son reigned in his stead." II Kings 19:37

Hezekiah's Prayer for Healing
"In those days was Hezekiah sick unto death. And the prophet Isaiah the son of Amoz came to him, and said unto him. . ." II Kings 20:1

God speaks
"Thus saith the Lord,

Set thine house in order; for thou shalt die, and not live.

Then he turned his face to the wall, and prayed unto the Lord, saying.

I beseech Thee, O Lord, remember now how I have walked before Thee in truth and with a perfect heart, and have done that which is good in Thy sight.

And Hezekiah wept sore." II Kings 20:1-3

Sometimes God gives us what we want because we won't take no for an answer; when it is not the best thing for us.

God speaks
"And it came to pass, afore Isaiah was gone out into the middle court, that the word of the Lord came to him, saying,

111

Turn again, and tell Hezekiah the captain of My people, Thus
saith the Lord, the God of David thy father,
I have heard thy prayer, I have seen thy tears:
behold, I will heal thee: on the third day thou shalt go up unto
the house of the Lord.
And I will add unto thy days fifteen years; and I will deliver
thee and this city out of the hand of the king of Assyria; and
I will defend this city for Mine own sake, and for My servant
David's sake." II Kings 20:4-6

God answers

"*And Isaiah said, Take a lump of figs. And they took and laid it on the*
boil, and he recovered. But to the king of Judah which sent you to inquire
of the Lord, thus shall ye say to him, Thus saith the Lord God of Israel,

as touching the words which thou hast heard; because thine
heart was tender, and thou hast humbled thyself before the
Lord, when thou heardest what I spake against this place,
and against the inhabitants thereof, that they should become
a desolation and a curse, and hast rent thy clothes, and wept
before Me; I also have heard thee,

saith the Lord." II Kings 22:18-19

Hezekiah later shows Nebuchadnezzar his entire kingdom, and the temple; this eventually leads to the Babylonian captivity.

1 & 2 Chronicles

Jabez

I first discovered this verse when we lived in North Dakota in 1983. I had it written out and put up on my wall to memorize and inspire me before it became famous.

"And Jabez was more honourable than his brethren: and his mother called his name Jabez saying, because I bare him with sorrow. And Jabez called on the God of Israel, saying. . ." I Chron. 4:9-10

Jabez prays

"Oh that Thou wouldest bless me indeed, and enlarge my coast, and that Thine hand might be with me, and that Thou wouldest keep me from evil, that it may not grieve me!"
I Chron. 4:10

God answers

"And God granted him that which he requested." I Chron. 4:10

Jabez asked for 4 things:
1. Bless me indeed.
2. Enlarge my coast (territory, borders).
3. Let Your hand be with me.
4. Keep me from evil so I won't have pain (or give pain).

The Peshitta Bible makes it more of a blessing, than a prayer

"And one of them was dear to his father and to his mother, so they called his name Our Eyes. And they said to him, The Lord shall surely

bless you and enlarge your territory, and His hand shall be with you and shall deliver you from evil, that it may not have power over you, and He shall grant you that which you request of Him." I Chron. 4:10

The NIV says,

"Jabez was more honoarable than his brothers. His mother had named him Jabez, saying, 'I gave birth to him in pain.'
Jabez cried out to the God of Israel,

'Oh, that You would bless me and enlarge my territory!
Let your hand be with me, and keep me from harm so that I
will be free from pain.'" I Chron. 4:10

The RSV says,

"Oh that Thou wouldest bless me and enlarge my border,
and that Thy hand might be with me,
and that Thou wouldst keep me from harm so that it might
not hurt me!" I Chron. 4:10

The LB says,

"Jabez was more distinguished than any of his brothers. His mother named him Jabez because she had such a hard time at his birth (Jabez means 'Distress'). *He was the one who prayed to the God of Israel,*

'Oh, that you would wonderfully bless me and help me in my work; please be with me in all that I do, and keep me from all evil and disaster!'" I Chron. 4:10

The NKJV says,

"Oh, that You would bless me indeed, and enlarge my territory, that Your hand would be with me, and that You

would keep me from evil, that I may not cause pain!"
I Chron. 4:10

God speaks

"Therefore David enquired again of God; and god said unto him,

Go not up after them; turn away from them and come upon
them over against the mulberry trees. And it shall be, when
thou shalt hear a sound of going in the tops of the mulberry
trees that then thou shalt go out to battle: for God is gone forth
before thee to smite the host of the Philistines.

David therefore did as God commanded him: and they smote the host
of the Philistines from GIbeon even to Gazer. I Chron. 14:14-16

David

David's 1st prayer in Chronicles
David prays and gives thanks to God through Psalms.

"Give thanks unto the Lord, call upon His name, make known His deeds among the people. Sing unto Him, sing psalms unto Him, talk ye of all His wondrous works. Glory ye in His holy name: let the heart of them rejoice that seek the Lord. Seek the Lord and His strength, seek His face continually." I Chron. 16:8-11

"...pray before Him continually" vs. 11 PB

"O give thanks unto the Lord; for He is good; for His mercy endureth for ever. And say ye,

> *Save us, O God of our salvation, and gather us together, and deliver us from the heathen, that we may give thanks to Thy holy name, and glory in Thy praise.*
> *Blessed be the Lord God of Israel for ever and ever. And all the people said, Amen, and praised the Lord."* I Chron. 16:34-36

David's 2nd prayer in Chronicles
"And David the king came and sat before the Lord, and said,

> *Who am I, O Lord God, and what is mine house, that Thou hast brought me hitherto?*
> *And yet this was a small thing in Thine eyes, O God; for Thou hast also spoken of Thy servant's house for a great while to come, and hast regarded me according to the estate*

of a man of high degree, O Lord God. What can David speak
more to Thee for the honour of Thy servant?
For Thou knowest Thy servant. O Lord, for Thy servant's sake,
and according to Thine own heart, hast Thou done all this
greatness, in making known all these great things.
O Lord, there is none like Thee, neither is there any God beside
Thee, according to all that we have heard with our ears. And
what one nation in the earth is like Thy people Israel,
whom God went to redeem to be His own people, to make
Thee a name of greatness and terribleness, by driving out
nations from before Thy people, whom Thou hast redeemed
out of Egypt?
For Thy people Israel didst Thou make Thine own people for
ever; and Thou, Lord, becamest their God. Therefore now,
Lord, let the thing that Thou hast spoken concerning Thy
servant and concerning his house be established for ever, and
do as Thou hast said.
Let it even be established, that Thy name may be magnified for
ever, saying, The Lord of hosts is the God of Israel, even a God
to Israel; and let the house of David Thy servant be established
before Thee. For Thou, O my God, hast told Thy servant that
Thou wilt build him an house: therefore Thy servant hath
found in his heart to pray before Thee. And now, Lord,
Thou art God, and hast promised this goodness unto Thy
servant: Now therefore let it please Thee to bless the house
of thy servant, that it may be before Thee for ever: for Thou
blessest, O Lord, and it shall be blessed for ever."
I Chron. 17:16-27

We are blessed also; because we are adopted into Israel. (Gal.
3:29; 4:5-7)

David's 3rd prayer in Chronicles

Satan temps David to number Israel – if David had done what was commanded in the law of Moses then he wouldn't have had any trouble; they were suppose to make a sacrifice for every male numbered so there would be no plague.

(*"When a census is taken a ransom must be paid for each one and then no plague will come upon them."* Ex. 30:12)

"And Satan stood up against Israel, and provoked David to number Israel. And David said to Joab and to the rulers of the people, Go, number Israel from Beersheba even to Dan; and bring the number of them to me, that I may know it." I Chron. 21:1

And Joab answered

"The Lord make His people an hundred times so many more as they be: but, my lord the king, are they not all my lord's servants? Why then doth my lord require this thing? Why will he be a cause of trespass to Israel? Nevertheless the king's word prevailed against Joab. Wherefore Joab departed, and went throughout all Israel, and came to Jerusalem ...and God was displeased with this thing; therefore He smote Israel." I Chron. 21:37

David confesses

"And David said unto God,

> *I have sinned greatly, because I have done this thing: but now,*
> *I beseech Thee, do away the iniquity of thy servant; for I have*
> *done very foolishly."* I Chron. 21:1-8

David's 4th prayer in Chronicles

David prays for God to deliver them from the plague.

"And David lifted up his eyes, and saw the angel of the Lord stand

between the earth and the heaven, having a drawn sword in his hand stretched out over Jerusalem. Then David and the elders of Israel, who were clothed in sackcloth, fell upon their faces.

And David said unto God,

> *Is it not I that commanded the people to be numbered? Even I it is that have sinned and done evil indeed; but as for these sheep, what have they done? Let Thine hand, I pray Thee, O Lord my God, be on me, and on my father's house; but not on Thy people, that they should be plagued.* I Chron. 21:16-17

Then the angel of the Lord commanded Gad to say to David, that David should go up, and set up an altar unto the Lord in the threshing floor of Ornan the Jebusaite… and called upon the Lord" I Chron. 21:16-18

David bought the threshing floor for the full price of 600 shekels of gold (I Chron. 21:24), and this became Jerusalem.

God answers

"…and He answered him from heaven by fire upon the altar of burnt offering. And the Lord commanded the angel; and he put up his sword again into the sheath thereof." I Chron. 21:26

And this is the place that the tabernacle was placed, and eventually Solomon built the temple here.

"For the Tabernacle of the Lord, which Moses made in the wilderness…" I Chron. 21:29

"Then David said, 'The house of the Lord God is to be here, and also the altar of burnt offering for Israel.'" I Chron.22:1 NIV

David's 5th prayer in Chronicles

"Then the people rejoiced, for that they offered willingly, because with perfect heart they offered willingly to the Lord: and David the king also rejoiced with great joy. Wherefore David blessed the Lord before all the congregation: and David said,

Blessed be Thou, Lord God of Israel our Father, for ever and ever. Thine, O Lord, is the greatness, and the power, and the glory, and the victory, and the majesty: for all that is in the heaven and in the earth is Thine; Thine is the kingdom, O Lord, and Thou art exalted as head above all. Both riches and honour come of Thee, and Thou reignest over all; and in Thine hand is power and might; and in Thine hand it is to make great, and to give strength unto all. Now therefore, our God, we thank Thee, and praise Thy glorious name.
But who am I, and what is my people, that we should be able to offer so willingly after this sort?
For all things come of Thee, and of Thine own have we given Thee. For we are strangers before Thee, and sojourners, and were all our fathers: our days on the earth are as a shadow, and there is none abiding. O Lord our God, all this store that we have prepared to build Thee an house for Thine holy name cometh of Thine hand, and is all Thine own. I know also, my God, that Thou triest the heart, and hast pleasure in uprightness. As for me, in the uprightness of mine heart I have willingly offered all these things: and now have I seen with joy Thy people, which are present here, to offer willingly unto Thee. O Lord God of Abraham, Isaac, and of Israel, our fathers, keep this for ever in the imagination of the thoughts of the heart of Thy people, and prepare their heart unto Thee: and give unto Solomon my son a perfect heart, to keep Thy Commandments, Thy testimonies, and Thy statutes, and to do

*all these things, and to build the palace, for the which I have
made provision.*

*And David said to all the congregation, Now bless the Lord your
God. And all the congregation blessed the Lord God of their fathers,
and bowed down their heads, and worshiped the Lord...*

*And they sacrificed sacrifices unto the Lord, and offered burnt offerings
unto the Lord, on the morrow after that day, even a thousand bullocks,
a thousand rams, and a thousand lambs, with their drink offerings, and
sacrifices in abundance for all Israel: and did eat and drink before the
Lord on that day with great gladness. And they made Solomon the son
of David king the second time, and anointed him unto the Lord to be the
chief governor, and Zadok to be priest. Then Solomon sat on the throne
of the Lord as king instead of David his father, and prospered; and all
Israel obeyed him."* I Chron. 29:9-23

Solomon

Scripture about Solomon.

Promise

Here is a promise in the Bible that uses Solomon as an example.

"Consider the lilies of the field, how they grow; they toil not, neither do they spin: and yet I say unto you, That even Solomon in all his glory was not arrayed like one of these. Wherefore, if God so clothe the grass of the field, which to day is, and to morrow is cast into the oven, shall He not much more clothe you, O ye of little faith? Therefore take no thought saying, What shall we eat? Or, What shall we drink? Or, Wherewithal shall we be clothed? ...for your heavenly Father knoweth that ye have need of all these things. But seek ye first the kingdom of God and His righteousness; and all these things shall be added unto you. Take therefore no thought for the morrow; for the morrow shall take thought for the things of itself. Sufficient unto the day is the evil thereof." Matt. 6:28-34; Lk.12:27

Solomon's 1ˢᵗ Prayer in Chronicles

Solomon went to the high place at Gibeon where the old Tabernacle of Moses was and offered 1000 sacrifices to God; that night God appeared to him,

"and (**God**) *said unto him,*

Ask what I shall give thee?" II Chron. 1:7

"And Solomon said unto God,

Thou hast shewed great mercy unto David my father, and hast made me to reign in his stead.
Now, O Lord God, let Thy promise unto David my father be established: for Thou hast made me king over a people like the dust of the earth in multitude.
Give me now wisdom and knowledge, that I may go out and come in before this people: and come in before this people: for who can judge this Thy people, that is so great?"
II Chron. 1:8-10

And God said to Solomon,

Because this was in thine heart, and thou hast not asked riches, wealth, or honour, nor the life of thine enemies, neither yet hast asked long life; but hast asked wisdom and knowledge for thyself, that thou mayest judge My people, over whom I have made thee king: wisdom and knowledge is granted unto thee; and I will give thee riches, and wealth, and honour, such as none of the kings have had that have been before thee, neither shall there any after thee have the like."
II Chron. 1:7-12

Solomon's 2nd Prayer in Chronicles
"O Lord God of Israel,

there is no God like Thee in the heaven, nor in the earth; which keepeth Covenant, and sheweth mercy unto Thy servants that walk before Thee with all their hearts: Thou which hast kept with Thy servant David my father that which Thou hast promised him; and spakest with Thy mouth, and hast fulfilled it with Thine hand, as it is this day.

Now therefore, O Lord God of Israel, keep with Thy servant
David my father that which Thou hast promised him, saying,
there shall not fail thee a man in my sight to sit upon the
throne of Israel; yet so that Thy children take heed to their
way to walk in My law, as Thou hast walked before Me. Now
then, O Lord God of Israel, let Thy word be verified,
which Thou hast spoken unto Thy servant David. But will
God in very deed dwell with men on the earth?
Behold, heaven and the heaven of heavens cannot contain
Thee; how much less this house which I have built!
Have respect therefore to the prayer of Thy servant, and to his
supplication. O Lord my God, to hearken unto the cry and the
prayer which Thy servant prayeth before Thee. That Thy eyes
may be open upon this house day and night, upon the place
whereof Thou hast said that Thou wouldest put Thy name
there; to hearken unto the prayer which Thy servant prayeth
toward this place.
Hearken therefore unto the supplications of Thy servant, and
of Thy people Israel, which they shall make toward this place:
hear Thou from Thy dwelling place, even from heaven:
and when Thou hearest, forgive. If a man sin against his
neighbor, and an oath be laid upon him to make him swear,
and the oath come before Thine altar in this house: then
hear Thou from heaven, and do, and judge Thy servants, by
requiting the wicked, by recompensing his way upon his
own head; and by justifying the righteous, by giving him
according to his righteousness.
And if Thy people Israel be put to the worse before the enemy,
because they have sinned against Thee; and shall return and
confess Thy name, and pray and make supplication before
Thee in this house; Then hear Thou from the heavens, and

*forgive the sin of Thy people Israel, and bring them again
unto the land which Thou gavest to them and to their fathers."*
II Chron. 6:14-25

God will hear if we:
1. Return to God
2. Confess His name
3. Turn from our sins
4. Pray — Ask God to forgive

*"When the heaven is shut up, and there is no rain, because
they have sinned against Thee; yet if they pray toward this
place, and confess Thy name, and turn from their sin, when
Thou dost afflict them; then hear Thou from heaven, and
forgive the sin of Thy servants, and of Thy people Israel, when
Thou hast taught them the good way, wherein they should
walk; and send rain upon Thy land, which Thou hast given
unto Thy people for an inheritance.
If there be dearth in the land, if there be pestilence, if there
be blasting, or mildew, locusts, or caterpillars; if their
enemies besiege them in the cities of their land; whatsoever
sore or whatever sickness there be: then what prayer or what
supplication soever shall be made of any man, or of all Thy
people Israel, when every one shall know his own sore and his
own grief, and shall spread forth his hands in the house: then
hear Thou from heaven Thy dwelling place, and forgive, and
render unto every man according unto all his ways, whose
heart Thou knowest; (for Thou only knowest the hearts of the
children of men:) That they may fear Thee, to walk in Thy
ways, so long as they live in the land which Thou gavest unto
our fathers. Moreover concerning the stranger, which is not of*

Thy people Israel, but is come from a far country for Thy great
name's sake, and Thy mighty hand, and Thy stretched out
arm; if they come and pray in this house; then hear
Thou from the heavens, even from Thy dwelling place, and
do according to all that the stranger calleth to Thee for; that
all people of the earth may know Thy name, and fear Thee,
as doth Thy people Israel, and may know that this house
which I have built is called by Thy name. If Thy people go
out to war against their enemies by the way that Thou shalt
send them, and they pray unto Thee toward this city which
Thou hast chosen, and the house which I have built for Thy
name: then hear Thou from the heavens their prayer and their
supplication, and maintain their cause.
If they sin against Thee, (for there is no man which sinneth
not), and Thou be angry with them, and deliver them over
before their enemies, and they carry them away captive unto a
land far off or near; yet if they bethink themselves in the land
whither they are carried captive, and turn and pray unto Thee
in the land of their captivity, saying, we have sinned,
we have done amiss, and have dealt wickedly; if they return to
Thee with all their heart and with all their soul in the land of
their captivity, whither they have carried them captives,
and pray toward their land, which Thou gavest unto their
fathers, and toward the city which Thou hast chosen, and
toward the house which I have built for Thy name:
then hear Thou from the heavens, even from Thy dwelling
place their prayer and their supplications, and maintain their
cause, and forgive Thy people which have sinned
against Thee. Now, my God, let, I beseech thee, Thine eyes
be open, and let Thy ears be attent unto the prayer that is
made in this place. Now therefore arise, O Lord God, unto

Thy resting place, Thou, and the Ark of Thy strength: let Thy priests, O Lord God, be clothed with salvation, and let Thy saints rejoice in goodness.
O Lord God, turn not away the face of Thine anointed: remember the mercies of David Thy servant."
II Chron. 6:26-42

God's answers

"*Now when Solomon had made an end of praying, the fire came down from heaven, and consumed the burnt offering and the sacrifices; and the glory of the Lord filled the house of the Lord, because the glory of the Lord had filled the Lord's house.*" II Chron. 7:1-2

God speaks

"*And the Lord appeared to Solomon by night, and said unto him,*

I have heard thy prayer, and have chosen this place to Myself for an house of sacrifice.
If I shut up heaven that there be no rain, or if I command the locusts to devour the land, or if I send pestilence among My people; If My people, which are called by My name, shall humble themselves, and pray, and seek My face, and turn from their wicked ways; then will I hear from heaven, and will forgive their sin, and will heal their land.
Now Mine eyes shall be open, and Mine ears attent unto the prayer that is made in this place.
(This was in the Old Testament; now we are to look to heaven where the New Jerusalem is) For now have I chosen and sanctified this house, that My name may be there for ever: and Mine eyes and mine heart shall be there perpetually. And

as for Thee, if Thou wilt walk before Me, as David thy father walked, and do according to all that I have commanded thee, and shalt observe My statues and My judgments; then will I stablish the throne of Thy kingdom, according as I have covenanted with David thy father, saying, there shall not fail thee a man to be ruler in Israel. But if ye turn away, and forsake My statues and My Commandments, which I have set before you, and shall go and serve other gods, and worship them; Then will I pluck them up by the roots out of My hand which I have given them; and this house, which I have sanctified for My name, will I cast out of My sight, and will make it to be a proverb and a byword among all nations.

And this house, which is high, shall be an astonishment to every one that passeth by it; so that he shall say, Why hath the Lord done thus unto this land, and unto this house?

And it shall be answered, Because they forsook the Lord God of their fathers, which brought them forth out of the land of Egypt, and laid hold on other gods, and worshiped them, and served them: therefore hath He brought all this evil upon them." II Chron. 7:12-22

Shemaiah the prophet to king Rehoboam

"Whereupon the princes of Israel and the king humbled themselves; and they said,

The Lord is righteous." II Chron. 12:6

God answered

God listened to them because they humbled themselves before

Him.

"And when the Lord saw that they humbled themselves, the Word of the Lord came to Shemaiah, saying,

> They have humbled themselves; therefore I will not destroy them, but I will grant them some deliverance; and My wrath shall not be poured out upon Jerusalem by the hand of Shishak." II Chron. 12:7

Asa

King Asa's 1st Prayer for help
"And Asa cried unto the Lord his God, and said,

> *Lord, it is nothing with Thee to help, whether with man, or with them that have no power: help us, O Lord our God: for we rest on Thee, and in Thy name we go against this multitude, O Lord, Thou art our God; let not man prevail against Thee."* II Chron. 14:11

Asa's 2nd prayer for help
> *"Thou art our Lord, Thou art the help of Thy people; and when Thou dost deliver a great army in the hands of a small force, then all the inhabitants of the earth shall know that it is good to rely on Thee; help us O Lord our God because in Thy name we have come against this great army. O Lord our God, delay not Thy might from us."* II Chron. 14:11 PB

God answers
"So the Lord smote the Ethiopians before Asa, and before Judah: and the Ethiopians fled... for the fear of the Lord came upon them: and they spoiled all the cities; for there was exceeding much spoil in them." II Chron. 14:12-14

Asa's 3rd prayer for help
"Then Asa cried out to the Lord his God,

> *O Lord, No one but You can help the powerless against the*

mighty! Help us, O Lord our God, For we trust in You alone.
It is in Your name that we have come against this vast horde.
O Lord, You are our God; do not let mere men prevail against
You!" II Chron. 14:11

God answers

"So the Lord defeated (them, and they) *fled…*

A vast amount of plunder was taken from these towns, too. They also… captured many sheep, goats, and camels before finally returning to Jerusalem." II Chron. 14:12-15 NLT

"And they entered into a Covenant to seek the Lord God of their fathers with all their heart and with all their soul…" II Chron. 15:12

God answered

"… and He was found of them: and the Lord gave them rest round about." II Chron. 15:15

Jehoshaphat

Jehoshaphat was very concerned when he learned that a large army was coming against them. He determined to seek God with prayer and fasting, and also proclaimed a fast for all the congregation of Judah. The people came from all over, and set themselves to seek God with king Jehoshaphat.

Fasting and prayer

"Jehoshaphat feared, and set himself to seek the Lord, and proclaimed a fast, throughout all Judah. And Judah gathered themselves together, to ask help of the Lord: even out of all the cities of Judah they came to seek the Lord. And Jehoshaphat stood in the congregation of Judah and Jerusalem, in the house of the Lord, before the new court, and said,

O Lord God of our fathers, art not Thou God in heaven? And rulest not Thou over all the kingdoms of the heathen? And in Thine hand is there not power and might, so that none is able to withstand Thee?
Art not Thou our God, who didst drive out the inhabitants of this land before Thy people Israel, and gavest it to the seed of Abraham Thy friend for ever? And they dwelt therein, and have built Thee a sanctuary therein for Thy name, saying,
If, when evil cometh upon us, as the sword, judgment, or pestilence, or famine (Ez.14:27), *we stand before this house, and in Thy presence,* (for Thy name is in this house,) *and cry unto Thee in our affliction, then Thou wilt hear and help. And now, behold, the children of Ammon and Moab and Mount Seir, whom Thou wouldest not let Israel invade, when they*

*came out of the land of Egypt, but they turned from them, and
destroyed them not; behold, I say, how they reward us, to come
to cast us out of Thy possession, which Thou hast given us to
inherit. O our God, wilt Thou not judge them? For we have
no might against this great company that cometh against us;
neither know we what to do: but our eyes are upon Thee."*
II Chron. 20:3-12

God answers

There are times we don't know what to do, but we keep our eyes
on Jesus.

"… Thus saith the Lord unto you,

*Be not afraid nor dismayed by reason of this great multitude;
for the battle is not yours, but God's… Ye shall not need to
fight in this battle: set yourselves, stand ye still, and see the
salvation of the Lord with you, O Judah and Jerusalem: fear
not, nor be dismayed; to morrow go out against them: for the
Lord will be with you* ("help you" PB)."

*"And Jehoshaphat bowed his head with his face to the ground: and all
Judah and the inhabitants of Jerusalem fell before the Lord, worshiping
the Lord. And the Levites… stood up to praise the Lord God of Israel
with a loud voice on high."* II Chron. 20:15-18

Sing and pray

Believe God; sing and praise God.

"Believe in the Lord your God, so shall ye be established ("you will
be able to stand firm" NLT); *believe His prophets, so shall ye prosper*
("you will succeed" NLT). *And when he had consulted with the people
he appointed singers unto the Lord, and that should praise the beauty of*

134

holiness, as they went out before the army, and to say,

Praise the Lord; for His mercy endureth for ever."
II Chron. 20:20-21

God answers

"And when they began to sing and to praise, the Lord set ambushments against (them)*... and they were smitten."* II Chron. 20:22

"... at the moment they began to sing and to praise, the Lord caused the armies... to begin fighting among themselves, and they destroyed each other!" II Chron. 20:21-23 LB

"... (they) went out to plunder... and came away loaded with money, garments, and jewels... so much that it took them three days to cart it all away ("collect it all" NLT)! *On the fourth day they gathered in the Valley of Blessing... and how they praised the Lord* ("which got its name that day because the people praised and thanked the Lord there" NLT)! *Then they returned... full of joy that the Lord had given them this marvelous rescue* ("victory" NLT) *from their enemies... when the surrounding kingdoms heard that the Lord Himself had fought against the enemies of Israel, the fear of God fell upon them. So Jehoshaphat's kingdom was quiet* ("at peace" NLT)*, for his God had given him rest* ("on every side" NLT")*."* II Chron. 20:25-30 LB

Hezekiah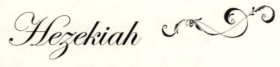

They bow to God and sing praises.

"And when they had made an end of offering, the king and all that were present with him bowed themselves, and worshiped. Moreover Hezekiah the king and the princes commanded the Levites to sing praise unto the Lord with the words of David, and Asaph the seer.

And they sang praises with gladness, and they bowed their heads and worshiped." II Chron. 29:29-30

Hezekiah calls people to celebrate Passover

Hezekiah sent letters to all the people and said,

"Ye children of Israel, turn again unto the Lord God of Abraham, Isaac, and Israel, and He will return to the remnant of you, that are escaped out of the hand of the kings of Assyria. And be not ye like your fathers, and like your brethren, which trespassed against the Lord God of their fathers, who therefore gave them up to desolation, as ye see. Now be ye not stiffnecked, as your fathers were, but yield yourselves unto the Lord, and enter into His sanctuary, which He hath sanctified for ever: and serve the Lord you God, that the fierceness of His wrath may turn away from you. For if ye turn again unto the Lord, your brethren and your children shall find compassion before them that lead them captive, so that they shall come again into this land: for the Lord your God is gracious and merciful, and will not turn away His face from you, if ye return unto Him. II Chron. 30:6-9

Prayer for pardon

"...But Hezekiah prayed for them, saying,

*The good Lord pardon every one that prepareth his heart
to seek God, the Lord God of his fathers, though He be not
cleansed according to the purification of the sanctuary."*
II Chron. 30:18-19

God answers

"And the Lord hearkened to Hezekiah, and healed the people." II
Chron. 30:20

God answers

They *"humbled themselves and came to Jerusalem"* and God gave
"them one heart" II Chron. 30:11-12

*"So there was great joy in Jerusalem: for since the time of Solomon
the son of David king of Israel there was not the like in Jerusalem. Then
the priests the Levites arose and blessed the people: and their voice was
heard, and their prayer came up to His holy dwelling place, even unto
heaven."* II Chron. 30:27

Hezekiah prays

*"Hezekiah the king, and the prophet Isaiah the son of Amoz, prayed
and cried to heaven."* II Chron. 32:20

God answers

*"And the Lord sent an angel, which cut off all the mighty men of
valour, and the leaders and captains in the camp of the king of Assyria.
So he returned with shame of face to his own land. And when he was
come into the house of his god, they that came forth of his own bowels
slew him there with the sword. Thus the Lord saved Hezekiah and
the inhabitants of Jerusalem from the hand of Sennacherib the king of
Assyria, and from the hand of all other, and builded them on every side."*

II Chron. 32:21-22

Hezekiah prays for healing

"In those days Hezekiah was sick to the death, and prayed unto the Lord..." II Chron. 32:24

God answers

"...and He spake unto him, and He gave him a sign.

But Hezekiah rendered not again according to the benefit done unto him; for his heart was lifted up: therefore there was wrath upon him, and upon Judah and Jerusalem.

Notwithstanding Hezekiah humbled himself for the pride of his heart, both he and the inhabitants of Jerusalem, so that the wrath of the Lord came not upon them in the days of Hezekiah." II Chron. 32:24-26

King Manasseh

Manasseh humbles himself

"And when he (Manasseh) was in affliction, he besought the Lord his God, and humbled himself greatly before the God of his fathers. And **prayed** unto Him..." II Chron. 33:12-13

God answers

". . .and He was **intreated** of him, and heard his supplication, and brought him again to Jerusalem into his kingdom. Then Manasseh knew that the Lord He was God." II Chron. 33:13

"Now the rest of the acts of Manasseh, and his **prayer** unto his God, and the words of the seers that spake to him in the name of the Lord God of Israel, behold, they are written in the book of the kings of Israel. His prayer also, and how God was intreated of him, and all his sin, and his trespass, and the places wherein he built high places, and set up groves and graven images, before he was humbled: behold, they are written among the sayings of the seers." II Chron. 33:18-19

King Josiah

King Josiah prays when king Josiah saw that the people were not following God, but Baal. He sought God, and *"inquired of the Lord."* II Chron. 34:21

God answers

"Thus saith the Lord,

> *Behold, I will bring evil upon this place, and upon the inhabitants thereof, even all the curses that are written in the book which they have read before the king of Judah: because they have forsaken Me, and have burned incense unto other gods, that they might provoke Me to anger with all the works of their hands; therefore My wrath shall be poured out upon this place, and shall not be quenched… because thine heart was tender, and thou didst humble thyself before God, when thou heardest His words against this place, and against the inhabitants thereof, and humbledst thyself before Me, and didst rend thy clothes, and weep before Me; I have even heard thee also, saith the Lord. Behold, I will gather thee to thy fathers, and thou shalt be gathered to thy grave in peace, neither shall thine eyes see all the evil that I will bring upon this place, and upon the inhabitants of the same."*
> II Chron. 34:23-28

Ezra

Ezra

Israel leaves Babylon and goes back to Jerusalem after the 70 yr. captivity.

Prayer for the king

"...*pray for the life of the king, and of his sons.*" Ezra 6:10

Ezra calls for Fasting and prayer

"*Then I proclaimed a fast there, at the river of Ahava, that we might afflict ourselves before our God, to seek of Him a right way for us, and for our little ones, and for all our substance. For I was ashamed to require of the king a band of soldiers and horsemen to help us against the enemy in the way: because we had spoken unto the king, saying, The hand of our God is upon all them for good that seek Him; but His power and His wrath is against all them that forsake Him. So we fasted and besought our God for this...*" Ezra 8:21-23

God answers

"...*and He was intreated of us.*" Ezra 8:23

"...*and the hand of our God was upon us, and He delivered us from the hand of the enemy, and of such as lay in wait by the way.*" Ezra 8:31

Ezra's prayer for forgiveness

Ezra didn't condemn them; but identified himself with his forefathers, and the people in confessing sin. He claimed responsibility along with the others — although he didn't actually participate in their sins.

*"O my God, I am ashamed and blush to lift up my face to
Thee, my God: for our iniquities are increased over our head,
and our trespass is grown up unto the heavens.
Since the days of our fathers have we been in a great trespass
unto this day; and for our iniquities have we, our kings, and
our priests, been delivered into the hand of the kings
of the lands, to the sword, to captivity, and to a spoil, and to
confusion of face, as it is this day.
And now for a little space grace hath been shewed from the
Lord our God, to leave us a remnant to escape, and to give us
a nail* ("pin" KJV fn – "firm place" NIV) *in His holy place,
that our God may lighten our eyes, and give us a little reviving
in our bondage.
For we were bondmen; yet our God hath not forsaken us in
our bondage, but hath extended mercy unto us in the sight of
the kings of Persia, to give us a reviving, to set up the house of
our God, and to repair the desolations thereof, and to give us a
wall in Judah and in Jerusalem. And now, O our God,
what shall we say after this? For we have forsaken Thy
Commandments.
Which Thou hast commanded by Thy servants the prophets,
saying, The land, unto which ye go to possess it, is an unclean
land with the filthiness of the people of the lands, with their
abominations, which have filled it from one end to another
with their uncleanness. Now therefore give not your daughters
unto their sons, neither take their daughters unto your sons,
nor seek their peace or their wealth for ever: that ye may
be strong, and eat the good of the land, and leave it for an
inheritance to your children for ever. And after all that is
come upon us for our evil deeds, and for our great trespass,
seeing that Thou our God hast punished us less than our*

iniquities deserve, and hast given us such deliverance as this;
should we again break Thy Commandments, and join in
affinity with the people of these abominations? Wouldest not
Thou be angry with us till Thou hadst consumed us, so that
there should be no remnant nor escaping? O Lord God of
Israel, Thou art righteous: for we remain yet escaped, as it is
this day: behold, we are before Thee in our trespasses: for we
cannot stand before Thee because of this." Ezra 9: 6-15

"Now when Ezra had **prayed**, and when he had confessed, weeping and casting himself down before the house of God, there assembled unto him out of Israel a very great congregation of men and women and children: for the people wept very sore. And Shechaniah the son of Jehiel... answered and said unto Ezra, We have trespassed against our God... yet now there is hope in Israel concerning this thing. Now therefore let us make a Covenant with our God... according to the counsel of my Lord, and of those that tremble at the Commandment of our God; and let it be done according to the law. Arise; for this matter belongeth unto Thee: we also will be with thee: be of good courage, and do it.

Then arose Ezra, and made the chief priests, the Levites, and all Israel, to swear that they should do according to this word. And they sware. Then Ezra rose up from before the house of God, and went into the chamber of Johonon... **(He fasted)** he did eat no bread, nor drink water: for he mourned because of the transgression of them that had been carried away. And they made proclamation throughout Judah and Jerusalem unto all the children of the captivity, that they should gather themselves together unto Jerusalem...Therefore make confession unto the Lord God of your fathers, and do His pleasure: and separate yourselves from the people of the land ... As Thou hast said, so must we do." Ezra 10:1-9,11-12

Nehemiah

Nehemiah

Nehemiah led a caravan of Israelites back from Babylon after the 70 yr. captivity to rebuild the wall around Jerusalem. There are nine prayers from Nehemiah to God in this book. When Nehemiah prays, he includes himself and his family in confession as having sinned against God.

When the Israelites were taken captive in Babylon, they had set aside certain fast days to commemorate Jerusalem falling to the Babylonian's, and the murder of Gedaliah. When they came back to Jerusalem, they wondered if they should continue these fasts. God tells them that their fasting was not done for Him all along, but for others to see and to make themselves look righteous before man. God would not hear that kind of prayer and fasting, and tells them how they should fast.

Nehemiah's 1st Prayer

"And it came to pass, when I heard these words, that I sat down and wept, and mourned certain days, and fasted, and prayed before the God of heaven, and said,

> *I beseech Thee, O Lord God of heaven, the great and terrible God, that keepeth Covenant and mercy for them that love Him and observe His Commandments: let Thine ear now be attentive, and Thine eyes open, that Thou mayest hear the prayer of Thy servant, which I pray before Thee now day and night, for the children of Israel Thy servants and confess the sins of the children of Israel, which we have sinned against Thee* ("we have acted very wickedly toward You" NIV)*: both*

146

*I and my father's house have sinned. We have dealt very
corruptly against Thee, and have not kept the
Commandments, nor the statues, nor the judgments, which
Thou commandest Thy servant Moses. Remember, I beseech
Thee, the word that Thou commandedest Thy servant
Moses, saying, If ye transgress, I will scatter you abroad
among the nations: but if ye turn unto Me, and keep My
Commandments, and do them;*
*though there were of you cast out unto the uttermost part of
the heaven, yet will I gather them from thence, and will bring
them unto the place that I have chosen to set My name there.
Now these are Thy servants and Thy people, whom Thou hast
redeemed by Thy great power, and by Thy strong* ("mighty"
NIV "great power" LB) *hand. O Lord, I beseech Thee,
let now Thine ear be attentive to the prayer of Thy servant,
and to the prayer of Thy servants, who desire to fear Thy
name: and prosper, I pray Thee, Thy servant this day*
("Give success to Your servant today" RSV), *and grant him
mercy* ("great favor" LB) *in the sight of this man. For I was
the king's cupbearer."* Neh. 1:4-11

The king asks for his request

*"Then the king said unto me, For what dost thou make request? So I
prayed to the God of Heaven."* Neh. 2:4

Nehemiah's 2nd Prayer

Nehemiah asks God to fight his battles for him.

*"Hear, O our God; for we are despised: and turn their reproach
upon their own head* ("...turn their insults back on their
own heads" NIV), *and give them for a prey in the land of*

captivity:
and cover not their iniquity, and let not their sin be blotted out
from before Thee: for they have provoked Thee to anger before
the builders." Neh. 4:4-6

"Nevertheless we made our prayer unto our God, and set a watch
against them day and night, because of them," Neh. 4:9

Nehemiah's 3rd Prayer
Nehemiah asks God to remember the good he's done.

"Think upon me, my God, for good, according to all that I
have done for this people." Neh. 5:19

Nehemiah's 4th Prayer
Prayer for strength.
"Now therefore, O God, strengthen my hands." Neh. 6:9

Nehemiah's 5th Prayer
Nehemiah asks God to remember the wrong done to him.

"My God, think Thou upon Tobiah and Sanballat according to
these their works, and on the prophetess Noadiah,
and the rest of the prophets, that would have put me in fear."
Neh. 6:14

Nehemiah's 6th Prayer
Nehemiah makes a confession to National sin and prays for God's
grace on His people.

"...and cried with a loud voice to the Lord their God...

stand up and bless the Lord your God for ever and ever: and blessed be Thy glorious name, which is exalted above all blessing and praise.
Thou, even Thou, art Lord alone; Thou hast made heaven, the heaven of heavens, with all their host, the earth, and all things that are therein, the seas, and all that is therein, and Thou preservest them all; and the host of heaven worshippeth Thee. Thou art the Lord, the God, who didst choose Abram, and broughtest him forth out of Ur of the Chaldees, and gavest him the name of Abraham; and foundest His heart faithful before thee, and madest a Covenant with him to give the land of the Canaanites, the Hittites, the Amorites, and the Perizzites, and the Jebusites, and the Girgashites, to give it, I say, to his seed, and hast performed Thy words; for Thou art righteous:and didst see the affliction of our fathers in Egypt, and heardest their cry by the Red Sea; and shewedst signs and wonders upon Pharaoh, and on all His servants, and on all the people of His land; for Thou knewest that they dealt proudly against them. So didst Thou get Thee a name, as it is this day. And Thou didst divide the sea before them, so that they went through the midst of the sea on the dry land; and their persecutors Thou threwest into the deeps, as a stone into the mighty waters. Moreover Thou leddest them in the day by a cloudy pillar; and in the night by a pillar of fire, to give them light in the way wherein they should go. Thou camest down also upon Mount Sinai, and spakest with them right judgments and true laws, good statues and Commandments: and madest known unto them Thy Holy Sabbath, and commandest them precepts, statutes, and laws, by the hand of Moses Thy servant: and gavest them bread from heaven for their hunger,

and broughtest forth water for them out of the rock for their
thirst, and promisedst them that they should go in to possess
the land which Thou hadst sworn to give them.
But they and our fathers dealt proudly, and hardened their necks,
and hearkened not to Thy Commandments, and refused to obey,
neither were mindful of Thy wonders that Thou didst among
them; but hardened their necks, and in their rebellion appointed
a captain to return to their bondage; but Thou art a God ready
to pardon, gracious and merciful, slow to anger, and of great
kindness, and forsookest them not. Yea, when they had made
them a molten calf, and said, This is thy god that brought thee up
out of Egypt, and had wrought great provocations;
yet Thou in Thy manifold mercies forsookest them not in the
wilderness: the pillar of the cloud departed not from them by day,
to lead them in the way: neither the pillar of fire by night, to shew
them light, and the way wherein they should go. Thou gavest also
Thy good Spirit to instruct them, and withheldest not Thy manna
from their mouth, and gavest them water for their thirst.
Yea, forty years didst Thou sustain them in the wilderness, so that
they lacked nothing; their clothes waxed not old, and their feet
swelled not. Moreover Thou gavest them kingdoms and
nations, and didst divide them into corners; so they possessed the
land of Sihon, and the land of the king of Heshbon, and the land of
Og king of Bashan. Their children also multipliedst Thou as
the stars of heaven, and broughtest them into the land, concerning
which Thou hadst promised to their fathers, that they should go in
to possess it. So the children went in and possessed the land, and
Thou subduedst before them the inhabitants of the land,
the Canaanites, and gavest them into their hands, with their kings,
and the people of the land, that they might do with them as they
would. And they took strong cities, and a fat land,

and possessed houses full of all goods, wells digged, vineyards,
and oliveyards, and fruit trees in abundance: so they did eat, and
were filled, and became fat and delighted themselves in Thy great
goodness. Nevertheless they were disobedient, and rebelled against
Thee, and cast Thy law behind their backs, and slew Thy prophets
which testified against them to turn them to Thee, and they
wrought great provocations.
Therefore Thou deliveredst them into the hand of their enemies,
who vexed them: and in the time of their trouble, when they cried
unto Thee, Thou heardst them from heaven; and according
to Thy manifold mercies Thou gavest them saviours, who saved
them out of the hand of their enemies. But after they had rest, they
did evil again before Thee: therefore leftest Thou them in the hand
of their enemies, so that they had the dominion over them:
yet when they returned, and cried unto Thee, Thou heardest
them from heaven; and many times didst Thou deliver them
according to Thy mercies; and testifiedst against them, that
Thou mightest bring them again unto Thy law: yet they dealt
proudly, and hearkened not unto Thy Commandments but
sinned against Thy judgments… and withdrew the shoulder,
and hardened their neck, and would not hear. Yet many years
didst Thou forbear them, and testifiedst against them by Thy
Spirit in Thy prophets: yet would they not give ear: therefore
gavest Thou them into the hand of the people of the lands.
Nevertheless for Thy great mercies' sake Thou dist not utterly
consume them, nor forsake them; for Thou art a gracious and
merciful God.
Now therefore, our God, the great, the mighty and the terrible
God, who keepest Covenant and Mercy let not all the trouble
seem little before Thee, that hath come upon us, on our kings,
on our princes, and on our priests, and on our prophets, and

on our fathers, and on all Thy people, since the time of the
kings of Assyria unto this day. Howbeit Thou art just in all
that is brought upon us; for Thou hast done right, but we have
done wickedly: neither have our kings, our princes,
our priests, nor our fathers, kept Thy law, nor hearkened unto
Thy Commandments and Thy testimonies, wherewith Thou
didst testify against them. For they have not served Thee in
their kingdom, and in Thy great goodness that Thou gavest
them, and the large and fat land which Thou gavest before
them, neither turned they from their wicked works. Behold,
we are servants this day, and for the land that Thou gavest
unto our fathers to eat the fruit thereof and the good
therof, behold, we are servants in it: and it yieldeth much
increase unto the kings whom Thou hast set over us because
of our sins: also they have dominion over our bodies, and over
our cattle, at their pleasure, and we are in great distress. And
because of all this we make a sure Covenant, and write it; and
our princes, Levites, and priests, seal unto it." Neh. 9:4-38

Thanksgiving in prayer

"And Mataniah the son of Micha, the son of Zabdi, the son of Asaph,
was the principal to begin the thanksgiving in prayer..." Neh. 11:17

Nehemiah's 7th Prayer

Remember my good deeds.

"Remember me, O my God, concerning this, and wipe not out
my good deeds that I have done for the house of my God, and
for the offices thereof." Neh. 13:14

Nehemiah's 8th Prayer

Prayer for mercy.

> "...*remember me, O my God, concerning this also, and spare me according to the greatness of Thy mercy* ("**great love**" NIV)." Neh. 13:22
>
> "*Have compassion... according to Your great and unfailing love.*" NLT

Nehemiah's 9th Prayer

Remember me with favor.

> "*Remember them, O my God,*
> *because they have defiled the priesthood, and the Covenant of the priesthood, and of the Levites. Thus cleansed I them from all strangers, and appointed the wards of the priests and the Levites, every one in his business; and for the wood offering, at times appointed, and for the firstfruits, remember me, O my God, for good.*" Neh. 13:29-31
>
> "*Remember me with favor...*" NIV

Esther

Esther

Fasting and praying

Esther is the only book in the Bible that doesn't actually mention the name of God. That may have been because they were afraid to identify themselves as being Israelites who worshiped the One true God.

Esther was a Jewish girl who was taken to be the queen of Persia by king Ahasuerus. Mordecai finds out that Hamaan is planning to kill them all.

He *"rent his clothes, and put on sackcloth with ashes, and went out into the midst of the city, and cried with a loud and a bitter cry; and came even before the king's gate: for none might enter into the king's gate clothed with sackcloth. And in every province, whithersoever the king's commandment and his decree came, there was great mourning among the Jews, and fasting, and weeping, and wailing; and many lay in sackcloth and ahses."*

Mordecai tells Esther that she needs to approach the king, but she could lose her life if she does that.

So Eshter tells Mordecai to fast and pray for her.

"Go, gather together all the Jews that are present in Shushan, and fast ye for me, and neither eat nor drink three days, night or day: I also and my maidens will fast likewise; and so will I go in unto the king, which is not according to the law: and if I perish, I perish. So Mordecai went his way, and did according to all that Esther had commanded him." Esther 4:15-17

God answers

God heard their prayers and Esther was received by the king and he listened to her. God gave them the victor over their enemies.

"But when Esther came before the king, he commanded by letters that his (Hamaan's) wicked device, which he devised against the Jews, should return upon his own head, and that he and his sons should be hanged on the gallows." Esther 9:25

 *Job*

Job

God's conversation with Satan about Job

"Now there was a day in Heaven when the sons of God came to present themselves before the Lord, and Satan came also among them" and had a conversation with God about Job. God pointed Job out as a godly man who would serve Him but Satan accused him without cause and asked God to take away the hedge of protection around Job that God had given. God allowed Satan to first take away his possessions and his children then afflict him with boils. God did this to prove to Satan that Job did not serve God just for what he could get from God; and to see that *"there is no none like him in the earth, a perfect and an upright man, one that feareth God, and escheweth* ("shuns") *evil?"* Job 1:6-8

Job was faithful through it all, and God blessed him with a double blessing in the end. Three of his friends came to comfort him through his ordeal, but they ended up being miserable comforters and Job had to end up praying for them.

Eliaphaz

If it were me,

"I would seek unto God, and unto God would I commit my cause..." Job 5:8

Job

"Oh that I might have my request; and that God would grant me the thing that I long for!" Job 6:8

*"I will say unto God
Do not condemn me; shew me wherefore Thou contendest*

with me.

Is it good unto Thee that Thou shouldest oppress, that Thou shouldest despise the work of Thine hands, and shine upon the counsel of the wicked?

Hast Thou eyes of flesh? Or seest Thou as man seeth? Are Thy days as the days of man are Thy years as man's days, that Thou inquirest after mine iniquity, and searchest after my sin? Thou knowest that I am not wicked; and there is none that can deliver out of Thine hand.

Thine hands have made me and fashioned me together round about; yet Thou dost destroy me. Remember, I beseech Thee, that Thou hast made me as the clay; and wilt Thou bring me into dust again.

Hast Thou not poured me out as milk, and curdled me like cheese? Thou hast clothed me with skin and flesh, and hast fenced me with bones and sinews.

Thou hast granted me life and favour, and Thy visitation hath preserved my spirit. And these things hast Thou hid in Thine heart: I know that this is with Thee.

If I sin, then Thou markest me; and if I be righteous, yet will I not lift up my head. I am full of confusion; therefore see Thou mine affliction; for it increaseth. Thou huntest me as a fierce lion: and again Thou shewest Thyself marvelous upon me. Thou renewest Thy witnesses against me, and increasest Thine indignation upon me; changes and war are against me. Wherefore then hast Thou brought me forth out of the womb? Oh that I had given up the ghost, and no eye had seen me! I should have been as though I had not been; I should have been carried from the womb to the grave. Are not my days few? Cease then, and let me alone, that I may take comfort a little. Before I go whence I shall not return, even to the land of

> darkness and the shadow of death;
> a land of darkness, as darkness itself; and of the shadow of
> death, without any order, and where the light is as darkness."
> Job 10:2-22

Eliaphaz

"Yea, thou castest off fear, and restrainest prayer before God..." Job 15:4,5

Job answers

"...my prayer is pure." Job 16:17
What profit is there in praying to God?
"But Job answered and said,

> Hear diligently my speech, and let this be your consolations...

Therefore they say unto God,

> Depart from us; for we desire not the knowledge of Thy ways.
> What is the Almighty? that we should serve Him? And what
> profit should we have, if we pray unto Him?" Job 21:1,14-15

God hears our prayers

"Thou shalt make thy prayer unto Him, and He shall hear thee, and thou shalt pay thy vows. Thou shalt also decree a thing, and it shall be established unto thee: and the light shall shine upon thy ways." Job 22:27-28

"Will God hear his cry when trouble cometh upon him? Will he always call upon God?" Job 27:9
"For though he has accumulated riches, what is the hope of the godless

at the time when God takes away his life. God will not hear his prayer when trouble comes upon him." Job 27:9 PB

God answers

"He shall pray unto God, and He will be favourable unto Him: and he shall see His face with joy: for He will render unto man his righteousness. He looketh upon men, and if any say, I have sinned (I Jn. 1:9), *and perverted that which was right, and it profited me not; He will deliver his soul from going into the pit, and his life shall see the light. Lo, all these things worketh God oftentimes with man, to bring back his soul from the pit, to be enlightened with the light of the living."* Job 33:26-30

"So that they cause the cry of the poor to come unto Him, and He heareth the cry of the afflicted." Job 34:28 RSV

"So they cause the poor to cry out, catching God's attention. Yes, He hears the cries of the needy." Job 34:28 NLT

God answers
1st time God speaks to Job

*"Then the Lord answered Job out of the whirlwind, and said,
Who is this that darkeneth counsel by words without knowledge?
Gird up now thy loins like a man: for I will demand of thee, and answer thou Me.
Where wast thou when I laid the foundations of the earth?
Declare, if thou hast understanding. Who hath laid the measures thereof, if thou knowest? Or who hath stretched the line upon it?
Whereupon are the foundations thereof fastened? Or who laid the corner stone thereof; when the morning stars sang together, and all the sons of God shouted for joy?
Or who shut up the sea with doors, when it brake forth, as if it*

had issued out of the womb?

When I made the cloud the garment thereof, and thick darkness a swaddling band for it.

And brake up for it My decreed place, and set bars and doors. And said,

Hitherto shalt thou come, but no further: and here shall thy proud waves be stayed?

Hast thou commanded the morning since thy days; and caused the dayspring to know his place; that it might take hold of the ends of the earth, that the wicked might be shaken out of it? It is turned as clay to the seal; and they stand as a garment. And from the wicked their light is withholden, and the high arm shall be broken.

Hast thou entered in the springs of the sea? Or hast thou walked in the search of the depth?

Have the gates of death been opened unto thee? Or hast thou seen the doors of the shadow of death?

Hast thou perceived the breadth of the earth?

Declare if thou knowest it all.

Where is the way where light dwelleth? And as for darkness, where is the place thereof, that thou shouldest take it to the bound thereof, and that thou shouldest know the paths to the house thereof?

Knowest thou it, because thou wast then born? Or because the number of thy days is great?

Hast thou entered into the treasures of the snow? Or hast thou seen the treasures of the hail, which I have reserved against the time of trouble, against the day of battle and war?

By what way is the light parted, which scattereth the east wind upon the earth? Who hath divided a watercourse for the overflowing of waters, or a way for the lightning of thunder;

to cause it to rain on the earth, where no man is; on the
wilderness, wherein there is no man; to satisfy the desolate
and waste ground; and to cause the bud of the tender herb to
spring forth? Hath the rain a father?
Or who hath begotten the drops of dew? Out of whose womb
came the ice?
And the hoary frost of heaven, who hath gendered it?
The waters are hid as with a stone, and the face of the deep is
frozen.
Canst thou bind the sweet influences of Pleiades, or loose the
bands of Orion? Canst thou bring forth Mazzaroth in his
season? Or canst thou guide Arcturus with his sons?
Knowest thou the ordinances of heaven? Canst thou set the
dominion thereof in the earth?
Canst thou lift up thy voice to the clouds, that abundance of
waters may cover thee? Canst thou send lightnings, that they
may go, and say unto thee, Here we are?
Who hath put wisdom in the inward parts? Or who hath given
understanding to the heart? Who can number the clouds in
wisdom? Or who can stay the bottles of heaven, when the dust
grows into hardness, and the clods cleave fast together?
Wilt thou hunt the prey for the lion? Or fill the appetite of the
young lions, when they couch in their dens, and abide in the
covert to lie in wait?
Who provideth for the raven his food? When his young ones
cry unto God, they wander for lack of meat." Job 38:1-41

2nd time God speaks to Job

"Knowest thou the time when the wild goats of the rock bring
forth? Or canst thou mark when the hinds do calve? Canst
thou number the mouths that they fulfil?

Or knowest thou the time when they bring forth? They bow themselves, they bring forth their young ones, they cast out their sorrows.

Their young ones are in good liking, they grow up with corn; they go forth, and return not unto them. Who hath sent out the wild (donkey-NIV) free?

Or who hath loosed the bands of the wild (donkey-NIV)? Whose house I have made the wilderness, and the barren land his dwellings. He scorneth the multitude of the city, neither regardeth he the crying of the driver. The range of the mountains is his pasture, and he searcheth after every green thing. Will the ("ox"-NIV) ...be willing to serve thee, or abide by thy crib? Canst thou bind the ("ox"-NIV) ...with his band in the furrow?

Or will he harrow the valleys after thee? Wilt thou trust him, because his strength is great?

Or wilt thou leave thy labour to him? Wilt thou believe him, that he will bring home thy seed, and gather it into thy barn? Gavest thou the goodly wings unto the peacocks?

Or wings and feathers unto the ostrich? Which leaveth her eggs in the earth, and warmeth them in dust, and forgetteth that the foot may crush them, or that the wild beast may break them. She is hardened against her young ones, as though they were not hers: her labour is in vain without fear; because God hath deprived her of wisdom, neither hath He imparted to her understanding.

What time she lifteth up herself on high, she scorneth the horse and his rider. Hast thou given the horse strength? Hast thou clothed his neck with thunder?

Canst thou make him afraid as a grasshopper? The glory of his nostrils is terrible. He paweth in the valley, and rejoiceth in

his strength: he goeth on to meet the armed men.
He mocketh at fear, and is not affrighted; neither turneth he
back from the sword. The quiver rattleth against him, the
glittering spear and the shield.
He swalloweth the ground with fierceness and rage: neither
believeth he that it is the sound of the trumpet. He saith
among the trumpets, Ha, ha; and he smelleth the battle afar
off, the thunder of the captains, and the shouting. Doth the
hawk fly by thy wisdom, and stretch her wings toward the
south? Doth the eagle mount up at thy command, and make
her nest on high?
She dwelleth and abideth on the rock, upon the crag of the
rock, and the strong place. From thence she seeketh the prey,
and her eyes behold afar off..." Job 39:1-29

God speaks

"Moreover the Lord answered Job, and said, shall he that
centendeth with the Almighty instruct Him? He that
reproveth God, let him answer it." Job 40:1-2

Job speaks

"Then Job answered the Lord, and said,

Behold I am vile; what shall I answer Thee? I will lay mine
hand upon my mouth. Once have I spoken; but I will not
answer: yea, twice; but I will proceed no further." Job 40:3-5

3rd time God speaks to Job

"Then answered the Lord unto Job out of the whirlwind, and said,

Gird up thy loins now like a man: I will demand of thee, and

declare thou unto Me. Wilt thou also disannul My judgment?
Wilt thou condemn Me, that thou mayest be righteous?
Hast thou an arm like God? Or canst thou thunder with a
voice like Him? Deck thyself now with majesty and excellency:
and array thyself with glory and beauty.
Cast abroad the rage of thy wrath: and behold every one that
is proud, and abase him. Look on every one that is proud,
and bring him low; and tread down the wicked in their place.
Hide them in the dust together; and bind their faces in secret.
Then will I also confess unto thee that thine own right hand
can save thee.
Behold now behemoth, which I made with thee; he eateth
grass as an ox. Lo now, his strength is in his loins, and his
force is in the navel of his belly.
He moveth his tail like a cedar: the sinews of his ("thighs" LB)
are wrapped together. His bones are as strong pieces of brass;
his bones are like bars of iron.
He is the chief of the ways of God: he that made him can make
his sword to approach unto him. Surely the mountains bring
him forth food, where all the beasts of the field play.
He lieth under the shady tree, in the covert of the reed, and
fens ("marsh" NIV).
The shady trees cover him with their shadow: the willows
of the brook compass him about. Behold, he drinketh up a
river, and hasteth not: he trusteth that he can draw up Jordan
into his mouth. He taketh it with his eyes: his nose pierceth
through snares." Job 40:6-24

God still speaking

"Canst thou draw out leviathan with an hook? Or his tongue
with a cord which thou lettest down? Canst thou put an hook

*into his nose? Or bore his jaw through with a thorn?
Will he make many supplications unto thee? Will he speak soft
words unto thee?
Will he make a covenant with thee? Wilt thou take him for a
servant for ever? Wilt thou play with him as with a bird? Or
wilt thou bind him for thy maidens?
Shall the companions make a banquet of him? Shall they
part him among the merchants? Canst thou fill his skin with
barbed irons? Or his head with fish spears?
Lay thine hand upon him, remember the battles, do no more.
Behold, the hope of him is in vain: shall not one be cast down
even at the sight of him?
None is so fierce that dare stir him up: who then is able to
stand before Me? Who hath prevented Me, that I should repay
him? Whatsoever is under the whole heaven is Mine.
I will not conceal his parts, nor his power, nor his comely
proportion.
Who can discover the face of his garment? Or who can come
to him with his double bridle? Who can open the doors of his
face? His teeth are terrible round about.
His scales are his pride, shut up together as with a close seal.
One is so near to another, that no air can come between them.
They are joined one to another, they stick together, that they
cannot be sundered. By his neesings a light doth shine,
and his eyes are like the eyelids of the morning* ("his sneezing
flash forth light" RSV).
*Out of his mouth go burning lamps, and sparks of fire leap
out. Out of his nostrils goeth smoke, as out of a seething pot or
caldron.
His breath kindleth coals, and a flame goeth out of his mouth.
In his neck remaineth strength, and sorrow is turned into joy*

before him. The flakes of his flesh are joined together: they are firm in themselves; they cannot be moved. His heart is as firm as a stone; yea, as hard as a piece of the nether millstone. When he raiseth up himself, the mighty are afraid: by reason of breakings they purify themselves.

The sword of him that layeth at him cannot hold: the spear, the dart, nor the habergeon ("javelin"). He esteemeth iron as straw, and brass as rotten wood. The arrow cannot make him flee: slingstones are turned with him into stubble. Darts are counted as stubble: he laugheth at the shaking of a spear. Sharp stones are under him: he spreadeth sharp pointed things upon the mire. He maketh the deep to boil like a pot: he maketh the sea like a pot of ointment. He maketh a path to shine after him; one would think the deep to be hoary ("white hair"). Upon earth there is not his like, who is made without fear. He beholdeth all high things: he is a king over all the children of pride." Job 41:1-34

Job answers God

"Then Job answered the Lord, and said,

> *I know that Thou canst do everything, and that no thought can be withholden from Thee. Who is he that hideth counsel without knowledge? Therefore have I uttered that I understood not; things too wonderful for me, which I knew not… Wherefore I abhor myself, and repent in dust and ashes. Hear, I beseech Thee, and I will speak: I will demand of Thee, and declare Thou unto me. I have heard of Thee by the hearing of the ear: but now mine eye seeth Thee. Wherefore I abhor myself, and repent in dust and ashes"* Job 42:1-3,6

God speaks

Job prays for his friends.

"God speaks to Eliphaz the Temanite,
My wrath is kindled against Thee, and against thy two friends
for ye have not spoken of Me the thing that is right, as My
servant Job hath... My servant Job shall pray for you:
for him will I accept: lest I deal with you after your folly,
in that ye have not spoken of Me the thing which is right, like
My servant Job.

... go to My servant Job ...Therefore take unto you now seven
bullocks and seven rams, and go to My servant Job, and offer
up for yourselves a burnt offering; and My servant Job shall
pray for you: for him will I accept: lest I deal with you after
your folly, in that ye have not spoken of Me the thing which is
right, like My servant Job." Job 42:7-8

God answers

God blesses Job and turns his captivity around when he prays for his friends.

"And the Lord turned the captivity of Job, when he prayed for his friends; also the Lord gave Job twice as much as he had before.

Then came there unto him all his brethren, and all his sisters, and all they that had been of his acquaintance before, and did eat bread with him in his house: and they bemoaned him, and comforted him over all the evil that the Lord had brought upon him: every man also gave him a piece of money, and every one an earring of gold. So the Lord blessed the latter end of Job more than his beginning: for he had fourteen thousand sheep, and six thousand camels, and a thousand yoke of oxen, and a thousand (female donkeys).

He had also seven sons and three daughters. And he called the name of the first, Jemima ("Dove" MB), *and the name of the second, Kezia*

("Cinnamon" MB) *and the name of the third, Kerenhappuch ("Dark-eyes" MB). And in all the land were no women found so fair ("beautiful" NIV; "lovely" LB) as the daughters of Job: and their father gave them inheritance among their brethren. After this lived Job an hundred and forty years, and saw his sons and his sons' sons even four generations. So Job died, being old and full of days." Job 42:10*

Psalms

Psalms

"Ask of me, and I shall give thee the heathen for thine inheritance, and the utteremost parts of the earth for thy possession." Ps. 2:8

David's 1st prayer in Psalms
David's prayer when he fled from Absalom (II Sam. 15,16).

"Lord, how are they increased that trouble me! Many are they that rise up against me. Many there be which say of my soul, there is no help for him in God.
Selah. But Thou, O Lord, art a shield for me; my glory, and the lifter up of mine head. I cried unto the Lord with my voice, and He heard me out of His holy hill.
Selah. I laid me down and slept; I awaked; for the Lord sustained me.
I will not be afraid of ten thousands of people, that have set themselves against me round about. Arise, O Lord; save me, O my God: for Thou hast smitten all mine enemies upon the cheek bone; Thou hast broken the teeth of the ungodly. Salvation belongeth unto the Lord: Thy blessing is upon Thy people. Selah (a musical term that means "rest")." Ps. 3:1-8

David's prayer
May have been written after David fled Jerusalem; when Absalom tried to take over his kingdom.

"Hear me when I call, O God of my righteousness: Thou hast enlarged me when I was in distress; have mercy upon me, and

hear my prayer." Ps. 4:1

God speaks
"O ye sons of men, how long will ye turn My glory into shame?
How long will ye love vanity, and seek after leasing ("lies"
ESV)*? Selah.*
But know that the Lord hath set apart him that is godly for
Himself: the Lord will hear when I call unto Him. Stand in
awe, and sin not: commune with your own heart upon your
bed, and be still. Selah." Ps. 4:6-8

"Offer the sacrifices of righteousness, and put your trust in the Lord.
There be many that say,

Who will shew us any good? Lord..." Ps. 4:5-6

Prayer
". . .lift Thou up the light of Thy countenance upon us. Thou
hast put gladness in my heart, more than in the time that
their corn and their wine increased. I will both lay me down
in peace, and sleep: for thou, Lord, only makest me dwell in
safety."
Ps. 4:1-8

David's prayer
Psalms 5 is traditionally said to be of David. Some say this isn't David because of the reference to the temple, but some say that he was calling the Sanctuary the temple. It is said that Jewish people prayed this prayer early in the morning.

"Give ear to my words, O Lord, consider my meditation. Hearken unto the voice of my cry, my King, and my God: for unto Thee will I pray. My voice shalt Thou hear in the morning, O Lord; in the morning, O Lord; in the morning will I direct my prayer unto Thee, and will look up. For Thou art not a God that hath pleasure in wickedness: neither shall evil dwell with Thee. The foolish shall not stand in Thy sight: Thou hatest all workers of iniquity (Those who won't repent and receive forgiveness from God).*
Thou shalt destroy them that speak leasing ("falsehood" PB – "speak lies" RSV): *the Lord will abhor the bloody and deceitful man. But as for me, I will come into Thy house in the multitude of Thy mercy: and in Thy fear will I worship toward the holy temple. Lead me, O Lord, in Thy righteousness because of mine enemies; make Thy way straight before my face.*
For there is no faithfulness in their mouth; their inward part is very wickedness; their throat is an open sepulcher; they flatter with their tongue. Destroy Thou them, O God; let them fall by their own counsels; cast them out in the multitude of their transgressions; for they have rebelled against Thee. But let all those that put their trust in Thee rejoice: let them ever shout for joy, because Thou defendest them: let them also that love Thy name be joyful in Thee. For Thou, Lord, wilt bless the righteous: with favour wilt Thou compass him as with a shield." Ps. 5:1-12

David's prayer

Some say that David wrote this before his baby boy died. This is one of seven Psalms of penitence: Ps.6; 32; 38; 51; 102; 130; and 143. The early church used these verses as a song, and sang the verses on

Ash Wednesday, along with Ps.32, 38, 51, 102, 130 and 143.

> "O Lord,
> rebuke me not in Thine anger, neither chasten me in Thy hot
> displeasure. Have mercy upon me, O Lord; for I am weak: O
> Lord, heal me; for my bones are vexed. My soul is also sore
> vexed: but Thou, O Lord, how long? Return, O Lord, deliver
> my soul: oh save me for Thy mercies' sake." Ps. 6:1-4

God hears our prayers

"… for the Lord has heard the voice of my weeping." Ps. 6:8 UKJV

"The Lord hath heard my supplication; the Lord will receive my prayer. Let all mine enemies be ashamed and sore vexed: let them return and be ashamed suddenly." Ps. 6:9-10

David's song prayer

Some think that this was written while King Saul was still alive; maybe while David was hiding in a cave.

> "O Lord my God,
> in Thee do I put my trust: save me from all them that
> persecute me, and deliver me: lest he tear my soul like a lion,
> rending it in pieces, while there is none to deliver. O Lord my
> God, I have done this; if there be iniquity in my hands; if I
> have rewarded evil unto him that was at peace with me; (yea, I
> have delivered him that without cause is mine enemy): Let
> the enemy persecute my soul, and take it, yea, let him tread
> down my life upon the earth, and lay mine honour in the dust.
> Selah. Arise, O Lord, in Thine anger, lift up Thyself because of
> the rage of mine enemies: and awake for me to the judgment

that Thou hast commanded." Ps. 7:1-7

David's prayer
Written during harvest time.

"*O Lord our Lord,*
how excellent is Thy name in all the earth! Who hast set Thy
glory above the heavens.
Out of the mouth of babes and sucklings hast Thou ordained
strength because of Thine enemies, that Thou mightest still the
enemy and the avenger. When I consider Thy heavens,
the work of Thy fingers, the moon and the stars, which Thou
hast ordained; what is man (**#582 "ordinary, mortal"**) *that*
Thou art mindful of him?
And the son of man, that Thou visitest him? For Thou hast
made him a little lower than the angels (**we will be equal**
to the angels at the resurrection Lk. 210:36), *and hast*
crowned him with glory and honour. Thou madest him to
have dominion over the works of Thy hands; Thou hast put all
things under his feet: all sheep and oxen, yea, and the beasts
of the field; the fowl of the air, and the fish of the sea, and
whatsoever passeth through the paths of the sea.
O Lord our Lord, how excellent is Thy name in all the earth!"
Ps. 8:1-9

"*The Lord looked down from heaven upon the children of men, to see*
if there were any that did understand, and seek (**pray to**) *God. They are*
all gone aside, they are all together become filthy: there is none that doeth
good, no, not one. Have all the workers of iniquity no knowledge… and
call not upon the Lord." Ps. 14:2-4

David's prayer

Prayer used as a song in worship.

> "I will praise Thee, O Lord, with my whole heart; I will shew
> forth all Thy marvelous works.
> I will be glad and rejoice in Thee: I will sing praise to Thy
> name O Thou most High.
> When mine enemies are turned back, they shall fall and perish
> at Thy presence.
> For Thou hast maintained my right and my cause; Thou
> sattest ("sat" ESV) in the throne judging right.
> Thou hast rebuked the heathen, Thou hast destroyed the
> wicked, Thou hast put out their name for ever and ever...
> Have mercy upon me, O Lord; consider my trouble which I
> suffer of them that hate me, Thou that liftest me up from the
> gates of death: that I may shew forth all Thy praise in the gates
> of the daughter of Zion: I will rejoice in Thy salvation.
> Arise, O Lord; let not man prevail: let the heathen be judged
> in Thy sight. Put them in fear, O Lord: that the nations may
> know themselves to be but men, Selah." Ps. 9:1-5,13-19

David's prayer

> "Why standest Thou afar off, O Lord? Why hidest Thou
> Thyself in times of trouble...
> Arise, O Lord; O God, lift up Thine hand: forget not the
> humble... Thou hast seen it; for Thou beholdest mischief and
> spite, to requite it with Thy hand: the poor committeth himself
> unto Thee; Thou art the helper of the fatherless.
> Break Thou the arm of the wicked and the evil man: seek out
> his wickedness till Thou find none...Lord, Thou hast heard
> the desire of the humble: Thou wilt prepare their heart, Thou
> wilt cause Thine ear to hear: to judge the fatherless and the

oppressed, that the man of the earth may no more oppress."
Ps. 10:1-15

David's prayer

Most think that David wrote Ps. 9 & 10 as one psalm; probably written while David was in the courts of King Saul, and saw wicked men on all sides.

> *"Help, Lord; for the godly man ceaseth; for the faithful fail*
> *from among the children of men.*
> *They speak vanity every one with his neighbour: with*
> *flattering lips and with a double heart do they speak... Thou*
> *shalt keep them, O Lord; Thou shalt preserve them from this*
> *generation for ever...." Ps. 12:1-2*

David's prayer

David being hunted by King Saul.

> *"How long wilt Thou forget me, O Lord? For ever? How*
> *long wilt Thou hide Thy face from me? How long shall I take*
> *counsel in my soul, having sorrow in my heart daily?*
> *How long shall mine enemy be exalted over me? Consider*
> *and hear me, O Lord my God:lighten mine eyes, lest I sleep the*
> *sleep of death; lest mine enemy say, I have prevailed against*
> *him; and those that trouble me rejoice when I am moved. But*
> *I have trusted in Thy mercy; my heart shall rejoice in Thy*
> *salvation. I will sing unto the Lord, because He hath dealt*
> *bountifully with me." Ps. 13:1-6*

> *"Out of the depths have I cried unto Thee, O Lord.*
> *Lord, hear my voice: let Thine ears be attentive to the voice of*

my supplications." Ps. 13:1-2

David's prayer
> *"Lord, who shall abide in Thy tabernacle? Who shall dwell in*
> *thy holy hill?"* Ps. 15:1

God's answer
Live righteously and God promises that He will never let you be moved.
* * Don't gossip.
* * Speak the truth.
* * Fear God.

> *"He that walketh uprightly, and worketh righteousness, and*
> *speaketh the truth in his heart.*
> *He that backbiteth not with his tongue, nor doeth evil to his*
> *neighbour, nor taketh up a reproach against his neighbour. In*
> *whose eyes a vile* (#3985 "reprobate") *person is contemned*
> (#959 "despised"); *but He honoureth them that fear* (#3373
> "yare = fearing, afraid, fearful, morally, reverent) *the Lord.*
> *He that sweareth to his own hurt, and changeth not. He*
> *that putteth not out his money to usury, nor taketh reward*
> *against the innocent. He that doeth these things shall never be*
> *moved."* Ps. 15:2-5

David's prayer
David running from King Saul during this prayer. Those who serve other gods will have sorrows multiplied.

> *"Preserve me, O God: for in Thee do I put my trust. O my*
> *soul, thou hast said unto the Lord, Thou art my Lord: my*

goodness extendeth not to thee; but to the saints that are in the earth, and to the excellent, in whom is all my delight. Their sorrows shall be multiplied that hasten after another god... Thou wilt shew me the path of life: in Thy presence is fullness of joy; at Thy right hand there are pleasures for evermore."

Ps. 16:1-4,11

David's prayer

Prayer of David used in worship. It is a prayer he said when king Saul died (II Sam. 1:1-27).

"Hear the right, O Lord, attend unto my cry, give ear unto my prayer, that goeth not out of feigned lips.
Let my sentence come forth from Thy presence; let Thine eyes behold the things that are equal. Thou hast proved mine heart; Thou hast visited me in the night; Thou hast tried me, and shalt find nothing; I am purposed that my mouth shall not transgress. Concerning the works of men, by the word of Thy lips I have kept me from the paths of the Destroyer. Hold up my goings in Thy paths, that my footsteps slip not. I have called upon Thee, for Thou wilt hear me, O God: incline Thine ear unto me, and hear my speech.
Shew Thy marvelous loving kindness, O Thou that savest by Thy right hand them which put their trust in Thee from those that rise up against them. Keep me as the apple of the eye, hide me under the shadow of Thy wings (Ps. 91:1). *From the wicked that oppress me, from my deadly enemies, who compass me about. They are inclosed in their own fat: with their mouth they speak proudly. They have now compassed us in our steps: they have set their eyes bowing down to the earth: like as a lion that is greedy of his prey, and as it were a young*

lion lurking in secret places. Arise, O Lord, disappoint him, cast him down: deliver my soul from the wicked, which is Thy sword: from men which are Thy hand, O Lord, from men of the world, which have their portion in this life, and whose belly Thou fillest with Thy hid treasure: they are full of children, and leave the rest of their substance to their babes. As for me, I will behold Thy face in righteousness: I shall be satisfied, when I awake, with Thy likeness (at the resurrection)." Ps. 17:1-15

David's prayer

Written after David's victory over Goliath.

"I will love Thee, O Lord, my strength... I will call upon the Lord, who is worthy to be praised: so shall I be saved from mine enemies... In my distress I called upon the Lord, and cried unto my God: He heard my voice out of His temple, and my cry came before him, even into His ears... Thou hast also given me the shield of Thy salvation: and Thy right hand hath holden me up, and Thy gentleness hath made me great. Thou hast enlarged my steps under me, that my feet did not slip... For Thou hast girded me with strength unto the battle: Thou hast subdued under me those that rose up against me, Thou hast also given me the necks of mine enemies; that I might destroy them that hate me... Thou hast delivered me from the strivings of the people; and Thou hast made me the head of the heathen: a people whom I have not known shall serve me... Therefore will I give thanks unto Thee, O Lord, among the heathen, and sing praises unto Thy name."
Ps. 18:1,4,6,35,36,39,43,49

"I will call upon the Lord, who is worthy to be praised: so shall I be saved from my enemies." Ps. 18:3 UKJV

David's prayer
Save and cleanse me from sin.

"They cried, but there was none to save them: even unto the Lord, but He answered them not." Ps. 18:41 ("He will not answer them" PB)

"Thou hast delivered me from the strivings of the people; and Thou hast made me the head of the heathen: a people whom I have not known shall serve me. As soon as they hear of me, they shall obey me: the strangers shall submit themselves unto me." Ps. 18:43-44

"Who can understand his errors (Heb. word "Shigiah" sins of ignorance) *cleanse Thou me from secret faults. Keep back Thy servant also from presumptuous* (#2086 "insolent, arrogant" we know it's a sin but we do it anyway) *sins; let them not have dominion over me: then shall I be upright* (having integrity), *and I shall be innocent from* ("of" NIV) *the great transgression* (a big sin with terrible consequences). *Let the words of my mouth, and the meditation of my heart, be acceptable in Thy sight, O Lord, my strength, and my redeemer."* Ps. 19:12-14

"How can I know all the sins lurking in my heart? Cleanse me from hidden faults. Keep me from deliberate sins! Don't let them control me. Then I will be free of guilt and innocent of great sin" Ps. 19:12-14
NLT "much wickedness" 1599
Geneva Bible "great transgression" NIV

David's prayer

David prayed before going to war.

"*The Lord hear thee in the day of trouble; the name of the God of Jacob defend thee; send thee help from the sanctuary, and strengthen thee out of Zion; remember all thy offerings, and accept thy burnt sacrifice; Selah. Grant thee according to thine own heart, and fulfil all thy counsel. We will rejoice in Thy salvation, and in the name of our God we will set up our banners: the Lord fulfil all Thy petitions. Now know I that the Lord saveth His anointed; He will hear him from His holy heaven with the saving strength of his right hand. Some trust in chariots, and some in horses: but we will remember the name of the Lord our God. They are brought down and fallen: but we are risen, and stand upright.*

Save, Lord:

let the king hear us when we call." Ps. 20 1-9
("…let our King answer us in the day we call upon Him." PB)

David's prayer

"*The king shall joy in Thy strength, O Lord; and in Thy salvation how greatly shall he rejoice!*
Thou hast given him his heart's desire, and hast not withholden the request of his lips. Selah.
For Thou preventest him with the blessings of goodness: Thou settest a crown of pure gold on his head.
He asked life of Thee, and Thou gavest it him, even length of days for ever and ever. His glory is great in Thy salvation: honour and majesty hast Thou laid upon him.
For Thou hast made him most blessed for ever: Thou hast made him exceeding glad with Thy countenance. For the king trusteth in the Lord, and through the mercy of the Most

183

High he shall not be moved.
Thine hand shall find out all Thine enemies: Thy right hand
shall find out those that hate Thee. Thou shalt make them as
a fiery oven in the time of Thine anger: the Lord shall swallow
them up in His wrath, and the fire shall devour them. Their
fruit shalt Thou destroy from the earth, and their seed from
among the children of men.
For they intended evil against Thee: they imagined a
mischievous device, which they are not able to perform.
Therefore shalt Thou make them turn their back, when Thou
shalt make ready Thine arrows upon Thy strings against the
face of them. Be Thou exalted, Lord, in Thine own strength: so
will we sing and praise Thy power." Ps. 21:1-13

"... when he cried unto Him, He heard." Ps. 22:24

David's prayer

A prophecy of Jesus is in this prayer.

"My God, my God, why hast Thou forsaken me (Jesus spoke
these words on the cross)?

Why art Thou so far from helping me, and from the words of
my roaring? O my God, I cry in the daytime, but Thou hearest
not; and in the night season, and am not silent.
But Thou art holy, O Thou that inhabitest the praises of Israel.
Our fathers trusted in Thee: they trusted, and Thou didst
deliver them. They cried unto Thee, and were delivered: they
trusted in Thee, and were not confounded. But I am a worm,
and no man; a reproach of men, and despised of the people.
All they that see me laugh me to scorn: they shoot out the lip,
they shake the head saying, He trusted on the Lord that He
would deliver Him: let Him deliver Him, seeing He delighted

in Him (**They said this to Jesus on the cross**). *But Thou art He that took me out of the womb: Thou didst make me hope when I was upon my mother's breasts. I was cast upon Thee from the womb: Thou art my God from my mother's belly. Be not far from me; for trouble is near; for there is none to help. Many bulls have compassed me: strong bulls of Bashan have beset me round.*
They gaped upon me with their mouths, as a ravening and a roaring lion.
I am poured out like water, and all my bones are out of joint: my heart is like wax; it is melted in the midst of my bowels.
My strength is dried up like a potsherd: and my tongue cleaveth to my jaws; and Thou hast brought me into the dust of death. For dogs have compassed me:
the assembly of the wicked have inclosed Me: they pierced my hands and my feet.
I may tell all my bones: they look and stare upon me. They part my garments among them, and cast lots upon my vesture (**prophecy of Jesus**). *But be not Thou far from me, O Lord: O my strength, haste Thee to help me. Deliver my soul from the sword:*
my darling ("**my only one." KJV fn**) *from the power of the dog. Save me from the lion's mouth: for Thou hast heard me from the horns of the…* (**#7214 "wild bull"**).
I will declare Thy name unto my brethren: in the midst of the congregation will I praise Thee." Ps. 22:1-22

David's prayer

"Unto Thee, O Lord, do I lift up my soul. O my God, I trust in Thee: let me not be ashamed, let not mine enemies triumph over me. Yea, let none that wait on Thee be ashamed;

let them be ashamed which transgress without cause.
Shew me Thy ways, O Lord; teach me Thy paths. Lead me in
Thy truth, and teach me:
for Thou art the God of my salvation; on Thee do I wait all the
day. Remember, O Lord, Thy tender mercies and Thy loving
kindnesses; for they have been ever of old.
Remember not the sins of my youth, nor my transgressions:
according to Thy mercy remember Thou me for Thy goodness'
sake, O Lord. Good and upright is the Lord:
Therefore will He teach sinners in the way. The meek will He
guide in judgment:
and the meek will He teach His way. All the paths of the Lord,
are mercy and truth, unto such as keep His Covenant and
His testimonies. For Thy name's sake, O Lord, pardon mine
iniquity; for it is great... Turn Thee unto me, and have mercy
upon me; for I am desolate and afflicted.
The troubles of my heart are enlarged:
O bring Thou me out of my distresses. Look upon mine
affliction and my pain; and forgive all my sins. Consider mine
enemies; for they are many; and they hate me with cruel
hatred.
O keep my soul, and deliver me: let me not be ashamed; for I
put my trust in Thee. Let integrity and uprightness preserve
me; for I wait on thee. Redeem Israel, O God, out of all his
troubles." Ps. 25:1-11,16-22

"Remember, O Lord,
Your tender mercies and Your loving kindnesses; for they have
been ever of old. Remember not the sins of my youth, nor my
transgressions: according to Your mercy remember You me for
Your goodness sake, O Lord." Ps. 25:6-7 UKJV

David's prayer

"Judge me, O Lord; for I have walked in mine integrity: I have trusted also in the Lord; therefore I shall not slide. Examine ("test" NIV) O Lord, and prove me; try my reins ("mind" NIV) and my heart. For Thy loving kindness is before mine eyes; and I have walked in Thy truth. I have not sat with vain persons, neither will I go in with dissemblers ("hypocrites"). I have hated the congregation of evil doers:
and will not sit with the wicked. I will wash mine hands in innocency:
so will I compass Thine altar, O Lord: that I may publish with the voice of thanksgiving, and tell of all Thy wondrous works. Lord, I have loved the habitation of Thy house, and the place where Thine honour dwelleth. Gather not my soul with sinners, nor my life with bloody men: in whose hands is mischief, and their right hand is full of bribes.
But as for me, I will walk in mine integrity: redeem me, and be merciful unto me. My foot standeth in an even place: in the congregations will I bless the Lord." Ps. 26:1-12

David's prayer

"Hear, O Lord, when I cry with my voice: have mercy also upon me, and answer me.
When Thou saidist, Seek ye My face, Lord, will I seek. Hide not Thy face far from me; put not Thy servant away in anger: Thou hast been my help; leave me not, neither forsake me, O God of my salvation." Ps. 27:7-9

David's prayer

"Teach me Thy way, O Lord,

and lead me in a plain path, because of mine enemies. Deliver
me not over unto the will of mine enemies: for false witnesses
are risen up against me, and such as breathe out cruelty."
Ps. 27:11-12

David's prayer

"Unto Thee will I cry, O Lord my rock; be not silent to me: lest,
if Thou be silent to me, I become like them that go down into
the pit. Hear the voice of my supplications, when I cry unto
Thee, when I lift up my hands toward Thy holy oracle.
Draw me not away with the wicked, and with the workers of
iniquity, which speak peace to their neighbours, but mischief is
in their hearts.
Give **("repay" NIV)** *according to their deeds, and according to*
the wickedness of their endeavours: give them after the work of
their hands; render to them their desert.
Because they regard not the works of the Lord, nor the
operation of His hands, He shall destroy them, and not build
them up. Blessed be the Lord, because He hath heard the voice
of my supplications." Ps. 28:1-6
("Pay them back for all their evil deeds. Give them a taste
of what they have done to others." Ps. 28:4 LB)

David's prayer

"I will extol Thee, O Lord; for Thou hast lifted me up, and hast
not made my foes to rejoice over me. O Lord my God I cried
unto Thee..." Ps. 30:1-2

God answers

"... and Thou hast healed me. O Lord, Thou hast brought up
my soul from the grave; Thou hast kept me alive, that I should

188

not go down to the pit…" Ps. 30:2-3

"Lord, by Thy favour Thou hast made my mountain to stand strong: Thou didst hide Thy face, and I was troubled." Ps. 30:7

David's prayer

"I cried to Thee, O Lord; and unto the Lord I made supplication.
What profit is there in my blood, when I go down to the pit?
Shall the dust praise Thee? Shall it declare Thy truth? Hear, O Lord, and have mercy upon me:
Lord, be Thou my helper. Thou hast turned for me my mourning into dancing:
Thou hast put off my sackcloth, and girded me with gladness; to the end that my glory may sing praise to Thee, and not be silent. O Lord my God, I will give thanks unto Thee for ever."
Ps. 30:8-12

David's prayer

Prayer of David sent to the chief muscician.

"In Thee, O Lord, do I put my trust; let me never be ashamed: deliver me in Thy righteousness.
Bow down Thine ear to me; deliver me speedily: be Thou my strong rock, for an house of defence to save me. For Thou art my rock and my fortress; therefore for Thy name's sake lead me, and guide me. Pull me out of the net that they have laid privily for me: for Thou art my strength. Into Thine hand I commit my spirit **(Jesus said on the cross)***: Thou hast redeemed me, O Lord God of truth.*
I have hated them that regard lying vanities: but I trust in the

Lord.

I will be glad and rejoice in Thy mercy: for Thou hast considered my trouble; Thou hast known my soul in adversities; and hast not shut me up into the hand of the enemy:

Thou hast set my feet in a large room. Have mercy upon me, O Lord, for I am in trouble: mine eye is consumed with grief, yea, my soul and my belly.

For my life is spent with grief, and my years with sighing: my strength faileth because of mine iniquity, and my bones are consumed.

I was a reproach among all mine enemies, but especially among my neighbours, and a fear to mine acquaintance: they that did see me without fled from me.

I am forgotten as a dead man out of mind: I am like a broken vessel.

For I have heard the slander of many: fear was on every side; while they took counsel together against me, they devised to take away my life. But I trusted in Thee,

O Lord: I said, Thou art my God. My times are in Thy hand: deliver me from the hand of mine enemies, and from them that persecute me. Make Thy face to shine upon Thy servant: save me for Thy mercies' sake.

Let me not be ashamed, O Lord; for I have called upon thee: let the wicked be ashamed, and let them be silent in the grave.

Let the lying lips be put to silence; which speak grievous things proudly and contemptuously against the righteous.

Oh how great is Thy goodness, which Thou hast laid up for them that fear Thee; which Thou hast wrought for them that trust in thee before the sons of men!

Thou shalt hide them in the secret of Thy presence from the

pride of man: Thou shalt keep them secretly in a pavilion from
the strife of tongues.
Blessed be the Lord: for He hath shewed me His marvelous
kindness in a strong city. For I said in my haste, I am cut off
from before Thine eyes: nevertheless Thou heardest the voice of
my supplications when I cried unto Thee. O love the Lord, all
ye His saints:
for the Lord preserveth the faithful, and plentifully rewardeth
the proud doer. Be of good courage, and He shall strengthen
your heart, all ye that hope in the Lord." Ps. 31:1-24

David's prayer

Prayer after committing adultery with Bathsheba. David didn't hide
his sin, but acknowledged it – that is how we receive forgiveness: by
turning away from our sins. When we acknowledge our sins, it opens
the door to God's amazing grace, mercy and forgiveness.

"I acknowledged my sin unto Thee, and mine iniquity have I
not hid. I said, I will confess my transgressions unto the Lord;
and Thou forgavest the iniquity of my sin. Selah.
For this shall every one that is godly pray unto Thee in a time;
when Thou mayest be found:
surely in the floods of great waters they shall not come nigh
unto Him. Thou art my hiding place; Thou shalt preserve
me from trouble; Thou shalt compass me about with songs of
deliverance. Selah." Ps. 32:5-7

God speaks

"I will instruct thee and teach thee in the way which Thou
shalt go: I will guide thee with Mine eye." Ps. 32:8

"I sought the Lord and He heard me, and delivered me from all my fears... this poor man cried, and the Lord heard him, and saved him out of all his troubles." Ps. 34:4-6

"The righteous cry, and the Lord hears and delivers them out of all their troubles." Ps. 34:17 UKJV

David's prayer

"Plead my cause, O Lord, with them that strive with me: fight against them that fight against me.
Take hold of shield and buckler, and stand up for mine help.
Draw out also the spear, and stop the way against them that persecute me: say unto my soul, I am thy salvation.
Let them be confounded and put to shame that seek after my soul: let them be turned back and brought to confusion that devise my hurt. Let them be as chaff before the wind: and let the angel of the Lord chase them. Let their way be dark and slippery: and let the angel of the Lord persecute them. For without cause have they laid for me their net in a pit, which without cause they have digged for my soul. Let destruction come upon him at unawares; and let his net that he hath hid catch himself: into that very destruction let him fall.
And my soul shall be joyful in the Lord: it shall rejoice in His salvation.
All my bones shall say, Lord, who is like unto Thee, which deliverest the poor from him that is too strong for him, yea, the poor and the needy from him that spoileth him?
False witnesses did rise up; they laid to my charge things that I knew not.
They rewarded me evil for good to the spoiling of my soul.
But as for me, when they were sick my clothing was sackcloth:

*I humbled my soul with fasting; and my prayer returned into
mine own bosom. I behaved myself as though he had been
my friend or brother: I bowed down heavily, as one that
mourneth for his mother.*
But in mine adversity they rejoiced ("they are glad now that I
am in trouble" NLT), *and gathered themselves together: yea,
the abjects gathered themselves together against me,
and I knew it not; they did tear me, and ceased not: with
hypocritical mockers in feasts, they gnashed upon me with
their teeth. Lord, how long wilt Thou look on?*
Rescue my soul from their destructions, my darling ("My
precious life" NIV) *from the lions. I will give Thee thanks in
the great congregation: I will praise Thee among much people.
Let not them that are mine enemies wrongfully
rejoice over me: neither let them wink with the eye that hate
me without a cause.*
*For they speak not peace; but they devise deceitful matters
against them that are quiet in the land.*
*Yea, they opened their mouth wide against me, and said,
Aha, aha, our eye hath seen it. This Thou hast seen, O Lord:
keep not silence: O Lord, be not far from me. Stir up Thyself,
and awake to my judgment, even unto my cause, my God and
my Lord. Judge me (*judge in my favor),
*O Lord my God, according to Thy righteousness; and let them
not rejoice over me.*
*Let them not say in their hearts, Ha, so would we have it:
let them not say, We have swallowed him up. Let them be
ashamed and brought to confusion together that rejoice at
mine hurt: let them be clothed with shame and dishonour that
magnify themselves against me.*
Let them shout for joy, and be glad, that favor my righteous

cause: yea, let them say continually, Let the Lord be magnified,
which hath pleasure in the prosperity of His servant. And my
tongue shall speak of Thy righteousness and of Thy praise all
the day long." Ps. 35:1-28

"Seek the Lord, and pray before Him…" Ps. 37:7 PB

David's prayer

"O Lord, rebuke me not in Thy wrath: neither chasten me in
Thy hot displeasure. For Thine arrows stick fast in me, and
Thy hand presseth me sore.
There is no soundness in my flesh because of Thine anger;
neither is there any rest in my bones because of my sin.
For mine iniquities are gone over mine head: as an heavy
burden they are too heavy for me.
My wounds stink and are corrupt because of my foolishness. I
am troubled; I am bowed down greatly; I go mourning all the
day long.
For my loins are filled with a loathsome disease
("my back is filled with searing pain there is no health in
my body" NIV): *and there is no soundness in my flesh. I*
am feeble and sore broken; I have roared by reason of the
disquietness of my heart ("I groan in anguish of heart" NIV).
Lord, all my desire is before Thee: and my groaning is not hid
from Thee. My heart panteth, my strength faileth me: as for
the light of mine eyes, it also is gone from me.
My lovers and my friends stand aloof from my sore ("avoid
me because of my wounds" NIV); *and my kinsmen stand*
afar off. They also that seek after my life lay snares for me:
and they that seek my hurt speak mischievous things, and
imagine deceits all the day long.

But I, as a deaf man, heard not; and I was as a dumb man
that openeth not his mouth. Thus I was as a man that heareth
not, and in whose mouth are no reproofs.
For in Thee, O Lord, do I hope: Thou wilt hear, O Lord my
God. For I said, Hear me, lest otherwise they should rejoice
over me; when my foot slippeth they magnify themselves
against me. For I am ready to halt, and my sorrow is
continually before me.
For I will declare mine iniquity; I will be sorry of my sin. But
mine enemies are lively, and they are strong: and they that
hate me wrongfully are multiplied.
They also that render evil for good are mine adversaries;
because I follow the thing that is good. Forsake me not, O
Lord; O my God, be not far from me. Make haste to help me,
O Lord my salvation." Ps. 38:1-21

David's prayer

Some think this chapter was written while David was still a boy
tending the sheep.

"Lord, make me to know mine end, and the measure of my
days, what it is; that I may know how frail I am. Behold,
Thou hast made my days as an handbreadth; and mine age is
as nothing before Thee: verily every man at his best state
is altogether vanity. Selah. Surely every man walketh in a vain
shew: surely they are disquieted in vain: he heapeth up riches,
and knoweth not who shall gather them.
And now, Lord, what wait I for? My hope is in Thee. Deliver
me from all my transgressions: make me not the reproach
of the foolish. I was dumb, I opened not my mouth (a
prophecy of Jesus); *because Thou didst it. Remove Thy stroke*

195

("scourge" NIV) *away from me: I am consumed by the blow of Thine hand. When Thou with rebukes dost correct man for iniquity,*

Thou makest his beauty to consume away like a moth: surely every man is vanity.

Selah. Hear my prayer, O Lord, and give ear unto my cry; hold not Thy peace at my tears: for I am a stranger with Thee, and a sojourner, as all my fathers were.

O spare me, that I may recover strength, before I go hence, and be no more." Ps. 39:4-13

David's prayer

Written after Absalom was killed and David was sitting on the throne again. He praised God for those who heard his prayer.

"I waited patiently for the Lord; and He inclined unto me, and heard my cry, He brought me up out of an horrible pit, out of the miry clay, and set my feet upon a rock (Jesus), *and established my goings. And He hath put a new song in my mouth, even praise unto our God; many shall see it, and fear, and shall trust in the Lord."* Ps. 40:1-3

"Many, O Lord my God, are the wonders which You have done, and Your thoughts toward us; there is none to compare with You. If I would declare and speak of them, they would be too numerous to count. Sacrifice and meal offering You have not desired; my ears You have opened; burnt offering and sin offering You have not required." Ps. 40:5-6 NASB

"Many, O Lord my God, are Thy wonderful works which Thou hast done, and Thy thoughts which are usward: they cannot be reckoned up in order unto Thee: if I would declare and speak

of them, they are more than can be numbered." Ps. 40:5-6

"I delight to do Thy will, O my God:
yea, Thy law is within my heart. I have preached
righteousness in the great congregation: Lo, I have not
refrained my lips,

O Lord,
Thou knowest. I have not hid Thy righteousness within my
heart; I have declared Thy faithfulness and Thy salvation: I
have not concealed Thy lovingkindness and Thy truth from the
great congregation. Withhold not Thou Thy tender mercies
from me,
O Lord: let Thy lovingkindess and Thy truth continually
preserve me. For innumerable evils have compassed me
about: mine iniquities have taken hold upon me, so that I am
not able to look up; they are more than the hairs of mine head:
therefore my heart faileth me." Ps. 40:8-12

David's prayer

Psalm 40:6-8 is quoted in Heb. 10:5-7.

"Be pleased, O Lord, to deliver me: O Lord, make haste to help
me. Let them be ashamed and confounded together that seek
after my soul to destroy it; let them be driven backward and
put to shame that wish me evil.
Let them be desolate for a reward of their shame that say unto
me, Aha, aha. Let all those that seek Thee rejoice and be glad
in Thee: let such as love Thy salvation say continually, The
Lord be magnified.
But I am poor and needy: yet the Lord thinkest upon me:
Thou art my help and my deliverer; make no tarrying, O my

God." Ps. 40:13-17

David's prayer

This chapter is written after his friend Ahithophel betrayed him. Ahithophel was Bathsheba's uncle, and a trusted friend of David's. Maybe, Ahithophel resented David's affair with Bathsheba.

"I said, Lord,

> *Be merciful unto me: heal my soul; for I have sinned against Thee. Mine enemies speak evil of me, when shall he die, and his name perish? And if he come to see me, he speaketh vanity: his heart gathereth iniquity to itself; when he goeth abroad, he telleth it. All that hate me whisper together against me: against me do they devise my hurt. An evil disease, say they, cleaveth fast unto him: and now that he lieth he shall rise up no more. Yea, mine own familiar friend, in whom I trusted, which did eat of my bread, hath lift up heel against me."* Ps. 41:4-9

> *"But Thou, O Lord, be merciful unto me, and raise me up, that I may requite them. By this I know that Thou favourest me, because mine enemy doth not triumph over me. And as for me, thou upholdest me in mine integrity, and settest me before Thy face for ever. Blessed be the Lord God of Israel from everlasting, and to everlasting. Amen, and Amen."*
> Ps. 41:10-13

David's prayer

"When I remember these things, I pour out my soul in me... " Ps. 42:4

David's prayer
To the chief musician Maschil – for the sons of Korah.

"O my God, my soul is cast down within me; therefore will I
remember Thee from the land of Jordan..." Ps. 42:6

"Yet the Lord will command His loving kindness in the
daytime, and in the night His song shall be with me, and my
prayer unto the God of my life.
I will say unto God my Rock, Why hast Thou forgotten me?
why go I mourning because of the oppression of the enemy?"
Ps. 42:8-9

Sons of Korah
"Judge me, O God, and plead my cause against an ungodly
nation: O deliver me from the deceitful and unjust man. For
Thou art the God of my strength: why dost Thou cast me off?
Why go I mourning because of the oppression of the enemy?
O send out Thy light and thy truth: let them lead me; let them
bring me unto Thy holy hill, and to Thy tabernacles. Then will
I go unto the altar of God, unto God my exceeding joy; yea,
upon the harp will I praise Thee, O God my God." Ps. 43:1-4

Sons of Korah
This may have been written by someone in the Babylonian captivity.
Used in worship after a military defeat - To the chief musician – for
the sons of Korah – Maschil
"We have heard with our ears, O God, our fathers have told
us, what work Thou didst in their days, in the times of old.
How Thou didst drive out the heathen with Thy hand, and
plantedst them ("With Your hand You drove out the nations

and planted our ancestors" NIV); *how Thou didst afflict the people, and cast them out.*

For they got not the land in possession by their own sword, neither did their own arm save them: but Thy right hand, and Thine arm, and the light of Thy countenance, because Thou hadst a favour unto them. Thou art my King, O God: command deliverances for Jacob. Through Thee will we push down our enemies: through Thy name will we tread them under that rise up against us.

For I will not trust in my bow, neither shall my sword save me. But Thou hast saved us from our enemies, and hast put them to shame that hated us.

In God we boast all the day long, and praise Thy name for ever. Selah. But Thou hast cast off, and put us to shame; and goest not forth with our armies.

Thou makest us to turn back from the enemy: and they which hate us spoil for themselves. Thou hast given us like sheep appointed for meat; and hast scattered us among the heathen. Thou sellest Thy people for nought, and dost not increase Thy wealth by their price.

Thou makest us a reproach to our neighbours, a scorn and a derision to them that are round about us. Thou makest us a byword among the heathen, a shaking of the head among the people. My confusion is continually before me, and the shame of my face hath covered me, for the voice of him that reproacheth and blasphemeth; by reason of the enemy and avenger.

All this is come upon us; yet have we not forgotten Thee, neither have we dealt falsely in Thy Covenant.

Our heart is not turned back, neither have our steps declined from Thy way; though Thou hast sore broken us in the place of

dragons, and covered us with the shadow of death.
If we have forgotten the name of our God or stretched out our
hands to a strange god; Shall not God search this out? For He
knoweth the secrets of the heart. Yea, for Thy sake are we killed
all the day long; we are counted as sheep for the slaughter.
Awake, why sleepest Thou, O Lord? Arise, cast us not off
for ever. Wherefore hidest Thou Thy face, and forgettest our
affliction and our oppression?
For our soul is bowed down to the dust: our belly cleaveth unto
the earth. Arise for our help, and redeem us for Thy mercies'
sake." Ps. 44:1-26

This was originally written about Solomon but is symbolically about Jesus and His Bride. In Heb. 1;8 it says,

"But unto the Son he saith,
Thy throne, O God, is for ever and ever: a sceptre of
righteousness is the sceptre of thy kingdom."

This is quoting from Ps. 45:6.

"Thou art fairer than the children of men: grace is poured into
Thy lips: therefore God hath blessed Thee for ever. Gird Thy
sword upon Thy thigh, O most mighty, with Thy glory and Thy
majesty. And in Thy majesty ride prosperously because of truth
and meekness and righteousness; and Thy right hand shall
teach Thee terrible things. Thine arrows are sharp in the heart
of the king's enemies; whereby the people fall under Thee. Thy
throne, O God, is for ever and ever: the scepter of Thy kingdom
is a right scepter. Thou lovest righteousness, and hatest
wickedness: therefore God, Thy God, hath anointed Thee

with the oil of gladness above Thy fellows. All Thy garments smell of myrrh, and aloes, and cassia, out of the ivory palaces, whereby they have made Thee glad. Kings' daughters were among Thy honourable women: upon Thy right hand did stand the queen in gold of Ophir.

Hearken, O daughter, and consider, and incline thine ear; forget also thine own people, and thy father's house; so shall the king greatly desire thy beauty: for He is thy Lord; and worship thou Him. And the daughter of Tyre shall be there with a gift; even the rich among the people shall intreat thy favour. The king's daughter is all glorious within: her clothing is of wrought gold. She shall be brought unto the king in raiment of needlework: the virgins her companions that follow her shall be brought unto Thee with gladness and rejoicing shall they be brought: they shall enter into the king's palace. Instead of thy fathers shall be thy children, whom thou mayest make princes in all the earth. I will make Thy name to be remembered in all generations: therefore shall the people praise Thee for ever and ever." Ps. 45:2-17

Sons of Korah

"Thou breakest the ships of Tarshish with an east wind. As we have heard, so have we seen in the city of the Lord of hosts, in the city of our God: God will establish it for ever. Selah. We have thought of Thy lovingkindness, O God, in the midst of Thy temple.

According to Thy name, O God, so is Thy praise unto the ends of the earth: Thy right hand is full of righteousness. Let mount Zion rejoice, let the daughters of Judah be glad, because of Thy judgments. Walk about Zion, and go round about her: tell the towers thereof.

Mark Ye well her bulwarks, consider her palaces; that ye may
tell it to the generation following. For this God is our God for
ever and ever; He will be our guide even unto death."

Ps. 48:9-14

Asaph
God speaks

God tells Asaph to pay his vows and call on Him in the day of
trouble.

"Hear, O My people, and I will speak; O Israel, and I will
testify against thee: I am God, even thy God. I will not reprove
thee for thy sacrifices or thy burnt offerings, to have been
continually before Me. I will take no bullock out of thy house,
nor he goats out of thy folds. For every beast of the forest is
Mine, and the cattle upon a thousand hills.
I know all the fowls of the mountains: and the wild beasts of
the field are Mine.
If I were hungry, I would not tell thee: for the world is Mine,
and the fullness thereof… Offer unto God thanksgiving; and
pay thy vows unto the Most High: and call upon Me in the day
of trouble: I will deliver thee, and thou shalt glorify Me.
But unto the wicked God saith, What hast thou to do to
declare My statues, or that thou shouldest take My Covenant
in thy mouth. Seeing thou hatest instruction, and castest
my words behind thee. When thou sawest a thief, then thou
consentedst with him, and hast been partaker with adulterers.
Thou givest thy mouth to evil, and thy tongue frameth deceit.
Thou sittest and speakest against thy brother; thou slanderest
thine own mother's son. These things hast thou done,
and I kept silence; thou thoughtest that I was altogether such
an one as thyself: but I will reprove thee, and set them in order
before thine eyes.

*Now consider this, ye that forget God, lest I tear you in pieces,
and there be none to deliver.
Whoso offereth praise glorifiest Me: and to him that ordereth
his conversation aright will I shew the salvation of God."*
Ps. 50:7-23

"What right have you to recite My statues ("laws" NIV), *or
take My Covenant on your lips? For you hate* ("My" NIV)
*discipline, and you cast My words behind you.
If you see a thief, you are a friend of his* ("you join with him"
NIV); *and you keep company with adulterers. You give your
mouth free rein for evil, and your tongue frames deceit. You
sit and speak against your brother; you slander your own
mother's son. These things you have done and I have been
silent; you thought that I was… like* ("you" NIV). *But now I
rebuke you, and lay the charge before you.
Mark this, then, you who forget God, lest I rend, and there be
none to deliver… to him who orders his way aright* ("If you
keep to My path" NLT) *I will show the salvation of God!"*
Ps. 50:17-23 RSV

David's prayer

A confession used as a song in worship. This is a Prayer of David
after Nathan the prophet confronts him about the death of Uriah,
and his adultery with Bathsheba.

*"Have mercy upon me, O God, according to Thy loving
kindness: according unto the multitude of Thy tender mercies
blot out my transgressions.
Wash me thoroughly from mine iniquity, and cleanse me from
my sin. For I acknowledge my transgressions: and my sin is*

ever before me.

Against Thee, Thee only, have I sinned, and done this evil in Thy sight: that Thou mightest be justified when Thou speakest, and be clear when Thou judgest.

Behold, I was shapen in iniquity; and in sin did my mother conceive me.

Behold, Thou desirest truth in the inward parts: and in the hidden part Thou shalt make me to know wisdom. Purge me with hyssop, and I shall be clean: wash me, and I shall be whiter than snow. Make me to hear joy and gladness; that the bones which Thou hast broken may rejoice. Hide Thy face from my sins, and blot out all mine iniquities.

Create in me a clean heart, O God; and renew a right Spirit within me. Cast me not away from Thy presence; and take not Thy Holy Spirit from me. Restore unto me the joy of Thy salvation; and uphold me with Thy free Spirit ("a willing spirit" NIV) *Then will I teach transgressors Thy ways; and sinners shall be converted unto Thee.*

Deliver me from blood-guiltiness (Because he had Uriah killed), *O God, Thou God of my salvation: and my tongue shall sing aloud of Thy righteousness. O Lord, open Thou my lips; and my mouth shall shew forth Thy praise.*

For Thou desirest not sacrifice: else would I give it: Thou delightest not in burnt offering.

The sacrifices of God are a broken spirit: a broken and a contrite heart, O God, Thou wilt not despise.

Do good in Thy good pleasure unto Zion: build Thou the walls of Jerusalem. Then shalt Thou be pleased with the sacrifices of righteousness with burnt offering and whole burnt offering: then shall they offer bullocks upon Thine altar." Ps. 51:1-19

David's prayer

Written after being betrayed by the people of Keilah of Judah, whom David had saved from the Philistines.

> *"I will praise Thee for ever, because Thou hast done it:*
> *and I will wait on Thy name; for it is good before Thy saints."*
> Ps. 52:9

David's prayer

> *"Save me, O God, by Thy name, and judge me by Thy strength.*
> *Hear my prayer, O God; give ear to the words of my mouth.*
> *For strangers are risen up against me, and oppressors seek after my*
> *soul: they have not set God before them. Selah. Behold, God is*
> *mine helper: the Lord is with them that uphold my soul. He shall*
> *reward evil unto mine enemies: cut them off in Thy truth. I will*
> *freely sacrifice unto Thee: I will praise Thy name, O Lord; for it is*
> *good. For He hath delivered me out of all trouble: and mine eye*
> *hath seen His desire upon mine enemies: cut them off in Thy truth.*
> *I will freely sacrifice unto Thee: I will praise Thy name, O Lord;*
> *for it is good."* Ps. 54:1-6

David's prayer

Pray morning – noon – night (same as Daniel). While David was hiding in a cave fleeing, a friend betrayed him to king Saul (I Sam. 21:24).

> *"Give ear to my prayer, O God; and hide not Thyself from*
> *my supplication. Attend unto me, and hear me: I mourn in*
> *my complaint, and make a noise; because of the voice of the*
> *enemy, because of the oppression of the wicked: for they cast*
> *iniquity upon me, and in wrath they hate me.*

My heart is sore pained within me: and the terrors of death are
fallen upon me. And I said, Oh that I had wings like a dove!
For then would I fly away, and be at rest. Lo, then would I
wander far off, and remain in the wilderness. Selah. I would
hasten my escape from the windy storm and tempest.
Destroy, O Lord, and divide their tongues: for I have seen
violence and strife in the city.
Day and night they go about it upon the walls thereof:
mischief also and sorrow are in the midst of it. Wickedness
is in the midst thereof: deceit and guile depart not from her
streets. For it was not an enemy that reproached me; then I
could have borne it: neither was it he that hated me that did
magnify himself against me; then I would have hid myself
from him: but it was thou, a man mine equal, my guide,
and mine acquaintance. We took sweet counsel together,
and walked unto the house of God in company. Let death
seize upon them, and let them go down quick into hell: for
wickedness is in their dwellings, and among them. As for me,
I will call upon God; and the Lord shall save me.
Evening, and morning, and at noon, will I pray, and cry
aloud: and He shall hear my voice..." Ps. 55:1-17
"...and the Lord will rescue me." vs. 16 NLT

God answers
David speaks.

"He hath delivered my soul in peace from the battle that was
against me: for there were many with me.
God shall hear, and afflict them, even He that abideth of old.
Selah. Because they have no changes, therefore they fear not
God. He hath put forth his hands against such as be at peace

with Him ("my friend acts violently against those at peace with him" HCSB): *He hath broken his covenant."* Ps. 55:18-20

"The words of his mouth were smoother than butter, but war was in his heart: his words were softer than oil, yet were they drawn swords. Cast thy burden upon the Lord, and He shall sustain thee: He shall never suffer the righteous to be moved." Ps. 55:21-22

David's prayer

"But Thou, O God, shalt bring them down into the pit of destruction: bloody and deceitful men shall not live out half their days; but I will trust in Thee." Ps. 55:23

David's prayer

God puts our tears in a bottle, and writes them in a book.

"Be merciful unto me, O God: for man would swallow me up; he fighting daily oppresseth me ("press their attack" NIV).
*Mine enemies would daily swallow me up:
for they be many that fight against me, O Thou most High.
What time I am afraid, I will trust in Thee. In God I will praise His Word, in God I have put my trust; I will not fear what flesh can do unto me. Every day they wrest my words: all their thoughts are against me for evil. They gather themselves together, they hide themselves, they mark my steps, when they wait for my soul. Shall they escape by iniquity? In Thine anger cast down the people O God. Thou tellest my wanderings: put Thou my tears into Thy bottle; are they not in Thy book? When I cry unto Thee, then shall mine enemies turn back: this I know; for God is for me. In God will I praise His word: in the Lord will I praise His word.*

In God have I put my trust: I will not be afraid what man can do unto me. Thy vows are upon me, O God: I will render praises unto Thee. For Thou hast delivered my soul from death: wilt not Thou deliver my feet from falling, that I may walk before God in the light of the living ("life" **ESV**)?"
Ps. 56:1-13

David's prayer

"Be merciful unto me, O God, be merciful unto me: for my soul trusteth in Thee: yea, in the shadow of Thy wings (**Ps.91:1**) *will I make my refuge, until these calamities be overpast.*

I will cry unto God Most High; unto God that performeth all things for me...Be Thou exalted, O God, above the heavens; let Thy glory be above all the earth.

They have prepared a net for my steps; my soul is bowed down: they have digged a pit before me, into the midst whereof they are fallen themselves.

Selah. My heart is fixed, O God, my heart is fixed: I will sing and give praise. Awake up, my glory; awake, psaltery and harp: I myself will awake early.

I will praise Thee, O Lord, among the people: I will sing unto Thee among the nations. For Thy mercy is great unto the heavens, and Thy truth unto the clouds.

Be Thou exalted, O God, above the heavens; let Thy glory be above all the earth." Ps. 57:1-11

David's prayer

"Break their teeth, O God, in their mouth: break out the great teeth of the young lions, O Lord. Let them melt away as waters which run continually:

when He bendeth His bow to shoot His arrows, let them be as
cut in pieces.
As a snail which melteth, let every one of them pass away: like
the untimely birth of a woman, that they may not see the sun.
Before Your pots can feel the thorns He shall take them away
as with a whirlwind, both living, and in His wrath. The
righteous shall rejoice when He seeth the vengeance: He shall
wash His feet in the blood of the wicked.

So that a man shall say, Verily there is a reward for the righteous:
verily He is a God that judgeth in the earth." Ps. 58:6-11

David's prayer
A prayer when Saul sent soldiers to kill David while at home with
his wife, Michael.

"Deliver me from mine enemies, O my God: defend me from
them that rise up against me. Deliver me from the workers of
iniquity, and save me from bloody men.
For, lo, they lie in wait for my soul: the mighty are gathered
against me; not for my transgression, nor for my sin, O Lord.
They run and prepare themselves without my fault: awake to
help me,and behold. Thou therefore, O Lord God of hosts, the
God of Israel, awake to visit all the heathen: be not merciful to
any wicked transgressors. Selah.
They return at evening: they make a noise like a dog, and go
round about the city.
Behold, they belch out with their mouth: swords are in their
lips: for who, say they, doth hear? But Thou,O Lord, shalt
laugh at them; Thou shalt have all the heathen in derision.
Because of His strength will I wait upon thee: for God is my

defence. The God of my mercy shall prevent me: God shall let
me see my desire upon mine enemies.
Slay them not, lest my people forget: scatter them by Thy
power; and bring them down,O Lord our shield. For the sin of
their mouth and the words of their lips let them even
be taken in their pride: and for cursing and lying which they
speak.
Consume them in wrath, consume them, that they may not be:
and let them know that God ruleth in Jacob unto the ends of
the earth. Selah.
And at evening let them return; and let them make a noise like
a dog, and go round about the city. Let them wander up and
down for meat, and grudge if they be not satisfied. But I will
sing of Thy power; yea, I will sing aloud of Thy mercy in the
morning; for Thou hast been my defence and refuge in the day
of my trouble.
Unto Thee, O my strength, will I sing: for God is my defence,
and the God of my mercy." Ps. 59:1-17

David's prayer

"O God, Thou hast cast us off, Thou hast scattered us, Thou
hast been displeased; O turn Thyself to us again. Thou hast
made the earth to tremble; Thou hast broken it:
heal the breaches thereof; for it shaketh. Thou hast shewed
Thy people hard things:
Thou hast made us to drink the wine of astonishment. Thou
hast given a banner to them that fear Thee.
That it may be displayed because of the truth. Selah.
That Thy beloved may be delivered; save with Thy right hand,
and hear me." Ps. 60:1-5

God speaks

"God hath spoken in His holiness;

I will rejoice, I will divide Shechem, and mete out the valley
of Succoth. Gilead is Mine, and Manasseh is Mine; Ephraim
also is the strength of Mine head; Judah is My lawgiver; Moab
is My washpot; over Edom will I cast out My shoe: Philistia,
triumph thou because of Me.
Who will bring Me into the strong city? Who will lead me into
Edom?" Ps. 60:6-9

David responds to God

"Wilt not Thou, O God, which hadst cast us off?
And Thou, O God, which didst not go out with our armies?
Give us help from trouble: for vain is the help of man.
Through God we shall do valiantly: for He it is that shall tread
down our enemies." Ps. 60:10-12

David's prayer

"Hear my cry, O God; attend unto my prayer. From the end of
the earth will I cry unto Thee, when my heart is overwhelmed:
lead me to the rock that is higher than I.
For Thou hast been a shelter for me, and a strong tower from
the enemy. I will abide in Thy tabernacle for ever: I will trust
in the covert of Thy wings. Selah.
For Thou, O God, hast heard my vows: Thou hast given me
the heritage of those that fear Thy name. Thou wilt prolong the
king's life: and his years as many generations.
He shall abide before God for ever: O prepare mercy and
truth, which may preserve him.
So will I sing praise unto Thy name for ever, that I may daily

perform my vows." Ps. 61:1-8

"… pour out your heart before Him; God is a refuge for us.
Selah" Ps. 62:8 UKJV

God answers

Power and Mercy belong to God.

"God hath spoken once; twice have I heard this; that power
belongeth unto God." Ps. 62:11

David's prayer

"Also unto Thee, O Lord,
belongeth mercy: for Thou renderest to every man
According to His work." Ps. 62:12

David's prayer

"O God, Thou art my God; early will I seek Thee: my soul
thirsteth for Thee, my flesh longeth for Thee in a dry and
thirsty land, where no water is; to see Thy power and thy glory,
so as I have seen Thee in the sanctuary.
Because Thy loving kindness is better than life, my lips shall
praise thee. Thus will I bless Thee while I live: I will lift up my
hands in Thy name.
My soul shall be satisfied as with marrow and fatness; and my
mouth shall praise Thee with joyful lips: when I remember
Thee upon my bed, and meditate on thee in the night watches.
Because Thou hast been my help, therefore in the shadow of
Thy wings will I rejoice.
My soul followeth hard after Thee: Thy right hand upholdeth
me. But those that seek my soul, to destroy it, shall go into
the lower parts of the earth. They shall fall by the sword: they

shall be a portion for foxes.
But the king shall rejoice in God; every one that sweareth by
Him shall glory: but the mouth of them that speak lies shall be
stopped." Ps. 63:1-11

David's prayer

"Hear my voice, O God, in my prayer: preserve my life from
fear of the enemy. Hide me from the secret counsel of the
wicked; from the insurrection of the workers of iniquity: who
whet their tongue like a sword, and bend their bows to shoot
their arrows, even bitter words: that they may shoot in secret
at the perfect: suddenly do they shoot at him, and fear not.
They encourage themselves in an evil matter: they commune of
laying snares privily; they say, Who shall see them..."
Ps. 64:1-5

David's song prayer

"Praise waiteth for thee, O God, in Sion:
and unto Thee shall the vow be performed. O Thou that
hearest prayer, unto Thee shall all flesh come. Iniquities prevail
against me: as for our transgressions, Thou shalt purge them
away. Blessed is the man whom Thou choosest, and causest to
approach unto Thee, that he may dwell in Thy courts: we shall
be satisfied with the goodness of Thy house, even of Thy holy
temple.
By terrible things in righteousness wilt Thou answer us, O God
of our salvation; who art the confidence of all the ends of the
earth, and of them that are afar off upon the sea: which by His
strength setteth fast the mountains; being girded with power:
which stilleth the noise of the seas, the noise of their waves,
and the tumult of the people.
They also that dwell in the uttermost parts are afraid at Thy

tokens: Thou makest the outgoings of the morning and evening to rejoice.
Thou visitest the earth, and waterest it: Thou greatly enrichest it with the river of God, which is full of water: Thou preparest them corn, when Thou hast so provided for it.
Thou waterest the ridges thereof abundantly: Thou settlest the furrows thereof: Thou makest it soft with showers: Thou blessest the springing thereof.
Thou crownest the year with Thy goodness; and Thy paths drop fatness. They drop upon the pastures of the wilderness: and the little hills rejoice on every side.
The pastures are clothed with flocks: the valleys also are covered over with corn: they shout for joy, they also sing."
Ps. 65:1-13

David's song prayer

"Say unto God, How terrible art Thou in Thy works ("How awesome are Your deeds" NLT*)!*
Through the greatness of Thy power shall Thine enemies submit themselves unto Thee. All the earth shall worship Thee, and shall sing unto Thee; they shall sing to Thy name. Selah."
Ps. 66:3-7

Prayer of David

You have tried us like gold in the fire.

"For Thou, O God, hast proved us: Thou hast tried us, as silver is tried. Thou broughtest us into the net; Thou laidst affliction upon our loins. Thou hast caused men to ride over our heads; we went through fire and through water: but Thou broughtest us out into a wealthy place ("of abundance" NIV*).*

I will go into Thy house with burnt offerings: I will pay Thee
my vows, which my lips have uttered, and my mouth hath
spoken, when I was in trouble.
I will offer unto Thee burnt sacrifices of fatlings, with the
incense of rams; I will offer bullocks with goats.
Selah." Ps. 66:10-15

"*I cried unto Him with my mouth, and he was extolled with my*
tongue. If I regard iniquity in my heart, the Lord will not hear me: but
verily God hath heard me; He hath attended to the voice of my prayer.
Blessed be God, which hath not turned away my prayer, nor His mercy
from me." Ps. 66:17-20
"*...God did listen*" Ps. 66:19 NLT
"*...God has heard*" Ps. 66:19 NASB

"*But verily God has heard me; He has attended to the voice of my*
prayer. Blessed be God, which has not turned away my prayer, nor His
mercy from me." Ps. 66:19-20 UKJV

David's song prayer

"*God*
be merciful unto us, and bless us; and cause Your face to shine
upon us; Selah. That Thy way may be known upon earth, Thy
saving health among all nations.
Let the people praise Thee, O God; let all the people praise
Thee. O let the nations be glad and sing for joy: for Thou
shalt judge the people righteously, and govern the nations
upon earth. Selah.
Let the people praise Thee, O God; let all the people praise
Thee. Then shall the earth yield her increase; and God, even
our own God, shall bless us. God shall bless us; and all the

ends of the earths shall fear Him." Ps. 67:1-7

Prayer of David

"O God,
when Thou wentest forth before Thy people, when Thou didst
march through the wilderness; Selah:
The earth shook, the heavens also dropped at the presence of God:
even Sinai itself was moved at the presence of God, the God of Israel.

Thou, O God, didst send a plentiful rain, whereby Thou
didst confirm Thine inheritance, when it was weary. Thy
congregation hath dwelt therein: Thou, O God, hast prepared
of Thy goodness for the poor." Ps. 68:7-10

Prayer of David

Lord,
"Thou hast ascended on high, Thou hast led captivity captive:
Thou hast received gifts for men;
yea, for the rebellious also, that the Lord God might dwell
among them." Ps. 68:18

Fulfilled at Jesus' resurrection, Mt. 27:52-53.

God answers

"The Lord said,
I will bring again from Bashan, I will bring My people again
from the depths of the sea: that thy foot may be dipped in
the blood of thine enemies, and the tongue of thy dogs in the
same." Ps. 68:22-23

"... strengthen, O God, that which Thou hast wrought for us."

Ps. 68:28
"O God, Thou art terrible out of Thy holy places: the God of Israel is He that giveth strength and power unto His people. Blessed be God." Ps. 68:35

Prayer of David

Prayer songs of David used in worship. We are to restore what we steal.

"Save me, O God; for the waters are come in unto my soul. I sink in deep mire, where there is no standing: I am come into deep waters, where the floods overflow me. I am weary of my crying: my throat is dried: mine eyes fail while I wait for my God. They that hate me without a cause are more than the hairs of mine head: they that would destroy me, being mine enemies wrongfully, are mighty: then I restored that which I took not away.

O God, Thou knowest my foolishness; and my sins are not hid from Thee. Let not them that wait on Thee, O Lord God of hosts, be ashamed for my sake: let not those that seek Thee be confounded for my sake, O God of Israel. Because for Thy sake I have borne reproach; shame hath covered my face. I am become a stranger unto my brethren, and an alien unto my mother's children.

For the zeal of Thine house hath eaten me up (Jesus); *and the reproaches of them that reproached Thee are fallen upon me. When I wept, and chastened my soul with fasting, that was to my reproach. I made sackcloth also my garment; and I became a proverb to them. They that sit in the gate speak against me; and I was the song of the drunkards.*

But as for me, my prayer is unto Thee,
O Lord, in an acceptable time: O God, in the multitude of Thy
mercy hear me, in the truth of Thy salvation.Deliver me out of
the mire, and let me not sink: let me be delivered from
them that hate me, and out of the deep waters. Let not the
waterflood overflow me, neither let the deep swallow me up,
and let not the pit shut her mouth upon me.
Hear me, O Lord; for Thy loving kindness is good: turn unto
me according to the multitude of Thy tender mercies. And
hide not Thy face from Thy servant; for I am in trouble:
hear me speedily. Draw nigh unto my soul, and redeem it:
deliver me because of mine enemies.
Thou hast known my reproach, and my shame, and my
dishonour: mine adversaries are all before Thee. Reproach
hath broken my heart; and I am full of heaviness: and I looked
for some to take pity, but there was none; and for comforters
but I found none.
They gave me also gall for my meat; and in my thirst they
gave me vinegar to drink **(prophecy of Jesus)***. Let their table*
become a snare before them: and that which should have
been for their welfare, let it become a trap. Let their eyes be
darkened, that they see not; and make their loins continually
to shake. Pour out Thine indignation upon them, and let
Thy wrathful anger take hold of them. Let their habitation be
desolate; and let none dwell in their tents. For they persecute
him whom Thou hast smitten; and they talk to the grief of
those whom Thou hast wounded. Add iniquity unto their
iniquity: and let them not come into Thy righteousness. Let
them be blotted out of the book of the living, and not be
written with the righteous. But I am poor and sorrowful: let
Thy salvation, O God, set me up on high." Ps. 69:1-29

Prayer of David

David's prayer – to remind us of our dependence on God.

"Make haste, O God to deliver me; make haste to help me,
O Lord. Let them be ashamed and confounded that seek after
my soul: let them be turned backward, and put to confusion,
that desire my hurt.

Let them be turned back for a reward of their shame that say,
Aha, aha. Let all those that seek Thee rejoice and be glad in
Thee: and let such as love Thy salvation say continually, Let
God be magnified. But I am poor and needy: make haste unto
me, O God: Thou art my help and my deliverer; O Lord, make
no tarrying." Ps. 70:1-5

Prayer of David

"In Thee, O Lord, do I put my trust: let me never be put to
confusion.

Deliver me in Thy righteousness, and cause me to escape:
incline Thine ear unto me, and save me. Be Thou my strong
habitation, whereunto I may continually resort: Thou hast
given commandment to save me; for Thou art my rock and my
fortress.

Deliver me, O my God, and of the hand of the wicked, out of
the hand of the unrighteous and cruel man. For Thou art my
hope, O Lord God: Thou art my trust from my youth.

By Thee have I been holden up from the womb; Thou art He
that took me out of my mother's bowels: my praise shall be
continually of Thee. I am as a wonder unto many; but Thou
art my strong refuge. Let my mouth be filled with Thy praise
and with Thy honour all the day. Cast me not off in the time
of old age; forsake me not when my strength faileth. For mine

enemies speak against me; and they that lay wait for my soul take counsel together, saying God hath forsaken him: persecute and take him; for there is none to deliver him, O God, be not far from me: O my God, make haste for my help. Let them be confounded and consumed that are adversaries to my soul; let them be covered with reproach and dishonour that seek my hurt. But I will hope continually, and will yet praise Thee more and more.

My mouth shall shew forth Thy righteousness and Thy salvation all the day; for I know not the numbers thereof. I will go in the strength of the Lord God: I will make mention of Thy righteousness, even of Thine only. O God, Thou hast taught me from my youth: and hitherto have I declared Thy wondrous works.

Now also when I am old and grayheaded, O God, forsake me not; until I have shewed Thy strength unto this generation, and thy power to everyone that is to come.

Thy righteousness also, O God, is very high, who hast done great things: O God, who is like unto Thee! Thou, which hast shewed me great and sore troubles, shalt quicken me again, and shalt bring me up again from the depths of the earth. Thou shalt increase my greatness, and comfort me on every side.

I will also praise Thee with the psaltery, even Thy truth, O my God:unto Thee will I sing with the harp, O Thou Holy One of Israel. My lips shall greatly rejoice when I sing unto Thee; and my soul, which Thou hast redeemed.

My tongue also shall talk of Thy righteousness all the day long: for they are confounded, for they are brought unto shame, that seek my hurt." Ps. 71:1-24

Prayer of David
For Solomon.

"Give the king Thy judgments, O God, and Thy righteousness unto the king's son... prayer also shall be made for him continually; and daily shall He be praised...
Blessed be the Lord God, the God of Israel, who only doeth wondrous things.
And blessed be His glorious name for ever; and let the whole earth be filled with his glory; Amen, and Amen.

The prayers of David the son of Jesse are ended." Ps. 72:1,15,18-20

Asaph

1ˢᵗ **Prayer of Asaph**

The man of God sees what God has in store for the wicked.

"Until I went into the sanctuary of God; then understood I their end ("final destiny" NIV). *Surely Thou didst set them in slippery places* ("slippery ground" NIV): *Thou castedst them down into destruction.*

How are they brought into desolation, as in a moment! They are utterly consumed with terrors. As a dream when one awaketh; so, O Lord, when Thou wakest, Thou shalt despise their image ("as a fantasy"). *Thus my heart was grieved, and I was pricked in my reins.*

So foolish was I, and ignorant: I was as a beast before Thee. Nevertheless I am continually with Thee: Thou hast holden me by my right hand. Thou shalt guide me with Thy counsel, and afterward receive me to glory.

Whom have I in heaven but Thee? And there is none upon earth that I desire beside Thee. My flesh and my heart faileth: but God is the strength of my heart, and my portion for ever.

For, lo, they that are far from Thee shall perish: Thou hast destroyed all them that go a whoring from Thee.

But it is good for me to draw near to God: I have put my trust in the Lord God, that I may declare all Thy works."

Ps. 73:17-28

2ⁿᵈ **Prayer of Asaph**

"O God,

why hast Thou cast us off for ever? Why doth Thine anger smoke against the sheep of Thy pasture?

Remember Thy congregation, which Thou hast purchased of old; the rod of Thine inheritance, which Thou hast redeemed; this Mount Zion, wherein Thou hast dwelt.

Lift up Thy feet unto the perpetual desolations; even all that the enemy hath done wickedly in the sanctuary. Thine enemies roar in the midst of Thy congregations; they set up their ensigns for signs. A man was famous according as he had lifted up axes upon the thick trees. But now they break down the caved work thereof at once with axes and hammers. They have cast fire into Thy sanctuary, they have defiled by casting down the dwelling place of Thy name to the ground. They said in their hearts, Let us destroy them together: they have burned up all the synagogues of God in the land.

We see not our signs: there is no more any prophet: neither is there among us any that knoweth how long. O God, how long shall the adversary reproach?

Shall the enemy blaspheme Thy name for ever? Why withdrawest Thou Thy hand, even Thy right hand? Pluck it out of Thy bosom. For God is my King of old, working salvation in the midst of the earth. Thou didst divide the sea by Thy strength: Thou brakest the heads of the dragons in the waters. Thou brakest the heads of leviathan in pieces, and gavest him to be meat to the people inhabiting the wilderness. Thou didst cleave the fountain and the flood:

Thou driedst up mighty rivers. The day is Thine, the night also is Thine: Thou hast prepared the light and the sun. Thou hast set all the borders of the earth: Thou hast made summer and winter. Remember this, that the enemy hath reproached, O Lord, and that the foolish people have blasphemed Thy name.

O deliver not the soul of Thy turtledove unto the multitude
of the wicked: forget not the congregation of Thy poor for
ever. Have respect unto the Covenant: for the dark places of
the earth are full of the habitations of cruelty. O let not the
oppressed return ashamed: let the poor and needy praise Thy
name. Arise, O God, plead Thine own cause: remember how
the foolish man reproacheth Thee daily.
Forget not the voice of Thine enemies: the tumult of those that
rise up against Thee increaseth continually." Ps. 74:1-23

3ʳᵈ **Prayer of Asaph**

"Unto Thee, O God, do we give thanks, unto Thee do we
give thanks: for that Thy name is near Thy wondrous works
declare. When I shall receive the congregation
I will judge uprightly." Ps. 75:1,2

4ᵗʰ **Prayer of Asaph**

"Thou art more glorious and excellent than the mountains
of prey ("rich with game" NIV)*... At Thy rebuke, O God of*
Jacob, both the chariot and horse are cast into a dead sleep.
Thou, even Thou, art to be feared: and who may stand in Thy
sight when once Thou art angry? Thou didst cause judgment
to be heard from heaven... surely the wrath of man shall
praise Thee:" Ps. 76:4,6-8

5ᵗʰ **Prayer of Asaph**

"I cried unto God with my voice, even unto God with my voice; and he
gave ear unto me. In the day of my trouble I sought the Lord... my soul
refused to be comforted." Ps. 77:1,2

"I meditated far into the night" Ps. 77:6 PB

"Thy way, O God, is in the Sanctuary: who is so great a God as our God? Thou art the God that doest wonders: Thou hast declared Thy strength among the people.
Thou hast with Thine arm redeemed Thy people, the sons of Jacob and Joseph. Selah.
The waters saw Thee, O God, the waters saw Thee; they were afraid: the depths also were troubled. The clouds poured out water: the skies sent out a sound: Thine arrows also went abroad. The voice of Thy thunder was in the heaven: the lightnings lightened the world: the earth trembled and shook. Thy way is in the sea, and Thy path in the great waters, and Thy footsteps are not known. Thou leddest Thy people like a flock by the hand of Moses and Aaron." Ps. 77:13-20

God answers

"Give ear, O My people, to My law: incline your ears to the words of My mouth. I will open My mouth in a parable (this is a prophecy of Jesus)*: I will utter dark sayings of old."*
Ps. 78:1-2

6th Prayer of Asaph

"O God, the heathen are come into Thine inheritance; Thy Holy Temple have they defiled; they have laid Jerusalem on heaps. The dead bodies of Thy servants have they given to be meat unto the fowls of the heaven (Matt.24:28;Lk.17:37 ;Rev.19:17,18)*, the flesh of Thy saints unto the beasts of the earth. Their blood have they shed like water round about Jerusalem* (Rev.14:20)*; and there was none to bury them. We are become a reproach to our neighbours, a scorn and derision to them that are round about us. How long, Lord? Wilt Thou be angry for ever? Shall Thy jealousy burn like fire? Pour out*

Thy wrath upon the heathen that have not known Thee, and upon the kingdoms that have not called upon Thy name. For they have devoured Jacob, and laid waste his dwelling place. O remember not against us former iniquities: let Thy tender mercies speedily prevent us; for we are brought very low. Help us, O God of our salvation, for the glory of Thy name: and deliver us, and purge away our sins, for Thy name's sake. Wherefore should the heathen say, Where is their God? Let Him be known among the heathen in our sight by the revenging of the blood of Thy servants which is shed. Let the sighing of the prisoner come before Thee; according to the greatness of Thy power; preserve Thou those that are appointed to die; and render unto our neighbours sevenfold into their bosom their reproach, wherewith they have reproached Thee, O Lord. So we Thy people and sheep of Thy pasture will give Thee thanks for ever: we will shew forth Thy praise to all generations." Ps. 79:1-13

7th Prayer of Asaph used as a song in worship

"Give ear, O Shepherd of Israel, Thou that leadest Joseph like a flock; Thou that dwellest between the Cherubim's (I Sam.4:4; Ps.80:1;99:1;Is.37:16); *shine forth.*

Before Ephraim and Benjamin and Manasseh stir up Thy strength, and come and save us. Turn us again, O God, and cause Thy face to shine; and we shall be saved.

O Lord God of hosts, how long wilt Thou be angry against the prayer of Thy people? Thou feedest them with the bread of tears; and givest them tears to drink in great measure.

Thou makest us a strife unto our neighbours: and our enemies laugh among themselves. Turn us again, O God of hosts, and cause Thy face to shine: and we shall be saved.

Thou hast brought a vine out of Egypt: Thou hast cast out the
heathen, and planted it. Thou preparedst room before it, and
didst cause it to take deep root, and it filled the land.
The hills were covered with the shadow of it, and the boughs
thereof were like the goodly cedars. She sent out her boughs
unto the sea, and her branches unto the river. Why hast Thou
then broken down her hedges, so that all they which pass by
the way do pluck her? The boar out of the wood doth waste
it, and the wild beast of the field doth devour it. Return, we
beseech Thee, O God of hosts:
look down from heaven, and behold, and visit this vine; and
the vineyard which Thy right hand hath planted, and the
branch that Thou madest strong for thyself. It is burned with
fire, it is cut down:
they perish at the rebuke of Thy countenance. Let Thy hand be
upon the man of Thy right hand, upon the son of man whom
thou madest strong for thyself. So will not we go back from
Thee: quicken us, and we will call upon Thy name. Turn us
again, O Lord God of hosts, cause Thy face to shine;
and we shall be saved." Ps. 80:1-19

God answers

"Thou calledst in trouble, and I delivered thee; I answered thee
in the secret place of thunder: I proved thee at the waters of
Meribah. Selah.
Hear, O My people, and I will testify unto thee: O Israel, if
thou wilt hearken unto Me; there shall no strange god be in
thee; neither shalt thou worship any strange god. I am the
Lord thy God, which brought thee out of the land of Egypt:
open thy mouth wide, and I will fill it. But My people would
not hearken unto My voice, and Israel would none of Me!

So I gave them up unto their own hearts lust; and they walked in their own counsels ("So I gave them over to the stubbornness of their heart." NASB). *O that My people had hearkened unto Me and Israel had walked in My ways! I should soon have subdued their enemies, and turned My hand against their adversaries."* Ps. 81:7-14

8th Prayer of Asaph

"How long will Ye judge unjustly, and accept the persons of the wicked? Selah.
Defend the poor and fatherless: do justice to the afflicted and needy. Deliver the poor and needy: rid them out of the hand of the wicked. They know not, neither will they understand; they walk on in darkness: all the foundations of the earth are out of course.
I have said, Ye are gods (quoted by Jesus Jn.10:34); *and all of you are children of the most High. But ye shall die like men, and fall like one of the princes. Arise, O God, judge the earth: for Thou shalt inherit all nations."* Ps. 82:1-8

9th Prayer of Asaph

"Keep not Thou silence, O God: hold not Thy peace, and be not still, O God. For, lo, Thine enemies make a tumult: and they that hate Thee have lifted up the head.
They have taken crafty counsel against Thy people, and consulted against Thy hidden ones.
They have said, Come, and let us cut them off from being a nation; that the name of Israel may be no more in remembrance. For they have consulted together with one consent: they are confederate against Thee... Selah.
Do unto them as unto the Midianites; as to Sisera, as to Jabin,

at the brook of Kison: which perished at Endor: they became as dung for the earth. Make their nobles like Oreb, and like Zeeb: yea, all their princes as Zebah, and as Zalmunna: who said, Let us take to ourselves the houses of God in possession. O my God, make them like a wheel; as the stubble before the wind. As the fire burneth a wood, and as the flame setteth the mountains of fire; so persecute them with Thy tempest, and make them afraid with Thy storm. Fill their faces with shame; that they may seek Thy name, O Lord. Let them be confounded and troubled for ever; yea, let them be put to shame, and perish: that men may know that Thou, whose name alone is JEHOVAH, art the Most High over all the earth." Ps. 83:1-18

1st prayer of the sons of Korah (temple singers) used as a song in worship

"How amiable are Thy tabernacles, O Lord of hosts! My soul longeth, yea, even fainteth for the courts of the Lord: my heart and my flesh crieth out for the living God.

Yea, the sparrow hath found an house, and the swallow a nest for herself, where she may lay her young (God sees the sparrow Mt.10:29), *even Thine altars,O Lord of hosts, my King, and my God. Blessed are they that dwell in Thy house; they will be still praising Thee. Selah. Blessed is the man whose strength is in Thee; in whose heart are the ways of them* ("the high ways the Israelites took to observe the religious festivals" NIV fn).

("Happy are those who are strong in the Lord, who want above all else to follow Your steps." LB)

("in whose heart are the highways to Zion." RSV)

Who passing through the valley of Baca (weeping) *make it a well; the rain also filleth the pools* (blessings).

They go from strength to strength, every one of them in Zion appeareth before God. O Lord God of hosts, hear my prayer: give ear, O God of Jacob. Selah.

Behold, O God our shield, and look upon the face of Thine anointed. For a day in Thy courts is better than a thousand. I had rather be a doorkeeper in the house of my God, than to dwell in the tents of wickedness. For the Lord God is a sun and shield: the Lord will give grace and glory: no good thing will He withhold from them that walk uprightly. O Lord of hosts, blessed is the man that trusteth in Thee." Ps. 84:1-12,17

2nd prayer of the sons of Korah (temple singers) used as a song in worship

"Lord, Thou hast been favourable unto Thy land: Thou hast brought back the captivity of Jacob. Thou hast forgiven the iniquity of Thy people, Thou hast covered all their sin (In the OT by blood of animals; in the NT by the blood of Jesus). *Selah.*

Thou hast taken away all Thy wrath: Thou hast turned Thyself from the fierceness of Thine anger. Turn us, O God of our salvation, and cause Thine anger toward us to cease. Wilt Thou be angry with us for ever?

Wilt Thou draw out Thine anger to all generations? Wilt Thou not revive us again: that Thy people may rejoice in Thee? Shew us Thy mercy, O Lord, and grant us Thy salvation. I will hear what God the Lord will speak: for He will speak peace unto His people, and to His saints: but let them not turn again to folly. Surely His salvation is nigh them that fear Him: that glory may dwell in our land. Mercy and truth are met together; righteousness and peace have kissed each other. Truth shall spring out of the earth (on the New Earth)*: and* *righteousness shall look down from heaven. Yea, the Lord shall give that which is good: and our land shall yield her increase. Righteousness shall go before Him; and shall set us in the way of His steps."* Ps. 85:1-13

Prayer of David

We pray to God every day.

"Bow down Thine ear, O Lord, hear me: for I am poor and needy. Preserve my soul: for I am holy: O Thou my God, save Thy servant that trusteth in Thee. Be merciful unto me, O Lord: for I cry unto Thee daily. Rejoice the soul of Thy servant that trusteth in Thee. Be merciful unto me, O Lord: for I cry unto Thee daily. Rejoice the soul of Thy servant: for unto Thee, O Lord, do I lift up my soul.

For Thou, Lord, art good, and ready to forgive; and plenteous in mercy unto all them that call upon Thee. Give ear, O Lord, unto my prayer; and attend to the voice of my supplications. In the day of my trouble I will call upon Thee: for Thou wilt answer me. Among the gods there is none like unto Thee, O Lord; neither are there any works like unto Thy works. All nations whom Thou hast made shall come and worship before Thee, O Lord; and shall glorify Thy name. For Thou art great, and doest wondrous things: Thou art God alone.

Teach me Thy way, O Lord; I will walk in Thy truth: unite my heart to fear Thy name.

I will praise Thee, O Lord my God, with all my heart: and I will glorify Thy name for evermore. For great is Thy mercy toward me: and Thou hast delivered my soul from the lowest hell. O God, the proud are risen against me, and the assemblies of violent men have sought after my soul; and have not set Thee before them.

But Thou, O Lord, art a God full of compassion, and gracious, longsuffering, and plenteous in mercy and truth. O turn unto me, and have mercy upon me; give Thy strength unto Thy servant, and save the son of Thine handmaid. Shew me a token for good; that they which hate me may see it, and be ashamed: because Thou, Lord, Hast... (helped) *me, and comforted me."* Ps. 86:1-17

3rd prayer for the sons of Korah

Ethan the Levite – I Kings 4:31 during a time of decline in Judah wrote this psalm.

"O Lord God of my salvation, I have cried day and night before Thee: let my prayer come before Thee: incline Thine ear unto my cry; for my soul is full of troubles: and my life draweth nigh unto the grave. I am counted with them that go down into the pit. I am as a man that hath no strength: free among the dead, like the slain that lie in the grave, whom Thou rememberest no more: and they are cut off from Thy hand. Thou hast laid me in the lowest pit, in darkness, in the deeps. Thy wrath lieth hard upon me, and Thou hast afflicted me with all Thy waves. Selah. Thou hast put away mine acquaintance far from me; Thou hast made me an abomination unto them: I am shut up, and I cannot come forth. Mine eye mourneth by reason of affliction: Lord, I have called daily upon Thee, I have stretched out my hands unto Thee. Wilt Thou shew wonders to the dead? Shall the dead arise and praise Thee? Selah. Shall Thy loving kindness be declared in the grave? Or thy faithfulness in destruction? Shall Thy wonders be known in the dark? And Thy righteousness in the land of forgetfulness? But unto Thee have I cried, O

Lord; and in the morning shall my prayer prevent thee. Lord, why castest Thou off my soul? Why hidest Thou Thy face from me? I am afflicted and ready to die from my youth up: while I suffer Thy terrors I am distracted. Thy fierce wrath goeth over me; Thy terrors have cut me off. They came round about me daily like water; they compassed me about together. Lover and friend hast Thou put far from me, and mine acquaintance into darkness." Ps. 88:1-18

Ethan

The word Faithful(ness) is used seven times in Psalm 89

Seven is the number of the Holy Spirit, Rev. 1:4.

"A prayer that mourns the downfall of the Davidic dynasty and pleads for its restoration" NIV fn

The Prayer of Ethan, a Levite, to remember that he made a covenant with David.

> *"I will sing of the mercies of the Lord for ever: with my mouth will I make known Thy <u>faithfulness</u> to all generations. For I have said, Mercy shall be built up for ever: Thy <u>faithfulness</u> shalt Thou establish in the very heavens."* Ps. 89:1-2

God speaks

> *"I have made a Covenant with My chosen, I have sworn unto David My servant. Thy seed (Jesus) will I establish for ever, and build up Thy throne to all generations. Selah."* Ps. 89:3-4

Ethan's prayer

> *"And the heavens shall praise Thy wonder, O Lord: Thy <u>faithfulness</u> also in the congregation of the saints. For who in the heaven can be compared unto the Lord? Who among the sons of the mighty can be likened unto the Lord? God is greatly to be feared in the assembly of the saints, and to be had in reverence of all them that are about Him. O Lord God of hosts, who is a strong Lord like unto Thee? Or to Thy <u>faithfulness</u> round about Thee? Thou rulest the raging of the*

sea: when the waves thereof arise, Thou stillest them.
Thou hast broken Rahab ("Egypt" KJV fn; or a "mythical
monster of the deep... probably another name for
Leviathan" NIV fn) *in pieces, as one that is slain; Thou hast*
scattered Thine enemies with Thy strong arm. The heavens
are Thine, the earth also is Thine: as for the world and the
fullness thereof, Thou hast founded them. The north and the
south Thou hast created them: Tabor and Hermon shall rejoice
in Thy name. Thou hast a mighty arm: strong is Thy hand,
and high is Thy right hand. Justice and judgment are the
habitation of Thy throne: mercy and truth shall go before Thy
face. Blessed is the people that know the joyful sound: they
shall walk, O Lord, in the light of Thy countenance. In Thy
name shall they rejoice all the day: and in Thy righteousness
shall they be exalted. For Thou art the glory of their strength:
and in Thy favour our horn ("symbolizes strong one" NIV
fn) *shall be exalted. For the Lord is our defence; and the holy*
One of Israel is our king. PS. 89:5-18

God speaks

Then Thou spakest in vision to Thy Holy One, and saidest,
I have laid help upon one that is mighty; I have exalted one
chosen out of the people. I have found David My servant; with
My holy oil have I anointed him: with whom My hand shall be
established: Mine arm also shall strengthen him. The enemy
shall not exact upon him; nor the son of wickedness afflict
him. And I will beat down his foes before his face, and plague
them that hate him. But My faithfulness and My mercy shall
be with him: and in My name shall his horn ("strength" NIV
fn) *be exalted. I will set his hand also in the sea, and his right*
hand in the rivers. He shall cry unto Me, Thou art my Father,

my God, and the Rock of my salvation. Also I will make Him
(Jesus) My first born, higher than the king's of the earth. My
mercy will I keep for Him for evermore, and My Covenant
shall stand fast with Him. His seed also will I make to endure
for ever, and His throne as the days of heaven. If his children
forsake My law, and walk not in My judgments; if they break
My statutes, and keep not My Commandments; then will I
visit their transgression with the rod (Rev. 19:15), *and their*
iniquity with stripes. Nevertheless My loving kindness will I
not utterly take from him, nor suffer My <u>faithfulness</u> to fail.
My Covenant will I not break, nor alter the thing that is gone
out of My lips. Once have I sworn by My holiness that I will
not lie unto David. His Seed (Jesus) *shall endure for ever, and*
His throne as the sun before Me. It shall be established for ever
as the moon, and as a <u>faithful</u> witness in heaven. Selah.
Ps. 89:19-37

Ethan's prayer that

("God will remember His Covenant with David" NIV fn)
But thou hast cast off and abhorred, thou hast been wroth
with Thine anointed. Thou hast made void the Covenant of
Thy servant: Thou hast profaned his crown by casting it to
the ground. Thou hast broken down all his hedges; Thou hast
brought his strong holds to ruin. All that pass by the way spoil
him: he is a reproach to his neighbours. Thou hast set up the
right hand of his adversaries; Thou hast made all his enemies
to rejoice. Thou hast also turned the edge of his sword, and
hast not made him to stand in the battle. Thou hast made his
glory to cease, and cast his throne down to the ground. The
days of his youth hast Thou shortened: Thou hast covered him

with shame. Selah. How long, Lord? Wilt Thou hide Thyself
for ever? Shall Thy wrath burn like fire? Remember how short
My time is: wherefore hast Thou made all men in vain?
What man is he that liveth, and shall not see death? Shall he
deliver his soul from the hand of the grave?
Selah. Lord, where are Thy former loving kindnesses, which
Thou swarest unto David in Thy truth? Remember, Lord, the
reproach of Thy servants; how I do bear in my bosom
the reproach of all the mighty people; wherewith Thine
enemies have reproached, O Lord; wherewith they have
reproached the footsteps of Thine anointed. Blessed be the
Lord for evermore. Amen, and Amen." Ps. 89: 38-59

"... they have mocked every step of Your anointed One (Jesus)"
NIV Ps. 89:51

Prayer of Moses
The only prayer of Moses in the Psalms.

"Lord, Thou hast been our dwelling place in all generations.
Before the mountains were brought forth, or ever Thou hadst
formed the earth and the world, even from everlasting to
everlasting, Thou art God. Thou turnest man to destruction;
and sayest, Return, ye children of men. For a thousand years
in Thy sight are but as yesterday when it is past, and as a
watch in the night. Thou carriest them away as with a flood;
they are as a sleep: in the morning they are like grass which
growth up.
In the morning it flourisheth, and groweth up; in the evening it
is cut down, and withereth (Is.40:8;Ps.103:15,16). For we are
consumed by Thine anger, and by Thy wrath are we troubled.

*Thou hast set our iniquities before Thee, our secret sins in the
light of Thy countenance. For all our days are passed away in
Thy wrath: we spend our years as a tale that is told.
The days of our years are threescore years and ten (70 yrs.);
and if by reason of strength they be fourscore years (80), yet
is their strength, labour, and sorrow; for it is soon cut off, and
we fly away. Who knoweth the power of Thine anger? Even
according to Thy fear, so is Thy wrath.
So teach us to number our days, that we may apply our hearts
unto wisdom. Return, O Lord, how long? And let it repent
Thee concerning Thy servants. O satisfy us early with Thy
mercy; that we may rejoice and be glad all our days. Make
us glad according to the days wherein Thou hast afflicted us,
and the years wherein we have seen evil. Let Thy work appear
unto Thy servants, and Thy glory unto their children. And let
the beauty of the Lord our God be upon us: and establish Thou
the work of our hands upon us; yea, the work of our hands
establish Thou it."* Ps. 90:1-17

God speaking

*"Because he hath set his love upon Me, therefore will I deliver
him: I will set him on high, because he hath known My name.
He shall call upon Me, and I will answer him: I will be with
him in trouble; I will deliver him, and honour him. With long
life will I satisfy him, and shew him My salvation."*
Ps. 91:15-16

A Psalm dedicated to the Sabbath Day

Some say that, Psalm 92 is recited three times on the Sabbath Day.
*"For Thou, Lord, hast made me glad through Thy work: I will
triumph in the works of Thy hands.*

O Lord, how great are Thy works! And Thy thoughts are very deep. A brutish man knoweth not; neither doth a fool understand this. When the wicked spring as the grass (**Ps.9:5; 92:7;103:15,16;Is.40:8**), *and when all the workers of iniquity do flourish; it is that they shall be destroyed for ever: but Thou, Lord, art Most High for evermore. For, lo, Thine enemies, O Lord, for, lo, Thine enemies shall perish; all the workers of iniquity shall be scattered. But my horn shalt Thou exalt like the horn of an* (**#7214 "from raam, rehame, ram" meaning "ox"**): *I shall be anointed with fresh oil."* Ps. 92:4-10

We don't know who wrote this psalm; it may have been written after the Babylonian Captivity

"Thy throne is established of old: Thou art from everlasting. The floods have lifted up, O Lord, the floods have lifted up their voice; the floods lift up their waves. The Lord on high is mightier than the noise of many waters, yea, than the mighty waves of the sea. Thy testimonies are very sure: holiness becometh Thine house, O Lord, for ever." Ps. 93:2-5

How long will the wicked triumph?

We're not sure who wrote this psalm. Some think David; others think it comes after him.

"O Lord God, to whom vengeance belongeth; O God, to whom vengeance belongeth, shew Thyself.
Lift up Thyself, Thou judge of the earth: render a reward to the proud. Lord, how long shall the wicked, how long shall the wicked triumph? How long shall they utter and speak hard things? And all the workers of iniquity boast themselves? They break in pieces Thy people, O Lord, and afflict Thine heritage.

*They slay the widow and the stranger, and murder
the fatherless. Yet they say, The Lord shall not see, neither shall
the God of Jacob regard it.
Understand, ye brutish among the people: and ye fools, when
will ye be wise? He that planted the ear, shall He not hear?
He that formed the eye, shall He not see? He that chastiseth
the heathen, shall not He correct? He that teacheth man
knowledge, shall not He know? The Lord knoweth the thoughts
of man, that they are vanity. Blessed is the man whom Thou
chastenest, O Lord, and teachest him out of Thy law; that
Thou mayest give him rest from the days of adversity, until the
pit be digged for the wicked. For the Lord will not cast off His
people, neither will He forsake His inheritance. But judgment
shall return unto righteousness: and all the upright in heart
shall follow it. Who will rise up for Me against the evildoers?
Or who will stand up for Me against the workers of iniquity?
Unless the Lord had been my help, my soul had almost dwelt
in silence. When I said, My foot slippeth; Thy mercy, O Lord,
held me up. In the multitude of my thoughts within me Thy
comforts delight my soul. Shall the throne of iniquity have
fellowship with Thee, which frameth mischief by a law? They
gather themselves together against the soul of the righteous
and condemn the innocent blood. But the Lord is my defence;
and my God is the rock of my refuge. And he shall bring upon
them their own iniquity, and shall cut them off in their own
wickedness; yea, the Lord our God shall cut them off."*
Ps. 94:1-23

God is exalted! Again, we don't know who wrote this psalm. Some
think David.

"For Thou, Lord, art high above all the earth: Thou art exalted far above all gods." Ps. 97:9

Unknown psalm

"Thou answeredst them, O Lord our God: Thou wast a God that forgavest them, though Thou tookest vengeance of their inventions." Ps. 99:8

"...You were a forgiving God, but You punished them when they went wrong." NLT

Prayer of David when he was sworn king

"I will sing of mercy and judgment: unto Thee, O Lord, will I sing. I will behave myself wisely in a perfect way, O when will Thou come unto me? I will walk within my house with a perfect heart. I will set no wicked thing before mine eyes; I hate the work of them that turn aside; it shall not cleave to me. A forward heart shall depart from me: I will not know a wicked person. Ps. 101:1-4

God speaks

"Whoso privily slandereth his neighbour, him will I cut off: him that hath an high look and a proud heart will not I suffer. Mine eyes shall be upon the faithful of the land, that they may dwell with Me: he that walketh in a perfect way, he shall serve Me. He that worketh deceit shall not dwell within My house: he that telleth lies shall not tarry in My sight. I will early destroy all the wicked of the land: that I may cut off all wicked doers from the city of the Lord." Ps. 101:1-8

The prayer of the afflicted

Thought to be written when Jerusalem was under distress.

"Hear my prayer, O Lord, and let my cry come unto Thee. Hide not Thy face from me in the day when I am in trouble; incline Thine ear unto me: in the day when I call answer me speedily. For my days are consumed like smoke, and my bones are burned as an hearth. My heart is smitten, and withered like grass (Ps.90:5;92:7;102:4;103:15,16;Is.40:8); *so that I forget to eat my bread. By reason of the voice of my groaning my bones cleave to my skin. I am like a pelican of the wilderness: I am like an owl of the desert. I watch, and am as a sparrow alone upon the house top. Mine enemies reproach them all the day; and they that are mad against me are sworn against me. For I have eaten ashes like bread, and mingled my drink with weeping, because of Thine indignation and Thy wrath: for Thou hast lifted me up, and cast me down. My days are like a shadow that declineth; and I am withered like grass. But Thou, O Lord, shalt endure for ever; and Thy remembrance unto all generations.*

Thou shalt arise, and have mercy upon Zion: for the time to favor her, yea, the set time, is come. For Thy servants take pleasure in her stones, and favour the dust thereof. So the heathen shall fear the name of the Lord, and all the kings of the earth Thy glory. When the Lord shall build up Zion, He shall appear in His glory. He will regard the prayer of the destitute, and not despise their prayer...

I said, O my God, take me not away in the midst of my days: Thy years are throughout all generations. Of old hast Thou laid the foundation of the earth: and the heavens are the work of Thy hands (quoted in Heb.1:10). *They shall perish, but Thou shalt endure: yea, all of them shall wax old like a garment; as a vesture shalt Thou change them. And they shall* be changed: But Thou art the same, and Thy years shall have no end. The children of Thy servants shall continue, and their seed shall be established before Thee." Ps. 102:1-28

Prayer of David

Evening prayer.

"Bless the Lord, O my soul, O Lord my God, Thou art very great; Thou art clothed with honour and majesty. Who coverest Thyself with light as with a garment: who stretchest out the heavens like a curtain: who layeth the beams of His chambers in the waters: who maketh the clouds His chariot: who walketh upon the wings of the wind: who maketh His angels spirits; His ministers a flaming fire (Rev. 1:20): Who laid the foundations of the earth, that it should not be removed for ever. Thou coveredst it with the deep as with a garment: the waters stood above the mountains. At Thy rebuke they fled; at the voice of Thy thunder they hasted away. They go up by the mountains; they go down by the valleys unto the place which Thou hast founded for them. Thou hast set a bound that they may not pass over; that they turn not again to cover the earth." Ps. 104:1-9

"Thou makest darkness, and it is night: wherein all the beasts of the forest do creep forth. The young lions roar after their prey, and seek their meat from God. The sun ariseth they gather themselves together, and lay them down in their dens. Man goeth forth unto his work and to his labour until the evening. O Lord, how manifold are Thy works! In wisdom hast Thou made them all: the earth is full of Thy riches. So is this great and wide sea, wherein are things creeping innumerable, both small and great beasts. There go the ships: there is that

Leviathan, whom Thou hast made to play therein. These wait all upon Thee; that Thou mayest give them their meat in due season. That Thou givest them they gather: Thou openest Thine hand, they are filled with good. Thou hidest Thy face, they are troubled: Thou takest away their breath, thy die, and return to their dust. Thou sendest forth Thy Spirit, they are created: and Thou renewest the face of the earth." Ps. 104:20-30

A Levite

He's asking God to once again save His people.

Prayer

"Remember me, O Lord, with the favour that Thou bearest unto Thy people: O visit me with Thy salvation; that I may see the good of Thy chosen, that I may rejoice in the gladness of Thy nation, that I may glory with Thine inheritance. We have sinned with our fathers, we have committed iniquity, we have done wickedly. Our fathers understood not Thy wonders in Egypt; they remembered not the multitude of Thy mercies; but provoked Him at the sea, even at the Red Sea." Ps. 106:4-7

It is unclear who wrote Ps. 106.; 1 Chron. 16:34 is the same as Ps. 106:1. Some think it could be David.

"He... heard their ("prayer" – PB) *cry"* Ps. 106:44

Prayer

"Save us, O Lord our God, and gather us from among the heathen, to give thanks unto Thy holy name, and to triumph in Thy praise." Ps. 106:47

"Then they cried unto the Lord in their trouble, and He saved them out of their distresses. He brought them out of darkness and the shadow of death, and brake their bands in sunder." Ps. 107:6, 13-14

"Then they cry unto the Lord in their trouble, He saveth them out of

their distresses." Ps. 107:19

"Then they cried unto the Lord in their trouble, and He bringeth them out of their trouble, and He bringeth them out of their distresses." Ps. 107:28

Prayer

This Psalm has some of the most severe curses in the Bible.

> *"O God,*
> *my heart is fixed; I will sing and give praise, even with my glory. Awake, psaltery and harp: I myself will awake early. I will praise Thee, O Lord, among the people: and I will sing praises unto Thee among the nations. For Thy mercy is great above the heavens: and Thy truth reacheth unto the clouds. Be Thou exalted, O God, above the heavens: and Thy glory above all the earth; that Thy beloved may be delivered: save with Thy right hand, and answer me. God hath spoken in His holiness; I will rejoice, I will divide Shechem, and mete out the valley of Succoth. Gilead is Mine; Manasseh is Mine; Ephraim also is the strength of Mine head; Judah is My lawgiver; Moab is My washpot; over Edom will I cast out My shoe; over Philistia will I triumph. Who will bring me into the strong city? Who will lead me into Edom? Wilt not Thou, O God, who hast cast us off? And wilt not Thou, O God, go forth with our hosts? Give us help from trouble: for vain is the help of man."*
> Ps. 108:1-12

Prayer of David

"To the chief musician" means it was to be sung at a worship service

in the temple.

"Hold not Thy peace, O God of my praise; for the mouth
of the wicked and the mouth of the deceitful are opened
against me: they have spoken against me with a lying tongue.
They compassed me about also with words of hatred; and
fought against me without a cause. For my love they are my
adversaries ("They bring charges against me, even though I
love them and pray for them..." NIV): but I give myself
unto prayer. And they have rewarded me evil for good, and
hatred for my love. Set Thou a wicked man over him: and let
Satan stand at his right hand. When he shall be judged, let
him be condemned:and let his prayer become sin. Let his days
be few; and let another take his office (quoted in Acts 1:20
about Judas). Let his children be fatherless, and his wife a
widow. Let his children be continually vagabonds, and beg: let
them seek their bread also out of their desolate places. Let the
extortioner catch all that he hath; and let the strangers spoil
his labour. Let there be none to extend mercy unto him:
neither let there be any to favour his fatherless children. Let
his posterity be cut off; and in the generation following let
their name be blotted out. Let the iniquity of his fathers be
remembered with the Lord; and let not the sin of his mother be
blotted out. Let them be before the Lord continually, that he
may cut off the memory of them from the earth. Because that
he remembered not to shew mercy, but persecuted the poor
and needy man, that he might even slay the broken in heart.
As he loved cursing, so let it come unto him: as he delighted
not in blessing, so let it be far from him. As he clothed
himself with cursing like as with his garment, so let it come
into his bowels like water, and like oil into his bones. Let it be

unto him as the garment which covereth him, and for a girdle wherewith he is girded continually. Let this be the reward of mine adversaries from the Lord, and of them that speak evil against my soul. But do thou for me, O God the Lord, for Thy name's sake: because Thy mercy is good, deliver Thou me. For I am poor and needy, and my heart is wounded within me. I am gone like the shadow when it declineth: I am tossed up and down as the locust. My knees are weak through fasting; and my flesh faileth of fatness. I became also a reproach unto them: when they looked upon me they shaked their heads. Help me, O Lord my God: O save me according to Thy mercy: that they may know that this is Thy hand; that Thou, Lord, hast done it. Let them curse, but bless Thou: when they arise, let them be ashamed; but let Thy servant rejoice. Let mine adversaries be clothed with shame, and let them cover themselves with their own confusion, as with a mantle. I will greatly praise the Lord with my mouth; yea, I will praise Him among the multitude. For He shall stand at the right hand of the poor, to save him from those that condemn his soul." Ps. 109:1-31

The Hallel (joyful praises) consisted of six psalms; Ps. 113-118. Hallel's were recited as part of the morning worship service. Psalm 136 is called "*The Great Hallel*" and is recited at Passover.

Prayer
We do not know who wrote this psalm.

"Not unto us, O Lord, not unto us, but unto Thy name give glory, for Thy mercy, and for Thy truth's sake." Ps. 115:1

Prayer

Some think David wrote this psalm.

"Then called I upon the name of the Lord;
O Lord, I beseech Thee, deliver my soul." Ps. 116:4

Prayer

"O Lord,
truly I am Thy servant; I am Thy servant, and the son of Thine
handmaid: Thou hast loosed my bonds. I will offer to Thee the
sacrifice of thanksgiving, and will call upon the name of the
Lord." Ps. 116:16,17

Prayer

Some attribute this psalm to David. Psalm 118 is the middle chapter of the Bible; Psalm 117 is the shortest chapter in the Bible and Psalm 119 is the longest. There are 594 chapters before this chapter and 154 chapters after. Psalm 118:18 *("it is better to take refuge in the Lord than in man")* is the middle verse of the Bible. If you add all the chapters of the bible except for Ps. 118, you get 1188 chapters.

Written about Psalm 118

"When the Psalmist was in distress, he called upon the Lord. People who do not pray will stay in the grip of distress. We cannot depend on our own resources when in distress. They are too easily and quickly dispended. We cannot depend on others. Often they are unwilling or unable to help. We can however, turn to the Lord who always stands ready to help and has resources and strength that cannot be exhausted." Taken from **www. bibleteachingnotes.com** on Ps. 118.

"I called upon the Lord in my distress, the Lord answered me..." Ps. 118:5

"From the straitness I called Jah, Jah answered me in a broad place." Ps. 118:5 YLT

"When I was really hurting, I prayed to the Lord. He answered my prayer, and took my worries away." Ps. 118:6 CEV
This verse is referred to in Heb. 13:6.

"I thank You for answering my prayer and saving me!" Ps. 118:21 NLT

"Save now, I beseech Thee, O Lord: O Lord, I beseech Thee, send now prosperity ("let us win" CEV "give us success" NLT)." Ps. 118:25

"You are my God, and I will praise You! You are my God, and I will exalt You!" Ps. 118:28

Psalm 119

They sang this prayer as they ascended to the temple

This is the longest psalm and the longest chapter in the Bible. This is the prayer of one who delights in God's law! Some think that David wrote this prayer, but they don't know for sure.

This psalm is called an "*alphabetic acrostic*" poem. The 176 verses are divided into 22 stanzas; one stanza for each letter of the Hebrew alphabet. Each of the eight verses begins with a Hebrew letter of the alphabet. Twenty-four times we see the name of God (Jehovah or Yahweh) in this chapter.

"*The first eight lines of the psalm all begin with the letter aleph, the first letter of the Hebrew alphabet. The next eight lines begin with beth, the second letter. And so on for 176 verses until we reach the end of the matter at the last tav. No wonder the psalm is so long. Each of the letters must have its turn... Elsewhere in the Bible, acrostics which are complete or nearly so are found in seven more psalms, in the poem in the praise of the good wife in the last chapter of Proverbs, and in each of the first four chapters of Lamentations, bemoaning the overthrow of Jerusalem. The book of Nahum begins as an acrostic, but the plan is not carried out to the end. Some enterprising scholar has even discovered Ps.4 contains an acrostic which, when read backwards, spells:'Unto a lamp for Zerubbabel'.*"
http://www.andreascenter.org/articles/psalm%20119.htm

"*Thou hast commanded us to keep Thy Precepts diligently. O that my ways were directed to keep Thy Statutes! Then shall I not be ashamed, when I have respect unto all Thy Commandments. I will praise Thee with uprightness of heart, when I shall have learned Thy righteous Judgments. I will keep Thy Statutes: O forsake me not utterly. Wherewithal shall a young man cleanse his way? By taking heed thereto according to Thy word. With my whole heart have I sought Thee: O let me not wander from Thy Commandments. Thy Word have I hid in mine heart, that I might not sin against Thee. Blessed art Thou, O Lord: teach me Thy Statutes. With my lips have I declared all the Judgments of Thy mouth.*

I have rejoiced in the way of Thy Testimonies, as much as in all riches. I will meditate in Thy Precepts, and have respect unto thy ways. I will delight myself in Thy Statutes: I will not forget Thy Word. Deal bountifully with Thy servant, that I may live, and keep Thy Word. Open Thou mine eyes, that I may behold wondrous things out of Thy law. I am a stranger in the earth: hide not Thy Commandments from me. My soul breaketh for the longing that it hath unto Thy Judgments at all times. Thou hast rebuked the proud that are cursed, which do err from Thy Commandments. Remove from me reproach and contempt; for I have kept Thy Testimonies. Princes also did sit and speak against me: but Thy servant did meditate in Thy Statues. Thy Testimonies also are my delight and my counselors.

My soul cleaveth unto the dust: quicken Thou me according to Thy Word. I have declared my ways, and Thou heardest me: teach me Thy Statutes. Make me to understand the way of Thy Precepts; so shall I talk of Thy wondrous works. My soul melteth for heaviness: strengthen Thou me according unto Thy Word. Remove from me the way of lying: and grant me Thy law graciously. I have chosen the way of truth: Thy Judgments have I laid before me. I have stuck unto Thy Testimonies: O Lord, put me not to shame. I will run the way of Thy Commandments, when Thou shalt enlarge my heart.

Teach me, O Lord, the way of Thy Statutes; and I shall keep it unto the end. Give me understanding, and I shall keep Thy law; yea, I shall observe it with my whole heart. Make me to go in the path of Thy Commandments (Here the Bible tells us that the Commandments are the path)*; for therein do I delight. Incline my heart unto Thy testimonies, and not to covetousness. Turn away mine eyes from beholding vanity; and quicken Thou me in Thy way. Stablish Thy Word unto Thy servant, who is devoted to Thy fear. Turn away my reproach which I fear: for Thy Judgments are good. Behold, I have longed after Thy Precepts: quicken me in Thy righteousness. Let Thy mercies come also unto me, O Lord, even Thy salvation, according to Thy Word. So shall I have wherewith to answer him that reproacheth me: for I trust in Thy Word. And take not the Word of truth utterly out of my mouth; for I have hoped in Thy Judgments. So shall I keep Thy law continually for ever and ever. And I will walk at liberty* (Called the perfect law of liberty Jms. 1:25)*: for I seek Thy precepts. I will speak of Thy Testimonies also before kings, and will not be ashamed. And I will delight myself in Thy Commandments, which I have loved. My hands also will I lift up unto Thy Commandments, which I have loved; and I will meditate in Thy Statutes. Remember the Word unto Thy servant, upon which Thou hast caused me to hope. This is my comfort in my affliction: for Thy Word hath quickened me. The proud have had me greatly in derision: yet have I not declined from Thy law. I remembered Thy Judgments of old, O Lord; and have comforted myself. Horror hath taken hold upon me because of the wicked that forsake Thy law. Thy Statutes have been my songs in the house of my pilgrimage. I have remembered Thy name, O Lord, in the night, and have* kept Thy law. This I had, because I kept Thy Precepts. Thou art my portion, O Lord: I have said that I would keep Thy words. I entreated Thy favour with my whole heart: be merciful unto me according to Thy Word. I thought on my ways, and turned my feet unto Thy Testimonies. I made haste, and delayed not to keep Thy Commandments. The bands of the wicked have robbed me: but I have not forgotten Thy law. At midnight I will rise to give thanks unto Thee because of Thy righteous Judgments. I am a companion of all them that fear Thee, and of them that keep Thy precepts. The earth, O Lord, is full of Thy mercy: teach me Thy Statutes. Thou hast dealt well with Thy servant, O Lord, according unto Thy Word. Teach me good judgment and knowledge: for I have believed Thy Commandments. Before I was afflicted I went astray: but now have I kept Thy Word. Thou art good, and doest good; teach me Thy Statutes. The proud have forged a lie against me: but I will keep Thy precepts with my whole heart. Their heart is as fat as grease; but I delight in Thy law. It is good for me that I have been afflicted; that I might learn Thy statutes. The law of Thy mouth is better unto me than thousands of gold and silver. Thy hands have made me and fashioned me: give me understanding, that I may learn Thy Commandments. They that fear Thee will be glad when they see me; because I have hoped in Thy Word. I know, O Lord, that Thy Judgments are right, and that Thou in faithfulness hast afflicted me. Let, I pray Thee, Thy merciful kindness be for my comfort, according to Thy Word unto Thy servant. Let Thy tender mercies come unto me, that I may live: for

Thy law is my delight. Let the proud be ashamed; for they dealt perversely with me without a cause: but I will meditate in Thy precepts. Let those that fear Thee turn unto me, and those that have known Thy Testimonies. Let my heart be sound in Thy Statutes; that I be not ashamed. My soul fainteth for Thy salvation: but I hope in Thy Word. Mine eyes fail for Thy Word, saying, When wilt Thou comfort me? For I am become like a bottle in the smoke; yet do I not forget Thy statutes. How many are the days of Thy servant? When wilt Thou execute judgment on them that persecute me? The proud have digged pits for me, which are not after Thy law. All Thy Commandments are faithful: they persecute me wrongfully; help Thou me. They had almost consumed me upon earth; but I forsook not Thy Precepts. Quicken me after Thy lovingkindness; so shall I keep the Testimony of Thy mouth. For ever, O Lord, Thy Word is settled in heaven. Thy faithfulness is unto all generations: Thou hast established the earth, and it abideth. They continue this day according to Thine ordinances: for all are Thy servants. Unless Thy law had been my delights, I should then have perished in mine affliction. I will never forget Thy Precepts: for with them Thou hast quickened me. I am Thine, save me; for I have sought Thy Precepts. The wicked have waited for me to destroy me: but I will consider Thy Testimonies. I have seen an end of all perfection: but Thy Commandments is exceeding broad. O how love I Thy law! It is my meditation all the day. Thou through Thy Commandments hast made me wiser than mine enemies: for they are ever with me. I have more understanding than all my teachers: for Thy Testimonies are my meditation. I understand more than the ancients, because I keep Thy Precepts. I have refrained my feet from every evil

way, that I might keep Thy Word.
I have not departed from Thy Judgments: for Thou hast
taught me. How sweet are Thy words unto my taste! Yea,
sweeter than honey to my mouth! Through Thy Precepts I get
understanding: therefore I hate every false way. Thy Word is
a lamp unto my feet, and a light unto my path. I have sworn,
and I will perform it, that I will keep Thy righteous Judgments.
I am afflicted very much: quicken me, O Lord, according unto
Thy Word. Accept, I beseech Thee, the freewill offerings of my
mouth, O Lord, and teach me Thy Judgments. My soul is
continually in my hand: yet do I not forget Thy law. The
wicked have laid a snare for me: yet I erred not from Thy
Precepts. Thy Testimonies have I taken as an heritage for ever:
for they are the rejoicing of my heart. I have inclined mine
heart to perform Thy Statutes always, even unto the end. I
hate vain thoughts: but Thy law do I love. Thou art my hiding
place and my shield: I hope in Thy Word. Depart from me,
ye evildoers: for I will keep the Commandments of my God.
Uphold me according unto Thy Word, that I may live: and let
me not be ashamed of my hope. Hold Thou me up, and I shall
be safe: and I will have respect unto Thy Statutes continually.
Thou hast trodden down all them that err from Thy Statutes:
for their deceit is falsehood. Thou puttest away all the wicked
of the earth like dross; therefore I love Thy Testimonies.
My flesh trembleth for fear of Thee; and I am afraid of Thy
Judgments. I have done judgment and justice: leave me not to
mine oppressors. Be surety for thy servant for good: let not the
proud oppress me. Mine eyes fail for Thy salvation, and for the
Word of Thy righteousness. Deal with Thy servant according
unto Thy mercy, and teach me Thy Statues. I am Thy servant;
give me understanding, that I may know Thy Testimonies. It is

time for Thee, Lord, to work: for they have made void Thy law. Therefore I love Thy Commandments above gold; yea, above fine gold. Therefore I esteem all Thy Precepts concerning all things to be right; and I hate every false way. Thy Testimonies are wonderful; therefore doth my soul keep them. The entrance of Thy Words giveth light; it giveth understanding unto the simple. I opened my mouth, and panted: for I longed for Thy Commandments.

Look Thou upon me, and be merciful unto me, as Thou usest to do unto those that love Thy name. Order my steps in Thy Word: and let not any iniquity have dominion over me. Deliver me from the oppression of man: so will I keep Thy precepts. Make Thy face to shine upon Thy servant; and teach me Thy statutes. Rivers of waters run down mine eyes, because they keep not Thy law. Righteous art Thou, O Lord, and upright are Thy judgments. Thy Testimonies that Thou hast commanded are righteous and very faithful.

My zeal hath consumed me, because mine enemies have forgotten Thy words. Thy Word is very pure: therefore Thy servant loveth it. I am small and despised: yet do not I forget Thy precepts. Thy righteousness is an everlasting righteousness, and Thy law is the truth. Trouble and anguish have taken hold on me: yet Thy Commandments are my delights. The righteousness of Thy Testimonies is everlasting: give me understanding, and I shall live. I cried with my whole heart: hear me, O Lord: I will keep Thy Statutes. I cried unto Thee: save me, and I shall keep Thy Testimonies.

I prevented the dawning of the morning, and cried: I hoped in Thy Word. Mine eyes prevent the night watches, that I might meditate in Thy Word. Hear my voice according unto Thy lovingkindness: O Lord, quicken me according to Thy

Judgment. They draw nigh that follow after mischief: they are far from Thy law. Thou art near, O Lord; and all Thy Commandments are truth. Concerning Thy Testimonies, I have known of old that Thou hast founded them for ever. Consider mine affliction, and deliver me: for I do not forget Thy law. Plead my cause, and deliver me: quicken me according to Thy Word. Salvation is far from the wicked: for they seek not Thy Statutes. Great are Thy tender mercies, O Lord: quicken me according to Thy Judgments. Many are my persecutors and mine enemies; yet do I not decline from Thy Testimonies. I beheld the transgressors, and was grieved; because they kept not Thy Word. Consider how I love Thy Precepts: quicken me, O Lord, according to Thy loving kindness. Thy Word is true from the beginning: and every one of Thy righteous judgments endureth for ever. Princes have persecuted me without a cause: but my heart standeth in awe of Thy Word. I rejoice at Thy Word, as one that findeth great spoil. I hate and abhor lying: but Thy law do I love. Seven times a day do I praise Thee because of Thy righteous Judgments. Great peace have they which love Thy law: and nothing shall offend them. Lord, I have hoped for Thy salvation, and done Thy Commandments. My soul hath kept Thy Testimonies; and I love them exceedingly. I have kept Thy Precepts and Thy Testimonies: for all my ways are before Thee. Let my cry come near before Thee, O Lord: give me understanding according to Thy Word. Let my supplication come before Thee: deliver me according to Thy Word. My lips shall utter praise, when Thou hast taught me Thy Statutes. My tongue shall speak of Thy Word: for all Thy Commandments are righteousness. Let Thine hand help me; for I have chosen Thy Precepts. I have longed for Thy salvation, O Lord; and

Thy law is my delight. Let my soul live, and it shall praise Thee; and let Thy Judgments help me. I have gone astray like a lost sheep; seek Thy servant; for I do not forget Thy Commandments." Ps. 119:4-176

Ps. 119 mentions the law 125 times and used "Word/ Words" 40 times.

Commandments - Statues - Precepts - Testimonies - Judgments - Law

This psalm tells us:

God's law is Righteous judgments.

We are not to wander from the Commandments.

We should want God to Teach us His Statues.

We should meditate on His Precepts.

We should delight in the Statues.

We should ask God not to hide His Commandments from us.

We should Meditate on His Statues.

That the Testimonies are my delight.

To ask God to help us to understand His Precepts.

To ask, "Grant me Thy law."

We should stick to His Testimonies.

To run in the way of His Commandments.

To ask God to teach me the way of His Statues.

We should want to keep His law and observe it with our hearts.

To ask God to make us walk in the path of His Commandments.

His Judgments are good.

To long for His precepts.

To keep His law forever.

That if we keep His Precepts we will walk in liberty.

To delight in His Commandments.

Prayers of ascent

Prayer of ascent #1

This chapter is one of 15 psalms that begin with "*a song of ascents*"; Psalms 120 – 134. It is not known who wrote them. Some think they were written by David, others think that they were written after the Babylonian captivity.

"A song for the ascent to Jerusalem"
"a song of degrees" (KJV)

> *In my distress I cried unto the Lord, and He heard me.*
> *Deliver my soul, O Lord, from lying lips, and from a deceitful*
> *tongue."* Ps. 120:1-2

Prayer of ascent #2

"A song for the ascent to Jerusalem.
> *Unto Thee lift I up mine eyes, O Thou that dwellest in the*
> *heavens…*
> *Have mercy upon us, O Lord, have mercy upon us: for we are*
> *exceedingly filled with contempt.*
> *Our soul is exceedingly filled with the scorning of those that*
> *are at ease, and with the contempt*
> *of the proud."* Ps. 123:1,3-4

Prayer of Ascent #3

"A song for the ascent to Jerusalem.
> *Do good, O Lord, unto those that be good, and to them that*
> *are upright in their hearts."* Ps. 125:4

Prayer of ascent #4

"A song for the ascent to Jerusalem.
Turn again our captivity, O Lord, as the streams in the
south." Ps. 126:4

Prayer of ascent #5

"A song for the ascent to Jerusalem.
Out of the depths have I cried unto Thee, O Lord. Lord,
hear my voice: let Thine ears be attentive to the voice of my
supplications. If Thou, Lord, shouldest mark iniquities, O
Lord, who shall stand? But there is forgiveness with Thee, that
Thou mayest be feared." Ps. 130:1-4

Prayer of ascent #6

"A song for the ascent to Jerusalem.
Lord, my heart is not haughty, nor mine eyes lofty: neither do
I exercise myself in great matters, or in things too high for me."
Ps. 131:1

Prayer of ascent #7

"A song for the ascent to Jerusalem.
Lord, remember David, and all his afflictions: How he sware
unto the Lord, and vowed unto the mighty God of Jacob;
Surely I will not come into the tabernacle of my house, nor go
up into my bed; I will not give sleep to mine eyes, or slumber
to mine eyelids, until I find out a place for the Lord, an
habitation for the mighty God of Jacob.
Lo, we heard of it at Ephratah: we found it in the fields of the
wood. We will go into His tabernacles: we will worship at His
footstool. Arise, O Lord, into Thy rest; Thou, and the ark of
Thy strength. Let Thy priests be clothed with righteousness;

and let Thy saints shout for joy. For Thy servant David's sake turn not away the face of Thine anointed. …" Ps. 132:1-10

God answers

"If Thy children will keep My Covenant and My Testimony that I shall teach them, their children shall also sit upon Thy throne for evermore… Zion… This is my rest forever here will I dwell; for I have desired it. I will abundantly bless her provision: I will satisfy her poor with bread. I will also clothe her priests with salvation: and her saints shall shout aloud for joy. There will I make the horn of David to bud: I have ordained a lamp for Mine anointed. His enemies will I clothe with shame: but upon himself shall his crown flourish."
Ps. 132:12-18

"Thy name, O Lord, endureth for ever; and Thy memorial, O Lord, through out all generations." Ps. 135:13

Prayer

Some think that this is a series of eight prayers by David.
"Remember, O Lord, the children of Edom in the day of Jerusalem; who said, Rase it, rase it, even to the foundation thereof." Ps. 137:7
(*"Tear it down"* NIV)

"I will praise Thee with my whole heart: before the gods will I sing praise unto Thee. I will worship toward Thy holy temple, and praise Thy name for Thy loving kindness and for Thy truth: for Thou hast magnified Thy Word above all Thy name. In the day when I cried Thou answeredst me, and strengthenedst me with strength in my soul. All the kings of the earth shall praise Thee,O Lord, when they hear the words

of Thy mouth. Yea, they shall sing in the ways of the Lord: for great is the glory of the Lord. Though the Lord be high, yet hath he respect unto the lowly: but the proud He knoweth afar off. Though I walk in the midst of trouble, Thou wilt revive me: Thou shalt stretch forth Thine hand against the wrath of mine enemies, and Thy right hand shall save me...Thy mercy, O Lord, endureth for ever: forsake not the works of Thine own hands." Ps. 138:1-8

Prayer

Thought to be from David.

"O Lord, Thou hast searched me, and known me. Thou knowest my downsitting and mine uprising, Thou understandest my thought afar off. Thou compassest my path and my lying down, and art acquainted with all my ways. For there is not a word in my tongue, but, lo, O Lord, Thou knowest it altogether. Thou hast beset me behind and before, and laid Thine hand upon me.

Such knowledge is too wonderful for me; it is high, I cannot attain unto it. Whither shall I go from Thy Spirit? Or whither shall I flee from Thy presence? If I ascend up into heaven, Thou art there: if I make my bed in hell, behold, Thou art there (Ps.16:10;Acts 13:35). *If I take the wings of the morning, and dwell in the uttermost parts of the sea; even there shall Thy hand lead me, and thy right hand shall hold me. If I say, Surely the darkness shall cover me; even the night shall be light about me.*

Yea, the darkness hideth not from Thee; but the night shineth as the day: the darkness and the light are both alike to Thee.

For Thou hast possessed my reins ("created my inmost being" NIV): *Thou hast covered me in my mother's womb.*

I will praise Thee; for I am fearfully and wonderfully made: marvelous are Thy works; and that my soul knoweth right well. My substance was not hid from Thee, when I was made in secret, and curiously wrought in the lowest parts of the earth (similar to the womb which is like the depths of the earth). *Thine eyes did see my substance, yet being imperfect; and in Thy book all my members were written* ("You saw me before I was born. Every day of my life was recorded in Your book" NLT), *which in continuance were fashioned, when as yet there was none of them. How precious also are Thy thoughts unto me, O God! How great is the sum of them! If I should count them, they are more in number than the sand: when I awake, I am still with Thee. Surely Thou wilt slay the wicked, O God: depart from me therefore, ye bloody men. For they speak against Thee wickedly, and Thine enemies take Thy name in vain. Do not I hate them, O Lord, that hate Thee? And am not I grieved with those that rise up against Thee? I hate them with perfect hatred: I count them mine enemies. Search me, O God, and know my heart: try me, and know my thoughts: and see if there be any wicked way in me, and lead me in the way everlasting."* Ps. 139:1-24

Prayer

Thought to be of David; used as a song in worship.

"Deliver me, O Lord, from the evil man: preserve me from the violent man; which imagine mischief's in their heart; continually are they gathered together for war. They have sharpened their tongues like a serpent; adders' poison is under their lips. Selah. Keep me, O Lord, from the hands of the wicked; preserve me from the violent man; who have purposed to overthrow my goings. The proud have hid a snare for me,

and cords; they have spread a net by the wayside; they have set... ("traps" NIV) *for me. Selah. I said unto the Lord, Thou art my God: hear the voice of my supplications, O Lord. O God the Lord, the strength of my salvation, Thou hast covered my head in the day of battle. Grant not, O Lord, the desires of the wicked: further not his wicked device; lest they exalt themselves. Selah. As for the head of those that compass me about, let the mischief of their own lips cover them. Let burning coals fall upon them: let them be cast into the fire; into deep pits, that they rise not up again. Let not an evil speaker be established in the earth: evil shall hunt the violent man to overthrow him. I know that the Lord will maintain the cause of the afflicted, and the right of the poor. Surely the righteous shall give thanks unto Thy name: the upright shall dwell in Thy presence."* Ps. 140:1-13

Prayer
Thought to be of David.

"Lord, I cry unto Thee: make haste unto me; give ear unto my voice, when I cry unto Thee. Let my prayer be set forth before Thee as incense (Rev. 8:3); *and the lifting up of my hands as the evening sacrifice. Set a watch O Lord, before my mouth; keep the door of my lips. Incline not my heart to any evil thing, to practice wicked works with men that work iniquity: and let me not eat of their dainties. Let the righteous smite me; it shall be a kindness: and let him reprove me; it shall be an excellent oil, which shall not break my head: for yet my prayer also shall be in their calamities."* Ps. 141:1-5

"But mine eyes are unto Thee, O God the Lord: in Thee is my trust; leave not my soul destitute. Keep me from

the snare which they have laid for me, and the grins of the workers of iniquity. Let the wicked fall into their own nets, whilst that I withal escape." Ps. 141:8-10

Prayer

"I cried unto the Lord with my voice; with my voice unto the Lord did I make my supplication. I poured out my complaint before Him; I shewed before Him my trouble."

> *"When my spirit was overwhelmed within me, then Thou knewest my path. In the way wherein I walked have they privily laid a snare for me. I looked on my right hand, and beheld, but there was no man that would know me: refuge failed me; no man cared for my soul. I cried unto Thee, O Lord: I said, Thou art my refuge and my portion in the land of the living. Attend unto my cry; for I am brought very low: deliver me from my persecutors: for they are stronger than I. Bring my soul out of prison, that I may praise Thy name: the righteous shall compass me about; for Thou shalt deal bountifully with me." Ps. 142:1-7*

Prayer
Thought to be of David

> *"Hear my prayer, O Lord, give ear to my supplications: in Thy faithfulness answer me, and in Thy righteousness. And enter not into judgment with Thy servant: for in Thy sight shall no man living be justified. For the enemy hath persecuted my soul; he hath smitten my life down to the ground; he hath made me to dwell in darkness, as those that have been long dead. herefore is my spirit overwhelmed within me; my heart within me is desolate. I remember the days of old; I meditate*

on all Thy works; I muse on the work of Thy hands. I stretch forth my hands. I stretch forth my hands unto Thee: my soul thirsteth after Thee, as a thirsty land. Selah. Hear me speedily, O Lord: my spirit faileth: hide not Thy face from me, lest I be like unto them that go down into the pit. Cause me to hear Thy loving kindness in the morning; for in Thee do I trust: cause me to know the way wherein I should walk; for I lift up my soul unto Thee. Deliver me, O Lord, from mine enemies: I flee unto Thee to hide me. Teach me to do Thy will; for Thou art my God: Thy Spirit is good; lead me into the land of uprightness. Quicken me, O Lord, for Thy name's sake: for Thy righteousness' sake bring my soul out of trouble. And of Thy mercy cut off mine enemies, and destroy all them that afflict my soul: for I am Thy servant." Ps. 143:1-12

Prayer

Thought to be of David.

"Lord, what is man, that Thou takest knowledge of him! Or the son of man, that Thou makest account of him! Man is like to vanity: his days are as a shadow that passeth away. Bow Thy heavens, O Lord, and come down: touch the mountains, and they shall smoke. Cast forth lightning, and scatter them: shoot out Thine arrows, and destroy them. Send Thine hand from above; rid me, and deliver me out of great waters, from the hand of strange children; whose mouth speaketh vanity, and their right hand is a right hand of falsehood. I will sing a new song unto Thee, O God: upon a psaltery and an instrument of ten strings will I sing praises unto Thee. It is He that giveth salvation unto kings; who delivereth David His servant from the hurtful sword. Rid me, and deliver me from the hand of strange children, whose mouth speaketh vanity,

*and their right hand is a right hand of falsehood: that our sons
may be as plants grown up in their youth; that our daughters
may be as corner stones, polished after the similitude of a
palace: that our garners may be full, affording all manner
of store: that our sheep may bring forth thousands and ten
thousands in our streets: that our oxen may be strong to
labour; that there be no breaking in, nor going out; that there
be no complaining in our streets. Happy is that people, that is
such a case: yea, happy is that people whose God is the Lord."*
Ps. 144:1-15

Prayer
Thought to be of David.

*"I will extol Thee, my God, O king; and I will bless Thy name
for ever and ever. Every day will I bless Thee; and I will praise
Thy name for ever and ever. Great is the Lord, and greatly to
be praised; and His greatness is unsearchable. One generation
shall praise Thy works to another, and shall declare Thy
mighty acts. I will speak of the glorious honour of Thy majesty,
and of Thy wondrous works. And men shall speak of the might
of Thy terrible acts: and I will declare Thy greatness. They shall
abundantly utter the memory of Thy great goodness, and shall
sing of Thy righteousness… All Thy works shall praise Thee, O
Lord; and Thy saints shall bless Thee. They shall speak of Thy
kingdom, and talk of Thy power; to make known to the sons
of men His kingdom. Thy kingdom is an everlasting kingdom,
and Thy dominion endureth throughout all generations. The
Lord upholdeth all that fall, and raiseth up all those that be
bowed down. The eyes of all wait upon Thee; and Thou givest
them their meat in due season. Thou openest Thine hand, and
satisfiest the desire of every living thing."* Ps. 145:1-7,10-16

Proverbs

Proverbs

Don't reject Wisdom when she speaks for wisdom represents the Holy Spirit. We better listen to God's reproofs now, and turn from our wicked ways, or God says there will come a time when He will not listen because we wouldn't listen.

Wisdom speaks

"*Wisdom crieth without; she uttereth her voice in the streets: She crieth in the chief place of concourse* ("noisy streets" NIV), *in the openings of the gates: in the city she uttereth her words, saying,*

> *How long, ye simple ones, will ye love simplicity? And the scorners delight in their scorning, and fools hate knowledge? Turn you at My reproof: behold, I will pour out My Spirit unto you, I will make known My words unto you. Because I have called, and ye refused; I have stretched out My hand, and no man regarded; but ye have set at nought all my counsel, and would none of My reproof: I also will laugh at your calamity; I will mock when your fear cometh; when your fear cometh as desolation, and your destruction cometh as a whirlwind; when distress and anguish cometh upon you. Then shall they call upon me, but I will not answer; they shall seek me early, but they shall not find Me: for that they hated knowledge, and did not choose the fear of the Lord: they would none of My counsel: they despised all My reproof. Therefore shall they eat of the fruit of their own way, and be filled with their own devices. For the turning away of the simple shall slay them, and the prosperity of fools shall destroy them. But whoso*

hearkeneth unto Me shall dwell safely, and shall be quiet from fear of evil." Prov. 1:20-33

God answers

"My son, if thou wilt receive My words, and hide My Commandments with thee; so that thou incline thine ear unto wisdom, and apply thine heart to understanding; yea, if thou criest after knowledge, and liftest up thy voice for understanding; if thou seekest her as silver, and searchest for her ("seek and ye shall find" Matt.7:7) *as for hid treasures; then shalt thou understand the fear of the Lord, and find the knowledge of God.* Prov. 2:1-5

Isaiah

Isaiah

Warning to repent

God wants us to stop doing evil and learn to do good. God is warning Israel that if they don't repent and turn from their evil ways, He won't hear their prayers.

God speaks

"And when ye spread forth your hands, I will hide Mine eyes from you: yea, when ye make many prayers, I will not hear: your hands are full of blood. Wash you, make you clean; put away the evil of your doings from before Mine eyes; cease to do evil; learn to do well; seek judgment, relieve the oppressed, judge the fatherless, plead for the widow. Come now, and let us reason together, saith the Lord:though your sins be as scarlet they shall be as white as snow; though they be red like crimson, they shall be as wool. If ye be willing and obedient, ye shall eat the good of the land: but if ye refuse and rebel, ye shall be devoured with the sword: for the mouth of the Lord hath spoken it." Is. 1:15-20

They make vows

"...yea, they shall vow a vow unto the Lord, and perform it. And the Lord shall smite Egypt: He shall smite and heal it: and they shall return even to the Lord, and He shall be intreated of them, and shall heal them." Is. 19:21-22

Seek God early in the morning

"With my soul have I desired Thee (O God) in the night; yea,

274

with my spirit within me will I seek Thee (O God) early: for
when Thy judgments are in the earth, the inhabitants
of the world will learn righteousness." Is. 26:9

Isaiah prayer #1

"Lord, in trouble have they visited Thee, they poured out a
prayer when Thy chastening was upon them.
Like as a woman with child, that draweth near the time of her
delivery, is in pain, and crieth out in her pangs; so have we
been in Thy sight, O Lord." Is. 26:16-17

Hezekiah's prayer

Hezekiah prays that God helps him against Sennacherib.

"And Hezekiah prayed unto the Lord, saying,
O Lord of hosts, God of Israel, that dwellest between the
cherubims (I Sam.4:4;II Kings 19:15;Ps.80:1;99:1;Is.37:16),
Thou art the God, even Thou alone, of all the kingdoms of the
earth: Thou hast made heaven and earth.
Incline Thine ear, O Lord, and hear; open Thine eyes, O Lord,
and see: and hear all the words of Sennacherib, which hath
sent to reproach the living God.
Of a truth, Lord, the kings of Assyria have laid waste all the
nations, and their countries, and have cast their gods into the
fire: for they were no gods, but the work of men's hands, wood
and stone: therefore they have destroyed them. Now therefore,
O Lord our God, save us from his hand that all the kingdoms
of the earth may know that Thou art the Lord, even Thou
only." Is. 37:15-20

God answers

"Thus saith the Lord God of Israel,

Whereas thou hast prayed to Me against Sennacherib king of Assyria: This is the word which the Lord hath spoken concerning him; the virgin, the daughter of Zion, hath despised thee and laughed thee to scorn; the daughter of Jerusalem hath shaken her head at thee. Whom hast thou reproached and blasphemed? And against whom hast thou exalted thy voice, and lifted up thine eyes on high? Even against the Holy One of Israel. By thy servants hast thou reproached the Lord, and hast said, By the multitude of my chariots am I come up to the height of the mountains, to the sides of Lebanon; and I will cut down the tall cedars thereof, and the choice fir trees thereof; and I will enter into the height of his border, and the forest of his Carmel. I have digged, and drunk water; and with the sole of my feet have I dried up all the rivers of the besieged places. Hast thou not heard long ago, how I have done it; and of ancient times, that I have formed it? Now have I brought it to pass, that thou shouldest be to lay waste defenced cities into ruinous heaps. Therefore their inhabitants were of small power, they were dismayed and confounded: they were as the grass of the field, and as the green herb, as the grass on the housetops, and as corn blasted before it be grown up. But I know thy abode, and thy going out, and thy coming in, and thy rage against Me. Because thy rage against Me, and thy tumult, is come up into Mine ears, therefore will I put My hook in thy nose, and my bridle in thy lips, and I will turn thee back by the way by which thou camest. And this shall be a sign unto thee, Ye shall eat this year such as groweth of itself; and the second year that which springeth of the same: and in the third year sow ye, and reap, and plant vineyards, and eat the fruit thereof. And the remnant that escaped of the house of Judah shall again

take root downward, and bear fruit upward: for out of Jerusalem shall go forth a remnant, and they that escape out of mount Zion: the zeal for the Lord of hosts shall do this. Therefore thus saith the Lord concerning the king of Assyria, He shall not come into this city, nor shoot an arrow there, nor come before it with shields, nor cast a bank against it. By the way that he came, by the same shall he return, and shall not come into this city, saith the Lord.
For I will defend this city to save it for Mine own sake, and for My servant David's sake.

God answers
Then the angel of the Lord went forth, and smote in the camp of the Assyrians a hundred and fourscore and five thousand (185,000): and when they arose early in the morning, behold, they were all dead corpses." Is. 37:21-38

In the end, King Sennacharib's sons kill him with the sword. (II Kings 19:37)

Hezekiah's Prayer for healing while lying in bed
The sun goes backward.
"Then Hezekiah turned his face toward the wall, and prayed unto the Lord, and said,

Remember now, O Lord, I beseech Thee, how I have walked before Thee in truth and with a perfect heart, and have done that which is good in Thy sight.

And Hezekiah wept sore." Is. 38:2-3

God answers

"Then came the word of the Lord to Isaiah, saying,
Go, and say to Hezekiah, Thus saith the Lord, the God of David thy father, I have heard thy prayer, I have seen thy tears: behold, I will add unto thy days fifteen years. And will deliver thee, and this city out of the hand of the king of Assyria: and I will defend this city. And this shall be a sign unto thee from the Lord, that the Lord will do this thing that He hath spoken; Behold, I will bring again the shadow of the degrees, which is gone down in the sun dial of Ahaz, ten degrees backward. So the sun returned ten degrees, by which degrees it was gone down." Is. 38:5-8

Isaiah prayer #2

"... O Lord, I am oppressed; undertake for me ... O Lord, by these things men live, and in all these things is the life of my spirit: so wilt Thou recover me, and make me to live. Behold, for peace I had great bitterness: but Thou hast in love to my soul delivered it from the pit of corruption: for Thou hast cast all my sins behind Thy back. For the grave cannot praise Thee, death cannot celebrate Thee: they that go down into the pit cannot hope for Thy truth. The living, the living, he shall praise Thee, as I do this day: the father to the children shall make known Thy truth. The Lord was ready to save me: therefore we will sing my songs to the stringed instruments all the days of our life in the house of the Lord." Is. 38:14-20

Israel made other gods and prayed to them; this is what angered God to the point that He would not hear or answer their prayers even when they fasted and wept (Is. 44:15-21).

God speaks

God warns that they were praying to idols that could not save them; seek the true God who can save!

"For thus saith the Lord that created the heavens; God Himself that formed the earth and made it; He hath established it, He created it not in vain, He formed it to be inhabited:

I am the Lord; and there is none else. I have not spoken in secret, in a dark place of the earth: I said not unto the seed of Jacob, Seek ye Me in vain: I, the Lord, speak righteousness, I declare things that are right. Assemble yourselves and come; draw near together, ye that are escaped of the nations: they have no knowledge that set up the wood of their graven image, and pray unto a god that cannot save. Tell ye, and bring them near; yea, let them take counsel together: who hath declared this from ancient time? Who hath told it from that time? Have not I the Lord? And there is no God else beside Me. Look unto Me, and be ye saved all the ends of the earth: for I am God, and there is none else. I have sworn by Myself, the word is gone out of My mouth in righteousness, and shall not return, that unto Me every knee shall bow, every tongue shall swear **(Rev.5:13)**. *Surely, shall one say, in the Lord have I righteousness and strength: even to Him shall men come; and all that are incensed against Him shall be ashamed. In the Lord shall all the seed of Israel be justified, and shall glory."* Is. 45:18-25

"Hearken to Me, ye that follow after righteousness, ye that seek the Lord: look unto the Rock **(Jesus)** *whence ye are hewn, and to the hole of the pit whence ye are digged."* Is. 51:1

279

"Even them will I bring to My holy mountain, and make them joyful in My house of prayer: their burnt offerings and their sacrifices shall be accepted upon Mine alter; for Mine house shall be called an house of prayer for all people." Is. 56:7

Jesus said in the New Testament,
"My house shall be called a house of prayer" Matt. 21:13

Jeremiah

Jeremiah

The weeping prophet

"A voice was heard upon the high places, weeping and supplications of the children of Israel: for they have perverted their way, and they have forgotten the Lord their God. Jer. 3:21

God speaks

"Return, ye backsliding children, and I will heal your backslidings." Jer. 3:22

Prayer

"Behold, we come unto Thee; for Thou art the Lord our God... for we have sinned... and have not obeyed..." Jer. 3:22-25

God speaks

"... I spake unto you, rising up early and speaking, but ye heard not; and I called you, but ye answered not: therefore will I do unto this house, which is called by My name, wherein ye trust, and unto the place which I gave to you and to your fathers, as I have done to Shiloh. And I will cast you out of My sight, as I have cast out all your brethren, even the whole seed of Ephraim. Therefore pray not thou for this people, neither lift up cry nor prayer for them, neither make intercession to Me: for I will not hear thee." Jer. 7:13-16

God would not hear because they chose other gods and did abominable things.

"*Therefore thus saith the Lord,*

Behold, I will bring evil upon them, which they shall not be able to escape; and though they shall cry unto Me, I will not hearken unto them. Then shall the cities of Judah and inhabitants of Jerusalem go, and cry unto the gods unto whom they offer incense: but they shall not save them at all in the time of their trouble. For according to the number of thy cities were thy gods, O Judah; and according to the number of the streets of Jerusalem have ye set up altars to that shameful thing, even altars to burn incense unto Baal. Therefore pray not thou for this people, neither lift up a cry or prayer for them: for I will not hear them in the time that they cry unto Me for their trouble. What hath My beloved to do in Mine house, seeing she hath wrought lewdness with many, and the holy flesh is passed from thee? When thou doest evil, then thou rejoicest… But, O Lord of hosts, that judgest righteously, that triest the reins and the heart ("You examine the deepest thoughts of the hearts and minds" NLT), *let me see Thy vengeance on them: for unto Thee have I revealed my cause. Therefore thus saith the Lord of the men of Anathoth, that seek thy life, saying, Prophesy not in the name of the Lord, that thou die not by our hand: therefore thus saith the Lord of hosts, Behold, I will punish them: the young men shall die by the sword; their sons and their daughters shall die by famine: and there shall be no remnant of them: for I will bring evil upon the men of Anathoth, even the year of their visitation.*" Jer. 11:11-15;20-23

#1 Jeremiah's Prayer

Prayer against his enemies.

"*Righteous art Thou, O Lord, when I plead with Thee: yet let*

me talk with Thee of Thy judgments: Wherefore doth the way
of the wicked prosper? Wherefore are all they happy that deal
very treacherously? Thou hast planted them, yea, they have
taken root: they grow, yea, they bring forth fruit:
Thou art near in their mouth, and far from their reins
("hearts" NIV – "mind" NASB – "conscience" HCSB).
But Thou, O Lord, knowest me: Thou hast seen me, and tried
mine heart toward Thee: pull them out like sheep for the
slaughter, and prepare them for the day of slaughter. How
long shall the land mourn, and the herbs of every field wither,
for the wickedness of them that dwell therein? The beasts are
consumed, and the birds; because they said, He shall not see
our last end." Jer. 12:1-3

God answers

God's answer to Jeremiah's Prayer shows God is angry with the
pastors, who have destroyed the vineyard. He will destroy those
pastors who won't obey Him.

"If thou hast run with the footmen, and they have wearied
thee, then how canst thou contend with horses?
And if in the land of peace, wherein thou trustedst, they
wearied thee, then how wilt Thou do in the swelling of Jordan?
For even thy brethren, and the house of thy father, even they
have dealt treacherously with Thee; yea, they have called a
multitude after Thee: believe them not, though they speak fair
words unto thee. I have forsaken Mine house, I have left Mine
heritage; I have given the dearly beloved of My soul into the
hand of her enemies. Mine heritage is unto Me as a lion in the
forest; crieth out against Me: therefore have I hated it. Mine

heritage is unto Me as a speckled bird, the birds round about are against her; come ye, assemble all the beasts of the field, come to devour. Many pastors have destroyed My vineyard, they have trodden My portion under foot, they have made My pleasant portion a desolate wilderness. They have made it desolate, and being desolate it mourneth unto Me; the whole land is made desolate, because no man layeth it to heart. The spoilers are come upon all high places through the wilderness: for the sword of the Lord shall devour from the one end of the land even to the other end of the land: no flesh shall have peace. They have sown wheat, but shall reap thorns: they have put themselves to pain, but shall not profit: and they shall be ashamed of your revenues because of the fierce anger of the Lord. Thus saith the Lord against all mine evil neighbours, that touch the inheritance which I have caused My people Israel to inherit; Behold, I will pluck them out of their land, and pluck out the house of Judah from among them. And it shall come to pass, after that I have plucked them out I will return, and have compassion on them, and will bring them again, every man to his heritage, and every man to his land. And it shall come to pass, if they will diligently learn the ways of My people, to swear by My name, The Lord liveth; as they taught My people to swear by Baal; then shall they be built in the midst of My people. But if they will not obey, I will utterly pluck up and destroy that nation, saith the Lord." Jer. 12:5-17

God is against false prophets

"Thus saith the Lord unto this people,
Thus have they loved to wander, they have not refrained their feet, therefore the Lord doth not accept them; He will not remember their iniquity, and visit their sins." Jer. 14:10

God will not hear even though they fast and pray, because they turned to idols instead of God and did wickedly. They didn't listen to God after many warnings, and now God won't listen to them.

"*Then said the Lord unto me,*
Pray not for this people for their good. When they
fast, I will not hear their cry; and when they offer burn
offering and an oblation, I will not accept them: but I will
consume them by the sword, and by the famine, and by the
pestilence. (Ez.14:21)." Jer. 14:11-12

Prayer
"*Then said I, Ah, Lord God!*
Behold, the prophets say unto them, ye shall not see the sword,
neither shall ye have famine; but I will give you assured peace
in this place." Jer. 14:13

The false prophets are prophesying lies, but God did not send them.

God speaks
"*Then the Lord said unto me,*
The prophets prophesy lies in My name: I sent them not,
neither have I commanded them, neither spake unto them:
they prophecy unto you a false vision and divination, and a
thing of nought, and the deceit of their heart. Therefore thus
saith the Lord concerning the prophets that prophesy in My
name, and I sent them not, yet they say, Sword and famine
shall not be in this land; By sword and famine shall those
prophets be consumed... I will pour their wickedness upon
them..." Jer. 14:14-16

Prayer

*"We look for peace, and there is not good; and for the time of
healing, and behold trouble!
We acknowledge, O Lord, our wickedness, and the iniquity of
our fathers: for we have sinned against Thee."* Jer. 14:19-20

#2 Prayer of Jeremiah

"Hast Thou utterly rejected (us)? *Hath Thy soul loathed* (us)?
*Why hast Thou smitten us, and there is no healing for us?
We looked for peace, and there is no good; and for the time
of healing, and behold trouble! We acknowledge, O Lord, our
wickedness, and the iniquity of our fathers: for we have
sinned against Thee. Do not abhor us, for Thy name's sake,
do not disgrace the throne of Thy glory: remember, break not
Thy covenant with us. Are there any among the vanities of the
Gentiles that can cause rain? Or can the heavens give showers?
Art not Thou He, O Lord our God? Therefore we will wait
upon Thee: for Thou hast made all these things."* Jer. 14:19-22

God speaks

God speaks to Jeremiah. Because they forsook God, God would
now forsake them.

"Then said the Lord unto me,
*Though Moses and Samuel stood before Me, yet My mind
could not be toward this people: cast them out of My sight, and
let them go forth. And it shall come to pass, if they say unto
thee. Whither shall we go forth? Then thou shalt tell them,
Thus saith the Lord; Such as are for death, to death; and such
as are for the sword, to the sword and such as are for the
captivity, to the captivity* (Mt.26:52;Rev.13:10). . .*And I will
cause them to be removed into all kingdoms of the earth,*

because of Manasseh the son of Hezekiah king of Judah, for
that which he did in Jerusalem. For who shall have pity upon
thee, O Jerusalem? Or who shall bemoan thee? Or who shall
go aside to ask how thou doest? Thou hast forsaken Me, saith
the Lord, thou art gone backward: therefore will I stretch out
my hand against thee, and destroy thee; I am weary with
repenting (because they won't change). *And I will fan them*
with a fan in the gates of the land; I will bereave them of
children, I will destroy My people, since they return not from
their ways. Their widows are increased to Me above the sand
of the seas: I have brought upon them against the mother
of the young men a spoiler at noonday: I have caused him to
fall upon it suddenly, and terrors upon the city. She that hath
borne seven languisheth: she hath given up the ghost; her sun
is gone down while it was yet day: she hath been ashamed and
confounded: and the residue of them will I deliver to the
sword before their enemies, saith the Lord... The Lord said,
Verily it shall be well with thy remnant; verily I will cause the
enemy to entreat thee well in the time of evil and in the time
of affliction. Shall iron break the northern iron and the
steel? Thy substance and thy treasures will I give to the
spoil without price, and that for all thy sins, even in all thy
borders. And I will make thee to pass with thine enemies
into a land which thou knowest not: for a fire is kindled in
Mine anger, which shall burn upon you." Jer. 15:1-14

#3 Prayer of Jeremiah
If they return to God, He will return to them.

"O Lord,
Thou knowest: remember me, and visit me, and revenge me
of my persecutors; take me not away in Thy longsuffering:

288

know that for *Thy* sake I have suffered rebuke. *Thy* words were
found, and I did eat them (Ez.2:9,10;3:1; Rev.10:9); and *Thy*
word was unto me the joy and rejoicing of mine heart: for I
am called by *Thy* name, O Lord God of hosts. I sat not in the
assembly of the mockers, nor rejoiced; I sat alone because of
Thy hand: for *Thou* hast filled me with indignation. Why is
my pain perpetual, and my wound incurable, which refuseth
to be healed? Wilt *Thou* be altogether unto me as a liar, and
as waters that fail?" Jer. 15:15-18

God answers

"*Therefore thus saith the Lord,*
If thou return, then will I bring thee again, and thou shalt
stand before Me; and if thou take forth the precious from the
vile, thou shalt be as My mouth: let them return unto thee;
but return not thou unto them. And I will make thee unto this
people a fenced brazen wall: and they shall fight against
thee, but they shall not prevail against thee: for I am with
thee to save thee and to deliver thee, saith the Lord. And I will
deliver thee out of the hand of the wicked, and I will redeem
thee out of the hand of the terrible." Jer. 15:19-21

God speaks

God used Jeremiah as an object lesson.

"*The word of the Lord came also unto me, saying,*
Thou shalt not take thee a wife, neither shalt thou have sons or
daughters in this place. For thus saith the Lord concerning the
sons and concerning the daughters that are born
in this place, and concerning their mothers that bare them,
and concerning their fathers that begat them in this land; They
shall die of grievous deaths; they shall not be lamented;

neither shall they be buried; but they shall be as dung upon the face of the earth: and they shall be consumed by the sword, and by famine; and their carcasses shall be meat for the fowls of heaven (Matt.24:28;Lk.17:37;Rev.19:17,18), *and for the beasts of the earth. For thus saith the Lord, Enter not into the house of mourning, neither go to lament nor bemoan them: for I have taken away My peace from this people, saith the Lord, even loving kindness and mercies. Both the great and the small shall die in this land: they shall not be buried, neither shall men lament for them. . .Thou shalt not also go into the house of feasting, to sit with them to eat and to drink. For thus saith the Lord of hosts, the God of Israel; Behold, I will cause to cease out of this place in your eyes, and in your days, the voice of mirth, and the voice of gladness, the voice of the bridegroom, and the voice of the bride. And it shall come to pass, when thou shalt shew this people all these words, and they shall say unto thee, Wherefore hath the Lord pronounced all this great evil against us? Or what is our iniquity? Or what is our sin that we have committed against the Lord our God?*

Then shalt thou say unto them Because your fathers have forsaken Me, saith the Lord, and have walked after other gods, and have served them, and have worshiped them, and have forsaken Me, and have not kept My law; and ye have done worse than your fathers; for, behold, ye walk every one after the imagination of his evil heart, that they may not hearken unto Me: therefore will I cast you out of this land into a land that ye know not, neither ye nor your fathers; and there shall ye serve other gods day and night; where I will not shew you favour. Therefore, behold, the days come, saith the Lord, that it shall no more be said, The Lord liveth, that brought up the children of Israel out of the land of Egypt; but the Lord liveth, that brought up the children of Israel from the land of the north, and from all the lands whither He had driven them: and I will bring them again into their land that I gave unto their fathers. Behold, I will send for many fishers, saith the Lord, and they shall fish them; and after will I send for many hunters, and they shall hunt them from every mountain, and from every hill, and out of the holes of the rocks. For Mine eyes are upon all their ways; they are not hid from My face, neither is their iniquity hid from Mine eyes. And first I will recompense their iniquity and their sin double; because they have defiled My land, they have filled Mine inheritance with the carcasses of their detestable and abominable things. Jer. 16:1-18

#4 prayer of Jeremiah

"O Lord,
my strength, and my fortress, and my refuge in the day of affliction, the Gentiles shall come unto Thee from the ends of the earth, and shall say, Surely our fathers have inherited lies, vanity, and the things wherein there is no profit. Shall a man make gods unto himself, and they are no gods? Therefore, behold, I will this once cause them to know, I will cause them to know Mine hand and My might; and they shall know that My name is The Lord." Jer. 16:19-21

#5 prayer of Jeremiah

"O Lord,
the hope of Israel, all that forsake Thee shall be ashamed, and they that depart from Me shall be written in the earth, because they have forsaken the Lord, the fountain of living waters. Heal me, O Lord, and I shall be healed; save me, and I shall

be saved: for Thou art my praise. Behold, they say unto me,
Where is the word of the Lord? Let it come now. As for me, I
have not hastened from being a pastor to follow Thee: neither
have I desired the woeful day; Thou knowest: that which came
out of my lips was right before Thee. Be not a terror unto me:
Thou art my hope in the day of evil. Let them be confounded
that persecute me, but let not me be confounded: let them be
dismayed, but let not me be dismayed: bring upon them the
day of evil, and destroy them with double destruction."
Jer. 17:13-18

God speaks

"The Word which came to Jeremiah from the Lord, saying,

Arise and go down to the potter's house, and there I will cause
thee to hear My Words.
Then I went to the potter's house, and, behold he wrought a work on
the wheels. And the vessel that he made of clay was marred in the hand
of the potter: so he made it again another vessel, as seemed good to the
potter to make it.

Then the Word of the Lord came to me, saying,

O house of Israel, cannot I do with you as this potter?

Saith the Lord,
Behold, as the clay is in the potter's hand, so are ye in hand,
O house of Israel. At what instant I shall speak concerning a
nation, and concerning a kingdom, to build and to plant it;
if it do evil in My sight that it obey not My voice, then I will
repent of the good, wherewith I said I would benefit them.

Now therefore go to, speak to the men of Judah, and to the
inhabitants of Jerusalem, saying,

Thus saith the Lord;
Behold, I frame evil against you, and devise a device against
you: return ye now every one from his evil way, and make
your ways and your doings good.

And they said,
There is no hope: but we will walk after our own devices, and we will
every one do the imagination of his evil heart.

Therefore thus saith the Lord;
Ask ye now among the heathen, who hath heard such things:
the virgin of Israel hath done a very horrible thing. Will a
man leave the snow of Lebanon which cometh from the rock
of the field? Or shall the cold flowing waters that come from
another place be forsaken? Because My people hath forgotten
Me, they have burned incense to vanity, and they have caused
them to stumble in their ways from the ancient paths, in a
way not cast up; to make their land desolate, and a perpetual
hissing; every one that passeth thereby shall be astonished, and
wag his head. I will scatter them as with an east wind before
the enemy; I will shew them the back, and not the face, in the
day of their calamity.

Then said they,
Come, and let us devise devices against Jeremiah; for the law shall not
perish from the priest, nor counsel from the wise, nor the word from the
prophet. Come, and let us smite him with the tongue, and let us not give
heed to any of his words." Jer. 18:1-18

#6 prayer of Jeremiah

"Give heed to me, O Lord, and hearken to the voice of them that contend with me. Shall evil be recompensed for good? For they have digged a pit for my soul. Remember that I stood before Thee to speak good for them, and to turn away Thy wrath from them. Thou shalt bring a troop suddenly upon them: for they have digged a pit to take me, and hid snares for my feet. Yet, Lord, Thou knowest all their counsel against me to slay me: forgive not their iniquity, neither blot out their sin from Thy sight, but let them be overthrown before Thee; deal thus with them in the time of Thine anger." Jer. 18:19-23

#7 prayer of Jeremiah

"O Lord,
Thou hast deceived me, and I was deceived: Thou art stronger than I, and hast prevailed: I am in derision daily, every one mocketh me. For since I spake, I cried out, I cried violence and spoil; because the word of the Lord was made a reproach unto me, and a derision, daily. Then I said, I will not make mention of Him, nor speak any more in His name. But His word was in mine heart as a burning fire shut up in my bones, and I was weary with forbearing, and I could not stay." Jer. 20:7-9

#8 prayer of Jeremiah

"But the Lord is with me as a mighty terrible One: therefore my persecutors shall stumble, and they shall stumble, and they shall not prevail: they shall be greatly ashamed; for they shall not prosper: their everlasting confusion shall never be forgotten. But, O Lord of hosts, that triest the righteous, and seest the reins and the heart ("You examine the deepest thought of hearts and minds" NLT), *let me see Thy vengeance*

on them: for unto Thee have I opened my cause. Sing unto the
Lord, praise ye the Lord: for He hath delivered the soul of the
poor from the hand of evildoers." Jer. 20:11-13

Warning from the Lord about the Babylonian captivity

"The word which came unto Jeremiah from the Lord, when king
Zedekiah sent unto him Pashur the son of Melchiah, and Zephaniah the
son of Maaseiah the priest, saying, Inquire, I pray thee, of the Lord for
us; for Nebuchadnezzar king of Babylon maketh war against us; if so be
that the Lord will deal with us according to all His wondrous works, that
He may go up from us. Then said Jeremiah unto them, Thus shall ye say
to Zedekiah. . ." Jer. 21:1-3

God speaks

"Thus saith the Lord God of Israel;
Behold, I will turn back the weapons of war that are in your
hands, where with ye fight against the king of Babylon, and
against the Chaldeans, which besiege you without the walls,
and I will assemble them into the midst of this city. And I
Myself will fight against you with an outstretched hand and
with a strong arm, even in anger, and in fury, and in great
wrath. And I will smite the inhabitants of this city, both man
and beast: they shall die of a great pestilence.
And afterward, Saith the Lord, I will deliver Zedekiah king of
Judah, and his servants, and the people, and such as are left
in this city from the pestilence, from the sword, and from the
famine (Ez.14:21), into the hand of Nebuchadnezzar king of
Babylon, and into the hand of their enemies, and into the
hand of those that seek their life: and he shall smite them with
the edge of the sword; he shall not spare them, neither have

pity, nor have mercy. And unto this people thou shalt say. . ."
Jer. 21:4-8

God speaks

A warning to Jerusalem before the Babylonian captivity because of their evil doings.

"Thus saith the Lord;
Behold, I set before you the way of life, and the way of death.
He that abideth in this city shall die by the sword, and by the
famine, and by the pestilence (Ez.14:21): but he that goeth
out, and falleth to the Chaldeans that besiege you, he shall
live, and his life shall be unto him for a prey. For I have set My
face against this city for evil, and not for good, Saith the Lord:
it shall be given into the hand of the king of Babylon, and he
shall burn it with fire. And touching the house of the king of
Judah, say, Hear ye the word of the Lord; O house of David,
thus saith the Lord; Execute judgment in the morning, and
deliver him that is spoiled out of the hand of the oppressor, elst
My fury go out like fire, and burn that none can quench it,
because of the evil of your doings. Behold, I am against thee, O
inhabitant of the valley, and rock of the plain, saith the Lord;
which say, Who shall come down against us? Or who shall
enter into our habitations? But I will punish you according to
the fruit of your doings, Saith the Lord: And I will kindle a fire
in the forest thereof, and it shall devour all things round about
it." Jer. 21:8-14

God speaks

Don't provoke God by worshiping idols.

"And the Lord hath sent unto you all His servants the prophets, rising
early and sending them; but ye have not hearkened, nor inclined your

ear to hear. They said, Turn ye again now every one from his evil way, and from the evil of your doings, and dwell in the land that the Lord hath given unto you and to your fathers for ever and ever:

> *and go not after other gods to serve them, and to worship them, and provoke Me not to anger with the works of your hands; and I will do you no hurt. Yet ye have not hearkened unto Me, saith the Lord..." Jer. 25:5-7*

God speaking to those taken captive to Babylon; they are to pray for the cities they live in.

"Now these are the words of the letter that Jeremiah the prophet sent from Jerusalem unto the residue of the elders which were carried away captives, and to the priests, and to the prophets, and to all the people whom Nebuchadnezzar had carried away captive from Jerusalem to Babylon; ...

saying, Thus saith the Lord of hosts, the God of Israel,

> *unto all that are carried away captives, whom I have caused to be carried away from Jerusalem unto Babylon; build ye houses, and dwell in them; and plant gardens, and eat the fruit of them; take ye wives, and beget sons and daughters; and take wives for your sons, and give your daughters to husbands, that they may bear sons and daughters; that ye may be increased there, and not diminished.*
>
> *And seek the peace of the city whither I have caused you to be carried away captives, and pray unto the Lord for it: for in the peace thereof shall ye have peace. For thus saith the Lord of hosts, the God of Israel; Let not your prophets and your diviners, that be in the midst of you, deceive you, neither hearken to your dreams which ye cause to be dreamed.*

*For they prophesy falsely unto you in My name: I have not
sent them, saith the Lord. For thus saith the Lord, That
after seventy years be accomplished at Babylon* (this is the
prophecy Daniel read about in Dan. 9:2) *I will visit you, and
perform my good word toward you, in causing you to return
to this place.*

After 70 yrs. in Babylon, God promises that he will be there for
them again.

*"For I know the thoughts that I think toward you, saith
the Lord, thoughts of peace, and not of evil, to give you an
expected end* ("to give you a hope and a future" NIV).
*Then shall ye call upon Me, and ye shall go and pray unto Me,
and I will hearken unto you. And ye shall seek Me, and find
Me, when ye shall search for Me with all your heart.
And I will be found of you, saith the Lord:
and I will turn away your captivity, and I will gather you from
all the nations, and from all the places whither I have driven
you, saith the Lord; and I will bring you again in the place
whence I caused you to be carried away captive.*

*Because ye have said,
The Lord hath raised us up prophets in Babylon; know that
thus saith the Lord of the king that sitteth upon the throne
of David, and of all the people that dwelleth in this city,
and of your brethren that are not gone forth with you into
captivity; Thus saith the Lord of hosts; Behold, I will send upon
them the sword, the famine, and the pestilence* (Ez. 14:21),
*and will make them like vile figs, that cannot be eaten, they
are so evil. And I will persecute them with the sword, and
with the famine, and with the pestilence* (Ez.14:21), *and will*

deliver them to be removed to all the kingdoms of the earth,
to be a curse, and an astonishment, and an hissing, and a
reproach, among all the nations whither I have driven them:
because they have not hearkened to My words,

Saith the Lord,
Which I sent unto them by My servants the prophets,
rising up early and sending them; but ye would not hear,

Saith the Lord.
Hear ye therefore the Word of the Lord all ye of the captivity,
whom I have sent from Jerusalem to Babylon:

Thus saith the Lord of hosts, the God of Israel... **(to those)**
which prophesy a lie unto you in My name;
Behold, I will deliver them into the hand of Nebuchadnezzar
king of Babylon...

Saying, The Lord make thee like Zedekiah and like Ahab...
(who) *have committed adultery with their neighbours' wives,*
and have spoken lying words in My name, which I have not
commanded them; even I know, and am a witness,

Saith the Lord. Thus shalt thou also speak to Shemaiah the
Nehlamite, saying, Thus speaketh the Lord of hosts, the God of
Israel, saying, Because thou hast sent letters in thy name unto
all the people that are at Jerusalem, and to Zephaniah the son
of Maaseah the priest, and to all the priests, saying,

The Lord hath made thee priest in the stead of Jehoiada the
priest, that ye should be officers in the house of the Lord, for

every man that is mad, maketh himself a prophet, that thou shouldest put him in prison, and in the stocks. Now therefore why hast thou not reproved Jeremiah of Anathoth, which maketh himself a prophet to you? For therefore he sent unto us in Babylon, saying, This captivity is long: build ye houses, and dwell in them; and plant gardens, and eat the fruit of them.

And Zephaniah the priest read this letter in the ears of Jeremiah the prophet. Then came the Word of the Lord unto Jeremiah, saying, Send to all them of the captivity, saying,

Thus saith the Lord concerning Shemaiah the Nehelamite; because that Shemaiah hath prophesied unto you, and I sent him not, and he caused you to trust in a life: therefore thus saith the Lord;
Behold, I will punish Shemaiah the Nehlamite, and his seed: he shall not have a man to dwell among this people; neither shall he behold the good that I will do for My people, Saith the Lord; Because he hath taught rebellion against the Lord."
Jer. 29:1-32

God speaks

"At the same time, saith the Lord,
will I be the God of all the families of Israel, and they shall be My people. Thus saith the Lord, The people which were left of the sword found grace in the wilderness; even Israel, when I went to cause him to rest. The Lord hath appeared of old unto me, saying, Yea, I have loved thee with an everlasting love: therefore with lovingkindness have I drawn thee.
Again I will build thee, and thou shalt be built, O virgin of Israel (**Rev.7 & 14**): *thou shalt again be adorned with thy tabrets, and shalt go forth in the dances of them that make*

300

merry. Thou shalt yet plant vines upon the mountains of
Samaria: the planters shall plant, and shall eat them as
common things. For there shall be a day, that the watchmen
upon the mount Ephraim shall cry, Arise ye, and let us go
up to Zion unto the Lord our God. For thus saith the Lord;
Sing with gladness for Jacob, and shout among the chief of the
nations. . ." Jer. 31:1-7

Prayer

"publish ye, praise ye, and say, O Lord,
save Thy people, the remnant of Israel." Jer. 31:7

God speaks

"Behold, I will bring them from the north country,
and gather them from the coasts, of the earth, and with them
the blind and the lame, the woman with child
and her that travaileth with child together; a great company
shall return thither. They shall come with weeping, and with
supplications will I lead them: I will cause them to walk
by the rivers of waters in a straight way, wherein they shall
not stumble: for I am a father to Israel, and Ephraim is my
firstborn.Hear the word of the Lord, O ye nations, and declare
it in the isles afar off, and say, He that scattered Israel
will gather him, and keep him, as a shepherd doth His flock.
For the Lord hath redeemed Jacob,and ransomed him from the
hand of him that was stronger than he. Therefore they shall
come and sing in the height of Zion, and shall flow together to
the goodness of the Lord, for wheat, and for wine, and for oil,
and for the young of the flock and of the herd: and their soul
shall be as a watered garden; and they shall not sorrow any
more at all. Then shall the virgin rejoice in the dance, both

*young men and old together: for I will turn their mourning
into joy, and will comfort them, and make them rejoice from
their sorrow. And I will satiate the soul of the priests with
fatness, and My people shall be satisfied with My goodness,
saith the Lord. Thus saith the Lord; A voice was heard in
Ramah, lamentation, and bitter weeping; (Rachel) weeping
for her children refused to be comforted for her children,
because they were not. Thus saith the Lord; Refrain thy voice
from weeping, and thine eyes from tears: for thy work shall be
rewarded, Saith the Lord; And they shall come again from the
land of the enemy. And there is hope in thine end, Saith the
Lord, that thy children shall come again to their own border."*
Jer. 31:8-17

Ephraim speaks

*"I have surely heard Ephraim bemoaning himself thus;
Thou hast chastised me, and I was chastised, as a bullock
unaccustomed to the yoke: turn Thou me, and I shall be
turned; for Thou art the Lord my God. Surely after that
I was turned, I repented; and after that I was instructed,
I smote upon my thigh; I was ashamed, yea, even
confounded, because I did bear the reproach of my youth."*
Jer. 31:18-19

God speaks

*Is Ephraim My dear son? Is he a pleasant child? For since I
spake against him, I do earnestly remember him still: therefore
My bowels are troubled for him; I will surely have mercy upon
him, Saith the Lord. Set thee up waymarks, make thee high
heaps: set thine heart toward the highway, even the way, which
thou wentest: turn again, O virgin of Israel, turn again to these
thy cities. How long wilt thou go about, O thou backsliding*

daughter? For the Lord hath created a new thing in the earth,
a woman shall compass a man. Thus saith the Lord of hosts,
the God of Israel; as yet they shall use this speech in the land
of Judah and in the cities thereof, when I shall bring again
their captivity; the Lord bless thee, O habitation of justice, and
mountain of holiness. And there shall dwell in Judah itself,
and in all the cities thereof together, husbandmen, and
they that go forth with flocks. For I have satiated the weary
soul, and I have replenished every sorrowful soul. Upon this
I awaked, and beheld; and my sleep was sweet unto me.
Behold the days come, Saith the Lord, that I will sow the house
of Israel and the house of Judah with the seed of man, and
with the seed of beast. And it shall come to pass, that like as
I have watched over them, to pluck up, and to break down,
and to throw down, and to destroy, and to afflict;
so will I watch over them, to build and to plant, saith the
Lord. In those days they shall say no more,
The fathers have eaten a sour grape, and the children's teeth
are set on edge. But every one shall die for his own iniquity:
every man that eateth the sour grape, his teeth shall be set
on edge. Behold, the days come, Saith the Lord, That I will
make a new Covenant with the house of Israel, and with the
house of Judah: not according to the Covenant that I made
with their fathers in the day that I took them by the hand to
bring them out of the land of Egypt; which My Covenant they
brake, although I was an husband unto them, Saith the Lord:
But this shall be the covenant that I will make with the house
of Israel; after those days, Saith the Lord, I will put My law
in their inward parts, and write it in their hearts; and will be
their God, and they shall be My people. And they shall teach
no more every man his neighbour, and every man his brother,

303

*saying, Know the Lord: for they shall all know Me, from the
least of them unto the greatest of them, Saith the Lord: For I
will forgive their iniquity, and I will remember their sin
no more. Thus saith the Lord, Which giveth the sun for a
light by day, and the ordinances of the moon and of the stars
for a light by night, which divideth the sea when the waves
thereof roar; the Lord of hosts is His name; if those ordinances
depart from before Me, Saith the Lord, Then the seed of Israel
also shall cease from being a nation before me for ever. Thus
saith the Lord; If heaven above can be measured, and the
foundations of the earth searched out beneath, I will also cast
off all the seed of Israel for all that they have done, Saith the
Lord. That the city shall be built to the Lord from the tower of
Hananeel unto the gate of the corner. And the measuring line
shall yet go forth over against it upon the hill Gareb, and shall
compass about to Goath. And the whole valley of the dead
bodies, and of the ashes, and all the fields unto the brook of
Kidron, unto the corner of the horse gate toward the east, shall
be holy unto the Lord; it shall not be plucked up, nor thrown
down any more for ever."* Jer. 31:20-40

#9 prayer of Jeremiah

God allowed evil to come upon them because they did not obey
His Commandments.

"I prayed unto the Lord, saying,

Ah Lord God!

*Behold, Thou hast made the heaven and the earth by Thy
great power and stretched out arm, and there is nothing too
hard for Thee; Thou shewest loving kindness unto thousands,
and recompensest the iniquity of the fathers into the bosom of
their children after them: the Great, the mighty God, the Lord*

of hosts, is His name, Great in counsel and mighty in work: for Thine eyes are open upon all the ways of the sons of men: to give every one according to His ways, and according to the fruit of his doing: which hast made Thee a name, as at this day; and hast brought forth Thy people Israel out of the land of Egypt with signs, and with wonders, and with a strong hand, and with a stretched out arm, and with great terror; and hast given them this land, which Thou didst swear to their fathers to give them, a land flowing with milk and honey; and they came in, and possessed it; but they obeyed not Thy voice, neither walked in Thy law; they have done nothing of all that Thou commandest them to do: therefore Thou hast caused all this evil to come upon them: Behold the mounts, they are come unto the city to take it; and the city is given into the hand of the Chaldeans, that fight against it, because of the sword, and of the famine, and of the pestilence (Ez. 14:21): and what Thou hast spoken is come to pass and, behold, Thou seest it. And Thou hast said unto me, O Lord God, Buy thee the field for money, and take witnesses; for the city is given into the hand of the Chaldeans." Jer. 32:16-25

God speaks

"Then came the Word of the Lord unto Jeremiah, saying,

Behold, I am the Lord, the God of all flesh: is there anything too hard for Me?
Therefore thus saith the Lord;
Behold, I will give this city into the hand of the Chaldeans, and in the hand of Nebuchadnezzar king of Babylon, and he shall take it: and the Chaldeans, that fight against this city, shall come and set fire on this city, and burn it with the

houses, upon whose roofs they have offered incense unto Baal,
and poured out drink offerings unto other gods, to provoke
Me to anger. For the children of Israel and the children of
Judah have only done evil before Me from their youth: for the
children of Israel have only provoked Me to anger
with the work of their hands,
Saith the Lord.
For this city hath been to Me as a provocation of Mine anger
and of My fury from the day that they built it even unto this
day; that I should remove it from before My face, because
of all the evil of the children of Israel and of the children of
Judah, which they have done to provoke Me to anger, they,
their kings, their princes, their priests, and their prophets,
and the men of Judah, and the inhabitants of Jerusalem. And
they have turned unto Me the back, and not the face: though I
taught them, rising up early and teaching them, yet they have
not hearkened to receive instruction.

But they caused "Judah to sin."
And now therefore thus saith the Lord, the God of Israel,
concerning this city, whereof ye say,

It shall be delivered into the hand of the king of Babylon by the
sword, and by the famine, and by the pestilence (**Ez.14:21**);
Behold, I will gather them out of all countries, whither I have
driven them in Mine anger, and in My fury, and in great
wrath; and I will bring them again unto this place and I will
cause them to dwell safely: and they shall be My people, and
I will be their God. And I will give them one heart, and one
way, that they may fear Me for ever, for the good of them, and
of their children after them: and I will make an everlasting

*Covenant with them, that I will not turn away from them, to
do them good; but I will put My fear in their hearts, that they
shall not depart from Me. Yea, I will rejoice over them to do
them good, and I will plant them in this land assuredly with
My whole heart and with My whole soul.*

For thus saith the Lord:

*Like as I have brought all this great evil upon this people,
so will I bring upon them all the good that I have promised
them. And fields shall be bought in this land, Whereof ye say,*

*It is desolate without man or beast; it is given into the hand of
the Chaldeans. Men shall buy fields for money, and subscribe
evidences, and seal them, and take witnesses in the land of
Benjamin, and in the places about Jerusalem, and in the cities
of Judah, and in the cities of the mountains, and in the cities
of the valley, and in the cities of the soul: for I will cause their
captivity to return, Saith the Lord."* Jer. 32:26-44

The people speak to Jeremiah

*"All the captains and "all the people from the least even unto the
greatest, came near, and said unto Jeremiah the prophet, Let, we beseech
thee, our supplication be accepted before thee, and pray for us unto the
Lord thy God, even for all this remnant… that the Lord thy God may
shew us the way wherein we may walk, and the thing that we may do.*

*Then Jeremiah the prophet said unto them, I have heard you; behold,
I will pray unto the Lord your God according to your words; and it shall
come to pass, that whatsoever thing the Lord shall answer you, I will
declare it unto you; I will keep nothing back from you… whether it be
good, or whether it be evil, we will obey the voice of the Lord our God, to*

whom we send thee; that it may be well with us, when we obey the voice of the Lord our God." Jer. 42:1-6

God answers

"And it came to pass after ten days, that the Word of the Lord came unto Jeremiah… Thus saith the Lord, the God of Israel, unto whom ye sent me to present your supplication before Him;

> if ye will still abide in this land, then will I build you and not pull you down, and I will plant you, and not pluck you up: for I repent Me of the evil that I have done unto you. Be not afraid of the king of Babylon, of whom ye are afraid; be not afraid of him, saith the Lord: For I am with you to save you, and to deliver you from his hand. And I will shew mercies unto you, that He may have mercy upon you, and cause you to return to your own land." Jer. 42:7-12

Lamentations

Lamentations

Jeremiah feels God is not listening. and there may be times that we feel that God doesn't hear us.

"Also when I cry and shout, he shutteth out my prayer...
(O God)
Thou hast covered Thyself with a cloud, that our prayer should not pass through" Lam. 3:8,44

"Remember, O Lord, What is come upon us: consider, and behold our reproach.
Our inheritance is turned to strangers, our houses to aliens.
We are orphans and fatherless, our mothers are as widows.
We have drunken our water for money; our wood is sold unto us. Our necks are under persecution: we labour, and have no rest. We have given the hand to the Egyptians, and to the Assyrians, to be satisfied with bread. Our fathers have sinned, and are not; and we have borne their iniquities. Servants have ruled over us: there is none that doth deliver us out of their hand. We (got) our bread with the peril of our lives because of the sword of the wilderness. Our skin was black like an oven because of the terrible famine. ... the faces of elders were not honoured. They took the young men to grind, and the children fell under the wood. The elders have ceased from the gate, the young men from their musick. The joy of our heart is ceased; our dance is turned into mourning. The crown is fallen from our head: woe unto us, that we have sinned! For this our heart is faint; for these things our eyes are dim.
Because of the mountain of Zion, which is desolate, the foxes

walk upon it. Thou, O Lord, Remainest for ever; Thy throne from generation to generation. Wherefore dost Thou forget us for ever, and forsake us so long time? Turn Thou us unto Thee, O Lord, and we shall be turned; renew our days as of old. But Thou hast utterly rejected us; Thou art very wroth against us."

Lam. 5:1-22

Daniel

Daniel

Daniel asks God to reveal the kings dream

Daniel and his three friends find out that they will be killed with all the magicians, astrologers, and sorcerers if they don't interpret the king's dream about the statue.

"Then Daniel went to his house, and made the thing known to Hananiah, Mishael, and Azariah, his companions: that they would desire mercies of the God of heaven concerning this secret **(they would pray to God)**_; that Daniel and his fellows should not perish with the rest of the wise men of Babylon."_ Dan. 2:17-18

God answers

"Then was the secret revealed unto Daniel in a night vision. Then Daniel blessed the God of heaven." Dan. 2:19

Daniel praises God

"Daniel answered and said,

> _Blessed be the name of God for ever and ever: for wisdom and might are His: and He changeth the times and the season: He removeth kings, and setteth up kings: He giveth wisdom unto the wise, and knowledge to them that know understanding: He revealeth the deep and secret things: He knoweth what is in the darkness, and the light dwelleth with Him."_ Dan. 2:20-22

God answered.

> _"The king answered and said,_

> _Lo, I see four men loose, walking in the midst of the fire, and_

they have no hurt; and the form of the fourth is like the Son of God." Dan. 3:25

Daniel prays three times a day

The princes in Babylon were jealous of Daniel and conspired to have him killed if he prayed to his God, but Daniel continued to pray three times a day facing toward Jerusalem as it was his custom to do. Remember Solomon's prayer asking God to hear when they faced toward Jerusalem.

". . . When Daniel knew that the document had been signed, he went to his house where he had windows in his upper chamber open toward Jerusalem. He got down on his knees three times a day and prayed and gave thanks before his God, as he had done previously. Then these men came by agreement and found Daniel making petition and plea before his God." Dan. 6:10-11

Daniel was thrown into the lion's den for praying to the One true God; but God shut the lions mouth and saved him.

Daniel keeps praying regardless of the king's decree

"Then they came near, and spake before the king concerning the king's decree;

Hast thou not signed a decree, that every man that shall ask a petition of any God or man within thirty days, save of thee, O king, shall be cast into the den of lions? The king answered and said, The thing is true, according to the law of the Medes and Persians, which altereth not. Then answered they and said before the king, That Daniel, which is of the children of the captivity of Judah, regardeth not thee, O king, nor the decree that thou hast signed, but maketh his petition three times a day. Then the king, when he heard these words, was sore displeased with himself, and set his heart on Daniel to deliver him: and he laboured till the going down of the sun to deliver him." Dan. 6:12-14

God saves Daniel

The king:

1. Fasted
2. Didn't listen to music
3. Stayed up all night

"Then the king went to his palace, and passed the night fasting: neither were instruments of musick brought before him: and his sleep went from him. Then the king arose very early in the morning, and went in haste unto the den of lions. And when he came to the den, he cried with a lamentable voice unto Daniel: and the king spake and said to Daniel, O Daniel, servant of the living God, is thy God, whom thou servest continually, able to deliver thee from the lions?" Dan. 6:18-20

God answered prayer because Daniel was innocent, and because he believed in his God.

God answers

"Then said Daniel unto the king, O king, live for ever. My God hath sent his angel, and hath shut the lions' mouths, that they have not hurt me: forasmuch as before Him innocency was found in me; and also before thee, O king, have I done no hurt. Then was the king exceeding glad for him, and commanded that they should take Daniel up out of the den. So Daniel was taken up out of the den, and no manner of hurt was found upon him, because he believed in his God." Dan. 6:21-23

Daniel read the prophecies of Jeremiah (Dan.9:2) and knew that it was time for God to bring Israel back to Jerusalem.

Daniel pleaded in prayer - Fasted in sackcloth and ashes – and confessed. We don't ask because we are righteous, but because God is merciful.

"And I set my face unto the Lord God, to seek by prayer and supplications, with fasting, and sackcloth, and ashes; and I prayed unto the Lord my God, and made my confession, and said, O Lord,

the great and dreadful ("**awesome**" NIV) *God, keeping the covenant* ("**of love**" NIV) *and mercy to them that love Him and to them that keep* ("**obey**" NIV) *His Commandments; we have sinned, and have committed iniquity* ("**done wrong**" NIV), *and have done wickedly, and have rebelled, even by departing* ("**turned away**" NIV) *from Thy precepts and from Thy judgments: neither have we hearkened unto Thy servants the prophets, which spake in Thy name to our kings, our princes, and our fathers, and to all the people of the land. O Lord, righteousness belongeth unto Thee, but unto us confusion of faces* ("**we are covered with shame**" NIV), *as at this day; to the men of Judah, and to the inhabitants of Jerusalem, and unto all Israel, that are near, and that are far off, through all the countries whither Thou hast driven them, because of their trespass* ("**unfaithfulness to You**" NIV) *that they have trespassed against Thee. O Lord, to us belongeth confusion of face, to our kings, to our princes, and to our fathers, because we have sinned against Thee.*
To the Lord our God belong mercies and forgiveness, though we have rebelled against Him; neither have we obeyed the voice of the Lord our God, to walk in His laws, which He set before us by His servants the prophets. Yea, all Israel have transgressed Thy law, even by departing, that they might not ("**refusing to**" NIV) *obey Thy voice; therefore the curse is poured upon us, and the oath that is written in the law of Moses the servant of God, because we have sinned against Him. And He hath confirmed His words, which He spake against us, and against our judges that judged us, by bringing upon us a great evil: for under the whole heaven hath not been done as hath been done upon Jerusalem. As it is written in the law of Moses, all this evil is come upon us: yet made we not*

our prayer before the Lord our God, that we might turn from our iniquities, and understand Thy truth. Therefore hath the Lord watched upon the evil, and brought it upon us: for the Lord our God is righteous in all His works which He doeth: for we obeyed not His voice.

And now, O Lord our God, that hast brought Thy people forth out of the land of Egypt with a mighty hand, and hast gotten Thee renown, as at this day; we have sinned, we have done wickedly. O Lord, according to all Thy righteousness, I beseech Thee, let Thine anger and Thy fury be turned away from Thy city Jerusalem, Thy holy mountain: because for our sins, and for the iniquities of our fathers, Jerusalem and Thy people are become a reproach to all that are about us.

Now therefore, O our God, hear the prayer of Thy servant, and His supplications, and cause Thy face to shine upon Thy sanctuary that is desolate, for the Lord's sake. O my God, incline Thine ear, and hear ("Your servant's prayers" LB)*; open Thine eyes, and behold our desolations, and the city which is called by Thy name: for we do not present our supplications before Thee for our righteousness, but for Thy great mercies. O Lord hear; O Lord forgive; O Lord, hearken and do; defer not* ("don't delay"LB)*, for Thine own sake, O my God: for Thy city and Thy people are called by Thy name."*

Dan. 9:3-20

God answers

Daniel confesses his sins and the sins of his people. God sent an angel in response to Daniel's Prayer.

"Yea, whiles I was speaking, and praying, and confessing my sin and the sin of my people Israel, and presenting my supplication before the Lord my God, for the holy mountain of my God; yea, whiles I was speaking

in prayer, even the man Gabriel, whom I had seen in the vision at the beginning, being caused to fly swiftly, touched me about the time of the evening oblation. And he informed me, and talked with me, and said, O Daniel, I am now come forth to give thee skill and understanding. At the beginning of thy supplications the commandment came forth, and I am come to shew thee; for thou art greatly beloved: therefore understand the matter, and consider the vision." Dan. 9:21-23

 *Hosea*

Hosea

Hosea tells us to pray this prayer.

"O Israel, return unto the Lord thy God; for thou hast fallen by thine iniquity. Take with you words, and turn to the Lord: say unto Him. . ." Hosea 14:1-2

Prayer

> *"Take away all iniquity, and receive us graciously: so will we render the calves of our lips." Hosea 14:2*
> *"...and we will render the fruit of our lips" RSV*
> *"...and we will offer You the sacrifice of praise" LB*

Joel

Jonah

Habakkuk

Joel

God speaks

"*Therefore also now, says the Lord,*

Turn all of you even to Me with all your heart, and with fasting, and with weeping, and with mourning. And rend your heart, and not your garments. . ." Joel 2:12-13

and turn unto the Lord your God: for He is gracious and merciful, slow to anger, and of great kindness, and repents Him of the evil." Joel 2:12-13 UKJV

Jonah

God told Jonah to go to Nineveh but he ran away. God sent a terrible storm and they cast Jonah into the sea where he was swallowed up by a large fish.

Prayer of the men who threw Jonah overboard.

"Wherefore they cried unto the Lord, and said,

> *We beseech Thee, O Lord, we beseech Thee, let us not perish*
> *for this man's life, and lay not upon us innocent blood:*
> *for Thou, O Lord, hast done as it pleased Thee."* Jonah 1:14

Jonah's prayer from the belly of a fish

"Then Jonah prayed unto the Lord his God out of the fish's belly, and said,

> *I cried by reason of mine affliction unto the Lord, and He*
> *heard me: out of the belly of hell cried I, and Thou heardest my*
> *voice. For Thou hadst cast me into the deep, in the midst of*
> *the seas; and the floods compassed me about: all Thy billows*
> *and Thy waves passed over me. Then I said, I am cast out of*
> *Thy sight; yet I will look again toward Thy holy temple* (now
> we are to look to the New Jerusalem in Heaven). *The*
> *waters compassed me about, even to the souls; the depth closed*
> *me round about, the weeds were wrapped about my head. I*
> *went down to the bottoms of the mountains; the earth with*
> *her bars was about me for ever: yet hast Thou brought up my*
> *life from corruption, O Lord my God.*

When my soul fainted within me I remembered the Lord: and my prayer came in unto Thee, into Thine holy temple. They that observe lying vanities forsake their own mercy. But I will sacrifice unto Thee with the voice of thanksgiving; I will pay that that I have vowed. Salvation is of the Lord." Jonah 2:1-9

God answers

"And the Lord spake unto the fish, and it vomited out Jonah upon the dry land." Jonah 2:10

Jonah went to Ninevah and preached for three days. He must have been a great Evangelist with God's help because the whole city repented with fasting and sackcloth; but that didn't make Jonah happy. Maybe the Assyrians had hurt his family or friends. He may have had a good reason to resent the Ninevites, but God had a plan to use Jonah in spite of himself to save a very large city.

"When the news reached the king of Nineveh, he got up from his throne, took off his robe, put on sackcloth, and sat in ashes. Then he made this announcement and sent it throughout the city:

*'This is an order from the king and his nobles: No one is to eat or drink anything. This includes all people, animals, cattle, and sheep. Every person and animal must put on sackcloth. Cry loudly (***"pray earnestly"** NLT*) to God for help. Turn from your wicked ways and your acts of violence. Who knows? God may reconsider his plans and turn from his burning anger so that we won't die.' God saw what they did. He saw that they turned from their wicked ways."* Jonah 3:6-10

God answers

So God reconsidered his threat to destroy them, and he didn't do it." Jonah 3:6-10 GWT

God spared Nineveh because they repented with sackcloth and fasting and turned from their wicked ways but eventually the

Assyrians (which Nineveh was the capitol of) became very wicked again and God used them to punish Israel by capturing them and dispersing the 10 tribes; which were never brought back to their land again. Nineveh was destroyed around 612 BC; probably around 100 yrs. after Jonah preached there, but soon they became worse than before and God punished them by wiping them out completely.

Jonah prays in anger

Jonah should have been happy to see such a great revival, but he really didn't want Nineveh to be saved; in fact, he accused God of being too merciful and gracious. That says a lot about God.

"*But it displeased Jonah exceedingly, and he was very angry. And he prayed unto the Lord, and said,*

> *I pray Thee, O Lord, was not this my saying, when I was yet in my country? Therefore I fled before unto Tarshish: for I knew that Thou art a gracious God, and merciful, slow to anger, and of great kindness, and repentest Thee of the evil. Therefore now, O Lord, take, I beseech Thee, my life from me; for it is better for me to die than to live.*

God speaks

Then said the Lord,
> *Doest thou well to be angry?"* Jonah 4:1-4

Jonah speaks

God made a gourd to grow so that Jonah would have shade in the heat, but then God prepared a Crimson Worm, "*tola ot*," to destroy it and take it away from Jonah. You can see this worm all through the Bible (You can buy my book on www.thecrimsonworm.com).

"*And it came to pass, when the sun did arise, that God prepared a*

325

vehement east wind; and the sun beat upon the head of Jonah, that he fainted, and wished in himself to die, and said,

> *It is better for me to die than to live."* Jonah 4:3,8

Jonah speaks

"And he said,

> *I do well to be angry, even unto death"* Jonah 4:9

God speaks

"Then said the Lord,

> *Thou hast had pity on the gourd* (but really he pitied himself), *for the which thou hast not laboured, neither madest it grow: which came up in a night, and perished in a night: and should not I spare Nineveh, that great city, wherein are more than sixscore thousand* (120,000) *persons that cannot discern between their right hand and their left hand; and also much cattle?"* Jonah 4:9-11

Habakkuk

Prayer

"A prayer of Habakkuk the prophet upon Shigionoth. ("variable songs, or tunes, called in Hebrew, Shigioroth" KJV fn)

O Lord,
I have heard Thy speech, and was afraid:
O Lord, revive Thy work in the midst of the years,
in the midst of the years make known; in wrath remember
mercy." Hab. 3:1-2

New Testament Prayers

Matthew

Matthew

The Lord's Prayer
Jesus teaches the disciples how to pray.

"And when thou prayest, thou shalt not be as the hypocrites are: for they love to pray standing in the synagogues and in the corners of the streets, that they may be seen of men. Verily I say unto you, They have their reward. But thou, when thou prayest, enter into thy closet, and when thou hast shut thy door, pray to thy Father which is in secret; and thy Father which seeth in secret shall reward thee openly. But when ye pray, use not vain repetitions, as the heathen do; for they think that they shall be heard for their much speaking. Be not ye therefore like unto them: for your Father knoweth what things ye have need of before ye ask Him. After this manner therefore pray ye:

Our Father which art in heaven, Hallowed be Thy name.
Thy kingdom come.
Thy will be done in earth, as it is in heaven.
Give us this day our daily bread.
And forgive us our debts, as we forgive our debtors.
And lead us not into temptation,
but deliver us from evil: for Thine is the kingdom, and the power, and the glory, for ever. Amen." Matt. 6:5-13

Believe
"... Jesus saith unto them,
Believe ye that I am able to do this?

330

"They said unto Him,

Yea, Lord..."

Jesus said to them:
". . .according to your faith be it unto you." Matt. 9:28-29

Jesus' prayer
"At that time Jesus answered and said,
I thank Thee, O Father, Lord of heaven and earth, because
Thou hast hid these things from the wise and prudent, and
hast revealed them unto babes. Even so, Father; for so it
seemed good in Thy sight. All things are delivered unto Me
of My Father: and no man knoweth the Son, but the Father;
neither knoweth any man the Father, save the Son, and he to
whomsoever the Son will reveal Him." Matt. 11:25-27

Jesus' prayer
"At that time Jesus answered and said,
I thank Thee, O Father, Lord of Heaven and earth, because
Thou hast hid these things from the wise and prudent, and
hast revealed them unto babes. Father; for so it seemed good
in Thy sight." Matt. 11:25

The Father speaks
"While He yet spake, behold, a bright cloud overshadowed them: and
behold a voice out of the cloud, which said,

This is My beloved Son, in whom I am well-pleased;
Hear ye Him." Matt. 17:5

If you do not forgive others, then your Father will not forgive you your trespasses, Matt. 6:15.

Peter asked, How many times should I forgive? Jesus answered, seventy times seven, Matt. 18:21-22.

In the parable of the unforgiving servant, he asks for mercy and forgiveness and the ruler forgave him by paying his huge debt. God forgives us a huge debt also so we ought to forgive others as He forgave us, Matt. 18:23-35.

Jesus said to them,
> "It is written (Is.56:7), *My house shall be called the house of prayer; but ye have made it a den of thieves.*" Matt. 21:13

Jesus' Prayer before the cross
"Then cometh Jesus with them unto a place called Gethsemane, and saith unto the disciples, Sit ye here, while I go and pray yonder. And He took with Him Peter and the two sons of Zebedee, and began to be sorrowful and very heavy. Then saith He unto them,

My soul is exceeding sorrowful, even unto death: tarry ye here, and watch with Me. And He went a little further, and fell on His face..."
Matt. 26:36

1ˢᵗ prayer in the garden
"...and prayed, saying,

> *O My Father,*
> *if it be possible, let this cup pass from Me; nevertheless, not as I will but as Thou wilt."* Matt. 26:36-39

"Watch and pray, that ye enter not into temptation: the spirit indeed is willing, but the flesh is weak." Matt. 26:41

2ⁿᵈ prayer in the garden
Even Jesus asked the Father to give Him what He wanted, but the

bottom line is that He (Jesus) wanted "*God's will*" to be done in the end.

"*He went away again the second time and prayed, saying, O My Father,*

> *if this cup may not pass away from Me, except I drink it,*
> *Thy will be done.*" Matt. 26:41-42

3rd prayer in the garden

"*And He left them, and went away again, and prayed the third time, saying the same words.*" Matt. 26:44

"*Thinkest thou not that I cannot now pray to My Father, and He shall presently give Me more than twelve legions of angels?*" Matt. 26:53

Jesus' 4th and last prayer at the cross

"*And about the 9th hour* (**3** p.m.) *Jesus cried with a loud voice, saying,*

> *Eli, Eli, lama, Sabachthani?*

That is to say,

> *My God, My God, why hast Thou forsaken Me?*" Matt. 27:46

Mark

 *Mark*

Jesus' 1ˢᵗ prayer in the garden

"Sit ye here, while I shall pray... and began to be sore amazed, and to be very heavy; and saith unto them, My soul is exceeding sorrowful unto death: tarry ye here, and watch. And He went forward a little, and fell on the ground, and prayed that, if it were possible, the hour might pass from Him." Mk. 14:32-35

Jesus' 1ˢᵗ prayer - God's will be done

"And He said,

> *Abba, Father, all things are possible unto Thee; take away this cup from Me: nevertheless not what I will, but what Thou wilt."* Mk. 14:36

Jesus' 2ⁿᵈ prayer in garden (same as 1ˢᵗ)

"Watch ye and pray, lest ye enter into temptation... And again He went away, and prayed, and spake the same words." Mk. 14:38-39

Jesus' 3ʳᵈ prayer (on the cross)

"And at the 9ᵗʰ hour (3 p.m.) Jesus cried with a loud voice, saying,

> *Eloi, Eloi, lama, sabachthani?*

Which is, being interpreted,

> *My God, My God, why hast Thou forsaken Me?"* Mk. 15:35

335

Luke

Luke

Jesus prays to the Father in Heaven

"In that hour Jesus rejoiced in Spirit, and said,

*I thank Thee, O Father, Lord of Heaven and earth, that Thou
hast hid these things from the wise and prudent; and hast
revealed them unto babes: even so, Father, for so it seemed
good in Thy sight."* Lk. 10:21

The Lord's Prayer

Jesus taught the disciples how to pray.

*"And it came to pass, that, as He was praying in a certain place, when
He ceased, one of His disciples said unto Him, Lord, teach us to pray, as
John also taught his disciples. And He said unto them, When ye pray,
say,*

Our Father which art in Heaven, Hallowed be Thy name,
Thy kingdom come.
Thy will be done, as in Heaven, so in earth.
Give us day by day our daily bread.
*And forgive us our sins; for we also forgive every one that is
indebted to us.*
And lead us not into temptation;
but deliver us from evil." Lk. 11:1-4

To have our prayers answered and to be forgiven, we must forgive
as God forgave us; no exceptions! God can forgive any sin but the
condition is, we must also forgive others.

"And forgive us our debts; as we forgive our debtors."
Matt. 6:12

"So likewise shall My heavenly Father do also unto you, if ye from your hearts forgive not every one his brother their trespasses." Matt. 18:3

"… Forgive, and ye shall be forgiven:" Lk. 6:37

Jesus *"in whom we have redemption through His blood, even the forgiveness of sins…"* Col. 1:14

If you wrong someone, you should make restitution. See Lev. 6:4-6

"And He spake a parable unto them to this end, that men ought always to pray, and not to faint" Lk. 18:1

Prayer of the publican and sinner

"Two men went up into the temple to pray; the one a Pharisee, and the other a publican. The Pharisee stood and prayed thus with himself. . ." Lk. 18:10-11

Pharisees self-righteous prayer

"God,

I thank Thee, that I am not as other men are, extortioners, unjust, adulterers, or even as this publican. I fast twice in the week, I give tithes of all that I possess.

And the publican, standing afar off, would not lift up so much as his eyes unto heaven, but smote upon his breast, saying. . ."
Lk. 18:13

Publican's humble prayer

God,
be merciful to me a sinner.

I tell you, this man went down to his house justified rather than the other: for every one that exalteth himself shall be abased; and he that humbleth himself shall be exalted." Lk. 18:13-14

It wasn't the fasting that was bad, but having pride over others; fasting should be accompanied by humility.

"In that hour, Jesus rejoiced in spirit, and said,
> *I thank Thee, O Father, Lord of heaven and earth, that Thou hast hid these things from the wise and prudent, and hast revealed them unto babes: even so, Father; for so it seemed good in Thy sight.*

All things are delivered to Me of My Father: and no man knoweth who the Son is, but the Father; and who the Father is, but the Son, and he to whom the Son will reveal Him." Lk. 10:21-22

Jesus' Prayer in the Garden of Gethsemane

"... Pray that ye enter not into temptation. And He was withdrawn from them about a stone's cast, and kneeled down, and prayed, Saying,

Father,
> *if Thou be willing, remove this cup from Me: nevertheless not My will, but Thine, be done.*

And there appeared an angel unto Him from heaven strengthening Him. And being in an agony He prayed more earnestly: and His sweat was as it were great drops of blood falling down to the ground. And when He rose up from prayer, and was come to His disciples, He found them sleeping for sorrow, and said unto them, Why sleep ye? Rise and pray, lest ye enter into temptation." Lk. 22:40-46

Jesus' Prayer on the cross

Jesus begins to intercede.

"Then Jesus said,

Father
forgive them; for they know not what they do.

And when Jesus had cried with a loud voice and He having said this, He gave up the ghost." Lk. 23:34

"And when Jesus had cried with a loud voice and He said,
Father,
unto Thy hands I commend ("commit" NIV) My Spirit: and having said thus, He gave up the ghost." Lk. 23:46

John

John 🙞

Jesus' Prayer
When Jesus raised Lazarus from the grave.
"Jesus lifted up His eyes and said,

Father,
I thank Thee that Thou hast heard Me, and I knew that Thou
hearest Me always, but because of the people which stand by I
said it; that they may believe that Thou hast sent Me."
Jn. 11:41-42

Jesus' prayer in the Garden of Gethsemane
"Now is My soul troubled; and what shall I say?

Father,
save Me from this hour: but for this cause came I unto this
hour. Father glorify Thy name."

The Father in heaven answers
Then came a voice from Heaven saying,
I have both glorified it, and will glorify it again." Jn. 12:28

Jesus' Prayer
Prayer for His disciples and those who would follow Him; to
protect His disciples.
"These words spake Jesus, and lifted up His eyes to heaven, and said,
Father,
the hour is come; glorify Thy Son, that Thy Son also may

glorify Thee: as Thou hast given Him power ("authority" NIV)
over all flesh, that He should give eternal life to as many as
Thou hast given him.
And this is life eternal, that they might know Thee the only
true God, and Jesus Christ, whom Thou hast sent.
I have glorified Thee on the earth: I have finished the work
which Thou gavest Me to do. And now, O Father, glorify Thou
Me with Thine own self with the glory which I had with Thee
before the world was (We see here that Jesus was with God
before the world was created.)

"In the beginning was the Word, and the Word was with God, and
the Word was God. The same was in the beginning with God. All things
were made by Him; and without Him was not anything made that was
made. In Him was life; and the life was the light of men... And the Word
was made flesh (Jesus)*, and dwelt among us..."* Jn. 1:1-14
(We see here that Jesus is the Word, Jesus is God, and He
created the world).

I have manifested Thy name unto the men which Thou gavest
Me out of the world: Thine they were, and Thou gavest them
Me; and they have kept ("obeyed" NIV) *Thy word. Now they*
have known that all things whatsoever Thou hast given Me
are of Thee. For I have given unto them the words which Thou
gavest Me; and they have received them, and have known
surely that I came out from Thee, and they have believed that
Thou didst send Me. I pray for them; I pray not for the world,
but for them which thou hast given Me; for they are Thine.
And all Mine are Thine, and Thine are Mine; and I am
glorified in them. And now I am no more in the world, but
these are in the world, and I come to Thee. Holy Father, keep

through Thine own name those whom Thou hast given Me,
that they may be one, as we are. While I was with them in
the world, I kept ("protected" NIV) *them in Thy name: those*
that Thou gavest Me I have kept, and none of them is lost, but
the son of perdition; that the scripture might be fulfilled. And
now come I to Thee; and these things I speak in the world, that
they might have My ("full" NIV) *joy fulfilled in themselves. I*
have given them Thy Word; and the world hath hated them,
because they are not of the world, even as I am not of the
world. I pray not that Thou shouldest take them out of the
world, but that Thou shouldest keep ("protect" NIV) *them*
from the evil. They are not of the world, even as I am not
of the world. Sanctify them through Thy truth; Thy Word is
truth. As Thou hast sent Me into the world, even so have I
also sent them into the world. And for their sakes, I sanctify
Myself, that they also might be sanctified through the truth.
Neither pray I for these alone, but for them also which shall
believe on Me through their Word; that they all may be one; as
Thou, Father, art in Me, and I in Thee, that they also may be
one in us: that the world may believe that Thou hast
sent Me. And the glory which Thou gavest Me I have given
them; that they may be one, even as we are one: I in them, and
Thou in Me, that they may be made perfect in one; and that
the world may know that Thou hast sent Me, and hast loved
them, as Thou hast loved Me.
Father, I will that they also, whom Thou hast given Me,
be with Me where I am; that they may behold My glory,
which Thou hast given Me: for Thou lovedst Me before the
foundation of the world.
O righteous Father, the world hath not known Thee: but I
have known thee, and these have known that Thou hast sent

Me. And I have declared unto them Thy name ("I have made You known to them" NIV), and will declare it: that the love herewith Thou hast loved Me may be in them, and I in them.

When Jesus had spoken these words, He went forth with his disciples over the brook Cedron, where was a garden, into the which He entered, and His disciples." Jn. 17:1-26;18:1

Acts

2 Corinthians

Jude

Acts

Prayer of disciples to replace Judas

"And they prayed, and said,

Thou, Lord,

which knowest the hearts of all men, shew whether of these
two Thou hast chosen, that he may take part of this ministry
and Apostleship, from which Judas by transgression fell, that
he might go to his own place.

And they gave forth their lots; and the lot fell upon Matthias; and he
was numbered with the eleven Apostles." Acts 1:24-26

Prayer for Holy Spirit

"... they lifted up their voice (out loud) to God with one accord, and
said,

Lord,

Thou art God, which hast made heaven, and earth, and the
sea, and all that in them is: who by the mouth of Thy servant
David hast said, Why did the heathen rage, and the people
imagine vain things? The kings of the earth stood up, and the
rulers were gathered together against the Lord, and against
His Christ. For of a truth against Thy holy child Jesus, whom
Thou hast anointed, both Herod, and Pontius Pilate, with the
Gentiles, and the people of Israel, were gathered together. For
to do whatsoever Thy hand and Thy counsel determined
before to be done. And now, Lord, behold their threatenings:
and grant unto Thy servants, that with all boldness they may
speak Thy word. By stretching forth Thine hand to heal; and
that signs and wonders may be done by the name of Thy holy

347

child Jesus." Acts 4:24-30

God answers

"And when they had prayed, the place was shaken where they were assembled together; and they were all filled with the Holy Ghost, and they spake the word of God with boldness. And the multitude of them that believed were of one heart and of one soul: neither said any of them that ought of the things which he possessed was his own; but they had all things common. And with great power gave the apostles witness of the resurrection of the Lord Jesus: and great grace was upon them all. Neither was there any among them that lacked: for as many as were possessors of lands or houses sold them, and brought the prices of the things that were sold, and laid them down at the apostles' feet: and distribution was made unto every man according as he had need." Acts 4:31-35

Stephen's Prayer

Stephen was stoned for believing in Jesus and while they were stoning him, he saw Jesus standing at the right hand of God. Just before he died he prayed,

"Lord Jesus, Receive my spirit.

And he kneeled down, and cried with a loud voice,

Lord,
Lay not this sin to their charge.

And when he had said this, he fell asleep." Acts. 7:59-60

Prayer for Peter

"Peter therefore was kept in prison: but prayer was made without ceasing of the church unto God for him." Acts 12:5

God answered

"And when Peter was come to himself, he said, Now I know of a surety, that the Lord hath sent his angel, and hath delivered me out of the hand of Herod, and from all the expectation of the people of the Jews. And when he had considered the thing, he came to the house of Mary the mother of John...where many were gathered together praying." Acts 12:12

Apostolic Benediction

"The grace of the Lord Jesus Christ, and the love of God, and the communion of the Holy Ghost, be with you all. Amen." II Cor. 13:11-14

Jude's Doxology

"Now unto Him that is able to keep you from falling, and to present you faultless before the presence of His glory with exceeding joy, to the only wise God our Saviour, be glory and majesty, dominion and power, both now and ever. Amen."
Jude 24-25

Revelation

Revelation

The 24 elders praise God in song

Our prayers are always before God's throne; the incense in heaven is our prayers.

"And when He had taken the book, the four and twenty elders fell down before the Lamb, having everyone of them harps and golden vials full of odours ("incense" KJV fn) *which are the prayers of the saints and they sung a new song..."* Rev. 5:8

"Thou art worthy, O Lord, to receive glory and honour and power: for Thou hast created all things, and for Thy pleasure they are and were created." Rev. 4:11

Every creature in heaven, and earth and under the earth and in the sea praised God

"Blessing, and honour, and glory, and power, be unto Him that sitteth upon the throne, and unto the Lamb for ever and ever."
Rev. 5:13

Souls under altar

In the 5th Seal the souls under the altar in heaven ask God,

"How long, O Lord, holy and true,
dost Thou not judge and avenge our blood on them that dwell
on the earth?

Answer

"And it was said, unto them, that they should rest yet for a little season,

until their fellow servants also and their brethren, that should be killed as they were, should be fulfilled." Rev. 6:11

A great multitude in heaven cried with a loud voice,

"Salvation to our God which sitteth upon the throne, and unto the Lamb." Rev. 7:10

A voice from heaven in answer to prayers

After the cross, there was war in heaven Rev. 12:7

"And I heard a loud voice saying in heaven, Now is come salvation, and strength, and the kingdom of our God, and the power of His Christ: for the accuser of our brethren is cast down, which accused them before our God day and night." Rev. 12:10

Because Satan was cast out of heaven and to the earth, we are told to:

"Be sober, be vigilant; because your adversary the devil, as a roaring lion, walketh about, seeking whom he may devour..." I Pet. 5:8

Many people in heaven praise God

"...and after these things I heard a great voice of much people in heaven, saying,

Alleluia; Salvation, and glory, and honour, and power, unto the Lord our God: for true and righteous are His judgments..." Rev. 19:1-2

A voice from the throne in answer to prayer

"And a voice came out of the throne, saying,

Praise our God, all ye His servants, and ye that fear Him, both small and great." Rev. 19:5

The last prayer of the Bible
> *"... Even so, come, Lord Jesus."* Rev. 22:20

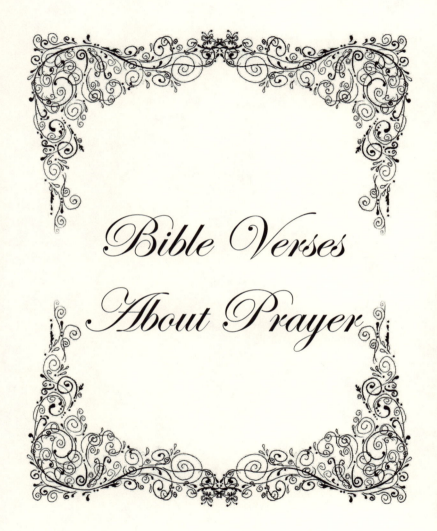

Bible Verses
About Prayer

Old Testament

"...God had listened to Abraham's request and kept Lot safe..." Gen. 19:29 NIV

Jacob wrestled with God and said, *"I will not let You go except You bless me."* Gen. 32:26

"But if from thence thou shalt seek the LORD thy God, thou shalt find Him, if thou seek Him with all thy heart and with all thy soul. But if from thence thou shalt seek the LORD thy God, thou shalt find Him, if thou seek Him with all thy heart and with all thy soul. (For the LORD thy God is a merciful God;) He will not forsake thee, neither destroy thee, nor forget the Covenant of thy fathers which He sware unto them." Deut. 4:29-31

God asked the Israelites, *"Has any people heard the voice of God speaking from the midst of the fire, as you have heard it, and survived?"* Deut. 4:33 NASB

"Now after the death of Joshua it came to pass, that the children of Israel asked the LORD..." Judges 1:1

"And they said unto him, Ask counsel, we pray thee, of God, that we may know whether our way which we go shall be prosperous. And the priest said unto them, Go in peace: before the Lord is your way wherein ye go." Judges 18:5-6

"And the children of Israel arose, and went up to the house of God, and asked counsel of God... (And the children of Israel went up and wept *before the LORD until even, and asked counsel of the LORD,.. and the Lord said...)"* Judges 20:18,23

"...and the God of Israel grant thee thy petition that thou hast asked of him... And she said **(to Eli, the priest),** *Oh my lord, as thy soul liveth, my lord, I am the woman that stood by thee here, praying unto the LORD. For this child I prayed; and the LORD hath given me my petition which I asked of him..."* I Sam. 1:17,26,27

"If one man sin against another, the judge shall judge him: but if a man sin against the Lord, who shall intreat for him..." I Sam. 2:25

"And Saul asked counsel of God, ...But he answered him not that day." I Sam. 14:37

"...and after that God was intreated for the land." II Sam. 21:14

"And the king answered and said unto the man of God, Intreat now the face of the Lord thy God, and pray for me, that my hand may be restored me again, and the man of God besought the Lord..." I Kings 13:6

God answers
"... and the king's hand was restored him again, and became as it was before. became as it was before." I Kings 13:6

God spoke to the prophet Ahijah, I Kings 14:5.

God answers
God heard them because they trusted in Him.
"They cried to God in the battle, and He was intreated of them:

because they put their trust in Him." I Chron. 5:20

"Seek the LORD and his strength, seek his face continually." I Chron. 16:11

"Now set your heart and your soul to seek the LORD your God..." I Chron. 22:19

"And thou, Solomon my son, know thou the God of thy father, and serve Him with a perfect heart and with a willing mind: for the LORD searcheth all hearts, and understandeth all the imaginations of the thoughts: if thou seek Him, He will be found of thee; but if thou forsake Him, He will cast thee off for ever." I Chron. 28:9

Humble yourself and pray

"If My people, which are called by My name, shall humble themselves, and pray, and seek My face, and turn from their wicked ways; then will I hear from heaven, and will forgive their sin, and will heal their land." II Chron. 7:14

"And after them out of all the tribes of Israel such as set their hearts to seek the LORD God of Israel came to Jerusalem, to sacrifice unto the LORD God of their fathers." II Chron. 11:16

"And he did evil, because he prepared not his heart to seek the LORD." II Chron. 12:14

"And commanded Judah to seek the LORD God of their fathers, and to do the law and the Commandment." II Chron. 14:4

*"And he (**Azariah**) went out to meet Asa, and said unto him, Hear ye*

me, Asa, and all Judah and Benjamin; The LORD is with you, while ye be with Him; and if ye seek Him, He will be found of you; but if ye forsake Him, He will forsake you... And they entered into a covenant to seek the LORD God of their fathers with all their heart and with all their soul..." II Chron. 15:2,12

God answers

In battle the chariots encompassed king Jehoshaphat and:

"He cried out, and the Lord helped him; and God moved them to depart from him." II Chron. 18:31

The prophet, Jehu, talking to king Jehoshaphat

"Nevertheless there are good things found in thee, in that thou hast taken away the groves out of the land, and hast prepared thine heart to seek God." II Chron. 19:3

People came from every town in Judah to Jerusalem to seek the Lord and inquire of Him with prayer and fasting.

"And Jehoshaphat feared, and set himself to seek the LORD, and proclaimed a fast throughout all Judah. And Judah gathered themselves together, to ask help of the LORD: even out of all the cities of Judah they came to seek the LORD." II Chron. 20:3,4

"But Hezekiah prayed for them, saying, The good LORD pardon every one that prepareth his heart to seek God, the LORD God of his fathers... And the LORD hearkened to Hezekiah, and healed the people." II Chron. 30:19,20

"And in every work that he began in the service of the house of God, and in the law, and in the Commandments, to seek his God, he did it

with all his heart, and prospered." II Chron. 31:21

"... while he (King Josiah) *was yet young, he began to seek after the God of David his father..."* II Chron. 34:3

"And the children of Israel, which were come again out of captivity, and all such as had separated themselves unto them from the filthiness of the heathen of the land, to seek the LORD God of Israel..." Ezra 6:21

"Then I proclaimed a fast there, at the river of Ahava, that we might afflict ourselves before our God, to seek of him a right way for us, and for our little ones, and for all our substance... So we fasted and besought our God for this: and he was intreated of us." Ezra 8:21,23

"I would seek unto God, and unto God would I commit my cause: Which doeth great things and unsearchable; marvellous things without number: Who giveth rain upon the earth, and sendeth waters upon the fields: To set up on high those that be low; that those which mourn may be exalted to safety." Job 5:8-11

"I have sinned; what shall I do unto thee, O Thou preserver of men? why hast Thou set me as a mark against Thee, so that I am a burden to myself? And why dost Thou not pardon my transgression, and take away mine iniquity? for now shall I sleep in the dust; and Thou shalt seek me in the morning, but I shall not be." Job 7:21-22

"If thou wouldest seek unto God betimes, and make thy supplication to the Almighty..." Job 8:5

"Whom, though I were righteous, yet would I not answer, but I would make supplication to my Judge. If I had called, and He had answered

me; yet would I not believe that He had hearkened unto my voice." Job 9:15-16

"Oh that one would hear me! Behold, my desire is, that the Almighty would answer me, and that mine adversary had written a book. Surely I would take it upon my shoulder, and bind it as a crown to me." Job 31:35-36

"Ask of me, and I shall give thee the heathen for thine inheritance, and the uttermost parts of the earth for thy possession. Thou (Jesus) *shalt break them with a rod of iron; Thou shalt dash them in pieces like a potter's vessel."* Ps. 2:8-9 *"What joy for all who take refuge* (find protection) *in Him!"* Ps. 2:12 NLT

"And they that know Thy name will put their trust in Thee: for Thou, LORD, hast not forsaken them that seek Thee. When he maketh inquisition for blood, He remembereth them: He forgetteth not the cry of the humble. Have mercy upon me, O LORD; consider my trouble which I suffer of them that hate me, Thou that liftest me up from the gates of death" Ps. 9:10,12,13

"The wicked, through the pride of his countenance, will not seek after God: God is not in all his thoughts." Ps. 10:4

"The LORD looked down from heaven upon the children of men, to see if there were any that did understand, and seek God. They are all gone aside ("astray"), *they are all together become filthy: there is none that doeth good, no, not one."* Ps. 14:2-3

"The meek shall eat and be satisfied: they shall praise the LORD that seek him: your heart shall live for ever." Ps. 22:26

"This is the generation of them that seek Him, that seek Thy face, O Jacob. Selah." Ps. 24:6

"One thing have I desired of the LORD, that will I seek after; that I may dwell in the house of the LORD all the days of my life, to behold the beauty of the LORD, and to inquire in His temple... When thou saidst, Seek ye My face; my heart said unto Thee, Thy face, LORD, will I seek. Hide not Thy face far from me; put not Thy servant away in anger: thou hast been my help; leave me not, neither forsake me, O God of my salvation." Ps. 27:4,8,9

"I cried to Thee, O Lord; and unto the Lord I made supplication." Ps. 30:8

"...they that seek the LORD shall not want any good thing." Ps. 34:10

"The righteous cry, and the Lord heareth, and delivereth them out of all their troubles." Ps. 34:17

"Let all those that seek Thee rejoice and be glad in Thee: let such as love Thy salvation say continually, The LORD be magnified. But I am poor and needy; yet the Lord thinketh upon me: Thou art my help and my deliverer; make no tarrying, O my God." Ps. 40:16-17

"God looked down from heaven upon the children of men, to see if there were any that did understand, that did seek God. Every one of them is gone back: they are altogether become filthy; there is none that doeth good, no, not one." Ps. 53:2-3

Pray morning, noon, and night

"As for me, I will call upon God; and the Lord shall save me. Evening, *and morning, and at noon, will I pray, and cry aloud: and He shall hear my voice. He hath delivered my soul in peace from the battle that was against me: for there were many with me. God shall hear..."* Ps. 55:16-18

Psalm of David, when he was in the wilderness of Judah

O God, thou art my God; early will I seek Thee: my soul thirsteth for Thee, my flesh longeth for Thee in a dry and thirsty land, where no water is; To see Thy power and Thy glory, so as I have seen Thee in the Sanctuary. Because Thy lovingkindness is better than life, my lips shall praise Thee. Thus will I bless Thee while I live: I will lift up my hands in Thy name. My soul shall be satisfied as with marrow and fatness; and my mouth shall praise Thee with joyful lips: When I remember Thee upon my bed, and meditate on Thee in the night watches. Because Thou hast been my help, therefore in the shadow of Thy wings will I rejoice." Ps. 63:1-7

If I cherish sin in my heart – God will not hear me (I can repent and turn away from my sins and God will then hear my prayers)

"I cried unto Him with my mouth, and He was extolled with my tongue. If I regard iniquity in my heart, the Lord will not hear me: but verily God hath heard me; He hath attended to the voice of my prayer. Blessed be God, which hath not turned away my prayer, nor His mercy from me." Ps. 66:17-20

"If I had cherished iniquity in my heart, the Lord would not have listened" vs. 18 RSV

I like the way the Living Bible puts it because we all sin, but we should acknowledge our sins and confess it; asking God to forgive and cleanse by His blood; God never leaves us without a remedy, I Jn. 1:9.

"He would not have listened if I had not confessed my sin." LB Ps. 66:18

"Because Thou hast been my help, therefore in the shadow of Thy wings will I rejoice." Ps. 69:6

"The humble shall see this, and be glad: and your heart shall live that seek God. The Lord heareth the poor ("needy" NIV) *and despiseth not His prisoners* ("captive people"NIV)*"* Ps. 69:32-33

"Let all those that seek Thee rejoice and be glad in Thee: and let such as love Thy salvation say continually, Let God be magnified. But I am poor and needy: make haste unto me, O God: Thou art my help and my deliverer; O LORD, make no tarrying." Ps. 70:4-5

"...that they may seek thy name, O LORD." Ps. 83:16

"O come, let us worship and bow down: let us kneel before the Lord our Maker, for He is our God; and we are the people of His pasture, and the sheep of His hand. Today if ye will hear His voice, harden not your heart, as in the provocation, and as in the day of temptation in the wilderness..." Ps. 95:3-8

"He will regard the prayer of the destitute, and not despise their prayer." Ps. 102:17

"Glory ye in His holy name: let the heart of them rejoice that seek the LORD. Seek the LORD, and His strength: seek His face evermore." Ps. 105:3-4

"Blessed are they that keep his Testimonies, and that seek him with the whole heart." Ps. 119:2

"I will lift up mine eyes unto the hills, from whence cometh my help? My help cometh from the Lord, which made heaven and earth (**our Creator God**)." Ps. 121:1-2

"Pray for the peace of Jerusalem: they shall prosper that love thee." Ps. 122:6

"Out of the depths have I cried unto Thee, O Lord. Lord, hear my voice: let Thine ears be attentive to the voice of my supplications." Ps. 13:1-2

"Then shall they call upon me, but I will not answer; they shall seek me early, but they shall not find me: For that they hated knowledge, and did not choose the fear of the LORD…" Prov. 1:28-29

"I love them that love me; and those that seek me early shall find me." Prov. 8:17

"The Lord is far from the wicked and close to the righteous (**who are righteous in Christ's righteousness**).
"The sacrifice of the wicked is an abomination to the Lord: but the prayer of the upright is His delight. The Lord is far from the wicked: but He heareth the prayer of the righteous." Prov. 15:8,29

"Evil men understand not judgment: but they that seek the LORD understand all things." Prov. 28:5

"He that turneth away his ear from hearing the law, ("**ignores the law**" NLT; "**turns away his ear from listening to the law**" NASB), *even his prayer shall be abomination* ("**detestable**" NIV; "**despised**" NLT)." Prov. 28:9

The Lord sent this message to king Ahaz, *"Ask Me for a sign"* but he wouldn't do it. Is. 7:10-12

"And when they shall say unto you, Seek unto them that have familiar spirits, and unto wizards that peep, and that mutter: should not a people seek unto their God? for the living to the dead?" Is. 8:19

"For the people turneth not unto Him that smiteth them, neither do they seek the LORD of hosts." Is. 9:13

"And it shall come to pass when it is seen that Moab is weary on the high place, that he shall come to his sanctuary to pray; but he shall not prevail." Is. 16:12

Seek God early

"With my soul have I desired Thee in the night; yea, with my spirit within me will I seek Thee early: for when Thy Judgments are in the earth, the inhabitants of the world will learn righteousness." Is 26:9

God said, *"Ask me of things to come…"* Is. 45:11

"Hearken to me, ye that follow after righteousness, ye that seek the LORD: look unto the Rock whence ye are hewn, and to the hole of the pit whence ye are digged." Is. 51:1

"Seek ye the LORD while He may be found, call ye upon Him while He is near: Let the wicked forsake his way, and the unrighteous man his thoughts: and let him return unto the LORD, and He will have mercy upon him; and to our God, for He will abundantly pardon." Is. 55:6-7

How to fast
God speaks

"Cry aloud, spare not, lift up thy voice like a trumpet, and shew My people their transgression, and the house of Jacob their sins. Yet they seek Me daily, and delight to know My ways, as a nation that did righteousness, and forsook not the ordinance of their God: they ask of Me the ordinances of justice; they take delight in approaching to God. Wherefore have we fasted, say they, and Thou seest not? wherefore have we afflicted our soul, and Thou takest no knowledge? Behold, in the day of your fast ye find pleasure, and exact all your labours. Behold, ye fast for strife and debate, and to smite with the fist of wickedness: ye shall not fast as ye do this day, to make your voice to be heard on high. Is it such a fast that I have chosen? a day for a man to afflict his soul? is it to bow down his head as a bulrush, and to spread sackcloth and ashes under him? wilt thou call this a fast, and an acceptable day to the LORD? Is not this the fast that I have chosen? to loose the bands of wickedness, to undo the heavy burdens, and to let the oppressed go free, and that ye break every yoke? Is it not to deal thy bread to the hungry, and that thou bring the poor that are cast out to thy house? when thou seest the naked, that thou cover him; and that thou hide not thyself from thine own flesh? Then shall thy light break forth as the morning, and thine health shall spring forth speedily: and thy righteousness shall go before thee; the glory of the LORD shall be thy rereward. Then shalt thou call, and the LORD shall answer; thou shalt cry, and He shall say, Here I am. If thou take away from the midst of thee the yoke, the putting forth of the finger, and speaking vanity; And if thou draw out thy soul to the hungry, and satisfy the afflicted soul; then shall thy light rise in obscurity, and thy darkness be as the noonday And the LORD shall guide thee continually, and satisfy thy soul in drought, and make fat thy bones: and thou shalt be like a watered garden, and like a spring of water, whose waters fail not. And they that shall be of thee shall build the old waste places: thou shalt raise up the foundations of many generations; and thou shalt be called, The repairer of the breach, The restorer of paths to dwell in." Is. 58:1-12

Our sins separate us from God

"Behold, the Lord's hand is not shortened, that it cannot save; neither His ear heavy, that it cannot hear (your prayers): but your iniquities have separated between you and your God, and your sins have hid His face from you, that He will not hear." Is. 59:1-2

"Woe to them that go down to Egypt for help; and stay on horses, and trust in chariots, because they are many; and in horsemen, because they are very strong; but they look not unto the Holy One of Israel, neither seek the Lord!" Is. 31:1

"... lift up thy prayer for the remnant that is left." Is. 37:4

"Even those I will bring to My holy mountain And make them joyful in My house of prayer. Their burnt offerings and their sacrifices will be acceptable on My altar; For My house will be called a house of prayer for all the peoples." Is. 56:7

"Thus saith the LORD, Stand ye in the ways, and see, and ask for the old paths, where is the good way, and walk therein, and ye shall find rest for your souls. But they said, We will not walk therein." Jer. 6:16

"Then shall ye call upon me, and ye shall go and pray unto me, and I will hearken unto you. And ye shall seek me, and find me, when ye shall search for me with all your heart and I will be found of you. And I will be found of you, saith the LORD..." Jer. 29:11-14

"They shall come with weeping, and with supplications will I lead them: I will cause them to walk by the rivers of waters in a straight way, wherein they shall not stumble: for I am a father to Israel, and Ephraim is my firstborn. Hear the Word of the Lord... Therefore they shall come and sing in the height of Zion" Jer. 31:9,12

"It may be they will present their supplication before the Lord, and will return every one from his evil way: for great is the anger and the fury that the Lord hath pronounced against this people." Jer. 36:7

King Zedekiah asked Jeremiah the prophet *"...pray now unto the Lord our God for us."* Jer. 37:3

Jeremiah pleads with king Zedekiah
This scripture could be used as a prayer to God.
"Therefore hear now, I pray thee, O my lord the king: Let my supplication, I pray thee be accepted before thee... I presented my supplication before the king..." Jer. 37:20; 38:26

Zedekiah answers the people
"For you have only deceived yourselves; for it is you who sent me to the LORD your God, saying, 'Pray for us to the LORD our God; and whatever the LORD our God says, tell us so, and we will do it. So I have told you today, but you have not obeyed the LORD your God, even in whatever He has sent me to tell you. Therefore you should now clearly understand that you will die by the sword, by famine and by pestilence (Ez.14:21), *in the place where you wish to go to reside."* Jer. 42:19-22 NASB

"In those days, and in that time, saith the LORD, the children of Israel shall come, they and the children of Judah together, going and

weeping: they shall go, and seek the LORD their God. They shall ask the way to Zion with their faces thitherward, saying, Come, and let us join ourselves to the LORD in a perpetual Covenant that shall not be forgotten." Jer. 50:4-5

"*And I sought for a man among them, that should make up the hedge, and stand in the gap before me for the land, that I should not destroy it: but I found none.*" Ez. 22:30

Daniel fasted and prayed for understanding

"*Then said he* (the angel) *unto me, Fear not, Daniel: for from the first day that thou didst set thine heart to understand, and to chasten thyself before thy God, thy words were heard, and I am come for thy words.*" Dan. 10:11-12

"*Afterward shall the children of Israel return, and seek the LORD their God, and David their king; and shall fear the LORD and his goodness in the latter days.*" Hosea 3:5

Instead of asking God, Israel was now asking their idols

"*My people ask counsel at their stocks* (idols), *and their staff* (divining rods) *declareth unto them: for the spirit of whoredoms hath caused them to err, and they have gone a whoring from under their God.*" Hosea 4:12

"*They shall go with their flocks and with their herds to seek the LORD; but they shall not find Him; He hath withdrawn Himself from them…* (God said) *I will go and return to my place, till they acknowledge their offence, and seek My face: in their affliction they will seek Me early.*" Hosea 5:6

"*And the pride of Israel testifieth to his face: and they do not return to the LORD their God, nor seek Him for all this.*" Hosea 7:10

"Sow to yourselves in righteousness, reap in mercy; break up your fallow ground: for it is time to seek the LORD, till He come and rain righteousness upon you." Hosea 10:12

"...Jacob... took his brother by the heel in the womb, and by his strength he had power with God: Yea, he had power over the angel, and prevailed: he wept, and made supplication unto Him: he found Him in Bethel, and there He spake with us; even the Lord God of hosts; the Lord is his memorial." Hosea 12:2-5

"For thus saith the LORD unto the house of Israel, Seek ye Me, and ye shall live... Seek the LORD, and ye shall live; lest He break out like fire in the house of Joseph, and devour it, and there be none to quench it in Bethel... Seek Him that maketh the seven stars and Orion, and turneth the shadow of death into the morning, and maketh the day dark with night: that calleth for the waters of the sea, and poureth them out upon the face of the earth: The LORD is His name..." Amos 5:4,6,8

"And they shall wander from sea to sea, and from the north even to the east, they shall run to and fro to seek the Word of the LORD, and shall not find it." Amos 8:12

"Seek ye the LORD, all ye meek of the earth, which have wrought His judgment; seek righteousness, seek meekness: it may be ye shall be hid in the day of the LORD'S anger." Zeph. 2:3

"When they had sent unto the house of God... their men, to pray before the Lord." Zech. 7:2-3

"... Let us go speedily to pray before the Lord, and to seek the Lord of hosts: I will go also. Yea, many people and strong nations shall come to

370

seek the Lord of hosts in Jerusalem, and to pray before the Lord." Zech. 8:21-22

"Ask ye of the LORD rain in the time of the latter rain; so the LORD shall make bright clouds, and give them showers of rain, to every one grass in the field. For the idols have spoken vanity, and the diviners have seen a lie, and have told false dreams; they comfort in vain: therefore they went their way as a flock, they were troubled, because there was no shepherd. Mine anger was kindled against the shepherds, and I punished the goats: for the LORD of hosts hath visited his flock the house of Judah, and hath made them as his goodly horse in the battle." Zech. 10:1-3

"... beseech God that He will be gracious unto us..." Mal. 1:9

"... and the Lord, whom ye seek, shall suddenly come to His temple, even the messenger of the Covenant, whom ye delight in: behold, He shall come, saith the LORD of hosts." Mal. 3:1

New Testament

Sometimes prayer is worship and sometimes we offer gifts with our prayers

The Wisemen saw Jesus and fell down to worship Him.

"And when they were come into the house, they saw the young child with Mary His mother, and fell down, and worshiped Him: and when they had opened their treasures, they presented unto Him gifts; gold, and frankincense, and myrrh." Matt. 2:11

He asks Jesus, Let me go with You

"And when He was come into the ship, he that had been possessed with the devil prayed him that He might be with him." Mk. 5:18

Jesus answers

"Howbeit Jesus suffered him not, but saith unto him, Go home to thy friends, and tell them how great things the Lord hath done for thee, and hath had compassion on thee." Mk. 5:19

First be reconciled

"Therefore if thou bring thy gift to the altar, and there rememberest that thy brother hath ought against thee; leave there thy gift before the altar, and go thy way; first be reconciled to thy brother, and then come and offer thy gift (or prayer to God)." Matt. 5:23-24

Pray for others

"...pray for them that despitefully use you and persecute you: that ye may be the children of your Father which is in heaven: for He maketh His sun to rise on the evil and on the good, and sendeth rain on the just

and on the unjust." Matt. 5:44

"Ask, and it shall be given you; seek, and ye shall find; knock, and it shall be opened unto you: For every one that asketh receiveth; and he that seeketh findeth; and to him that knocketh it shall be opened. Or what man is there of you, whom if his son ask bread, will he give him a stone? Or if he ask a fish, will he give him a serpent? If ye then, being evil, know how to give good gifts unto your children, how much more shall your Father which is in heaven give good things to them that ask Him?" Matt. 7:7-11

Don't worry about what you will eat, what you will drink, or what you will wear

"For your heavenly Father knoweth that ye have need of all these things. But seek ye first the kingdom of God, and His righteousness; and all these things shall be added unto you. Take therefore no thought for the morrow: for the morrow shall take thought for the things of itself. Sufficient unto the day is the evil thereof." Matt. 6:33-34

We seek God through prayer, fasting, obedience, reading the Word, and spending time with Him, etc.

Ask

The key is to ask for things that won't harm us and are good for us.

"Ask, and it shall be given you; seek, and ye shall find; knock, and it shall be opened unto you: for every one that asketh receiveth; and he that seeketh findeth; and to him that knocketh it shall be opened. Or what man is there of you, whom if his son ask bread, will he give him a stone? Or, if he ask a fish, will he give him a serpent? If ye then, being evil, know how to give good gifts unto your children, how much more shall your Father which is in heaven give good things to them that ask Him?" Matt. 7:7-11

Sometimes we just need to speak the word out loud

The centurion understood Jesus' authority and asked Jesus to just, *"speak the word"*.

Jesus said,

"I have not found so great faith, no, not in in Israel." Matt. 8:5-10

Believe

"... Jesus saith unto them, Believe ye that I am able to do this? They said unto Him, Yea, Lord... (Jesus said to them) *according to your faith be it unto you."* Matt. 9:28-29

Pray for more laborers

Jesus said that the harvest was ripe and the labourers were few.

"Pray ye therefore the Lord of the harvest, that He will send forth labourers into His harvest." Matt. 9:38

Jesus blessed the food

"... looking up to Heaven, He blessed (the loaves and fish)*"* Matt. 14:19

Jesus prays

"And when He had sent the multitudes away, He went up into a mountain apart to pray: and when the evening was come, He was there alone." Matt. 14:23

We have the keys of the Kingdom to use in our prayers and spiritual warfare

"And I will give unto thee the keys of the kingdom of heaven: and whatsoever thou shalt bind on earth shall be bound in heaven: and whatsoever thou shalt loose on earth shall be loosed in heaven." Matt. 16:19

The Father loves us because we love Jesus

"And in that day ye shall ask Me nothing. Verily, verily, I say unto you, Whatsoever ye shall ask the Father in My name, He will give it you. Hitherto have ye asked nothing in My name: ask, and ye shall receive, that your joy may be full. These things have I spoken unto you in proverbs: but the time cometh, when I shall no more speak unto you in proverbs, but I shall shew you plainly of the Father. At that day ye shall ask in My name: and I say not unto you, that I will pray the Father for you: For the Father Himself loveth you, because ye have loved Me, and have believed that I came out from God." Jn. 16:23-27

The disciples couldn't cast out the demons because of their unbelief

Faith comes by prayer and fasting and some prayers need fasting with them to increase our faith.

"Then came the disciples to Jesus apart, and said, Why could not we cast him out? And Jesus said unto them, Because of your unbelief: for verily I say unto you, If ye have faith as a grain of mustard seed, ye shall say unto this mountain, Remove hence to yonder place; and it shall move; and nothing shall be impossible unto you. Howbeit this kind goeth not out but by prayer and fasting." Matt. 17:21

When two or three agree on earth, God answers their prayers

"Verily I say unto you Whatsoever ye shall bind on earth shall be bound in heaven: and whatsoever ye shall loose on earth shall be loosed in heaven. Again I say unto you, that if two of you shall agree on earth as touching any thing that they shall ask, it shall be done for them of My Father which is in heaven. For where two or three are gathered together in My name, there am I in the midst of them." Matt. 18:19-20

Jesus prays for the children

"Then were there brought unto Him little children, that He should put His hands on them, and pray: and the disciples rebuked them." Matt. 19:13

Jesus speaks

Jesus said,

"Suffer little children, and forbid them not, to come unto Me; for of such is the Kingdom of Heaven." Matt. 19:14

James and John ask to sit on Jesus' right and left in His Kingdom

"'What is it you want?'

He asked.

She said,

'Grant that one of these two sons of mine may sit at your right and the other at your left in your kingdom.'" Matt. 20:21

"But Jesus answered and said,

Ye know not what ye ask. Are ye able to drink of the cup that I shall drink of, and to be baptized with the baptism that I am baptized with? They say unto him, We are able. And he saith unto them, Ye shall drink indeed of my cup, and be baptized with the baptism that I am baptized with: but to sit on my right hand, and on my left, is not mine to give, but it shall be given to them for whom it is prepared of My Father."

Matt. 20:22-23

My house is a house of prayer

"And said unto them, It is written, My house shall be called the house of prayer; but ye have made it a den of thieves." Matt. 21:13

Believe and you will receive

Jesus cursed the fig tree and the disciples were amazed that the next day it withered.

"Jesus answered and said unto them, Verily I say unto you, If ye have faith, and doubt not, ye shall not only do this which is done to the fig tree, but also if ye shall say unto this mountain, Be thou removed, and be thou cast into the sea; it shall be done. And all things whatsoever ye shall ask in prayer believing ye shall receive." Matt. 21:21-22

The Pharisees prayed long prayers for pretense

"Woe unto you, scribes and Pharisees, hypocrites! For ye devour widows' houses, and for a pretence make long prayer: therefore ye shall receive the greater damnation." Matt. 23:14

"But pray ye that your flight be not in the winter, neither on the Sabbath day... Watch therefore: for ye know not what hour your Lord doth come. But know this, that if the Goodman of the house had known in what watch the thief would come, he would have watched, and would not have suffered his house to be broken up.... Blessed is that servant, whom his Lord when he cometh shall find so doing (watching and praying) *Verily I say unto you, That He shall make him ruler over all His goods."* Matt. 24:20,42-47

Rise before daybreak

"And in the morning, rising up a great while before day, He went out, and departed into a solitary place, and there prayed." Mk. 1:35

Jesus blessed the food looking up to Heaven

"He looked up to Heaven and blessed (the loaves and fish)*"* Mk. 6:38

"And when He had sent them away, He departed into a mountain to pray." Mk. 6:46

If we want God to answer our prayers, we cannot be ashamed to stand up for Him

"Whosoever therefore shall be ashamed of Me and of My words in this adulterous and sinful generation; of him also shall the Son of man be ashamed, when He cometh in the glory of His Father with the holy angels." Mk. 8:38

The disciples could not cast the demon out from the child without prayer and fasting

"And one of the multitude answered and said, Master, I have brought unto Thee my son, which hath a dumb spirit… and I spake to Thy disciples that they should cast him out; and they could not. He answereth him, and saith, O faithless generation, how long shall I be with you? how long shall I suffer you? bring him unto Me.

And they brought him unto Him: and when He saw him, straightway the spirit tare him: and he fell on the ground, and wallowed foaming. And He asked his father, How long is it ago since this came unto him? And he said, Of a child. And oft times it hath cast him into the fire, and into the waters, to destroy him: but if thou canst do any thing, have compassion on us, and help us.

By saying, *"If you can"* he showed his unbelief; we must believe if we want Jesus to answer our prayers. He could do very little miracles in His hometown because of their unbelief.

Jesus said unto him, If thou canst believe, all things are possible to him that believeth. And straightway the father of the child cried out, and said with tears, Lord, I believe; help Thou mine unbelief. And when Jesus saw that the people came running together, He rebuked the foul spirit, saying unto him, Thou dumb and deaf spirit, I charge thee, come

out of him, and enter no more into him. And the spirit cried, and rent
him sore, and came out of him: and he was as one dead; insomuch that
many said, He is dead. But Jesus took him by the hand, and lifted him
up: and he arose. And when He was come into the house, His disciples
asked Him privately, Why could not we cast him out? And He said unto
them. . ." Mk 9:17-29

Prayer and fasting

"This kind can come forth by nothing, but by prayer and fasting." Mk.
9:29

"And James and John, the sons of Zebedee, come unto Him (Jesus)
saying, Master, we would that Thou shouldest do for us whatsoever we
shall desire. And He said unto them,
    What would ye that I should do for you?
They said unto him,
    Grant unto us that we may sit, one on Thy right hand, and the
    other on Thy left hand, in Thy glory.

But Jesus said unto them,
    Ye know not what ye ask: can ye drink of the cup that I drink
    of? and be baptized with the baptism that I am baptized with?

And they said unto him,
    We can.

And Jesus said unto them, Ye shall indeed drink of the cup that I drink
of; and with the baptism that I am baptized withal shall ye be baptized:
But to sit on my right hand and on my left hand is not mine to give; but
it shall be given to them for whom it is prepared." Mk. 20:38-40

"And He taught, saying unto them,

Is it not written, My house shall be called of all nations the house of prayer? But ye have made it a den of thieves... Therefore I say unto you, What things soever ye desire, when ye pray, believe that ye receive them, and ye shall have them. And when ye stand praying, forgive, if ye have ought against any: that your Father also which is in heaven may forgive you your trespasses." Mk. 11:17,24-25

Believe

Jesus curses the fig tree - Believing is when we have no doubt.

"And in the morning, as they passed by, they saw the fig tree dried up from the roots. And Peter calling to remembrance saith unto him, Master, behold, the fig tree which Thou cursedst is withered away. And Jesus answering saith unto them, Have faith in God. For verily I say unto you, That whosoever shall say unto this mountain, Be thou removed, and be thou cast into the sea; and shall not doubt in his heart, but shall believe that those things which he saith shall come to pass; he shall have whatsoever he saith. Therefore I say unto you, What things soever ye desire, when ye pray, believe that ye receive them, and ye shall have them. And when ye stand praying, forgive, if ye have ought against any: that your Father also which is in heaven may forgive you your trespasses. But if ye do not forgive, neither will your Father which is in heaven forgive your trespasses." Mk. 11:24-26

"Beware of the scribes, which love to go in long clothing, and love salutations in the marketplaces, and the chief seats in the synagogues, and the uppermost rooms at feasts: which devour widows' houses, and for a pretence make long prayers: these shall receive greater damnation." Mk. 12:38-40

"...pray ye that your flight be not in the winter." Mk. 13:18

Watch and pray

"Take ye heed, watch and pray: for ye know not when the time is. For the Son of man is as a man taking a far journey... Watch ye therefore: for ye know not when the master of the house cometh, at even, or at midnight, or at the cockcrowing, or in the morning: lest coming suddenly He find you sleeping. And what I say unto you I say unto all, Watch." Mk. 13:33-36

"Watch ye and pray, lest ye enter into temptation. The spirit truly is ready, but the flesh is weak. And again He went away, and prayed, and spake the same words." Mk. 14:38-39

"And the whole multitude of the people were praying without at the time of incense... for thy prayer is heard..." Lk. 1:10,13

"And there was one Anna, a prophetess, the daughter of Phanuel, of the tribe of Asher: she was of a great age, and had lived with an husband seven years... and she was a widow of about fourscore and four years (84 yrs.), which departed not from the temple, but served God with fastings and prayers night and day." Lk. 2:36-37

"Now when all the people were baptized, it came to pass, that Jesus also being baptized, and praying..." Lk. 3:21

Prayer answered

"... the heaven was opened. And the Holy Ghost descended in a bodily shape like a dove upon Him, and a voice came from heaven, which said, Thou art My beloved Son; in Thee I am well pleased." Lk. 3:21

Jesus is willing

"...a man full of leprosy: who seeing Jesus fell on his face, and besought

Him, saying, Lord, if Thou wilt, Thou canst make me clean. And He put forth His hand, and touched him, saying, I will; be thou clean. And immediately the leprosy departed from him." Lk. 5:12-13

We can have the confidence that Jesus is willing and able to answer our prayers!

Go to a quiet place

"And He withdrew Himself into the wilderness, and prayed." Lk. 5:16

Fast and pray

"And they said unto him, Why do the disciples of John fast often, and make prayers, and likewise the disciples of the Pharisees; but Thine eat and drink? And He said unto them, Can ye make the children of the bridechamber fast, while the bridegroom is with them? But the days will come, when the bridegroom shall be taken away from them, and then shall they fast in those days." Lk. 5:33-35

Jesus prayed all night

"He went out into a mountain to pray, and continued all night in prayer to God." Lk. 6:12

We are to pray for those who misuse us

"Pray for them which despitefully use you…" Lk. 6:28

Jesus prayed for the food

"… looking up to Heaven, He blessed them (the loaves and fish)." Lk. 9:16

Praying alone

"And it came to pass, as He was alone praying, His disciples were with Him…" Lk. 9:18

"Once when Jesus was praying by Himself, the disciples joined him, and he asked them, 'Who do the crowds say that I am?'" CEB

Prayed on a mountain

"...and went up into a mountain to pray. And as He prayed, the fashion of His countenance was altered, and His raiment was white and glistering." Lk. 9:28-29

The harvest is ready - pray for the labourers

"... the harvest truly is great, but the labourers are few: pray ye therefore the Lord of the harvest, that He would send forth labourers into His harvest." Lk. 10:2

Parable of friend asking for bread

Persistent prayer is not the same as repetitive prayer. Jesus tells a story about a neighbor or friend who keeps asking for bread in the middle of the night and even though the man doesn't want to get up or be troubled he gets up and gives his friend what he asks for because he is persistent.

"I say unto you, Though he will not rise and give him, because he is his friend, yet because of his importunity (Dict. "to press – demand with urgency or persistence; to beg for urgently or persistenly – to annoy – relentless") *he will rise and give him as many as he needeth."*

(Importunity #335 means, *"shamelessness,impudence"*)

And I say unto you, ask, and it shall be given you; seek, and ye shall find; knock, and it shall be opened unto you. For every one that asketh receiveth; and he that seeketh findeth; and to him that knocketh it shall be opened.

If a son shall ask bread of any of you that is a father, will he give him a stone? Or if he ask a fish, will he for a fish give him a serpent? Or if he shall ask an egg, will he offer him a scorpion? If ye then, being evil, know

how to give good gifts unto your children; how much more shall your heavenly Father give the Holy Spirit to them that ask Him?" Lk. 11:5-13

"When once the master of the house is risen up, and hath shut to the door, and ye begin to stand without, and to knock at the door, saying, Lord, Lord, open unto us; and He shall answer and say unto you, I know you not whence ye are" Lk. 13:25

"For all these things do the nations of the world seek after: and your Father knoweth that ye have need of these things. But rather seek ye the kingdom of God; and all these things shall be added unto you." Lk. 12:30-31

Men ought to pray
"And He spake a parable unto them to this end, that men ought always to pray, and not to faint..." Lk. 18:1

Parable of widow going before judge - Persistent prayer
Jesus tells the story of a woman who kept asking the judge to avenge her. The judge didn't want to be bothered with her, but he did avenge her because he was getting weary of her continually coming to him.

"And the Lord said, Hear what the unjust judge saith. And shall not God avenge His own elect, which cry day and night unto Him, though He bear long with them? I tell you that He will avenge them speedily. Nevertheless when the Son of man cometh, shall He find faith on the earth?" Lk. 18:6-8

House of prayer
"My house is a house of prayer" Lk. 19:46

Beware of scribes who make long prayers for show

"Beware of the scribes, which desire to walk in long robes, and love greetings in the markets, and the highest seats in the synagogues, and the chief rooms at feasts; Which devour widows' houses, and for a shew make long prayers: the same shall receive greater damnation." Lk. 20:46-47

Watch and pray

"Watch ye therefore, and pray always, that ye may be accounted worthy to escape all these things that shall come to pass, and to stand before the Son of man." Lk. 21:36

"And the Lord said, Simon, Simon, behold, Satan hath desired to have you, that he may sift you as wheat: but I have prayed for thee, that thy faith fail not: and when thou art converted, strengthen thy brethren." Lk. 22:31-32

Jesus blesses the food (prays over it)

"When He was at the table with them, He took bread, gave thanks, broke it and began to give it to them. Then their eyes were opened and they recognized Him." Lk. 24:30 NIV

Jesus cleanses the temple for the 2nd time

"...make not My Father's house an house of merchandise" Jn. 2:16
He called it a *"house of prayer"* in Mt. 21:13.

Jesus blesses the food

"And Jesus took the loaves; and when He had given thanks (for the loaves and fish)..." Jn. 6:11

Do we seek Jesus for the right reasons?

"Jesus answered them and said, 'Truly, truly, I say to you, you seek Me, not because you saw signs, but because you ate of the loaves and were filled.'" Jn. 6:26

"Ye shall seek me, and shall not find me: and where I am, thither ye cannot come… What manner of saying is this that he said, Ye shall seek me, and shall not find me: and where I am, thither ye cannot come?" Jn. 7:34,36

God doesn't hear sinners but those who worship God and do His will

Jesus opened the eyes of a blind man and then the he was questioned by the Pharisees. The healed man said to the Pharisees,

"Now we know that God heareth not sinners: but if any man be a worshipper of God, and doeth His will, him He heareth… If this man were not of God, He could do nothing." Jn. 9:31-33

What do we do if God doesn't hear sinners (and we know that we are sinners)? We ask God to forgive us. Cleanse us by His blood; then we strive to do His will.

"And whatsoever we ask, we receive of Him, because we keep His Commandments, and do those things that are pleasing in His sight." I Jn. 3:22

Martha told Jesus, *"But I know, that even now, whatsoever Thou wilt ask of God, God will give it thee."* Jn. 11:22

We are to ask in Jesus' name

"And whatsoever ye shall ask in My name, that will I do, that the Father may be glorified in the Son. If ye shall ask any thing in My name,

I will do it. If ye love Me, keep My Commandments. And I will pray the Father, and He shall give you another Comforter (#3875 Gr."paraclete" means, "advocate, intercessor, consoler, comforter, helper"), *that He may abide with you for ever; Even the Spirit of truth; whom the world cannot receive, because it seeth Him not, neither knoweth Him: but ye know Him; for He dwelleth with you, and shall be in you. I will not leave you comfortless: I will come to You."* Jn. 14:13-18

"If ye abide in me, and My words abide in you, ye shall ask what ye will, and it shall be done unto you." Jn. 15:7

If we love God, we obey Him; not to earn salvation, which is free to all who believe Him, but to show Him how much we love Him. He will reward us someday for our works even though all our righteousness is as filthy rags. Even our works are rewarded by grace. We are saved by grace to do good works.

"For we are God's handiwork, created in Christ Jesus to do good works, which God prepared in advance for us to do." Eph. 2:10

"If ye love Me, keep My Commandments. And I will pray the Father, and he shall give you another Comforter, that he may abide with you for ever; even the Spirit of truth; whom the world cannot receive, because it seeth him not, neither knoweth Him: but ye know Him; for He dwelleth with you, and shall be in you. I will not leave you comfortless: I will come to you." Jn. 14:15-18

Abide in Me

We bear fruit in our lives by staying connected to Jesus.

"Now ye are clean through the Word which I have spoken unto you. Abide in Me, and I in you. As the branch cannot bear fruit of itself, except it abide in the vine; no more can ye, except ye abide in Me. I am the vine, ye are the branches: He that abideth in Me, and I in him, the

same bringeth forth much fruit: for without Me ye can do nothing. If a man abide not in Me, he is cast forth as a branch, and is withered; and men gather them, and cast them into the fire, and they are burned. If ye abide in Me, and My words abide in you, ye shall ask what ye will, and it shall be done unto you... If ye keep My Commandments, ye shall abide in My love: even as I have kept My Father's Commandments, and abide in His love... This is My Commandment, that ye love one another, as I have loved you. Greater love hath no man than this, that a man lay down his life for his friends. Ye are My friends, if ye do whatsoever I command you... Ye have not chosen Me, but I have chosen you, and ordained you, that ye should go and bring forth fruit, and that your fruit should remain: that whatsoever ye shall ask of the Father in My name, He may give it you." Jn. 15:7,10

The Father loves you because you believe in Jesus and love Him

"And in that day ye shall ask me nothing. Verily, verily, I say unto you, Whatsoever ye shall ask the Father in My name, He will give it you. Hitherto have ye asked nothing in My name: ask, and ye shall receive, that your joy may be full... at that day ye shall ask in My name: and I say not unto you, that I will pray the Father for you: for the Father Himself loveth you, because ye have loved me, and have believed that I came out from God." Jn. 16:23-27

I pray for you

"At that day ye shall ask in My name: and I say not unto you, that I will pray the Father for you: for the Father Himself loveth you, because ye have loved Me, and have believed that I came out from God. I came forth from the Father, and am come into the world: again, I leave the world, and go to the Father." Jn. 16:26-28

They were all in one accord

"These all continued with one accord in prayer and supplication, with the women, and Mary the mother of Jesus, and with His brethren." Acts 1:14

"And they continued stedfastly in the Apostles' doctrine and fellowship, and in breaking of bread, and in prayers." Acts 2:42

Hour of prayer

"Now Peter and John went up together into the temple at the hour of prayer, being the ninth hour (3 p.m.)." Acts 3:1

"But we will give ourselves continually to prayer, and to the ministry of the Word." Acts 6:4

"... and when they had prayed, they laid their hands on them." Acts 6:6

Prayer for Holy Spirit

"Who, when they were come down, prayed for them, that they might receive the Holy Ghost: (For as yet He was fallen upon none of them) ..." Acts 8:15-16

You cannot buy the Holy Spirit. He is freely given by God to those who believe and are baptized.

"But Peter said unto him, Thy money perish with thee, because thou hast thought that the gift of God may be purchased with money. Thou hast neither part nor lot in this matter: for thy heart is not right in the sight of God. Repent therefore of this thy wickedness, and pray God, if perhaps the thought of Thine heart may be forgiven thee. For I perceive that thou art in the gall of bitterness, and in the bond of iniquity. Then

answered Simon, and said, Pray ye to the Lord for me, that none of these things which ye have spoken come upon me." Acts 8:20-24

Saul converted and called Paul

"And the Lord said unto him, Arise, and go into the street which is called Straight, and inquire in the house of Judas for one called Saul, of Tarsus: for, behold, he prayeth, and hath seen in a vision a man..." Acts 9:11-12

Saul converted to Paul and baptized

"And Saul arose from the earth; and when his eyes were opened, he saw no man: but they led him by the hand, and brought him into Damascus. And he was three days without sight, and neither did eat nor drink. And there was a certain disciple at Damascus, named Ananias; and to him said the Lord in a vision, Ananias. And he said,

Behold, I am here, Lord. And the Lord said unto him, Arise, and go into the street which is called Straight, and inquire in the house of Judas for one called Saul, of Tarsus: for, behold, he prayeth, and hath seen in a vision a man named Ananias coming in, and putting his hand on him, that he might receive his sight. Then Ananias answered, Lord, I have heard by many of this man, how much evil he hath done to Thy saints at Jerusalem: and here he hath authority from the chief priests to bind all that call on Thy name. But the Lord said unto him,

Go thy way: for he is a chosen vessel unto Me, to bear My name before the Gentiles, and kings, and the children of Israel: for I will shew him how great things he must suffer for My name's sake. And Ananias went his way, and entered into the house; and putting his hands on him (Saul) said, Brother Saul, The Lord even Jesus,

that appeared unto thee in the way as thou camest, hath sent me, that thou mightest receive thy sight, and be filled with the Holy Ghost. And immediately there fell from his eyes as it had been scales: and he received *sight forthwith, and arose, and was baptized."* Acts 9:8-18

Dorcas (full of good works) raised to life and many believed because of it

"Now there was at Joppa a certain disciple named Tabitha, which by interpretation is called Dorcas: this woman was full of good works and almsdeeds which she did. And it came to pass in those days, that she was sick, and died: whom when they had washed, they laid her in an upper chamber. And forasmuch as Lydda was nigh to Joppa, and the disciples had heard that Peter was there, they sent unto him two men, desiring him that he would not delay to come to them. Then Peter arose and went with them. When he was come, they brought him into the upper chamber: and all the widows stood by him weeping, and shewing the coats and garments which Dorcas made, while she was with them." Acts 9:36-40

Peter prayed

But Peter put them all forth, and kneeled down, and prayed; and turning him to the body said, Tabitha, arise..." Acts 9:40

God answered

"And she opened her eyes: and when she saw Peter, she sat up. And he gave her his hand, and lifted her up, and when he had called the saints and widows, presented her alive. And it was known through out all Joppa; and many believed in the Lord." Acts 9:40-42

Conversion of Cornelius

His prayers and offerings are remembered by God.

"There was a certain man in Caesarea, called Cornelius, a centurion of the band called the Italian band, a devout man, and one that feared God with all his house, which gave much alms to the people, and prayed

to God always. He saw in a vision evidently about the ninth hour (**3 p.m.**) of the day an angel of God coming in to him, and saying unto him, Cornelius. And when he looked on him, he was afraid, and said, What is it, Lord? And he said unto him, Thy prayers and thine alms are come up for a memorial before God. And now send men to Joppa, and call for one Simon, whose surname is Peter: He lodgeth with one Simon a tanner, whose house is by the sea side: he shall tell thee what thou oughtest to do. And when the angel which spake unto Cornelius was departed, he called two of his household servants, and a devout soldier of them that waited on him continually;

and when he had declared all these things unto them, he sent them to Joppa. On the morrow, as they went on their journey, and drew nigh unto the city, Peter went up upon the housetop to Pray about the 6th hour (**noon**) and he became very hungry, and would have eaten: but while they made ready, he fell into a trance, and saw heaven opened, and a certain vessel descending unto him, as it had been a great sheet knit at the four corners, and let down to the earth: wherein were all manner of fourfooted beasts of the earth, and wild beasts, and creeping things, and fowls of the air. And there came a voice to him, Rise, Peter; kill and eat. But Peter said,

Not so, Lord; for I have never eaten any thing that is common or unclean. And the voice spake unto him again the second time, What God hath cleansed, that call not thou common. This was done thrice: and the vessel was received up again into heaven. Now while Peter doubted in himself what this vision which he had seen should mean, behold, the men which were sent from Cornelius had made inquiry for Simon's house, and stood before the gate, and called, and asked whether Simon, which was surnamed Peter, were lodged there. While Peter thought on the vision, the Spirit said unto him, Behold, three men seek thee. Arise therefore, and get thee down, and go with them, doubting nothing: for I have sent them." Acts 10:1-20

Peter went to Cornelius' house and proclaimed to him the gospel of Jesus Christ; Cornelius and his whole household were saved.

Cornelius fasts and prays

"And Cornelius said, Four days ago I was fasting until this hour; and at the ninth hour (3 p.m.) *I prayed in my house, and, behold, a man stood before me in bright clothing, and said,*

God answers

God heard his prayers and remembered his offerings.

Cornelius, thy prayer is heard, and thine alms are had in remembrance in the sight of God." Acts 10:30-31

"... Peter... was in the city of Joppa praying: and in a trance (he) *saw a vision..."* Acts 11:4-5

Prayer for Peter

"Peter therefore was kept in prison: but prayer was made without ceasing of the church unto God for him." Acts 12:5

God answers

"And when Herod would have brought him forth, the same night Peter was sleeping between two soldiers, bound with two chains; and the keepers before the door kept the prison, and behold the angel of the Lord said unto him, Gird thyself, and bind on thy sandals. And so he did. And he saith unto him, Cast thy garment about thee, and follow me. And he went out, and followed him; and wist not that it was true which was done by the angel; but thought he saw a vision. When they were past the first and the second ward, they came to the iron gate that leadeth unto the city; which opened to them of his own accord and they went out, and passed on through one street; and forthwith the angel

393

departed from him. And when Peter was come to himself,

he said, Now I know of a surety, that the Lord hath sent His angel, and hath delivered me out of the hand of Herod, and from all the expectation of the people of the Jews. And when he had considered the thing, he came to the house of Mary the mother of John, whose surname was Mark; where many were gathered together praying.

God answers

"And Peter knocked at the door of the gate, a damsel came to hearken, named Rhoda. And when she knew Peter's voice, she opened not the gate for gladness, but ran in, and told how Peter stood before the gate. And they said unto her, Thou art mad. But she constantly affirmed that it was even so. Then said they, It is his angel. As they ministered to the Lord, and fasted, the Holy Ghost said, Separate me Barnabas and Saul for the work whereunto I have called them. And when they had fasted and prayed, and laid their hands on them, they sent them away.

So they, being sent forth by the Holy Ghost, departed unto Seleucia; and from thence they sailed to Cyprus... As they ministered to the Lord, and fasted, the Holy Ghost said, Separate me Barnabas and Saul for the work whereunto I have called them And when they had fasted and prayed, and laid their hands on them, they sent them away. So they, being sent forth by the Holy Ghost, departed unto Seleucia; and from thence they sailed to Cyprus..." Acts. 12:13-13:4

Praying for Barnabus and Saul

"As they ministered to the Lord, and fasted, the Holy Ghost said, Separate Me Barnabas and Saul for the work whereunto I have called them. And when they had fasted and prayed, and laid their hands on them, they sent them away. So they, being sent forth by the Holy Ghost, departed..." Acts 13:3

Paul perceived that he had faith to be healed in Acts 14:9.

Prayer and fasting

"And when they had ordained them elders in every church, and had prayed with fasting, they commended them to the Lord, on whom they believed." Acts 14:23

"And on the Sabbath we went out of the city by a river side, where prayer was wont to be made; and we sat down, and spake unto the women which resorted thither." Acts 16:13

"And it came to pass, as we went to prayer, a certain damsel possessed with a spirit of divination met us, which brought her masters much gain by soothsaying..." Acts 16:16

"And at midnight Paul and Silas prayed, and sang praises unto God..." Acts 16:25

"And when he had thus spoken, he kneeled down, and prayed with them all." Acts 20:36

"... and we kneeled down on the shore, and prayed." Acts 21:5

"And it came to pass, that, when I was come again to Jerusalem, even while I prayed in the temple, I was in a trance; and saw Him saying unto me, Make haste, and get thee quickly out of Jerusalem: for they will not receive thy testimony concerning Me." Acts 22:17

Paul shipwrecked

Paul told them not to set sail that there would be a shipwreck. They set sail anyway and there was a storm; they were shipwrecked.

Paul fasted and an angel came and talked to him and said,

"Fear not, Paul; thou must be brought before Caesar: and, lo, God hath given thee all them that sail with thee.

Wherefore, sirs, be of good cheer: for I believe God, that it shall be even as it was told me... Then fearing lest we should have fallen upon rocks, they cast four anchors out of the stern, and wished ("prayed" LB) *for the* ("daylight" LB)." Acts 27:23-24,29

God helped them and they all made it safely to shore.

"And when he had thus spoken, he took bread, and gave thanks to God in the presence of them all: and when he had broken it, he began to eat." Acts 27:35

"And it came to pass, that the father of Publius lay sick of a fever... to whom Paul entered in, and prayed, and laid his hands on him, and healed him." Acts 28:8

"... Paul... thanked God, and took courage." Acts 28:15

"That they should seek the Lord, if haply they might feel after Him, and find him, though He be not far from every one of us" Acts 17:27

"First, I thank my God through Jesus Christ for you all, that your faith is spoken of throughout the whole world. For God is my witness, whom I serve with my spirit in the gospel of His Son, that without ceasing I make mention of you always in my prayers; making request, if by any means now at length I might have a prosperous journey by the will of God to come unto you." Rom. 1:8-10

"There is none that understandeth, there is none that seeketh after God. They are all gone out of the way, they are together become

unprofitable; there is none that doeth good, no, not one." Rom. 3:11-12

The Holy Spirit helps us pray

"Likewise the Spirit also helpeth our infirmities: for we know not what we should pray for as we ought: but the Spirit itself maketh intercession for us with groanings which cannot be uttered. And He that searcheth the hearts knoweth what is the mind of the Spirit, because He maketh intercession for the saints according to the will of God." Rom. 8:26-27

"Brethren, my heart's desire and prayer to God for Israel is, that they might be saved." Rom. 10:1

"Rejoicing in hope; patient in tribulation; continuing instant in prayer..." Rom. 12:12

Paul asked God to deliver him from unbelievers

"Now I beseech you, brethren, for the Lord Jesus Christ's sake, and for the love of the Spirit, that ye strive together with me in your prayers to God for me; that I may be delivered from them that do not believe..." Rom. 15:30-31

"Defraud ye not one the other, except it be with consent for a time, that ye may give yourselves to fasting and prayer; and come together again, that Satan tempt you not for your incontinency." I Cor. 7:5

Submit as unto the Lord

"But I would have you know, that the head of every man is Christ: and the head of the woman is the man **(who is under Christ)***; and the head of Christ is God. Every man praying or prophesying, having his head covered, dishonoureth his head. But every woman that prayeth or prophesieth with her head uncovered dishonoureth her head: for that*

*is even all one as if she were shaven, for if the woman be not covered,
let her also be shorn: but if it be a shame for a woman to be shorn or
shaved, let her be covered. For a man indeed ought not to cover his
head, forasmuch as he is the image and glory of God: but the woman
is the glory of the man. For the man is not of the woman; but the
woman of the man. Neither was the man created for the woman; but
the woman for the man. For this cause ought the woman to have power*
("a covering, in sign that she is under the power of her husband" KJV
fn) *on her head because of the angels. Nevertheless neither is the man
without the woman, neither the woman without the man, in the Lord.
For as the woman is of the man, even so is the man also by the woman;
but all things of God. Judge in yourselves: is it comely that a woman
pray unto God uncovered? Doth not even nature itself teach you, that,
if a man have long hair, it is a shame unto him? But if a woman have
long hair, it is a glory to her: for her hair is given her for a covering. But
if any man seem to be contentious, we have no such custom, neither the
churches of God."* I Cor. 11:3-16

A woman is under the authority of her husband if he is under the
authority of Jesus Christ. God would never want a woman to submit
to anything ungodly or against God.

When you pray, speak in a language everyone can understand

"Wherefore let him that speaketh in an unknown...(Gr. #1100 "a
language") *pray that he may interpret. For if I pray in an unknown...*
(Gr. #1100 "a language"), *my spirit prayeth, but my understanding is
unfruitful. What is it then? I will pray with the Spirit, and I will pray
with the understanding also: I will sing with the Spirit, and I will sing
with the understanding also. Else when thou shalt bless with the Spirit,
how shall he that occupieth the room of the unlearned say Amen at thy
giving of thanks, seeing he understandeth not what thou sayest? For*

thou verily givest thanks well, but the other is not edified." I Cor. 14:13-17

"Ye also helping together by prayer for us, that for the gift bestowed upon us by the means of many persons thanks may be given by many on our behalf." II Cor. 1:11

"Praying us with much intreaty that we would receive the gift, and take upon us the fellowship of the ministering to the saints." II Cor. 8:4

"And by their prayer for you, which long after you for the exceeding grace of God in you." II Cor. 9:14

We can do nothing against the truth.

"Now I pray to God that ye do no evil; not that we should appear approved, but that ye should do that which is honest, though we be as reprobates. For we can do nothing against the truth, but for the truth." II Cor. 13:7-8

Paul's prayer for the Ephesians

"Wherefore I also, after I heard of your faith in the Lord Jesus, and love unto all the saints, cease not to give thanks for you, making mention of you in my prayers; that the God of our Lord Jesus Christ, the Father of glory may give unto you the Spirit of wisdom and revelation in the knowledge of Him... Now unto Him that is able to do exceeding abundantly above all that we ask or think, according to the power that worketh in us. Unto Him be glory in the church by Christ Jesus throughout all ages, world without end. Amen." Eph. 1:15-17,20-21

"For this cause I bow my knees unto the Father of our Lord Jesus Christ.... That He would grant you, according to the riches of His glory,

to be strengthened with might by His Spirit in the inner man..." Eph. 3:14,16

God wants to give us more than we ask for according to how much the Holy Spirit works in us

"Now unto Him that is able to do exceeding abundantly above all that we ask or think, according to the power that worketh in us, unto Him be glory in the church by Christ Jesus throughout all ages, world without end. Amen." Eph. 3:20

Pray always

"Praying always with all prayer and supplication in the Spirit and watching thereunto with all perseverance and supplication for all saints; and for me, that utterance may be given unto me, that I may open my mouth boldly, to make known the mystery of the gospel, for which I am an ambassador..." Eph. 6:18

We want to glorify God in life and death

"Always in every prayer of mine for you all making request with joy, for your fellowship in the gospel from the first day until now... For I know that this shall turn to my salvation through your prayer, and the supply of the Spirit of Jesus Christ, according to my earnest expectation and my hope, that in nothing I shall be ashamed, but that with all boldness, as always, so now also Christ shall be magnified in my body, whether it be by life, or by death." Phil. 1:4,19

God will finish the work He started in you

"I thank my God upon every remembrance of you, always in every prayer of mine for you all making request with joy, for your fellowship in the gospel from the first day until now; being confident of this very thing, that He which hath begun a good work in you will perform it until the *day of Jesus Christ..."* Phil. 1:3-4

God wants your love to abound in knowledge and without offense

"And this I pray, that your love may abound yet more and more in knowledge and in all judgment; that ye may approve things that are excellent; that ye may be sincere and without offence till the day of Christ." Phil. 1:9-10

Through prayer

"For I know that this shall turn to my salvation through your prayer, and the supply of the Spirit of Jesus Christ, according to my earnest expectation and my hope, that in nothing I shall be ashamed, but that with all boldness, as always, so now also Christ shall be magnified in my body, whether it be by life, or by death." Phil. 1:19-20

Someday, every knee will bow to Jesus

"That at the name of Jesus every knee should bow, of things in heaven, and things in earth, and things under the earth; and that every tongue should confess that Jesus Christ is Lord, to the glory of God the Father." Phil. 2:10-11

Make your requests with thanksgiving

"Be careful for nothing; but in every thing by prayer and supplication with thanksgiving let your requests be made known unto God. And the peace of God, which passeth all understanding, shall keep your hearts and minds through Christ Jesus." Phil. 4:6

"If ye then be risen with Christ, seek those things which are above, where Christ sitteth on the right hand of God." Col. 3:1

Continue to pray and ask for open doors to proclaim the Gospel

"Continue in prayer, and watch in the same with thanksgiving; withal praying also for us, that God would open unto us a door of utterance, to speak the mystery of Christ... labouring fervently for you in prayers, that ye may stand perfect and complete in all the will of God" Col. 4:2-3,12

Paul's prayer for the Philippians

"But my God shall supply all your need according to His riches in glory by Christ Jesus. Now unto God and our Father be glory for ever and ever. Amen... The grace of our Lord Jesus Christ be with you all. Amen." Phil. 4:19-23

Pray always

"We give thanks to God and the Father of our Lord Jesus Christ, praying always for you... For this cause we also, since the day we heard it, do not cease to pray for you, and to desire that ye might be filled with the knowledge of His will in all wisdom and spiritual understanding; that ye might walk worthy of the Lord unto all pleasing, being fruitful in every good work, and increasing in the knowledge of God... giving thanks unto the Father which hath made us meet to be partakers of the inheritance of the saints in light..." Col. 1:3,9-12

Fervent prayer

"... always labouring fervently for you in prayers, that ye may stand perfect and complete in all the will of God." Col. 4:12

Give thanks

"We give thanks to God always for you all, making mention of you in our prayers; remembering without ceasing your work of faith, and

labour of love, and patience of hope in our Lord Jesus Christ, in the sight of God and our Father..." I Thess. 1:2-3

Pray night & Day
"Night and day praying exceedingly that we might see your face, and might perfect that which is lacking in your faith?" I Thess. 3:10

Paul's prayer for the Thessalonians
"For what thanks can we render to God again for you, for all the joy wherewith we joy for your sakes before our God; night and day praying exceedingly that we might see your face, and might perfect that which is lacking in your faith? Now God Himself and our Father, and our Lord Jesus Christ, direct our way unto you. And the Lord make you to increase and abound in love one toward another, and toward all men, even as we do toward you: to the end He may stablish your hears unblameable in holiness before God, even our Father, at the coming of our Lord Jesus Christ with all His saints." I Thess. 3:16

Pray without ceasing
"Pray without ceasing... And I pray God your whole spirit and soul and body be preserved blameless unto the coming of our Lord Jesus Christ. Faithful is He that calleth you, who also will do it. brethren, pray for us..." I Thess. 5:17,23,25

Pray always
"Wherefore also we pray always for you, that our God would count you worthy of this calling, and fulfil all the good pleasure of His goodness, and the work of faith with power: that the name of our Lord Jesus Christ may be glorified in you, and ye in Him, according to the grace of our God and the Lord Jesus Christ." II Thess. 1:11-12

Pray for us

"Finally, brethren, pray for us, that the Word of the Lord may have free course ("that the message spreads" NLT), *and be glorified, even as it is with you: and that we may be delivered from unreasonable and wicked men: for all men do not have faith. But the Lord is faithful"* II Thess. 3:1-2

Pray for all men

"I exhort therefore, that, first of all, supplications, prayers, intercessions, and giving of thanks be made for all men..." I Tim. 2:1

Pray everywhere

"I will therefore that men pray every where, lifting up holy hands, without wrath and doubting." I Tim. 2:8

They were to pray over foods offered to idols

"Forbidding... to abstain from meats, which God hath created to be received with thanksgiving of them which believe and know the truth. For every creature of God is good, and nothing to be refused, if it be received with thanksgiving: for it is sanctified by the word of God and prayer." I Tim. 4:4-5

Pray night & Day

"Now she that is a widow indeed, and desolate, trusteth in God, and continueth in supplications and prayers night and day." I Tim. 5:5

Pray without ceasing

"I thank God, whom I serve from my forefathers with pure conscience that without ceasing I have remembrance of thee in my prayers night and day..." II Tim. 1:3

God will stand with us and strengthen us even when no one else will

"At my first answer no man stood with me, but all men forsook me: I pray God that it may not be laid to their charge. Notwithstanding the Lord stood with me, and strengthened me..." I Tim. 4:17

I mention you in my prayers

"I thank my God, making mention of thee always in my prayers, hearing of thy love and faith, which thou hast toward the Lord Jesus, and toward all saints...I trust that through your prayers I shall be given unto you." Philemon 4,5,22

Jesus prayed with tears

"... when He (Jesus) had offered up prayers and supplications with strong crying and tears unto him that was able to save him from death, and was heard in that He feared; though He were a Son, yet learned He obedience by things which He suffered..." Heb. 5:7-8

Jesus our Intercessor

"But this man (Jesus), because He continueth ever, hath an unchangeable priesthood. Wherefore He is able also to save them to the uttermost that come unto God by Him, seeing He ever liveth to make intercession for them." Heb. 7:24-25

"And without faith it is impossible to please Him, for he who comes to God must believe that He is and that He is a rewarder of those who seek Him." Heb. 11:6

Pray for us

"Pray for us: for we trust we have a good conscience, in all things willing to live honestly." Heb. 13:18

Pray for wisdom

"If any of you lack wisdom, let him ask of God, that giveth to all men liberally, and upbraideth not (doesn't find fault); *and it shall be given him. But let him ask in faith, nothing wavering, for he that wavereth is like a wave of the sea driven with the wind and tossed. For let not that man think that he shall receive any thing of the Lord. A double minded man is unstable in all his ways."* Jms.. 1:5-8

You have not because you don't ask; don't ask to consume it on your lusts

"Ye lust, and have not: ye kill, and desire to have, and cannot obtain: ye fight and war, yet ye have not, because ye ask not. Ye ask, and receive not, because ye ask amiss, that ye may consume it upon your lusts." Jms.. 4:2-3

God doesn't want to give us something that would ultimately cause us to lose our soul.

"For what shall it profit a man, if he shall gain the whole world, and lose his own soul? Or what shall man give in exchange for his soul?" Mk. 8:36-37

Fervent prayer availeth much

"Is any among you afflicted? Let him pray. Is any merry? Let him sing psalms. Is any sick among you? let him call for the elders of the church; and let them pray over him, anointing him with oil in the name of the Lord; and the prayer of faith shall save the sick, and the Lord shall raise him up: and if he have committed sins, they shall be forgiven him. Confess your faults one to another, and pray one for another, that ye may be healed. The effectual fervent prayer of a righteous man availeth much. Elias was a man subject to like passions as we are, and he prayed earnestly that it might not rain: and it rained not on the earth by the

space of three years and six months. And he prayed again, and the heaven gave rain, and the earth brought forth her fruit." Jms.. 5:13-18

Husbands, don't let your prayers be hindered

"Likewise, ye husbands, dwell with them (your wives) according to knowledge, giving honour unto the wife, as unto the weaker vessel, and as being heirs together of the grace of life; that your prayers be not hindered... For the eyes of the Lord are over the righteous, and His ears are open unto their prayers: but the face of the Lord is against them that do evil." I Pet. 3:7,12

Watch and pray

"But the end of all things is at hand: be ye therefore sober, and watch unto prayer." I Pet. 4:7

Jesus intercedes for us to the Father

"My little children, these things write I unto you, that ye sin not. And if any man sin, we have an advocate with the Father, Jesus Christ the righteous: and He is the propitiation for our sins; and not for ours only, but also for the sins of the whole world." I Jn. 2:1-2

("Advocate" is #3875 "paraclete" Gr. Int. means "intercessor, consoler, comforter, helper, of the Holy Spirit".

"propitiation" #2434 means "atoning sacrifice, atonement, expiator")

God hears our prayers if we do what pleases Him

"And whatsoever we ask, we receive of Him, because we keep His Commandments, and do those things that are pleasing in His sight." I Jn. 3:22

Keeping God's Commandments pleases Him.

Pray life for others

If we ask according to His will, He hears us.

"This is the confidence that we have in Him, that, if we ask any thing according to His will, He heareth us: and if we know that He hear us, whatsoever we ask, we know that we have the petition that we desired of him. If any man see his brother sin a sin which is not unto death, he shall ask, and He shall give him life for them that sin not unto death. There is a sin unto death: I do not say that he shall pray for it." I Jn. 5:14-16

"And if we know that He hear us, whatsoever we ask, we know that we have the petitions that we desired of Him." II Jn. 5:15

"And if we beseech Him to hear us concerning the things that we ask of Him, we are assured that we have already received from Him those things that we desire." II Jn. 5:15 PB

Pray in the power of the Holy Spirit

"But ye, beloved, building up yourselves on your most holy faith, praying in the Holy Ghost. Keep yourselves in the love of God, looking for the mercy of our Lord Jesus Christ unto eternal life." Jude 20-21

The incense in Heaven is our prayers

"And another angel came and stood at the altar, having a golden censer; and there was given unto him much incense, that he should offer it with the prayers of all saints upon the golden altar which was before the throne. And the smoke of the incense, which came with the prayers of the saints, ascended up before God out of the angel's hand." Rev. 8:3-4

"And when He had taken the book, the four beasts and four and twenty elders fell down before the Lamb, having every one of them harps, and golden vials full of odours, which are the prayers of saints. And they

sung a new song, saying Thou art worthy to take the book, and to open the seals thereof: for Thou wast slain, and hast redeemed us to God by Thy blood out of every kindred, and tongue, and people, and nation; And hast made us unto our God kings and priests: and we shall reign on the earth." Rev. 5:8-10

Prayer Promises

Promises that God will hear and answer our Prayers

Jesus always came against Satan with **"*It is written*"** and we can too (Matt. 4:4).

> May God grant whatever you ask - I Sam.1:17
> They called... He answered - Ps.99:6
> When I call, answer me quickly - Ps.102:2
> He will respond to the prayer of the destitute; He will not despise their plea - Ps.102:17
> I call on the Lord - Ps.120:1
> The Lord is faithful to all His promises - Ps. 145:13
> You shall pray & I will hearken to you - Jer. 29:12
> Call & I will answer - Jer.33:3
> Ask and you shall receive - Matt.7:7,8
> With God all things are possible - Matt.19:26;Mk.9:23;10:27
> Have faith in God - Mk.11:22
> God will give you whatever you ask for - Jn.11:22; Jms.15:7
> Ask anything in My name & I will do it - Jn.14:12,13
> If we abide in Him and He abides in us we can receive from Him - Jn.15:7,16
> I will give you the holy & sure blessings - Acts 13:34
> All things are yours - Rom.8:32
> All the promises are yes in Christ Jesus - II Cor.1:20
> He is able to do more than we ask or think - Eph.3:20
> If we ask according to His will - I Jn.5:14 (Never be afraid of God's will, He wants what's best for you)

"I will hasten My word to perform it." Jer. 1:12

"For the Word of God is quick and powerful" Heb. 4:12

"The words I speak to you are Spirit and life" Jn. 6:63

We must have faith when we come to God

They believed His promises - Ps.103:3-6,14,17;106:12.

"But without faith it is impossible to please God; for He that cometh to God must believe that He is, and that He is a rewarder of them that diligently seek Him." Heb. 11:6

"This is the victory that overcometh the world, even our faith." I Jn. 5:4

Coming Soon

Look for my next book, "All the Promises" for more promises from the Bible and prayers using the promises.

Personal answers to prayer

I want to share a few prayers that God has answered for me and my family.

The first answers to prayer is about my mother. Because if my mother had died as a child, I wouldn't even be here.

When she was quite young, around 5 yrs. old, she had gotten very sick with what they thought was Rheumatic fever. They thought she might die. My grandparents had just accepted Jesus and they had read in the Bible that if you were sick, you should call the elders in the church and anoint the sick person with oil and pray.

"Is any sick among you? Let him call for the elders of the church; and let them pray over him, anointing him with oil in the name of the Lord..." Jms. 5:14

So that is what they did. They called the elders of the church, who anointed her with oil and prayed over her. She was healed that very day, and is still living today at 80 yrs. old.

The second answer to prayer I would like to tell you about in my mother's life came when she was around 13. She had decided that she would take a walk in the woods with her friend. It was a beautiful day and they were having a lovely time picking flowers and singing and enjoying themselves. They had been in the woods for a while when the fog rolled in and they decided they better go home. They walked and walked but after a few hours they realized that they were just going around in circles.

Meanwhile, at home, her parents had decided that they should be home by now and had looked and looked for them, but couldn't find them. It was starting to get late so they decided to ask for help. Many people came over and were scouring the woods looking for them, but they wondered if they would ever find them.

Back in the woods, my mother realized that if God didn't help her, she wasn't going to find her way home. She decided to pray. She told God that she was lost and couldn't find her way home. She was going to put her hand out and ask God to take a hold of her hand and lead her home. After saying Amen, she put her hand out into the air as though someone was holding it and started walking. In a very short while, they were nearing home and they heard people yelling their names. By this time it was quite dark and everyone had their flashlights on looking for them.

Needless to say, her parents (my grandparents) were very happy to see them and she knew that God had taken hold of her hand that day and led her safely home. She was very grateful to God for this miracle in her life and so am I.

Thank You Jesus for keeping my mother safe and well so that I could be born!

God provides blankets

Do what God asks and He will provide.

When we first got married in 1974, my husband, George, was in the service and we didn't make much money back then. We got to Italy with just a suitcase full of clothes and nothing else. George found a small apartment for us to live in and it was furnished but we didn't have any blankets and sometimes it got very cold in the winter. Well, he decided he would borrow some blankets and return them when we left. One day God convicted me that we should return those blankets immediately, that very day. So when George got home I told him that God wanted us to take the blankets back.

We didn't have any heat and we didn't have any money for blankets.

It would be a couple of weeks before he got paid but we did what God told us to do not knowing how God would provide. I wasn't worried because I knew that God had told us to do this. George wasn't sure what would happen but he knew he could always sleep on the ship and be warm.; he didn't know what I would do.

Well, that day God had a surprise for both of us. After George left for work, the landlady came down. Now she didn't know what we had done; she lived above our apartment but she didn't speak English. She came with an arm load of blankets and she stitched the two single mattresses together so the wind couldn't come up between them. She gave us a small heater and put a towel under the door so the wind wouldn't come in.

Now while all this was happening at home, George got an unexpected check for $400 which we didn't even need to use because we had blankets enough to keep us till we moved but God wanted him to know, "I can take care of you if you do what I ask." When George came home, I couldn't wait to tell him what had happened and he couldn't wait to tell me what he received in the mail!

God is happy when we obey Him and He's there to help us when we need Him.

Thank you Jesus!

The miracle watermelon
The Promise:

Before you ask God gives.
"Before they call, I will answer." Is. 65:24

Our first year of marriage was in Gaeta, Italy in 1974. One day we were walking around town (because we had no car) and we were feeling a little sad because we were missing our families. We hadn't seen them in quite a while and there was no way to go to the states and see them. We wished we had stamps to write to them but it was toward the end of the month when the money would always run out. If we didn't write, then we usually didn't get letters and we looked forward to those letters so much.

One day, we saw a man selling slices of watermelon for $.25 but we didn't even have a quarter between us and we sure wished we could have a piece of watermelon. So we walked back to our apartment with a heavy heart. When we got to our apartment, there on the doorstep was a very large watermelon with the words, "*From the Lord*" carved on the side in large letters. Wow, we couldn't believe our eyes. Where did it come from? We asked all our friends if they knew anything about it but they all were just as surprised as we were. We invited all our friends over and shared it with them.

We were so happy that God saw two kids feeling bad one day and gave us a watermelon to cheer us up.

Thank you Jesus for the watermelon!

God tells me to send a Bible to my sister

While we were in Italy, I had a small pocket Bible that I was planning to take with me everywhere I went. I wanted to mark all the special verses in the Bible so that I could find them easily if I met someone and got into a discussion with them about Biblical themes. I worked very hard on this Bible for about two months; every chance I got. When the day came that it was all finished, I was very excited. I loved this Bible very much because I had put so much work into it; but the day I finished it, to my surprise, I felt God telling me to send it to my sister. I said,

Lord, are you sure? She may not appreciate it or she may even be mad at me for sending it to her.

She might think that I'm trying to preach to her.

But God made it very clear to me that He wanted me to send it to her and send it now! So I wrapped it up and sent it to my sister immediately; she was living with my dad in San Francisco at the time. She was a teenager and going through a difficult time I think. So I sent it just like God told me to and never thought another thing about it. I never heard anything from my sister so just put it out of my mind. After a year, it was time to come home. I came home first while George was processing out of the Navy. When I got home, I saw my sister and asked her if she got the Bible I had sent to her. She told me yes she had; and that at the time, she had been sitting on her bed in her bedroom alone in the house and asking God,

Do You see me? Do You care about me?

And just then the mail came and there was a package for her in the mail. She wondered what it could be and when she opened it, there was that Bible I had sent to her. And not just a Bible but a Bible that had been all marked up, which made her feel that God really did see her and care about her to send a Bible with such a personal touch and right at the exact time of her prayer. I'm glad that I listened to God that day and did what He told me to do. When I think about it; it's amazing to me that it took me about two months to work on putting all the notes in that Bible and that it got there on the exact day, the exact hour, and the exact minute that it was needed but that is how God works; that was a miracle that only God can do.

Thank you Jesus for letting me know to send that Bible and thank you for answering my sister's prayer.

God delivered us from the fierce dog

The first year after we returned from Italy we moved to Arizona near my husband's uncle and decided to sell Christian books for the summer. We were going door to door and had been pretty successful when one day, on a Friday, we went up to this house that was off by itself. We got up to the door and realized that no one was home so we started to leave when a very large German Shepherd dog came around from the back, growling and blocked us from leaving the door. He wasn't going to bite us as long as we didn't try to move off that entryway. I began to think, What if these people don't come home for hours or what if they don't come home for the weekend? What were we going to do? There was no way that the dog was going to let us move and I knew he wasn't going to budge until his owners came home. So I prayed in my mind,

"Lord, You closed the lion's mouths for Daniel so I know that You can close this dog's mouth so that we can get off this porch and go home."

No sooner had I said, "Amen", then that dog turned around and went back into the back yard and lay down. I can tell you that we got off that porch in a hurry and got back into our car and headed home. I was so grateful that God answered that prayer that day and closed the dog's mouth. If He did it in the Bible, than I know He can do it for me and that day He did!

"Thank You Jesus for closing the dog's mouth."

The first miracle
God provides $20 (3 times)

When we got back from Italy, we moved to Portland, Oregon in

1975 and took a job helping people in need. When we started that job we knew that we wouldn't have any money for a whole month. Well, toward the end of the month we got to the place where we didn't have any food except a bottle of hot sauce and a jar of wheat germ.

The first miracle occurred when our car ran out of gas just as we pulled into a gas station. George took his credit card out and there was no money in his wallet (he had looked in every nook and cranny) but when he went to put the credit card back in his wallet, there was a twenty dollar bill sticking out.

The second miracle

The next week we ran out of food again down to that bottle of hot sauce and jar of wheat germ. We went to the park a few blocks from our house and were jogging and when we got within two blocks of home, I heard the phone ringing; but George couldn't hear it. He didn't know how I could hear it but I guess God wanted me to hear it. He ran to the house and the phone was still ringing. It was my mother and she figured we couldn't be too far away at 6 in the morning so she let the phone keep ringing until George answered it. She said God had told her to send us a twenty.

The third miracle

The next week George's grandmother called and said she had a dream that God told her to send us a twenty. After that we got paid regularly and we had enough to live on.

"Thank You Jesus for slipping us a twenty three times!"

George healed

This happened while we were living in Portland in 1975. One

morning when George got up out of bed, I noticed some small round brown spots on his backside. He went to the Dr. to see what it was and the Dr. sent him to the VA in Portland. All the nurses and Dr.'s were coming and going - looking at George's back side, which was a little embarrassing for him. They all concluded that he had what is called, "*Piokiloderma*".

We didn't know anything about that but were told you didn't die from it directly but you would get a lot of little tumors under the skin and could have other complications and there was no cure but there was medicine to contain it; not a very promising diagnosis!

Well, we decided to pray with a pastor friend in 10 days. I fasted those 10 days and at the end of that time we went to our friend, who had a special room where you only went when you prayed and you had to take your shoes off because it was used only for prayer and he called it holy ground. We prayed that day for George's healing and the next time he went to the Dr. he was completely well and it has, by the grace of God, never come back. The Dr. did not know why it was gone only that it was gone.

Well, we know why; God did a miracle!

"Thank You Jesus for healing George!"

George fell asleep at the wheel

This time we were living in Myrtle Creek Oregon in 1981 and we were thinking of moving to North Dakota. George had to drive to Portland then fly to Fargo and stay for a couple of days looking the situation over; where we would live and what the church looked like. After checking everything out and taking a few pictures for me, he flew home and then drove from Portland to Myrtle Creek to get home.

It was late that night so I went to bed; I had just fallen asleep when I woke up and felt that God wanted me to pray; I had a strong impression that George's life was in danger. So I looked at the clock to see what time it was and then started praying fervently that God would be with him and help him in whatever situation he was in. I felt so strongly that something was wrong that I started crying because I didn't know if he was going to make it home safely or not.

When George came through that door, I was so happy to see him that I hugged him crying. He was a little surprised to see my reaction because he didn't know I knew anything had happened. He told me that he had fallen asleep at the wheel and I asked him what time that had happened and the time he told me was the exact time that God had wakened me to pray. He had stopped at a rest stop and slep for a little while before finishing his trip home.

"Thank you, Jesus, for watching over George and keeping him safe."

Our daughter healed of a perforated eardrum

When our daughter, Rebecca was about 3 yrs. old (1983), she had a weakness for ear infections; she usually had them several times a year. One time while she was sitting on the couch, all of a sudden she screamed out in pain. I ran over to see what was wrong and she was holding her ear and crying and stuff was oozing out of her ear. We took her as quickly as we could to the emergency Dr. who also happened to be a friend of ours. He looked in her ear and said,

"Yes, she has a perforated ear drum."

He gave us some Amoxicillin and told us to make an appointment with another Dr. on Monday since this was Friday, which we did.

When we got home, I said to our daughter,

"Let's pray and ask God to heal you."

So we prayed together and asked that God would heal her ear.

After we prayed, I put her to bed and was sitting on the couch reading when about an hour later Rebecca came running out of her bedroom shouting,

"My ear doesn't hurt, my ear doesn't hurt."

Well, that was wonderful and the rest of the weekend she seemed fine. We still went to our appointment on Monday to see how she was doing and the Dr. said,

"No, she doesn't have a perforated ear drum."

I said,

"Well, could a perforated eardrum heal between Friday and Monday?"

And he said,

"Oh no, she never did have a perforated ear drum."

Well, I knew that she really did have a perforated eardrum and I also knew that God had healed her.

Thank you Jesus for healing Rebecca's ear!

Healed

One time while we were living in N. Dakota, we went home to Oregon for a visit. We stayed with my mom and step-dad for about a week. I got very sick and felt like I might even die; I don't think anyone knew how sick I really was. I got achy and swollen and I felt nauseous all the time and threw up for seven days in a row; not being able to eat anything.

My brother-in-law came to visit while we were there and saw how sick I was and in need of prayer so he had everyone gather around and pray for me. He had a very strong faith and I could sense that there was no doubt in him. His faith inspired my faith and I remember thinking, "*I really believe*"; and when I had that thought, ("*I really believe*") I felt a funny sensation in my gut and the nausea instantly stopped (the first time in 7 days) and in three days I was back to normal. I didn't feel something come from him to me but he inspired my faith and when my faith came to life, I felt something coming from within me. His faith inspired my faith and it was just like Jesus said, *"Your faith has made you whole"* Matt.9:22;Mk.5:34;10:52;Lk.8:48;17:19.

I'm thankful that my brother-in-law cared enough to pray for me that day.

"Thank you Jesus for healing me!"

Lawsuit

Quite a few years ago, not by our choosing, we got involved in a lawsuit. The first day in court things seemed to be going badly and when we got back into our motel room and got ready for bed, I couldn't sleep so I got up and knelt down beside the bed. Sometimes I'll just kneel and humble myself before the Lord and not say anything; I just let the emotions flow out to God and let the Holy Spirit intercede for me as it says in the Bible.

The Promise

"Likewise the Spirit also helpeth our infirmities; for we know not what we should pray for as we ought: but the Spirit itself maketh intercession for us with groanings which cannot be uttered. And He that searcheth the hearts knoweth what is the mind of the Spirit, because He maketh intercession for the saints according to the will of God" Rom. 8:26-27.

The Bible says that the Holy Spirit makes groans for us to the Father.

Well, every time I tried to get up I just couldn't. The heaviness of the lawsuit was crushing me but it felt like I couldn't get up so I just stayed there in prayer on my knees not saying anything; just letting my soul cry out to God.

I would stay on my knees for a few hours and then try to get up but I couldn't; so I stayed down on my knees and kept crying out to God with my heart. I stayed that way most of the night and finally, at 6 a.m. in the morning the burden completely lifted and I knew that no matter what happened it was going to be O.K.; that God was in control of the situation. All worry and fear and doubt were gone and I had complete assurance and confidence in God that everything would work out. The battle was won that night and the next day when I went into that courtroom I had strength now that hadn't been there before; even the lawyers saw it and I think even the judge could tell.

Well, as you can imagine, God won that lawsuit for us - praise to God! I know He heard me that night and helped us in our troubles.

"Thank you Jesus for hearing me!"

Flood in N. Dakota – God promised the water to come this far & no further

When we moved to Fargo, North Dakota in 1981, we lived right on the Red River. The Red River flooded most years because it thaws out in the South before the North thaws out and this is one of very few rivers that runs North. Since I knew that the river usually flooded into the basement of our house, I prayed and claimed the verse in the Bible that says, God speaks to the waters and says, "*This far and no further*" Job 38;Ps.104:9. We lived there four years and it flooded the year before we moved in and the year after we moved out but it never flooded for the four years that we lived there. The waters would come halfway into the yard but never up to the basement as long as we were there.

"Thank you Jesus for keeping Your promise!"

423

George breaks his ribs

We moved to Myrtle Creek again in 1988 and one day George decided to get up real early and go fishing on the coast. After he left, I was in a deep sleep when I woke me up and again I felt God telling me to pray; that George's life was in danger. I started praying fervently that God would watch over him and keep him safe. I looked at the clock to see what time it was.

In the meantime, George was with his friend in his friend's boat. When they got to what is called "*the bar*" on the ocean there was a yellow light flashing which meant that they shouldn't go out; the water was too rough. Well, his friend decided they would go out anyway, being that he was skipper of the boat. On the way out a large sneaker wave lifted the boat up very high then dropped it on the water. Unknown to anyone in the boat, George had fallen off the chair and hit his ribs and was in a lot of pain.

The skipper said, "Wow, that was a close one" and then he saw George writhing on the floor in agony. If that boat had capsized at that point, George would probably have died not being able to swim or even keep his head up.

The waves were very rough and they had to figure out how to get back over "*the bar*" and back to shore. God was with them, though, and gave them a series of waves they could ride to get to shore safely. They took George to the Dr. and found out that he had a few broken ribs. They gave George pain medication which took the pain away and then they went back out fishing all day. By the time they were ready to come home, the pain medication had worn off and George was in a lot of pain coming back.

When he got home and told me he had broken his ribs, I asked him what time that was and the time he told me was exactly the time God had awakened me to start praying. Thank you Jesus for watching over George again!

Cyst on my elbow

While we were living in Myrtle Creek around 1989, it was raining and I was going into a store when for some strange reason I could see the lady in the store moving the rug away from the door. I walked into the store and when I hit that slick floor with my wet shoes, I went flying and landed on my elbow. I had to have three stitches. Well, he stitched me up and everything went normal until after the stitches came out and it had healed; a little cyst had developed where the stitches had been. It was an irritation and mildly painful all the time.

One day after I was tired of this pain, I said in my head, *"Lord, this is a little thing and I know that You can do this; would you please take this cyst off"*! And no sooner did I say, *"Amen"* than our daughter who was in the back seat of the car needed my attention and called, mommy, and as I turned to see what she wanted my elbow hit the seat hard right on the cyst and it burst and that was the end of that.

> *"Thank you Lord for removing that cyst! I knew it was a no big thing for You, and I knew You could do it."*

Singing Evangelist testifies how God gave him money for car

Again, while we were living in Myrtle Creek around 1989, my husband and I were driving cars that cost about $200 each. The brakes didn't work right and you had to pump the gas peddle to get it going and they just weren't very safe or reliable.

Well, one day we went to listen to a singing Evangelist and he was talking about how God had given them a van that they needed so badly as they traveled a lot. I remember thinking,

> *"Lord, You know that we need safe, reliable cars also.*

If you can give that guy a car, I know You can give us a car?"

Not long after that George went down to go hunting at Mt. Shasta with his family and while he was down there, his car went out permanently and my car couldn't even make the trip down so I had to borrow someone's car to go get him. While George was waiting for me to pick him up, he heard God speaking to him that he would get a new car.

There had been a lady in the hospital that George had gone to pray over months before that God had healed and unknown to us she had promised that she would give God $10,000 but she hadn't done it yet. After our car went out God reminded her of her promise and told her that He wanted her to give the money to George for a new car. She called us to come over to her home and said, "If it doesn't offend you, I would like to give you this money that I promised to give to God, for a new car."

George said, "I don't know what to say but it sure won't offend me. Thank you!"

And with that money we were able to get two cars, a good reliable car for George and a nicer car for me than I had had.

"Thank you Jesus for providing for our needs out of Your riches in glory!"

God started waking me up to study and pray

We moved to Florence, Oregon in 1990 where George pastored a church and after a few years, we started an A.C.E. school. I taught grades 1 through 6 and George was the Principal, as well as pastor, for six years. One night as I was getting up to go to the bathroom, I heard God speak so clearly to my heart. I knew that He wanted me to start getting up in the middle of the night to spend time with Him in prayer and Bible study; that I would be going through a lot of things and would need special help from Him.

"Well, Lord, I am so tired at night that I don't even want to get up to go to the bathroom and if I do get up, I keep my eyes shut so that I can go right back to sleep."

But I knew that the Lord still wanted me to get up so I prayed, *"Lord, I'll make a deal with You. If You make me so wide awake in the middle of the night that I can't go to sleep, then I will get up."*

Well, the very next night at 2 a.m. I was wide awake; I tossed and turned but couldn't go back to sleep. This had never happened to me before; O.K. Lord, I'll get up.

So from that night on the Lord would wake me up in the middle of the night and I would spend time with Him. Sometimes it was just a couple of times in the week and sometimes it was four or five times a week. He would let me know when He wanted to spend time with me by waking me and I have had some of my best times with God in the middle of the night. The nice thing about being with God at night is that there are no distractions; no need to clean, no phone ringing, etc.

When I knew that I had to work the next day, I would limit my time to one hour but if I didn't have anything pressing the next day, I would spend up to two hours with God. I have enjoyed my time with God in the early morning hours like nothing I could have ever imagined!

"I love them that love Me and Those who seek Me early, will find me!"
Prov. 8:17

Praying for George when he was in a canoe

One day while I was working in a Stationery supply store in Florence, Oregon, I felt God telling me to pray for George; his life was in danger (again)!

I didn't even know where George was or what he was doing but, of course, I prayed that God would keep him safe and help him in whatever trouble he was in.

A few hours later George told me this story.

His friend had taken him out in the middle of the lake to hunt ducks in a canoe. He left George in the canoe hunting while he took off in his boat driving around the lake but he planned on coming back after a few hours to check on him.

George had been hunting for a while when he saw a duck overhead and shot. Well, the shot made him lose his balance and he went flying backwards out of the canoe. That time of year the lake was freezing cold and try as hard as he could, he couldn't get back into the canoe. He lifted the canoe over his head and flipped it over which got most of the water out but he didn't have the strength to get inside. He was getting colder and colder and he said that it felt like his organs were shutting down.

Finally, he got at the back of the canoe and pushed the canoe under him as he jumped on the squared off back end. He was barely in with his belly over the edge but couldn't get all the way in and the canoe had taken in some water during all this.

It just so happened that his friend was driving around in his boat but was still quite a ways away and when he looked in George's direction. He could see in the distance that the canoe looked a little funny; kind of low in the water and leaning to one side so he thought, I better go and check that out. He wanted to see what was the matter.

When he got there, George was shaking uncontrollably and his friend helped into the boat and wrapped a thermal blanket around him. He drove the boat as fast as he could and got him back to the house and put him in a hot shower; but he didn't know that you aren't suppose to put someone with hypothermia in a hot shower; you're suppose to start out with cool water and work your way up to warm water. I think that because he had used the thermal blanket and the amount of time it took to get to the house, that it put George just past the danger point so that the hot water didn't kill him.

I'm thankful that God watched over my husband that day and kept him alive through all of that.

"Thank you Jesus!"

God clothes me like He promised

Another time not too long ago in 2013; I was thinking of that verse in the Bible that says,

"Therefore I say unto you, Take no thought for ...your body, what ye shall put on.... And why take ye thought for raiment? Consider the lilies of the field, how they grow; they toil not, neither do they spin: and yet I say unto you, that even Solomon in all his glory was not arrayed like one of these. Wherefore, if God so clothe the grass of the field, which today is, and to morrow is cast into the oven, shall He not much more clothe you, O ye of little faith... Therefore take no thought, saying... Wherewithal shall we be clothed... for your heavenly Father knoweth that ye have need of all these things? But seek first the kingdom of God, and His righteousness; and all these things shall be added unto you." Matt. 6:25-32

My clothes were getting old and I didn't have any money to buy new ones so I prayed,

"Lord, You promised in Your Word that you would give clothing to those who need it! I can't afford to buy any shirts

and I need them. I know that verse is for me as well as anyone else."

Well, in the next few days my sister (without knowing what I had prayed) gave me a large green trash bag full of clothes! And I mean full! It took me a few weeks before I had the time to go through them but when I did, I saw beautiful blouses and shirts of all colors and description. Some had embroidery on them and some had rhinestones; they all fit and were very beautiful.

The people in the church said, "Wow, what nice shirts you have! Where did you get them?" and I would tell them that my sister gave them to me but really God gave them to me through my sister!

I'm thankful that my sister gave these clothes to me and I thank Jesus for working through my sister to fulfill His word to me!

I have had so many answers to prayer that I could write another book just on that but I will close with these. God is willing and able to answer our prayers if we come to Him, asking in faith and believing that He is able to do what He has promised. Test Him today and see what He is willing to do for you. I don't know what prayers God is going to answer for you. God is the same today as He was in the Bible but sometimes He says, "Yes"; sometimes, "*Maybe*"; and sometimes, "*No*". Sometimes we need to search our hearts and life to see if there is anything separating us from God and blocking the answers to our prayers.

"Behold, The Lord's hand is not shortened, that it cannot save; neither His ear heavy ("dull" NIV) *that it cannot hear but your iniquities have separated between you and your God, and your sins have hid His face from you, that He will not hear."* Is. 59:1,2

One time God showed me that He had already said "yes" to my

prayer but there was someone inspired by the Devil to prevent me from receiving the answer to my prayer. I needed to pray and ask God to rebuke the Devourer who was stealing my blessings from me.

There is also a promise in Mal.3:4 that if we give God 10%, He will rebuke the Devourer.

God bless you as you seek answers to your prayers from God!

All the promises are Yes in Christ Jesus!

"For all the promises of God in Him are yea, and in Him Amen, unto the glory of God by us." II Cor. 1:20

"For no matter how many promises God has made, they are "Yes" in Christ..." NIV

Sample prayers

We should try to pray every morning and every evening; they don't have to be long prayers. We can set aside special times for longer prayers. We should always pray over our food. The Bible says that our food is sanctified through prayer. We can also intercede for others. Here are some sample prayers that I have provided with an empty page at the end of this book to write down a prayer of your own. You can look through the prayers and promises in this book and incorporate them into your own. You can also get a journal and keep a record of your prayers and write down the answers when they come and the date. That can be very encouraging when you look back and see God answering.

Sample Prayer #1
Claiming the promises.

Father in Heaven,
You said in Your Word that _____ *(quote vs.)* _.
Please let it be according to Your Word and I thank You that
You have heard and answered my prayers
In the name of Your dear Son, Jesus Christ, my Creator,
Redeemer, Amen!

Sample Prayer #2
Victory over sin.

Jesus,
You said in Jn. 16:33 that You have already overcome the
world. I ask that You give me Your victory over _____ *(identify*
the sin) _.

I claim Your promises in the Bible and believe that I receive
In Your name I pray.
Amen!

Sample Prayer #3

Binding the Strong man.

The Promise

"I will give unto thee the keys of the kingdom of heaven; and whatsoever thou shalt bind on earth shall be bound in heaven: and whatsoever thou shalt loose on earth shall be loosed in heaven." Matt. 16:19 (#3089 *"loosen, break-up, destroy, dissolve, melt"*)

"Or else how can one enter into a strong man's house, and spoil his goods, except he first bind the strong man? And then he will spoil his house." Matt. 12:29;Mk.3:27

"For the weapons of our warfare are not carnal, but mighty through God to the pulling down of strongholds..." II Cor. 10:5

Lord,
I ask You to bind the strong man over this situation with Your precious blood & I take back ___(name it)___ that he stole from me. In Jesus' name
Amen!

The blood of Jesus condemns Satan. We are cleansed by the blood in Rev.1:5;7:14. We are justified by the blood in Rom.5:9. We are given the keys of the Kingdom; binding and loosing in Matt. 16:19.

Sample prayer #4

When you read through the Bible, make a list of the things that God wants you to do and ask Him to help you do them. Start with one thing at a time and try to incorporate them into your life.

Lord,
I see that these ____(list)____are the things that You require of
me and it would please You if I did them.
Please help me to do these things in my life through the power
of Your Holy Spirit and in the name of Your Son, Jesus Christ.
Thank you!

Sample prayer #5

When I have done everything I can do in a situation and there is nothing more I can do; instead of feeling worried or anxious I will commit it to the Lord.

"casting all your care upon Him; for He careth for you." I Pet. 5:7

Lord,
I commit this situation to You. I thank You that I can trust
You to take care of this problem for me. Amen!

Sample prayer #6

This is a good prayer to pray every morning.

"Lord,
Thank you for this day. I give it to You.
I ask that Your will be done today in my life and the lives
of my loved ones. Please send me and my family a double
measure of Your grace and mercy today.
Come and be with me all day today and every day.
Thank You for hearing and answering my prayer. In Jesus'
name, Amen!"

The Promise:
"Your mercy is new every morning" Lam. 3:22-23

Sample prayer #7

This is a good prayer to pray every night before going to bed.

"Lord,

*Thank you for this day. Please forgive me for where I fell
short today and please accept my efforts. Help me to do better
tomorrow. I love You, Lord – Amen!"*

Sample prayer #8

Here is a sample prayer of how you can write verses into your own
prayers. I take words from the Bible and put it in my own words to
form a prayer.

"Lord,

*Let Your ear be attentive to my prayers and hear me. Redeem
me by Your great power!*

*And strong hand because I desire to fear Your name;
Please prosper me, and grant me Your mercy* (taken from
Neh.1:4-11).

*Lord, You said in Your Word that it is Your pleasure to prosper
me* (taken from Ps.35:28) *Therefore, let Your will be done!*

*It is nothing for You to help me; so please help me, O Lord, for
I rest in You and in Your name I come against those who are
coming against me. For You are Lord, let not man
prevail against me* (taken from II Chron. 14:11-13).

You are my help!

*Help me from my enemies (Satan and those he uses)
Redeem me and turn their reproach on their own heads*
(taken from Neh.4:4-6)

*When they made a golden calf in the wilderness, You did not
forsake them* (taken from Neh.9:4-38)

*You heard from heaven and in Your mercy You saved them
from their enemies. So please, don't forsake me but save me*

435

from my enemies. I thank You that Your hand is against those who come against me but upon me for good because I seek You. You delivered me from my enemies and broke their power over me.
(taken from Ps.10:1-15;Ezra 8:31)
Please don't let them oppress me anymore!
Please consider my situation and hear my prayer. Don't let them boast that they have prevailed over me! because I trust in Your mercy (taken from Ps.13:1-6).
Deliver me from the wicked (taken from Ps.17:1-15).
Don't let my trouble seem little and insignificant to You. You are just and we do wickedly; But in my distress I call to You. Don't deliver me to the will of my enemies. Let them be ashamed who come against me but don't let me be ashamed (taken from Ps.31:1-24).
Fight against them that fight against me (taken from Ps.35:1).
Lord, put a hedge of protection around me and everything that I have; and around my family in Jesus' name, my Creator, Redeemer, like you did for Job in the beginning and end of his life. Hear me lest they rejoice over me (taken from Ps.38). *Make haste to help me!*
When I am afraid, I will trust in You (taken from Ps.56:1-13).
You are my only defense (taken from Ps.59:1-17).
Let all their words and decrees against me come to nothing because You said, Woe to those who decree unrighteous decrees (taken from Is.10:1).
Lord, grant me the thing I long for (taken from Job 22:27,28).
Save me by Your right hand of power because I put my trust in You – keep me as the apple of Your eye and hide me under the shadow of Your wings (taken from Ps. 91:1).

Lord, lead me in Your path of righteousness and please don't forsake me (taken from Ps.27:11,12).
I thank You that You have brought me up out of a pit and set my feet on the Rock, Christ Jesus.
I ask that You will put a new song in my mouth so I can praise You (taken from Ps.40:1-3).
I ask that You command my deliverance and in Your name push down my enemies; in Your name tread them under that rise up against me (taken from Ps.44:1-26).
I cast my all my burdens on You, Lord, for You will sustain me. You will never let the righteous be moved (taken from Ps.55:1-23)*I thank You, Lord, that You hear me and answer my prayers. In Jesus' name, Amen!"*

God answers

I claim these promises as an answer to my prayer.

The Lord sent help from His sanctuary in heaven and He heard me. He subdued under me those that rose up against me and delivered me. The Lord says, Do not be afraid or discouraged for the battle is not yours, but God's... You will not even have to fight this battle. Take your positions; then stand still and watch the Lord's victory. He is with you... Go out... for the Lord is with you! Amen! (Taken from Ps.20;Ps.18)

Steps of Salvation

We are all sinners and need a Savior.

"For all have sinned and come short of the glory of God." Rom. 3:23

"While we were sinners Christ died for us." Rom. 5:8

If we repent (turn from our sins) and receive Jesus, God will not turn us away!

"Repent ye therefore, and be converted (changed) *that your sins may*

be blotted out..." Acts 3:19

"... and him that cometh to Me I will in no way cast out." Jms.. 6:37

Believe

First we must believe that Jesus is God and that He died on the cross for us. There is no other way to God but through Jesus because He is the only One who never sinned! And He is our Creator, Redeemer.

"No man cometh unto the Father, but by Me." Jn. 14:6

"Neither is there salvation in any other: for there is none other name under heaven given among men, whereby we must be saved." Acts 4:12

"That if thou shalt confess with thy mouth the Lord Jesus, and shalt believe in thine heart that God hath raised him from the dead, thou shalt be saved." Rom. 10:9

"But God, who is rich in mercy, for His great love wherewith He loved us, even when we were dead in sins, hath quickened us together with Christ, (by grace ye are we saved;) and hath raised us up together... For by grace are ye saved through faith; and that not of yourselves: it is the gift of God: not of works, lest any man should boast..." Eph. 2:4-9

"Whoever calls on the name of the Lord shall be saved... that if thou shalt confess with thy mouth the Lord Jesus, and shalt believe in thine heart that God hath raised Him from the dead, thou shalt be saved." Rom. 10:13

Receive

Then we receive Him as our Lord and Savior.

"But as many as received him, to them gave He power to become the sons of God, even to them that believe on His name..." Jn. 1:12

"For he hath made him to be sin for us, who knew no sin; that we might be made the righteousness of God in Him." II Cor. 5;21

Sample Prayer #9

Prayer of Salvation

" Dear Father in Heaven, I confess that I am a sinner and need a Savior.
I repent of my sins; please forgive me and wash me clean by Your blood (Rev. 1:5). I believe that Jesus is God and came to earth to die for my sins. I receive You, Jesus, as my Lord, Master, and Savior.
Thank you for Your great work on the cross for me.
Teach me Your will and help me to do it.
In Jesus' name - Amen!"

Now that you are saved, you need to learn what it is that God wants you to do. God saved you by grace but he saved you to do good works. If Jesus is your Lord, then you'll do what He asks.

"For by grace are you saved… created in Christ Jesus unto good works, which God hath before ordained that we should walk in them." Eph. 2:8

Sometimes people say it's too hard. Well, it's easy to be saved (Jesus did that for you — it's a free gift) but it's true that it's hard to get the rewards. If it was easy, then everyone would have the same reward. Matthew 5:19 tells us that some are least and some are great in the Kingdom of heaven. I heard someone say once at a funeral, *"Oh, he'll have a great reward in heaven because he made so many people happy."* But it's not our place to say what his reward is; only God knows that. We are not to go around judging other people but only to do our part and wait for the reward. In fact, we will probably be quite surprised when God passes out the rewards because He sees things differently then we do. He judges the motives of the heart and He sees what is done in secret.

"Some men's sins are open (obvious) *beforehand, going before to judgment; and some men they follow after."* I Tim. 5:24 **(The NIV says,** *"…the sins of others trail behind them."***)**

439

Someone once said to me, "You mean to tell me we're not all the same in heaven?" And I said, "That's true but it's based on humility not pride".

When we see the pain and suffering and endurance some people have had to go through, we'll know that they deserve whatever God gives to them. The thing to do now is your best; you don't want to come up short in the rewards department.

But be clear about one thing, you can't serve God and the Devil at the same time. You have to choose.

"No man can serve two masters: for either he will hate the one, and love the other; or else he will hold to the one, and despise the other..." Matt. 6:24

"Doth a fountain send forth at the same place sweet water and bitter? Can the fig tree, my brethren, bear olive berries? either a vine, figs? so can no fountain both yield salt water and fresh." Jms.. 3:11

You can have a little fruit or a lot of fruit in your life but if you have no fruit, you'll be thrown out. The dead branches are thrown into the fire, Matt. 7:19;Jn.15:6. There will be some who think they know Jesus but He says to them, "*I don't know you*" Matt. 7:21-23.

Read the Word! Just do it!

How do we know what God wants us to do? The Word tells us what pleases God and what we are commanded to do. We need to read the Word and do the Word like the parable of the wise man in the Bible, Matt. 7:24-27.

"Study to shew thyself approved unto God, a workman that needeth not to be ashamed, rightly dividing the word of truth." II Tim. 2:15

"As newborn babes, desire the sincere milk of the word, that ye may grow thereby..." 1 Peter 2:2

We need to read the Bible to learn what pleases Him and do it with His help; He will reward us someday in Heaven. After all, if you've made Him Lord, then you will be willing to do what He says or He isn't really your Lord! God the Father showed us how much he loved us by letting His Son die for us. Jesus showed us how much He loved us by dying on the cross (even while we were still sinners Christ died for us, Rom. 5:8).

Even though we are saved by grace, we show God how much we love Him by our obedience. In fact, obedience is the highest form of worship. The Bible says, "*to obey is better than sacrifice*" I Sam. 15:22. (Of course, we aren't perfect yet but we are willing and we strive to do what pleases Him with the help of the Holy Spirit. God sees us as perfect in Jesus while we're striving to overcome. It's easy to be saved – Jesus paid the price. But it's hard to earn the rewards. That's why we just keep trying with the help of the Holy Spirit). The Bible tells us that those who obey will be greater in heaven than those who don't, Matt. 5:19.

Paul says that when we accept Jesus, we enter into the race.

"*I have fought the good fight, I have finished the race*" II Tim. 4:7
"*...run in such a way as to get the prize...*" I Cor. 9:24 NIV

Even though I might be saved, I don't want to be disqualified to win the prize.

"*...so that after I have preached to others, I myself will not be disqualified for the prize.*" I Cor. 9:27

At the Judgment, our works will go through the fire to see what they are made of and what reward we will receive; did we do our good works for God or for man to see?

"*Every man shall receive his own award according to his own labor... Now if any man build upon this foundation gold, silver, precious stone, wood, hay, or stubble. Every man's work shall be made manifest: for the day shall declare it, because it shall be revealed by fire; and the fire shall try every man's work of what sort it is. If any man's work abide which he hath built thereupon, he shall receive a reward. If any man's work shall be burned, he shall suffer loss: but he himself shall be saved; yet so as by fire.*" I Cor. 3:8,12-15

You see that this verse doesn't say that we are lost, it says our works are lost. Some people want their reward now; they want their pleasures now and the Bible says that they already have their reward so they won't be getting one in heaven.

"*Therefore when thou doest thine alms, do not sound a trumpet before thee, as the hypocrites do in the synagogues and in the streets, that they may have glory of men. Verily I say unto you, They have their reward (already).*" Matt. 6:2

Some don't get a reward in heaven because they already got their reward on earth.

"*So when you give to the poor, don't announce it with trumpet fanfare. This is what hypocrites do in the synagogues and on the streets in order to be praised by people. I can guarantee this truth: That will be their only reward.*" Matt. 6:2 (God's Word Translation)

The next step is baptism by immersion

"*Go ye therefore, and teach all nations, baptizing them in the name of the Father, and of the Son, and of the Holy Ghost: teaching them to observe all things whatsoever I have commanded you: and lo, I am with you always, even unto the end of the world. Amen.*" Matt. 28:19

"*...repent, and be baptized every one of you in the name of Jesus Christ for the remission of sins, and ye shall receive the gift of the Holy Ghost...*" Acts 2:38

Bible baptism is by immersion. Jesus came up out of the water and He is our example.

"*And Jesus, when He was baptized, went up straightway* **out of the water.**" Matt. 3:16-17

Philip went down into the water with the Ethiopian and they came up out of the water.

"And as they went on their way, they came unto a certain water: and the eunuch said, See, here is water; what doth hinder me to be baptized? And Philip said, If thou believest with all thine heart, thou mayest. And he answered and said, I believe that Jesus Christ is the Son of God. And he commanded the chariot to stand still: and they went down both **into the water,** *both Philip and the eunuch; and he baptized him. And when they were* **come up out of the water,** *the Spirit of the Lord caught away Philip, that the eunuch saw him no more: and he went on his way rejoicing."* Acts 8:36-39

Remember the story of Namaan. Elijah told Naaman to *"Go and wash yourself seven times in the Jordan River."* But he became angry and walked away. He wanted Elijah to wave his hands over him or tell him to wash in the rivers at home. He wanted to do things his own way but if we want the blessing, we have to do things God's way.

"...his officers tried to reason with him and said, Sir, if the prophet had told you to do some great thing, wouldn't you have done it? So you should certainly obey him when he says simply to go and wash and be cured! So Naaman went down to the Jordan River and dipped himself seven times, as the man of God had instructed him. And his flesh became as healthy as a young child's and he was healed!" II Kings 5:10-14. Being baptized by immersion is not that hard to do; God tells you to do it, so just do it!

After baptism, take Communion regularly
"...this do in remembrance of Me" Lk. 22:20
"For as often as ye eat this bread, and drink this cup, ye do shew the Lord's death till He come." 1 Cor. 11:26

Learn to pray
"Lord, teach us to pray" Lk. 11:1
"Is any among you afflicted ("suffering" NASV "suffering hardships"

NLT "in trouble" NIV)? *Let him pray"* Jms..5;13

If you suffer, endure it!

"For our light affliction, which but for a moment, worketh for us a far more exceeding and eternal weight of glory" II Cor. 4:17 KJV

"These troubles and sufferings of ours are, after all, quite small and won't last very long. Yet this short time of distress will result in God's richest blessing upon us forever and ever!" LB

"For this slight momentary affliction is preparing for us an eternal weight of glory beyond all comparison" RSV

"For our light and momentary troubles are achieving for us an eternal glory that far outweighs them all." NIV

In the parable of the Sower and the four soils, the soil with rocks represented that their faith withered up because of persecution, Matt.13;Mk.4:1-20;Lk.8:4-21.

Topical Prayers

Some of these are not actual prayers for these topics but these topics are mentioned in the prayers; you can find all these prayers written out in this book if you want to read them; just look them up in that section of this book.

Prayer Jesus taught Disciples
Matt.6:5-13;Lk.11:1-4

Prayers Jesus prayed
Mt.11:25-27;17:5;26:41,42,53;27:46;Mk.14:32-39;15:35
Lk.10:21;22:40-6; 23:34,46; Jn.12:27,28;17:1-26;18:1

Don't remember our sins
II Sam.7;Ps. 79:1-13

Hear our prayer
II Chron.6:19

I have heard your prayer
II Chron.7:12;II Cor.6:2

Prayer for Children
Gen.25:21,22
Hannah's prayer for a son in I Sam.1:9-29

Prayer of confession
Judges 13;I Chron.21:1-8; Neh.1:4-11;9:5-38; Job 33:26-30;Ps.32:5

7;51:1-19

Prayer for deliverance
Jacob's prayer for deliverance from Esau in Gen.32:9-12
Judges 15:8;13:1,22;15:18;I Sam.12:10;II Kings 19:20-37;Ps.7:1-7;17:1-15;22:1-22;31:1-24;40:13-17;44:1015;59:1-17;91:15,16;120:1,2;140:1-13;142:1-7;143:1-12; Micah 5:6; Jer.42:11

Prayer for forgiveness
Ps.25:1-22;86:1-17;99:8;130:1-4;Dan.9:3-20

Prayer for Healing
Ps.103:3;Hosea6:1;11:3;Is.38:2,3;Jer.3:21-25;17:13-18;33:6;Mal.4:2;
Matt.8:17; 9:22;Acts 4:24-35; I Pet.2:24;Jms.5:13-16;

Prayer for Help
I Sam.10:19;II Sam.7:10,11;II Chron.14:11-13;20:3-12;II Cor.6:2;
Ps.12:1,2;20:1-9;40:13-17;60:10-12;79:1-13

Prayer for Holy Spirit
II Sam.22;23:5;I Kings 2:2;8:56;II Kings 2:9-15

Prayer for Latter Rain
Zech.10:1

Prayers for life
Abraham prays life for king Abimelech in Gen.20:7

You can pray life for a brother
I Kings 17:20-22;Ps.21:1-13

Prayer for mercy
Ps.6:1-4;27:7-9;30:1-12;56:1-13;57:1-11;67:1-7;86:1-17;90:1-17

Prayer for redemption
Ps.44:1-26

Prayer for protection
Jn.17:1-26;18:1

Prayer for safety
Ps.4:8

Prayers for salvation
Ex.14:13; Ps.3:1-8;35:1-28;54:1-6;69:1-29;80:1-19;106:4-7;118:25
Save us Is.37:15-20;Jer.17:13-18

Prayer for Strength
Duet.3:22;20:4;33:29;Josh.1;Neh.6:9;Ps.68:28,35;70:1-5;108:12;109:1-31;Phil.4:13

Prayer of Thanks & Praise
I Chron.16:8-11,34-36; II Chron.20:21, 22s; 8:1-9;9:1-13;18:1;35:1-28;48:9-14;52:9;54:1-6;56:1-13;57:1-11;65:1-13;66:3-7;86:1-17;71:1-24;79:1-20;79:13;106:47;116:16,17;145:1-7;Rev.4:11;5:13;7:10;12:10;19:1,2,5

Prayer to Open their eyes
II Kings 6:17

Prayer for a wife
Eliezer prays to find a wife for Isaac. Gen.24:15-19

Prayer for wisdom
I Kings 3:3-15;II Chron. 1:7-12;Ps.82:1-8

Preserve me
Ps.16:1-11

Teach me
Ps.25:1-22;27:11,12

Check out my web page www.thecrimsonworm.com. Be my friend on facebook "*Crimson Worm.*"

Your prayers

Write out your own prayers.

Additional Prayers

Old Testament

Gen. 4:13,14 *Cain talks to God*
Gen.15:2 *prayer*
Gen. 15:18-21 *God makes a Covenant with Abraham*
Gen. 17:17 *fell on face*
Gen. 17:18 *Prayer*
Gen 17:1-16 *God talks to Abraham*
Gen. 18:23,24 *Abraham pleads for Sodom & Gomorrah*
Gen. 20:17 *Abraham prays to God*
  vs. 18 *God's answer*
Gen. 21:12 *God speaks to Abraham*
Gen. 26:24 *God speaks*
Gen. 26:25 *Isaac "called upon the Lord"*
Gen. 35:1-3, 7, 9-15 *God speaks*
Ex. 2:23 *Israelites cry out to God*
Ex. 15:6,7,11 *Moses' song to God*
Ex. 12:25 *Moses cried to God*
Ex. 12:27 *bowed & worshipped*
Ex. 17:4 *Moses cried to God*
Ex. 19:9,19 *God speaks*

Ex. 20:22-*God spoke from heaven*
Num. 3:14-16 *God speaks*
Num. 11:10-15 *Moses speaks to God*
Num. 23:1-7 *God meets with Balaam*
Num. 27:15-17 *Moses speaks to God*
Deut. 4:7
Duet. 21:6-9 *Lord be merciful*
Duet. 33:11 *Prayer for blessing*
Josh. 24:7 *They cried to the Lord*
  Answer - He put darkness between them & the Egyptians
Judges 1:1,2 *Asked the Lord*
Judges 6:12-23 *Gideon & the angel of the Lord*
Judges 6:17-18
Judges 6:36-40 *Gideon talks to God*
Judges 11:30 *Jephthah's rash vow and prayer*
  God answers vs. 32,33
Judges 15:18 *Samson cries out to God*

vs. 19 God's answer
Judges 16:28 *prayer of Samson*
Answer vs. 22 hair begins to grow
Judges 20:23,28 *Wept & asked counsel of God*
Judges 21:3 *Prayer for Benjamites*
I Sam. 2:30 *God speaks to Eli*
I Sam. 5:23
I Sam. 7:9 *Samuel cried to the Lord for Israel*
Answer - and the Lord heard him.
I Sam. 14:37 *Saul asks God*
I Sam. 22:4, 7, 42, 50
I Sam. 23:10-13 *David's prayer*
I Sam. 28:6 *Saul prays but God won't answer*
I Sam. 30:8 *David's prayer*
II Sam. 5:23 *David prays – God answers*
II Sam. 12:16 *David fasts and prays*
II Sam. 21:1 *David prays & God answers*
II Sam. 22:4
II Samuel 22:7
II Sam. 22:42
II Sam. 24:10 *David's prayer - God answers*
II Sam. 24:11-13 *Prophet speaks*

to David for God
II Sam. 24:14-16 – *David answers*
II Sam. 24:17 *David's prayer*
II Sam. 24:20-25 *David builds altar & entreats God*
I Kings 8:12,13 *Solomon speaks to God*
I Kings 17:21-22-*prayer*
I Kings 17:24 *"...the Word of the Lord in thy mouth..."*
I Kings 18:38 *God answers*
II Kings 13:4 *Jehoahaz' prayer*
I Chron 5:20
I Chron 14:14-16 *God speaks*
I Chron. 17:7 *God speaks to David*
I Chron. 23:20
II Chron. 13:14 *They cried unto the Lord with trumpets* Neh. 8:6 *Ezra blessed the Lord*
II Chron. 14:7
Job 6:22-7:21 *Job speaks to God*
Job 9:25-10:22 *Job speaks to God*
Job 14:3-22 *Job speaks to God*
Job 23:3-16 NLT *If only I knew where to find God I would talk to Him*
Ps. 9:12 NIV *"... He does not ignore the cry of the afflicted."*
Ps. 9:13-14 NIV *Prayer*

Ps. 10:17 *Lord You hear the humble*
Ps. 18:41
Ps. 34:4
Ps. 36:5-11 *Prayer of David*
Ps. 37:4 *He will give you the desires of your heart*
Ps. 42:1-5 *Prayer of sons of Korah*
Ps. 66:19-20 *God heard me*
Ps. 79:5-10 *Prayer of Asaph*
Ps. 99:6 PB *"Zion heard, and was glad; and the daughters of Judah rejoiced because of Thy judgment, O Lord. They called on the Lord and He answered them."*
Ps. 99:7 *He spoke to them in the cloudy pillar*
Ps. 104:1-4 *Prayer "...Lord ... hears my prayers and listens"* LB
Ps. 116:1-7 *"I love the Lord, because He hath heard my voice"*
Is. 6:5-7 *God speaks*
Is. 6:11 *prayer*
   Answer Is. 6:12,13
Is. 25 *Prayer of praise*
Is. 26:8-19 *prayer*
   God answers Is. 26:20,21
Jer. 1:4,5 *God speaks*
Jer. 1:6 *Jeremiah speaks*
Jer. 1:7-19 *God speaks*
Jer. 4:1-9 *God speaks*

Jer. 4:10 *Jeremiah's prayer*
Jer. 10:23-25 *Jeremiah's prayer*
Jer. 21:23 *Inquire of the Lord for us*
Jer. 33:2-3 *Call unto Me & I will answer you*
Lam. 1:20-22 *Jeremiah's prayer*
Lam. 2:18,19 *Their heart cried to the Lord*
Lam. 2:20-22 *Jeremiah's prayer*
Lam. 3:55-66 *Jeremiah's prayer*
Ez. 4:14 *Ezekiel's prayer*
   Ez. 4:15-17 *God answers*
Ez. 9:8-10 *Ezekiel fell on face & prayed*
   vs. 11 *God's answer*
Ez. 11:13 *Ezekiel fell on face & prayed*
   vs. 14-21 *God's answer*
Ez. 12:1-18:32 *God speaks*
Dan. 12:8 *Daniel's prayer*
   vs. 9-13 *God's answer*
Hosea 7:7 *none calleth to Me*
Amos 7:2-6 *Amos' prayer*
Amos 7:4 *God answers*
Amos 7:5 *Amos' prayer*
Amos 7:7-9 *God speaks & Amos answers*
Hab. 1:2-4,12-17 *Habakkuk's prayer*
Hab. 3:2 *God answers*

452

Joel 2:12,13 UKJV *God speaks*
"therefore also now, says the Lord,
turn all of you even to Me with
all your heart, and with fasting,
and with weeping, and with
mourning.

Joel 2:19 *Lord will answer*
Mal. 1:6-2:9 *God speaks*
Mal. 7:18-19 - *confess sins*
Zech. 10:1 *Ask the Lord for rain*

New Testament

Matt. 5:18
Matt. 7:11 *Father gives good to*
those who ask
Conversations with Jesus
Matt. 8:2-3,6-9,13,25,26-
32;9:18,21,22,25,27-30;14:28-
31;15:22-28;17:15-18;20:23,30-34
Mk. 1:23-25, 40-42; 7:34,35
Sometimes we need to pray this
prayer: Lord, "I believe, help my
unbelief."
Mk. 1:35 *Jesus prayed early*
Mk.1:40-*Lord if you are willing*
you can make me clean
Mk. 5:18
Mk. 6:41 *Jesus looked up to*
heaven and blessed the bread
Mk. 6:46 *Jesus prayed*
Mk. 9:24
Mk. 18:21-35
Lk. 1:13 *Angel tells Zacharias,*
your prayer was heard

Lk. 1:46-55 *Mary's Song of praise*
to God
Lk. 1:68-70 *Song of Zacharias*
Lk. 2:29-32 *Prayer of Simeon*
Lk. 3:21 *Jesus prayed at baptism-*
God sent H.S.
Lk. 5:12-13, *Lord, if You're*
willing, You can make me clean
   vs.16 *Jesus went to wilderness*
to pray
Lk. 6:12 *Jesus went to mountain*
to pray
Lk. 9:28,29 *Jesus took Peter,*
James, & John to pray
Lk. 11:1-13 *Lord's prayer*
Lk. 17:5,14,19 *Lord, increase our*
faith
Lk. 18:1-18 *Woman's persistent*
prayer
And rend your heart, and not
your garments, and turn unto the
Lord your God. For He is gracious

and merciful, slow to anger, and
of great kindness, and repents
Him of the evil."
Lk. 18:11-14 *Pharisees &
publican's prayer*
Lk. 18:41 *Lord, that I might
receive my sight*
Lk. 21:36
Lk. 22:31,32 *Jesus said, I prayed
for you, Peter*
Lk. 23:42 *Thief on the cross*
Jn. 6:34 *Lord always give us this
bread*
Jn. 11:41-42 *Jesus' prayer*
Jn. 14:16 *Jesus' prayer to Father to
give H.S.*
Acts 6:7-8 *God answers*
Acts 9:5-6 *Saul/Paul speaks to
Jesus*
Acts 13:3 *Fasted & prayed*
Acts 22:10 *What should I do,
Lord?*
Rom. 12:12 *"...faithful in prayer"*
NIV
Rom. 15:5 *May God grant you*
Rom. 16:27 *To only wise God be
glory through Jesus*
I Cor. 1:2
II Cor. 13:7 *I pray to God you do
no evil*
II Cor. 12:8-9 *Paul prayed 3 times*

Eph. 3:14-21 *I bow my knees to
the Father*
Phil. 1:9-11 *I pray your love
abounds*
Col. 1:3,12-14 *Giving thanks to
the Father*
Col. 1:9 *we do not cease to pray
for you*
Col. 1:12-14
Col. 2:2 LB *This is what I have
asked God for you*
I Thess. 3:9 *pray night & day for
you*
I Thess. 3:11-13 *Paul's prayer
about Thessalonians*
I Thess. 5:25 *brethren, pray for us*
II Tim. 1:3,4 *without ceasing pray
for you night & day*
Heb. 4:16 *Come boldly to the
throne*
Heb. 13:15 *offer a sacrifice of
praise*
Jms. 4:7-10 NLT *when you
bow down to God, admit your
dependence on Him*
Jms. 5:13-16
I Jn. 1:9 *prayer of confession
If we confess our sins, He is
faithful and just to forgive us
our sins and purify us from all
unrighteousness* – NIV

Famous Prayers

"Lord Jesus, You are medicine to me when I am sick, strength to me when I need help, life itself when I fear death, the way when I long for heaven, the light when all is dark, and food when I need nourishment. Glory be to You forever. Amen."

Ambrose

"When the darkness appears and the night draws near, and the day is past and gone, at the river I stand, guide my feet, hold my hand; take my hand, precious Lord, lead me home."

Thomas Andrew Dorsey

"Lord, grant me a holy heart that sees always what is fine and pure and is not frightened at the sight of sin but creates order wherever it goes. Grant me a heart that knows nothing of boredom, weeping, and sighing. Let me not be too concerned with the bothersome thing I call 'myself'. Lord, give me a sense of humor and I will find happiness in life and profit for others."

Thomas Moore

"Dear Father, we thank Thee for what Thou art going to give us to eat."

George Muller

God answered

George Muller prayed this prayer when he had nothing to feed the children in the orphanage and soon after this prayer God sent a milkman who needed to get rid of all his milk before it spoiled and he left it at the orphanage without knowing of about his prayer.

In 1830 George Muller had decided to never ask people for help but would ask help only from God in prayer. It is said that he helped more than 10,000 children and claimed that God had answered more than 50,000 of his prayers. He had read the Bible through some 200 times. He said this,

> "I live in the Spirit of prayer, I pray as I walk about, when I lie down, and when I rise up. And the answers are always coming. Thousands and tens of thousands of times have my prayers been answered! When once I am persuaded that a thing is right and for the glory of God, I go on praying for it until the answer comes."
>
> George Muller

> "Lord, I give up all my own plans and purposes, all my own desires and hopes, and accept Thy will for my life. I give myself, my life, my all utterly to Thee to be Thine forever."
>
> Amy Carmichael

Amy Carmichael prayed this prayer while facing toward Jerusalem. She was a missionary to India and purchased girls being sold for prostitution. She helped more than 10,000 girls and had a vision of Jesus weeping over the children.

> "Almighty God, unto whom all hearts are open, all desires known, and from whom no secrets are hid: cleanse the thoughts of our hearts, by the inspiration of Thy H.S. that we may perfectly love Thee, and worthily magnify Thy holy name."
>
> Book of Common Prayer

"Most merciful God, we confess" Book of Common Prayer

The Irish Blessing

> *"May the road rise to meet you,*
> *May the wind be always at your back,*
> *May the sun shine warm upon your face,*
> *The rains fall soft upon your fields and,*
> *Until we meet again,*
> *May God hold you in the palm of His hand."*
> --- Anonymous

> *"Lord, make me an instrument of your peace.*
> *Where there is hatred, let me sow love,*
> *Where there is injury, pardon*
> *Where there is doubt, faith,*
> *Where there is despair, hope,*
> *Where there is darkness, light,*
> *Where there is sadness, joy.*
> *O Divine Master, grant that I may not so much*
> *seek to be consoled as to console,*
> *not so much to be understood as to understand,*
> *not so much to be loved, as to love;*
> *for it is in giving that we receive,*
> *it is in pardoning that we are pardoned,*
> *it is in dying that we awake to eternal life."*
> --- Francis of Assisi

Amy Carmichael speaking of prayer:

1. Don't get into bondage about place, or position of the body... sometimes, at least, [our Lord] went into the open air to a hillside; to

a garden...I have known some who could kneel hours by a chair... walking up and down; this was Bishop Moule's way. Some go into their rooms and shut the door...let the learning of your mind lead you, a God-directed mind leans to what helps the spirit most.

2. Don't be discouraged if at first you seem to get nowhere...no command in the bible is so difficult to obey and so penetrating in power...[as] *'Be still and know that I am God.'* Many have found this so....

3. Don't feel it necessary to pray all the time; listen...And read God's words of Life. Let them enter into you.

4. Don't forget there is one other person interested in you— extremely interested...there is no truer word than the old couplet: Satan trembles when he sees the weakest saint upon his knees.

5. Don't give up in despair if no thoughts and no words come, but only distractions and inward confusions. Often if helps to use the words of others...Psalm, hymn, song—use what helps most.

6. Don't worry if you fall asleep. *"He giveth his beloved in sleep."*

7. And if the day ends in what seems failure, don't fret. Tell Him you're sorry. Even so, don't be discouraged. All discouragement is of the devil...

Poem about Prayer

"Father,
hear us we are praying.
Hear the words our hearts are saying.
We are praying for our children.
Keep them from the powers of evil,
from the secret hidden peril,
from the whirlpool that would suck them,
from the treacherous quicksand pluck them
From the worldings hollow gladness,
from the sting of faithless sadness,
Holy Father, save our children.
Through life's troubled waters steer them,
through life's bitter battle cheer them;
Father, Father, be Thou near them.
Read the language of our longing,
Read the wordless pleadings thronging,
Holy Father, for our children.
And wherever they may bide, lead them home at eventide."

Amy Carmichael

A Hymn of Prayer

"Precious Lord, take my hand;
lead me on, let me stand;
I am tired, I am weak, I am worn.
Thru the storm, thru the night,
lead me on to the light,
take my hand, precious Lord, lead me home"

Thomas A. Dorsey

Index

About The Author

Lori Pagel is a pastor's wife who taught at an A.C.E. for 7 years. She teaches Children's Church and currently serves as the church secretary. She gives piano and voice lessons in her spare time. She loves photography and recently wrote a book about the Crimson Worm.

Lori loves Jesus and is looking forward to His soon return. She loves to read her Bible and learn about the wonderful things that God has done.

Publisher ∽❧

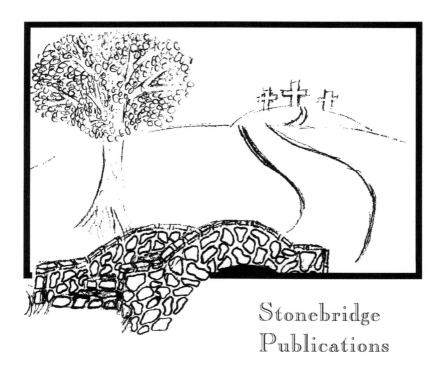

Stonebridge
Publications

For more great titles, visit Stonebridgepublications.com

CORPORATIZING CANADA

"This exceptional collection reveals the profound influence of neoliberal corporatization on the management, mission, and delivery of public services in contemporary Canada. The essays clearly demonstrate the many subtle ways in which the boundaries between the public and private have become progressively blurred, narrowing the scope of democratic decision-making, and the very idea of the public itself."

—**Janine Brodie**, Distinguished University Professor and Canada Research Chair, Political Economy and Social Governance, University of Alberta

"Corporatization is commonly misunderstood as a dimension of monolithic global forces associated with neoliberalism, advancing marketization while eroding state autonomy and welfare state capacity. *Corporatizing Canada* highlights several contemporary examples, often framed in a broader historical context, that demonstrate the multifaceted nature of corporatization, while providing insight into alternative approaches that may maintain or revive collective interests, commitments to public oversight of essential services, and approaches oriented to equity and social justice. This is an indispensable offering for anyone seeking to understand the nature of the Canadian state, offering deep insights into the complex, changing dynamics of the intersections between public and private interests."

—**Terry Wotherspoon**, Department of Sociology, University of Saskatchewan

CORPORATIZING CANADA

CANADA

Making Business
Out of Public
Service

Edited by Jamie Brownlee, Chris Hurl, and Kevin Walby

BETWEEN THE LINES
Toronto

Corporatizing Canada

First published in 2018 by
Between the Lines
401 Richmond Street West
Studio 281
Toronto, Ontario M5V 3A8
Canada
1-800-718-7201
www.btlbooks.com

Every reasonable effort has been made to identify copyright holders. Between the Lines would be pleased to have any errors or omissions brought to its attention.

Library and Archives Canada Cataloguing in Publication

Corporatizing Canada : making business out of public service / edited by Jamie Brownlee, Chris Hurl, and Kevin Walby.

Includes bibliographical references and index.
Issued in print and electronic formats.
ISBN 978-1-77113-358-6 (softcover).--ISBN 978-1-77113-360-9 (PDF).--
ISBN 978-1-77113-359-3 (EPUB)

1. Corporatization--Canada. 2. Public administration--Canada. I. Brownlee, Jamie, editor II. Hurl, Chris, 1978-, editor III. Walby, Kevin, 1981-, editor

| HD3850.C67 2018 | 351.71 | C2017-907772-4 |
| | | C2017-907773-2 |

Text and cover design by David Vereschagin, Quadrat Communications
Printed in Canada

We acknowledge for their financial support of our publishing activities: the Government of Canada; the Canada Council for the Arts, which last year invested $153 million to bring the arts to Canadians throughout the country; and the Government of Ontario through the Ontario Arts Council, the Ontario Book Publishers Tax Credit program, and the Ontario Media Development Corporation.

Contents

Acknowledgements

Jamie Brownlee and Chris Hurl thank Bill Carrol and Wally Clement for all their support over the years, and for their inspiration in undertaking critical corporate research. Kevin Walby would like to thank Bilguundari Enkhtugs, Antigoni Lampovitiadi, and Brendan Anthony Roziere for their assistance. He dedicates this book to Terry Wotherspoon and Eric Kempthorne for getting him interested in sociology, as well as Dorothy E. Smith and Bill Carroll for their teachings, writings, and guidance. We thank everyone at BTL as well.

Introduction

Critical Perspectives on Corporatization

Jamie Brownlee, Chris Hurl, and Kevin Walby

Social activists and critical scholars have often used the concept of "corporatization" to describe the changing nature of the Canadian state over the past thirty years. The concept evokes the image of economic elites controlling public institutions and using business metrics to evaluate their performance. Corporatization is also used to describe the expanding discretion of senior managers to set priorities in health and social services, the creation of market-friendly public sector cultures, the development of new contractual arrangements between the public and private sector, and the "capture" of regulatory agencies by industry. In the popular press, the term corporatization is invoked to explain changes in areas as diverse as mental health, foreign aid, LGBTQ pride events, and the funeral industry.[1] Clearly, corporatization means different things to different people, with it becoming a sort of catch-all concept to describe a multifaceted set of political and economic processes associated with neoliberalism and growing corporate power. However, little attention has been devoted to exploring what corporatization means, to assessing its process and impacts, or to investigating how it is taken up across different types of public agencies and institutions. A small body of research has examined the effects of corporatization around the world, initially looking at North America and Western Europe, and, more recently, the Global South.[2] Much of this literature focuses on public utilities, such as electricity and water, as well as health care and higher education, although research has increasingly focused on other areas of service delivery. Some researchers have also examined the growing impact of corporatization on civil society. For instance, recent scholarship has exposed how social activist organizations increasingly look and act like multinational corporations, and how non-governmental and non-profit organizations are pursuing partnerships with the same corporations they ostensibly oppose.[3]

Corporatizing Canada: Making Business Out of Public Service critically examines how corporatization has been implemented in different ways across the Canadian public sector—from schools, to criminal justice organizations, to utilities, hospitals, and food banks. What becomes clear is that there is no universal blueprint or master plan that is applied across these different areas. While the notion of corporatization might conjure the image of boardroom decisions being orchestrated by shadowy corporate leaders, the contributions in this volume show how corporatization involves a constellation of policies, programs, and practices that play out differently across institutional settings, shaped by distinctive histories, geographies, and forms of resistance.

In this introduction, we begin by highlighting three distinct but interlocking processes that our authors—including activists and scholars—touch on as aspects of corporatization that are implemented within government agencies, public institutions, and community organizations across Canada. These are: (i) corporatization as arm's length administration; (ii) corporatization as expanding managerial control and "business-like" organization; and (iii) corporatization as public-private integration. By focusing on these three processes, we are not suggesting that there are no other practices that are part of corporatization or that these three aspects operate independently. Rather, we have focused on what appear to be the most prominent themes in this volume. We conclude with a discussion of "neoliberal" corporatization, including how it operates as a political and ideological process, and the threat it poses to democratic decision-making and the public at large.

Corporatization as Arm's Length Administration

Corporatization involves implementing institutional arrangements positioned at a distance from the realm of formal politics. As David McDonald notes, this process creates "arm's length enterprises with independent managers responsible solely for the operation of their own immediate organization, and where all costs and revenues are accounted for as though it were a stand-alone company."[4] Corporatized institutions are granted a degree of autonomy from politicians and the realm of political discourse in setting priorities. They typically have a separate legal status from other public agencies and an organizational structure—such as a board of directors—similar to that of private sector companies. According to McDonald, these corporatized entities now comprise "the bulk of the public sphere in many Western European countries," and recent studies suggest that corporatization is becoming a dominant form of service delivery around the world.[5]

In Canada, there are many examples of arm's length administrative arrangements in the delivery of public services. For example, EPCOR Utilities Inc. recently assumed control over water services in Edmonton. Whereas the municipality previously provided water services, EPCOR is organized through a board of directors that acts autonomously from the city. They are financially ring fenced and responsible for managing their own revenues, and politicians and political parties consequently have little say over how water services in Edmonton are managed, how rates are set, or how decisions about this vital public utility are made (see Lui, Chapter 15 in this volume). Other examples include BC Hydro, the Toronto Transit Commission, and Infrastructure Ontario. Each of these agencies operates at arm's length from government, with decisions concentrated in the hands of a board of directors who act with a degree of autonomy in setting service priorities. It is the responsibility of these officials to ensure that the services continue to function and generate enough revenue to stay financially solvent.

The forms of corporatization that most deeply entrench private interests and result in commodification and commercialization reflect a distinct neoliberal character. "Neoliberal corporatization" represents the pinnacle of arm's length services being run like businesses or being operated to create private profit. However, it is important to note that some researchers (see McDonald, Chapter 16 in this volume) argue that corporatized "stand alone" agencies can also operate in a more progressive way. With a focus on the Global South, McDonald argues that many corporatized utilities have "bucked the neoliberal trend ... openly resisting marketized forms of public management" and retain a commitment to universality and equity.[6]

Organizing public services through arm's length forms of administration is not limited to neoliberal regimes. These forms of management have a long lineage, with variants of corporatization evident in liberal welfare, social democratic, and socialist regimes over the past century. Consider the movement towards public ownership by Canadian municipalities in the late nineteenth and early twentieth centuries—initially through assuming public ownership over water and gas services, and culminating in the formation of larger provincial bodies and provincial and federal agencies such as Ontario Hydro and the Liquor Control Board of Ontario.[7] The formation of stand-alone public agencies in the wake of the Second World War was thought to depoliticize service delivery, making it a matter of technical administration, which could be implemented uniformly. Corporatization in this context involved the establishment of public agencies that stood at arm's length from the corrupt patronage networks of political machines, and were managed by a body of impartial managers who were concerned with running services as cleanly and efficiently as possible.

In the midst of economic crisis and fiscal restraint, the form of corporatization adopted from the 1970s onwards has had an increased emphasis on profitability at the expense of national goals and public welfare commitments.[8] For example, the public, non-commercial objectives of Canadian National Railways (CNR) (i.e., transporting passengers along unprofitable routes, transporting grain in western Canada at discounted prices) were largely abandoned after 1975 when the organization was redefined as a profit-seeking enterprise. Similarly, the public service mission of Air Canada (i.e., extend transportation to remote areas of the country, "unify" Canada) was modified in 1978 after a new law required the firm to become a profit-generating organization. Predictably, Air Canada's public commitments were jettisoned, and its non-profitable routes abandoned. The reorientation of these kinds of state-owned enterprises "away from break-even operations providing an essential public service toward profit-seeking enterprises" proved to be a foundational element of the corporatization process in the years ahead.[9] Today, many corporatized entities appear to be just as commercially oriented as their private sector counterparts.

While it is important to consider the evolution of corporatization in Canada, this volume makes clear that one of the consistent, distinctive aspects of the process is the linking of "market-oriented operating principles" with stand-alone, state-owned entities.[10] In the Canadian context, the separation of public agencies from formal political structures is paralleled by a tendency to treat them like businesses. It is this "business-like" operation of public agencies that is a key component of corporatization today.

Corporatization as Expanding Managerial Control and "Business-Like" Organization

Corresponding with arm's length forms of administration, corporatization in Canada has involved efforts to increase managerial control over public services. The emphasis on arm's length forms of control is based on the capacity of managers to achieve a degree of autonomy to direct public services. As John Clarke and Janet Newman note, managers must be given the "right to manage" and "the freedom to make decisions about the use of organizational resources to achieve desired outcomes."[11] Moreover, corporatization not only increases market-based logic in the public sector, it creates new forms of public management and auditing by subjecting public services to techniques of "good financial housekeeping." As

Clarke and Newman point out, "what services are to be provided to whom, and according to what order of priorities, become part of the business decisions of managers subject to the logics of strategic positioning and financial survival."[12] The needs of the public are then subordinated to the economic bottom line, as managers try to increase efficiency and cut costs.

In Canada, as in other countries, this form of corporatization is often associated with the principles of New Public Management (NPM), which emerged as a hegemonic managerial paradigm in the late 1980s and early 1990s. However, an emphasis on managerial control was also evident after the First World War, when American management consultants were brought in to develop job classifications and scientific management schema, enabling the co-ordination of public services through centralized administration. In the early 1960s, the influential Glassco Commission famously urged Ottawa to embrace the latest corporate personnel policies in "letting managers manage."[13] Proponents of NPM today see corporatization as a way to usher in a more "business-like" approach to public service organization and delivery, and to facilitate market-friendly public sector cultures and ideologies. Public institutions increasingly use market-like mechanisms to deliver services and are being run according to market-oriented principles, such as competition, cost-reflexive pricing, financialized performance indicators, and competitive outsourcing. Public services are cast as commodities to be bought and sold, and service users are treated more as "customers" than citizens. The result is publicly owned entities that mimic business discourses and practices, with a short-term focus on financial ends.

To practice good financial housekeeping and achieve a state of business-like service delivery, managers use a range of management schema, and auditing and performance metrics. Indeed, a central aspect of the corporatization process in Canada has involved the development of new kinds of institutional arrangements for the measurement of economic performance, as well as new technologies that appraise value-for-money and identify opportunities for cost-savings and "efficiencies." This shift is reflected, for example, in the rise of programs such as the Ontario Municipal Benchmarking Initiative, through which municipal officials delivering services are evaluated according to the degree to which they are competitive with other jurisdictions.

The implementation of these managerial programs enables the concentration of power in the hands of senior managers, fashioning themselves after corporate CEOs. In this role, many of these managers have reduced the discretion of front line workers and public professionals to decide on the organization's needs and priorities (see Baines, Chapter 12 in this volume), thereby displacing professional knowledge with management priorities focused on the "best use of public resources based on deployment of calculative power."[14]

Corporatization as Public-Private Integration

In line with a focus on the economic bottom line and business-like service delivery, corporatization involves the growing influence of private corporations on public decision-making and service delivery. Increasingly, corporate representatives are embedded in public agencies, as advisors, partners, stakeholders, auditors, and independent managers. Research in this area shows how elite networks and their interconnections operate in different spheres of power. For instance, the Canadian Association of University Teachers recently reported that bankers, lawyers, corporate executives, and other players in the business world make up nearly half of the membership of the boards of governors at Canada's fifteen largest research universities. This network has considerable sway in setting the priorities for research and learning in these institutions.[15] Several authors in this volume look at the position of economic elites and other private sector managers on the boards of public institutions, including Bill Carroll and his colleagues (Chapter 4), who identify ties between carbon capital, universities, and research institutes, and Jamie Brownlee (Chapter 14), who examines Canada's National Energy Board as a site of regulatory capture.

The nature of the relationship between the public and private sector is an ongoing subject of debate. Some scholars emphasize the tendency of private corporations to colonize the public sector. Following Daniel Guttman and Barry Willner's classic 1976 study, this conceptualization of corporatization involves the "surrender of governmental powers to corporate enterprises."[16] Where public officials previously presided, we now find a "corporatocracy" composed of private elites who act as a cartel in setting the political agenda. In this sense, as journalist Murray Dobbin notes, "[c]orporate influence and control has infiltrated almost every dimension of democratic governance and citizen protection in Canada."[17] Others, including Greg McElligott (see Chapter 8 in this volume), emphasize that the public sector was never fully removed from private sector interests. From Confederation onwards, business interests have had a powerful voice in setting the state's agenda through membership on government boards and royal commissions. In his work on the nature of the Canadian state, Leo Panitch identified a longtime "confraternity of power"—an ideological hegemony emanating from both the bourgeoisie and the state cultivating the "view that the national interest and the business interests are at one."[18] Similarly, H.V. Nelles has described the prominence in Canada of what he describes as "state-enterprise capitalism," with government enterprises "run by businessmen, for businessmen, in what was always referred to as a 'businesslike' manner."[19]

From this perspective, the Canadian state may be distinct in its relative lack of autonomy from business interests. The question, then, is not so much the degree to which outside business interests have colonized the state, but the kinds of relationships that are generated through the corporatization process. Rather than looking at who is "pulling the strings," the focus shifts to the "ties that bind" these actors together. Here, corporatization can be viewed as a process of "state-corporate symbiosis,"[20] involving a thickening of ties between private and public agencies. This new relationship is reflected, for example, in the emergence of institutional frameworks for the governance of public-private partnerships, discussed by Heather Whiteside (see Chapter 1 in this volume), and in the development of police foundations, described by Kevin Walby and Randy K. Lippert (see Chapter 7 in this volume). How these new institutional arrangements integrate public and private interests (and seemingly keep them at arm's length) remains a subject of investigation for corporatization researchers in Canada. For instance, a range of recent research has highlighted the role of private sector auditors, management consultants, and competitiveness experts in generating "a common global language through which business and political leaders could discuss how public policy influenced corporate and entrepreneurial performance, and a measurement framework through which all public policy, public investment and executive political decision making could be subjected to a blanket economic audit."[21] Private sector actors have become entrenched as intermediaries across policy networks (see Hurl, Chapter 11 in this volume).

Public-private partnerships (P3s) are a key form of "symbiotic" corporatization that brings together public and private sector actors. There are over 200 infrastructure P3s operating across Canada today, including in areas such as water, health care, transportation, and prisons. Many researchers have been critical of P3 expansion, concluding that these arrangements are something of a "Trojan Horse" in infrastructure development that allow the insertion of market forces and the profit motive in the provision of public goods and services.[22] Although P3s are often touted as lowering risks and costs to the public, they are also associated with cost overruns, higher bills and user fees, layoffs, reductions in service quality, and even threats to public health. In 2016, a poll conducted for the Ontario Public Service Employees Union found that public support for public-private partnerships had dropped from 70 percent to 25 percent following a 2014 auditor general's report showing that P3s had resulted in $8 billion in extra costs for the province.[23] Most Ontarians (71 percent) also said that P3s give up too much control to corporations and that investors have too much say in how public money is spent.

While the three processes introduced here—corporatization as arm's length administration, as expanding managerial control and "business-like" organization, and as public-private integration—are consistent themes throughout this volume, we also recognize that corporatization is not a homogenous process. It takes different forms depending on the institutional setting, with these processes emerging and combining in different ways. In some cases, corporatization involves a greater degree of professional autonomy in generating priorities and making decisions, while in others there will be little distance from private sector business interests. Moreover, how boundaries are negotiated between the public and private is variable. While private companies may directly provide input on public priorities through sitting on the boards of public agencies, their involvement may also be managed through arm's length contractual arrangements. How these processes have evolved also depends on historical factors. While some services—such as hydroelectricity—have been corporatized for a long time, the development of arm's length structures are more recent in other areas. Moreover, the claim that public agencies "stand apart" from the formal realm of politics is always open to contestation, as citizens, public professionals, labour unions, and community groups continue to challenge the various manifestations of corporatization.

The Public-Private Divide:
Neoliberal Corporatization as a Deeply Political Process

Corporatization, especially its neoliberal varieties that are the focus of this volume, is an ideological and deeply political process, one that raises critical questions about the nature and meaning of "public" ownership in Canada. Corporatization is not the same as privatization, although the terms are often used interchangeably. Privatization involves transferring ownership from the public to the private sector, whereas neoliberal corporatization is generally associated with public sector organizations integrating with, or becoming more like, private firms.

As opposition to neoliberalism continues to grow around the world, many citizens and even governments are turning against privatization. Today, privatized public services in many domains—including water, energy, transportation, housing, health care, and waste management—are reverting to public hands through processes such as re-municipalization.[24] With this opposition to privatization mounting, corporatized public entities are being viewed as the preferred vehicle for transforming the public sector. Corporatization is presented as a way to enhance corporate profits and maintain economic growth—or to achieve the same goals of privatization without the political and economic risks associated with it. Public-private partnerships, for example, are sold on notions of transparency and efficiency, but also on progressive principles like "co-operation" and "teamwork." This type of framing confers legitimacy and helps politicians and policy-makers avoid the pitfalls of privatization and outsourcing (though the results may be just as damaging from a public interest perspective). The introduction of market mechanisms (e.g., cost-reflexive pricing) into services that are still in public hands can also spare corporations the anger of consumers once they are privatized. In some cases, corporatized public agencies will even "celebrate their 'public' status at home while aggressively seeking for-profit contracts outside of their jurisdictions."[25] Manitoba Hydro, for example, has a contract to privatize the electricity transmission network in Nigeria "while it fights off privatization attempts at home by citing the merits of public control."

Although corporatization is often viewed as a less offensive "alternative" to privatization, it can be just as commercially oriented as outright privatization (e.g., cutting off services to poor households and institutionalizing moral codes of conduct around the "responsibility to pay" for market-oriented services). Moreover, its intent is sometimes to act as precursor to future privatization. All of this suggests that corporatized institutions may be "public" in name only, functioning as little more than a ploy to commodify and commercialize service delivery while deceiving the public into believing that the threats of privatization have been averted. In this way, corporatization is the "proverbial wolf in sheep's clothing, offering a façade of public ownership while propagating market ideology and advancing capital accumulation."[26]

Another way that neoliberal corporatization has been taken up as a political and ideological project involves its claimed advantages in public sector management. Neoliberal ideology suggests that governments are irrational and "inefficient" institutions that should be limited and downgraded so as not to interfere with market principles. Market-based instruments are said to reduce costs through competitive pressures and be inherently responsive to consumer demand. Unlike "politicized" public agencies, only the private sector is—or can be—responsive and accountable to the public. Yet, evidence suggests that private providers of public services are no more efficient than public ones.[27] There is also little evidence that privatization leads to better quality or more cost-effective services, especially for essential services like health care and utilities.[28] The same is true of the supposed efficiencies associated with corporatized entities that remain "public." Neoliberal corporatization may (or may not) be "efficient" according to a narrow set of finance-oriented criteria, but there are often huge ancillary costs, including less equitable forms of service delivery, precarious work environments, lack of affordability, and a decline in universal coverage and provision. These points are not lost on our authors, many of whom take aim at the political and ideological underpinnings of neoliberal corporatization.

At the same time, the purpose of this volume is not to pit defenders of "traditional" state management against advocates of corporatized, market, or private sector management models. The Canadian state has always used practices that serve and emulate business, and has routinely worked to restrict the influence of organized labour and the public in decision-making. But unlike private corporations (and, increasingly, corporatized public agencies), Canada's public sector remains at least partially accountable to the general population. Indeed, one of the reasons why proponents of corporatization want to weaken the public or popular aspects of government is to reduce the threat of popular involvement in decision-making, and turn those decisions over to corporations and corporatized state agencies far removed from public control.

The primary goal of this volume is to demonstrate how the process of neoliberal corporatization is detrimental from a public interest perspective. As our authors show, corporatization has made labour and working conditions in the public and non-governmental sectors more precarious. Corporatization has made public planning and the provision of public services less democratic and less equitable, and has reduced the accountability of governments and the capacity of the population to influence decision-making through formal democratic channels. It has transformed public programs into assets managed as if they were corporate revenue streams. Above all, neoliberal corporatization in Canada has elevated financial and corporate interests ahead of the public, collective good, and social justice.

Volume Outline

This volume is divided into six sections, each one focusing on a different area of service delivery. The first section focuses on the corporatization of health care, which has been an epicentre for corporatized institutional arrangements for the past thirty years. A central component of these new arrangements is public-private partnerships. In her chapter, Heather Whiteside examines the institutional architecture of public-private partnerships and how they have changed the ways that health care in Canada is delivered. Natalie Mehra of the Ontario Health Coalition puts this process in a broader historical perspective. Looking at Ontario, she explores how corporate business models, arm's length management practices, and public-private ownership structures have emerged in the health sector over the past three decades.

The second section examines the corporatization of education. While the focus of this literature is often on higher education, Erika Shaker explores how corporations can also be found setting primary- and secondary-level public education curriculums and educational priorities. Larry Kuehn highlights the growing market for international students as a catalyst for corporatization and the shifting priorities of schools and school boards at all levels of education. In the realm of higher learning, Bill Carroll, Nicolas Graham, and Zoë Yunker examine the growing network of interlocks that link the directorates of fossil fuel companies with the governance boards of universities and research institutes, and discuss the implications for higher education in the context of climate change and carbon divestment. Lastly, Claire Polster discusses resistance to corporatization that can build from a fundamentally different understanding of public institutions, one that focuses on social relations within the university.

The third section explores the corporatization of criminal justice, including the police, courts, and prisons. While the police position themselves as an ostensibly public organization, Kevin Walby and Randy K. Lippert highlight the emergence of police foundations as private arm's length fundraising instruments for police departments. Likewise, Kelly Gorkoff looks at corporatized forms of justice with the development of networked and arm's length administrative arrangements in drug treatment courts. In his discussion of the public-private relationships that have developed in prisons and prison construction, Greg McElligott argues that there has always been a tight relationship between public agencies and private developers. According to McElligott, corporatization has not changed the character of the Canadian state, even if it has further insulated it from true democratic control.

The fourth section investigates the corporatization of policy-making and assesses the extent to which policy-making in Canada is modeled after decision-making practices in the private sector. Peter Graefe explores how corporatization has taken a distinctive form in Canada based on the changing federal-provincial negotiation of jurisdiction, while Chris Hurl examines how private sector actors are embedded in the municipal policy-making process through new forms of auditing and evaluation.

The fifth section focuses on the corporatization of social services in the non-profit sector and civil society. Donna Baines highlights the impact of corporatized institutional arrangements on front line workers in Canada's non-profit social services sector, and Graham Riches looks at how food charities in Canada are increasingly organized according to corporate models. Riches asserts that the corporatization of charitable food banking is threatening aspects of Canadian welfare state provision, such as income security and a publicly funded social safety net.

The sixth section examines the corporatization of public utilities and resource governance in Canada. Jamie Brownlee discusses the degree to which private sector models and actors have shaped the policies and structure of the National Energy Board, and how industry has effectively "captured" the agency. Emma Lui discusses the corporatization of water management, which is increasingly organized according to market-based principles aimed at maximizing revenues and minimizing costs. Finally, David McDonald concludes by discussing the prospects for corporatization more broadly through a comparison of Canada with other parts of the world. As McDonald argues, there is nothing inherently neoliberal about the corporatization process, especially in the area of public utilities. He emphasizes the multiple ways in which policy-makers, managers, and employees of corporatized entities can shape more progressive narratives of public sector reform, and maintain commitments to universality and equity.

Looking Ahead

Given the scope of corporatization in Canada, this volume is just scratching the surface of the areas that need to be investigated. There is a range of fields that remains unexplored, including transit and waste management, paramedical services and the pharmaceutical industry, new green forms of energy such as wind and solar power, postal services, airports, sports, marijuana, child and elderly care, and recreation infrastructure. We hope that by beginning a conversation on corporatization through a comparative analysis of service areas, we can contribute to the development of a comprehensive assessment of how corporatization is operating in Canada, and to strategies for resisting corporatization where it entrenches domination and inequality.

Health Care

Healthy Profit

Private Finance and Public Hospitals

Heather Whiteside

Introduction

Over the past decade, ninety for-profit public-private partnerships (P3s) have been launched to design, build, finance, and operate hospitals within the Canadian public health care system. Over half of Canada's provinces and territories have become P3 enthusiasts: Ontario, British Columbia, Quebec, New Brunswick, Nova Scotia, Saskatchewan, Alberta, and Northwest Territories. P3s are present in nearly all public sectors and jurisdictions across Canada, but health care has been particularly targeted. "Better, faster, cheaper" is the motto underpinning P3 use both here and abroad, but their empirical record on all fronts has proven dismal.[1] Healthy returns on investment of at least 10 percent contrast with pro forma building designs, rampant delays, and repayment burdens added to the public purse through profit seeking and higher-priced debt. P3s are at best insurance policies against risk, with project elements shifted to corporate actors, but all costs are fully paid for by the public in the end. Along the way, corporate management and the profit motive become entrenched within sensitive areas like public health care.

This chapter uncovers and analyzes the corporate entities involved in making a healthy profit off Canadian health care. It examines how public hospitals are being corporatized through P3s' indirect encouragement of "business-like" practices in the public sector, and the direct involvement of corporate/private partners like equity-holding construction and engineering firms, private service providers, and creditors ranging from Wall Street investment banks, to pension funds, to offshore tax-haven registered companies. The chapter also details how the corporatization of public hospitals affects hospital staff, planning and service delivery, and the Canadian health care system more broadly.

Corporatization and the Canadian Health Care System

Corporatization and privatization are distinct, but often interrelated, processes. As Jamie Brownlee argues, whereas privatization involves the act or process of transferring ownership from the public to the private sector, corporatization involves the integration of public and corporate institutions and the adoption of "business-like" practices within the public sector.[2] P3s cover all bases: transferring control from public to private hands, institutional integration of the corporate and public sectors, and the re-orientation of public sector decision-making along corporate lines.

P3s are most often structured as lease agreements, where the state retains formal ownership of the newly created asset (like a hospital). Given that these are multi-decade leases, and that leases transfer rights, control, and decision-making, private partners become de facto owners for thirty-plus years. The corporate profit motive permeates all aspects of P3 projects and market social relations are expanded throughout their lifetime. P3s are deep "partnerships" involving the institutional integration of corporations and governments, making them distinct from more limited forms of alternative service delivery (such as contracting out) because private partner decision-making is far wider in scope and duration. P3-induced restructuring intensifies the dependence of the public sector on the market by awarding authority and decision-making power over the formulation and execution of public policy to private for-profit investors. In sum, corporate design, management, and support service providers, along with private finance, now play key roles within P3 hospitals and public health care, and public decision-makers are often chosen for their business acumen.

P3s are hardly the only source of corporate influence in Canada's public health care system, and medicare has never been entirely free from market pressures. In many ways, the scope of the public system has always accommodated private interests. For instance, medicare does not cover several important aspects of health care delivery related to home care, long-term residential care, and dentistry. Further, Canadian doctors are not fully absorbed in the public system and continue to make their own decisions about where and what they practice.[3] Rather than being salaried employees of the state, doctors are paid on a fee-for-service basis by provincial governments. In addition, the uneasy federal-provincial division of responsibilities and costs that hindered the initial development of public health care has never been adequately resolved. The federal government became responsible for national oversight and a large portion of the funding, whereas the provinces were left to administer provincial medicare insurance programs and oversee associated aspects, such as hospital infrastructure and service planning and delivery. As a result, there is some inter-provincial variation in terms of the role of the market and the breadth and depth of health service coverage. These variations have only widened under neoliberalism and corporatization.

Thirty years of corporate and market forces vying for access to the relatively untapped profit streams promised by public health care have fundamentally transformed the system, despite widespread public support for medicare. While core elements of the system remain relatively protected (e.g., hospital stays, doctor's visits), medicare has been eroded from the inside. A for-profit corporate presence has emerged through fiscal austerity and spending reforms at the federal level, provincial funding changes imposed on local authorities, and the privatization of hospital infrastructure and ancillary services (such as cleaning, dietary, and linen services).

Federal spending cuts and program reforms over the past few decades have downloaded far greater responsibility and oversight onto the shoulders of the provinces, and provinces have in turn shifted the burden of neoliberal adjustment onto local health authorities, such as Regional Health Authorities (RHAs) or hospital boards. For example, many RHAs and hospital boards are subject to performance agreements that necessitate hospital restructuring and amalgamations, service cuts (e.g., cancelling elective surgeries), fee hikes (e.g., parking lot rates, private hospital rooms), and reduced labour costs (e.g., freezes on hiring and overtime, layoffs). Local agencies are forced to privilege the bottom line, often at the expense of service provision and a consideration of wider social needs. P3s are often used to address the vacuum created by fiscal austerity, filling gaps through private finance and corporate service providers.

Funding arrangements for hospital operating costs, such as "activity-based," "pay for results," and "pay for performance" schemes, now distribute funds and tie hospital board member compensation to corporatized metrics like efficiency, throughput, lowest price, and related performance measures.[4] To accommodate cuts and changes to public finance, the introduction of private finance and corporate decision-making, and the knowledge needed to partner with multinational consortia, we have seen the development of specialized government procurement agencies and the corporatization of RHAs and hospital boards. The boards are stocked with upper echelon public servants largely selected for their business background and expertise in areas like real estate and contract law, rather than experience in the health sector.[5]

P3s and Public Health Care Corporatization

Hospital P3s involve many components: agreements related to land, financing, infrastructure (design, construction), equipment procurement, and the operation and management of public services. While each P3 agreement is unique, most display a complicated public/private division among project tasks. For instance, (i) the land upon which P3 hospitals are built is not fully privatized but leased; (ii) private financing is used for construction purposes but not for hospital equipment (which is most often procured through local community ventures); (iii) design is private and subject to commercial confidentiality and proprietary laws, but public input and approval must be sought at key stages of development; and (iv) clinical services are publicly funded and managed, whereas non-clinical services in P3 hospitals are publicly funded but privately managed. The range of non-clinical care services subject to corporate control has also fluctuated over time and by project. Even when a P3 hospital agreement does not cover non-clinical services, these services may be subject to contracting out.

The implications of P3-induced corporatization can vary. Most obviously, it involves shifting work from the public sector to corporate employers, with wages and working conditions often deteriorating as a result. The women and visible minorities who predominantly provide these services are disproportionately burdened by lower wages, less secure employment and predictable shifts, as well as neo-Taylorist labour disciplining and monitoring techniques.[6] Ursula Huws describes this public to private employment shift as involving the expropriation of rights previously won by organized labour.[7] Not only are staff working for P3 private operators adversely affected, but the bargaining power of public sector unions and the labour movement is weakened. Past struggles for universal public services are undermined in the process.[8]

With P3s in the public health care system, government becomes the purchaser of services and infrastructure, not the public directly, and thus the universal nature of public services may not be undermined per se. Health services remain universally accessible to the public but their management, organization, and to some degree their future planning becomes dominated by large (often multinational) corporations, not community or competing public interests. The P3 model has reconceptualized support services (such as dietary, cleaning, and linen) so they are more akin to hotel services than health care services, or fundamental aspects of health care provision. However, given that support staff "ensure the cleanliness of rooms, furnishings, and equipment that are vital to infection control; they prepare and deliver meals; they dispose of garbage and bio-hazardous material; they do the laundry for patients and staff," crucial areas of health care such as hygiene, nutrition, infection control, and patient care are implicated.[9]

The introduction of the profit motive into public hospitals affects health outcomes, patients, and staff training. Cutting corners to reduce costs and increase profitability creates difficulties for service integration and planning,[10] and has been directly linked to illness and death. For example, in 2009, BC's Nanaimo Regional General Hospital developed the antibacterial-resistant super bug *C. difficile*, causing dozens to fall ill and five deaths. Though infection control is a problem in all hospitals, the BC Centre for Disease Control reports that due to understaffing and improper training by the private contractor, support staff made several crucial errors in their sanitization protocol, which greatly exacerbated later attempts at infection control.[11] This supports Marjorie Griffin Cohen and Marcy Cohen's contention that " because of the special requirements and dangers inherent in a hospital setting, this type of cleaning requires a level of knowledge and skill that is acquired through years of on-the-job experience as well as specialized training. Such training is not typically offered by the private sector."[12]

Business-like practices, the other key components of P3 corporatization, reorient public sector decision-making by adopting the logic and reasoning of the private sector. Market-based notions of risk and value for money inherent in P3 justification reconceptualize the public interest and become the basis upon which P3 proliferation is encouraged. In provinces with advanced P3 programs, the entrenchment of this model has involved multiple forms of public sector reorientation: enabling legislation and capital planning frameworks (e.g., BC's *Community Charter Act, Health Sector Partnerships Agreement Act,* and Capital Asset Management Framework; Ontario's *Municipal Act,* Infrastructure Planning, Financing, and Procurement Framework, and Alternative Financing and Procurement model); supportive secondary reforms (BC's restructured Regional Health Authorities, and the creation of Local Health Integration Networks in Ontario); and new forms of institutional support achieved via the activities of quasi-public government agencies (Partnerships BC and Infrastructure Ontario).[13] These P3 programs create a new "common sense" that alters public sector decision-making and procurement processes, leading to further support for corporatization. P3 enabling policies and practices *transform* government decision-making, they do not merely substitute older protocols with newer ones, and the P3 model is not a "neutral" addition to existing public management models.

Specialized government procurement agencies encourage the transformative impact of P3 corporatization. As public sector entities (usually Crown corporations), agencies like Partnerships BC appear to represent the public interest but in practice clearly represent business interests as well. In 2002, Partnerships BC was created to "[work] in the interests of government and taxpayers."[14] Four years later, former President and CEO Larry Blain was describing the deep integration of business interests within Partnerships BC's operations:

> There are two sides to a [P3] market. There is the province, which has an interest in procurement on an effective and least-cost basis. There is also the private partners who need to be interested in British Columbia and want to do business here and want to do business with us. We have to attract them, so we have to attract both sides … that's our role.[15]

Fulfilling this role has meant that staff are rarely recruited from within the bureaucracy; instead, accountants, engineers, lawyers, private sector consultants, and those with backgrounds in finance and commerce are targeted. Further, by earning revenue off other government departments using the P3 model, Partnerships BC has come to treat the Ministry of Health and others as its clients. A 2014 Internal Audit & Advisory Services report conducted for the Ministry of Finance found Partnerships BC to have a conflict of interest as a result.[16]

Leading P3 Corporate/Private Actors

P3 infrastructure appears to be fully "public." These projects are typically presented to Canadians as public infrastructure and services tied to their relevant government ministry or department. In reality, major roles are carved out for the private partners that form the project company (construction, engineering, service, management, and financial firms) along with a myriad of other private actors that make up the P3 industry (e.g., private consultants, lawyers, credit rating agencies, and accountants). Highlighting a few of the noteworthy corporate/private actors that form the private partners of Canadian P3s can illustrate corporatization's transformative nature.

Private Partners: Construction and Engineering Firms

Along with foreign companies now entrenched in Canadian P3 markets, Canada has a few homegrown construction and engineering firms that are active in the corporatization of public hospitals through their equity ownership stakes in P3s across the country. Canadian construction giant SNC Lavalin is the central private partner in Montreal's super-hospital project—the McGill University Health Centre, costing over $1 billion—along with Centre hospitalier universitaire projects in Montreal, such as St. Justine's pediatric hospital. SNC Lavalin is also an active P3 partner elsewhere, including in New Brunswick's first health sector P3 (the Restigouche Hospital Centre), BC's Canada Line (a light rail project linking Vancouver's airport to the downtown), and 407 International Inc., which owns and controls the tolls on Ontario's fully privatized Highway 407. In 2010, a series of scandals erupted relating to fraud, corruption, and bribery accusations involving many of the company's projects worldwide. In 2013, SNC Lavalin was added to the list of companies banned from bidding on World Bank projects. That same year, it divulged to Quebec's Charbonneau Commission inquiry into provincial corruption that it had made illegal political donations.

EllisDon, another leading Canadian construction firm and partner in twenty P3 deals (and counting) since 2004, is also an important player in Canada's P3 industry. With projects ranging from courthouses and hospitals to public transit, it is currently a member of the country's largest P3 project—the Eglinton Crosstown Light Rail Transit project in Toronto. In health care, EllisDon was part of the project company forming the private partner of the two pioneering P3 hospitals in Ontario (the Brampton Civic Hospital and Royal Ottawa Hospital), with a long list to follow: Ontario's St. Joseph's Hospital & Health Sciences Centre, South West Centre for Forensic Mental Health Care in St. Thomas, London Regional Mental Health Care facility, and Oakville Trafalgar Memorial Hospital; and in BC, the Penticton Regional Hospital Patient Care Tower and Surrey Memorial Hospital Critical Care Tower. EllisDon is a major financial contributor to the Liberal party and has had family connections to the party in the past. In 2013, it attempted to circumvent the Ontario Labour Relations Board by gaining political support to end its legally binding commitment to unionized workers dating back to a 1958 closed-shop working agreement. The controversial Bill 74 (the *Fairness and Competitiveness in Ontario's Construction Industry Act*) was ultimately defeated but the effort is instructive.

The role of SNC Lavalin, EllisDon, and other private partners in these hospitals is often forced upon local authorities against their wishes. For example, when the health authority board in charge of the Surrey hospital project reported to the province that a P3 was "not the first choice of the committee," the board was overruled and the P3 was pushed through.[17] Stellar records are hard to find once the P3 process gets going; the Brampton and Royal Ottawa projects were delayed and suffered significant cost overruns along with design and construction flaws.[18]

Private Partners: Financiers

P3 financing is typically secured in stages and through a number of different entities. Construction financing often relies on loans from private commercial or public investment banks, and, when the project is operational, bond financing is used, or some combination of the two. The entities that make up the engineering, construction, and service providers are usually the equity holders in the project—they make project decisions but are only paid once debts are repaid. The creditors (debt holders) that provide financing by purchasing bonds can be wealthy individuals who invest in infrastructure funds, but are more often institutional investors: banks, pension funds, life insurance companies, sovereign wealth funds, and superannuation funds.

Given that public infrastructure is a relatively low risk, high reward investment site, public sector pension money (and pension funds of all sorts) is frequently invested in P3 infrastructure. The Ontario Municipal Employees Retirement System and the Ontario Teachers' Pension Plan, for example, were involved in several Canadian P3s in the past. By wrapping up public sector workers' retirement savings with projects that challenge unions and public sector jobs, and may even undermine employees' working conditions and wages, the monetary benefits that come from investing in P3 projects can cut both ways. Beyond pension funds, Wall Street investment banks are also moving into infrastructure debt financing. Investment banks like Goldman Sachs, Morgan Stanley, the Carlyle Group, and Citigroup are now either buying into "infrastructure funds" or creating infrastructure funds themselves (i.e., generating their own form of pooled savings that seek out investment in P3 infrastructure assets).

The involvement of private finance in public infrastructure extends beyond P3 project companies. Offshore infrastructure funds are also being set up to move P3 revenue to tax haven-registered firms. Dexter Whitfield reports that a flourishing £17.1 billion global industry in secondary P3 market sales is now being churned up by the buying and selling of equity in P3 private partner project companies, with rates of return on investment coming in at upwards of 50 percent (five times the amount typically agreed to in an average P3 scheme).[19] These earnings flow to the original private partner, the secondary market investors (re)selling equity in the project company, and associated shareholders. Five of the largest offshore infrastructure funds made a total profit of £1.8 billion between 2011 and 2015, monies that would be of great benefit to cash-strapped governments, particularly the municipalities where these infrastructure projects are located. In Canada, where more than 200 P3s have been developed since the early 1990s, over twenty equity sales had occurred as of 2016. Given that most Canadian P3s were only launched in the past five to ten years, and are typically social (not commercialized) infrastructure, this secondary market in equity sales is set to grow. Along with its growth comes revenue loss through offshoring. Already we see tax haven-registered companies buying and selling Canadian public infrastructure assets. In health care, this includes Bilfinger Berger Global Infrastructure, registered in Luxembourg, that now owns the Kelowna and Vernon hospital projects, and John Laing Infrastructure Fund Limited, registered in Guernsey, that owns the Abbotsford Regional Hospital and Diamond Health Care Centre in BC.

Private Partners: Operations and Maintenance Providers

Sodexo has been involved with several P3 hospitals in Canada, including BC's Abbotsford Hospital and Cancer Centre and the Gordon and Leslie Diamond Health Care Centre. Workplace training, management, and staffing are vital components of a hospital's functioning and sanitation, so support staff can play an integral role in a hospital's overall service delivery. Whereas public employers specialize in public services and the relevant sector in particular, Sodexo is a multinational corporation that provides services ranging from food and maintenance within hospitals, schools, prisons, and all manner of other institutions. BC's Hospital Employees Union reports that in 2002, Sodexo hired teenagers from army camps as strikebreakers in a hospital dispute in Scotland.[20] It has also allegedly published a Union Avoidance Manual to discourage or prevent its employees from joining or forming unions.

Another major service provider in Canadian P3s, Carillion (a partner in Ontario's Brampton Civic Hospital and Royal Ottawa Hospital) was found guilty of equally unsavory activities in England in 2012. It created an illegal consulting association blacklist that targeted workers who raised safety concerns, refusing to hire those particular staff from employment agencies. Carillion is also a construction firm and that arm of the company is embroiled in scandal over its treatment of migrant workers in Qatar in association with World Cup 2022 projects. Staff complaints and workplace tensions have emerged in both Ontario and BC P3 hospitals under the management of Carillion and Sodexo—lines of public-private governance and accountability have become blurred, contract details around entitlements and responsibilities are hidden from staff, and low wages with precarious, flexibilized working conditions are endemic.[21]

Local Companies

Smaller municipal and provincial contractors are often excluded from P3 markets. Not only does this create a power imbalance when a local administration is negotiating with a consortium of large private firms, such as multinational banks and Canadian construction giants, but it also creates a power imbalance within the private sector. Smaller construction contractors, cleaners, caterers, and the like are now hired and fired by multinational P3 private partners, a practice seldom overseen or controlled by governments, despite these companies being on the front lines of public service provision.

John Knappett of Knappett Projects Inc., a construction contractor out of Victoria, BC, makes the compelling case that P3 has meant bigger construction projects rather than more construction projects.[22] In the early 2000s, the BC government promised that by using P3s the province's construction industry would flourish. More contracts and more construction would result from adding private finance to the mix, allowing for enhanced opportunities to bid on infrastructure projects. By 2008, the British Columbia and Yukon Territory Building and Construction Trades Council found that P3s were hurting small and medium-sized contractors in the province.[23] Though the council supports P3s in principle (being an obvious potential beneficiary of new construction projects), they argue that prime contractors are most often large firms, and once a contract is awarded it is entirely up to their discretion whether and how they subcontract to smaller local companies. The council also reports that there is no official oversight into how subcontracting is done or whether it is done, and that in some cases the prime contractors are not tendering bids fairly or openly.

Similar concerns around construction industry competition (or the lack thereof) exist in Ontario. Mike Sharp, chairman of the Ottawa Construction Association and vice-president of Black and McDonald Ltd., estimates that in 2008 there were only eight to ten general contractors in the province that were able to take on P3 projects.[24] Given that P3 contracts bundle all project elements together (design, construction, financing, operations, and maintenance), each company that forms a private partner must be able to bear the financial burden of surety and bonding amounting to the entire cost of a project, which squeezes out smaller firms and limits P3 bidding to only the largest companies. In construction, this might mean a redistribution of contracts from smaller to larger firms; in services, the introduction of the P3 model has meant the creation of a subcontracting industry in Canada for the delivery of public services that is often beyond the control of public administrators.

Conclusion

The aim of a P3 is to transform government from a provider of public services to the procurer of private commodities, and multi-decade contracts ensure that profit is extracted from the operation of crucial public infrastructure projects and services. P3s are therefore a central feature of public health care corporatization as they integrate corporate management and decision-making into nearly all elements of public hospital design, building, financing, management, and support service operations. Two decades of P3 policy in Canada has meant that public health sector administrators now manage a large portion of their affairs through private investment vehicles. As the process rolls forward, the P3 model begins to take on a life of its own. With the loss of in-house capacity and alterations to decision-making rationale, P3 corporatization is self-reinforcing. There is little left in the public sector to compare in an options appraisal, and P3 evaluation becomes self-referential with public hospitals increasingly adjusted to a corporate presence.

Justifications for the use of P3s in public health care often centre on the "need" to leverage private funds during times of fiscal austerity. In 2015, Canada elected a federal Liberal government with a platform offering alternatives to austerity. Unfortunately, campaign rhetoric proved fickle. Rather than using public funds to finance public works more cheaply, a soon-to-be-created Canada Infrastructure Bank will open its doors (and public assets) to private capital investment. Touted as a "win-win," Canada intends to attract institutional investors' sizeable supply of capital by "identify[ing] a pipeline of potential projects and ... investment opportunities that provide the biggest economic, social and environmental returns."[25] Public infrastructure will be reconfigured. Revenue-generating infrastructure projects—those that are "commercializable" through tolls and user fees—will be targeted and equity investments will be offered. Any benefits flowing from the Canada Infrastructure Bank will come with a price tag of at least a 7 to 9 percent return on investment for private equity holders and introduce greater commitments to corporatization than ever.

Alternatives that would avoid revenue leaching through profiteering, equity sales, and offshoring, and allow for greater democratic control and a wider range of policy options in the future, can draw upon the same sources that private finance does: pooled savings, debt, user fees, and taxes. As opposed to privatizing shares in Crown corporations, these assets could be leveraged by expanding operations into new commercial areas that remit dividends and generate revenue (e.g., marijuana). Rather than relying on private investment vehicles, public sectors could tap into new or existing forms of pooled savings, such as pension and superannuation funds and employment insurance. Resource-rich provinces could also establish or enhance sovereign wealth funds. Select user fees from certain projects (e.g., transit, highways) could ensure intergenerational repayment equity and be used as income streams for repaying "revenue" bonds backed by a project's operations. The Canadian federal government currently enjoys the lowest ratio of net debt to GDP in the G-7 (and will for some time), making direct public borrowing through bond markets a viable policy option.[26] Fiscal policy changes, such as creating a more progressive tax system to redistribute "dead money" hoarded by wealthy individuals and institutions, would enhance public sector budget revenue, as would allowing municipalities to collect new forms of tax revenue beyond the current reliance on property taxes. Whatever the fiscal solution, cutting P3s out of public health care would not only be cheaper, it would significantly dampen the negative impacts of corporatization in Canada's health care system.

Three Waves of Health Care Corporatization in Ontario Hospitals

Natalie Mehra

Introduction: A Mickey Mouse Idea

In 2010, the government-appointed health planning board in southwestern Ontario announced a conference for health care executives and leaders featuring a keynote address by the Disney Institute. Complete with a picture depicting statues of Walt Disney and Mickey Mouse in front of the towers of the theme park, the publicity e-brochure for the session declared:

> At the ESC LHIN [Erie St. Clair Local Health Integration Network] conference keynote session by *Disney Institute,* you have the opportunity to benchmark a world-class approach to leadership. Their professional facilitators will unveil the fundamental leadership philosophies behind Walt's great success . . . Learn successful Disney processes and the organizational structure that supports them . . . Examine the strategies Disney leaders employ to keep their teams constantly improving and reaching new goals.[1]

Public outrage was swift. The outcry spread to opposition party MPPs and was raised on the floor of the Ontario legislature. The Ontario Health Coalition, a public interest group dedicated to protecting public health care, was alerted to the LHIN's plans through a sudden slew of emails. Reactions ranged from incredulous to incensed and were sent in by disparate sources: the mayor of a large town, an MPP, a hospital union representative, several community members, and local health coalition advocates. Newspapers in the region's largest cities and its smallest villages excoriated the plan. Within a matter of days, the LHIN was forced to scrap the planned $9,500 Disney keynote.[2]

The episode provided an easily identifiable target around which public anger could coalesce, underlining the extent to which regional health and hospital administrators have strayed from the widely shared values and priorities of the community. It demonstrated that, despite the attitudes of the planners and managerial classes, the public still views public hospitals as places of care in which notions like customer loyalty and Disney's operating structures have no place. But the embrace of corporate approaches to health care management is not limited to a local health board in the far southwest region of the province. In fact, the LHIN had taken its inspiration from the Ontario Hospital Association, an organization led by the province's hospital CEOs, which had earlier that year also featured Disney at one of their conferences.[3]

This is by no means a new development. The adoption of corporate approaches to health care management and care has already advanced deeply into Ontario's health system. Starting in earnest in the 1990s, each wave of health cuts and neo-liberal restructuring has deepened the corporatization of our public health care system. Across the continuum of care from hospitals to home care, fundamental changes have been made to governance structures and processes by which care is planned, organized, and evaluated. An army of middle-managers, consultants, and technocrats have descended to manage the cuts, reforming institutions to fit new measurement techniques dominated by market modalities. Appointed boards of directors have replaced community control. Public input has been replaced with "community engagement"—controlled processes that limit opportunities to express opposition and provide meaningful input. A new cadre of corporate health executives has emerged, with values that are often in conflict with both clinical and public priorities. For-profit companies have had an impact on the culture of long-term care and home care, as work processes have changed in order to accommodate the requirements of new management approaches.

Corporatization, in this sense, involves the ascendance of business interests, values, and models within public institutions.[4] It refers to the ways in which changes in ownership alter the values and priorities of health care institutions and services, but also to the increasing influence of corporate models of organization, labour processes, and care in services that remain publicly owned. In this chapter, I explore how corporatization has taken shape in the Ontario health care system and, specifically, Ontario hospitals. I argue that there have been three "waves" of corporatization in Ontario's hospital system. While not entirely distinct from one another, each of these waves brought new elements of corporatization into play. While hospitals remain "non-profit" in Ontario, their methods of management, processes of work, and care have been fundamentally reconfigured on the basis of business-like principles. These changes pose a challenge to the foundational principles of equity and compassion upon which our public health system is based, and are often deeply opposed by the communities affected.

The First Wave: Distinguishing between "Core" and "Ancillary" Services

The first wave of corporatization in Ontario's hospitals was characterized by the outsourcing of "non-core" or "ancillary" contracts. Perhaps recognizing that the public would not tolerate the wholesale privatization of doctors and nurses, hospital executives adopted an approach that split services into "core" and "ancillary" functions, with ancillary services devalued and contracted out. As part of this process, community-based services such as hospital kitchens were closed and replaced with centralized supply factories, and work processes were altered to reflect the growing profit motive and a more casualized labour force. While enabling outright privatization, these processes also facilitated the importation of business-like rationalities in gauging the relative importance of different areas of service provision (see also Hurl, Chapter 11, in this volume).

The practice of separating out working-class-provided services, defining them as "non-clinical," "non-core," or "ancillary," gained momentum in the early 1990s under the leadership of Bob Rae's NDP government, and then accelerated under the Harris Conservatives. This split between services deemed to be "clinical" and those deemed to be "non-core" mirrored the corporate restructuring that had taken place in private industry over the previous decade, when large numbers of manufacturing firms began to contract out their production, maintenance, and janitorial services. It also followed a trend in the United States where public and non-profit hospital services were transferred to for-profit companies.[5] By 1995, US hospital outsourcing contracts were valued at $890 million and a growing army of private firms were looking for new expansion opportunities.[6] In 1993, the Toronto General Hospital (now the University Health Network) embarked on a plan to contract out its non-core services, including cleaning, food, and supplies. Overriding any concerns about service quality, the hospital believed that privatizing these services would increase efficiency and cost-effectiveness. The rationale for outsourcing was articulated by Michael Young, Chief Financial Officer of Toronto's Sunnybrook Hospital, revealing the extent to which business models were being embraced by hospital leadership at the time. According to Young, "[t]here are some aspects of health care that can be compared with a manufacturing organization ... The process is patient care; the output is, well ... patients."[7] Of course, for hospital patients, much of their quality of care (and prospects for recovery) depends upon support services (e.g., food services, cleaning services, information services) that are now deemed non-core or ancillary.

A study of the early Toronto General Hospital cleaning contract from the mid-1990s found that the number of housekeeping staff was reduced by 25 percent when the private company took over.[8] Staff morale plummeted and cleaning quality deteriorated. Across the province, hospital staff had reported that private cleaning companies had prioritized the economic bottom line by reducing the number of cleaning staff, imposing strict time limits on their work, and reducing the quality of cleaning supplies. One nurse in northern Ontario described the situation this way:

> When the private company came in, they brought in people to follow the cleaners around and calculate the exact amount of time each task would take. They laid off a number of the cleaners and gave the remaining staff time limits for each function: so many minutes to make a bed or clean a toilet and so on. They told them not to clean behind the furniture in the long-term care part of the hospital. The hospital became filthy.[9]

Since they began in the 1990s, these practices have reached epidemic levels. In 2013, the CBC's *The Fifth Estate* conducted an online survey asking participants to rate their hospitals. They received more than 3,500 responses. The largest proportion of respondents—one-third—complained that dirty hospitals were a chief concern.[10] Just a few years earlier in 2008, the BC Centre for Disease Control had published a study on an outbreak of *C. difficile*—a potentially fatal hospital superbug—that killed eight patients and infected more than sixty others. It found that the privatized cleaning service at the hospital had too few cleaners to provide the services required and that they were poorly trained in infection control. To make matters worse, cleaners were required to use a diluted bleach solution that was a hundred times weaker than required.[11]

Like cleaning services, the contracting out and factory production of hospital food started in the early to mid-1990s and subsequently spread across the country. Hospitals used to have in-house kitchens and food was prepared on site. When private food companies were brought in, they began to use industrial processes to mass produce and chill cooked food, then ship it to hospitals where it was reheated on carts and delivered to patients ("retherm" food).

Unlike hospital executives, the public has not supported the growth of factory food in hospitals, and "retherm" food is the subject of public debate wherever it is imposed. The public expects hospitals to be places of healing and hospital food is supposed to be wholesome and nourishing. Public trends supporting locally grown food run contrary to the widespread practice of centralized factory-produced hospital food, and dozens of campaigning groups from environmental-ists to consumer advocates are pushing for a return of the hospital kitchen and for fresh, local, culturally diverse, and healthier menus.

However, while fight-back campaigns around food services have made some inroads, the contracting out of hospital services continues to expand into new territory. Since the 1990s, public hospitals have entered into a dizzying array of joint ventures with transnational corporations, from laboratory compan-ies to drug and rehabilitation firms.[12] Along with it, corporate modalities have spread from so-called non-clinical services to virtually all aspects of patient care, including the management of clinical services. Increasingly, the bottom line is not defined by the quality of care, but the extent to which care provision can be stripped of its non-core operations.

The Second Wave: Consolidation, Consultancies, and the Loss of Community Control

Promising to open Ontario for business, the Harris government swept into power in 1994. His government's Common Sense Revolution campaign called for "gov-ernment to do business like a business—by focusing on results and putting the customer first."[13] In 1996, the Ontario Management Board adopted a new service delivery framework in which each ministry was directed to produce an annual "business plan" outlining restructuring proposals to generate "efficiencies."[14] Accordingly, the Ministry of Health began to create yearly business plans that referred to hospitals and other major program areas as "core businesses" and massive restructuring followed. A report commissioned by the Ontario Health Coalition and published by the Canadian Centre for Policy Alternatives (CCPA) in 2000 described some of the changes:

> The Harris government's Bill 26 ... enacted and modified many laws, including the Health Insurance Act, the Health Care Accessibility Act, the Ministry of Health Act, the Ontario Drug Benefit Act, the Prescription Drug Cost Regulation Act, the Public Hospitals Act, the Independent Health Facilities Act, the Regulated Health Professions

Act, and the Physician Services Delivery Management Act. Among its many provisions, this legislation empowered the Minister of Health to change the financing and operation of public hospitals, and even to order their shutdown or amalgamation; allowed private medical facilities, such as laboratories, to be established without tendering, and removed the requirement that preference be given to Canadian non-profit organizations, thus opening the door to U.S. for-profit firms.[15]

For public hospitals, this meant a wholesale transformation through restructuring and draconian cuts. Between 1989 and 1998, sixty-four Ontario hospitals were merged or closed outright, reducing the total number of hospitals in the province from 262 to 198.[16] Between 1996 and 2000, thirty-nine hospitals were ordered closed by the Health Services Restructuring Commission, which was established under Bill 26. The Minister of Health also shut down six psychiatric hospitals. Forty-four other hospitals were amalgamated into fourteen new multisite corporations, and the Health Services Restructuring Commission also proposed that one hundred more hospitals be combined in eighteen networks or clusters. Moreover, the total number of hospital beds was drastically reduced, with the elimination of more than 11,400 (one in four) beds over the span of a decade. This included more than one-third of Ontario's acute care and chronic care hospital beds.[17] While these numbers capture the extent to which hospitals were rationalized and services cut, less is known about the impacts of corporatization on community control and the culture of public hospitals.

In fact, the consolidation of public hospitals combined with the cuts of the 1990s had a profound impact on the workforce and the culture of care. Community hospitals that were built by residents through grassroots fundraising efforts were wrested from local control as services were centralized into fewer sites. With amalgamations and mergers, local governance was significantly eroded. Private consulting firms were brought in to manage the restructuring, which ushered in a wave of corporate workplace and care reforms. At the management level, clinicians were being replaced by executives with business degrees, deepening the corporatization of these institutions. Workloads increased considerably as "productivity" was stretched to new limits and services were provided by a shrinking and casualized workforce. Most importantly, the quality of care was increasingly subordinated to corporate restructuring. According to the 2000 CCPA report noted above:

> The hospitals still in operation have been forced to respond to the budget cuts inflicted on them by doing a lot of internal restructuring.

They have laid off staff, increased the use of temporary and part-time workers and volunteers, and contracted out services such as laundry, housekeeping and meals. Some have hired management consulting firms to advise them on how to cut costs and reorganize their operations. Entering into the "public-private partnerships" so favoured by the government—for laboratory services in particular—has also been a popular strategy for many hospital administrators.[18]

Hospital consolidations mirrored corporate horizontal integration plans in a bid to reap economies of scale. The cost savings were never realized.[19] But the consolidations fundamentally challenged the culture and community control of local public hospitals. Prior to the mergers, Ontario hospitals were freestanding public and charitable entities. Built either through fundraising efforts of local communities or by the Catholic church, most community hospitals had deep roots stretching back to World War II and even earlier. With the amalgamations and mergers, local hospitals lost their independence, services were "rationalized," a new tier of corporate managers were instituted in the new hospital corporations, and management consulting firms increasingly presided over hospital decision-making. Impacts on the workforce and the quality of patient care are outlined by the CCPA as follows:

> The nursing staff was cut by nearly 4,000 between 1994 and 1999, resulting in ... "lower levels of cleanliness, reduced patient supervision, increased stress, and less nursing time per patient" in most hospitals ... overall staff in the hospital sector dropped from 154,000 in 1995 to 128,000 in 1998 ... A major study published in the Canadian Medical Association Journal indicated that "reported errors" had increased significantly between 1992 and 1997: "Misadventures rose from 18 to 30 per 10,000 for in-patients and 5.2 to 11.6 for day surgeries. Complications rose from 330 to 500 per 10,000 for in-patients and from 65.2 to 95.1 per 10,000 for day surgeries. Adverse drug reactions rose from 104 to 162 per 10,000 for in-patients and from 8.1 to 10.8 for day surgeries."[20]

As hospitals grappled with funding cuts and management upheaval, an army of private consultants entered the scene, consolidating a public-private policy complex in generating policy advice. Looking at health, along with four other ministries, the provincial auditor general found that annual expenditures on consulting contracts had more than doubled over five years, increasing from $271 million in 1998 to $662 million in 2002. "Hundreds of consultants were engaged at per diem rates that were on average two to three times higher than those of ministry employees performing similar duties," he reported.[21] This was only the beginning. The subsequent proliferation of consulting contracts is evidenced in the Ontario Auditor General's Special Report of 2010, which found that the Ministry of Health alone spent $86.1 million on consulting services in the 2007–08 fiscal year, $102.2 million in 2008–09, and $35.4 million in 2009–10.[22] In addition, the auditor general reviewed the consulting practices of three Local Health Integration Networks (LHINs), which are the regional health boards appointed by government to manage their local health systems (there are fourteen in total). The auditor found that "[f]or the 2007/08 to 2009/10 fiscal years, the three LHINs we visited had annual expenditures on consultants ranging from $224,000 to $1.4 million per year."[23]

Within public hospitals as well, the use of consultants skyrocketed after the restructuring of the 1990s. A host of new consulting firms had opened up shop in Ontario and existing global firms had experienced more than a decade of significant growth (see Hurl, Chapter 11 in this volume). In the hospital section of Ontario's special audit, the auditor general provided examples of contracts that amounted to tens of millions of dollars. These were in addition to the consulting contracts in the ministry and LHINs noted above.[24] Rather than a publicly interested professional civil service guiding policy, and democratic local boards running hospitals, a whole industry of increasingly globalized middle managers was given contracts to generate advice at the local level and policy direction at the central level.

After restructuring and consolidation, a new cadre of corporate hospital executives was created. Physicians were replaced with business school graduates, and with the new management teams came new health care priorities and values. Similar to trends in the private sector, executive compensation soared to record levels. By 2010, the salaries of the largest five Ontario hospital CEOs ranged from a whopping $688,000 to $754,000 per year.[25] In comparison, by 2013, the annual billings of the highest paid specialists in Canada—ophthalmologists, who are themselves extremely well compensated—averaged $676,000, with the average general practitioner billing approximately $225,000.[26] Clearly, the health system no longer valued clinicians as its top priority. They were replaced by a new set of privileged executives supported by new tiers of highly compensated corporate administrators. Hospitals began to separate out their executive offices, referring to them as "corporate services," and clinical decision-making was increasingly controlled by people whose education and values were fundamentally different than in previous decades.

Across Canada, as Regional Health Authorities were brought in to replace elected boards of directors, Ontario's hospitals began to eliminate community control in a different way. When hospitals were amalgamated, new by-laws were written to govern the new non-profit corporations. Local hospital boards were dissolved, and centralized boards were created. In some amalgamations, a local advisory committee remained. Some were elected, but they had few powers to affect or influence the decisions of the new hospital corporations. Some hospitals eliminated community memberships entirely, opting to have only the hospital board members (and sometimes past hospital board members) constitute the membership. In doing so, hospital leadership exploited a provision in the *Not-for-profit Corporations Act* that allowed the hospital corporations to select their members (and then the hand-picked members would "elect" the board) in order to eliminate hospital democracy. Community activists soon discovered that they no longer had any avenue to influence the future of their hospitals. As the second wave of corporatization waned, a nearly one hundred-year history of local communities building and governing local hospitals was coming to an end.

The Third Wave: Market-Based Funding, Service Consolidation, Public-Private Partnerships, and Mega-Mergers

In 2000, eighteen-year-old Joshua Fluelling died of an asthma attack in an ambulance that had circled Toronto streets unable to find a hospital that was not at full capacity. Two weeks earlier, Toronto police had shot and killed a man who held a toy gun to a physician's head, demanding immediate medical attention for his infant son. Indeed, the news media was filled with horror stories around this time of people unable to access critical care. Community morals were crossed and the public uproar was too powerful to ignore. As a result, there was a short respite from funding cuts between 2000 to 2006.

When a new Liberal government was elected in Ontario in 2003, it promised to break from the Conservative government's restructuring mandate. During its first three years in office, the Liberals increased public hospital funding and began to reopen hospital beds. But the orders of the Conservatives' Health Services Restructuring Commission remained in place, unchallenged by any new plan, and the forms of corporatization that were previously instituted continued. By 2006, the influence of fiscal conservatism had again gained ascendance and a new wave of hospital restructuring began, pushing corporatization to new levels. This time, health care reforms followed the market-driven policy models previously adopted in Britain (initially under Thatcher's Conservatives and then under Blair's Labour Party). Planned underfunding put relentless pressure on hospitals' overhead budgets. So-called "public-private partnerships," which were used in the 1990s to corporatize discrete services, were expanded to entire hospitals under decades-long contracts. In a wholesale purge, local ministry offices that were staffed by professional civil servants and district health councils were shut down and replaced by cabinet-appointed LHINs. The "purchaser-provider split" was enshrined in legislation to ensure that services were contracted out rather than publicly owned. A new funding system for hospitals based on market-driven, pay-for-procedure methods cut the remaining threads of community control. Hospitals were increasingly required to follow rigorous measurement techniques and were put in competition with one another for funding and services. Hospital centralization and specialization were propelled to new extremes and rural hospitals were gutted.

Having learned the lessons of the 1990s, which saw widespread public backlash against funding cuts and restructuring, the new Liberal government moved to wipe out hospital democracy. Public planning methods were eradicated and the largest hospital executives were given lucrative consulting contracts. Consultants, administrators, and executives operating behind the scenes designed new care plans. Collection and publication of data on the impact of hospital cuts were severely curtailed. Municipal council representatives were ousted and the culture of hospital boards of directors changed. Without any public debate or input, a revolution in the control of planning and operating modalities of Ontario's hospitals was undertaken. Within ten years, the dreams and expectations of hundreds of communities—to have local hospitals housing a comprehensive set of services to meet local needs—were abandoned by hospital and political leadership.

Dalton McGuinty, Ontario's Liberal premier, described part of this approach in his 2015 autobiography:

> I was eager to engender public-sector entrepreneurialism. For example, we introduced "pay for performance" for hospitals. Hospitals that provided a procedure at lower cost were funded to do more of these procedures than their higher-cost counterparts. We were incenting outputs, and it didn't take long for hospital administrators to catch on and make productive changes.[27]

Beginning in 2006, the McGuinty government embarked on a decade-long plan to downsize and reform hospitals through planned underfunding and the introduction of "pay-for-performance," a fee-for-service funding formula. To maintain service levels, public hospitals require funding to meet inflation, population growth, ageing, and utilization pressures. From 2006 to 2016, successive provincial budgets set hospital funding below the rate of inflation (and included nothing for population growth and ageing), forcing hospitals to shrink the scope of the services they provided. By 2008, half of Ontario's hospitals were in deficit and 70 percent were projecting deficits for the following year. Despite major cuts to hospitals that had already been downsized for more than a decade, the real-dollar cuts to hospital funding grew more pronounced after the 2008 economic downturn. Between 2012 and 2016, budgets were frozen with 0 percent increases. As a result, hospitals systematically closed and privatized outpatient laboratory, rehabilitation, and other services, and cut staff and curtailed in-patient care.

At the same time, Ontario copied the market-oriented funding processes that were introduced in the UK. Prior to this, Ontario's hospitals were given global budgets and local hospitals distributed funds to services based on population need.[28] Euphemistically called "patient-based" and "quality-based-procedure" funding, the premise of the new system was simple: hospital services would be quantified, like widgets in a corporate factory. Hospitals would compete on a price basis for funding. Those hospitals that could meet the lowest price targets would get funding for certain volumes of procedures. Those that could not compete would lose funding for those procedures. With the introduction and subsequent expansion of the fee-for-service model, hospital care services were centralized to a new extreme. This represented the antithesis of the long-standing public notion of a community hospital with a comprehensive set of services geared to local needs.

There was no shortage of warnings that these changes would negatively impact community hospitals. In a 2007 news release, Canadian Doctors for Medicare warned that an "over-dependence on activity-based payments would ... erode hospitals' commitment to providing a full range of services to all patients and reduce efficiency through higher administrative costs." Likewise, the National Health Service Consultants' Association (the British organization representing public physicians) sent an open letter to Canadian doctors stating that: "These policies have fragmented health care, discouraged collaboration between health care professionals, and wasted money ... we have tried these policies and they have proved a mistake. We urge you to learn from our experience and to reconsider." In fact, the changes that the new funding formula wrought were far worse than expected. Between 2011 and 2014, the government phased in the new funding model. By 2014, one-third of hospitals' global budgets were converted to fee-for-service. Cataract surgeries, MRIs and CTs, hip and knee surgeries, and other services that fell under the funding model were quickly centralized to fewer hospital sites. Other hospitals, unable to compete in price, dropped these services altogether.

As the corporatized fee-for-service model took hold, a revolution in hospital planning and management occurred. Hospital executives moved to position their hospitals in the new funding "market." Hospital CEOs and administrators became consumed with "market share," "throughput" and "profit centres." Services that did not easily fit into measurable chunks were sidelined as hospitals focused on a plethora of new measurements and reporting procedures. Shadow billing was spread across clinical specialties that did not fit under the fee-for-service model, and pressure was put on clinicians to continually increase their volume units of various services.[29] Even care practices that are obviously not measurable by volume (psychology, for example) were contorted to meet the new maxims. Psych visits became measured—in six-minute, one-hour, two-hour chunks, and so on—and had to be reported meticulously for fear of losing programs or services, regardless of population need. Clinicians complained that planning for patients, peer consults, learning, and other vital elements of their work were left out because they were not easily measured or quantified. Clinicians also reported that they were driven to see more and more patients for smaller lengths of time, and time for their work became more and more scarce. Patients complained that they had become "numbers" in increasingly alienating hospital environments. Indeed, in a very literal sense, they had.

As a result of payment by volume methods and the drive to increase volume, access to care was deeply compromised. Rural hospitals were deemed "inefficient" and their services were systematically stripped, leaving entire towns to travel to the city for care. City hospitals also became dangerously overcrowded, but were nonetheless subject to round after round of deep cuts, and services were increasingly rationalized across ever-larger regions. Entire hospitals were closed down at rates unheard of in Canada. Patients were shocked and angered to find that their local community hospitals had become "sites" in multi-unit amalgamations, and each site was expected to specialize in fewer services.

Above all, the introduction of market-style funding and competition, and the attendant cultural changes within hospital management, decimated community hospitals and fundamentally altered access to patient care. For example, the Huron Perth Healthcare Alliance, located in Ontario's southwest, is a cluster of medium to small hospitals spread over an hour's drive in the summer time (longer in winter) with one hospital board centred in Stratford. During the decades of cuts, the smaller hospital "sites" in the alliance systematically lost services. Under pressure from shrinking real-dollar budgets and the trend toward specialization, virtually all rehabilitation was moved to Seaforth, a small town near Lake Huron. Medical beds were cut at St. Mary's and Seaforth and moved to Clinton. Surgeries were centralized in Stratford. Patients' families complained that they would drive to one hospital to see their loved ones only to find that they had been moved to another hospital, sometimes an hour away. Similarly, the Niagara Health System closed down all surgeries and emergency departments in two south Niagara hospitals, centralized all birthing from five hospitals to one, and moved most chronic care to the southern tier. With no transportation system to get them from town to town, more than half a million people were forced to drive across the entire Niagara peninsula to access different types of care. Even northern Ontario, where distances between towns are much greater, was not spared. Outpatient mental health services were cut from North Bay and centralized in Sudbury, leaving patients with an hour-and-a-half drive to access care. In Greater Toronto, patients in North York were dismayed to discover that their local hospital had given up cataract surgeries and they were now expected to drive an hour north to Newmarket.

These changes were accomplished without any legislation, with no parliamentary debate, without public hearings, and without any formal planning. In fact, to force through these changes that were overwhelmingly opposed by the public, the government created new structures for oversight and eradicated whatever semblance of democracy remained in hospital governance. New restructuring powers were given to LHINs. The minister of health was also given new powers to order hospital mergers and closures, with few if any procedural safeguards or opportunities for public input. LHINs were required to enforce funding cuts on local hospitals and find opportunities for "integration," including amalgamations and service consolidations. Only the barest requirements for public notice, often on obscure websites, were required for major service restructuring and the public was given no ability to require disclosure of documents. Consulting companies were routinely brought in to release high-cost reports or run controlled exercises to support what the public perceived as predetermined conclusions that resulted in further cuts and corporate-style changes to their local hospitals.

All of this proved to be a lightening rod for public anger. At every Ontario Health Coalition public forum and town hall meeting in recent years, a simmering fury at the ways in which our local hospitals have changed is readily apparent. Inevitably, the loudest applause will follow comments by participants about firing the executives with their bloated salaries and the army of consultants and technocrats that have disproportionate influence over—and take disproportionate resources away from—clinical care and vital patient support services.

Conclusion

Corporatization has become a dominant force in Ontario's hospitals and the broader health care system. While Ontarians have, for now, stymied the efforts of for-profit clinics and hospitals to assume outright ownership over health services, a revolution in the management and control of our hospitals has occurred. The market mechanisms used to corporatize Ontario's health care sector have profoundly changed the modalities of care and the structures that manage it. These processes have alienated and endangered the public, and are experienced as oppressive by clinical and support staff alike. The methods and impacts of corporatization are too little studied. But by naming it and by revealing its characteristics, we have an opportunity to challenge it. It is useful to remind ourselves that it took three decades of incremental (and sometimes radical) steps to arrive at this point. It is possible to, and indeed we must, find ways to reinstate democratic processes as the cornerstone of public hospital reform and governance.

Education

———————— *3* ————————

The Rise of the Corporate Cashroom

Corporatization and the Neoliberal Canadian School

Erika Shaker

Introduction

Commercialism is more prevalent than ever in most aspects of our lives, both in the sheer number of ads we are exposed to daily,[1] and in the increasingly creative ways in which spaces are redefined as marketing venues. However, it would be a mistake to suggest that Canadian classrooms have only recently become a venue for marketing, commercial branding, or corporate involvement.[2] Back in the 1930s, for example, the Copp Clark Company (Toronto) offered every school in the country a map of Canada or of the world "absolutely free" (maps and prepaid postage supplied by chocolate and candy manufacturer William Neilson Limited). The only condition: the advertising for Neilson's candy and chocolate was not to be obscured. A 1953 survey conducted by William Neilson Limited estimated that about 55,000 maps had been sent to Canadian schools. So, while not new, the visible presence of the corporate sector in Canadian schools has grown exponentially over the past few decades, but particularly since the 1990s. This chapter focuses on the degree to which the relentless pursuit of new profitable markets, coupled with a manufactured shift in attitudes toward public institutions in general (and public schools in particular), have converged, and the impact this has had on public education across the country.

All non-public education funding is ostensibly evidence of privatization, but for the purposes of this chapter I have differentiated between money, services, resources, and influence from individual sources and from corporate ones. Admittedly there is overlap—harnessing a community school fundraising campaign as part of a corporate PR initiative, for example—because both speak to a profound ideological shift in how we value and provide funding for public institutions. In this chapter, however, I focus on the corporatization of education in Canada and how it has evolved. More specifically, the chapter is concerned with the school as disseminator of educational content, rather than the physical infrastructure of the school as an institution.

In this context, corporatization includes a range of initiatives that seek to integrate the corporate presence directly into the school through the provision of sponsored materials or activities; the forging of "partnerships" between schools and corporate entities to provide programs or services for schools; and corporate-initiated school fundraising campaigns. In some cases, the effect is to replace public money with private (corporate) donations, and in others it is to integrate the public school into a broader corporate marketing strategy. Some initiatives are more commercial in nature, while others position themselves as compensating for something lacking in day-to-day school operations. Some of the least commercial initiatives take a more comprehensive, programming-based approach, ensuring that schools deliver curriculum that is developed in conjunction with corporate "stakeholders" and reinforcing a distinctly market-friendly set of priorities.

In this latter model, the school is positioned not in opposition to corporatization, but as the mechanism through which corporate priorities and the corporate mindset are naturalized and reinforced to and for "future workers and consumers" (also known as students). It is, as David McDonald describes, "a softer, less aggressive form of commercialization that grants a stronger role for the state than was being called for in the 1980s and 1990s, but one that does little to alter mainstream public administration's commitment to commoditization and its faith in the market."[3] Arguably, this "softer" approach has been much more successful in synthesizing corporate principles with educational priorities than any number of commercially branded sponsorship initiatives. In other words, while more traditional school marketing initiatives still exist, the overall emphasis has shifted from brand/product/logo visibility to ideological familiarity and naturalization (with corporate logos much more subtly placed).

Corporatization and Public Education

The systematic defunding of public education in Canada began in earnest in the mid-1990s, as budget deficit hysteria took hold at both the federal and provincial levels and public spending was slashed accordingly.[4] But the inconvenient truth about social programs is that the public need for and dependence on them does not decline as their funding is cut. In fact, as inequality has increased as a direct result of cuts to our social safety net,[5] the need for social programs to provide support to the most vulnerable grows ever greater, even as their ability to fulfil that need is financially and, eventually, structurally undermined.

Where schools are concerned, this has resulted in larger class sizes, fewer extracurricular activities, school closures, labour unrest, and delayed maintenance. It has also resulted in an increase in fundraising, "voluntary" user fees, and other private sources of revenue to compensate for inadequate public funding. As some schools are better positioned to raise more money because of the communities they represent or where they are located, it has also reinforced the very socio-economic inequities that universally well-funded and well-resourced schools can help overcome.

The corporate schoolhouse has evolved against the backdrop of several key trends: the exponential growth of the profitable global education market; the commercial power and influence of kids as consumers; and the election of provincial and federal governments committed to a neoliberal vision of education and an austerity-based view of budgeting (often with a dose of anti-union, anti-expertise rhetoric thrown in for good measure). The global education industry, which represents a broad range of education services at all levels, has been recently valued at nearly $5 trillion.[6] This industry is rapidly expanding, particularly with e-learning and the rise of "tech-ucation" (or "edu-tech," or "edu-tainment").

Private management of the physical infrastructure of schools and other formerly publicly funded buildings (often known as public-private partnerships or leasebacks) has also become an increasingly popular construction and management model for governments anxious to reduce the appearance of public spending on their books. The problems inherent in this form of alternative funding and management of public institutions have been well documented by the Canadian Centre for Policy Alternatives and others (see Whiteside, Chapter 1 in this volume).[7] In fall 2016, Nova Scotia announced that it would be purchasing twenty-five of the province's thirty-nine P3 schools[8] when their leases expire, because "purchasing is more affordable than extending the leases and provides the added benefit of ownership while providing a long-term solution to providing schools for these areas."[9] In short, education is a tremendously lucrative sector, which explains the lengthy list of corporations with an interest in the education market (from early childhood to post-secondary) in attendance at BMO's "Back to School" conference in 2016.

While the education industry's focus is generally on the physical structure, delivery, and content of education, there is another profitable rationale for business involvement in the education sector: the lucrative consumer market represented by the school community—teachers, students, families, and those who connect with their local school as a neighbourhood institution. And no wonder: kids aged nine to fourteen influence family spending decisions to the tune of $20 billion each year—the combined wealth of the world's twenty-eight poorest countries.[10] In addition, they are developing consumer preferences that can, if stoked correctly, last a lifetime. In other words, this is a long-term market base that is not to be taken for granted.

For marketers, the school is a goldmine because it is a marketing venue like few others. It offers access to a captive audience of young and evolving consumers whose shopping preferences are in the process of being formed, and an implicit endorsement of corporate products and images from a well-respected institution (that—bonus!—deals in "right" and "wrong"); it provides corporations with an immediate "in," piggybacking off the close relationship schools have with their communities; and where "educational" products are concerned, it ensures two markets for the price of one (parents purchasing their own version of an item their child finds useful).[11]

The relentless corporate push for new audiences and new marketing venues, however, can be met with resistance from "gatekeepers"[12] (i.e., parents or teachers), resistance that, through years of underfunding and dwindling resources, has steadily been worn down, resulting in a grudging acceptance and even a normalization of corporate branding of publicly owned spaces, including schools. This change in public attitudes corresponds with an uptick in both casual and institutional denigration of the public sector and its employees (or at least the unions that represent them), the pervasive fetishization of balanced budgets through spending cuts, and the ongoing naturalization of commercial branding in virtually all facets of daily life.

It is a confluence of trends that has made public schools exceedingly vulnerable to—and, consequently, dependent on—the demands and largesse of those willing to compensate (at a price) for inadequate public funding or resources. It also neatly limits the role of the school to one of training graduates to fit into the "real world," not challenge its inadequacies, and certainly not to change it.

Youth News Network: A Case Study in Commercialism

Probably the most notorious example of Canadian schoolhouse commercialism was Youth News Network (YNN),[13] modeled after the American Channel 1. YNN was incorporated in 1990 and in 1991–92 began offering to loan schools TV sets, closed-circuit cameras, and a computer lab, in return for the school committing (in a five-year contract) to its students watching a twelve-and-a-half minute news-and-infotainment show every day (ten minutes of news, two-and-a-half minutes of ads and public service announcements). If the school did not comply, the equipment would be taken back. The carrot was clearly the computer lab— and perhaps served to foreshadow the ways in which technology has facilitated corporate involvement in education—as Canadian schools already had access to several other commercial-free options through Cable in the Classroom.

After a shaky start and several failed attempts at convincing school boards of the educational benefits of YNN, in 1998 (and with a new parent company, Athena Educational Partners) the company finally gained a toe-hold in several schools across the country, including its flagship location, Meadowvale Secondary School in Mississauga, and a handful of others in Alberta and Quebec. The broader political context is of note: in Ontario, the Harris Conservatives had begun their campaign to cut over $2 billion out of public education, and school communities were feeling the pinch. This cost-cutting climate was referenced several times by Rod Macdonald, YNN's founder, as a rationale for schools accepting this "free" gift, which, after all, was not "that" commercial.[14] Resistance from parents, students, and teachers was swift and well-organized. Ministries of education were pressed on the issue: a number rejected YNN outright, and others indicated they would leave the decision up to their individual school boards. And, sometime in 2001, YNN's final attempt to make itself a permanent fixture of Canadian classrooms came to an underwhelming conclusion.

In retrospect, while the success of the grassroots-led campaign to defeat YNN was a positive outcome, it also, perhaps counterintuitively, reinforced the impression that Canadian schools (especially when compared to their American counterparts[15]) were commercial-free, and would remain so. This was patently not the case, as one Quebec teacher pointed out in defense of YNN: Students "come home with Scholastic book orders which advertise commercial books like

Star Wars, the Grade 10 math program calls for a Texas Instruments calculator, their books have to be Hilroy, and Crayola advertises in schools all the time."[16] This quote is indicative of two issues: (i) YNN, while perhaps the splashiest, was certainly not the *first* corporate attempt to market directly to the classroom (since its founding in 1920, Scholastic has been deeply engrained in classrooms, including in Canada since 1957[17]); and (ii) what has probably been one of the most prevalent arguments used to justify commercial and corporate involvement in public schools: in the "real world" we all, kids included, are exposed to advertising on a daily basis. Corporate logos are literally fashion statements. Why should the school remain untouched?

A Shift in Tactics

Product or logo placement is certainly easy to spot (that is, after all, the point of marketing) and, therefore, to track. There have been attempts to follow these trends both provincially and nationally.[18] Part of the difficulty, however, in accurately determining the pervasiveness of various initiatives is the relatively decentralized nature of our education system. Is a commercial venture board-wide (e.g., Toronto District School Board and Future Shop[19]), provincial (e.g., Chevron's BC-based "Fuel Your School"[20]), or national (e.g., Indigo's "For the Love of Reading"[21])? Is it framed as a community-based fundraiser, such as Campbell's "Labels for Education," which is currently winding down as the company moves towards more general "social responsibility" work?[22]

As important as these initiatives are, they do not represent the full extent of corporate involvement in education. Many of the more blatant commercial initiatives are being replaced by others that appear to be less about overtly branded, sponsored classroom content and more about a thematic approach. Take Chevron and Indigo, for example, which position themselves as solving the problem of education underfunding (the presence of which is taken as a given) by working with consumers to support their local school through a corporate fundraising vehicle. In Indigo's case, the focus is on a lack of funding for school libraries and reading resources; in Chevron's case, $1 from every fill-up of thirty litres or more at a Chevron station will be donated to "help support education in Greater Vancouver" (up to a maximum of $565,000). It is more of a "strategic philanthropy" approach, where the public's goodwill towards their local school and awareness of education underfunding becomes harnessed as part of a marketing strategy that positions these corporations as school benefactors—even though the vast majority of the money being donated is raised by members of the community.[23]

It also speaks to a broader trend: using identified needs that resonate with the public as themes through which to improve a corporate reputation. There is a reason that McDonald's has spent so much time post-*Supersize Me!* trying to rebrand itself as a company that promotes healthy living (Go Active!), using ingredients that Mom[24] (the ultimate gatekeeper) would approve of, and giving out fitness trackers in Happy Meals (which sadly had to be recalled after the wrist-strap caused an allergic reaction in several children).[25]

The corporatization of classroom management and monitoring of student behaviour is another growing trend, and a particularly interesting one because of how it intersects with data storage and school surveillance. Companies like ClassDojo,[26] founded in 2011, have positioned themselves as helping to facilitate a smoothly run classroom through their free app, which allows teachers to assign students points for "good behaviour" (thumbs up!) or take away points for behaviour deemed unhelpful (thumbs down!). Results can be displayed on a whiteboard in each class, and are also sent to parents via an app on their phones. It is an updated rewards system complete with cute monster avatars and sound effects, with a real-time parent alert thrown in for good measure. Not only does the outsourcing of classroom management and student motivation free up valuable time for overworked educators (ClassDojo can do it in "just one click!"[27]), "the data generated by the software can also be valuable in tracking a pupil's progress over time."[28]

Not surprisingly, pedagogical concerns have been raised about this form of motivation (or public shaming) and its effects on students, as well as privacy concerns.[29] The company insists it will not sell data for marketing purposes, and, as of 2015, agreed to dump the behaviour data after one year, but because ClassDojo is US-based, it means a "legal grey-zone"[30] for privacy laws and Canadian students whose teachers are using the app. Currently, ClassDojo is in two-thirds of all schools in the US (90 percent of school districts) and 180 countries around the world, according to the company's head of communications.[31] And Class Dojo has, incidentally, set its sights even higher, positioning itself as a tool to connect parents and teachers as a sort of mashup between Snapchat and Facebook that makes the need for face-to-face parent-teacher meetings "obsolete": "Communicating throughout the year, and even throughout the school day, means parents are apprised of what their kids are experiencing and how they are behaving at school all the time, not surprised by incidents that are only discussed in a once-a-semester parent-teacher meeting."[32] ClassDojo can "guide conversations at home" and help parents "support and enhance" their kids' learning development while sending photos of classroom activities and "student successes" to parents throughout the day through an app "purpose built for education." Eventually, the app could also manage all fundraising transactions and payments for school trips and lunches.[33]

In essence, ClassDojo has created a market based on segmenting several activities and priorities that once were considered integral to the education process—classroom behaviour, student engagement, communicating with parents—and repackaging them as a series of individualized transactions accessed through a free (for now) downloadable app. This is not a philanthropic endeavour: while there is no charge at the moment, there is tremendous profit potential that the company clarifies will be driven by parents who would be prepared to pay for premium features and content.[34] Lack of family time, lack of school resources, and lack of student attentiveness have been monetized by an enterprising start-up that has replaced pedagogy and authentic human interaction with a very public display of real-time rewards and punishments.

There is a common thread: all three of the initiatives discussed in this section position themselves as solving a problem that schools and educators (and, by extension, students and their families) are experiencing. Of course, the corporate "solutions" being proposed are not solutions at all. Even with fundraising campaigns, the chronic lack of school funding and resources is not being addressed and remedied with, say, a corporate-led call for increased public education funding—it is being, ironically, capitalized on to improve corporate profits and customer relations as part of a broader marketing strategy. Meanwhile, the time-consuming details of classroom management for already overburdened educators have been repackaged and gamified and presented to parents; where "three thumbs up and four thumbs down!" somehow becomes a perfectly valid response to "what did you learn in school today?"

Educating the Educators: Schools and the "Real World"

One of the most established organizations dedicated to facilitating school/corporate relationships in Canada is The Learning Partnership (TLP). According to its website, TLP is "dedicated to building stakeholder partnerships to support, promote and advance publicly funded education in Canada" and to "build lasting bridges between the education and business communities, and through these collaborations, enable students to strive for personal and academic excellence, and success in the workplace."[35] There is a significant focus on ensuring that student achievement is positively impacted, and that educators are "educated" about the "changing world of work."[36] It claims that since TLP was established in

1993, over 6.5 million students have participated in at least one of its programs (possibly the most well-known being "Take Our Kids to Work"). There are also resources on the website, including *Guiding Principles for Business and School Partnerships* from the Council for Corporate and School Partnerships (founded by Coca-Cola).

What is particularly striking about this well-established and well-funded (with revenues of almost $6.4 million in 2015–16[37]) charitable organization's promotional literature is the degree to which corporations are positioned as "helping" schools ensure the continued prosperity of our society (no pressure). "Innovative" programs are provided for students and educators to learn about leadership and networking.[38] There is also a lot of focus on building bridges, but it appears the traffic only flows one way: educators will learn to lead, students will "learn attitudes, relevant skills and are empowered to compete successfully in a complex global economy and drive Canada's continued competitive edge." Nowhere is there any discussion about what members of the business community might learn from listening to students or educators, other than some vague language about how business and education leaders can develop an understanding of each other's "roles, environments, challenges and opportunities."[39]

This type of business leadership narrative advanced by TLP underpins how corporate involvement in education is justified: public schools are responsible for ensuring our continued prosperity and lifelong civic engagement. But they cannot do it alone, and when it comes to "big-picture" issues like the global workplace and macroeconomics, we need to bring in the *real* experts with *real-world* expertise and *real-world* resources to ensure success (somehow suggesting that, left to their own devices, teachers would prefer an abacus to a tablet).

Anti-intellectualism as a political tactic is not new. John Snobelen, the minister of education under Ontario Conservative Premier Mike Harris, was famously a high school dropout who in 1995 voiced his intent to "create a crisis" in Ontario education to justify overhauling it as a cornerstone of the "Common Sense Revolution."[40] Despite significant public support for the Days of Action, which included a ten-day province-wide teachers' strike, deep funding cuts followed from which Ontario's education system has arguably not recovered. Of course, this was not limited to Ontario or even Canada, as anti-intellectualism is indicative of a much broader and more pervasive context.[41] The elevation of "Real World Experience" has become synonymous with a rising pseudo-populist distrust of intellectuals, experts, and bureaucrats. Long-time politicians (also referred to, usually derisively, as "career politicians"[42]) are routinely ridiculed for never having held a "real job."[43]

The underlying theme is the marginalizing of expertise and the elevation of "real" business experience over the "unreal" public sector, or at the very least the need for the public sector to internalize market-oriented practices to be more effective, efficient, and, ultimately, taken more seriously. In other words, schools have been enlisted in the project to reinforce the conditions that make a more pervasive corporate presence and mindset not only acceptable, but preferable, because our economic prosperity depends on it. Rather than providing a counterweight or challenge to the corporate perspective, or even to point out its contradictions, schools are expected to act (and teach, and grade)—literally—in the corporate interest. If the purpose of education is not to critique but rather to meet the needs of the market, then (logically) market "experts" must provide educators with the curriculum and coursework necessary to fulfil this new, conveniently synthesized mandate.

Financial Literacy

Public education has often been lectured about its responsibility to "meet the needs of business" since the business world is where many graduates will end up. There has also been an ongoing debate about whether the role of public education is to prepare students for the workplace, or provide them with the tools to critically evaluate assumptions and expectations about who we are and how we live. On the "real world" side, there has been a growing focus on curricular programs in Canadian schools that are explicitly designed to give students "practical" skills such as financial literacy and entrepreneurialism.

Promotion of the concept of financial literacy is not recent. The Canadian Foundation for Economic Education (CFEE) was established back in 1974 to "improve economic, financial and enterprising capability."[44] In 1998, the Bank of Montreal developed the *My Money Investment Club* educational materials, which *Jr. Jays Magazine* and Kids Club organizations in conjunction with the Canadian Association of Chiefs of Police distributed to schools across the country. The kit was designed to introduce students age eight and older to "money management and investing."[45]

But introducing school-aged kids to the concept of financial planning has become much more robust and integrated than a kit with a board game and teacher's guide that can be voluntarily used (or not) in class. In 2014, the Harper government created a national Financial Literacy Leader,[46] a position the Liberals continued when they were elected in 2015. This followed a recommendation from a 2011 task force on financial literacy, but no doubt was also a response to the widely reported increase in Canadian household debt levels, which reached 165 percent in 2013, "calling into question Bank of Canada Governor Mark Carney's assertion that families are listening to his warnings about the risks of borrowing too much."[47] The "obvious" solution: explain to Canadians already dealing with stagnant incomes and the rise of precarious work that they need additional training in how to make more money (if they can), spend less ("wants vs. needs"), and manage their finances more effectively.

And it is never too soon to start, right? Recently, the CFEE and Scotiabank partnered on "Talk With Our Kids About Money" Day (TWOKAM for short),[48] because "as more Canadians are faced with increasingly complex financial decisions at younger ages, learning the basics of money management is as important as numeracy."[49] This is not a one-off. Financial institutions are well-represented in the creation and promotion of financial literacy resources and programs both inside and outside of schools in partnership with organizations like the CFEE. The *Financial Post* recently compiled a list of financial literacy programs in each province "to get a handle on how well Canadians [well, Canadian public school students] are educated on everything from basic budgets to student loans and the stock markets."[50]

Obviously, there is nothing inherently wrong with learning about basic concepts of saving, spending, and money management. The concern, however, is that the individualistic framing of financial literacy is deeply *irresponsible* because these programs:

> promote a particular worldview in which we cannot collectively alter our economic practices; we can only modulate our individual consumption and investment, which, as if by an invisible hand, will help others ... As a public pedagogy, financial literacy education promotes a profound civic irresponsibility, limiting our obligations to others to ensuring they have a basic level of financial knowledge while delegitimizing effective and socially just collective solutions to financial insecurity.[51]

The focus here is not on structural change or collective and just remedies to a flawed economic system, but rather on individual consumerist solutions. As a result, these programs undermine the systemic change that is required to deal with and reverse financial insecurity that has been reinforced through neoliberal policies and practices. You do not eliminate student debt by teaching students how to eat less caviar, take on one more part-time job, or use single-ply toilet paper. You eliminate student debt by reversing the deep cuts to post-secondary education that started in the mid-1990s and resulted in an exponential increase in the user fees students were expected to bear.[52]

The trend towards "real-world" skills does not end with financial literacy. Schools are now expected to teach students moxie (otherwise known as entrepreneurialism) as the cure for what ails our economy, and "a must for Canada's youth, even those just starting to learn their ABCs."[53] Laura Pinto has documented what she calls the rise of the cultural myth of the entrepreneur in Canadian education, and the profound limitations of this panacea.[54] These programs have been feted as the solution to Canada's high youth unemployment rate, economically depressed regions and communities, and the "changing marketplace" young people are facing.[55] And that is not all. According to Pinto, "because small businesses represent 98% of Canadian companies, 30% GDP, and 45% of employment ... promoting entrepreneurship would result in more small businesses start-ups, higher GDP and lower unemployment."[56]

Problems solved, right? Why spend (public) money on a youth employment strategy, or a "good jobs" strategy, when schools can—as part of their role in furthering the "public interest"—reinforce the neoliberal mantra that rugged individualism, hard work, and a spirit of adventure are all students really need to ensure their, and ultimately our, economic security?

Well, not exactly. Pinto goes on to explain that this narrative conveys "a sub-myth of meritocracy" that paints an inherently inaccurate picture of what it means to be an entrepreneur, and who actually succeeds as one. High failure rates, lower pay, longer hours, and a reduced or limited access to benefits like employment insurance are conspicuously absent—or at best mentioned and then dismissed—from much of the curriculum content and available texts.[57] Furthermore, the "just work hard" mantra that pervades entrepreneurialism texts makes little to no mention of "the role of luck, and fails to acknowledge that the entrepreneur's social identity (predominantly white and male) had anything to do with their success."[58] In fact, research demonstrates that the common shared trait of entrepreneurs is: "access to financial capital—family money, an inheritance, or a pedigree and connections that allow for access to financial stability. While it seems that entrepreneurs tend to have an admirable penchant for risk, it's usually that access to money which allows them to take risks."[59] Because this context is absent from the way in which schools are expected to celebrate and teach entrepreneurialism, what is left is "roll-with-it neoliberalization," explains Pinto. As a result, "entrepreneurship curriculum encourages passive student acceptance of existing economic, labour market, and social conditions."[60]

In short, entrepreneurial education is not about doing better for all of us. It is about internalizing and individualizing all responsibility for (rare) success and (more prevalent) failure within a narrow market framework, despite all the evidence of who, exactly, our deeply inequitable system privileges and who it marginalizes. This is the corporatization of education carried to its logical conclusion, stripped of commercialism and branding, where the purpose and role of the school have been so conflated with the demands of the corporate sector that it is impossible to see where one ends and the other begins. "Good" schools prepare students to succeed, after all, not to point out flaws in the system or question the expertise of those who designed it.

Conclusion

While it is often the more visible examples of corporate intrusion into public education (Cola wars and exclusive marketing arrangements between school boards, or the previously discussed YNN) that attract attention and even outrage, that is by no means the extent of educational corporatization. If anything, it is only the (branded) tip of the neoliberal iceberg. The relentless search for new ad surfaces and new markets is synonymous with capitalism, and certainly the presence of advertising and sponsored content in public education is not new. However, its acceleration and expansion since the mid-1990s is a direct result of the rise of neoliberalism—in budgeting practices, and in mindset.

When balanced-budget rhetoric took hold at the federal and provincial levels in the 1990s, social spending became a key target. As a result, social programs and public institutions, and those who depend on them, became casualties of the neoliberal agenda. Where education was concerned, this resulted in insufficient funding and under-resourced schools, tangibly felt in overcrowded classrooms, fewer resources, delayed maintenance, and school closures. The political need to marginalize resistance to the neoliberal agenda also meant the scapegoating of teachers' unions to try and drive a wedge between the public (parents) and educators; it was often accompanied by an anti-intellectualism rooted in the belief that schools and teachers, left to their own devices, were ill-equipped to provide students with the skills and knowledge required by the workplaces of tomorrow. As a result, the "real" experts—business leaders—need to be consulted about what schools should be teaching, and what (and how) students should be learning.

Often, the corporate partner is positioned as helping schools solve a problem—underfunding, lack of books, literacy levels, teachers' time constraints—to take advantage of a growing "public concern" market, and to help mitigate some very real PR problems by donning the mantle of corporate social responsibility. Where priorities such as financial literacy and entrepreneurialism are concerned, however, the school itself has been enlisted in the goal of naturalizing (on behalf of the marketplace and financial and political elites) the ways in which neoliberalism has reinforced socio-economic inequality, telling students that they (and they alone) are responsible for how they respond to it. Collective solutions—a more progressive system of taxation, sustained funding for universal programs, a comprehensive anti-poverty strategy—are not up for consideration.

The school provides a silent and implicit endorsement of the messages and products associated with it, which is a key incentive for corporations anxious to access a lucrative target audience or associate themselves with a well-respected community institution as part of a PR strategy. But when educational goals are conflated with corporate priorities, and when educators are expected to defer to corporate expertise about what "the market" requires, the implications for the public good are compounded. Far from being in opposition to neoliberalism, the school is reconfigured as being the instrument, wielded by well-intentioned corporate supporters and benefactors, through which the requirements of neoliberalism will be fulfilled. Doing "well" in school becomes synonymous with doing well "for" neoliberalism—as consumers (directly or by parental proxy) of corporate products; as workers in corporate firms; and as boosters of free market ideology through internalized principles like "entrepreneurialism" and "sound financial investment."

Context, though, is key: household debt levels are at record-highs, 50 percent of working Canadians say they are living paycheque to paycheque, and precarious or insecure work has increased by 50 percent in the past twenty years in Hamilton and the Greater Toronto area.[61] The solutions to these problems go beyond "working harder" and "saving more"; they require broad economic policy at the political level, not teaching students self-starter-ism or how to design a balance sheet. But systemic critique of the current economic system and the collective solutions required to address its flaws have no place in the corporatized school, which is positioned as being responsible for national economic stability as well as inculcating in students the desire to succeed in a capitalist economy. This means that, rather than opening-up opportunities to critique the current system and propose alternatives to it, the school becomes complicit in shutting down analysis that potentially undermines the corporate agenda.

The outcome of corporatizing education goes beyond branding, beyond handouts, and beyond exclusive marketing to classrooms and captive student audiences. It is also, at its most effective and most insidious, about encouraging "partnerships" designed to allow corporate leaders to "help" education leaders learn how to better meet the country's economic needs, and teach students accordingly. It has resulted in a "shift in value priorities away from universalism, equity, security and resilience towards efficiency and individualism,"[62] where the school has been enlisted to naturalize Boot-strap Theory 101, under the guise of educating the next generation of leaders.

Carbon Capital and Corporate Influence

Mapping Elite Networks of Corporations, Universities, and Research Institutes[1]

William K. Carroll, Nicolas Graham, and Zoë Yunker

Introduction

Corporations have for many years exercised influence within Canadian universities, but since the 1980s their influence has broadened and deepened alongside trends in declining state funding.[2] Proponents of this shift justify university "corporatization" as good business logic in an increasingly competitive economic environment, but critics point to dangers in business's largely unchecked access to the academic arena.[3] Under the auspices of "academic capitalism," the goal posts of the academic institution have shifted towards profit-making. According to Jamie Brownlee, this reflects a cultural transformation spreading throughout academia, as course offerings, research funding, hiring, and enrolment "are assessed less in terms of academic criteria and more on whether or not they represent good business decisions."[4] Recent studies in North America have confirmed that corporate research funding and industry representation on academic governance boards can profoundly influence the direction and scope of research undertaken within the academy, sacrificing academic freedom and integrity.[5] When industry directs scientific research, rather than allowing the academic community to do so through peer review processes, "scientific horizons shrink" and knowledge that may portend alternative futures is diminished.[6]

Our focus in this chapter is on a specific sector of corporate capital—the carbon-extractive industries—and one specific vector of influence: the interlocks that link directorates of corporations with the governance boards of universities and research institutes. As a core sector of the Canadian economy, carbon capital has much to gain from its relationship with academia.[7] In a tangible sense, universities offer access to expert information tailored to corporate interests through funded and directed research projects.[8] By embedding itself in the university, industry can externalize their research costs, appropriating the institution's resources and talent at a fraction of what they would incur on their own. A corporation's alignment with universities can also carry legitimating benefits: when fossil fuel companies are represented at the helm of Canadian universities, they gain a privileged position from which to shape debates around climate change policy, sanctioning the continued (and often accelerated) use of fossil fuels. Facing an uphill battle to maintain social license amidst a rapidly changing climate, carbon capital is simultaneously able to draw on the veneer of academic prestige provided by its ties to higher education, polishing its reputation by employing the language of scientific validation, while cultivating a policy environment favourable to extractive interests.[9]

Here we explore the influence of carbon-extractive industries on university governance boards as an instance of corporatization. In contrast to privatization, which implies the outsourcing of state services to private capital, corporatization implies a renewed role for the state as an indispensable tool for advancing capital accumulation. The corporatized university offers an illuminating case: as carbon capital reaches into the academic sphere, it institutionalizes a "new climate denialism,"[11] whereby the climate crisis is acknowledged while effective climate action is forestalled in favour of increased fossil fuel production. The new denialism features policies that appear to be credible responses to the scientific consensus on climate change but do not hurt carbon capital—the most prevalent of these being the pursuit of more efficient carbon extraction and consumption, new technologies that reduce emissions, and policies to incent incremental change.[12] In mapping corporate linkages to academia, this chapter identifies sites where business influence over knowledge and research obstructs the shift towards a low-carbon future. We begin by providing an overview of directorate interlocks between carbon capital, universities, and research institutes. Next, we examine how research institutes in our sample interlock both with each other and with core fossil fuel firms. Finally, our analysis identifies a tightly woven, *carbon-centred scientific-industrial complex* emerging from the network of Alberta-based schools and their corporate ties, and highlights key locations within this complex where the reach of industry is unmistakable.

Mapping Carbon Capital's Reach
into Universities and Research Institutes

As Naomi Klein has argued, the increasing risks of runaway climate change now pit capitalism against the climate, with fossil fuel corporations and their allies on the front lines of a high-stakes ideological struggle.[13] In the context of these challenges, carbon capital's role in corporatizing universities and their research merits close scrutiny. We map the network of interlocking directorates through which carbon capital's influence enters the governance of universities and research institutes. Elite interlocks are a critical vector enabling industry's reach into academia, but corporatization, as intimated above, is also significantly bolstered by industry funding of academic research. The growing presence of corporate funding in universities is closely tied to shifts in government spending; in 1979, roughly 84 percent of funding for universities came from government, whereas by 2009 the percentage had dropped to 58 percent.[14] As government revenue streams decline and administrative budgets soar, universities are increasingly managed as entrepreneurial institutions, and corporate influence over the terms of the university-business relationship deepens. At the same time, as higher education is adjusted to the tune of neoliberal political economy, corporatization is galvanized from *within* the university.[15] Amidst a culture of entrepreneurialism and academic capitalism, institutions, departments, and faculty members are increasingly called on to maximize the university's revenues through research endeavours, and large injections of capital realized through corporate-university partnerships are welcomed as supports for academic achievement.

Representation on university governing boards operates in tandem with funding relations, enabling corporations to shape the agendas of university research in ways that mesh with corporate business strategies.[16] In contrast to a university's senate, where faculty members manage largely internal academic decisions such as scholarships and educational programming, a university's governing board is tasked with managing institutional resources and advancing the school's external relationships—giving it a considerable degree of influence over the school's positioning within civil society.[17] As the directors and executives of corporations participate in the governance of these institutions, their voices and values shape academic and research priorities, including the creation of programs sympathetic to the interests of carbon capital. Corporate representation thus creates a platform from which elite networking and consensus-building can take place. By mapping these networks, we reveal part of the social architecture of corporatization.

To represent the carbon-extractive corporate sector we selected 238 corporations in this industry, each based in Canada with 2014 assets of at least $50 million. To represent the academic/research sector we chose forty-six post-secondary institutions and schools and sixteen research institutes. Since the carbon-extractive sector is centred in western Canada, we prioritized the inclusion of western-based post-secondaries. Ten universities in the three western-most provinces were selected, along with four western-based polytechnic schools. Recognizing that corporate interests are particularly invested in sectors of post-secondary education that contribute directly to the world of business, we also included seven western-based business schools, two engineering schools, and the University of Calgary's School of Public Policy. Each of these schools has its own advisory board, potentially linking its governance practices into the corporate elite network. The other twenty-six post-secondaries in our sample include all non-western "research" and "comprehensive" universities listed in the 2016 *Maclean's* magazine University Ranking Survey.[18] For research institutes, our concern with the carbon-extractive corporate resource sector led us to include sixteen institutes whose mandates bear upon carbon extraction, plus the Canadian Foundation for Innovation and the Saskatchewan Research Council. These institutes are based in Calgary (five), Edmonton (five), other western-Canadian cities (four), and Ottawa (two).

Our sample echoes an emerging body of research identifying business schools housed within major Canadian universities as leading the charge in academic corporatization.[19] Indeed, while markers of corporatization extend throughout the disciplines, business schools are strikingly forthright about maintaining close ties to capital. From corporate-funded research chairs to campus buildings titled after prominent benefactors, the willingness of business schools to align with corporate capital grounds an academic culture where corporatization is accepted as a standard rule of practice.[20] These industry relationships generate a considerable amount of revenue, often outstripping the funding received through other institutional channels.[21] Faculty compensation is also often significantly higher.[22] This locates business schools at the vanguard of university corporatization, consolidating the internal pressure to corporatize by diffusing profit-oriented academic policy throughout the larger, more traditionally structured university.

To carry out our analysis, we gathered data on the names of the directors or governors of these sixty-two academic/research organizations and the directors and top executives of the 238 carbon-extractive corporations, as of year-end 2015.[23] Our interest was in identifying the organizations and individuals that participate in interlocking. A total of fifty-three individuals are networkers; i.e., they have multiple affiliations that include positions on university and research-institute boards. While thirty-seven of these are carbon-capital directors and executives, sixteen have no corporate affiliations in the carbon sector but have multiple affiliations with the university and research organizations. The affiliations of these fifty-three persons pull thirty-seven carbon-sector firms, fourteen universities, and eleven research institutes into an elite governance network, with a particularly high rate of participation among the research institutes. Although thirty-two of the forty-six post-secondary institutions do not engage in interlocking with other organizations in our sample, seven of eleven based in Alberta participate, as do two of five based in Saskatchewan. All but two of the corporations participating in the network are based in Calgary, underlining the centrality of that city to the carbon-extractive sector and its elite network, which is known to be highly integrated.[24]

Fully fifty-one of the sixty-two academic/research organizations belong to a single connected network, indicating that interlocks create a basis for elite cohesion among carbon-capital business leaders and others involved in university and research-institute governance. However, some organizations are far more integral to the network than others. On average, each organization is interlocked with three others, but nineteen of them have only one interlock while eighteen have two. At the other end of the centrality curve, five organizations share directors with at least eight other organizations, participating in forty-five of the 186 interlocks that knit the corporations and academic/research organizations together. Pride of place goes to Haskayne School of Business at the University of Calgary, with twelve interlocks, and the Edmonton-based Alberta Innovates-Technology Futures interlocks with nine organizations. The University of Calgary and its School of Public Policy each participate in eight interlocks, as does the Edwards School of Business at the University of Saskatchewan (U of S). These five academic and research organizations, all of them based in Alberta or Saskatchewan, pull the other organizations into a connected network. When the five are removed from the network it breaks into ten pieces, the largest of which contains eighteen organizations. And as Figure 3 shows below, the five most prominent organizations are surrounded by a host of carbon-extractive corporations, indicating the extensive participation of corporate directors and executives on the governance boards of these public institutions. Given that Alberta and Saskatchewan are far and away the two heaviest per capita emitters in Canada, their academic/research ties to carbon capital are not incidental. As the oil industry struggles to sustain social license in a policy environment increasingly attuned to climate change issues, its reach into focal sites of knowledge production suggests a strategic attempt at self-preservation.

Below, we investigate further by focusing on the elite individuals who carry the network and their affiliations. We first analyze affiliations with academic institutions and research institutes, followed by an examination of the carbon-centred scientific-industrial complex that is comprised of key university and research organizations with extensive ties to industry, based for the most part in Alberta.

University Governance and Corporate Elite

Figure 1 shows the network of university and carbon-capital elite affiliations. Individuals are depicted as squares, organizations as circles (with corporations coloured black and academic organizations light grey). The size of each node is proportionate to the centrality of the organization or individual within the network. We pay particular attention to academic boards bearing numerous ties to the fossil fuel sector—sites of carbon capital's selective, strategic reach into Canadian academia. As noted above, most of these ties are found within business schools that operate semi-autonomously from their host universities, as well as the University of Calgary School of Public Policy (U of C SPP). The U of C SPP—both a graduate school offering Masters degrees and a prominent neoliberal policy institute whose website boasts fifty peer-reviewed papers yearly—has seven carbon-capital firms represented on its board through four individuals. The SPP benefits from its host university's reputation for scholarship and independent research while simultaneously promoting a neoliberal ideology that trumpets the importance of the oil industry (discussed below).[25]

One of the SPP's key elite networkers, Nancy Southern, scion of the family that owns ATCO and Canadian Utilities (CAN_UTIL), sits on four carbon-capital boards. The U of C SPP's board is further linked to Arc Resources (ARC_RES) through Herbert Pinder (president of a Saskatoon-based private equity firm and a Fraser Institute Trustee) and Tim Hearn (retired president and CEO of Imperial Oil and former chairman of the C.D. Howe Institute).

Linking the School of Public Policy to Saskatoon-based Edwards School of Business (E_SB) is Daniel Halyk, who sits on both boards and is founding CEO of Calgary-based Total Energy Services (TOTAL_SR). The Edwards School represents a key node of fossil fuel influence in the university network. Its namesake alone is indicative: in 2007, the school was renamed after billionaire Murray Edwards.[27] Edwards' interests include over $1.3 billion in holdings in Canadian

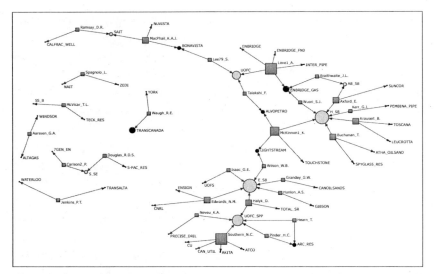

Figure 1: The network of affiliations with carbon-capital corporations and universities.[26]

Natural Resources, and large shares of Ensign Energy and Imperial Metals, among others. Edwards is the executive chair at Canadian Natural Resources Limited, and holds directorships in such nationally oriented elite organizations as the Business Council of Canada and the C.D. Howe Institute.[28] On the main floor of the school, the "Murray Edwards Stock Ticker" commemorates a donation from Edwards in 2002. Close by is the Murray Edwards Case Room, established through a donation in 2000.[29]

Murray Edwards sits among other oil elites on the Edwards School's Dean's Advisory Council, an "elite community of members" whose membership is secured solely through large donations to the school. Daphne Taras, the council's founder, explained that "Dean's Circle members have a true relationship with the Edwards School of Business," suggesting that Dean's Circle members are privy to elite influence within the university on a pay-per-seat basis.[30] Dean's Circle members carry ties to six major fossil fuel companies and to the U of S Board of Governors.

W. Brett Wilson, a Dean's Circle member at Edwards (and former panelist on CBC's hit show *Dragon's Den*), is also principal shareholder and a director of Lightstream Resources, which is chaired by Kenneth McKinnon, a carbon-capital networker who also helps govern the Haskayne School of Business (H_SB) at the University of Calgary. Lauded by *Canadian Business* magazine as the "go-to school for students eager to work in the energy industry," Haskayne is the most central institution in the university network, with ten carbon-capital corporations linked into its board through six well-connected board members.[31] Pipeline giant Enbridge—the largest pipeline and energy infrastructure company in North America—is represented on Haskayne's Management Advisory Council by Stephen Wuori, president of Liquids, Pipelines and Major Projects.[32] Another Haskayne Council member, Eric Axford, is executive vice-president of Suncor (and Suncor's representative on the board of the Canadian Association of Petroleum Producers), but also serves as a senator at U of C and on the Advisory Council at the Alberta School of Business (AB_SB).[33] Enbridge is also represented on the Council by J. Lorne Braithwaite, a shopping-centre magnate who has been an Enbridge director since 1989 and additionally serves on the Advisory Board of the Ivey School of Business at Western University in London, Ontario (not shown in the sociogram).

Affiliations with Enbridge also lead to the University of Calgary's governance board via Interpipeline Corp (INTER_PIPE) chair, Alison Love. In addition, the U of C's board includes directors of mid-sized oil companies, such as Firoz Talakshi, who sits with Kenneth McKinnon on the Alvopetro board, and Sue Lee, formerly senior vice-president at Suncor and now a director of Bonavista Energy. Keith McPhail, another Bonavista board member, also sits on the board of the Southern Alberta Institute of Technology (SAIT), one of Alberta's largest polytechnic institutes that boasts of its "close partnerships with industry."[34]

Beyond this connected configuration of Alberta- and Saskatchewan-based schools, eastern- and BC-based universities populate the small, disconnected netlets on the left of the sociogram. At York University, Rick Waugh chairs the board of governors while serving on the board of TransCanada Corporation, the principal for the Energy East pipeline proposal.[35] British Columbia's academic landscape is peripheral to the larger university network, but Tracey McVicar's affiliations link Vancouver-based mining giant Teck Resources (TECK_RES) to UBC's Sauder School of Business (SS_B). McVicar also sits on the board of the Fraser Institute and was, until 2015, a director of BC Hydro. With extensive coal, zinc, and copper mining operations throughout the province, Teck Resources has a strategic interest in exerting influence within BC's academic and climate policy-focused institutions.

Drawing on a total sample of forty-six institutions, the seven universities and schools mentioned above show particularly close ties to carbon capital. Within these sites, the carbon-extractive industry is well positioned to shape carbon-friendly research environments, while benefitting from the university's historic position as a site of social legitimation.

Research Institutes

Research institutes knit together university researchers, state officials and corporate directors, helping to form an elite governance network. The institutes in our sample produce knowledge that bears upon the operations of carbon capital, but they also direct the flow of public funding for scientific and technological research and development. As noted earlier, several of the research institutes in our sample interlock with each other, as well as with the carbon-extractive sector (see Figure 2). Prominent in this network are Alberta-based research and development organizations, Alberta Innovates-Technology Futures (AITF) and Alberta Innovates-Energy and Environment Solutions (AIEES). The main function of these institutes, which were created in 2010 by the government of Alberta but operate at arm's length, is to fund and facilitate applied research and development and to assist in commercializing research discoveries. Both AITF and AIEES are governed by boards of directors that participate in the allocation of funding and, as we find, are interlocked extensively with the fossil fuel sector.[36] The AITF alone is directly connected to five fossil fuel companies. Three of these ties are carried by the ubiquitous Ken McKinnon. The chair of AITF, Judy Fairburn, is also executive vice-president of oil major Cenovus Energy and a director of Ottawa-based Sustainable Development Technology Canada. Corporate representation at AIEES includes Enbridge director Charles Fischer and Margaret Byl

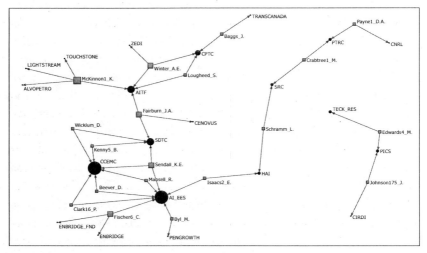

Figure 2: The network of affiliations with carbon-capital corporations and research institutes.[37]

of Pengrowth Energy. As we see in Figure 2, additional corporate interlocks with research institutes are carried by TransCanada Executive Vice-President James Baggs (a director at the Canadian Pipeline Technology Collaborative (CPTC), which partners with AIEES to co-ordinate and fund innovation in the pipeline sector) and David Payne, who directs both Canadian Natural Resources (CNRL) and Regina's Petroleum Technology Research Centre (PTRC).

Carbon capital's efforts to embed itself in "energy institutes" that have pro-liferated with the deepening climate crisis are evidenced at the University of Victoria's Pacific Institute for Climate Science (PICS), shown on the right of the sociogram. PICS's mandate is to undertake research on the impacts of climate change and develop and promote mitigation and adaptation policies. Beyond its connection to the Canadian International Resources and Development Institute (CIRDI), PICS is relatively isolated from the network of research institutes, but its advisory board includes Mark Edwards, director of coal giant Teck Resources—an environmental award-winning corporation *and* a major carbon polluter.[38]

In addition to these corporate ties, research institutes also interlock extensively with each other, forming a networked research infrastructure supporting carbon extraction, especially in Alberta but also on a national basis. AIEES, for example, shares three directors with the Climate Change and Emissions Management Corporation (CCEMC)—an Alberta-based and provincially funded organization that works as a research funding steering committee directed at reducing emis-sions and improving the energy efficiency of carbon-extractive development.[39] AITF, AIEES, and CPTC all share directors with Ottawa's Sustainable Development Technology Canada (SDTC), a foundation that is partly funded by the govern-ment of Canada and finances Canada's "clean tech" sector—especially innova-tions focused on addressing issues of climate change, clean air, water quality, and soil. While some of these interlocking research-institute directors do not hold current positions in carbon-capital firms, their other affiliations, past and present, mark them as influential networkers in the world of corporate capital, often involving "revolving door" relations between corporations and government agencies, boards, and commissions. Kathleen Sendall, for example, who directs AIEES, CPTC, and SDTC, also directs French-based geosciences and information technology corporation CGG and was formerly chair of the Canadian Association of Petroleum Producers. Dan Wicklum of CCEMC and SDTC is CEO of Canada's Oil Sands Innovation Alliance—an industry association that co-ordinates techno-logical development—and has previously held senior positions at Environment Canada and Natural Resources Canada. Brenda Kenny, also of CCEMC and SDTC, stands out as a key networker. Beyond her research-institute affiliations, she sits on the board of governors of the University of Calgary and was president and CEO of the Canadian Energy Pipeline Association—a group representing Canada's transmission pipeline companies—from 2008 to 2015.[40]

By participating in the governance of research institutes, carbon capital is strategically positioned to influence the flow of public funds for research and innovation. The sector's funding of and participation in the governance of university-based institutes serves a further legitimation function. It helps contain potential sources of opposition from these institutions while allowing business to oversee climate policy and technology research within an academic context that offers a veneer of arm's length, scientific prestige.

Mapping Fossil Knowledge Networks in Alberta

When we examine the academic and research organizations that interlock with big carbon, we find a *carbon-centred scientific-industrial complex*—a densely connected network of research institutions based primarily in Alberta that are extensively tied to carbon capital. Our findings complement recent political-ecological analyses that view Alberta as a first world "petro-state."[41] In such states, a carbon-intensive economic structure and heavy reliance on oil rents has far-reaching implications for knowledge production, powerfully shaping research infrastructures and priorities. Indeed, in regions like Alberta, the immense pressure put on higher education and research organizations by carbon capital has led to concerns about research and university "capture" by the fossil fuel industry.[42]

To simplify the presentation, Figure 3 displays the interlocks, leaving aside the individuals whose multiple affiliations create them. All told, ten universities and schools, eight research institutes, and thirty-two carbon-extractive firms participate in this connected component. The size of each organization's node is proportionate to the centrality of the organization within the network; the thickness of a line indicates the number of shared directors between a pair of organizations.

The dual Alberta Innovates institutes are again central in this network, along with the Haskayne and Alberta business schools, the University of Calgary, and the Ottawa-based Sustainable Development Technology Canada. The Enbridge group of companies is a corporate focal point, with several elite ties into university governance in Alberta. Saskatoon-based Edwards School of Business is linked to the research institutes only indirectly, through interlocks with Lightstream Resources, Canadian Natural Resources, and Ensign. The University of Calgary's School of Public Policy interlocks with the Edwards School but is detached from

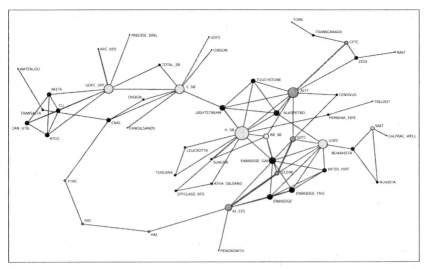

Figure 3: Interlocking directorates in the carbon-centred scientific-industrial complex.[43]

the other academic and research bodies, although it interlocks extensively with a host of Alberta-based carbon-extractive firms. The interlocks that link carbon firms into universities are found primarily in business schools as well as the U of C School of Public Policy. This enables industry to shape key sites of business and policy development through both the socialization of budding managers and the policy perspectives they and others take up, especially on issues of energy. Below, we highlight some of the practices of corporatization at key sites in and around the University of Calgary, arguably ground zero for carbon capital's influence on ostensibly "public" institutions.

The University of Calgary School of Public Policy (U OF C_SPP) provides a clear example of the impacts of this influence. The school was founded in 2008 through a $4 million donation from James Palmer, a well-connected oil and gas lawyer who formerly lobbied on behalf of Exxon Mobil and Imperial Oil. Besides its numerous elite interlocks, described previously, SPP's porous relationship with carbon-sector interests can be read through its research and academic program offerings. The "National Infrastructure and Market Access Program," launched in 2015, "investigates the feasibility" of installing pipeline routes from east to west as well as through a northern route—shipping oil to the Arctic Ocean through the Northwest Territories. Meanwhile, its "Extractive Resource Governance" program aims to "provide policy education and analysis to regions with newly discovered or evolving extractive industries."[44]

In fact, the U OF C_SPP is much more than an academic unit; it is a neo-liberal think tank embedded within a research university. Among ongoing initiatives, it convenes the behind-the-scenes Canadian Network for Energy Policy Research and Analysis (CNEPRA), a forum that brings together prominent academics from around the country to advance energy policy research. CNEPRA is funded by the Energy Council of Canada, an industry association with board ties to the Canadian Association of Petroleum Producers (CAPP), the Canadian Gas Association, and the Canadian Energy Pipeline Association, among others. CNEPRA hosts conferences whose themes match its major annual research initiatives. Its 2015 conference focused on helping "regulators and the energy sector understand and manage the social license phenomena threatening the energy industry,"[45] perhaps one of the most important strategic issues of concern for carbon capital. The conference was followed by a white paper advising governments to lean on the regulator to defuse controversy, further advocating steps to bolster the appearance of more comprehensive consultation processes in order to gain social acceptance for energy project approvals.[46] Another report counseled governments to minimize controversy around energy projects by communicating the issues through strategic frames of economic self-interest and national security.[47]

As shown in Figure 3, the Haskayne School of Business (H_SB) is a key site for carbon capital's strategic reach into academia. Its oil-drenched board helps explain its fleetness in navigating the shifting landscape of climate change denial. Its "Global Energy Executive MBA" program, initiated in 2015, shows an acute awareness of the challenges ahead for oil and gas, promising to prepare students to manage the "escalating demand imbalances and political instability in key energy producing regions and ever-increasing scrutiny from a diverse array of stakeholders."[48] The program was launched through a $1 million donation from the institution's namesake, Richard F. Haskayne—former chair of TransCanada Corporation—and is currently funded by Arc Resources and Talisman Energy.[49] The Haskayne School reports that most of the program's students hold executive positions in the oil and gas industry, and alumni include the Senior VP of Cenovus, Drew Zieglgansberger, and Senior VP of Kiewit Energy Group, Dan Lumma.[50] Its instructors include Daniel Yergin, who sits on the US Secretary of Energy Advisory Board and formerly chaired the US Department of Energy's Task Force on Strategic Energy Research and Development.[51] Oil and gas companies frequently host field visits at Haskayne; indeed, the school encourages corporations to sponsor the $105,000 tuition for particularly promising staff, guaranteeing to "deliver a return on your investment" by increasing the value of personnel viewed as human capital.[52]

Housed within the Haskayne School is the Centre for Corporate Sustainability (CCS), a research institute whose operations are significantly shaped by industry. The CCS—originally called the Enbridge Centre for Corporate Sustainability—was launched in 2011 with a $1.25 million donation from the company.[53] Controversy emerged when faculty members spoke out against Enbridge's attempts to shape inter-university partnerships to bolster their flagging reputation in US markets, while exerting influence over student selection and award processes. Following its renaming, the school has largely removed itself from the spotlight, but continues to create and disseminate knowledge and policy recommendations pertaining to the Canadian energy sector. It addresses key business and environmental challenges faced by industry, including policies surrounding corporate social responsibility and the reduction of carbon emissions. Directing research at CCS is an "external advisory board" that includes carbon-capital executives such as Linda Coady (Chief Sustainability Officer at Enbridge), Neil Symington (Senior Advisor of Sustainable Integration at Suncor Energy), and John Van Ham (Manager of Environment and Sustainable Development Oil Sands at ConocoPhillips Canada).[55] In addition to corporate advisors, and the initial donation from Enbridge, CCS receives ongoing sponsorship and funding from a host of fossil fuel firms, including ConocoPhillips, Nexen Energy, Shell Canada, Chevron Canada, and British Petroleum.[56] The centre funds undergraduate, graduate, post-doctorate, and faculty research, and grants for research projects are sponsored by industry (including the Enbridge Sustainability Scholarship and the Suncor Energy Postdoctoral Fellowship), as are seminars and outreach efforts, such as the ConocoPhillips IRIS Seminar Series.[57]

Beyond shaping business practices and policy, the fossil fuel sector is helping to guide the agendas of the hard sciences, producing technological and scientific research that is directly applied to the carbon extraction process. Five out of eight university-based research institutes in our sample are in Alberta. In comparison to business schools and policy institutes, these organizations are less integrated into the network of interlocking directors. Corporatization in this field tends to be driven more by the funding of applied research.[58]

In the face of mounting pressures to respond to the extractive industry's environmental impacts, fossil fuel corporations increasingly fund technological and scientific research aimed at lowering the costs of production *and* reducing the environmental impact of fossil fuel extraction and transport. This is seen, for example, at the U of C's Consortium for Heavy Oil Research by University Scientists. The consortium is an "oil industrial sponsored program," located in the Geology/Geophysics/Petroleum Engineering Departments.[59] It conducts research on the geological aspects of reservoir production, engineering, and simulation, and aims to develop technologies that simultaneously maximize the production and energy efficiency of extraction from heavy oil fields. Industry sponsors include ConocoPhillips, Nexen Energy, Shell Canada, British Petroleum, Japan Oil and Gas, Chevron Canada, and Kuwait Oil.[60] Similarly—and also at the U of C—the Hydrocarbon Metagenomics Lab conducts exploratory research surrounding the potential to harness naturally occurring organisms and bio-processes present in Canada's tar sands, oilfields, and coal beds in an effort to decrease the environmental impact of carbon extraction. While not governed by an advisory board, it also receives funding from a host of fossil fuel companies, including ConocoPhillips, Encana, Nexen, ARC Resources, Quick Silver Resources, Shell Canada, Suncor, Syncrude, and Trident Exploration.[61]

Development of reputedly "clean technologies" constitutes a dominant approach to reducing greenhouse gas emissions. While some research funding in this area comes directly from industry, it is also publicly subsidized. The Hydrocarbon Metagenomics Lab, for example, receives funding from the Canada Foundation for Innovation—a research-institute and funding body created by the government of Canada, but which operates as an independent, non-governmental entity.[62] AIEES, whose board of directors includes a number of representatives from the fossil fuel sector, is also listed as a sponsor/funder for the Canadian Centre for Clean Coal.[63] Meanwhile, the Centre for Intelligent Mining Systems and the Helmholtz-Alberta Initiative receive funding from the government of Alberta.[64] While investment in technology to achieve greater efficiency in carbon extraction and reduce the carbon footprint of fossil fuels has a practical benefit for the environment, the effectiveness of this approach is limited: these initiatives are not intended to reduce hydrocarbon dependence, nor are they capable of doing so. Masquerading as credible responses to the climate crisis, they instead serve to legitimize continued expansion of carbon extraction. The ongoing public subsidization of such research, especially in Alberta—and the comparative failure to invest in alternative, green initiatives—suits the interests of big carbon.[65]

The carbon-centred scientific-industrial complex identified above reveals the social architecture through which carbon capital exerts continuous pressure on higher education and research organizations. This complex is consistent with (and further entrenches) "petro-state" priorities and imperatives. Indeed, carbon capital's reach into academic and research organizations has far-reaching implications for those working to challenge existing models of fossil-based economic development and to advance alternatives.

Conclusion

Working within a quickly moving field of university corporatization, carbon capital is reshaping the operational and cultural boundaries of academia. As fossil fuel companies quietly oversee climate policy and technology research, the public—helping to foot the bill for research that exacerbates the climate crisis—pays twice. The guiding principles of the "new climate denialism" are simple: climate change science is topically acknowledged without substantially addressing the root problem, which is rising carbon emissions.[66] As the impact of climate change becomes increasingly apparent, this denialism gains pace. Global carbon trading markets and technological innovations to "green" the tar sands help populate a field of new policy tools that enable carbon capital to "talk the talk" of climate policy while continuing to increase fossil fuel production. In Canada's business schools and research institutes, these complicated but ultimately inadequate policy responses are legitimized through academic affiliation. The situation in Canada, while deeply concerning, is not exceptional. A recent study of carbon capital's influence at leading American universities concludes: "Fossil fuel interests—oil, gas, and coal companies, fossil-fueled utilities, and fossil fuel investors—have colonized nearly every nook and cranny of energy and climate policy research in American universities, and much of energy science too. And they have done so quietly, without the general public's knowledge."[67]

However, our research also shows that the university cannot be read as a homogenous entity. Some schools—and even departments and programs within schools—reflect distinct cultural terrains that shape differential patterns of corporatized practice. One of the most controversial forms of corporatization—the transfusion of market values into the public sphere—is highly contingent on a university's institutional culture, which shapes normative expectations around the ethics of corporate ties. These cultures exist as moving targets rather than discrete policies. Business schools, often the most advanced sites of "hybrid" private-public partnership, are a harbinger of what may come if the trend towards corporatization continues on its current path. Our analysis calls for further research to expose the threats that elite networks and private research funding pose to academic integrity. In the context of the unfolding climate crisis, this work will support a deeper understanding of the reach of carbon capital into civil and political society—a reach that inhibits the just transition to sustainable energy that is vitally needed.

5

International Students as a Market in Canadian Public Education

Larry Kuehn

Introduction

On the night of the November 2016 US election, the University of British Columbia reported that its web section on international students received 30,000 hits. Presumably, many of these hits were from potential international students concerned about how they would be welcomed in a Trump-ruled America. In the corporatized context of educational marketing, this could be seen as a competitive advantage for Canada. The idea of competitive advantage fits well with the promotion and growth of Canadian public education as a commodity in the international marketplace, as the dominance of neoliberal policies emphasizing cost-savings, budget reductions, and austerity has led institutions to seek alternative sources of revenue. At the post-secondary level, colleges and universities are encouraged to seek grants from private corporations, frequently with directions attached to their use. At all levels of education, tuition from international students and international programs makes up a growing proportion of budgetary resources available to Canadian schools and universities. Both corporate influence and government policy have pushed educational institutions to make academic programs subservient to preparing workers for the global economy and providing service functions for the corporate marketplace.

This chapter explores one aspect of the corporatization of education in Canada—the transformation of education as a globally traded commodity. Through processes of commodification, where students (redefined as customers or consumers) are transformed into revenue-generating goods, the growing market for international students has helped to transform educational institutions into corporate-like actors. As part of this process, public education providers are increasingly behaving like private companies, mimicking business discourse and adopting market-oriented styles and practices. I outline the global institutional framework within which an international market for education has emerged, and show how Canadian educational institutions have reframed their mandates to attract new revenue streams via international student recruitment. This includes altering institutional priorities to both attract international students to attend schools in Canada, and roll out international schools abroad that are managed by Canadian institutions. For the purposes of this chapter, a case study of British Columbia is used to examine the issue of international students as a business enterprise and the corporatization of Canadian education more broadly.

Education as a Global Commodity

Historically, education has been seen as an essential element of nation-building, aiming to establish and cultivate a national citizenry, with a secondary objective of training young people for employment within the local economy. Globalization presents a challenge to this nation-centred view, as increasingly education is framed as preparing youth for competition in the global economy and education itself is seen as a globally tradeable commodity. When viewed as a tradeable commodity, education is the product and the international student (or their parents) is the customer. A 2016 Global Affairs Canada report states that

> total annual expenditure of international students including their visiting families and friends, contributed almost $11.4 billion to economic activities in Canada in 2014 ... The amount of overall annual spending by international students translates to 122,700 jobs (equivalent to 104,100 FTE) supported in the Canadian economy ... Canada's international education services ($11.4 billion) amount to 11% of Canada's total service exports to the world, and are equivalent to 2.2% of Canada's total merchandise exports.[1]

The conception of education as a commodity has been established in global trade negotiations and agreements. Before the last quarter century, international trade was thought of primarily as exchanges of goods. However, as advanced capitalist economies have matured, services such as education have challenged the production of manufactured commodities as key economic activities. Developing countries have also seen services increase as a share of their economies, becoming potential markets for global corporations. In this context, trade agreements came to focus on rules around what constitutes services and how they could be commodified and traded. The World Trade Organization (WTO) has adopted a definition of trade in services, including education, which is centred around commodification and commercialization. Unnoticed by most, this was formulated in the WTO's General Agreement on Trade in Services (GATS) that applied to all its members when the organization was created in the mid-1990s.[2] Education was also covered in multilateral and regional trade agreements beginning with the North American Free Trade Agreement in 1994 (unless it was explicitly excluded). Generally speaking, these trade agreements have been negotiated by trade officials and corporate lawyers who have little direct experience in the specific service areas now included, and education officials were not involved in the process of creating these agreements.

How could inclusion in this trade regime make a difference to education? A central assumption of these agreements is one of transnational rights to compete for the service products. A nation does not have the right to adopt rules that exclude foreign entities from competing in offering services, unless a restriction was reserved when the agreement was negotiated. Even if, in a few cases, countries try to block foreign businesses, this represents a sharp break from the conception of education as informing citizenship, maintaining national identity, and improving the health and well-being of the general population. Three major trade agreements under consideration today would further limit the ability of governments to protect services such as education from foreign corporate competition: the Canada-European Union Comprehensive Economic and Trade Agreement (CETA), the Trans-Pacific Partnership (TPP), and the Trade in Services Agreement (TiSA). All of these agreements have been negotiated in secret, with terms available to the public through Wikileaks.[3]

While education may not be the central concern of these trade agreements, that could change. Indeed, public educational institutions are already restructuring themselves along corporate lines in order to enter into trading relationships. Universities, for example, have created departments to assist in claiming patents and turning publicly funded research into for-profit companies that are expected to compete in the global marketplace. As well, digital technologies aimed at all aspects of education are expanding, including learning resources, online education, learning management systems, assessments and testing, and e-portfolios. Venture capital is investing heavily in these technologies. As a result, education has become the most significant area of non-privatized government expenditures that corporations want opened up to global competition. One transnational corporation in particular, Pearson Education, is seeking to become the leading global education provider, branding itself as "the world's learning company."[4] Pearson markets in all areas of education and has contracts with the Organisation for Economic Co-operation and Development (OECD) to define the frameworks of the PISA (Program for International Student Assessment) exams. PISA exam results now influence education policy and marketing on a global scale. They have become a de facto international standard for defining educational quality among the seventy-plus countries now using the exams. According to the OECD, these tests are a measure of how successful national economies are in preparing students for the global economy. Corporate influence in framing the content of the PISA exams provides direction on how national education systems should define and sell "success" in this regard.

Corporatizing International Student Recruitment in British Columbia

In the context of these emerging international arrangements for trade in education, Canadian educational institutions have reframed their mandates, restructuring their business practices to attract new revenue streams from international students. Education in British Columbia is primarily public, with approximately 89 percent of K–12 students in the public school system. All but one of the province's chartered universities are public. Private post-secondary schools offering English as an additional language are aimed primarily at international students. However, with the emergence of these new markets, public institutions—both K–12 and post-secondary—have come to operate much like private corporations when it comes to recruiting and enrolling international students.

One growing area of educational marketing involves the recruitment and hiring of private agents who operate in foreign countries to "sell" Canadian institutions. Thompson Rivers University, for example, states that its "global network of Marketing Services Representatives (MSRs) are based in key markets and regions around the world. They provide local support to agents and students, including training, counselling, and general marketing support." Educational institutions also send representatives to participate in global trade missions organized by federal and provincial governments. For example, in 2014, a delegation of nine BC post-secondary officials, including several university presidents, accompanied Premier Christy Clark to India to promote the growth of international students as part of the "BC Jobs Plan."[5]

Monetary value is prioritized in Canadian public school districts as they attempt to maximize revenue from their international customers. Typically, these districts charge international students at least $14,000 a year in tuition fees. In addition, families pay around $800 per month for homestay with Canadian families. Some school districts offer short-term or summer programs that have a combination of English language development and cultural programs. At roughly $25,000 a year in direct costs, most of these international students are from families in the higher income brackets of their countries of origin.

The number of international students in BC public schools and the income derived from them has grown from 4,000 students and $55.5 million in 2001–02 to nearly 15,000 students and $216.5 million in 2015–16.[6] Most of the school districts that attract international students are in the Metro Vancouver and Vancouver Island areas, with a diversity of languages and ethnicities reflected in the student populations. The rural, more isolated, and less diverse districts attract few international students, and consequently suffer from inequities in funding. The rationale for recruiting international students is often framed in terms of multiculturalism and encouraging global awareness among Canadian youth. However, the income from student tuition is clearly the driving force, with each international student bringing approximately twice as many dollars to the district as the per student grant from the provincial government for Canadian students.

BC school district online promotion gives a sense of what the province is offering. School district websites often mirror corporate marketing promotions, selling the recreational and social elements of Canadian education as much as academic offerings. A central draw, of course, is education in English. High quality education in BC is claimed by referencing the PISA results. Canada is one of the top performers on the international PISA league tables, and BC scores are among the highest in the country. For those who earn a BC secondary school diploma (called the Dogwood after the provincial flower), easier access is promised to BC post-secondary education. The districts also promote "The Canadian Advantage," which includes a "safe, beautiful environment and plenty of choice."[7]

In a more corporatized educational environment, BC schools and school districts have embraced a market-oriented outlook and vigorously compete with one another in seeking international students, developing links to overseas agents and building relationships in specialized market niches. The suburban Coquitlam school district, for example, has developed a network of relationships in China, sending administrators and school board members overseas and welcoming the Confucius Institute into its schools. While the Toronto school board and some universities have rejected the Confucius Institute amid concerns about

Communist government control, the Coquitlam board is prepared to ignore these concerns to gain a competitive market advantage. In contrast, the competitive advantage promoted by another suburban school district (until it was removed following public complaints) emphasizes that the district has "Low Immigration and is Caucasian-centric for an Optimal English Immersion Experience."

Turning Overseas Schools into Profitable Businesses—Or Not

Not only has the market for international students contributed to the corporatization of education at home, Canadian institutions are increasingly marketing their services abroad. "International schools" have expanded rapidly in recent years. In 2014, they involved "almost 350,000 educators in over 7,000 English-medium schools in non-English-speaking countries."[8] Canadian international schools currently constitute a small portion of this educational sector: Alberta (seventeen schools), Manitoba (six), New Brunswick (twenty-two), Ontario (twenty), and Nova Scotia (seventeen). British Columbia has the largest number, with forty-six schools (thirty-four in China, five in Korea, and seven in other countries, with the most recent in France). Most of these schools have been developed since 2000. An Asia-Pacific Foundation report notes that "Canada remains unique for having implemented an offshore schools model in the Asia-Pacific market with governments accrediting, regulating, earning fees and inspecting these programs."[9] These practices are a response to criticisms over the quality of instruction offered in some international schools. Overseas schools in what the province calls the "BC Global Education Program," for example, use the British Columbia curriculum and require the same provincial exams given to students in BC. The teachers of the BC courses are required to have a BC teaching certificate and the BC Ministry of Education inspects the schools. These schools have been able to attract qualified teachers without much difficulty because BC universities have been graduating more teachers than there are available positions in BC schools. One attraction for students is that receiving a graduation certificate from one of these schools provides easier access to Canadian universities.

When the BC Liberal government was elected in 2001, it aimed to reduce expenditures on public education and create an environment of school "choice" and competition. It also sought to cultivate an entrepreneurial approach among public school boards, encouraging them to compete for outside revenue to make up for reduced government funding. New legislation allowed school boards to set up school district business companies. Gerald Fallon and Sonya Pancucci describe the intention:

It enables public school districts to incorporate private companies to set up offshore schools and to market educational services and programs locally, nationally, and internationally. Policy-makers introduced this Bill with the assumption that public educational institutions must compete with other "providers," to sell their services and programs effectively in order to keep revenues at a healthy level to ensure their institutional viability and relevancy.[10]

Several district business companies started overseas schools, but "customer" complaints led the province to change the regulations and adopt private for-profit ownership, with revenues for curriculum and testing going to the provincial government rather than to the business companies. Some of the business companies tried to sell learning resources developed by teachers or offer online tutoring of international students in English. Several business companies were also used to co-ordinate the international students in their schools and collect tuition fees, but districts soon discovered they could run these student programs within the regular operations of the school district.

The business companies were generally failures, and most were dissolved within a few years. BC school districts did not have the marketing experience or connections to sell education services globally, and some lost funds loaned to the companies as upfront capital. Crucially, business companies failed because the impetus for publicly owned, for-profit corporations was based on an ideology and did not take into account that elected school trustees are primarily focused on public education in their communities (not on building profitable educational corporations to make up for inadequate public funding). In the end, the number of BC overseas schools did grow, but as schools owned by entrepreneurs in the countries where they were located. One educational entrepreneur, for instance, owns ten of the thirty-four BC schools in China. Today, BC overseas schools do earn some additional revenue for the provincial government, estimated at about $15 million, but most of the profits go to the owners.

International Students Increasingly Fund Public Universities and Colleges

Government funding of BC post-secondary education has fallen well behind the cost of offering quality education. To maintain programs, institutions have turned to other sources of income—corporate funding, and increasing domestic and international student tuition. International students provide a considerable influx of new money. The province set a target for increasing international students in 2012 with its "BC Jobs Plan goal of a 50% increase in the number of international students studying in BC by 2016," and later reported that this target had been achieved. The government also promoted BC higher education as part of its trade missions to China, India, and Japan (the largest number of international students comes from these countries, as well as South Korea), and it actively supports international student recruitment through the province's "education marketing managers." In 2017, the government claimed that international students are considered an "export" (based on WTO definitions), making it the third largest export from the province, behind only forestry products, minerals, and fuels. It is defined as an export "since funds that support the industry come from outside Canada."[11]

The specific impact that international students can have on an institution was explained by Kathy Denton, President of Douglas College, a suburban public college in the Metro Vancouver region. Responding to a previous article in the *Vancouver Sun* claiming that the financial contributions of international students are over-estimated, Denton writes that:

> ... international students must create educational opportunities for domestic students. Although Douglas College effectively operates as a non-profit institution, offering educational programming costs money. For our business to be sustainable, each course we offer has to cover its costs through a combination of government grants, student tuition and other income. Because international students pay many times the tuition fees of their domestic counterparts, it only takes a few in a given class to "break even." So demand for courses that would otherwise be wait-listed becomes economically viable with the addition of a few international students.[12]

Denton also addressed an issue raised privately by some faculty members, but seldom in any public forum: academic rigour. As the number of international students increases, students with a wider set of abilities and skills are accepted. Denton's response is that "at Douglas, we work hard to ensure that the international students we accept are academically prepared for college life in Canada."[13] However, teachers of international students in BC (at all levels) have informed me that the high fees paid by international students can create an expectation that they should receive credits for every course they take—or even the high grades required for entry into further programs—regardless of academic performance. In other words, these students have adopted a "degree purchasing" orientation where educational credentials are viewed as purchasable commodities, a trend that has also been noted in the academic literature.[14]

Simon Fraser University provides a compelling example of just how many international students are being admitted to BC universities. According to the university's Fall 2015 International Student Report:[15]

- 4,457 undergraduate international students were registered at SFU, representing 17.6 percent of the total undergraduate population (56.7 percent of international undergraduates were from China).

- 1,281 graduate international students were registered at SFU, an increase of 3.9 percent over 2014—representing 29.3 percent of the total graduate population.

- 19 percent of undergraduates attending SFU graduated from a foreign high school.

- 28 percent of graduate students attending SFU earned their bachelor's degree outside of Canada.

To increase international student numbers, SFU co-ordinates with an institution called Fraser International College. This is essentially a private college, run by Navitas, a private Australian-based education provider, that offers courses to improve language and math skills to a level where the student may be successful in a university academic program. After completing two semesters of courses with qualifying grades, the student is then granted admission to SFU and can move directly into second year university programs. About 1,500 students pay fees of approximately $20,000 for these private services (plus extras) and are told to expect living costs of about $15,000.[16] Navitas provides the university with a share of the tuition revenue it receives in exchange for being allowed to use university facilities, as well as university names and logos in its marketing campaigns. The company's corporate strategy acknowledges that public funding cuts and the increasing reliance on full-fee-paying international students are essential to its success.

Similar initiatives are evident at the University of British Columbia (UBC), the largest post-secondary institution in BC, which advertises itself as "North America's most international university." UBC offers an "International Undergraduate Study Preparation Program" that is aimed at preparing students for UBC or other North American universities. The full extended program can cost more than $50,000. This program does not guarantee admission to UBC, but claims that "after this program, you can expect to be fully prepared for the rigours of a Canadian or American university curriculum."[17] UBC also faced criticism after it created a special school for international students called Vantage College, which included a 1,000-capacity student residence. The residence was initially available only to international students, even though 5,000 domestic UBC students were on housing waiting lists (UBC eventually changed the policy).[18] These private international offerings and incentives are one of the ways that public institutions are attempting to deal with financial pressures.

Private English language schools for international adult students, primarily short-term students, range in size from a handful to several thousand students. In 2014, it was estimated that 42,000 students in BC were attending one of these programs (along with 46,000 in Ontario). The total income for BC was estimated to be some $330 million, including tuition and other living expenditures.[19] Some public colleges and universities now compete with these private schools for students, but register a minority of the English language students studying in the province. One consequence of this competition is that public institutions are restructuring their programs by offering a laddering into undergraduate or graduate programs (including to students whose academic qualifications may be suspect) and on-campus residence rather than homestay programs.

Weighing Benefits—Or Not

The figures speak for themselves. Recruiting and educating international students produces a positive economic return for Canada. It subsidizes public education, providing additional resources for Canadian students over and above those provided from government coffers and domestic tuition. It provides jobs for teachers and support service workers. In calculating the economic return, governments even include spending by students' families when they visit their children in Canada. Moreover, the expectations of the US political scene with Donald Trump's presidency present an optimistic scenario for further growth. Educator and journalist Crawford Kilian makes the case for "imagining Canada as an education superpower":

> Education is a very low-emissions export. Kids fly in, you fill their heads with words and numbers and ideas, and they fly out again. No ravaged watersheds, no oil spills, no poisoned salmon streams. What's more, if you do your job right you create lifetime customers. They will come back not only as tourists but as purchasers of any other goods and services we may want to offer.[20]

Government promotion in support of an international student strategy sells the stability and safety of Canada, its beauty, and, of course, its education quality.

Canadian scores on the OECD PISA exams are among the highest in the international league table rankings, and are useful in recruiting international students and their tuition dollars. Indeed, PISA is intended by the OECD to be a measure of the preparedness of students to take part in a global economy—a strong product selling point.[21]

But beware. Treating international students as a business enterprise, in part to compensate for austerity in the public system, also has negative consequences and implications. For one, when the business is tuition, it is subject to social and economic trends and crises. Economic downturns and fear of epidemics can have a major impact on domestic public institutions. The two years after the Great Recession of 2008 were the only years that the tuition intake from international students in BC K–12 schools declined since the promotion and growth of international student recruitment began. Similarly, the SARS scare in 2003 had finance departments in Canadian public institutions afraid of the potential revenue losses from students being kept at home to avoid disease.

There are also cultural and citizenship considerations. In setting recent objectives for curriculum reform, the BC Ministry of Education explicitly included international students among those whose needs must be met.[22] One consistent element of the BC curriculum is a course on Canada in Grade 11, based on the belief that every student graduating from BC secondary schools should have a substantial course on Canada in their last two years of education. However, the Chinese or Egyptian students working for a BC graduation certificate could understandably have less interest in the specifics of Canadian history and government. The new social studies curriculum introduces many courses as alternatives, and removes the requirement for a Canadian history and geography social studies course.[23]

Clearly, education as a corporatized international product can shape the nature of the education being offered. At the time of this writing, major curriculum revision is taking place across the province, focusing on "competencies" rather than content as the base for curriculum reform. Despite BC's position at the top of OECD PISA scores in 2015, the claim is that changes need to be made in order to stay competitive globally. Whatever other advantages "competencies" may have as an organizer for education, they are less focused on content specific to BC and Canada, making them easier to use in BC's overseas "global" schools and for the international students studying in BC schools.

The normalization of education as private and focused on individual competitive advantage is an underlying threat to public education. Public education has public purposes beyond those of the individual, such as socialization into civic responsibilities and participation in a democratic society. Public financial support for education produces a legitimate claim on students beyond just developing individualized skills. Once education becomes a commodity, however, its goals and purposes change. Relying on the wealthy classes from other countries to subsidize Canadian public education can result in very different educational structures and outcomes, including a much more corporatized educational landscape.

The Education World Is Not Flat

The conception that education is a global product needs to be challenged. In his praise of globalization in 2005, Thomas Friedman named his book *The World is Flat*. It was based on him traveling the globe and finding similarities everywhere. He was, of course, only seeing the world from the perspective of a transnational elite. Several years ago, in an article entitled "The Education World is Not Flat," I identified some of what Friedman was missing in his analysis:

> It is certainly true that global brands and global media reach even into seemingly isolated villages almost everywhere. What Friedman omits is that while commodities, including cultural commodities, travel across borders, most people do not and cannot. They still live in communities. Those communities need to be able to maintain education systems that reflect their needs for social cohesion and democratic development and not just be dependent on global markets, cultural "products," and the "anonymous socialization" of the Web 2.0 tools.[24]

Pressures to harmonize internationally are powerful. The OECD PISA results and related research reports are aimed at providing governments with models for education policy based on neoliberal assumptions that preparing young people for the global economy is the central purpose of education everywhere. According to this view, all schools, not just those incorporating international students, should internalize these assumptions. As Hans Schuetze asks, "Is the world heading for, or are Western countries imposing, a global (Western) model of schooling that ... becomes the benchmark of schooling in less developed countries?"[25]

Beyond generating a common set of "skills" and "competencies," international education is also contributing to the formation of a transnational elite class that has more in common with each other than with most of the people in their own countries or even communities. One take on this division is characterized by David Goodhart as "people who see the world from Anywhere and the people who see it from Somewhere."[26] Tristan Bunnell suggests that "one possible out-come of greater global self-identification and affinity is that the elite 'class-in-itself' served by 'international schooling' might develop a class consciousness, forming a 'class-for-itself.' This new elite formation could use its position and networks to exert even more power over education systems, leading to further economic and social advantage."[27]

Of course, there are alternatives. For instance, international education could also be oriented around "global citizenship," building from an assumption of cross-national interests and responsibilities. It could incorporate the idea of environmental stewardship, recognizing the linked fate of environmental and global survival in the context of ecological challenges. This carries with it an altruistic sense of commonality, mitigating inequality, and seeking justice—the development of a socially responsible global class.

The first statement of Internationalization Principles for Canadian Institutions of the Canadian Bureau for International Education reads: "Internationalization is a vital means to achieving global-level civic engagement, social justice and social responsibility, and ultimately is vital to the common good."[28] Although there may be some lip service paid to this vision (there are benefits to internation-alization), it pales in comparison to the dominant, corporatized models of educa-tional commodification described in this chapter. In the real world, international education is primarily about subsidizing public institutions imperilled by auster-ity measures, producing individual advantages and "competencies" to take part in the global economy, and providing a vehicle for transnational elite formation. These priorities push governments and educational providers to adopt policies that make public institutions look and act more like private corporations, with a range of negative social and educational consequences. Corporatization is help-ing to turn international education into little more than a private consumable commodity and, ultimately, an agent of global inequality.

Canada can offer high quality education at all levels—for its own students and others—because of its privileged position. And it can afford to put global social justice at the centre of its role in international education, rather than con-tinuing to develop it primarily as a profit centre in the economy.

6

How and Why to Change the Ways We Try to Change the Corporatization of Canada's Universities[1]

Claire Polster

Introduction

For those of us who have long been concerned about the corporatization of Canada's universities, now is a hopeful time. After trying for decades to raise awareness about the nature and implications of this process, through which our universities come to work more for, with, and as businesses, many people now are not only conscious of corporatization, but are concerned about and mobilizing against it. Things are especially exciting in some places, such as Alberta, where a government that may be open to progressives' concerns and wishes has come to power.[2] At this promise-filled moment, it is crucial that we think carefully not only about what corporatization is, but also about how to resist it. That is why I articulate and defend an approach to change-making that can help bring us closer to this goal. This approach, which I call the social relations approach and elaborate on below, aims always to *transform* the underlying relations that give rise to the institution we wish to change, rather than *reform* the apparent causes of the institution's state.[3]

I have decided to give you my punch line first. It is that even though, when it is presented to them, most people agree that a social relations approach makes sense and may even be obvious, this approach seems notoriously absent and elusive when it comes to actions to oppose corporatization. When devising and implementing strategies for change, people almost invariably revert to attacking the apparent causes of corporatization, which leaves the process intact and activists disappointed and demobilized. My goal is not to explain why people tend to slip out of a social relations approach and into what I call a cause-and-effect approach, but to show both that they do this and how adopting the social relations approach can make better use of our energies and opportunities. To conclude, I offer some suggestions to help us stay grounded in a social relations approach when trying to make progressive change in our universities.

What Is a Social Relations Approach?

To begin, let me lay the groundwork for my argument by addressing what social relations are, what a social relations approach involves, and how it differs from a cause-and-effect approach. Social relations are those ongoing courses or patterns of human activity that give any institution its particular shape and form. The difference between an art gallery versus an art auction or between a basketball game and a football game lies in the patterns of interaction, the terms of engagement, or the social relations that make them what they are. All social relations have a two-way dynamic. They are produced and sustained by people's activity, but they also shape and constrain their activity. Like a complex game or a dance, such as a square dance, they make it possible for people to come together and interact in certain ways while at the same time restricting or preventing other possibilities.

An approach to changing social relations aims to reconfigure or redirect how people connect and interact at a fundamental rather than surface level. The goal is not to reform what people do, but to radically transform the patterns of action in which they are engaged. If we take the analogy of the square dance, our aim would not be to change the particular people who do the dance or the tempo of the music to which they dance. Rather, it would be to establish new patterns of movement and interaction that put a fundamentally new kind of dance, like a waltz or a line dance, into place.[4]

To successfully transform the social relations that constitute a complex institution such as a university, we need two things. First, we need a solid understanding of how the institution is actually put together. This kind of understanding does not come from cause-and-effect thinking or trying to explain *why* the institution is as it is. It comes from ecological or systemic analysis that aims to map *how* the institution is organized. Second, we need strategies that help shift or reconstitute the institutional terrain or ground, rather than target any single, specific cause of that institution's condition.

To help clarify what this means and how a social relations approach differs from a cause-and-effect approach, consider two different ways we might understand and respond to a child's illness. A cause-and-effect approach would lead us to ask why the child got sick and to explain the child's illness as the effect of their catching a bug. In response, this approach would lead us to give the child a pill to kill the bug that is the cause of the disease. In contrast, a social relations approach would have us explore or map how the child's illness arises out of various interacting factors or conditions, including the quality of their nutrition, the state of their immune system, the health of those in their community, and environmental conditions around them. This more systemic understanding would lead us to develop strategies to shift the ground or conditions that underlie the child's ill-health—improving their nutrition, strengthening their immune system, and so on—to diminish the possibility, and not only that particular instance, of disease.

Three Strategies Based in Cause-and-Effect Thinking

My belief—or at least my hope—is that most people can see the virtues of the social relations approach. Nonetheless, when it comes to making change, many if not most of us revert to cause-and-effect thinking and action, seeking to attack the apparent causes of our universities' problems, rather than to reorganize its constitutive social relations. In what follows, I give three examples of popular strategies that people have taken up to resist corporatization that exemplify this cause-and-effect approach. I do not offer these examples to disparage the people who put valuable time and energies into them. On the contrary, I do this out of respect for their efforts and intentions and a desire to improve their outcomes.

The first and probably most popular strategy people adopt to oppose corporatization is to lobby for more public funding for higher education.[5] This strategy stems from the belief that lack of funds caused our universities to turn to the corporate sector for support, and to service corporations in return for that support. The solution that follows from this explanation is to lobby for increased public funding so that our universities can regain their independence from industry and revitalize their public service mission.

Rather than seeking and targeting the reason why our universities are oriented towards serving industry, the approach I advocate would have us explore how university/industry relations are actually organized. When we look for this, we see that over the last three decades or so, governments and others have established various practices and programs that hook up or bring university and industry people closer together. For example, they have increased the number of corporate executives that sit on higher education policy-making bodies, and the amount of public money and programs that support industrially oriented academic research (see Carroll et al., Chapter 4 in this volume). They have also created new positions on and off campus that promote university/industry partnerships, and various institutions like centres of excellence and research parks to enhance universities' contributions to industrial innovation and competitiveness.[6] Taken together, these developments bring university and industry people into contact more often and in new ways that progressively cede control over university resources to the private sector at the public's expense.

When we attend to how university/industry relations are actually organized, we can see that putting more money into higher education as it is presently constituted is an ineffective if not counterproductive strategy. More money will not fundamentally undo the new relations between universities and corporations. On the contrary, it may entrench and intensify them, much as pouring more water down a mountain entrenches existing streams and channels. If we want to resist corporatization, we need first to redirect the patterns or pathways through which those in the university are hooked up to those outside of it, so that they are reoriented to serving public needs and interests rather than private ones.

There are many possible ways to do this. These include transforming government research funding programs and councils so that they support more basic and undirected research, and restricting universities' involvement in the various entrepreneurial ventures of others and of their own. These also include creating new positions and bodies, such as the Dutch science shops, to increase universities' openness to and partnerships with community and public interest groups.[7] The point is that once, and only once, we have reorganized this terrain, or transformed the politics of the use of university funds, will it be a good idea to seek more public funding for higher education, because only then will funds flow through channels and support actions that we intend rather than oppose.

A second increasingly popular strategy to oppose corporatization is to alter the indicators that are used to assess academics' and universities' performance. This strategy stems from the belief that the reason why academics are prioritizing private over public needs and interests is because the measures by which they are assessed do so as well. The solution that follows from this explanation is to alter these indicators so that they accord more value to public-serving activities, and thereby to get academics to do the same.[8]

Rather than seeking to explain and address the reason why academics are favouring certain kinds of work over others, the approach I advocate would have us examine how academic decision-making, or how academic autonomy and accountability, are actually organized. When we do this, we see that over the last three decades or so, various policies, practices, and technologies have been put into place that transform faculty from publicly oriented professionals into nervous employees who increasingly focus on their own interests and the interests of those on whom their well-being depends—managers, funders, etc.[9] Indeed, performance indicators are themselves one such technology. These indicators limit academics' ability to autonomously define and pursue their own agendas by forcing them to account to management for what they do, and to do this on management's terms, and according to managerial—not academic—priorities. Further, because they are used not just to assess but also to rank faculty and universities, these indicators convert academics from colleagues into competitors, who are increasingly insecure and preoccupied with their own well-being. This alters, in turn, how academics relate to and interact with various constituencies outside the university. Rather than asking, "what can I do for others?", faculty are increasingly asking, "what can others do for me?" and opting for choices that produce the best outcomes for themselves.[10]

When we attend to how the context of academic decision-making is actually organized, we can see that changing the particular indicators used in the university is not a helpful strategy. While different indicators might make some academics more comfortable or successful in their work, they do nothing to alter faculty's subjection to managerial exigencies and values, to ease competition between and insecurity among academics, or to diminish academics' instrumentalism. On the contrary, by focusing only on altering these indicators, our actions actually serve to entrench and legitimize them and the social relations they put in place.

If we want to restore a public-serving ethic to our universities, we need to reorganize the ground or the context of academics' decisions and actions. There are many possible ways of doing this. These include limiting the production and use of performance indicators and/or replacing them with more robust, creative, and socially beneficial means of accounting for academic work.[11] These also include establishing programs, positions, and institutions whose mandate is to enhance rather than to measure academics' performance, so that faculty may focus on better serving the broader society rather than on performing for their bosses in order to protect themselves.

The point again is that if we wish to get rid of corporatization, we must not reform what people do—even if it is with a progressive twist (like creating "public serving" performance indicators); we must transform the underlying organization of the institution. We will not restore a public service ethic to the university by convincing university managers to compel academics to uphold it (or to appear to uphold it). We will restore it by establishing new relations in the institution that support and nurture a public-serving culture.

My final example of a strategy to resist corporatization, which has been taken up in several universities in recent years, is to attempt to oust or "re-educate" its senior administrators.[12] This strategy stems from the belief that the reason why our universities are increasingly corporate and undemocratic is because their leaders are unfamiliar with or unfaithful to academic norms and values and treat universities like any other private corporation. The solution that stems from this explanation is to replace these leaders with less corrupt or more enlightened ones who will respect our universities' public and democratic values.

Rather than seeking to explain and address the reason why our universities have become so corporate and undemocratic, the approach I advocate would have us examine how university governance is organized. When we do this, we see that over the last three decades or so, policies and practices have been put into place that progressively diminish the ability of faculty, students, staff, and community members to shape and influence institutional decision- and policy-making. These changes include the displacement of collegial with documentary forms of decision-making whose parameters and products are controlled by administrators, and the stacking of collegial bodies with representatives of management. They also include the definition of more spheres of university activity as "purely administrative" (and therefore not requiring faculty or others' input or approval), and the growing use of various consultative and other practices—like town halls and coffee breaks with the president—that give people a "say" but no real power.[13] Taken together, these changes narrow the range of voices and considerations that may be entered into university deliberations. When you add into the mix the closer relations between universities and corporations that I noted earlier, you can see how conditions that allow corporate values and practices to predominate are created.

When we attend to how university governance is actually organized, we can see that replacing individual administrators with others is not an effective strategy. More enlightened administrators may be nicer to have around, but they are subject to the same pressures and bound by the same rules and procedures as their less popular counterparts. If we want less corporate and more democratic universities, we must change not the individuals that lead them but the patterns of action through which decisions and policies are made. As I implied earlier, we should not change the dancers: we need to change the dance.

There are many ways that this may be done. For instance, university workers and students could collectively boycott institutional decision-making and policy processes that restrict meaningful participation, and initiate new ones, like alternative budgeting processes, that do.[14] They could also revitalize and co-ordinate the operations of collegial bodies so that more voices and values may inform institutional policies and decisions, and create new bodies—like the University of Toronto General Assembly[15]—to open up new avenues and opportunities for university and community groups to shape university decisions and agendas. I would further note that investing our hopes and energies in changing social relations rather than individuals will not only increase the likelihood that our universities become less corporate and more democratic, but that they stay this way. For these new relations will constrain all future administrators to operate in the ways we have institutionalized, regardless of their particular personalities and preferences.[16]

Staying Grounded in a Social Relations Approach

I could provide several other examples of flawed strategies that support the argument I am making. However, I hope that these three are sufficient to show why we should adopt a social relations approach when trying to resist corporatization in our universities—and in other public institutions as well. In closing, I want to offer four suggestions or safeguards to help opponents of university corporatization stay grounded in this approach, and avoid the easy and tempting slide into cause-and-effect thinking and action.

The first suggestion is to begin always by asking *how* the institution we want to change is organized rather than *why* it is as it is. Answering this question requires thorough research and investigation rather than speculation or theorizing.[17] A helpful way to remember this is to always look towards the ground to discover the underlying relations that give rise to the institution we wish to change, rather than casting our eyes towards the heavens to ask for explanations of why things are thus and so. If we do this, we are more likely to orient towards reconstructing the institution's terrain than to take aim at any single cause of its problems.

A reason we often avoid or slip out of a social relations approach is because it seems overwhelming to try to reconstruct the many complex patterns of interaction that constitute our universities. My second suggestion is that we accept that we cannot change university relations all at once, and focus our efforts on changing those relations that will have the most significant impact. If we think of social relations as various interwoven threads that make up the fabric of the university, we should seek to pull on those threads whose extraction alters the fabric as much as possible. An excellent example of one such thread is to prevent, by law or other means, the university's involvement in the privatization or commercialization of publicly funded research. Making this one change would help weaken or challenge various features of our corporate universities, including greater managerialism, increased secrecy and competition in research, escalating tuition fees, and the suppression of alternative knowledge. Pulling out this thread would also loosen up various others, making it easier to extract them when their time comes.

Third, when putting new strategies into place to help alter institutional relations, we need also to remain vigilant and create safeguards to protect them from institutional capture; that is, from being reabsorbed into existing institutional relations, which neutralizes their transformative effects. A quick example illustrates the point. Years ago, some of us created a community research unit in our faculty to serve the needs of disadvantaged groups who could not afford to pay people to do research for them. The idea was not just that the unit would do different kinds of research, but that it would transform university/community relations and help reverse corporatization. It would do this by providing a vehicle for faculty and others to revitalize their public-serving activities and commitments, and by encouraging the public to see the university as their resource, which they were free and encouraged to draw upon. Over time, however, the unit has been incorporated into—and has incorporated into itself—various university funding, auditing, reporting, and other practices that divert its time and energy from more transformative activities and goals. Although it still does very valuable research, it is fair to say that the research unit has been changed by the university more than the university has been changed by it.

My final suggestion is that we resist the temptation to seek the immediate or quicker gratification that comes from targeting causes, especially as we get daunted by the hard and slow work that the social relations approach often involves. For although reconstructing social relations is far more difficult and fraught than shooting magic bullets, I hope I have shown that it yields far greater and more lasting returns. This suggestion may be especially pertinent in some contexts, such as in Alberta where the NDP's rise to power seems to open a potentially brief window for progressives to finally have their wishes heard and perhaps granted, and they do not want to squander the opportunity. Progressives across the country may be feeling a similar pressure to quickly repair and reverse the damage done by the Conservatives to our public institutions while the Liberals' (apparent) open-mindedness and receptivity last. While I certainly understand the sentiment, I would suggest that right now it is all the more important that we take our time to do the slow and careful analysis to ensure that we pursue the right things, and the slow and careful work to ensure that we mobilize in the most effective ways. This will not only maximize the opportunity that having more progressive governments in power affords us, but will also allow us to transform our universities and society in fundamental ways that stand a better chance of outlasting any particular government's lifetime.

Criminal Justice

Police Foundations and the Corporatization of Criminal Justice in Canada

Kevin Walby and Randy K. Lippert

Introduction

The core of social control and state legitimacy in liberal democracies is non-biased, impartial public policing.[1] As Julie Ayling and Clifford Shearing put it, "public policing is a public service ... provided by government to the public at large, to which each member of the public has equal access regardless of income."[2] Yet, since the 1960s, a multitude of private security entities have emerged to profit from new crime control markets while catering to specific interests.[3] This shift challenges the so-called monopoly police and the state have over the means of social control in Western societies.

Public policing entities have responded to this challenge in many ways, depending on jurisdiction and economic context. Across the United States, private security's role in public policing has expanded. In the United Kingdom (UK), public-private partnerships in policing are also well established.[4] Yet privatization of public policing in Canada would appear to be an anomaly, not a trend. Rather than adopting policies that encourage the privatization of policing, public police in Canada have managed to maintain citizen and government support for the idea that they are the experts in security provision and, more significantly, maintain support for high and rising levels of public funding.[5] A case in point is the recent announcement by the City of Toronto to hire eighty new officers for the Toronto Police Service, Canada's largest municipal police service,[6] amidst an earlier hiring freeze and calls among other Ontario municipalities for "modernization" to reduce spending on municipal policing in Canada's largest province.[7]

When push comes to shove, Canadian governments tend to find funding for public police salaries. These results reflect the fact that public police managers have begun to embrace a new "corporate consciousness."[8] Revitalized police unions and top brass have started importing business principles and management practices into public police organizations across North America. As with corporatization elsewhere in government, this development in public policing is resulting in most large- and medium-sized police departments becoming more like business enterprises in management style and fundraising.[9] These changes depart from the idea of policing for the public good. As Pat O'Malley and Steve Hutchinson note, such changes have "unintentionally produced a ... corporate structure."[10] Yet, there is almost no research on the corporatization of public policing in Canada.

The corporatization of public police has spurred internal and external shifts in these organizations. Internally, performance management and subjection of budgets to cost-benefit analysis associated with New Public Management have made some minor inroads.[11] Externally, corporatization is changing the way public police interact with and derive funds from private, corporate entities. In this chapter, we examine private sponsorship of public policing in Canada as a form of corporatization in the criminal justice system. As we reveal, private sponsorships mean business interests are becoming more prominent in Canadian policing, as these departments (i) operate more like market-based organizations, and (ii) create stand-alone, legally separate, arm's length entities with different core mandates. We explore the emergence of police foundations as funnels for private sponsorship. These foundations act as shell corporations that allow public police to operate outside existing accountability structures. The corporatization of public police is thus strikingly different from the privatization of public police in the UK. Whereas in the UK privatization has eroded public police management and funding, in Canada corporatization has strengthened and augmented the reach of public police practices and financial operations. We demonstrate how police foundations in Canada are a key element of this process and parallel corporatization in other public sector realms.

The chapter is organized into three parts. First, we review literature on corporatization and argue that the emergence of the police foundation should be conceptualized as corporatization. Second, we analyze empirical material on police foundations in Canada. We assert these foundations exemplify a "state-corporate symbiosis"[12] or linking of police and corporate power that is reflective of corporatization. In conclusion, we assess the implications of growing embeddedness of public policing agents in arrangements of private influence, raising questions about police legitimacy and the public interest.

Corporatization in Context

Raymond Dart has studied how non-profit organizations are becoming more business-like in their goals, service-delivery, and management styles.[13] Similarly, Florentine Maier and her colleagues have explored how non-profit organizations become market-oriented and begin to resemble businesses.[14] But is becoming "business-like" synonymous with corporatization? What forms does corporatization take? Being more precise is important analytically and conceptually, but is also crucial for activists, academics, and policy-makers hoping to challenge the corporatization process and its effects.

David McDonald has provided key insights into how to think about corporatization. As McDonald notes, corporatization is analytically and empirically distinct from privatization.[15] Corporatization refers to a restructuring of state and government entities occurring since the late 1950s at least. For McDonald, corporatization involves two main processes.[16] First, corporatization generates new forms of management in the public sector that "create arm's length enterprises with independent managers responsible solely for the operation of their own immediate organization, and where all costs and revenues are accounted for as though it were a stand-alone company."[17] This approach to corporatization is associated with "New Public Management," and is accompanied by new performance measures for workers, including police.[18] Second, McDonald argues that corporatization is associated with market-friendly public sector cultures, ideologies, and policies.[19] This process involves a trend towards commodification and commercialization, which is not necessarily marketization or privatization. Marketization entails more direct private sector participation, and privatization entails large-scale sell-offs of public services and assets. Corporatization as a concept highlights the restructuring of state and government bodies, a process that neither automatically nor inevitably entails (and sometimes rebuffs) private sector participation and sell-offs of public assets. In other words, marketization and privatization involve the unbundling or splintering[20] of public assets, rather than a new management and expansion of them.

Corporatization is uneven and takes several forms. Neoliberal corporatization involves applying "market-oriented operating principles" to stand-alone, state-owned entities.[21] This approach leans the furthest towards market intervention in state projects. However, the distinction is that corporatization entails state agencies functioning with a business model, not a business appropriating goods from the state. Under these conditions, commodification and commercialization are common. An off-shoot of neoliberal corporatization involves commodification of the goods and services provided by state agencies. As McDonald puts it, "this commodification process allows utility managers to argue that the only way to truly 'appreciate' a service is to pay for it (ideally at full market cost)."[22] This means government practices and services can become commodified and monetized, and offered at a cost, which sometimes erodes the public accessibility of the good or service. This erosion happens because the emphasis is less that the good or service be equitably distributed and more that it is somehow paid for in these new arrangements. Most literature on these forms of corporatization has focused on public utilities; however, we argue the process is also relevant to public policing.

As McDonald notes, no single example is likely to meet all criteria in these definitions.[23] We argue that an overlooked marker of corporatization is the creation of foundations used to channel private donations and sponsorships into government operations. Universities and hospitals have long used foundations to raise money outside public funding and legal structures. Our focus is on police foundations as one indicator of corporatization in the criminal justice sector. McDonald argues that corporatized government entities "typically have a separate legal status from other public service providers and a corporate structure similar to publicly traded private sector companies, such as a board of directors."[24] Police foundations are registered as private charities and are not public entities under Canadian law, and thus have a legal status separate from public police. Police foundations also have a board of directors. According to McDonald, the goal of these new organizations is to "create arm's length enterprises" that can help "reduce political interference."[25] We show that police foundations meet McDonald's criteria for corporatization.[26]

Public Policing and Corporatization:
The Case of Police Foundations

Public police in Canada are establishing private, seemingly arm's length foundations that can receive large donations and in turn spend the acquired money on police initiatives. In Canada, there are strict police department-level rules for direct private sponsorship of and donation to public police, as well as laws that prevent police services from becoming business enterprises or altering their organizational structure (e.g., Ontario's *Police Services Act*). One foundation representative we interviewed compared public firefighters raising donations to what the public police can do: "Police cannot stand there and take money … So that's another reason for the foundation. Our police department under the Police Act ... can't do what firefighters do ... their charitable society can do much more." However, foundations allow private funds to be channelled indirectly, circumventing these rules and laws. Police foundations operate like what David Jancsics terms "domestic shell corporations."[27] As official independent charities, these entities must disclose financial information to the Canada Revenue Agency (CRA), but this information is limited. The private dimension allows much information about foundation activities to remain obscured under its "shell" as well as for the foundation to act as a go-between for private donors and public police.

Not all police foundations in Canada operate similarly. There is a bifurcation between philanthropic and corporate models.[28] Thus, some police foundations operate on a model of charity or philanthropy, such as those in London, Winnipeg, Montreal, Waterloo, Hamilton, and, to a lesser extent, the RCMP Foundation.[29] These foundations relay funds to other charities or social services and rarely seem to channel funds towards police practices directly. They appear to leverage their legitimacy as public police agencies to raise funds mostly for underfunded organizations. There is, however, another set of police foundations that have adopted a corporate model that raises private funds primarily for public police equipment or programming. This is precisely how these foundation representatives describe their main aim: "We have been driven by the need for pieces of equipment or the need by our police department" (Foundation Rep. 1). These foundations are in Vancouver, Delta, Abbotsford, Edmonton, and Calgary. Regardless of whether they are more philanthropic or corporate in character (there is overlap), police services in Canada now desire foundations and are endeavouring to create them. Donations and sponsorships can be filtered through these shell corporations, whereas similar funds passed directly to police would raise questions about corruption or bias.[30] Operating with a different legal status and a board of directors comprising corporate CEOs, foundations broker relations between private sponsors or donors and the public sphere, buffering police agencies and their top brass from accusations of impropriety.

Based on information acquired from the CRA, the first police foundation was established as a charitable organization in Vancouver in 1995, though the Vancouver Police Foundation claims to have commenced operations in 1976. Edmonton Police Foundation was created in 2000, Delta Police Foundation in 2002, and Abbotsford Police Foundation in 2005. Calgary Police Foundation was formed in 2010 and received charitable status in 2011. Typical of other police foundations, the Calgary Police Foundation's board of directors includes members from major corporations, such as Cenovus, Nexen, Shaw, and

PricewaterhouseCoopers. These police foundations continue to grow in number and annual budget.

We examined charitable donations, revenues, and expenditures from five police foundations for the last five years as reported to the CRA. What these figures demonstrate is a trend towards large corporate donations being funneled to public police through police foundations. The figures also reveal that public police tend to be the primary donee of foundation funds. In 2011, the Vancouver Police Department (VPD) received $435,898 from Vancouver Police Foundation, and they received $593,255 in 2012. In 2013, total revenues of Vancouver Police Foundation were $1,085,733, with $816,151 in donations and $647,902 in expenses. The VPD (the primary donee) received $226,841. These figures increased to a total revenue of $3 million in 2014, a year in which total expenses were $1,574,498 and total donations were just over $1 million. The total amount of gifts to VPD (the primary donee) in 2014 was $290,668. In 2015, total fundraising revenue for Vancouver Police Foundation was $8,198,426, with over $7 million in donations and total expenses of $1,147,417. The VPD received $258,725. These figures suggest that the foundation is stashing cash to spend later. The trends here are evident in other police foundations. In 2012, total fundraising revenue for Calgary Police Foundation was $3,283,157, with over $3 million in donations and total expenses of $1,727,435. Calgary Police Service (CPS) received $220,907. In 2014, total fundraising revenue for Calgary Police Foundation was $2,502,442, with over $2 million in donations and total expenses sitting at $1,788,385. CPS received $400,000. Edmonton Police Foundation raised $615,050 in 2014, and Edmonton Police Service (EPS) was the primary donee, receiving $287,992. In fact, EPS is the primary donee in each year for which there are records.

Donations to police foundations can be sizeable, and foundations can direct donations and sponsorships in ways that public police cannot. For example, in one year, Edmonton Police Foundation accepted donations from Enbridge ($25,000), Northlands ($10,000), and several other $10,000 donations from provincially based companies. In 2014, Calgary Police Foundation embarked on a funding drive that secured large donations from energy companies in Calgary totalling more than $1 million.

Foundations must also spend money to make money. In 2016, Vancouver Police Foundation spent $60,231 on advertising and $133,782 on fundraising. Calgary Police Foundation similarly spent $139,512 and $88,262 respectively. Edmonton Police Foundation spent $240,983 on fundraising alone. Galas in particular cost money to host. Each year Edmonton Police Foundation hosts the True Blue Gala. For a table of eight persons, the cost ranges from $2,200 to

$2,700. At these galas, donors contribute monies, but also gain privileged access to key public police decision-makers at their tables or the event. One police foundation's representative indicated: "We're doing a joint professional sports team-police foundation in the fall ... and we expect this will bring in 500k to $600,000 as opposed to the 150k ... level that we have [been] normally getting from our annual gala" (Foundation Rep. 2). Other fundraising includes selling police calendars, such as in Calgary in 2014 when all sales of the Police Service Canine Unit charity calendar went to Calgary Police Foundation. These sales raised more than $30,000 for this foundation the previous year. Like other police foundations, Vancouver's displays a "corporate consciousness"[31] in how it raises funds through print and radio ads, fundraising dinners, galas, targeted corporate initiatives, and targeted personal contacts. As one foundation representative bluntly stated: "We just phoned up people that we thought had deep pockets ... and that's how we started" (Foundation Rep. 1). But he added that there was a new, more targeted approach, too: "Now ... we'll have to go and sit down ... and try and convince different businesses, that we don't know, that are big ... to be on board and be annual givers."

Some expenditures by police foundations are philanthropic (though still police- or criminal justice-oriented). For example, in 2016, Vancouver Police Foundation funded VPD Women's Safety Fair ($4,480), Lunch with the Chief ($3,600), the Fentanyl Awareness Campaign ($20,000), and numerous athletics and youth programs, including the Youth Police Academy ($20,000). Other events or items catered more to public police members, such as the Vulnerable Person Registry ($10,000), the VPD Member Appreciation and Promotion Event ($21,000), and the VPD Family Day ($9,000). Calgary Police Foundation funded the Calgary Police Cadet Corp, and YouthLink, a massive police museum collection of exhibits and mock forensics labs for kids. Abbotsford Police Foundation funded the Abbotsford Police Camp, operated in conjunction with Abbotsford Police Department and Central Abbotsford Community School. Abbotsford Police Foundation website allows donors to give to Abbotsford Police Foundation generally or to specific projects.

However, as corporate police foundations operate more like domestic shell corporations, these funds are increasingly being directed towards police equipment or initiatives. Vancouver Police Foundation has been behind several major recent procurements for the Vancouver Police Department (VPD). In 2016, this foundation allocated $12,950 for special medical kits and $30,000 for binocular night vision devices. In 2015, it allocated $47,000 for a boat, engine, and trailer for the Marine Unit; $40,797 for a canine-mounted video camera system; and

$75,000 for enhanced video surveillance for the Mobile Command Vehicle. In 2014, it allocated $24,000 for an aiming laser for the Emergency Response Team. In 2013, it allocated $7,000 to a VPD Crime Alerts system that would update subscribers on crimes in specific neighbourhoods, and $15,000 for the VPD Ceremonial Unit, which sends delegations to public events and police funerals. In 2013, Vancouver Police Foundation also spent $25,725 on an arm for a robot that the foundation had purchased for the VPD's Emergency Response Team the year prior. Vancouver Police Foundation raised $250,000 for a bullet-proof, armoured rescue vehicle in 2008–2009,[32] and raised funds for infra-red cameras for the Marine Unit in 2009. Also in BC, in 2013, Delta Police Foundation raised $120,000 for a mobile command unit, a satellite police station complete with computer workstations and toilets that co-ordinates video surveillance at public events.[33] Delta Police Foundation raised funds for three motor vehicles for community policing initiatives in the city, too. In 2013, Edmonton Police Foundation raised $85,000 towards the purchase of police helicopters. In 2015–2016, Abbotsford Police Foundation helped to generate monies for an all-terrain vehicle for Abbotsford Police Department.

Some fundraising efforts of police foundations tend to resemble the strategies of for-profit companies rather than public agencies. Fundraising is one aspect of the work of police foundations where their activities would appear to be corporate in nature. Vancouver Police Foundation has been pushing the boundaries of police fundraising. In 2011, the organization partnered with the drugstore chain London Drugs, whose customers could donate to the Foundation or purchase a $20 "I Love Vancouver" T-shirt, with proceeds to the foundation.[34] London Drugs and Vancouver Police Foundation partnered on the Kops Shades for Kids Campaign. Aviator sunglasses—"a signature look inherently tied to police"—were sold for $20, with proceeds to the foundation.[35] In 2016, Calgary Police Foundation copied the aviator fundraising strategy, according to their foundation website. Enrolling a corporation to collect funds for a police foundation in a commercial context shows how foundations broker police legitimacy to arrange this, and how foundations reach deep into the private realm.

Donations to police foundations are evidence of the corporate world's growing influence on public police. Calgary Police Foundation literally framed the names and faces of its biggest donors on a wall at Calgary Police Headquarters. The donor wall included framed acknowledgements for Cenovus, Enbridge, Encana, MEG Energy, Talisman Energy, and more.[36] Together these corporate entities donated over $1 million to the foundation in just one year. Their donations must be funneled through the foundation, due to the rules for private sponsorship of public police. However, clearly the Calgary Police see themselves as the benefactor of corporate funding and strategies, although the display must tip-toe around the issue, since the wall does not indicate that these corporate entities donated directly to police. These corporate ties raise questions about conflicts of interest and bias or partiality in policing.

As McDonald argues, having a board of directors is one criterion for the corporatization of government agencies.[37] This governance model is clearly more common in the corporate sector. Interlocking boards of directors reveal police foundations as a form of "state-corporate symbiosis."[38] CEOs are regulars on police foundation boards. One foundation board member related extensive previous corporate board experience: "I've sat on a lot of boards … multi-billion-dollar boards" and indicated that he was "able to work to bring in a lot of A-list people who are from these kinds of enterprises that are connected" (Foundation Rep. 2).

Board composition is another aspect of the work of police foundations where interpenetration of public police and the corporate world is evident. One foundation member remarked: "We're composed mainly … [of] business people" (Foundation Rep. 1). There is also often considerable interpenetration of the police foundation and police service, such as when a member of a police foundation will be appointed an honorary chief constable for a day as a way to express appreciation. Although the foundation's board members are supposed to be independent, most foundation representatives we interviewed indicated that the chief makes recommendations or has final say about who will be on the supposedly independent foundation board. This interpenetration raises the spectre of conflict of interest. Yet some police foundation boards comprise police officers or administrators, too. The Edmonton Police Service Chief sits on the Edmonton Police Foundation board. A chief constable and police sergeant sit on the board of Abbotsford Police Foundation. With corporate-style police foundations that fundraise to provide money for police gear and operations, the presence of sworn officers on these foundation boards would seem to transgress the very boundary that the foundation is established to bridge. For this reason, Charles Walters argues that police foundations should be subject to ethical guidelines and standards.[39] The presence of corporate CEOs and other private business persons on foundation boards is a crucial aspect of fund solicitation. As described by one foundation board member we interviewed, the private connections of board members are invaluable to the foundation's fundraising, allowing a deep reach into plump private coffers: "It's not because you want to be on the foundation [that] you get to be on the foundation … we want people that are connected so that we can get into the different … areas" (Foundation Rep. 1).

These foundations are only growing in the level of expenditures for police services. Thus, one representative referring to a major upcoming fundraising initiative for their adjacent police service indicated: "It's a big city; we gotta do something that's major. And well, we did it." Later, this representative added somewhat cryptically: "We'll have somebody at the airport looking for this guy to see is he really a problem? ... We're just building that capacity, that's a multi-million-dollar thing and so we made a commitment ... we will fund this over the next three years at about a million bucks a year." Another representative kept referring to his foundation moving away from "money in, money out," and the need instead for a "war chest" so that "we won't be hit up with this 'okay we want to help the police, but we don't have any money'" (Foundation Rep. 1). The corporatization of policing raises questions of transparency, accountability, and justice that should resonate with scholars and activists who are examining and challenging corporatization elsewhere in the public sector.

Conclusion

As McDonald indicates, corporatization is "seen by many as an 'alternative to privatization.'"[40] The creation of foundations by public police to extend their own operations and reach without taking on "the political and economic risks of direct private sector participation" is evidence, we have argued, of corporatization.[41] We have suggested that police foundations are an overlooked but expanding form for the corporatization of public policing in Canada. Police foundations meet McDonald's criteria of corporatization in several ways. This is because police foundations are registered charities and therefore are not public entities under Canadian law. Police foundations' boards typically include many corporate CEOs. These "arm's length enterprises ... reduce political interference"[42] and controversies that would stem from corporate encroachment on the public police mission that sponsorship entails. Foundations allow public police to create a corporate veil to camouflage these exchanges of capital that could raise questions about collusion, bribery, or corruption.[43]

The corporatization process varies by form and context. In some government sectors, including policing, "state intervention is being *withdrawn*, in other areas it is *redrawn*, and in still others it is being *extended*."[44] Though it has not yielded a "straightforward shift from the logic of the public good to the logic of the market,"[45] privatization of public police in the UK has expanded public-private partnerships and the unbundling of police organizations, transferring operations to companies such as G4S as the state withdraws. Meanwhile, corporatization of public police in Canada is redrawing and extending public police operations rather than splintering and selling its security services to private agencies. Corporatization entrenches and further institutionalizes public police power, syphoning private resources to augment it. Yet, to the extent that private influence via these means is surfaced and rendered visibly biased or partial, these new arrangements may also reduce the police legitimacy that buttresses police power in the first instance. Quite aside from issues of actual bias and influence resulting from these new foundation arrangements, they may well entail robbing Police Officer Peter (police legitimacy) to pay Police Officer Paul (more funds for operations that may or may not maintain police legitimacy). Put differently, what is the price for police of bad optics when, for example, citizens protesting a corporate development threatening their neighbourhoods and environment see large corporate logos covering the new police foundation-purchased mobile command unit as public police wheel it into place to monitor and direct operations against protestors? It is indeed legitimacy that is among the central aspects at stake in the politics of these foundations' ascendency across Canada.

Police foundations are only one element of the corporatization process in the criminal justice sector. The consequences of this corporatized approach to public policing deserves more study, for instance, the implications for policing mandates and policing styles, and the association of policing with the public good. Future research should not only investigate flows of funds via overlapping corporate and police foundation boards, but should compare these to university and hospital foundations as part of a broader examination of corporatization in Canada. Academics, activists, and even policy-makers concerned with the impacts of foundations and the corporatization process should develop strategies to challenge corporatization and find synergies with other social movements and mobilizations.

Do Construction Companies Create Criminal Justice Policy?

Reflections on the Nature of Corporate Power in the Canadian State

Greg McElligott

Introduction

Criminologists and other social scientists often advocate "evidence-based" approaches to public policy. These presumably contrast with less sensible or "ideological" ones that are unlikely to achieve their stated ends, and may impose excessive costs or unacceptable collateral damage. The "tough on crime" policies that have filled our prisons, for example, may hurt prisoners and their home communities without producing a net reduction in crime rates. Viewed from the perspective of their effect on crime, such policies seem irrational in the face of relevant evidence. What evidence-based critiques expose, however, is a startling naiveté on the part of their proponents about the nature of policy and policy-making.[1] Especially troubling here is the notion that the official goals of public policy are the same as the state's actual aims, and the related assumption that policy fields are discrete and self-contained enough to prevent "contamination" by other priorities. Thus, the supermax prison may be an irrational approach to reducing crime, but a perfectly reasonable way of subsidizing corporate profits in the construction industry and elsewhere.

Many readers of this collection will share deeply embedded preconceptions about the state's ability to act in the public interest, or on behalf of other abstractions like "justice" or "equality." But, on a daily basis, the reality is much messier. It may be argued that nearly every field of public policy is shaped by the need to support private profit-making, and that such pressures have intensified in recent years. Labels like "corporatization" are often used to explain structural changes that seem to exacerbate this trend. Advocates and opponents agree that corporatization is something "less" than outright privatization, an attempt to "mimic the structure and efficiency of private corporations while ensuring continued emphasis on social objectives through public ownership."[2] Writers on corporatization may prefer mimicry or social objectives, and may doubt a particular state's commitment to either, but both sides of the field assume that corporatization represents some kind of break with the past.[3] This break is often depicted as a violation of fundamental boundaries (as in some of the works discussed in this book), which see the state as increasingly colonized by private interests. But what was the baseline to begin with? How can we tell what has changed?

To answer these questions, this chapter traces developments related to Canada's federal prisons. It begins with a discussion of state theory, which tried to pinpoint some essential features of capitalist states just as the latter began to cast off their welfare responsibilities. It then examines management practices in the Canadian state. How were these connected to shifting fashions in management theory more generally? How did they affect prison design, prison construction, and the private contractors involved in both? Finally, the chapter considers how the reorientation of the state might support business indirectly, by helping to erode workers' power in the labour market. In the end, it should be clear that corporatization has not changed the essential nature of the Canadian state, even if it has further insulated the latter from true democratic control.

State Theories and the "Grey Zone of Publicness"[4]

Under the Harper Conservatives (2006–2015), the government of Canada paid out at least $730 million to private companies that were expanding federal prisons run by Correctional Service Canada (CSC), and many millions more to those working on construction projects for other federal departments.[5] The value of CSC contracting out rose dramatically under the Conservatives, mostly because of the construction projects, and contracts went disproportionately to companies with headquarters in the Greater Toronto Area (GTA) and other large regional "metropoles."[6] GTA-based Bird Construction and Bondfield Construction each won CSC tenders worth over $60 million, for example.[7] Construction companies do not usually get such a large share of CSC contracts, but the department has traditionally relied on private suppliers for a wide range of services—food, laundry, medical, counseling, and so on—despite the fact that Canada's prisons are said to be publicly run.[8] Contracts beyond construction are smaller and more dispersed, with the two largest winners here (food supplier GFI Prairies and dentist Dr. Gayle Church) each securing contracts worth roughly $2 million, or about one-thirtieth of what Bird and Bondfield won.[9]

What can this example tell us about corporatization in Canada? Public-private boundaries are clearly more porous than is sometimes assumed. Talk of corporations colonizing the state is confusing in this context, because such "colonies" already seem to be well established, albeit by a slightly different set of companies. And even if CSC prisons are not directly owned by corporations, or staffed by corporate personnel, they need to be attentive to the market—if only to satisfy their own basic operational requirements. Controversy has surrounded the private management of prisons, but history shows a long-standing pattern of state-corporate co-operation in the development and operation of legal punishments.[10] Scandals of corruption and abuse stain this history, of course. Yet today both public and private operators use brutal, impersonal, supermax prison designs that may do more damage on their own than any particular ownership structure.[11]

While governments increasingly rely on corporate providers, some of these providers rely heavily on government contracts. The mingling of interests that might be expected here features prominently in discussions of the Prison-Industrial Complex (PIC), where it is used to explain why US prison growth seems to exceed any rational policy objective.[12] Prisons continue to spread because PIC interests benefit from them, and prisons are chosen over other crime-fighting tools (like schools) because the latter are seen as offering fewer benefits to the corporate and political interests that have coalesced around prisons.[13] Adopting the arm's length management forms associated with corporatization may facilitate this process by drawing prisons into what David McDonald calls the "grey zone of publicness," and hiding the extent of corporate influence.[14] In Ontario, public-private partnership (P3) financing deals for prisons and other projects became more prevalent after privatization was discredited, yet they often cede just as much control and revenue to private actors.[15]

Strangely, construction companies do not feature prominently in the PIC literature, but their influence over criminal justice policy might be expressed in this way: favouring built solutions to social problems rather than "softer" preventative approaches that do not involve construction (such as hiring more addiction counselors, or rebuilding the social safety net). Their preferences also coincide with a longer tradition of "Tory High Modernism" that has united Canadian business and (particularly conservative) political interests behind megaprisons and other megaprojects since the nineteenth century at least.[16] The builders of Kingston Penitentiary, which opened in 1835, dreamed that properly designed walls might themselves reform prisoners and help control surrounding populations.[17] A similar rationale, embodying what James Scott calls a "hyperfaith" in mechanically enforced control, was still being expressed some 165 years later to describe Ontario's new high-tech "superjails."[18] From the "moral architecture" of Kingston Pen, to superjail control rooms that evoked "the bridge of the Starship Enterprise," the common threads were a convenient need for privately supplied construction, and a shared understanding that reliance on human staff should be kept to an absolute minimum.[19]

In this example, the interests and ideologies of top government and corporate personnel are so intertwined that it is hard to distinguish them as separate actors. One would expect, then, that public policy would tend to follow their preferences, rather than those of groups excluded from the mix.[20] Shared interests and ideologies lead to common purpose and, if democratic controls are weak enough, that purpose can consistently run counter to the interests of most citizens.[21] More elaborate versions of this kind of argument stress that elite consensus is cemented by shared backgrounds and management career paths that traverse public/private boundaries (and so encourage opportunistic conformity). None of these explanations are new, and their significance was addressed at a deeper level by the "state theory" debates initiated by neo-Marxist scholars in the late 1960s.[22]

One of the more important insights to emerge from this literature was that states in a capitalist context had to achieve "relative autonomy" from narrow business interests if they were to produce "hegemonic" policy that responded to the general needs of the capitalist class as a whole.[23] So direct rule by business, either within one policy field, or in something like US President Trump's cabinet of billionaires, was not necessarily good for capital, since it tended to make politically stabilizing concessions to subordinate interests (whether workers or other businesses) less likely. Still, the state's position was only *relatively* autonomous because it was tied to the needs of business as a whole, not those of particular corporations or capitalists.

In this explanation, the key roles of the state were to facilitate the *accumulation* of private capital (through infrastructure investment, tax expenditures, etc.) while arranging minimal concessions (symbolic or material) to other interests to help *legitimize* the destructive impact of market-based growth.[24] Where legitimization failed to secure the acquiescence or passivity of subordinate interests, the state was charged with strategically deploying *coercion* to keep them in line.[25]

From this perspective, the shift to the "penal management of poverty" is a massive strategic swing toward coercion at the expense of legitimization, to police and prisons at the expense of welfare.[26] Yet there are signs that neoconservative strategies based on mass incarceration are hitting the same limits that ultimately doomed the welfare state. Just as spiraling costs and related taxation rendered the welfare state unsustainable from a business perspective, these same factors now seem to be overwhelming the promise of profit through incarceration.

Many state theorists underlined the state's role in tending to the "common affairs of the whole bourgeoisie," which meant helping business construct a common political line on key issues, and reconciling weaker sectors of capital to the leadership of the stronger.[27] In the example above, most benefits from prison expansion went to the GTA and other metropoles, but some contracts went to smaller operators, and construction was spread across the prison system so that it appeared to benefit many local prison communities.[28] The state arranged this politically palatable distribution with a fair degree of autonomy from capital, but it served the interests of capital nonetheless. What, then, does it mean to say, as McDonald does, that some corporatized entities "represent the possibility of operating state agencies with considerable autonomy from the market"?[29] Certainly it may be possible for such agencies to do less harm than others, and administer policies that offer more benefits to subordinate groups. But is it likely that such arrangements would threaten the interests of "the whole bourgeoisie," and thus attack injustice more fundamentally?

Again, history is not very consoling in this regard. As long as prisons are connected to law, they will be linked to a system whose "absurd formalism" and claims of equal treatment remain essential ideological props for capitalist rule, at least in Anglophone democracies.[30] This means that there are real limits to how far any individual, company, or agency can deviate from the common ruling-class line. As Douglas Hay says in another, much earlier, context: "gentlemen were very sensitive to opinion in their neighborhoods, for there might be serious consequences if the show of force was either not quite impressive enough, or so brutal that it outraged men and destroyed the mystique of justice."[31] Preserving the "mystique of justice" became more complicated as capitalist states took on democratic forms, but the apparent commitment to legal equality still coexists with the selective application of terror and a deep commitment to the perpetuation of class inequality. Prisons obviously remain central to the state's coercive role, but outright terror is now restrained by the legitimating importance of "the rule of law," and by the need to warehouse "surplus" populations and undergird labour market discipline on behalf of capital as a whole.[32] So any particular corporate interest—even one as big as the private prison industry—must ultimately defer to the current hegemonic line, or be reined in.

The question of how the state knows or creates capital's core class interests was the subject of some contention among state theorists. Ralph Miliband stressed the impact of shared personnel with shared backgrounds, while Nicos Poulantzas and others focused on the constraining effect of the surrounding capitalist economy.[33] While either path conceivably leaves room for miscommunication or misjudgment (since state actors are human and do not automatically know how to proceed), the fallibility of the state as a whole did not receive much attention in most of this literature.

However, the central message here is the most crucial—that the state in a capitalist society must be a capitalist state, committed at its core to the perpetuation of corporate rule.[34] If we follow this line, the corporatization of the state sounds a lot less novel, and a lot more like the continuation of long-standing practices of "adjustment," meant to address "slippage" between different organizations committed to the same goals. McDonald notes that transforming parts of the state into stand-alone agencies has many virtues from a managerialist point of view, but it can also "be used to create market-friendly public sector cultures and ideologies."[35] From the perspective of the theories noted above, that is always a central purpose of a capitalist state, and not just with respect to its own internal operations. Nevertheless, so long as business and the state maintain some organizational separation, inconsistencies in aim and practice will occasionally need to be ironed out.[36] In Canada, this has usually been accomplished by soliciting advice through special task forces and royal commissions.

Keeping Up with Management Fads[37]

Attempts to have "businesslike" behaviours and attitudes extend into the realm of government are hardly novel in the Canadian context. After the First World War, the Canadian state engaged American consultants to help it bring job classifications and scientific management into its formerly patronage-based bureaucracy. In 1962, consultants in the influential Glassco Commission famously urged Ottawa to "let managers manage" and embrace the latest corporate personnel policies. Glassco also voiced the deeper logic of contracting out, noting that private suppliers should be preferred not because they might be cheaper or more efficient, but because "other things being equal, it is preferable to buy rather than to make, in order to restrain the continuing spread of government and to strengthen the private sector."[38]

As neoconservatives took control in the late 1970s, a permanent lobby for corporate emulation was set up inside the state in the form of a wide network of auditors who employed politically charged "value for money" techniques to judge public expenditures. All of these promoted efficiency standards and workplace reorganization to encourage harder work among public employees. Later efforts would employ the softer "human relations" methods that were in vogue at that time. In the 1980s and 1990s, federal employees were asked to search for "excellence," embrace "total quality management," and discover their "governing values." As the new millennium approached, they were told they would be "empowered to serve." In each case, outside corporate expertise was tapped to push for the intensification of arbitrary management power inside the state, and deference to the market outside it.[39] In this light, the adoption of arm's length managerial arrangements seems like an extension of previous trends. Arbitrary managerial power is boosted once again, and still defers to the market, only now it is placed at a slight remove from the state bureaucracy.

Obviously, there is a great deal of hype and faddishness in the sorts of management theories that are sold (at considerable profit) to governments in these situations. As Jim Silver points out, many of these approaches merely repackage old ideas, all of which "seek the managerial Holy Grail: a means of stimulating or energizing workers, 'motivating' them to increased production without higher pay or improved conditions."[40] Anyone who has experienced a corporate reorganization knows how frustrating they can appear to those on the front line.[41] So, while there clearly has been consistent pressure to make the Canadian state run more like a business, that does not mean the suggested methods are rational, even in the narrow corporate context. And if the state theorists are right, capitalist states may be trapped in a series of fundamental contradictions—absorbing more and more costs of production while reaping fewer of its benefits in order to keep corporate tax rates "competitive."[42] It may simply be impossible to act rationally given these competing demands.

It is true that the ethos of "lean production"—embedded in works such as David Osborne and Ted Gaebler's *Reinventing Government*[43]—has had particularly destructive consequences for people both within and beyond the state. The belief that practically all state-provided services could instead be handled by private contractors "steered" by state elites has frequently led to a two-stage process of degradation and substitution. First, publicly provided services are starved and diminished, then private sector intervention is heralded as the key to improving service delivery. By this point, expectations are low enough that the public may be willing to accept what corporations can deliver on a for-profit basis. Efficiency is trumpeted after defining "service" in cold, quantifiable terms that erase human contact and deprive it of its essential meaning. Thus huge, centralized, high-tech production—the "big-box" model pioneered by Walmart, et al.—can be portrayed as a reasonable way of serving human needs, even if it is just a capitulation to trendy management theory.[44]

Ontario's experiment with a privately run "superjail" (the Central North Correctional Centre, in Penetanguishene, from 2001–2006) was a typical case. The design was a product of big-box thinking, and its operation embodied lean production values by farming out management—and other services, such as health care—to an American multinational prison company (Management and Training Corp.). The superjail was also an integral part of plans to reshape most of the provincial state.[45] The experiment failed, because the prison's operator skimped on staffing, food, and other expenses in ways that provoked both prisoners and guards, and made the superjail a dangerous place for all involved.[46] Direct corporate rule was thereby discredited.

But the Harris government's Liberal successors began to experiment with more elaborate forms of public-private partnerships (P3s) that allowed the state to retain apparent control while funneling huge amounts of money to corporate builders and financiers. Ontario taxpayers are now committed to paying $1.1 billion over thirty years to cover the cost of building just one superjail—the Toronto South Detention Centre (TSDC).[47] The P3 form in this case has the virtues of hiding business influence (and business subsidies) more efficiently. But the Liberal version distributed funds in what was a more hegemonic way, with a bigger share going to the banks and finance industry—the traditional core of the capitalist class in Canada.[48] So, again the structural distance involved in corporatization does not necessarily disturb the commitment of state agencies to organizing on behalf of the wider interests of capital.

When the Conservatives took power federally in 2006, they once more took the task force route as a way of meshing CSC reorganization with their purportedly "tough on crime" approach. The CSC Review Panel was staffed and advised by politicians who had been part of Ontario's militantly pro-business "Common Sense Revolution," and the panel's report essentially recommended that the struggle be continued at the federal level. The 2007 *Roadmap to Public Safety* merged the traditional preference for built solutions with an attempt to instill "market values" and labour market discipline in prisoners. The first took the form of a proposed multi-billion-dollar building project that would have consolidated CSC prisons into a series of "regional complexes"—essentially megaprisons.[49]

This design had disciplinary justifications, but it would have been a massive boon to construction and other companies that served prisons. While the panel was warned by its own consultants that each regional complex would cost about $1 billion just to build, and was not likely to save any money, both parties felt it was reasonable to expect that the nature of this new approach would produce unpredictable new benefits.[50] This relatively casual dismissal of cost concerns echoes the "common sense" articulated by Glassco many years before: it is simply assumed that subsidizing private profits should be a natural part of anything governments do. That attitude, it should be remembered, seems to be a variable thing in the corporatization literature, whereas the evidence suggests it has been a constant in Canada since at least the 1960s.[51]

CSC's chief bureaucrat, Commissioner Don Head, told his department in 2008 that they were committed to a P3 model for the design and construction of the new regional complexes.[52] The review panel had suggested that CSC expansion begin with the consolidation of all Ontario's federal prisons in Kingston, which was already a hub housing many of them. P3 financing would have made such a project more plausible, but it still would have involved a huge investment in a Liberal riding and the closing of many prisons elsewhere.

The Harper Conservatives, then a minority government facing re-election, clearly found this prospect unpalatable. They remained committed to a major building project as the foundation of their tough on crime approach, but decided to spread the funding more evenly and develop smaller versions of the regional complex more gradually. So, just prior to the 2011 federal election, Conservative politicians fanned out across the country, promising construction contracts worth over $600 million to twenty-four prison towns in eight different provinces, and touting the potential for local economic spinoffs.[53] While this distribution seemed more equitable (at least to those who could ignore the social cost of prisons), when construction contracts were actually tendered, they went massively to large companies in the GTA and other urban centres, and only rarely to locally owned concerns.[54] Perhaps because total outlays were smaller and more dispersed than the panel had anticipated, P3 financing was not arranged, and the prison projects took on the form of a traditional pre-election spending spree. Whatever notions were initially present about how prisons might be ideally designed or financed, these were compromised in the end for the sake of hegemonic appearances, and potential partisan gains.

This example sets in relief the inadequacy of an approach to policy that accepts formal structures and relies on using "objective" evidence to affect change in a discrete field—even one as broad as criminal justice. Prisons were part of a larger coercive agenda linked to the destruction of old welfare state protections, the ramping up of work expectations (discussed below), and the creation of new opportunities for private profit-making. Actual crime reduction could only be a priority if efforts to achieve it contributed to these larger goals. Once we acknowledge the influence of such political/partisan factors, and the essential constraints of a capitalist state, the preference for built "solutions" to social problems becomes easier to explain. All that remains is the division of spoils. As CSC prison expansion moved from the realm of grand ideas into one of petty bribes and false promises, this was demonstrated quite clearly.

The ongoing attachment to the private sector's needs and methods—mediated by the occasional corrective consultation—is revealed in the form that the retrofitted prisons eventually took. Faithful to the spirit, if not the dimensions, of the review panel's original vision, the additions involved large, alienating hi-tech "pod" designs of the sort favoured by private prisons and now available in pre-fab form.[55] CSC Commissioner Head argued in 2008 that "there is an over reliance on technology in Corrections. Don't let technology define policy."[56] However, there is little in the prison expansion program to suggest that he has followed his own advice.

Prisons and Labour Market Discipline

The techniques of lean production are now deeply embedded in many work organizations and in the labour market itself. Employers are much less likely to do everything in-house, and they have easier access to global sources of goods, services, and labour. Large buyers like Walmart use their purchasing power to drive costs down around the globe, forcing suppliers and host governments to engage in a "race to the bottom" in terms of wages, work conditions, and environmental standards.[57]

One consequence is that worker expectations about job security and related benefits have had to be severely reduced. This is obviously a huge project that has involved decades of re-education and fear mongering. States that once were committed to softening the impact of volatile market forces now undercut protection for the unemployed while liberalizing trade and encouraging automation. Magnifying the threat of job loss and touting the inevitability of globalization has helped to produce new generations of workers for whom precarious work is the new norm. Lower expectations and a divided workforce have in turn allowed most employers to implement increasingly alienating and exploitive work arrangements. Yet not everyone is willing to accept the degraded work options now on offer, and the CSC Review Panel—like many before them—felt that prisons should play a greater role in correcting such attitudes.

In Ontario, the Harris Conservatives had launched a wide-ranging assault on workers' labour market power, and the gains they had won since 1945. While many of these efforts were intended to disrupt unions and collective bargaining, the Conservatives also tried to force poorer, unorganized workers to expect less. The social safety net was shredded as welfare rates and eligibility were rolled back, and benefits were made conditional on forced labour in a "workfare" scheme. Thousands of former welfare recipients were pressed into the lower reaches of the labour market just as rent controls were abolished, and homelessness was criminalized through laws curbing "aggressive panhandling."[58] Perhaps the most retrograde step of all was the loosening of overtime regulations, which made legal working hours longer than they had been in generations. Overall, this was an attempt to ratchet up the work ethic and increase prevailing levels of exploitation.

The Ontario experience seems to have influenced the CSC Review Panel, for their recommendations about how prisoners should be treated in the reconstructed prisons paralleled many of the measures undertaken by the Harris government. The panel suggested that prisoners' "structured work day" be increased by 50 percent—from eight to twelve hours daily.[59] This was part of an explicit effort to "promote a positive work ethic" among prisoners, which would also involve curtailing their legal rights (especially to refuse participation in programming), and making decent living conditions contingent on how hard they worked, and how hard they worked to rehabilitate themselves.[60]

Despite all the evidence that prisoners needed better access to addiction counseling, anger management, and so on, the CSC Panel advised that existing rehabilitation programs be reoriented toward employment and job readiness training.[61] CORCAN, the prisoner work and training program, should produce not for internal government needs, but to supply "fully trained and job-ready offenders ready for release to positions in the community."[62] The panel felt that the construction industry might be keen to arrange apprenticeship programs with CORCAN, and proposed that it and other businesses be allowed to shape the content of training programs to better meet their own needs.[63] Prisoners would have to be attentive to the needs of employers as well, because the system of "earned parole" advocated by the panel would have made a prisoner's early release conditional on them having found an outside job—presumably with the apprentice's "master."[64]

Like the Harris government, the panel chose to enforce participation in the growing low-wage workforce. This push was needed because the slim pickings on offer were less able to pull workers in on their own. The young men who tend to populate prisons were a particularly hard sell in this regard. Uniformly poor, usually undereducated (most finished only up to Grade 7), and disproportionally Indigenous and Black, prisoners tend to have checkered employment histories, addiction issues, and an aversion to many kinds of authority—often rooted in previous victimization and abuse.[65] These disadvantages were magnified in the new job market, and the disappearance of many decent working-class jobs made participation in the legal economy increasingly frustrating and humiliating.

Nominally, prison programming would be rejigged on behalf of prisoners re-entering society, and employment was known to be a key part of such transitions. But the limits to such supply-side approaches to unemployment are ably captured in the title of a 2011 article by Michael Hallett. It asks simply, "re-entry to what?"[66] The panel's vision for prisoners never established that there were actually jobs (much less good jobs) for which to be trained. Given that the absence of such jobs probably helped send many people to prison in the first place, this was an egregious oversight—if the employability shift was truly aimed at serving prisoners. But from the perspective of employers, this shift would undoubtedly be welcome. Some (such as construction companies) might get access to custom-trained workers, with the state once again absorbing the cost. And all employers would benefit from measures that flooded the labour market and undercut workers' bargaining power. In this respect, Canadian prisons would act like corporatized neoliberal utilities, providing services in areas seen as essential to business needs, and constantly pressing (or pressed) for cuts elsewhere.

Similar transitions have occurred throughout the old welfare state, as services formerly focused on subordinate groups have been repurposed to better support capital accumulation. This case is slightly more complicated because it affected legitimate services (rehab programs) within a coercive branch of the state. But, again, the shift is not fundamental—more like a reclamation of territory lost during the unique conditions of the post-war boom.

Conclusion: Saving the State?

Using a term like corporatization implies that some identifiably corporate thing has crossed into the realm of the public sphere, where it is alien and perhaps unsuitable. In the introduction to this collection, the authors discern at least three variations, involving "new" organizational forms, intensified management control, and boardroom-like integration of elite personnel.[67] But, as can be seen from the discussion above, the Canadian state has always been enmeshed in practices that serve and emulate business, and the boundaries between the two are fuzzy at best. In any case, structural separation does not mean that organizations are pursuing distinct ends, even if it does make things more complicated. As I have shown elsewhere, state organizations are not distinguished by any real democratic accountability, and governments across the political spectrum have abused and exploited their own workers, following the same beat that guides employers around the world.[68]

When states fall out of step, and adjustments seem necessary, corporate advice is solicited, usually from the special task forces or internal auditors described above. However, because this advice is inevitably drawn from faddish management theories, and because the role of the capitalist state is essentially impossible, following corporate advice does not necessarily improve efficiency, no matter how that word is defined. Adjustments can only hope to preserve a comfortable degree of consistency between the two realms. It is true that some adjustments are more wrenching and far reaching than others. The "Common Sense Revolution" in Ontario caused ripples well beyond its borders, and pioneered the intense application of lean and "big-box" production inside the state. It later found indirect expression in the CSC Review Panel's report, and helped shape and justify similar changes at the federal level.

Analyses of federal prison policy that ignore such developments (and the demands of the state's accumulation imperative more generally) can offer only a blinkered view of what is happening in this field. Institutions nominally devoted to fighting crime are increasingly being used to subsidize the construction industry, and to undermine workers' power.[69] Justin Trudeau's Liberal government has not reversed this approach; in fact, they seem poised to expand it with a vast, new infrastructure spending program, guided more closely by direct business participation.[70]

So, do construction companies create criminal justice policy? The available evidence suggests that they have more influence than most in its development, and may exert power in a wide and growing range of policy fields.[71] Such influence is not necessarily a product of direct lobbying, or direct corporate rule, for relatively autonomous structures are generally better at producing hegemonic policy in the long run. The Liberals' P3 approach seems to be slightly more sensitive to the needs of finance capital, for example, and it favours different parts of the construction industry.

What remains noteworthy is the degree to which interconnection, ideological consensus, and material interest unite all sides. Deference to the market is a crucial part of all of these, and it will constrain "progressive" corporatized agencies just as much as it constrains traditional state bureaucracies. The Canadian government cannot be "saved" from corporatization—at least not without a thoroughgoing transformation and democratization of the state itself.[72]

Corporatizing Therapeutic Justice

The Case of the Winnipeg Drug Treatment Court

Kelly S. Gorkoff

Introduction

For the past ten years, the Winnipeg Drug Treatment Court (WDTC) has operated in Manitoba's capital city, offering a specialized criminal court for people
charged under the *Controlled Drugs and Substances Act (CDSA)* and the *Criminal
Code*. Comparing its original proposal, stated goals, and planned mandate with
several of the court's evaluations, this chapter assesses the court as a case study
in the corporatization of criminal justice. To date, most of the critiques of drug
treatment courts have analyzed their use as part of a neoliberal turn in punishment or explored their more coercive aspects, such as the violation of due process
rights.[1] This chapter maintains that risk-based therapeutic drug treatment courts
are part of a larger shift in crime control, where penal welfare and liberal models
of justice give way to corporate, managerial strategies for governing offenders.

I begin by discussing different conceptions of corporatization from political
economy and security governance literatures. I analyse the WDTC's justification
under the therapeutic justice label and the market of addictions and crime produced therein. I then examine the governance structure—including the steering committee, budget, and staffing arrangements—with a focus on the ways in
which the court has been corporatized. A number of indicators are discussed,
including the use of partnerships, governmental steering, managerial accountability, the role of consumers and clients, budgetization, and performance indicators, as well as the impacts of corporatization on offenders and criminal justice
professionals. I find that the corporatized court model exemplified by the WDTC

shifts the notion of justice for addicted individuals away from liberal ideals of equality and human rights towards efficiency/budgetary concerns and a neo-liberal model centred around the management of risk.

Theorizing Corporatization

Corporatization is often identified as a management form that prioritizes market concerns over social concerns, producing a service or product that is reduced to an economic exchange.[2] While studies of markets and marketization typically address the economic component of a program or policy, studies of corporatization emphasize the governance structure.[3] Though difficult to tease apart, indicators of a corporatized model of governance include partnerships with private enterprises, use of performance assessments and economic indicators, and an accountancy-based conception of transparency, accountability, and efficiency.

In looking at public services, David McDonald claims that corporate governance involves the creation of arm's length entities that, while derived from state ministries and owned and operated by the state, have a degree of autonomy from it.[4] However, the corporatization process does not take one form. Per Laegrrid, Paul Ronness, and Vidar Rolland claim that there are numerous quasi-autonomous state bodies that assume different organizational forms over time. They suggest two processes of corporate governance: *agencification* and *corporatization*.[5] While corporatization refers to externally automated, state-owned companies (for example, Crown corporations such as Manitoba Hydro or Autopac), agencification involves an internal automatization or delegation of a particular policy area within the public administration (such as Manitoba Child Advocate or Women's Advisory Council).[6] Automatization creates civil service organizations/agencies that are formally separate from but subordinated to a parent ministry. Thus, they are less structurally devolved from central political authorities than are state-owned companies. McDonald argues that agencification enables greater financial transparency, reduced political interference, and strong managerial accountability.[7] This process resembles the concept of anchored pluralism used in studies of security governance to explain justice processes whereby the state takes an arm's length *steering* function, focused on directing services from a distance, while agencies are empowered with *rowing,* directly operating these services.[8] We can think of these justice processes as examples of agencification because they perform regulatory tasks but have been given extended authority, most often in the form of managerial discretion, to direct technical tasks. For instance, the Fine Option Program in Manitoba is run by a separate agency that organizes the technical aspects of cases where individuals are sentenced to fines but cannot pay them. This agency directs the place and space for the sentence to be satisfied. It defines the number of hours, the regularity of work, and so on. In the language of anchored pluralism, it rows the operation of the court's sentence.

Corporatization, as a second form of corporate governance, is the external automatization or delegation to bodies outside the public administration but still within the public sector.[9] Corporatization is most often found in state-owned companies that exhibit higher degrees of structural devolution from central political authorities than do state agencies operating under agencification. This could include the creation of separate entities not part of the civil service and a range of companies established by separate laws (Manitoba Liquor and Lotteries) or government-owned enterprises (Manitoba Hydro). While these companies are usually legally owned by the state and created to address a strategic area of state interest, they are separate in terms of institutionalization, organization, and authority. The corporatization process is comparable to Clifford Shearing's analysis of police governance. Shearing argues that under policing boards, policing operates as a regulated network of participatory nodes, each with authority, capacity, and knowledge (that the state alone does not possess).[10] This is similar to Laegrrid, Ronness, and Rolland's claim that corporatized entities often take the form of state-governed administrative enterprises or foundations that operate under specialized sets of laws. Policing boards could be conceived under this corporate framework because they are responsible for specific legislation related to policing, and while owned by the government to address a strategic area of the state (security), they are separate in terms of their organization, authority, and institutionalization.

Public organizations are not static and can go through circular processes of agencification and de-agencification/corporatization and de-corporatization, depending on party constellations and administrative doctrines (at the international, national, and sub-national levels).[11] The case of the WDTC provides an example of a public sector organization going through this circular process.[12] The WDTC is neither a true state-owned company (corporatized/nodal network) nor is it a simple example of agencification. Examining the WDTC over its ten-year lifespan, we can note that while it began as an arm's length agency of the state, and was a good example of agencification, it slowly progressed into a leaner, flatter, more autonomous organization that can be considered an emerging participatory or institutional node, its own form of a corporate court. Thus, it appears the court is anchored to the state (via funding and its location in the department of justice) but rowed by twenty-four initially, now two, external bodies. As its funding and organizational structure has stabilized, the court has gained organizational independence. It is fair to say that the WDTC now has autonomy and (especially when paired with similar specialized courts) has changed from a traditional ministry-governed court to a node of directed/specialized legal and punitive power.

The following sections discuss how the Winnipeg Drug Treatment Court has shifted away from the parent ministry of the Manitoba Department of Justice to become a relatively autonomous agency through an examination of its initial proposal and justification and its mechanisms of governance. I then examine how the court's governance structure aligns with the components of a corporatized agency. Specifically, I will show that the WDTC addresses a market concern, produces an economically viable product, partners with actors outside the ministry (yet still part of the public administration), is rowed by outside agencies, and negotiates funding dependent on performance indicators.

The Winnipeg Drug Treatment Court

Criminal courts in Canada are traditionally governed by the liberal democratic state, subordinated to the ministries of justice both provincially and federally. They are governed via the Constitution, rule of law, and principles of democracy. This is evidenced in the appointment of judges by elected officials, and the actions of the courts themselves, which adhere primarily to the rights-based framework of statute, procedural, and common law. David Garland argues that this governance framework has given way to a modernist superstructure operating on a correctionalist motif and supported by more specialist arrangements.[13] According to Garland, criminal justice is now a hybrid penal-welfare structure, combining liberal legalism of due process and proportionate punishment with a correctionalist commitment to rehabilitation, welfare, and criminological expertise. However, even within this correctionalist penal-welfare orientation, the operation and ministry governance of the court has not been fundamentally modified. Change from the traditional criminal court model to the WDTC appears to happen through a combination of interest group pressure and a risk-based ideology of criminal justice, allowing for the adoption of corporate modes of governance.

Drug treatment courts were first introduced in the Canadian justice landscape in 1998 and the WDTC was established in 2005. These courts represent a significant shift in court processes away from liberal models of justice to therapeutic ones, and embody changes in the cultural task-specific characteristics of public sector justice organizations. Therapeutic jurisprudence represents a shift in law and court processes towards promoting the psychological and physical well-being of offenders by treating the criminogenic risks associated with a particular behaviour, in this case addiction. Therapeutic justice began with critiques from advocacy groups and the general public who questioned the use and effectiveness of traditional punitive justice practices for those addicted to alcohol and drugs.[14] These groups asserted that traditional criminal court outcomes were costly to society as well as to offenders, and did little to curb recidivism.[15] Drug treatment courts are steeped in this therapeutic approach, with the goals of reducing recidivism (and therefore harm) and offering greater cost effectiveness than the standard legal model for dealing with offenders whose crimes are related to addiction. The overarching purpose of the WDTC was to couple the strengths of the criminal justice system with the strengths of a focused addictions treatment program using existing community services. According to the proposed vision, the court

> exists to break the cycle of drug use, criminal behaviour, and incarceration by establishing a partnership between courts, treatment agencies, and community agencies. The WDTC will do so in an inclusive way but will be specifically cognizant of the over-representation of aboriginal men and women incarcerated in Manitoba. The WDTC will tailor its program to address the specific needs of groups such as young aboriginal men and women with children in culturally appropriate ways.[16]

The short- and long-term goals of the WDTC are to increase knowledge about addictions, to provide information on community resources, and to improve the life skills of clients through employment, vocational, and interpersonal support. These strategies have been linked to social benefits, such as reducing addiction-related crime and other harms associated with drug use.[17]

This critique of traditional modes of criminal justice mirrored a shift in public discourse concerning the social and economic harms associated with addiction generally, which culminated in the Canadian Drug Treatment Strategy (CDTS).[18] While addiction has been considered a disease since the 1930s, it was reinvented in the 1990s and early 2000s as a public health issue.[19] The CDTS addressed problematic substance use via capacity building (funding additional programs in established organizations) and the use of a tiered model of services and support. It reinforced existing support services and incorporated a host of new recommendations regarding knowledge exchange, co-ordinated leadership, evidence-based practice, and the measuring and monitoring of system performance. This included the development of a best practices toolkit and the targeting of knowledge exchange between jurisdictional levels. It also included the development of a national knowledge exchange network to ensure co-ordination between knowledge users and producers, and to promote the implementation of therapeutic strategies.

Moving away from ministry governance, the CDTS's final report advocates "partnerships across health care, public health, social service and justice to address the risks and harms associated with these problems."[20] The report also adopts a harms reduction approach that aims to "minimize risks and harms associated with substance use and related behaviours (e.g., sharing needles and other drug paraphernalia, unsafe sexual practices), and reaches out to encourage engagement in services and supports without requiring an immediate commitment to abstinence."[21] The CDTS, carried out by twelve federal departments and headed by the Department of Justice, has three components—prevention, treatment, and enforcement. Several Canadian DTCs (including Toronto, Vancouver, and Winnipeg) are supported by the treatment component of the CDTS. These twelve partners are required to assist in research and data collection, including the development of a national database for clients who use services in multiple jurisdictions.

Drawing on this new public health discourse and its connection to crime, the issue of problematic substance use has been reframed in the legal sphere as both a criminal and public health issue. This coincides with a larger shift in criminal justice practices that David Garland identifies at the nexus of civil society concerns and the commercialization of crime control. Here, the contours of officially co-ordinated crime control extend beyond the institutional boundaries of the state.[22] Put another way, the state begins to de-differentiate its response and spreads out its crime control efforts beyond the criminal justice organizations that previously sought to monopolize it.[23] Through this kind of discursive reframing and organizational restructuring, the addiction/crime nexus is now framed as a *criminogenic market*, and addicts are conceptualized according to the risks and harms associated with their drug use. It is within this space that agencification occurs, and it is here where we see the devolution of the state's welfare function and traditional justice court system to non-state service providers and the creation of new agencies to govern the issue of addictions. Indeed, the traditional court process can be considered a market failure because traditional courts produced outcomes that were costly (high recidivism rates) and insecure (continuation of the harms associated with addictive behaviour). In this process of devolution, the lines between public and private are blurred and public service agencies are remodelled in ways that emulate the values and practices of private industry (or, in this case, the national working group).[24]

The WDTC as a form of agencification takes place within and among these processes. Corporate technologies of governance focus on addressing risks and producing economically viable outcomes; in other words, creating market efficiency. DTCs have specifically been framed around practices of customer orientation, adhering to specific funding requirements, activating agencies/partnerships, and prudentialism (a precautionary logic aimed at pragmatic prevention of harm, not a cure).[25] The DTC model seeks to merge treatment and justice to achieve desired outcomes—the reduction of risk and cost-savings. Through collaboration and partnerships, new techniques of corporate governance are constituted under the semblance of harms reduction, which promise to reduce the costly physical and social harms of addiction. The WDTC's mandate claims exactly this:

> to reduce recidivism through judicially-supervised drug treatment programs; to break the cycle of drug use, crime and incarceration; and to provide information on community supports and improve a participant's life through employment, vocational and interpersonal support . . . this is associated with the goal of reducing the number of crimes associated with addiction; and to reduce harm due to drug use and addiction; and to provide the participant with the tools for vocation and educational success, positive mental and physical health, appropriate housing, and improved family relationships.[26]

Robin Mackenzie argues that harms reduction is a realistic goal of crime control for this market and becomes embedded in governing practices such as DTCs.[27] He claims that DTCs are "feel good" courts where success is defined as clients managing their risky addictions. He further asserts that this addiction management pairs with health discourses to dissuade excessive public consumption of anything that endangers health, thereby reducing health to a set of risks that need to be managed.[28]

The establishment and organization of the WDTC, based on the failure of traditional courts and the merits of therapeutic justice, took a form we can define as agencification. However, as I argue below, over the course of its ten-year existence, the court has been modified into a flatter, more stable organizational form that we can call a node, or corporatized model of governance.

Mechanisms of Corporate Governance in the WDTC

Three primary mechanisms of WDTC governance reveal the structural aspects of the court's corporate organization: the organizational structure of the court, the role of performance indicators, and the corporate culture of front line work. This analysis reveals that after its inception and turn away from traditional models of justice, the court has become a leaner, flatter, and more autonomous organization opposed to the large multi-purpose hierarchal bureaucracy it once was. David McDonald claims these processes are typical pathways for New Public Management, in which public sector organizations go through circular processes of agencification and de-agencification/corporatization and de-corporatization.[29] The WDTC has not been fully de-agencified or fully corporatized. While it has moved towards a corporatization model, it remains part of a circle-like pattern in corporate governance, fluctuating between elements of agencification and corporatization.[30]

Organizational Structure

The corporate organizational form includes a variety of mechanisms. As McDonald claims about agencification, one of the most important corporate forms is its independent operation, governed by a board of directors or steering committee, with autonomy from formal structures of state governance.[31] The board of directors or steering committee is corporate in nature because it provides a space wherein market needs take precedence over central political authority. It is thus evidence of structural devolution characterized in agencification. For public service agencies, this often takes the form of partnerships and stakeholders, which are reflected in the WDTC's steering committee. Congruent with the philosophy of therapeutic justice, the first few years of the WDTC were overseen by a group of third party partnerships/stakeholders. These partnerships were meant to address the limitations of traditional criminal justice courts by producing more efficient outcomes and broadening the purview of the court into civil society. The initial steering committee or governance board of the WDTC involved numerous community agencies and stakeholders including: (i) the two major addictions programs in Winnipeg: Addictions Foundation of Manitoba (AFM) and Behavioural Health Foundation; (ii) ten justice-related government bodies: provincial court judiciary, federal crown prosecutions, Winnipeg prosecutions, Winnipeg police service, RCMP, legal aid, defense bar, national crime prevention centre, Manitoba housing, and probation services; and (iii) a host of crime prevention, prostitution, and health agencies: Tamarack rehabilitation, Forward House Ministries, Aboriginal Court program, Elizabeth Fry Society, Sage House, Klinic, Prichard House, Onashowewin Inc., Aboriginal Health and Wellness, First Nations and Inuit Health Branch, Thunderbird House, and a group of Aboriginal elders. There are also connections with Winnipeg

Regional Health Authority (WRHA) and CODI (co-occurring disorders initiative with WRHA).[32]

The primary goal of the steering committee was to link up the activities of existing actors and agencies and direct their efforts towards addiction services and crime reduction through the operation of the court. The committee oversaw the development of programming, client flow through the court, and reduction in the use of overlapping agencies. Partnerships and stakeholders are said to be corporate because they create a new leadership and decision-making model free from political interference, and are guided by the needs of the knowledge experts and market of addicted offenders. This was the dominant model of governance for the court's first four years, with partners slowly leaving the steering committee in subsequent years. The initial organization of the court was clearly an example of agencification, as it represented internal automatization or delegation of a policy area within an existing ministry.

Despite the existence of a broad-based steering committee, funding was provided solely by the state. The initial funding ($516,000) from various bodies of the federal government was matched with in-kind support ($450,000) from the provincial government, and for three years was supported by a $599,000 transition house and support worker from Human Skills and Development Canada. However, while relying on state funding for operations, the committee represents a more corporatized arrangement to the extent that the state steers (fiscal component) and agencies row (market component). The corporatization process becomes more established as the WDTC begins to develop as a networked node of governance around which knowledge from various base organizations is mobilized. This is what Laegreid, Roness, and Rolland would call structural devolution, and what Shearing would call a nodal network.

Organizing DTCs in this way permits a shift in criminal justice that allows concrete markets to solidify and a corporate model to take hold. Moreover, it enables the absorption of multiple groups' knowledge claims into a governmental technology of risk and harms reduction, displacing other forms of addictions intervention, including abstinence-based programs. However, while the steering committee appears to be akin to corporate diversification (i.e., the numerous stakeholders), the funding model suggests that the court itself is a more centralized organization in which separate bodies become part of one larger-scale model. This organizational structure has significant autonomy from traditional court governance and extends the authority of the court to other civil service bodies. Although stakeholders are plentiful and diverse, and partnerships broad, the management tasks of the program/court are disciplined by market outcomes and government budgets.

While the WDTC is networked and indeed "rows" the program, it is dependent on the budgetary discretion of the provincial and federal governments. The budget of the WDTC has varied over its ten-year history. Shearing claims that in corporate domains, budgets can be used as the corporation sees fit and are therefore flexible.[33] The WDTC does have some flexibility, but it appears to have adopted fiscal management strategies where budgets/income dictate staffing arrangements, program elements, and service provision. For instance, the WDTC could not operate its transition house without funding from Human Skills and Development Canada. Therefore, a more precise indicator of agencified governance is the negotiation of a budget planned around "most efficient outcomes" as defined by funders. As such, the negotiation of the funding appears to be tied into performance indicators not set by the WDTC and its stakeholders, but by its funders. The federal money is tied to the treatment component of CDTS outcomes and performance indicators, the provincial money is tied to provincial court outcomes, and the transition house funds are tied to Human Skills and Development Canada outcomes. It is clear that the program direction of the WDTC depends on its own financial stability. As evidenced in shifting management structures and staffing as well as program elements, the WDTC can be said to operate like a corporation because its concern is its own survival as a corporate form. Dan Lang claims that these practices (program and staffing tied to financial outcomes) direct corporate organizations towards financial stability and growth of the corporation itself, and not always in directions of their own choosing.[34] Put another way, the WDTC will compromise its knowledge base to continue as an agency, which may explain why the steering committee lost numerous stakeholders over the years. Tying programming to fiscal outcomes has the effect of a smaller, more concentrated corporate form.[35]

Performance Indicators

Performance indicators are a foundational element of a corporate governance model. They emphasize return on investment with economic growth becoming both the end and the legitimation of public service.[36] Given the funding model of the WDTC, it must adhere to the Department of Justice's National Performance and Evaluation reporting requirements.[37] These requirements include output data (e.g., communication products, forums and workshops, information systems), service outputs (e.g., client information), program outputs (e.g., number of meetings attended, urinalysis reports, court appearances, time in custody, community referrals), and overall outcomes (e.g., progress reports on graduates, compliance, community impact, overall recidivism). Through such assessments, all the agencies involved in the therapeutic model are reduced to and subsumed by a corporate model focused on efficient outcomes. These governmental techniques of evaluation, accountability, and budgetary discipline provide a way to regulate and ensure responsibility and the fidelity of the workers, who, while remaining autonomous, are subjected to the budget and performance measures. As Nicolas Rose argues, these techniques represent the *budgetization* of an activity, where the old terms of calculation and decision are displaced and new diagrams of force and freedom are assembled.[38] Marino Regini suggests budgetary discipline establishes an exchange relationship, characterized by an agreement between the program/institution and the bureaucratic management of the funds that the government provides to the program/institution.[39] Consequently, programs are bound by this economic exchange and the mechanisms of governance and management are reduced to it.

Since its inception, the governance structure of the WDTC has been scaled back. A key recommendation of the 2008 interim process evaluation report was to "produce a governance structure that is moving toward more efficient management."[40] The 2015 evaluation shows that the steering committee, once populated by over twenty community groups, was eliminated in favour of direct supervision by the Manitoba Department of Justice, Court Division.[41] Indeed, a process evaluation in 2009 that included interviews with stakeholders found that many felt increasingly left out of the management structure, and were concerned with the harms reduction approach and the success indicators embedded in the court, but felt powerless to change it.[42] Opposed to this corporate model, many groups voluntarily left the court governance committee. This resistance highlights the disciplining effects of corporate governance, which, while ostensibly enabling more diverse representation, requires that all partners focus on meeting predetermined program goals (or leave the structure).

A consistent concern in the court evaluations is the role of staff with respect to court outcomes. The court was initially staffed by two primary teams—a court team and a treatment team.[43] While mostly working independently, the teams co-ordinated regarding clients' progression before the weekly court (court participants must appear before the judge weekly) and discussed in tandem the progress of each client prior to their court appearance. The judge, acting in a therapeutic fashion, rewarded or sanctioned the offender during their court appearance. Treatment workers ensured that clients attended regular individual and group therapy sessions, developed community contacts, and were supported in finding housing and skills training that (ideally) led to employment. Throughout its ten years, staffing was reduced and outsourced. Staffing began with a treatment team consisting of one manager, three counselors, one administrator, and one case manager, as well as a legal team comprised of one judge, organized through Justice Manitoba and a dedicated federal Crown, and supported by the Federal Department of Justice.[44] The 2015 evaluation reported a new treatment service model, characterized by greater distinctions between treatment and case management/supervision functions. The treatment component has been almost entirely taken over by the outside agency, Addictions Foundation of Manitoba (AFM). By 2015, the program was whittled down to two therapists/treatment workers hired by AFM and one case manager and support worker hired by the court itself.[45] These staffing changes were attributed to a streamlining of the court due to precarious funding. This is an interesting shift in the court's governance model. The agency itself becomes flatter and more streamlined, and even though it is linked back to the provincial government's court division, it gives the outside agency a more central role in the court's operation as a unit/node.

Although the court evaluations show a consistent rate of success in terms of performance indicators (e.g., recidivism rates stayed constant), the court did not accept clients in 2014 until the federal and provincial governments agreed to a new funding formula (in place until 2018). These staffing concerns are evidence of the budgetization of the court and its reduction to models of economic exchange and corporate orientation. Further examples include the court's focus on raising revenues and reducing expenses via the outsourcing of staffing to AFM. The change in staffing is also evidence of a myopic trajectory of the corporate court. Corporatization processes tend to create silos of activity, and this is exacerbated under neoliberalism with its emphasis on narrow financial performance criteria.[46] While traditional courts are horizontally organized, and all criminal courts operate equally, as a neoliberal corporate form the WDTC is separated from the other courts and myopically focused on its own service provision. It essentially operates in isolation from all other courts.

Front Line Service: Corporatizing Court Culture

Corporate structures impact the culture of the court as a workplace. The WDTC has altered the position, obligations, and relations between lawyers, judges, offenders, and the court system. While the traditional court culture is an adversarial one—where liberal, substantive, and common laws dictate the roles, obligations, and outcomes of court practices—corporate structures alter the actions of offenders and criminal justice workers. Within the operation of the WDTC, it is evident that the traditional roles of judge and defence counsel are modified, necessitating all team members to co-ordinate their activities and roles through the harms reduction approach and the performance indicator goals of the court.[47] For judges, their role as neutral arbitrators shifts to that of offender management, from guardians of the constitution to fathers of court participants.[48] The role of defence counsel shifts from gatekeeper of the system (check and balance on use of power by the state) to a therapist, where the duties are a mixture of healing and defending. Taken together, the workers under this corporate model are all directed towards managing a specific set of defined goals.

The restructuring of the court in this way forces individuals to take a more active role in their addiction/crime problem (or face a prison sentence), and they are reframed as clients as opposed to offenders.[49] The dominant discourse of harm reduction forces clients to be responsible for managing their own addiction within a myopic set of institutional parameters. Dan Malleck suggests that far from being productive and humane, this harms reduction ideology has become a public business, evidenced by addiction services such as twenty-eight day treatment programs and short-term residences, and the marketing of drugs such as Naloxone and Naltrexone, all of which frame the solution to addictions within a neoliberal model centred around the management of risk.[50] Likewise, Neil Hunt and Alex Stevens argue that these corporatized neoliberal models place the solution on the body of the client, and social issues like housing and the economy are sidelined to the actable problem of addictions and crime.[51] According to Malleck, solutions directed at the level of the addict do little to address issues of drug distribution and the social and political reasons why people become addicted in the first place.[52] Corporate models create sobriety as a commodity to be purchased or achieved, with the hope that therapeutic intervention will prevent addicts from becoming career criminals.

Under a corporate organizational form/node of governance populated by addiction experts, and with staff who are disciplined by budgetary concerns and performance outcomes, the court and its participants operate within a culture of economic reasoning. While seemingly more humane in terms of a less punitive experience, the WDTC—through weekly meetings, court requirements, drug testing, and multiple required behavioural stages (orientation stabilization, intensive treatment, maintenance, and graduation)—adopts much stronger measures of surveillance and monitoring than traditional incarceration.[53] This "addict gaze" reduces the client to a managed one who is, in Robin Mackenzie's words, a moralized subject forced to displace alternative forms of intervention.[54] This harms reduction construct, while aligning with the efficiency goals of the corporate structure, becomes a form of oppressive knowledge and fixes itself on the public body.[55] Justice is presumably dependent on this economic exchange, arranging its work to fit performance indicators through the language of cost-benefit, budgetary constraints, and efficient outcomes. While traditional discretionary power still exists in the court and most agencies of justice are increasingly subject to budgetary constraints, the corporate mechanisms of the WDTC entrench detailed specifications of performance and evaluation. What is lost in this process is traditional due process. Drug treatment courts now amount to coerced treatment, which may or may not produce positive outcomes (i.e., harms reduction), and are at odds with fundamental human rights which represent the backbone of traditional courts.[56]

Conclusion

Corporatization is identified as a management form that prioritizes market concerns over social concerns, producing a service or product that is reduced to an economic exchange. The management model, steering committee, staffing, and organizational structure of the WDTC reveal that the court operates, in part, under a model of agencification, enabling greater financial transparency, reduced political interference, and strong managerial accountability. Over its ten-year history, however, it has taken on a more corporatized structure, evidenced by its current management by AFM, an addictions service operating outside of the ministry of justice but with significant impacts on justice outcomes. Given its autonomy from the state, the court can be thought of as a participatory node with independent authority, capacity, and knowledge. As such, it represents a good case study of the corporatization of Canadian criminal justice. The corporatized court model exemplified by the WDTC shifts justice away from liberal ideals of equality and human rights towards efficiency and budgetary concerns. Although the court claims to help addicted individuals, it effectively modifies what constitutes help away from public service ideals and towards economic outcomes.

Policy-Making

―――――――― *10* ――――――――

Corporatization and Federal-Provincial Relations

Peter Graefe

Introduction

Canada's welfare state programs are distinctive in the degree to which they have been delivered through negotiations and agreements between federal and provincial governments. In examining these relations, analysts have often conflated the growth of social programs with the capacity of the federal government to impose national standards on the provinces, and to therefore see periods of retrenchment or stagnation, such as witnessed over the past quarter century, as reflecting a process of regrettable "decentralization." With the construction of the neoliberal state in the 1980s, for instance, many argued it was creating a more decentralized Canada. To the extent that the federal government played a role in developing pan-Canadian social rights through the enforcement of national standards in health and social assistance, there is likewise a tendency to see the federal government as the locus of progress and the claims of provinces for greater power as a reactionary undermining of those rights.

How has the restructuring of the state in a period of corporatization affected this federal-provincial dynamic? If corporatization is understood in a broad sense of remaking the public sector along the lines of corporate values, cultures, and perspectives, it has not involved a significant change in the federal government's power. Rather, we observe federal and provincial states that have both embraced corporate values and attempted to create market-friendly public sector cultures, and which then renegotiate their relationship in the context of this change. Instead of taking the form of decentralization, corporatization has been reflected in three trends. First, it has involved a narrowing of social policy discourse and ambitions in intergovernmental forums. Second, when the Liberals are in power federally, they have implemented, over partial provincial resistance, New Public Management-inspired forms of intergovernmental reporting and accountability. Third, when the Conservatives are in power federally, the trend is to federal-provincial disentanglement based on efforts to increase executive control over policy outputs. To reiterate, these three trends can be seen as related to the corporatization of the state in boxing social policy thinking within the realm of market-friendly ideologies (in the case of narrowing social policy discourse), and in trying to remake the public sector along the lines of private sector management strategies (in the case of the Liberal and Conservative trends).

Forms of State and Forms of Federalism

In terms of thinking through how federalism and intergovernmental relations change through time, it can be useful to pull apart the form of the state (say, Keynesian or neoliberal) from the form of the political regime (say, a unitary state or a federal one).[1] Clearly, the form of state and of regime are not fully separate from one another. The development of new state institutions and programs associated with Keynesianism in the 1940s and 1950s necessarily affected intergovernmental relations, as the federal government and the provinces had to negotiate how services were structured and how taxes were shared to pay for them. Yet, both the federal and provincial governments were undergoing a similar transformation in state forms at the time. There might have been conflicts, as when the neoliberal orientation of the federal government in the 1980s and early 1990s ran into provinces continuing to cling to parts of Keynesian social democracy, such as in Ontario and British Columbia. Most of the time, though, there was consensus over the broad philosophies to guide policy.

It might seem naive to assume that significant shifts in the form of the state would not greatly upset the federal-provincial dynamic. After all, the move to Keynesianism did legitimize the federal government intervening widely in areas of provincial jurisdiction, and in the process developing a much stronger sense of pan-Canadian citizenship. As well, the social forces supporting neoliberalism deliberately attempted to shift sites of authority within states (for instance, through devolution to regions or municipalities) as a means of breaking down welfarist institutions and restructuring the state.[2]

In the Canadian case, however, the understanding of the appropriate roles of the federal and provincial governments is by now well entrenched. It is supported by a complex pattern of citizen loyalties and identities that render attempts to change the federal and provincial roles politically problematic. And there is an institutionalization of roles and responsibilities, both through constitutional jurisprudence and the sophistication of developed bureaucracies both federally and provincially. As such, social forces attempting to change the state in Canada are more likely to transform the state in both its federal and provincial forms. Social forces taking on the additional task of fundamentally redefining the division of power between them would consume a great deal of political capital trying to redraw maps of citizen loyalty and knock down walls of intergovernmental bureaucratic self-preservation.

Even when building the post-war welfare state, the primary line of conflict was between a federal government with an eye to maintaining a pan-Canadian citizenship through building an integrated Canadian economy and Canada-wide social policies, and provinces who wished to develop their own programs and policies in order to develop a stronger sense of provincial citizenship. In this conflict, the provinces have often held the card of the Constitution. Particularly in social policy areas, provincial governments often have the constitutional jurisdiction to legislate, and so their consent is needed to implement policy. The federal government, by contrast, has a stronger ability to raise money through taxes, and has used this financial strength since the 1940s to entice the provinces to engage in common policies. Using its "spending power," the federal government has offered to provide funds to provinces that offer services in a manner prescribed by the federal government.

This trading of jurisdictional autonomy for federal funds has mostly been negotiated between the federal and provincial governments, and lies at the core of Canadian intergovernmental relations. The spending power gives the federal government a hierarchical position in the federation, in that it allows it a central agenda-setting role in these negotiations. While the Quebec government has opposed the use of this spending power on principle (on the grounds that it is nowhere mentioned in the Constitution, yet in practice constrains the use of the provincial powers mentioned in the Constitution), the other provinces have instead tried to bargain its use: how much control will there be over provincial programs and for what amount of federal spending?

In times when the form of state is receptive to the growth of social rights, such as the post-war Keynesian state, this can lead to something like the 1966 Canada Assistance Plan (CAP), with its standards for social assistance. The federal government used its agenda-setting power in this period to get provinces to agree to this program, and the financial resources it delivered allowed some poorer provinces to develop stronger assistance programs. But this was a negotiated process. The end result had more to do with a pre-existing commonality of perspectives between federal and provincial bureaucrats about where social assistance needed to go, with federal money, and with leadership hammering it into the form of national standards. When the state form changed to neoliberalism in the 1980s, this agenda-setting worked in a different way. With the convergence of federal and provincial perspectives around developing approaches to push social assistance recipients more quickly into the labour market, the federal government adopted new programs and approaches to spur reforms that went in the direction of workfare. When the federal government ended the CAP in its 1995 budget, it was seen as "decentralizing," in the sense of the loss of the pan-Canadian social rights that were upheld, at least rhetorically, in that policy. But it was not the case that the federal government was no longer using its agenda-setting power to engage the provinces around social assistance.[3]

Thus, if we consider the current period as one of the corporatization of the state, the question when looking at intergovernmental relations is how the remaking of the federal and provincial states has transferred into how they engage in bargaining over joint policy directions. The corporatization of the state shows up in a variety of forms, reflecting different dimensions of the process. If corporatization is understood in a broad sense of remaking the public sector along the lines of corporate values and perspectives,[4] or of "creating market-friendly public sector cultures and ideologies,"[5] we can understand its impact in the narrowing of the intergovernmental social policy discourse over the past quarter century to neoliberal and social investment themes. If corporatization is understood more specifically as the adoption and translation of private sector management concepts, we can see its impact in the changes in federal government leadership and accountability strategies over the past twenty years.[6] A key aspect of this private sector managerial change is the emphasis on outcomes rather than outputs: managers are not judged simply on delivering a particular object or activity efficiently, but on delivering the sought-after outcome. In a public sector context, this might mean that a training organization is judged less on how many people they serve (the output), and more on how many people they place into jobs (a sought-after outcome).

There is a tension between the adoption of the corporate form, with a presumed hierarchy where the top management sets goals that the organization is expected to meet, and a federal state, where the federal and provincial governments are each sovereign in their areas of jurisdiction, and as such co-equals.[7] While the spending power traditionally has been the manner through which the federal government has exercised hierarchical control in this decentralized system, the adoption of a New Public Management (NPM) outlook by both federal and provincial governments has meant this control has been reproduced in a new form.[8] Finally, the emphasis on results can also take the form of trying to disentangle policy-making, removing the intergovernmental dimension in order to enable more direct control by executives.[9] In other words, if the goal for the federal government is to shape outcomes, an alternative approach to "steering the provinces" is to try to find ways to act directly. Liberal governments have tended to adopt a corporatization model based on developing instruments of hierarchical control, while Conservative governments have emphasized achieving outcomes through disentanglement, mirroring corporate strategies of "delayering" organizational structures.

Narrowing the Social Policy Discourse

Looking at the dismantling of parts of the post-war welfare state in the 1990s (increased market discipline in employment insurance; cuts to transfers to provinces for social assistance, health, and post-secondary education; defunding of policy advocates), as well as the limited ambition of the "social investments state" measures of the early 2000s, social policy advocates often fault a "decentralization" of federalism, where the federal government's attempts at leadership were foiled by conservative provincial governments.[10] However, before turning to the forms of intergovernmental bargaining of the past two decades, one needs to understand what the federal and provincial governments were pursuing in their negotiations. The shift from the post-war welfare state to neoliberalism undercut the notion of creating social policies to deliver "social rights" of citizenship through universal programs, and instead tended to take aim at economic and social "inefficiencies." In the 1990s and early 2000s these included, for example, the impact of childhood poverty on brain development and the costs occasioned by homelessness (e.g., costs of hospital visits, trauma beds, policing, etc.).

Narrowly framing these issues as problems of inefficiency led to solutions that were not based on social rights, but on a logic of social investment. Public policies that built human capital (like early childhood interventions) or that prevented specific social ills (like homelessness) could "pay off" in a narrow cost-benefit sense if they were targeted properly to at-risk populations.[11] In this context, where both orders of government largely rejected universal social programs and social rights in favour of targeted social investments, it is not surprising that the result of their bargaining and negotiating were limited programs. It was not a question of one order of government forcing these policies on another, but of negotiating the appropriate machinery to deliver their new vision of the welfare state.[12]

New Forms of Hierarchy

Within this narrower, investment-focused vision of social policy, the federal and provincial governments developed new tools to manage their relationships. For the federal government, the language of NPM provided a novel way of engaging the provinces. NPM is understood here as an ideological movement in public administration, influential in the 1990s, that sought to apply private sector management precepts to public administration, particularly in terms of breaking up traditional bureaucratic organizational models. Bureaucracies were portrayed as costly, rule-bound organizations that hindered innovation and became self-serving. They needed to be made more flexible to better respond to the demands of customers on the one hand, and to achieve the outcomes planned by senior management teams on the other.

The traditional way of thinking about federal "spending power" was centred on a "command and control" vision of management and organization. The federal government would set the rules for social and infrastructure programs, and provinces who could demonstrate conformity with the rules would receive matching federal funds. If provinces did not deliver programs in conformity with the rules, they would be punished by not having their costs matched. While this system of applying "national standards" worked in terms of ensuring a similarity of provincial programs, the standards were mostly procedural. For instance, in social assistance, provinces could not apply residency requirements, they needed to provide assistance based on need, and they needed to offer an appeals process. In health, provinces had to ensure that health care was publicly administered and did not engage user fees.

By the 1990s, this approach proved less interesting for the federal government. In part this was related to a change in the power dynamics. In trying to restrain spending, the federal government had unilaterally cut and limited its financial exposure to provincial spending increases in health, post-secondary education, and social assistance, to say nothing of offloading responsibility to provinces for serving Indigenous peoples living off-reserve. To the extent that the federal government was unilaterally reducing its contributions, it also lost some of the financial and moral leverage to compel provinces to follow national standards. This applied to existing programs, and indeed the federal government recognized as much when it removed conditions around social assistance in the 1995 budget, at the same time as it cut social cash transfers to the provinces by one-third. But it also meant that the application of standards in new program areas would be treated skeptically by the provinces.

However, even if "command and control" was still possible, it is not clear that it would have entirely satisfied the federal government. As noted above, national standards largely policed process. They governed outputs, but did not have a lot of tangible direct impact on outcomes. They could guarantee the public delivery of health care, but not specific outcomes, such as primary care reform or shorter waiting times. New Public Management, with the idea of senior public service management "steering" through setting goals and ensuring the delivery of outcomes, and a variety of public and private sector actors "rowing" to achieve those outcomes, was an attractive alternative. It suggested that the federal government might choose some "softer" tools than tying money to meeting conditions to get the provinces to deliver programs and services that met federal goals. The idea was that between setting the agenda and developing reporting mechanisms, the federal government could compensate for its absence in the formal planning and implementation phases.[13]

This pushed federal Liberal governments to experiment with new corporatized forms of engaging the provinces, in an effort to exert hierarchical control on outcomes without the more traditional procedural policing of whether provinces followed the correct standards in producing outputs. As in the past, the negotiations were about the exchange of money in return for some say over how the provinces used their constitutional jurisdiction. However, in the late 1990s and early 2000s, rather than setting firm conditions in lengthy and detailed agreements (concretized in federal and provincial statutes like the Canada Assistance Plan and the *Canada Health Act*), the governments instead issued press releases or signed relatively short accords that announced the broad objectives they were seeking to achieve, as well as providing relatively terse plans for evaluation and reporting procedures.[14]

This form of managerial control through agenda-setting did involve more direct forms of "corporatization," in terms of creating or supporting formally independent think tanks, networks, and foundations that could provide policy agendas for the federal government to engage the provinces. The field of health care holds the most examples. From the late 1990s to the early 2000s, the federal budget would allocate support to establish or sustain bodies like the National Health Surveillance Network and the Canadian Health Network. Two bigger moves to assert a federal role in the health field were the creation of the Public Health Agency of Canada in 2004 and the Mental Health Commission of Canada in 2007. In addition, the federal government supported the work of think tanks and research organizations, such as the Canadian Policy Research Networks and the Caledon Institute, which were producing work on Canadian social policy and social architecture, setting agendas around childcare, disability, and housing benefits. In this process of sponsoring research, the federal government engaged in sustained conversations with experts, and received a head start in thinking through policy solutions and policy strategies that were identified therein. By creating formally independent organizations to do this agenda-setting work, as opposed to doing it in-house, the federal government could claim that it did not set the agenda. As such, the broad strategy of adopting corporate approaches to maintaining hierarchical control through agenda-setting was married to a narrower corporatization by incorporating new independent bodies to produce public goods.

The point here is not that these bodies or think tanks were "pro-federal government." It is more that they provided a steady stream of work identifying problems and proposing solutions that the federal government could package together and place on the intergovernmental agenda. Even if most of the provinces were likely to independently come to address the same problems with similar solutions, the net impact was to provide the federal government with the opportunity to engage the problems in multilateral discussions that might shape some pan-Canadian integration in the solutions adopted. This had the twin benefits for the federal government of reducing the provincial fragmentation of social policy, and for some credit claiming for new policies in areas such as child and disability benefits, homelessness, and health.

If the creation of these bodies and the development of new interlocutors worked to strengthen the agenda-setting capacity of the federal government, the development of accountability mechanisms was likewise felt to ensure that provinces made progress on achieving priorities. In other words, if the federal government sought to corporatize intergovernmental relations in order to drive outcomes, setting the agenda had to be paired with measures to ensure delivery of those priorities. The very fact of having to report on spending and indicators was thought to ensure provinces used federal transfers for their intended purposes and would be driven to concentrate on delivering what was measured. If they failed, presumably the public could punish them at election time. Reports would also allow other provinces to learn from the successes of their peers.

In some cases, this accountability took a direct corporate form by creating new bodies to which provinces would report. The most significant example of this was the creation, in agreement with the provinces, other than Quebec and Alberta, of the Health Council of Canada in 2003. This body monitored provincial progress in implementing the health care reforms agreed to in the 2004 Health

Accord, and tried to act as a clearinghouse for best practices, but was closed by the federal government in 2014. In most cases, however, the provinces simply agreed to produce annual reports for the public on how and where they spent federal money, and on their performance on a limited set of indicators. While the experience varied across policy fields and over successive agreements, the general pattern was that the provinces produced reports for the public largely for the sake of show. They did not provide information that citizens could easily use to hold governments to account, nor was there sufficiently detailed information to enable interprovincial learning.[15]

The Harper government did not have the same vision of social policy as the preceding Chrétien and Martin governments, and so did not apply the Liberals' agenda-setting and accountability model of corporatization. In some cases, like childcare, the government canceled agreements and instead invested in its own childcare tax benefit. In others, it let existing agreements tick along, as in health, or repackaged money and policy in a slightly altered form, as in housing or policies for people with disabilities. In the longer run, this lack of interest in provincial social policy development and delivery led to some loss of capacity to use NPM tools to affect policy outcomes. This is particularly true in agenda-setting. With the decision to defund or shutter organizations like the National Council of Welfare or the Canadian Policy Research Networks, the Harper government weakened its capacity to use these arm's length bodies to identify new policy priorities and to craft pan-Canadian solutions that it could bring into discussions with the provinces. In addition, by eschewing multilateral meetings with the provinces, the government lost its opportunity to engage the provinces collectively around its agenda. Finally, in winding down the Health Council of Canada, the government removed the reporting institution that was meant to monitor provincial delivery on their commitments in the major 2004 Health Accord.

While one might suspect the Harper government would be disposed to pushing the provinces to retrench their social programs or making them more consistent with pushing people into the labour market, in practice it largely followed a strategy of avoiding getting caught in federal-provincial entanglements by sustaining the status quo, and instead focusing on reforms it could undertake unilaterally.[16] Thus, it did not deploy the existing corporatized forms of intergovernmental relations to set the agenda and ensure accountability for results around its own priorities. Instead, it pursued a different translation of corporatized principles, as will be discussed in the next section.

In its platform for the 2015 federal election, the Liberal party made many mentions of working in collaboration with the provinces on a variety of social policy issues, such as health and childcare. This signaled a return to the corporatized intergovernmental relations of the Chrétien-Martin period, albeit with a desire for stronger reporting requirements to ensure the achievement of desired outcomes. In health care, for instance, the federal government is negotiating bilateral deals with provinces, where in return for money earmarked for mental health and home care, the provinces "measure and report on results and performance to ensure a transformation in care and improvements in services to Canadians."[17] The press release for the bilateral deals reports that "governments will develop performance indicators and mechanisms for annual reporting to citizens, as well as a detailed plan on how these funds will be spent, over and above existing programs."[18] So far, the federal government appears to be in a stronger negotiating position than in the late 1990s and early 2000s. For these health deals, it was able to break the provincial common front that had tried to push for more health funding before discussing mental health and home care. In the longer run, it must work with fewer agenda-setting tools due to the arm's length organizations shuttered under Harper, which may hamper its ability to shape provincial plans.

Executive Control Over Outcomes

Part of the appeal of corporatization, particularly when translated through the application of NPM precepts, is to find new means of ensuring that the decisions and plans of executives are efficiently delivered by front line bureaucrats. Corporate management is seen as being able to maintain hierarchical control while countering some of the pathologies of bureaucracy (such as red tape, the tendency of bureaucrats to develop their own goals, emphasis on following rules rather than taking risks), in part by producing evidence-based outcomes. The discussion above of the new forms of reporting and accountability are consistent with this outlook.

However, one might ask, why not simply have the federal government stick to its constitutional powers, and the provinces stick to theirs, and each government raise their own money and deliver their own programs? In other words, why not "disentangle" the governments so that intergovernmental relations become far less important? This is similar to the corporate strategy of "delayering" bureaucracies by reducing the number of intermediaries between the goal setters and those responsible for executing and delivering the results. Disentanglement does not mean non-entanglement: given the complexity of modern policy issues, federal and provincial governments will always have to consult each other and find ways to jointly solve problems. Nevertheless, if one left the provinces and the federal government to "do their own thing," you would have less interaction and thus fewer co-ordination problems in translating the executives' wishes into policy outcomes.

This was the overall approach adopted by the 2006–2015 Conservative government under Stephen Harper. In his statement on "Open Federalism" during the 2005–2006 campaign, he promised to respect provincial jurisdiction and rein in the use of federal spending power. His government's first budget similarly contained an annex outlining a very classical understanding of federalism, where particular issues were identified as the sole constitutional preserve of either the federal or provincial governments. His government mostly stayed true to this approach, aided by an anti-welfare statist ideology that limited ambitions to spend money in areas of provincial jurisdiction. Harper's social policy was less about welfare state programs and more about using criminal law and the penal system to regulate social behaviour. Thus, the government could legislate or enforce existing laws around issues like assisted suicide, sex work, gun control, drugs, and safe injection sites, without having to negotiate with provinces.[19] In many cases, it acted against the vocal wishes of provinces, ignoring, for instance, BC Premier Christy Clark's support for safe injection sites, Quebec Premier Jean Charest's request to not destroy gun registry records, and Ontario Premier Kathleen Wynne's open concerns about the constitutionality of the prostitution law. In sum, the Harper government provided a Conservative version of corporatization: the federal government would control outcomes through changing the instruments it used, so as to have direct control over outcomes. Rather than attempting to "steer the provinces," the federal government would try to engineer solutions through its direct control over criminal law.

The Harper government also followed the Chrétien and Martin lead in doing an end run around the provinces by providing tax benefits or transfers directly to Canadians, organizations, and cities. Whether with the transfer of gas tax monies to municipalities, the infrastructure support for cities, or the use of an array of tax credits related to disability, children, or childcare, the federal government has tried to achieve some goals through direct spending rather than negotiating with provinces.

This direct approach nevertheless hit snags along the way. There were a number of points during Harper's term in office where achieving policy aims ran into provincial jurisdiction and stymied his plans. The highest profile example was trying to create a Canadian Securities Commission, despite long-standing provincial claims to jurisdiction in the area. This plan was blocked by a decision of the Supreme Court in 2011. Later in its term, the Harper government also attempted to revamp the training system by introducing a Canada Jobs Grant, which would direct federal training dollars directly to individuals seeking training. The provinces, however, did not want to see federal dollars pulled from training programs that they felt were working, and so withheld their co-operation. Much as with earlier direct transfers, such as the National Child Benefit Supplement, the Millennium Scholarship Foundation, or the green municipal funds, the attempt to provide direct funding often requires some negotiation with the provinces, to make sure that the latter do not treat it as a "windfall" and withdraw their own funding. In so doing, they tend to arrive at intergovernmental agreements that look like the others above, in terms of setting out shared objectives and public reporting mechanisms.

Conclusion

Changes in the form of the state in Canada have contributed to a change in the conduct of intergovernmental relations. The corporatization process has impacted these relations, as the emphasis on remaking the public sector along the lines of corporate values and perspectives has led to the rejection of command-and-control style interventions to create national standards. The corporatization of Canadian intergovernmental relations has meant translating NPM strategies to ensure top-down control over outcomes in delayered and decentralized environments. For the Liberals, the corporatization strategy has involved using agenda-setting and results-reporting accountability mechanisms to steer the provinces. For the Conservatives, corporatization has taken the form of disentangling or delayering the process, to allow for more direct control over outcomes. The fact that these changes have gone hand-in-hand with the retrenchment of health and social assistance, and with timid and variable innovations in childcare, housing, and disability policy, has led many social policy advocates to demand a return to strongly enforced "national standards" in social policy.

The problem with this view is that it puts the cart before the horse: such "standards" are at best imaginable only after the federal government is willing to make major new social investments, and after the provinces are sufficiently on the same policy page to negotiate them. With both orders of government keen to maintain low taxes and undertake narrow, income-targeted programs, "national standards" are likely to create narrow, targeted social rights. Put another way, the problem with corporatized intergovernmental relations, whether in the Conservative or Liberal version, is less the new processes for delivering outcomes, than the impact of corporatization on narrowing the social policy discourse. An alternative to corporatized intergovernmental relations might be better to start with the development of a program of social rights that pushes beyond the current market-friendly public sector ideologies to demand substantive social protections from the insecurities of precarious work. As with the earlier periods canvassed in this chapter, the translation of this agenda into federal and provincial action will undoubtedly involve a renegotiation of their relationship. This might mean national standards, it might mean some version of the Liberal or Conservative corporatized strategies, or it might involve creating new modes of interaction and compromise. However, in a period of sustained austerity in social policy, it seems quixotic to seek solutions in redesigned intergovernmental processes, rather than the larger debates over social rights and public budgeting.

Corporatizing Urban Policy-Making

Management Consultants, Service Reviews, and Municipal Restructuring

Chris Hurl

Introduction

Since the onset of the 2008 economic crisis, the "Big Four" professional service firms—KPMG, Deloitte, PricewaterhouseCoopers, and Ernst and Young—have aggressively targeted Canada's municipal sector with the aim of expanding their market in management consulting. As a part of these efforts, they have rolled out new evaluative programs, which set out to demonstrate how governments measure up against comparable jurisdictions. While such programs ostensibly assist civic officials in making tough decisions on cutbacks and cost-savings, their growing use has also raised concerns about the depoliticization of municipal decision-making and the growing influence of private sector actors in shaping public policy.

In this chapter, I examine how Municipal Service Delivery Reviews (MSDRs) have served as a vehicle for the neoliberal corporatization of urban policy-making across Canada, especially in Ontario. While some scholars in this volume advance a narrower conception of corporatization, which is taken to denote an arm's length institutional arrangement or a form of managerial control, I explore neoliberal corporatization as a multifaceted program of governmental reform. This entails policy frameworks that reimagine government agency as a form of corporate decision-making. It includes managerial programs that bring together public officials and private firms in setting policy priorities. And it involves new kinds of performance metrics and auditing technologies through which public services become governable as objects of managerial discretion.

Looking at KPMG's recent interventions in Ontario, I explore how service reviews have been rolled out as vehicles of neoliberal corporatization at the municipal level. Over the past decade, municipal governments across the province have often commissioned KPMG management consultants to evaluate the services that they provide. Between 2011 and 2016, the firm was hired by at least twenty-seven municipalities, ranging from large cities—including Toronto, Hamilton, and Waterloo—to smaller towns, such as Georgian Bay and Smooth Rock Falls.[1] Through commissioning these kinds of reviews, I contend that civic officials have not only set budget priorities, but also reframed the parameters of local government decision-making, enabling the consolidation of private markets for policy advice across the province.

Service reviews have contributed to the corporatization of urban policy-making in three ways: First, they have enabled the growing integration of private firms and public agencies in generating urban policy priorities, bringing corporate and governmental power together in a public-private policy complex. Second, these programs have facilitated the diffusion of "business-like" practices in urban governance through benchmarking, best practices, and assorted performance indicators. Third, these programs have enhanced the discretion of senior managers, who are then able to make decisions about municipal services at a distance from public service professionals, front line workers, and community stakeholders.

I conclude by discussing the implications for local democracy. As decisions about city services come to be reframed as techno-managerial issues evaluated at arm's length, the realm of possibilities for public decision-making is narrowed. Segmented and set apart from the demands articulated by front line workers and community groups, local needs risk being reduced to managerial prerogatives. However, such tendencies to depoliticization are by no means uncontested, as possibilities remain for critical engagement and resistance.

Management Consulting as State-Corporate Symbiosis

Over the past thirty years, state agencies at all levels have come to rely on the private sector for policy advice. Public sector spending on private management consultants in Canada has increased dramatically, growing at the federal level from $56 million in 1984 to nearly $1 billion by 2008.[2] At the provincial level, Ontario makes up the largest market, growing to $389 million per year by 2008.[3]

And while it is difficult to determine the exact figures, there is also evidence to suggest that as cities face fiscal pressures from stagnating tax revenues and the downloading of services from higher levels of government, management consultants are increasingly taken up in advising municipalities.[4]

How can we explain the tremendous growth of management consulting in the public sector over the past three decades? Often, critical scholars view this as a process of colonization, by which a corporate "consultocracy" infiltrates state institutions, effectively forming a "shadow government" that operates outside official channels of decision-making and accountability.[5] In the context of neoliberal restructuring, this consultocracy has skillfully and self-servingly interjected itself in areas of policy-making that were previously undertaken by in-house civil servants. For instance, in his investigations of state restructuring across the UK through the 1980s and 1990s, Christopher Hood views the rise of consultants as part of a "new class" who "colonized the public management from the outside." State reforms, he notes, were driven by a "privatization complex" comprised of "management consultants, accountants and IT specialists who form the equivalent of 'efficiency experts'," seeking to extend their influence across state institutions as a means of drawing in new business.[6] More recently, Mike Raco has explored how this complex of experts operates as part of an "expanding machine" in UK urban governance, reflecting a managerial agenda through which power is being "transferred from citizens and governments to regulators and a new breed of powerful global companies and investors," effectively removing decision-making from democratic oversight by elected political officials and their constituencies.[7]

While the notion of colonization sheds light on the growing influence of management consultants under neoliberal governance arrangements, this metaphor remains limited to the extent that it presumes that governments were somehow less porous and less driven by imperatives to be "business-like" in the past. However, as Greg McElligott (see Chapter 8 in this volume) notes, the use of management consultants in government restructuring is by no means new or unique to neoliberal governments.[8] In Canada, management consultants were heavily drawn upon in the 1960 Glassco Commission on the structure of government, which advised Ottawa to "let the managers manage." Going even further back to the early twentieth century, there is evidence that management consultants were taken up by reformers at different levels of government to reorganize state agencies according to the principles of scientific management—promising economy, efficiency, and an end to wasteful patronage-based employment practices.[9]

Rather than beginning from the presumption that state agencies are presently being colonized by private actors, the growing use of consultants is perhaps better framed as a double-sided process, co-produced, on the one hand, by market consolidation of large, transnational professional service firms, and on the other by the growing openness of public institutions to private consulting services. Conor O'Reilly describes this as "state-corporate symbiosis," which has involved thickening relationships between public agencies and private sector actors. From this perspective, it is not so much a matter of understanding "who is pulling the strings," as it is about "'the ties that bind' these actors together."[10]

The process of corporatization has not just involved a growing reliance on private management consultants for policy-making advice. It has also entailed a shift from *ad hoc* relationships towards the consolidation of more enduring and regular ties with Big Four firms. From the 1960 Glassco Commission onwards, Denis Saint-Martin notes thickening relationships between these firms and the federal government.[11] Many consultants hired to work on the commission ended up working in senior management positions in the Civil Service Commission and the newly formed Treasury Board Secretariat, solidifying channels through which management consultants garnered access to state agencies. This paved the way for a second wave of government reform, beginning in the early 1990s under Liberal policies of fiscal restraint promoted by finance minister Paul Martin, and has contributed to the expansion of management consulting into provincial and municipal jurisdictions.

The appeal of "outside" business experts has been especially important under neoliberal governments, as political leaders drew inspiration from philosophies of New Public Management (NPM), emphasizing the importance of private sector ideas in reforming state agencies and problematizing the influence of in-house professionals in manipulating the policy-making process for their own purposes. In Ontario, for example, spending on management consultants was spurred on by the Common Sense Revolution of Mike Harris, which aimed for smaller government, fewer regulations, and lower taxes. Between 1998 and 2002, provincial spending on outside consultants consequently rose from $271 million to $662 million, just as the public sector workforce was being downsized from 81,000 to 61,000 full-time equivalent (FTE) positions.[12] Moreover, management consultants were taken up in the municipal sector, as the Harris government targeted local governments as havens for profligate spending, inefficiencies, and red tape. Along these lines, the Ministry of Municipal Affairs commissioned KPMG in 1996 to assess the presumed "cost savings" that would come from amalgamating the

Municipality of Metropolitan Toronto, alongside several other large metropolitan areas across the province.[13]

Of course, the growing use of management consultants by public agencies does not necessarily entail corporatization in itself. Alongside the growing demand for private consultants, there have also been changes in how management consultancy services are provided. While small and independent firms continue to provide advice on a range of specialized issues—from organizing public consultations on bike-lanes to implementing new IT systems and payroll technologies—corporate power in the management consulting industry has grown. According to a recent report by the industry association, the largest firms (with over $250 million in revenue) have come to represent 70 percent of the Canadian market.[14] Revenues are increasingly concentrated through scale advantages, changing procurement practices, and industry consolidation through mergers and acquisitions. Indeed, while Big Four firms initially divested from management consulting in response to the conflicts of interest exposed during the 2001 Enron scandal, they have reversed course since 2005, acquiring dozens of smaller consulting firms working with public sector agencies across Canada, primarily in health and education, but also in the municipal sector.[15]

Moreover, the degree of contact between public agencies and Big Four firms has also grown. Beyond simply posing as occasional advisors, these firms now portray themselves as indispensable "partners in governance" whose services are required on an ongoing basis in confronting the pressures to both publicly demonstrate that services are being provided efficiently, and develop new management models in the context of declining revenues and rising operating expenses.[16] Over the past decade, Big Four firms have become increasingly embedded in regulatory regimes and public institutions, such as Infrastructure Ontario, where they are responsible for assessing Value for Money (VfM) in the financing, construction, operation, and maintenance of public infrastructure projects.[17] Likewise, the use of consultants has also been encouraged through the development of new programs for reporting and benchmarking, such as the Ontario Municipal Benchmarking Initiative and the Municipal Performance Measurement Program, which require each of Ontario's 445 municipalities to collect data on core municipal service areas, and to annually report this information via the local media and municipal websites. In addition, they have become increasingly influential as financial intermediaries in assisting governments in negotiating new public infrastructure contracts with private firms.

While Big Four firms have played an instrumental role as "impartial" auditors and consultants in assessing the value of public services and infrastructures, they have also played an active role as proponents of privatized models of service delivery, lobbying different levels of government for greater private sector participation in service provision through their promotional publications and membership in international and national trade associations. For instance, KPMG is a Sponsor Member of the Canadian Council for Public Private Partnerships, the chief lobbying group for public-private partnerships (P3s) in Canada.[18] Beyond simply selling their advisory services, these firms regularly engage with a range of federal, provincial, and municipal agencies in advancing privatized service delivery models through conferences, workshops, and seminars. At the meetings of the Ontario Municipal Administrators' Association, KPMG partners have presented on topics such as "labour market issues" and "Commissioning vs. Outsourcing: Finding the Right Model." Similarly, they identified municipal employee unions as the problem at a 2009 meeting of the Alberta Urban Municipalities Association, warning of "[i]ncreasing labour costs as a result of collective agreements that continue to support increasing costs … not just in terms of labour rates but also benefits!"[19]

In this context, the use of service reviews in assessing the performance of municipal services has facilitated the further integration of government and private corporations in urban policy-making. Through accumulating professional expertise across jurisdictions and generating centralized archives and databanks, professional service firms have achieved an economy of scale in selling their advice to state officials. Institutional ties between large consultancy firms and state agencies have consolidated as state agencies generate more enduring connections with corporations in the outsourcing of policy advice, and professional service firms concentrate their power in the consultancy market.

City Politics as Corporate Decision-Making

The corporatization of urban policy-making is also evident in the managerial discourses and calculative schema that are marketed by professional service firms to civic officials. Over the past three decades, the Big Four firms have each worked to establish branded forms of assessment that can be uniformly packaged and sold across jurisdictions. Through the application of benchmarking and best practices drawn from the private sector, consultants have worked to recast municipal politics in the mold of corporate decision-making. Corporatization, in this sense, involves extending "a specific formulation of economic values, practices, and metrics" to different aspects of urban governance.[20]

Big Four firms have assumed a prominent role in packaging and circulating performance metrics—around competitiveness, efficiency, and lean management—that promise to alleviate policy-makers' anxieties about their competitive position relative to other cities. From the late 1980s onwards, William Davies notes that these firms were central players in fabricating "a common global language through which business and political leaders could discuss how public policy influenced corporate and entrepreneurial performance, and a measurement framework through which all public policy, public investment and executive political decision making could be subjected to a blanket economic audit."[21] Along these lines, a range of studies have recently highlighted how rankings, benchmarking, and other performance metrics have been marketed to public agencies and governments as a means of setting policy priorities, establishing new accountability frameworks, and achieving economy in service provision.[22]

While these studies have noted the role of such technologies in fabricating moral economies of "excellence" in which institutions compete for top positions on league tables, civic officials have also commissioned such programs in operationalizing austerity policies. Rather than serving as a point of departure for urban coalitions that prioritize growth, city branding, and entrepreneurialism (which was the focus in the late 1990s), recent studies note that in the wake of the 2008 crisis these programs were taken up by local political and economic elites to "naturalise the contraction of the state as value free and without alternative."[23] Drawing from private sector management philosophies of "core business"—popularized in management strategy books from the late 1980s and early 1990s, such as Moss Kanter's *When Giants Learn to Dance*—consulting firms have recently developed benchmarking technologies that aim to achieve greater "focus" in service delivery through shedding activities that do not directly contribute to an agency's "primary goals" (see also Mehra, Chapter 2 in this volume). In the context of austerity, this kind of rationality was taken up as a means of circumscribing public sector imaginaries, embodying a "retreat from older expansive conceptions of public service" through "narrowing frameworks for the evaluation of services to assessments of their 'performance' and 'efficiency' as a business."[24]

In Ontario, Municipal Service Delivery Reviews (MSDRs) have served as a vehicle for the diffusion of economic metrics across local governments. Framed as a "fresh approach to managing municipal spending," these reviews have been encouraged by Ontario's Ministry of Municipal Affairs since 2004, when it first published its *Guide to Service Delivery Reviews for Municipal Managers*. Traditionally, the guide notes, managing spending meant "across-the-board cuts to all services, 'cherry picking' which services to cut, deferring capital projects, increasing user fees or dipping into reserves." Typically, budget cuts resulted in comparable reductions in the service. However, the service review process takes a different tack. "It focuses on setting priorities—*making choices*—and, where possible reducing the cost of delivery while maintaining or improving services and service levels."[25] The aim, then, is to make municipal governments "intelligent" in their capacity to implement cutbacks.

Drawing from the ministry's recommendations, large firms like KPMG and PricewaterhouseCoopers have recently marketed their own distinct brands of MSDRs to dozens of cities across the province in order to assist civic officials in making "tough decisions." The evaluation process includes practices and technologies that assess and rank services in terms of their relative necessity, efficiency, and standard of delivery. For instance, in Toronto, KPMG consultants applied a "Core Service Filter" to the city's 155 services, seeking to determine areas of potential cost-savings. This was framed as a matter of distinguishing "core and high priority" services from those that are considered to be expendable—what consultants describe as simply "nice-to-have" rather than "must haves." The apparent need for services was determined by the extent to which they were deemed common across jurisdictions and statutorily required by different levels of government.

Standards were set by comparing accounts with a select sample of other cities deemed to be similar "in terms of size, history, urban characteristics, demographics, geography."[26] For example, Toronto was compared to Montreal, Chicago, Boston, Philadelphia, Barcelona, and Melbourne, which were listed in a "jurisdictional examples" section of KPMG's final report. Here, consultants gauged the extent to which Toronto departed from the norm in the field of municipal service delivery by providing services that were deemed to be uncommon, or provided at higher than standard levels in comparison with these other cities. As KPMG noted, "available spaces in Toronto libraries are elevated" in comparison with other jurisdictions.[27] They also identified best practices in other cities that Toronto might consider adopting, such as offloading heritage work, which was provided by an independent agency in a number of cities, and selling off parking facilities, which was undertaken in Chicago.[28] By making the city comparable with other, previously distant, jurisdictions, its needs could be defined on the basis of outside norms.

Based on the application of these schemas, consultants are then able to identify "key opportunities by function, other departments or private organization comparisons." In the context of Toronto, KPMG suggested options such as closing public library branches and reducing hours of operation, cutting back on the city's "very aggressive" recycling targets, ending subsidized recreation activities for low-income residents and children, and cutting the Toronto Transit Commission's Wheel Trans service for people with disabilities. Moreover, in appraising these options, consultants developed a prospective timeline and identified potential costs and political, economic, and social risks that were associated with their implementation.

Following the 2011 Toronto review program, similar schemas were applied in dozens of cities and towns across the country as a means of facilitating cutbacks and restructuring. In Hamilton, KPMG consultants proposed privatizing food services at all recreation facilities, boosting parking and recreation fees, utilizing P3s for the construction of recreation facilities, and making the municipal workforce more "flexible." In the town of Whitby, Ontario, consultants recommended restructuring the municipal labour force through the use of "lean process re-engineering," outsourcing and privatizing municipal services, increasing recreation fees, and implementing a corporate performance measurement system. And in the municipality of Wawa, Ontario, civic officials were advised to consider offloading the costs of long-term disability premiums onto its employees, reducing the number of playgrounds, eliminating transit services, and discontinuing community subsidies for seniors' programs.

By reimagining local politics as an exercise in corporate bookkeeping, service reviews consequently risk depoliticizing municipal policy-making, as decisions about community needs and priorities are reduced to simple accounting practices. This logic was captured well by a KPMG presentation to the town of Midland, Ontario. Noting that service levels "are higher than minimum standards and higher than what other municipalities your size are delivering," the senior consultant argued that "[y]our services can still come down and be comparable to what others receive."[29] The *normative* frame, in terms of what services should be provided, is consequently conflated with what is *normal* in other cities. This puts considerable pressure on civic officials to reduce or eliminate services that are uncommon in other jurisdictions, regardless of how beneficial these services may be for local residents and communities.

Segmenting and Circulating Corporate Knowledge

Beyond focusing on the content of managerial discourses and modes of evaluation, it is also important to consider how Big Four firms facilitate the movement of policy in new ways. Management consultants play a critical role in packaging policy ideas and putting them into circulation across jurisdictions—facilitating what Jamie Peck and Nik Theodore describe as "fast policy," or a policy-making condition that is characterized by "the intensified and instantaneous connectivity of sites, channels, arenas, and nodes of policy development, evolution, and reproduction."[30] Corporatization, thus, entails not only the kinds of ideas that are brought into municipal decision-making, but also the way that consultants enlist expertise and policy-making information from different places and times, drawing them together in a framework that generates a sense of proximity across jurisdictions.[31]

In Ontario, for example, the review process has facilitated the institutional segmentation of knowledge, with evaluations being designed and implemented at arm's length from the delivery of front line services. Thus, consultants have not typically engaged with front line workers or community groups as significant constituencies in deciding on a city's core services or its standards of delivery.[32] This is considered outside of their remit and risks making their project unviable. As one KPMG consultant explains, investigating the impacts of service reductions on service delivery "will completely bog you down and you can get caught in analyzing a handful of services to the greatest degree possible and then dismiss everything else, because that's where your effort's going to go."[33] Rather than investigating how services are organized and delivered on the front lines, data is generated through a second-order process of commensuration that simply renders existing by-laws and statutes, financial statements, and managerial policies legible across jurisdictions. There is seldom public participation in the process and, if there is, input from workers and local residents is only taken into consideration after the fact and treated as testimony from special interests.

Determining community needs is consequently generated through a specific form of social organization, which sets apart those formulating the schema from those who are actively involved in implementing it. The segmentation of knowledge in this way contributes to the production of what Dorothy Smith describes as ideological circularity, which "insulates governing schema from encounters with the givens of local historical experience."[34] This circularity is reflected in the fact that consultants do not need to possess any knowledge of community needs or priorities in rendering their judgments on what is necessary. The necessity of a service is not determined through investigating its performance on the ground, so much as it is about taking existing financial and management records and translating them into a self-enclosed second-order world of comparisons through which service priorities can be disciplined. The discretion of public workers delivering services at the front line can then be supplanted by the prerogatives of public managers, who interrogate professional decisions according to the perceived priorities and capacities of the organization.

The segmentation of knowledge through the commensuration of second-order data has also enabled its packaging and circulation across jurisdictions.

Toronto in particular has served as an important beachhead from which the review process and its attendant modes of evaluation can be further taken up and rolled out in municipal agencies across the region. Since 2011, MSDRs have been commissioned in at least twenty-seven cities and towns across the province, which KPMG advertises as giving them "extensive insight into municipal operations and best practices" and enabling them to develop "a proven approach to reviewing municipal organizational structures, staffing levels and services."[35]

KPMG has been able to extend its influence by using each review as a basis for collecting further data, training staff, and generating networks with public officials. As reviews are rolled out across jurisdictions, private archives can be accumulated through which information about Toronto is stored alongside data collected from other municipalities and public agencies. Moreover, consultants gather experience and build reputations, with many of the same staff from Toronto going on to spearhead projects in Hamilton, Waterloo, Timmins, Moosonee, and North Bay. More enduring policy networks are generated, as KPMG consultants position themselves as reputable advisors in public administration circles and local austerity coalitions. For instance, consultants have subsequently marketed the Toronto experience at professional seminars organized by the Institute for Citizen-Centred Service, which is seeking to further extend inter-jurisdictional referencing and benchmarking practices across Canadian municipalities, and at the meetings of the Canadian Association of Municipal Administrators.[36] In the end, all of these resources can be added to their inventory, making the firm ever more credible as it sells its advisory services to municipalities across the region and around the world.

In fact, this program was so successful in Ontario that the talent has now been promoted to head up KPMG International's Center of Excellence in Cities. Alan Mitchell, who was a chief architect of inter-municipal referencing in Ontario, was appointed as the center's executive director in 2012.[37] He has since been actively promoting MSDRs as one of the firm's central products for local governments globally. According to a recent report, the program is now being promoted in Australia and France (among other places), with a series of case studies presented as evidence of their success.[38]

Conclusion

The growing influence of the Big Four firms in the evaluation of municipal services has significant implications for local politics. The integration of corporate and governmental power, the refashioning of local politics as corporate decision-making, and the packaging and circulation of managerial knowledge as fast policy risk contributing to what some scholars describe as a deepening post-political condition, in which the political aspects of service delivery are displaced by techno-managerial prerogatives. Erik Swyngedouw notes that this is politics "reduced to the administration and management of processes," replacing "debate, disagreement and dissensus with a series of technologies of governing that fuse around consensus, agreement, accountancy metrics and technocratic environmental management."[39]

The state-corporate symbiosis has generated economies of scale through which municipalities come to rely on Big Four firms for a range of different professional services, which include not only consulting but also auditing and accountancy services, and expertise in brokering new contracts. While these firms were previously commissioned on an *ad hoc* basis, increasingly they are being imagined as "partners in governance," providing the requisite expertise in the evaluation and delivery of public services.

Consequently, these firms have become positioned as powerful policy actors in negotiating the standards of service delivery. Through the application of private sector modes of assessment and ranking to the public sector, such as MSDRs, alongside other forms of benchmarking and evaluation, consultants play an essential role in easing civic officials' anxieties about where they stand in relation to other cities and actively work to define and disseminate the norms of public service delivery across jurisdictions. Assuming the role of impartial intermediaries, these firms can draw from the accumulated weight of comparisons, generated by expert networks and private databanks, in making their presence felt, contributing to the normalization of urban policy-making by targeting services that depart from the standards set by other jurisdictions.

The growing mediation of local government decisions by private firms raises questions of accountability and transparency, as the institutional channels through which policy ideas are generated and shared become increasingly commodified. Through the maintenance of private archives and professional networks, firms like KPMG effectively place the policy-making process out of reach from public service professionals, community groups, and local residents. While the process is ostensibly public, the metrics for evaluation are kept at arm's length, carefully guarded by these firms as property under copyright laws.

The corporatization of urban policy-making through these kinds of programs might suggest that opportunities for public participation are diminishing; however, there are openings for resistance. While consultants set out to generate credibility by appealing to their impartial business expertise, their claims can be contested. For instance, the efforts by KPMG consultants to present themselves as credible actors were widely contested in Toronto, with hundreds of people showing up for public consultations hosted by the city.[40] The process galvanized widespread opposition to a local agenda of cutbacks, and ultimately resulted in the overturning of the proposed budget for that year. Perhaps more importantly, it also facilitated the generation of grassroots networks through which different policy priorities could be imagined and more progressive benchmarks could be set. Likewise, such processes have been challenged in Hamilton, Prince George, Nanaimo, and Vernon.[41] Nevertheless, while there has been resistance at times, the strategies of knowledge production undertaken by local community actors are often forgotten as these programs are mobilized across jurisdictions. A central challenge for activists, then, is to develop the capacity to build connections and share knowledge across communities—documenting both the techniques through which Big Four firms make their case, and effective strategies through which their knowledge claims can be unpacked and contested.

Civil Society and the
Non-Profit Sector

Managerialism and Outsourcing:

Corporatizing Social Services in Canada's Non-Profit Sector

Donna Baines

Introduction

The non-profit sector in Canada includes more than 165,000 charities and non-profit organizations, contributes 7.8 percent of GDP, and forms 10.5 percent of the labour force.[1] This makes the sector a significant player in the Canadian economy, larger than professions and roughly the same size as manufacturing and private services.[2] By picking up and providing services offloaded by the state, the non-profit sector has also played a significant yet under-examined role in welfare state downsizing and corporatization. This chapter explores corporatization in the largest subsection of non-profits, namely non-profit social services (NPSS), which comprises roughly 6 percent of the Canadian labour force.[3] The NPSS sector is gendered with women composing the majority of employees, service users, and volunteers.[4] It provides social service programs and supports (such as counseling, support groups, case work, referrals, and life skills) to a range of populations, including the elderly, youth and children, families, people in conflict with the law, the poor and unemployed, and people with a range of physical and mental health challenges.

Originally a site of non-market social relations and democratic participation,[5] the NPSS now largely mimics lumbering state bureaucracies operating in the interests of the private market rather than agile, innovative advocates for care.[6] Neoliberal corporatization and contracting out policies have created the conditions for stripping the NPSS and civil society on several axes, including removing or reducing: social participation in agency programs and policies; flexibility and the ability to respond quickly to new and long-standing social needs; and the capacity to stand outside of government and offer critique. The primary force behind this transition can be traced to the ways in which corporatization processes operate within the NPSS.

The NPSS sector is not and never was monolithic. It contains faith-based organizations promoting a range of religious ideologies alongside much-needed services, and large multi-service, multi-site enterprises operating in hierarchical and bureaucratic ways. It also contains storefront operations closely tied to the communities they serve. These smaller organizations are often informal, sometimes explicitly political, and frequently operate in a grey area outside of state and bureaucratic practice. These various organizations reacted differently to corporatization. However, all who accepted government funding became reluctant extensions of the state in one way or another, and often unintentional conduits of neoliberalism and austerity into the lives of service users.

This chapter argues that although corporatization existed in the NPSS prior to the 1980s, it was a more "benevolent" corporatization that included participatory and social justice-oriented practices that reflected its civil society roots. The challenge for neoliberal governments was to reshape the non-profit ethos and model of corporatization to align more closely with private market, neoliberal goals. Neoliberal corporatization, in the years that followed, resolved these "problems" through the introduction of managerialism, in the form of New Public Management (NPM), as a requirement for receiving government funding. The chapter begins with an overview of NPM and managerialism in the context of NPSS corporatization, followed by a discussion drawn from qualitative research findings that reveal a pattern of gendered precarity and unpaid work in the non-profit sector. The chapter goes on to analyse the erosion of participatory practices in the NPSS and resistance to corporatization in the non-profit sector.

NPM and Managerialism in the Context of NPSS Corporatization

Beginning in the 1980s, governments around the Anglo-American world introduced increasingly aggressive policies of downsizing and privatizing public services. This was largely achieved through competitive tendering and contracting out or selling off public goods. The fact that non-profit organizations already existed as arm's length, independent corporations meant that the state did not have to initiate these enterprises, but could build from them for the purposes of corporatizing existing social services. As I will demonstrate, the non-profit ethos of democratic participation, advocacy, and critique of government policies presented certain dilemmas for governments that sought to manage services at arm's length, while at the same time seeking to maintain control over the direction of social service provision. These dilemmas were managed by changing the management model and activities of non-profit agencies through the requirements contained in government funding contracts.[7]

Under contracting out and competitive tendering processes, for-profit and non-profit organizations competed for government contracts to provide particular services at the lowest possible cost. This resulted in decades of underfunding, the implications of which will be discussed further below. The details of government contracts also introduced and reinforced the increasingly private market-compatible state form within agencies.[8] This included the adoption of NPM, process-directed metrics (also known as outcomes or targets), and competitive performance management. Failure to comply with these accountability requirements meant that contracts were not renewed, and agencies struggled to remain in operation.[9]

New Public Management is a putatively arm's length public sector governance model derived from the private sector and originally developed for retail work.[10] NPM shifts risk from the government to front line workers by requiring them to account for funding outcomes through a series of metrics, such as the number of cases opened, number of referrals or interventions provided, and number of cases closed.[11] NPM's purported benefits (e.g., efficiency, improved outcomes) exist alongside the managerialist tendency to standardize work practices and reduce or remove those that are difficult to quantify.[12] Open-ended, relationship-based, participatory practices once thought to form the backbone of NPSS work are easily displaced by short-term, easy-to-measure, technical interactions.[13]

Though they are difficult to standardize and count, democracy-enhancing and social justice-oriented practices nurture the link between civil society and the NPSS, and serve as the major source of its integrity and innovation. The literature suggests that the removal of these practices results in mission drift, or an organization's shift from social justice goals to market-based objectives and values.[14] As Angela Eikenberry argues, service delivery is undermined when the democratic values of participation and voice are eroded by an emphasis on meeting government targets rather than responding to the needs of increasingly desperate groups of service users.[15]

In effect, NPM has been a Trojan horse introducing new sets of neoliberal practices and policies that effectively remade the NPSS in "pro-market, non-market" ways. Pro-market refers to the way that NPM governance unobtrusively institutes market-based policies within a sector where they were once seen as antithetical.[16] These private market logics are introduced smoothly and without fanfare, through the terms of government contracts. This process extends state gravitas to claims that the private market is the best antidote to the problems facing society, including those addressed by the NPSS.[17] Private market practices such as outcome measures and competitive performance management are further legitimized in this process and established as the archetypical management model for every kind of enterprise, even non-profit services for society's most vulnerable and exploited populations.[18] The changes are simultaneously non-market because even though they attempt to introduce efficiencies and cost-savings, they do not turn a profit or generate surplus.[19] Hence, they remain outside of that defining aspect of the private market.

Precarity, Gender, and Unpaid Work

Since the 1980s, neoliberal policies have downsized the welfare state, resulting in the NPSS assuming an ever-greater share of social services and their costs. As a result, the NPSS has been under growing pressure to meet rising demand and address threats to service quality. As well, flexibility and the endless pursuit of cost "efficiencies" have provided the context for employers to replace permanent, full-time jobs with numerous forms of precarious work including part-time, contract, casual, on-call, and zero-hours contracts.[20] A number of authors argue that although precarious employment provides valuable flexibility to employers, its cumulative impacts are harmful in that it introduces instability and insecurity to individuals and the economy.[21] According to the OECD, precarity also increases social inequality, especially for women who face greater vulnerability to involuntary part-time employment and other forms of precarious work, as well as the triple burden of care in the home, community, and paid labour force.[22]

Gender inequity in the NPSS is also extended through processes that predate neoliberalism but have been transformed within the NPM corporatization model. Years of underfunding, accompanied by the lowest bid process of contracting out, have produced serious gaps in service, which are filled through the unpaid labour of predominantly female workers.[23] Unpaid work is undertaken as part of this workforce's social justice commitment to service users and communities, and is generally described as an act of solidarity or a gift freely given (for which thanks is not required).[24] However, recent research has found that the conditions for "pure" gift relationships in unpaid social service work are increasingly rare. Donna Baines and Ian Cunningham, for example, show that unpaid labour does not just supplement paid work in the NPSS.[25] On the contrary, some social service organizations use unpaid labour to undertake core functions, and most would have had to seriously reduce service levels without it.

While the NPSS has always relied on volunteers and its majority-female work-force to extend services and remain connected to communities, by consistently underfunding the NPSS, neoliberal funding models have embedded unpaid work deep into its core operations.[26] Indeed, the competitive tendering model of con-tracting out means that agencies are compelled to consistently constrain and reduce costs in order to win bids and retain service levels. This is a vicious circle and means that agencies receive less and less funding to provide the same levels of service, ultimately turning to their altruistically motivated staff and volunteers to fill in the gaps. The literature confirms that employers directly (and govern-ment funders indirectly) depend on unpaid work to extend cash-strapped organ-izations, meet outcome measures, and evaluate staff for additional hours of paid work or the rare full-time position that opens up.[27] There is also growing evidence that current levels of unpaid work are unsustainable, as workers reach a breaking point resulting in high rates of sick days and job turnover, as well as the tendency for both paid and unpaid workers (mostly women) to leave the sector entirely.[28]

Eroding Participatory Practices

Earlier it was noted that NPM and neoliberal corporatization policies have undermined the ethos and healthy functioning of the NPSS and civil society on several axes, including removing or reducing: social participation; flexibility and the ability to respond quickly to new and long-standing social needs; and advocacy and the capacity to stand outside of government and offer critique. This section will discuss each of these axes in turn, drawing on qualitative interview data.

Social Participation

Participation in decisions affecting service content, delivery, priorities, and direction were once considered to be part of the work of NPSS employees. Indeed, participation and a voice in the workplace were often thought to provide at least partial compensation for low wages and benefits.[29] Community members and service users were frequently drawn into debates and decision-making through public forums, agency-wide open discussions, "listening meetings" focused on particular issues with select populations, and door-to-door consultations with neighbours and other service providers. The adoption of new corporatization models has resulted in years of under-bidding in the NPSS sector in order to win government contracts. This, in turn, has led to reduced funding for infrastructure, overhead, and training, and the eventual elimination of most forms of staff and community participation.

Commenting on their sense that they had lost the right to workplace participation and control over agency priorities, one senior front line worker noted, "We don't have a voice. If the funder wants the numbers, we give them the numbers no matter what else we have going on at the time. No voice."[30] In another example, workers in an NPSS agency went on strike to protest heavy caseloads and lack of participation in decision-making, and to demand benefits for precarious workers. These workers viewed being on strike as a way of reclaiming the "voice we lost over the last few years when the agency began to shut us out of shared decision making."[31] They also saw the strike as a way of taking care of service users by protecting the services they needed, and by defending precarious workers less able to speak for themselves. As one long-time worker put it, "We have to be their voice because they, quite frankly, don't have one."[32]

Frustrated with this situation, some workers have sought out new venues for democratic participation—including social justice groups and union campaigns—to have a voice on issues within and outside of their agencies. These alternative avenues for participation will be discussed further below.

Flexibility and the Ability to Respond to New and Long-Standing Social Needs

One of the main arguments behind contracting out services to the NPSS is that non-profits are more flexible than state agencies. They are also assumed to have the ability to react quickly to emerging concerns in the community and to develop innovative responses to social needs. However, with the integration of the NPSS into a corporatized model of governance, such capacities have eroded. Burdened by heavy documentation requirements and years of underfunding, most NPSS agencies have little flexibility, a diminished ability to meet existing needs, and an uphill struggle to address new concerns and at-risk populations.

For example, research shows that after years of funding cuts and escalating client demand, the non-profit sector had a very difficult time responding to the accelerated pressures resulting from the 2008 economic crisis and austerity policies.[33] Echoing the concerns of many, one front line supervisor noted, "This is a sector-wide problem that we're struggling with. The economy is in the hole, so there are more people that need service and yet there's less money." She continued, "We are always in a position of having to do more with less, and the areas that we can work on are becoming fewer ... we all have to be careful not to fool ourselves into thinking that what we are doing is enough."[34] Another manager asserted that there was no time or resources for developing new service plans or figuring out the best ways to address growing service demands: "Opportunities for reflection, discussion and absorbing these issues are very difficult to achieve in services that have huge funding constraints."[35]

Rather than flexible and agile, NPSS work practices are increasingly standardized and agency structures are increasingly rigid. For example, emphasizing the alienation she felt in her Taylorised work environment, one worker claimed that "at best I'm just a piece of machinery in a factory. I just churn out the work."[36] Meeting the heavy documentation requirements inherent in government funding contracts is another way that workers experience rigidity rather than flexibility in their work. Contract compliance is seen to take up a growing portion of workers' days to the point that, in the words of one worker, she was no longer "providing service to anyone. I am just constantly pushing paper."[37] A worker in another study voiced similar sentiments regarding "endless paperwork."[38] She also commented on how the work of documenting outcome measures shapes other work content and the pace of work itself. As she put it, "Once I start falling behind, it all just falls apart, really. That is a nightmare, that. But it's all gotta be there. They [management] love all their stats and their bits of paper."[39]

Advocacy and the Capacity to Stand Outside of Government and Offer Critique

The NPSS sector and its originator, civil society, once played a leading role as advocates for social equity and fairness, and a crucible for democratic thought and practices.[40] Part of this advocacy took the form of policy critique, which permitted workers, service users, and community members to have a greater say on social issues and matters of public policy. However, both NPSS advocacy and policy critique have been reduced under NPM. This is partly because reducing policy critiques to standardized metrics is difficult. For example, it is not easy to monitor the diffuse impacts of a policy brief on a particular policy, as the targets of these briefs are generally multiple and diffuse, including elected officials, civil servants, the media, social advocates, service users, and the general public. Moreover, there is rarely a one-to-one correlation between policy critiques and policy reform. Instead, impacts are long-term, incremental, time-intensive, widely dispersed, and challenging to enact, quantify, confirm, and track.[41] As Andrea Phillipson notes, policy change is a lengthy process in which researchers and advocates may receive the opportunity to play a small role, but, in reality, most policy is market driven, not based on the best available evidence or well-reasoned analysis.[42]

Although many NPSS workers have tried to retain a role in advocacy and policy critique, research suggests that this predominantly female workforce feels that NPM outcome measures have removed their capacity to undertake them. For instance, one senior housing worker argued that her employers forbade her to undertake policy assessments, emphasizing instead that her highest priority should be to complete documentation on time and to accurately record statistics. As another senior social worker stated, her employers were "incredibly fanatical about the (government funding) contract ... it's pushed down your throat continually and they won't rock the boat."[43] She was particularly concerned about the cessation of advocacy and policy work, observing that "I feel totally gagged and totally suffocated."[44]

Resistance in the Non-Profit Sector

As previously stated, the NPSS sector is not monolithic. There are sections of it where workers comply with managerialism and have little interest in participatory processes or service user involvement.[45] In other sections of the NPSS, workers and some managers are actively resisting corporatization. This chapter uses an inclusive definition of dissent or resistance at work as including anything one is not supposed to be doing at work.[46] Sometimes this involves individual resistance, such as time wasting, pilfering, and performing non-work activities on work time. These practices may make individual workers feel less alienated or exhausted, but they do little to slow or challenge corporatization. Resistance that does challenge corporatization in the NPSS comes in three main forms: (i) shared oppositional analyses and identities; (ii) using unpaid work not to meet the core functions of an agency but to restore their more participatory, social justice-related aspects; and (iii) joining and building social movements and unions.[47]

Most people working in the NPSS are drawn to the opportunity to work in tandem with their values and "give back" to others.[48] Collective social analyses and oppositional identities often arise spontaneously in workplaces where workers assume that others share their value base and concerns. How social justice/altruism operates (or should operate) within the workplace and the larger society tends to be a topic of informal, ongoing, open-ended conversations and shared analysis and identity. As one long-term, part-time social service worker noted, "Everyone who works here is very progressive. We always talk about everything and learn from each other."[49] This practice of debate on social issues operates as a pathway for dissent and resistance within and outside the workplace, and can be turned against an employer, government, or even the corporatization process itself. In some cases, unions have tapped into these informal networks and successfully built activism and strike action over workplace and larger social justice issues.[50]

Resistance within the NPSS is often conceptualized as a moral project in which workers seek to reconcile their distress with "uncaring" governments with their personal and professional values of equity, social justice, and care.[51] As noted above, many NPSS workers undertake unpaid work in addition to their paid hours. Ironically, the altruistic values that many workers hold dear can be harnessed to extract significant amounts of unpaid labour from them in the name of keeping underfunded agencies in business and serving the needs of vulnerable service users. In this case, given that the unpaid work is an expectation of management (and a by-product of neoliberal corporatization) and generally subject to the same disciplines and logics enforced during working hours, this unpaid work is exploitation.

However, when unpaid work is aimed at resisting unjust policies, such as those associated with the corporatization process, it reinforces oppositional analyses and identities, and can provide a conduit to further resistance. One worker justified undertaking community activism during paid work hours: "We can't wait out this period of conservative politics and watch people suffer. We have to try to make things better."[52] A number of other workers resisted by engaging in activism during unpaid hours. As one of them put it, "I used to get to do all this stuff [community mobilization] on the job, but we don't have time for it anymore and the government won't fund it. But, I can't just pull the plug and tell the people 'my job won't pay me to do this anymore, so go away'."[53] Other workers used unpaid hours in their workplaces (working unpaid overtime, through lunch and coffee breaks, coming in on the weekend and during vacations) to undertake advocacy and provide additional support for individual service users. As one worker observed, "The wages are terrible here anyway so why not work even more hours for no pay if it means you can keep a program afloat or keep someone from having to put their kids to bed hungry."[54]

Some NPSS workers also join formal resistance organizations, such as unions, coalitions, and social justice organizations. Many of them explained these activities as providing a place where they could do the kinds of things that "used to make my job worth doing." Others commented that in unions and social justice organizations they were able to recover the voice they had lost on the job.[55]

Conclusion

When those advocating contracting out and public sector downsizing encountered social service corporations already in place in the non-profit sector, it may have seemed like a fortuitous moment. There was no need to establish independent, arm's length enterprises to take on the provision of public services; these enterprises already existed and operated in semi-autonomous ways (for centuries in some cases). In a less fortuitous vein for neoliberal proponents, many non-profit entities operated according to democratic, altruistic, participatory, and socially engaged logics derived from their links to civil society. These deep-seeded practices and the ethos that informed them had to be uprooted and replanted with logics and practices that were not based in challenging government policy and extending government provision. The new pro-market, non-market focus of NPM introduced managerial practices that conveniently remade the NPSS in the image of the private-market-friendly contract state.[56] In the process, the form of corporatization within the NPSS necessarily changed to align itself more closely with market priorities and neoliberal philosophy.

This transformation was achieved through the details of government funding contracts requiring the use of NPM governance and management models and processes of competitive tendering, which consistently leave agencies short on resources for basic programming and scrambling for core funding. Though not an explicitly intended outcome, collective forums like general staff meetings and community consultations were reduced or canceled due to lack of money and sizeable workloads, with little room left in them for policy analysis or social advocacy.

In addition to unraveling democratic practices, corporatization in this sector had to find ways to sever or weaken the social solidarity between workers and service users. The model of social participation originating in civil society and carried on in parts of the NPSS emphasized commonalities among and between people, and the need for all to have voice and equitable access to a decent life. Part of this weakening was achieved through the standardization of work tasks and the priority placed on documenting target outcomes, rather than treating service users as peers in a shared endeavour to expand fairness and equity. Another way that social solidarity between workers and service users was undermined was through measures that removed opportunities to think about service needs within a larger policy context.

Some of these impacts disproportionately affect women, suggesting that corporatization does have a gendered character. For example, unpaid work was an expectation of the predominantly female labour force within the NPSS, closely resembling gendered expectations of unpaid care in the home and community.[57] However, under neoliberal corporatization the unpaid work became a requirement of the job in terms of gaining and retaining paid employment. Thus, under the conditions created by corporatization it was transformed from a gendered act of altruism and solidarity to an act of self-exploitation.

The resistance practices discussed above suggest that corporatization is an uneven project that does not operate the same way in all contexts. In the NPSS, although NPM and government contracts introduce conformity and standardization, the history of individual agencies and the communities in which they are grounded provides space for resistance to exist alongside corporatized service delivery. It suggests that some of the older civil society-linked practices, such as participation and advocacy, have survived in some pockets, even though their form and impact may have changed significantly. Further research is needed to explore the conditions under which voice, innovation, advocacy, and participation still occur within the NPSS, and further theorization of resistance may highlight ways to rebuild this sector as a democratic, participatory space.

The Corporatization of Food Charity in Canada

Implications for Domestic Hunger, Poverty Reduction, and Public Policy

Graham Riches

Introduction

This chapter examines the corporatization of charitable food banking in Canada since the early 1980s, and the role of corporate food charity in the depoliticization of domestic hunger as a matter of human rights and welfare state obligations. It explores the processes and roles played by "Big Food," dominated by the US transnational food industry,[1] professional sports, the music industry, and the media (specifically the CBC), in facilitating the growth and corporatization of today's "food charity economy." It also investigates the effectiveness of this economy for alleviating poverty and addressing food insecurity in Canada.

Canada's first charitable food bank was established in 1981 in Edmonton, Alberta. It was a community response to the deep economic recession at that time, which contributed to the mushrooming of this and other food banks across the country. Ironically, five years earlier the federal government had ratified the right to food as a core element of the International Covenant on Economic, Social and Cultural Rights.[2] Under international law, governments are recognized as the "primary duty bearers" for ensuring that states meet their obligations to realize food security for all. The right to food is not about charity and being fed but the right to feed oneself and one's family with choice and dignity[3]—in other words, having sufficient income (from wages or benefits) to shop for food like everyone else. Yet, today, with over four million Canadians experiencing food insecurity,[4] food charity under the leadership of Food Banks Canada (FBC) is publicly recognized as the country's primary response to widespread domestic hunger. More than 550 food banks within FBC's ten affiliated provincial associations, along with 3,800 participating agencies (including unaffiliated food banks and meal programs), are feeding over 850,000 individuals per month, an increase of 26 percent since the Great Recession of 2008.[5]

Canadians have been led to believe that community compassion expressed through charitable food handouts is the most effective way to feed our hungry poor and homeless. While millennials were raised with food banks, only baby boomers in the second decade of the twenty-first century will remember a time before food banking became entrenched, indeed culturally embedded, as the customary response to food poverty. This stands in stark contrast to the post-WWII sentiment that we should reject the breadlines and soup kitchens of the 1930s in favour of a welfare state committed to full employment, income security, and a publicly funded social safety net.[6]

Corporate Food Charity and Public Policy

Community service agencies and faith-based charities such as the Salvation Army and St. Vincent de Paul have long provided inspiration for charitable food banking. Less acknowledged is that hunger in Canada has been socially constructed as a matter for corporate philanthropy, rather than a political and human rights issue necessitating the attention of governments. Although charitable food banking may be on the public's radar today, its national organization and management are largely invisible and seldom addressed. Scant attention is paid to the food bank industry's increasing reliance on Big Food for feeding hungry people. The corporatization of food charity in this chapter refers to the process by which the management of food banking, including the funding and supply of surplus or wasted food, has become controlled by, and principally dependent upon, the corporate sector. This process is largely mediated through the narrative of corporate social responsibility, and it reflects the increasing control and influence (direct and indirect, intended and unintended) of corporations in reshaping Canada's social welfare policy and social safety net.

The rise of corporate food banking has several important implications for addressing food insecurity and poverty reduction. These include the public perception that hunger is primarily a matter for food charity, which allows governments to look the other way. From this perspective, the public is encouraged to accept the corporate claim that "food banks are the link between food waste and hunger," implying that food charity is the best way to alleviate both.[7] At the same time, corporate-managed charitable food assistance is replacing income assistance as the primary strategy for addressing poverty and domestic hunger. It has also led to the establishment of a secondary tier of the welfare system and the creation of a parallel "charity economy."[8] When governments rely on food charity and refer welfare claimants to food banks, they evade their public obligations to ensure the adequacy of minimum wage policies and welfare benefits. Questions of social values also arise regarding the altruistic nature and ethics of providing wasted food (surplus to the needs of the food industry) to feed hungry people (surplus to the requirements of the labour market). Meanwhile, little attention is paid to increasing reliance on food transfers/food assistance as opposed to cash transfers/income assistance for addressing poverty reduction.

Is it the government, the private sector, or civil society that is in charge of food security in Canada? What is the role of public policy, informed by the right to food, in addressing food insecurity?[9] Who wins and who loses from the corporate capture of food charity and welfare policy through the redistribution of wasted and surplus food to hungry people? It is important to consider how this state of affairs has come about and who is actually in charge of Canada's social safety net. Tracing the historical development and corporatization of Canada's food bank movement provides some critical insights.

Origins and Institutionalization of Canada's Food Bank Movement

Charitable food banks emerged in Canada as a direct response to the deep recession and high unemployment of the early 1980s. It was the inadequacy of federal unemployment insurance and provincial social assistance benefits that sparked their arrival on the welfare scene. Food banking models in Canada were imported from the United States, where the movement had been active since the 1967 establishment of the St. Mary's Food Bank in Phoenix, Arizona. St. Mary's soon branched out, and by 1979 Second Harvest was formed. Second Harvest acted as a broker for sixty-one regional food banks forming the backbone of the US food charity system. The organization was re-branded in 2008 as Feeding America, the country's leading domestic anti-hunger organization, which in 2014 was feeding 46-million people.[10] Those who established the first Canadian food banks in Alberta (1981), BC (1982), and Saskatchewan (1983) had previously worked with US food banks. They were also advised by prominent US practitioners such as Bob McCarty, first director of Second Harvest, and John van Hengel, co-creator of St. Mary's Food Bank. The first national conference of

Canadian food banks took place in 1985.[11] One of the purposes of the conference was to create a national association of food banks in Canada. In 1987, the Canadian Association of Food Banks (CAFB) was formed.

Local community and faith-based charities buttressed by provincial and national institutionalization informed food banking's early development. The "globalization" of charitable food banking was not far behind. In 2006, the national food bank associations of Canada, Mexico, and the US founded the Global Foodbanking Network (GFN), based in Chicago.[12] A year later, the GFN's Food Bank Leadership Institute[13] was established in Houston, Texas, operating as a global forum for training food bank social entrepreneurs from around the world.

In 2008, the CAFB was restructured and rebranded as Food Banks Canada (FBC). Not all Canadian food banks are affiliated with Food Banks Canada. Indeed, community food programs have flourished at the local level where there has been a "proliferation of charitable meal programs, including initiatives for children, as well as a myriad of meal and snack programs for homeless and impoverished youth and adults. This work has been taken on by a wide variety of community organizations including multi-service agencies, faith groups and even health centres."[14] Likewise, local community food organizations, such as meal programs, community gardens, collective kitchens, and farmer's markets, have blossomed. However, a generation on from the founding of Canada's first food bank, the food industry along with professional sports organizations, the music industry, and the CBC have become persuasive public promoters of food charity. Corporate Canada exerts increasing control and influence in terms of managerial expertise, capacity building, and funding, and by shaping public attitudes toward food banking.

The Corporatization of Charitable Food Banking in Canada

National Restructuring, Management, and Funding

When the CAFB was rebranded as FBC in 2008 ("renewing our brand" was the term used in that year's annual report), the influence of corporate Canada became clear. Symbolic of this development during the transition period, the chair of the CAFB/FBC board was a staff member of the Conference Board of Canada, one of the nation's leading business-oriented think tanks.[15] The former CAFB board, comprised mainly of food bank directors from across the country, was disbanded and a two-tier management structure was introduced: a board of directors comprising fifteen members largely drawn from the world of business, and a separate advisory Members Council (renamed Network Council in 2014). Currently, two provincial food bank executives from the Network Council serve on the FBC board of directors.

Since 2008, representatives of Big Food transnationals, such as McCains, Kraft, Loblaw, and Pepsico Foods Ltd. Canada, as well as Farm Credit Canada and national transportation companies, such as Purolator, Canadian Pacific, and Canadian National, have served on the board. They provide corporate management skills, financial expertise, and direct aid in cash and kind to ensure the distribution of food across the country through the National Food Sharing System.[16] Today, more than one hundred large and medium-sized corporations, ranked at different levels of partnership according to the value of their donations, contribute a mix of financial support, gifts in kind, food, and consumer products. Some also partner in food drive campaigns. In addition to the companies represented on the board, these partners include transnational food and beverage conglomerates, such as Campbell's, Cargill, ConAgra Food Canada, French's, General Mills, Kellogg's, Mondolez, Nestlé Canada, Ocean Spray, Procter & Gamble, Quaker, 7-Eleven, Unilever, and Walmart. Between 2007–08 and 2015–16, FBC's corporate donations more than doubled from just under $1 million to over $2.6 million, and by 2016 the value of donated food products stood at over $30 million.[17]

It is worth noting that Canada's corporate model of food banking imitates but is out-classed by the system south of the border. Feeding America, the third largest US charity, co-ordinates a network of 200 food banks working with 60,000 participating food programs. In 2014, it fed 46-million people, or roughly one in seven Americans. Its twenty-two-member board of directors includes Big Food representatives from Con Agra, Kroger, Mondolez, Mars, General Mills, Procter & Gamble, and Walmart. Overall, its $2.1 billion budget in 2014–15 depended on food and funding donations from 117 corporate partners and 139 celebrity supporters.[18]

Professional Sports and the Music Industry

Food charity's public legitimacy is not just derived from the corporate social responsibility of Canada's food, finance, and transportation sectors. Professional sports and the music industry have also been active promoters. Each year during the CFL football season, fans are encouraged to donate food at Purolator's "Tackle Hunger" food bank drives during CTV televised games. Indeed, FBC's treasurer during the restructuring period was a representative of Purolator Courier Ltd.[19]

Likewise, NHL and WHL teams support food bank drives, make financial donations, host dinners for the poor, and organize gift programs for needy children, especially at Christmas time. The Victoria-based *Times Colonist* reported that the months-long NHL lockout in 2012 was not just frustrating for hockey fans—it certainly was, I remember it well—but also "penalized some food banks" as "food drives usually conducted during the holiday seasons by teams and sports bars" were put on hold.[20] Particularly affected were food banks in Montreal and Ottawa. The Toronto Maple Leafs did not respond to a request for comment, but in 2016 the Lady Jays, working on behalf of the MLB Toronto Blue Jays, organized their thirty-second successful annual food bank drive.

Additionally, the music industry publicly supports charities of all kinds and plays an important role in promoting food charity. One only has to conduct a quick Google search to uncover the names of rock stars and bands, such as David Myles, Justin Bieber, the Elastic Band, Rush, The Tragically Hip, Barenaked Ladies, Sarah McLachlan, and Neil Young, who have been associated over the years with food bank appeals and donated their concert or album proceeds to food charities.[21] Celebrity appeals to community compassion resonate with music lovers, young and old. Despite good intentions, however, both professional sports and the music industry feed into the corporatization of food charity by further depoliticizing hunger and diverting the public gaze from its root causes.

The Media and the CBC

While the media warrants attention in terms of its support for philanthropic causes, the CBC, as Canada's nationally funded public broadcaster, demands special scrutiny. It plays a significant role in the corporate construction of hunger as a matter for charity. For thirty years, the CBC's annual Christmas fundraising efforts on behalf of food banks have perpetuated the myth of food charity as the primary and appropriate response to domestic hunger. The CBC's national mandate enjoins it to "inform, enlighten and entertain" and to engage in "news, content and commentary." Fundraising for this or that external charity, however worthy, is not mentioned. Certainly, the CBC reports from time to time on food banking and the social issues that necessitate them. However, when it offers prizes to attract donations to feed hungry Canadians, one has to wonder whether the CBC regards itself as a fully fledged food bank partner.

The donation values of the prizes offered at the 2015 Vancouver CBC Open House & Food Bank Day ranged from $225 to $3,000. The twenty-four prizes included "Essential Victoria": Tea at The Empress and Treasures at the Royal BC Museum; Winter Storm or Whale Watching Season Getaway for Two at the Wickaninnish Inn; Whistler Dream Getaway; Private Gourmet Feast for Eight; and Backcountry Snowcats Adventure for Two.[22] Promoting such prizes raises awkward ethical questions not only for the winning donors but also for the CBC's interpretation of its own corporate social responsibility. Outrageously, the basic welfare rate in British Columbia was frozen between 2007 and 2017. For single employable people dependent on social assistance, $2.57 per day is what remains from the welfare cheque after non-food expenditures have been deducted.[23] While the CBC's 2015 BC food bank drive raised $630,000—a laudable sum— this amounts to only $6 per person when account is taken of the more than 100,000 food bank users across the province.[24] In the same year, 485,500 British Columbians experienced some level of food insecurity, including 91,100 who may go days without being able to put food on the table.[25]

There is no doubt a moral imperative to feed hungry people. But there is no evidence that such expressions of corporate social responsibility have resulted in adequate incomes or reduced poverty. Moreover, why is the largely publicly funded CBC using taxpayer dollars to promote food charity and corporate welfare? Why not also support campaigns for a living wage, adequate income security, affordable social housing and childcare, enhanced mental health services, together with an integrated national food policy? Such activism would, of course, be construed as political advocacy, but so too is fundraising for food charity, which helps to frame hunger and poverty as outside the purview of formal politics and human rights requirements. When the CBC functions as an institutionalized part of the food bank system, it weakens its presumed journalistic role of independent and unbiased reporting.

The Consequences of Corporatization for Poverty Reduction and Public Policy

With the erosion of Canada's welfare state over the past thirty years, it is not surprising that a powerful combination of business, financial, and cultural forces have created a parallel system of corporately managed food banking that has propped up Canada's battered social safety net. Indeed, by the late 1980s, research had already shown that food banks occupied a second tier of the welfare system.[26] Little wonder that food banks are now perceived as a practical community response to hunger, and governments at all levels lack any appetite for public intervention. Why bother when corporate Canada has stepped up to the hunger and food bank plate? Interestingly, in 2010, the Conference Board of Canada established an organization called the Centre for Food in Canada, which, in 2014, released its Canadian Food Strategy. Its approach to addressing household food insecurity included tax credits and incentives for food donations.[27]

Who has benefited from the corporate embrace of food charity? And from the perspective of the right to food, what have been the consequences, intended and unintended, for poverty reduction and public policy in Canada?

Public Perceptions: Governments Looking the Other Way

Perceptions are everything in politics. Food banking's socially constructed appeal feeds the public perception that hunger is primarily a matter for charity.[28] Certainly the corporatization of charity—with its assumption of managerial effectiveness and efficiency—has done much to entrench this view. Yet, as Bread for the World, the Christian anti-hunger organization, has calculated in the case of the US, "amongst meals based on food assistance, only one in twenty-four is derived from private giving; the other twenty-three come from government sources. That is, $4.1 billion worth of food was distributed through charities in 2011, while USDA [United States Department of Agriculture] spent $96.9 billion on food and benefits."[29]

Comparative data is lacking in Canada, but it is likely that a similar discrepancy exists north of the border when comparing financial expenditures on charitable food banks and meal programs with those on federal employment insurance and provincial social assistance. Yet, current employment insurance and social assistance programs remain insufficient. It is the engrained public perception of corporate food charity's legitimacy and effectiveness that enables governments to download their obligations to the corporate sector and the community, while deflecting political attention from the inadequacy of minimum wages, housing allowances, and social security benefits, resulting in hundreds of thousands of Canadian households being unable to pay the rent and feed their families.

Consequently, for the hungry poor, charitable food handouts have become the meal ticket of last resort, marking the retreat to residual welfare minded by the national food bank industry. In this way, corporate food bank sponsorship acts as a major obstacle to ending domestic hunger and advancing poverty reduction in Canada.

The Effectiveness of Corporate Food Charity

How effective has the business-driven food bank model proven to be? It is generally acknowledged by food banks in Canada that they are not the answer to long-term food insecurity. FBC clearly states that "while food banks provide an essential service in their communities they are nevertheless a partial and imperfect solution to the problem caused by widespread poverty and food insecurity."[30] Even America's food banks say charity will not end hunger.[31] The scale of the problem with its deep roots in poverty, material deprivation, and income inequality is far beyond the resources and capacity of charitable organizations to resolve. Indeed, food charities are often unable to meet their clients' needs on a day-to-day basis. Too often food banks lack funding, run out of food, resort to rationing, and close early. Despite the generosity of Canadians, demand consistently outstrips supply, necessitating the constant need for more food drives and more fundraising.

None of this is surprising. According to Statistics Canada's 2012 Canadian Community Health Survey (CCHS), food insecurity in Canada—defined as the "inadequate or insecure access to food because of financial constraints"—was experienced by four million individuals, comprising 11.5 percent of the population, an increase of over 600,000 people since 2007.[32] This hungry population includes the marginally food insecure, people who worry about not having enough food; the moderately food insecure, those relying on low-cost food and unable to afford balanced meals; and the severely food insecure, those who do not have enough food and sometimes go days without eating. Even the CCHS survey is an underestimate, as it excludes the homeless and on-reserve First Nations populations. In 2012, food banks across Canada reportedly fed 882,188 individuals.[33] Therefore, less than one in four food insecure individuals actually use food banks. The majority of the food insecure are working poor.[34]

Furthermore, the claim made by the Global Foodbanking Network that the effectiveness of food banking can be traced to "the link between food waste and hunger" is also troubling.[35] In Canada, this argument is currently advanced by the National Zero Waste Council[36] and FBC,[37] through a national campaign directed at municipalities to support federal tax exemptions incentivizing food retail stores to divert greater amounts of food waste from landfills to food banks. Is this really a "win-win" for reducing food waste and domestic hunger?

As Tim Lang has argued, such policies cannot deal with the countless problems associated with our modern food economy, including the "structured mismatch between production, consumption, environment, health and social values," of which food waste is just a symptom.[38] Nor will it address issues such as low wages in the food retail market or the unsustainable nature of industrial food systems.[39] As mentioned, charitable food banks are a symptom of dysfunctional welfare states unable to address the upstream causes of poverty and inequality. Linking two symptoms of dysfunctional systems together as an effective remedy for widespread food waste and insecurity is hardly good medicine (let alone long-term preventive care). Tax incentives might benefit transnational food giants and smaller food retailers, but they will also further institutional-ize "secondary welfare systems" and "secondary food markets" for "secondary food consumers."

Social Values and Corporate Social Responsibility

At any time, but particularly when austerity strikes, issues arise regarding the ethics and altruistic nature of the food industry supplying its surplus food to feed hungry people, who themselves are surplus to the requirements of the labour market and leading precarious lives. There are vexing questions about food access for financially insecure people dependent upon a profit-conscious food industry benefiting from tax incentivized savings by supplying charities with its unsellable food. It is true that FBC is involved in research and advocacy at the national level. The organization claims to work with the federal government in supporting food bank clients to "gain access to affordable housing, sufficient income and nutritious food through improved public policy and sufficient social services that ensure our most basic needs are being met nationwide."[40] In this way, FBC expresses its corporate social responsibility. Yet, as Pat Caplan notes in her study of UK food banking, the "charitable giving of surplus food and money by food retailers also confers considerable benefits on the corporate donors,"[41] perhaps more akin to "corporate social investment,"[42] market branding, and the search for competitive advantage.

We should be asking whether the social and political functions of food char-ity—both community and corporate—act as a moral safety valve that allows the public to feel good about doing their part.[43] Again, there is a moral imperative to feed hungry people. It is a fundamental expression of social solidarity and com-passion.[44] However, as Pérez de Armiño asks in his analysis of the Spanish food bank movement, to what extent is food charity a form of "uncritical" solidarity which fails to deal with the root causes of poverty?[45]

From Income Assistance to Food Assistance

Corporate food charity in Canada has quietly and successfully established itself as a parallel and secondary welfare system. Yet the longer-term implications of this shift for social policy, public health, and poverty reduction have attracted little political attention. The seamless and unquestioned way in which a US charitable food banking model has been adopted suggests public policy indifference to the shift from income assistance to food assistance in meeting the needs of vulnerable populations. Is it possible that corporate food relief might be legislated into publicly funded social programs in Canada? Perhaps some attention should be paid to the fact that "the US differs from virtually every other OECD nation in its heavy reliance on food assistance rather than income transfers to aid impoverished families. While both social insurance and modest cash income guarantees are available to elderly and disabled Americans, able-bodied adults and their dependent children receive very little cash assistance."[46] One clear difference between the two nations is that unlike Canada, the US, through its agricultural subsidies, has a significant stockpile of surplus food upon which it draws for overseas and domestic food aid. Yet, US public and charitable food assistance programs make little contribution to poverty reduction. In light of Canada adopting the US corporate food bank model, together with the mistaken public perception that domestic hunger is now being effectively addressed, Canada is sleepwalking its way to radically undermining its social safety net in favour of a mishmash of provincial food safety nets across the country.

Another worrying consequence of the corporatization of food charity is the implications for democratic governance and public accountability when addressing domestic hunger and poverty reduction. Who is responsible for ensuring that Canada's vulnerable populations can both pay the rent and feed themselves? While Canada's historical commitment to a publicly funded welfare state and its ratification of the right to food under international law suggest that governments (federal and provincial) are the "primary duty bearers," the corporatization of food charity has created ambiguity and confusion. Political and policy leadership have been lacking and cannot simply be blamed on the jurisdictional problem of passing the buck between different levels of government. The corporate food banking industry has allowed governments of all political stripes to hide behind the curtain of its presumed effectiveness, as well as ethical claims that charitable food assistance is the necessary course of action. Yet, charity is not a right that can be claimed. As Louise Arbour has written, "there will always be a place for charity, but charitable responses are not an effective, principled or sustainable substitute for enforceable human rights guarantees."[47]

Public Utilities and Resource Governance

Pipelines, Regulatory Capture, and Canada's National Energy Board

Jamie Brownlee

Introduction

In recent years, serious questions have been raised by activists, journalists, and others about the independence and impartiality of the National Energy Board, Canada's federal agency responsible for regulating interprovincial and international aspects of the country's oil, gas, and electric utility industries. These concerns have intensified in the midst of contentious national debates over new pipeline projects, Canada's climate change goals, and the expansion of the Alberta tar sands. Some claim that the agency's decision-making processes run in contradiction to its public service mandate, while others go further to say that it has been ostensibly "captured" by the very industry it purports to regulate. Is the National Energy Board simply an industry facilitator, or does it still have the capacity to act as a regulatory watchdog? In this chapter, I locate these discussions in the context of corporatization.

The National Energy Board (NEB) was established as an independent federal regulatory agency by the government of Canada in 1959. Its roles include providing regulatory oversight to the 73,000 kilometres of existing oil and gas pipelines that cross either provincial boundaries or the Canada-US border, and approving the construction of new pipelines. North American energy regulators like the NEB are among the continent's most powerful public servants. Federal legislation gives the agency the power to review and decide on major project applications. Like courts, NEB review panels can produce and inspect documents, examine witnesses, take evidence under oath, and compel attendance at hearings. The agency also has the capacity to investigate energy companies, police pipeline safety issues, and enforce sanctions within its jurisdiction.

The NEB is governed by politically appointed members who are to operate independently of industry and at arm's length from government. The agency's independence is vital because, in addition to approving energy-related infrastructure proposals, it is responsible for environmental stewardship and protecting the public interest. The link between the agency's independence and its ability to operate in the public interest was explicitly addressed by Prime Minister John Diefenbaker at the time of the NEB's creation. He said: "to make sure that this board will operate for the benefit of all Canadians it will operate beyond any suggestion of control in any way."[1] However, critics have questioned the NEB's independence, and I argue in this chapter that its changing role can be tied to the corporatization of the agency. Below, I explain how Canada's National Energy Board has been corporatized through: (i) its internal management style, which emphasizes increased managerial control and business-like service delivery, and (ii) a process of state-corporate integration where private sector representatives and outside corporate interests have assumed a greater degree of influence over priority setting and decision-making.

The Corporatization of the National Energy Board

The regulatory independence of the NEB has long been a public concern. In the 1970s, for example, there was a growing belief within the federal government that the NEB was "far too sympathetic" to the energy industry and, as a result, Ottawa was overly dependent on industry information channelled through the agency.[2] These concerns were exacerbated in the early 1990s when the NEB's head office was moved from Ottawa to Calgary and accompanying legislation required all permanent agency members to reside in the new location. Over two-thirds of NEB staff did not relocate, which meant that their positions were largely filled by local residents, many of whom were former employees of the oil and gas sector. Locating the NEB in the heart of Canada's oil patch helped to create a "revolving door" between the NEB and industry, thereby leading regulators to view their priorities and those of the industry as one and the same. Also in the early 1990s, the agency's source of funding shifted from taxpayer revenues to industry levies. As a result, 90 percent of its funding came from the corporations it was supposed to regulate. In effect, this meant that a few powerful pipeline companies—including Enbridge, TransCanada, and Kinder Morgan—accounted for most of the agency's budget.

The impacts of these changes were recognized at the time. For instance, a 2000 report on the board's effectiveness noted a "disturbing perception that the National Energy Board has in some sense been 'captured' by the western based producer and pipeline industries."[3] That same year, the Standing Senate Committee on Energy recommended an investigation into energy regulators like the NEB to determine if there was a "material conflict" between energy promotion and environmental stewardship.[4]

The Introduction of Bill C-38:
New Modes of Regulatory Efficiency and Managerial Control

Between 2006 and 2015, the Harper Conservatives accelerated the corporatization of the NEB, in part through legislation. In 2012, the federal government passed the *Jobs, Growth and Long-term Prosperity Act* (Bill C-38), which overhauled environmental assessment and energy permitting processes in Canada. These legislative changes, which were undertaken in response to oil industry lobbying, were part of the government's plan to fast-track pipeline approval and aggressively limit public participation in environmental governance.

Bill C-38 included a number of specific changes to the *National Energy Board Act* and other pieces of legislation related to the agency. First, the legislation empowered the federal Cabinet to order the certification of a pipeline, even if a NEB review panel recommended against it. This change gave the government, and its Big Oil allies, effective veto power over pipeline approval. Second, the legislation outlined that the environmental impact assessments of projects would now be conducted by the NEB as part of a single, integrated process, rather than through separate or joint panel reviews administered by the Canadian Environmental Assessment Agency.[5] Bill C-38 also exempted energy development projects regulated by the NEB from the requirement to assess (and minimize) the impacts on the habitats of species at risk. And, despite the government's constitutional duty to consult and accommodate First Nations on proposed activities, the legislation ensured that consulting with Indigenous peoples was not a mandatory factor in NEB decision-making.[6]

These legislative changes built on momentum through the 1990s that saw the NEB becoming more "business-like" under the ethos of New Public Management (NPM) and reinvented government, which included a greater emphasis on customer and client service.[7] NPM is a managerial paradigm that emphasizes private sector approaches to reforming public agencies. It aims to make the public sector more corporate or business-like, often by implementing private sector models that give new powers to senior managers to set priorities at a distance from public service professionals, front line workers, and the public at large. Under the Harper Conservatives, NPM principles were extended to bring about a greater emphasis on regulatory "efficiency" and managerial control within the agency. The logic was simple: regulatory efficiency requires that senior managers have the freedom and discretion to make decisions that will facilitate the rapid approval of tar sands and related infrastructure projects, with little interference from the public (or non-management professionals within the NEB).

While the power of NEB management executives was increased, the role of the public correspondingly declined. As part of its regulatory overhaul, the Harper government amended the *NEB Act* to restrict public participation in pipeline hearings. The new rules limited participation to those individuals and organizations deemed to be "directly affected" by a particular project, or who possessed "relevant" information or expertise. Joe Oliver, then-Minister of National Resources, explained that the changes would reduce the influence of environmental activists who were seeking to "game the system" (as he claimed they did during the Northern Gateway pipeline hearings).[8] This move mirrored what was taking place in some provinces, including Alberta.[9] Enbridge's Line 9B hearing in 2013 was the first pipeline proposal to come under the authority of the new regime. The NEB denied intervenor status to groups like the Council of Canadians, Environmental Justice Toronto, East End Against Line 9, and Sierra Club Canada because they failed to demonstrate a "specific interest" in the pipeline, and were only advancing issues of public interest and concern. The NEB also limited the issues that could be discussed by both "commentators" and "intervenors" in the hearing process, including the environmental and health-related impacts of tar sands expansion.

Similarly, in 2014, the NEB limited the participation of 1,250 Canadians in the Trans Mountain pipeline hearing process to "letter writing," while 468 others were told they had no right to participate whatsoever.[10] The latter group included twenty-seven climate experts who wanted to present evidence on the pipeline's impact on climate change (the pipeline would nearly triple the capacity of tar sands oil transport across BC, from 300,000 to 890,000 barrels per day). The NEB also broke precedent during the Trans Mountain hearing process by eliminating the oral cross-examination of witnesses, thereby limiting corporate transparency. This move flatly contradicted the position of the federal Department of Justice, who informed the NEB that "cross examination is necessary to ensure a proper evidentiary record" and serves a "vital role in testing the value of testimonial evidence."[11] In the absence of oral cross-examination, the agency relied on written information requests between intervenors and the pipeline's proponent,

Kinder Morgan. Of the 2,501 questions for which intervenors received insufficient information in the first round of requests, the NEB ordered that Kinder Morgan provide adequate responses for just 115 (or 4.5 percent).[12] This meant that participants could not meaningfully challenge the company's arguments and evidence, and that it could evade questions. In some cases, Kinder Morgan "assumed the regulator's role" by declaring certain questions out of bounds.[13]

Replacing cross-examinations with written requests was in part a time-saving strategy, as the government had imposed strict time limits on NEB decisions to streamline pipeline approval. Under the revised *NEB Act*, the agency's review of applications is not to exceed fifteen months from the date an application is deemed complete. In addition, the NEB chairperson (then Gaetan Caron) was granted sweeping new powers to intervene in panel processes to ensure time limits were met. This could include the replacement of any or all members of a review panel, or the designation of a single board member (the chair included) to summarily rule on an application. According to Rowland Harrison, a law professor who served as an NEB board member from 1997 to 2011, the extraordinary scope of the chair's authority could be interpreted "as empowering the Chairperson to direct a panel *how* to deal with a specific application beyond addressing time limits as such."[14]

Concentrating power in the hands of senior managers also had implications for management-staff relations. Most notably, it reduced the independence and influence of non-management professionals within the agency. According to an internal NEB survey in 2015, only one-third of NEB employees indicated that they understood the "reasons for management decisions and direction" (down from nearly one-half in 2012–13), while one in five did not believe their ideas and input were being heard or addressed by NEB leadership.[15] In response to these findings, management canceled its employee survey and hired consultants from Ernst & Young, offering the firm a $522,206 contract to help "fix its management problem."[16] This decision is particularly interesting in light of some of the other financial decisions by the agency around that time. In 2014–15, for example, the agency cut its anticipated spending on safety oversight by $17 million. At the same time, it allocated an additional $14 million (over-budget) for public relations and communications. The latter included a three-year "communications plan," designed to "inspire confidence" in the NEB and determine what the agency should be "marketing to the media as 'newsworthy'."[17] The NEB's public relations efforts also included a 2016 contract for Presidia Security Consulting to investigate whether NEB staff had been speaking to the media. According to Ian Bron, a whistleblower previously employed by Transport Canada, this action is reminiscent of a "mobster mentality," where the regulator is imposing a "culture of silence" on its employees to discourage them from questioning management misconduct.[18]

Under the guise of business-like expediency and organizational "efficiency," there has been a reduction of the public's ability to influence NEB decisions, the procedural fairness of NEB hearings, the independence and professional knowledge of NEB staff, and the quality of procedural outcomes. This is in addition to the agency's growing focus on public relations and institutional branding, a trait it shares with other image-conscious corporations.

Regulatory Capture and the Revolving Door

In line with expanding managerial control and business-like service delivery, the corporatization of the NEB can be seen in the growing influence of energy corporations and private sector managers on agency priorities and decision-making. Here, corporatization is associated with a process of public-private integration that facilitates a "revolving door" relationship between the NEB and industry, facilitating regulatory capture. According to Bruce Campbell, regulatory capture occurs

> ... when regulation is routinely designed to benefit the private interest of the regulated industry at the expense of the public interest. A regulator can be deemed captured when industry is routinely able to shape the regulations governing its operations, block or delay new regulations, and remove or dilute existing regulations.[19]

For instance, Campbell argues that regulatory capture was a contributing factor in the Lac-Mégantic rail disaster in Quebec, and others have pointed to similar trends involving energy regulators in British Columbia (e.g., BC Oil and Gas Commission), Alberta, and elsewhere.[20]

It was clear early in Harper's tenure that the NEB was too close to industry. In 2008, the agency even dropped the word regulator from its branding and began describing itself as an industry "partner."[21] More recently, charges of regulatory capture and industry bias have come to the fore. In 2015, for example, economist Robyn Allan—past president and CEO of the Insurance Company of British Columbia, former senior economist for the BC Central Credit Union, and an expert intervenor in the Trans Mountain pipeline hearing—withdrew from the Trans Mountain hearing process. Explaining her decision, Allan said that the NEB panel "is not an impartial referee. The game is rigged; its outcome pre-determined by a captured regulator ... The NEB is not a national energy board; it is a parochial board steeped in Calgary petro culture, run by corporate interests."[22] An even more vocal critic has been Marc Eliesen, whose past positions include President and CEO of BC Hydro, Chair and CEO of Ontario Hydro, Chair of Manitoba Hydro, board member of Suncor Energy, and Deputy Minister of Energy in the provinces of Ontario and Manitoba. Eliesen also withdrew as an intervenor in the Trans Mountain hearing, calling the NEB's review process "fraudulent" and a "public deception." According to Eliesen, "this board has a predetermined course of action to recommend approval of the project and a strong bias in favour of the proponent . . . a truly industry captured regulator."[23]

These kinds of critiques can be traced, in part, to the social composition of the NEB's executive leadership. Having a shared class background often correlates with a similarity in values and ideological positions, and helps to facilitate agreement on the goals and purposes of public policy and limit disagreement to ways of achieving them. While the NEB has never operated completely independently from industry, a large proportion of NEB board members are (or have been) immersed in private sector energy culture and employment, with little representation from other communities and interests. Brenda Kenny, for example, spent almost ten years at the NEB before becoming president of the Canadian Energy Pipeline Association (CEPA), Canada's powerful pro-pipeline lobby. Bob Vergette, an NEB board member from 2008 to 2015, formerly served as a vice-president of Trans Mountain Pipelines. A 2012 report by the Polaris Institute revealed that six employees and executives from the Canadian Association of Petroleum Producers (CAPP) have held positions at the NEB.[24] Andrew Nikiforuk, a journalist and author who has written extensively about the NEB, described the board's makeup in 2014:

> [T]here's no public health expert. There is no expert in environmental assessment, there is no pipeline safety expert, there is no representative from First Nations, there's no representative or expert from fisheries, no oil spill or contaminant expert . . . It's a board of white people, mostly Conservatives, all based in Calgary, all with very similar backgrounds, whose job is largely to facilitate pipeline approval.[25]

The NEB currently has eight permanent board members, each serving seven-year terms. Many of these individuals have extensive ties to the energy industry. Vice-Chair Lynn Mercier, a long-time industry insider, spent twenty-nine years at Gaz Métro, a major gas distribution and pipeline company (Gaz Métro is owned by Noverco, of which Enbridge owns a 39 percent interest). Energy consultant Murray Lytle has held senior positions in the oil, gas, and mining industries, including Imperial Oil. Before joining the NEB, Roland George worked in the private energy sector for over three decades, including positions at Gaz Métro and the international energy consulting firm Purvin & Gertz. Philip Davies has also held senior management positions in the energy sector, including Vice President, General Counsel, and Corporate Secretary of Encana Gas Storage, and Associate General Counsel of Encana Midstream and Marketing. Moreover, the NEB's current chair, Peter Watson, was named Alberta's "resource person of the year" in 2011, an award normally reserved for industry leaders (other winners include the CEO of Cenovus, the CEO of Enbridge, and a former chairman of CAPP).

Some former NEB officials have also been integrated into what William Carroll, Nicolas Graham, and Zoë Yunker (see Chapter 4 in this volume) describe as a carbon-centred, scientific-industrial complex—a densely connected platform for elite networking and consensus-building, and a means by which the fossil fuel industry can direct and shape academic and other research priorities. For example, in addition to her lengthy stints at the NEB and CEPA, Brenda Kenny is affiliated with Emissions Reduction Alberta and Sustainable Development Technology Canada. She also sits on the Board of Governors at the University of Calgary and is an adjunct professor in the Haskayne School of Business. Former Chair of the NEB from 2007 to 2014, Gaetan Caron is now an executive fellow at the University of Calgary's School of Public Policy, a key player in the complex. The school has extensive ties to Big Oil interests and functions more as a neoliberal think tank than a graduate school in an accredited public university.[26] Responding to recent pipeline controversy in the *Financial Post*, Caron lamented that it had "become cool to blame the NEB for being all sorts of things—such as being captured by those it regulates." As a nation, he said, we "have managed to become ashamed of our prosperity in natural resources," something the Calgary School makes every effort to correct.[27]

Harper and his Cabinet made sure that the incoming Trudeau government had little room to alter the makeup of the NEB's executive leadership. This is because they filled the full-time board positions and extended the terms of existing members before the Conservatives were defeated in the 2015 election. One of these late-term appointments was Steven Kelly, a Calgary-based oil executive. Two years earlier, Kelly's consulting firm, IHS Global Canada, was hired by Kinder Morgan to prepare a report justifying the Trans Mountain pipeline expansion. As vice-president of the firm, Kelly wrote the report and submitted it to the NEB.[28] So, after helping Kinder Morgan lobby for the Trans Mountain pipeline, Kelly now sits on the board that regulates pipeline construction. Although he was not a member of the three-person panel that reviewed Trans Mountain and his report was not allowed into evidence (because of public pressure), his proximity to other board members and potential involvement in future pipeline rulings place him in a clear conflict of interest.

Corporate lobbying is another important driver of NEB corporatization that has integrated the goals and priorities of the agency with those of industry. According to the Polaris Institute, between July 2008 and November 2012, twenty-seven energy companies and eight industry associations held 2,733 meetings with Canadian public officials.[29] CAPP was the most active, accounting for 536. In contrast, one of the largest environmental coalitions in Canada—the Climate Action Network—logged just six lobbying meetings during this period. Further, CAPP and CEPA recorded 367 percent more communications with public office holders than Canada's two major automotive industry associations, and 78 percent more than Canada's two major mining industry associations. These efforts have not let up. Between February 2012 and October 2016, Kinder Morgan initiated 368 lobbying meetings with federal officials (if similar lobbying efforts in BC are included, this number rises to 826), with members of the House of Commons receiving the most attention.[30] According to Mike Lang and Shannon Daub, one of the reasons this matters in the context of energy regulation is that "the NEB reports to Parliament and its members via the Ministry of Natural Resources, which in turn acts as an advocate for resource development within the federal government."[31] Not surprisingly, Natural Resources Canada was second in line for the most federal lobbying meetings. Throughout this period, the NEB's extensive and growing corporate ties, revolving door relationships, and close proximity to corporate lobbyists helped to corporatize the NEB to an unprecedented extent.

The "Pipeline Cops": Treating Companies as Customers

The corporatization of the NEB has facilitated an institutional bias where regulated companies are treated more like "customers" than potential offenders, and where the needs and interests of industry are prioritized over those of the public. Nowhere is this bias more evident than in public health and safety. While some NEB employees refer to themselves as "pipeline cops," and the agency has the power to impose significant fines and even prison sentences, these kinds of punishments are almost unheard of in the pipeline industry. Instead, as noted above, the NEB has erred on the side of catering to companies and ignoring public challenges. In the Trans Mountain hearings, many intervenors filed breach of process and other motions in an effort to compel corporate transparency. Of these motions, 89 percent were denied by the NEB, including one by the province of BC requesting that the company's emergency response plans be made public. In contrast, 80 percent of Kinder Morgan's motions were granted.[32] Others have pointed to the inherently biased and limited scope of the hearing process itself. For instance, while the financial implications of tar sands development and transport were front and centre, most of the health and environmental impacts were expressly excluded. Climate change, one of the biggest threats from a public interest perspective, was once again pushed to the side.

In his investigative series for the *National Observer*, journalist Mike De Souza found evidence of a "casual relationship" and "pattern of cooperation" between the NEB and industry, which one might expect where an agency has been corporatized. The NEB's code of conduct requires its staff to prepare an agenda and take minutes at all meetings that involve matters under review by the agency, but investigations revealed that the agency regularly conducts "off the record" meetings (e.g., in restaurants or coffee shops) with corporate leaders about regulatory and safety matters, including ongoing investigations.[33] More disturbingly, the *National Observer* found multiple instances where the NEB allowed companies to edit their own safety audits. Several years ago, for example, a whistleblower at TransCanada made serious safety allegations against the company. These allegations were investigated by NEB officials, and they provided TransCanada with a draft version of their findings. The company recommended thirty-six changes to the final report, many of which removed embarrassing examples of TransCanada's poor safety record. The NEB accepted thirty-four of the thirty-six changes and incorporated them into the final report one month later.[34] In another incident in 2015, the NEB concluded a fifteen-month investigation into pipeline safety at Enbridge. Access to information (ATI) requests showed that the agency had removed sensitive information from the report at the company's request. The deleted information outlined that Enbridge was struggling to monitor and repair corrosive ruptures on its aging pipelines, a key factor that led to two major spills in 2007 (Glenavon, Saskatchewan) and 2010 (Marshall, Michigan). It also revealed that the company does not know how to properly clean up oil spills.[35]

In February 2016, the NEB issued an emergency safety order against Kinder Morgan after it discovered that the company was using defective pipeline parts, as NEB engineers believed this could lead to pipeline failure. According to De Souza, Kinder Morgan was able to "walk around" the safety order simply by placing a call to the regulator and requesting an immediate six-month extension.[36] This ruling allowed the company to avoid negative publicity in the critical months leading up to the NEB's decision on the Trans Mountain pipeline. If NEB engineers were correct, the ruling also put the environment and the public at significant risk. Input from Kinder Morgan suggests the company is not overly concerned about oil spills. In its Trans Mountain application submitted to the NEB, the company stated that "[p]ipeline spills can have both positive and nega- tive effects on local and regional economies, both in the short- and long-term ... Spill response and cleanup creates business and employment opportunities."[37]

These exposés by the *National Observer* are supported by the Office of the Auditor General of Canada. A 2011 report by the Commissioner of the Environment and Sustainable Development found that the NEB rarely follows up on identified pipeline problems. In twenty-seven of twenty-nine cases reviewed, the report found no evidence that the agency took measures to ensure the prob- lems had been addressed.[38] Some have argued that this lack of oversight was a contributing factor in the disastrous Enbridge pipeline spill in Michigan's Kalamazoo River.[39] A second audit in 2016 by Environment Commissioner Julie Gelfand found that the agency does not adequately track whether companies are complying with pipeline approval conditions (inadequate in twenty-four of the forty-nine cases examined), nor does it consistently follow up on deficien- cies in company compliance with regulatory requirements (e.g., that a company actually repairs a leaky or corrosive pipeline as ordered).[40] Many of the safety issues outlined in these audits have also been raised by the Canadian Association of Energy and Pipeline Landowner Associations (CAEPLA). For years, CAEPLA has argued that the NEB ignores the safety dangers in Canada's aging pipeline sys- tem.[41] Although pipeline companies are responsible for all conditions that have the potential to harm people, property, or the environment throughout a pipe- line's entire life-cycle, CAEPLA asserts that the NEB has let industry off the hook for billions of dollars in pipeline abandonment liabilities.

The "pipeline cops" may not be policing industry, but they are helping to police activists. Several years ago, ATI investigations revealed that the Harper government had been spying on anti-tar sands activists, as well as independent Indigenous and environmental organizations. This domestic intelligence and surveillance program involved a broad-based alliance between the Canadian Security Intelligence Service (CSIS), the RCMP, the National Energy Board, sev- eral energy corporations (including Enbridge and TransCanada), as well as other police and private security firms. The purpose was to track activist opposition to so called "critical infrastructure" projects. Not only did the NEB receive regular intelligence briefings on pipeline activism, the agency was (and remains) act- ively involved in intelligence gathering and surveillance, often in alliance with pipeline companies. According to Jeff Monaghan and Kevin Walby, NEB security personnel engage in widespread, open source surveillance of pipeline opponents. "Merely speaking in public about opposition to energy development" is sufficient grounds for surveillance, according to the researchers.[42] The NEB has also been involved in covert operations against environmental groups, including organizations that request participation in NEB hearings. Some of these groups argue that these surveillance tactics have compromised their ability to participate before the NEB in a fair and unbiased way, in part because the agency "may be made privy to unproven yet highly prejudicial allegations" against them.[43]

Ensuring regulatory compliance and protecting public health and safety is one of the most important tasks of the NEB or any other public regulator. However, the agency appears unable or unwilling to properly investigate corporate malfeasance, enforce sanctions, or otherwise hold energy and pipeline companies to account. Clearly, this corporatized regulator would rather please industry than police it.

Business as Usual Under the Trudeau Liberals?

Justin Trudeau's election campaign was replete with promises of fossil fuel subsidy phase-outs, renewable energy investments, and repaired environmental assessments. He proudly proclaimed that "Canada is back" on the issue of climate change. He pledged that the Crown would fully execute its constitutional duty to consult and respect Indigenous peoples on major project reviews. And he insisted he would not be a "cheerleader" for new pipelines like the previous government had been. According to Joe Oliver, Trudeau's 2016 mandate letter to the minster of natural resources was "like a manifesto from Ecojustice."[44] To help achieve these objectives, Trudeau promised to modernize and reform the NEB. Canada's pipeline approval process was broken, he said, and a major overhaul was in the works.

The Trudeau government had every opportunity to demonstrate that it was committed to this new mandate by putting TransCanada's Energy East pipeline review on hold until legislative amendments could repair the damage done by the Harper government. Instead, under Trudeau's watch, evidence continues to mount that the NEB cannot be trusted to evaluate pipeline proposals in a fair and unbiased way. The agency came under fire in August 2016 after it was discovered, through ATI requests, that senior NEB officials—Chair Peter Watson, Jacques Gauthier, and Lynn Mercier—had met with former Quebec premier Jean Charest to discuss the Energy East pipeline. At the time, Charest was a paid consultant for TransCanada. Notes taken at the meeting reveal that the primary subject of discussion was Energy East, and that Charest gave the regulator political advice on how it could garner public support for the pipeline. The parties also discussed "public relations and political strategies for promoting pipelines in Quebec."[45]

The "Charest Affair" is telling on many levels. For one, it exposes impropriety and public deception on the part of the agency. Under NEB rules, employees are not allowed to privately discuss matters that are before the agency, and it must make public the contents of any meeting related to an ongoing review. Not only was the meeting not disclosed, but NEB officials initially stated that they had *not* discussed the pipeline with Charest. They were later forced to apologize after ATI documents revealed otherwise (but they continued to maintain they were unaware that Charest was a TransCanada lobbyist). The incident also reflects a double standard that perhaps should be expected of a corporatized regulator. NEB officials tried to downplay the incident by claiming they had undertaken "similar meetings" with environmental groups, but the groups who attended these meetings were told in advance that they would not be allowed to discuss ongoing reviews like Energy East.[46]

Following public outrage over allegations of bias, the Energy East hearings were halted in August 2016. Less than a month later, Watson and the entire Energy East panel recused themselves from the pipeline review. The new panel, appointed in January 2017, restarted the process. According to Alberta Premier Rachel Notley, the recusals demonstrate that the NEB process is "transparent and respects the rule of law."[47] But this was no *mea culpa*. The members only recused themselves after intense media scrutiny and multiple legal challenges were filed. It did not help matters that Nature Canada was already investigating panel member Jacques Gauthier for conflicts of interest—Gauthier is the former CEO of an energy services company (LVM Inc.) that has done business with TransCanada related to Energy East.[48] Notably, just two weeks after Mercier and Gauthier recused themselves, they were assigned (by Chair Peter Watson) to review another application from Nova Gas Transmission, a wholly owned subsidiary of TransCanada.[49]

In November 2016, the Trudeau government announced that it was moving forward with its promised modernization of the NEB. To this end, Minister of Natural Resources Jim Carr created a five-member "expert panel" tasked with reviewing the NEB's structure, role, and mandate. This was a step in the right direction and long overdue, but the appointment of the modernization panel did little to appease critics. In particular, three of the five panel members tasked with reforming the NEB have close ties to the pipeline and oil industries, which place them in a significant conflict of interest with the panel's mandate.

One of the panel's co-chairs, Hélène Lauzon, is the president of the Quebec Business Council on the Environment, a pro-pipeline business association representing oil, gas, and pipeline companies, including TransCanada and Enbridge. The council's board of directors includes executives from Gaz Métro and the Canadian Fuels Association, which is the industry association for the petroleum distribution, refining, and marketing sector. The panel's other co-chair, Gary Merasty, serves as a director of the Canada West Foundation—a Calgary-based think tank known for its promotion of tar sands extraction and its unwavering pro-pipeline stance. Enbridge is one of the foundation's "champion" level sponsors. The third panelist, Brenda Kenny, is also on the board of directors of the Canada West Foundation. She was the president of CEPA from 2008 to 2015 (following her stint with the NEB). In 2011, Kenny, along with the presidents of CAPP, the Canadian Gas Association, and Canadian Petroleum Products Institute (representing the Energy Framework Initiative, a "who's who" of fossil fuel traffickers in Canada), sent a letter to key Cabinet ministers petitioning for regulatory overhaul. They urged the government to modify a series of laws (including the *NEB Act*) because the current approach of "prohibiting harm" embodied in existing environmental legislation was "outdated."[50] One of the things these laws had in common is that they all posed some kind of obstacle to pipelines and mining projects. These lobbying efforts led to the now infamous omnibus bills passed by the Harper government in 2012, which, as outlined earlier, gutted Canada's environmental protections and helped to corporatize the NEB.

In the end, hundreds of individuals, NGOs, academics, industry groups, and Indigenous communities provided feedback to the modernization panel. Its report, released in May 2017, recommended sweeping changes to the NEB. Predictably, the report takes for granted industry claims that pipelines are critical drivers of economic prosperity and the "social good." But to its credit, the panel also recommended that climate impact assessments be incorporated into federal project reviews (the NEB announced in August 2017 that it would expand the scope of its Energy East review to include, for the first time, the impact of both upstream and downstream greenhouse gas emissions). It also acknowledged that regulatory capture was a significant issue of public concern. To help counter the perception that the NEB was too close to industry, the report recommended relocating the regulator from Calgary to Ottawa, where it would be replaced with a new organization called the Canadian Energy Transmission Commission. Jason Kenney, leader of Alberta's Conservative Party, called parts of the report "absurd," which is a good indication the panelists drew further attention to issues that critics have been raising for some time.[51]

The future of the NEB remains uncertain. Many of Trudeau's promises were an illusion. The Liberal government has taken limited action to restore environmental protections and strengthen regulatory assessments, and they have been ardent supporters of tar sands and pipeline expansion projects. In terms of NEB reform, the government has reneged on its assurance that all pending pipeline applications would be evaluated by a new and independent energy regulator, one that would take a broad view of the public interest and have sufficient expertise in fields like environmental science and traditional Indigenous knowledge. The pending applications proceeded and, following NEB recommendations, Enbridge's Line 3 pipeline and Kinder Morgan's Trans Mountain pipeline were approved by the federal government on November 29, 2016. At the same time, the modernization panel has called into question some of the most troubling practices of the NEB, suggesting there may be some appetite to force the agency to pull back on the corporatization agenda.

Conclusion

Evidence of this potential pull back has begun to permeate the Canadian press. In early October 2017, at the time of this writing, TransCanada announced it would be withdrawing its application to build the Energy East pipeline. This decision was the result of many factors, including changes to world markets and the price of oil, as well as fierce opposition from environmental, community, and Indigenous groups across the country. In addition, one of the most important factors appears to be the expanded NEB environmental assessment process, which would consider the pipeline's indirect contributions to upstream and downstream greenhouse gas emissions. Indeed, some pipeline advocates have placed the onus for jeopardizing the pipeline squarely on the NEB's shoulders.[52]

While this news is a significant victory for tar sands and pipeline opponents, it is not enough to alleviate public concerns over the NEB's role as a corporatized and captured regulator. After six months of public consultations, the modernization panel exposed that Canadians no longer trust the NEB. According to the panel's report: "In our consultations we heard of a National Energy Board that has fundamentally lost the confidence of many Canadians ... We heard that Canadians have serious concerns that the NEB has been 'captured' by the oil and gas industry."[53] Another cross-national poll by EKOS found that only 10 percent of Canadians have "a lot of confidence" in the agency.[54] Although enhanced environmental assessments may be a first step and an early signal of improvements at the NEB, more robust, consistent measures are needed to address the impacts of corporatization. These include the overwhelming presence of industry person-nel within regulatory bodies, and the decreasing capacity of professionals and the public to provide input into regulatory decision-making. There are few areas where the corporatization process poses a greater threat than energy and pipe-line regulation. This process needs to be opposed in order to restore the integrity of regulatory practitioners and their vital role as guardians of the public interest.

Murky Waters

When Governments Turn Water Management into a Business

Emma Lui

The Growing Water Crisis in Canada

Canada holds roughly 6.5 percent of the planet's renewable freshwater, ranking third in the world for freshwater resources. However, 60 percent of this water flows northward, leaving only 2.6 percent of the world's water to southern Canada, where most of the population lives.[1] A 2015 Canadian-led study found that only 6 percent of groundwater worldwide is renewable.[2] These statistics only begin to dispel the myth of abundance about water in Canada. Yet, in continuing to approve water takings and thirsty industrial projects, governments across the country act as if there were an infinite supply.

Weakened environmental legislation, pollution from industries, and processes of corporatization are all putting water sources at risk. Canada does not have national drinking water standards, and groundwater sources—which one-third of the population relies on—have not been properly mapped. In 2015, there were 1,838 Drinking Water Advisories (DWAs) in effect across Canada.[3] As of January 2017, there were 148 DWAs in ninety-nine First Nations,[4] with more than 100 routinely in effect, some lasting for up to twenty years. Many oil, gas, and other industrial projects are located on the traditional territories of Indigenous nations, threatening their water rights, cultures, and ways of life.

The former Harper government put water at even greater risk when it gutted freshwater and environmental legislation. In 2012, the government stripped protections from 99 percent of lakes and rivers, leaving only three oceans, ninety-seven lakes, and sixty-two rivers under the purview of the *Navigation Protection Act*. It also exempted large pipelines and powerlines from scrutiny, so the impacts of these projects are no longer assessed for any navigable waterway. The *Fisheries Act* was arguably the most crucial piece of anti-pollution legislation in Canada, but the changes removed protections for fish and fish habitats. The government altered the *Canadian Environmental Assessment Act*, which resulted in the cancellation of nearly 3,000 environmental assessments. It not only washed its hands of protecting lakes and rivers, it ignored its obligations under the UN *Declaration on the Rights of Indigenous Peoples* to obtain free, prior, and informed consent. Despite the Trudeau government's election promises to restore the modest protections that the Harper government eliminated, not all protections under these Acts have been restored, much less strengthened. Alarmingly, over 99 percent of lakes and rivers remain unprotected under the *Navigation Protection Act*.

As is the case around the world, our governments and industries are promoting neoliberal policies that commodify and corporatize water. Neoliberal policies that turn water management into a business have become deeply entrenched in water governance, whether for bulk water withdrawals or the provision of water and wastewater services. Municipalities and Indigenous communities will face a water crisis—some an even deeper crisis—if governments and communities do not take bold action immediately.

This chapter argues that the corporatization of freshwater in Canada has only exacerbated this crisis. Corporatization entails the introduction of private sector norms and business models to water services and management. In the first section, I define several core facets of corporatization, which include commoditization, myopia, and productivism (the theory that increasing productivity is the primary goal of socio-economic activity). In the next three sections, I illustrate these facets through a study of three key trends in Canada. First, I examine the emerging aspirations of different levels of government towards full cost recovery, and how this has led to the commercialization of water in different ways. Second, I examine the emergence of new organizational models in the form of public-private partnerships (P3s) in the management of community water resources. Third, I examine the impact of international trade agreements on water governance. I conclude by stressing the importance of commons and public trust principles in protecting water in Canada, with inspiring examples of how communities are taking back control and protecting water as a human right.

The Corporatization of Water

Drawing from David McDonald's work, I highlight three key trends in neoliberal corporatization, all of which have impacted water services around the world: (i) commoditization, (ii) myopia, and (iii) productivism.[5] First, commoditization involves prioritizing monetary performance, creating public agencies that function as private companies, reframing citizens as consumers, and implementing cost-reflexive pricing, such as full cost recovery for water and wastewater services.[6] Jørgen Eiken Magdahl points out that "these services behave like, and imitate, private companies."[7] They have a corporate structure, including a board of directors, and can operate on a for-profit basis. Second, neoliberal corporatization is "myopic" in that it creates and exacerbates silos. Corporatization involves the creation of autonomous government agencies that own and operate a service, while having a separate legal status from other public services. These agencies are arm's length and costs and revenues are managed separately from other government departments.[8] Thus, water and wastewater services are planned and operated in isolation from other public services, such as health or waste management.[9] Finally, corporatization is centered on productivism, where corporatized services are geared towards the creation of new infrastructure for market-oriented economic growth. In the case of water, this often distracts from the challenges of over-consumption, unequal access to water services across regions, and public health impacts.[10]

Corporatization has been used as a neoliberal strategy to introduce market-friendly models to water services. By passing responsibility to an arm's length agency that is not necessarily accountable to the public, the corporatization of water services changes and, in some cases, absolves a government of its obligation to provide essential services and uphold fundamental human rights. In many countries, including Canada, the corporatization of water is also deeply embedded in public-private partnerships, discussed below. Corporatization also changes organizations and municipalities in ways that can open them up to deeper commercialization and privatization. Among other consequences, this can lead to strategies of revenue generation based on cost-reflexive pricing, introducing a "responsibility to pay" orientation to water services, and even cutting off services to poor households.

Proponents of corporatization models laud them for their purported efficiency. Some even suggest that corporatized water services help to ensure access. However, little attention is paid to questions of equity, affordability, conservation, or public health in these formulations, and evidence suggests that the impacts of corporatization can be just as harmful for low-income households as privatization.[11] In what follows, I discuss concrete examples of water corporatization in Canada and elsewhere, and their impacts on residents and communities.

Commercializing Canadian Water
Services and Nestlé's Bottled Water Takings

The commercialization and commoditization of water are similar in that they both involve treating water as something that can be bought and sold in the marketplace, like any other commodity. These processes have been facilitated in some municipalities and provinces in Canada through the adoption of full cost-recovery models, which involve the elimination or reduction of state subsidies for water supply and, in some cases, private models of delivery. It is important to contrast pricing for water services within a private sector model, or a market-oriented pricing model such as full cost recovery, with water fees that fund sources to ensure adequate water services within the public sector.[12] Models like full cost recovery commercialize and commoditize water and can pave the way to further corporatization or even privatization.

Full cost recovery entails financially "ring fencing" water services—so that revenue and costs are isolated from other public services—and creating user fees to recoup the full cost of the service. This can be problematic, because it makes water access conditional on payment, which violates the human right to water in the case of many low-income households and neighbourhoods. If residents cannot afford water rates, the government (agency) is justified in disconnecting services. In 2002, for instance, Ontario passed the *Sustainable Water and Sewage Systems Act*, which required municipalities to develop reports and plans on the "full cost" of providing water and wastewater services and eventually to adopt a full cost-recovery approach. The subsequent Expert Panel on Water and Wastewater Strategy released *Watertight: The Case for Change in Ontario's Water and Wastewater Sector* (2005), which recommended contracting out—a form of privatization—as well as corporatizing water utilities because, according to the panel, they have the "greatest benefits in terms of governance, transparency, financial sustainability and accountability."[13] Likewise, at the municipal level, major Canadian cities such as Toronto, Calgary, Ottawa, Vancouver, and Hamilton have all moved to a commoditized approach based on operating water services on a cost-recovery basis.

At the federal level, the Harper government passed the *Safe Drinking Water for First Nations Act* in 2013, establishing a framework from which to regulate drinking water for First Nations in Canada. However, the Act does not require free, prior, and informed consent of Indigenous communities, fails to make concrete funding commitments, and creates conditions where some First Nations may be required to enter into public-private partnerships. The legislation allows for "any person or body" to operate or manage water systems in First Nations, which opens the door for private companies to commercialize water in these communities.[14] The Act also stipulates that costs be recovered for work on water and wastewater systems, and that penalties (including fines and imprisonment) be implemented if regulations are violated. In 2015, the Assembly of First Nations passed a resolution calling for the repeal of the Act.

Water justice activists around the world have sounded the alarm about full cost-recovery policies, which have led to skyrocketing fee rates and public health impacts. The 2000 cholera epidemic in rural KwaZulu-Natal, South Africa, for example, was linked to the government's policy of full cost recovery. Residents could not afford the new connection fees and resorted to using polluted ponds and rivers for drinking and bathing.[15] Our Water Commons co-ordinator Daniel Moss asserts that full cost-recovery strategies are often applied selectively and put a disproportionate share of the cost on poor users who use the least amount of water.[16] In Canada, several municipalities from the Association of Municipalities of Ontario have also spoken out against full cost pricing, because of its impact on water rates and residents' "ability to afford further increases to their bills."[17]

Some Canadian provinces also run on a cost-recovery model when it comes to issuing water permits for bulk water takings. In 2015, the BC government released new water rates for groundwater, ranging from $0.02 to $2.25 per million litres, depending on the industry. According to the government's *Water Sustainability Act* website, one of the purposes of the new fees was to "generate sufficient revenue to recover the costs necessary to fully implement the *Water Sustainability Act* and associated programs."[18] Similarly, in his 2014–2015 Annual Report, then-Environmental Commissioner of Ontario, Gord Miller, recommended that the Ministry of Environment increase water taking fees and expand the application of fees to other water users "with a goal of recovering the full cost of the ministry's water management responsibilities."[19] While it is important for businesses to pay for water use, governments still must prohibit companies from pilfering these resources. Hinging water extraction rates on the capacity to effectively implement water legislation raises serious questions about a government's ability to promote water conservation. Does the government's fear of losing revenue lead to reluctance in limiting the number of high volume licences? Indeed, municipal councillors in Ontario have already expressed reluctance to conserve water because it "reduced overall revenues to run the system."[20]

Fees for "raw water" takings are generally low in Canada, but vary depending on the province and sector. For example, bottled water withdrawal fees were $2.25 in BC and $3.71 in Ontario for every million litres. In June 2017, the Ontario government increased bottled water taking fees from $3.71 to $503.71 after public opposition intensified in response to Nestlé's water grabs in southern Ontario. Even then, this only amounts to one-twentieth of a penny per litre, which sells for roughly $2 in stores. While there is a range of industries that have water taking permits, bottled water is particularly controversial because it is consumptive (water permanently leaves the watershed), and water permits for these extractions allow water to be commodified and sold for profit.

Nestlé has been bottling water in southern Ontario since the late 1980s. Every year, it draws up to 4.7 million litres from two wells in Aberfoyle and Hillsburgh in Wellington County, near Guelph. In August 2016, Nestlé purchased the Middlebrook well in Elora, despite the local municipality's attempt to buy the well to safeguard its water supply, sparking a national outcry. The well draws water from the Grand River Watershed, the traditional territory of the Six Nations of the Grand River (SNGR). Yet many people in Six Nations do not have clean running water. In 2016, Human Rights Watch reported that

> the majority of SNGR residents still get their water from private wells or cisterns ... Approximately 300 to 400 households on the reserve lack access to household water and wastewater services, and rely on trucked water and private outhouses or portable toilets.

The band council has also issued a boil-water advisory for most residents of Six Nations.

Nestlé's bottled water operations in BC have also stirred opposition. Despite the droughts in 2015, Nestlé continues to extract 265 million litres annually from a well in Hope, located on Sto:lo Territory. The well connects to an aquifer that six thousand nearby residents rely on.[21] Nestlé is not the only corporation putting local watersheds at risk in the province. Agriculture Canada reports that 83 percent of Canada's bottled water exports come from BC.[22] BC's 2015 *Water Sustainability Act* keeps in place an antiquated system known as "first in time, first in right" (FITFIR). The FITFIR system gives priority to those who used water in a region first. During times of water scarcity, it cuts off access to newer users. The Act supports business as usual (and Nestlé's profits) at the peril of Indigenous peoples and other residents of British Columbia, whose water resources are being drained at unsustainable rates.

The provision of water services and management does require funding. However, residential use only accounts for 9 percent of all water use in Canada, and raising rates for residential users will not adequately address the massive loss of clean water from industrial agriculture, extreme energy development, or bottled water takings. In terms of municipal water fees, most cities in Canada charge residents and businesses by volume use, though there are some municipalities that charge flat rates, and others that implement tiered systems.[23] However, to uphold the human right to water and ensure affordability and fairness, water services should be paid for through a progressive tax system.[24] Examples of progressive taxation include systems where governments generate funds for essential services (like water) through property or income taxes, which require lower-income earners to pay a smaller share of their income while higher-income earners pay a larger share. This type of system would go a long way to providing clean water services to residents without direct cost, and stagger the overall costs of the system based on the ability to pay.

Public-Private Partnerships (P3s)

Public private partnerships (P3s) are multi-decade contracts between a private party and a government entity, where the private sector plays a key role in financing, designing, building, operating, or even owning facilities and infrastructure that are otherwise designed to be public services. These agreements are usually negotiated in secret, inhibiting public input and stifling democratic debate on important social and economic issues.[25] The Canadian Union of Public Employees notes that "P3 contracts are often protected by commercial confidentiality and exempt from freedom of information legislation."[26] P3s can also result in higher costs, lower quality services, and loss of accountability and community control. Water justice movements around the world have often criticized P3s as a form of privatization. In the present context, however, P3s can also be thought of as an effect or outcome of corporatization, where water and sanitation services are turned into a commodity, and financed/operated separately from other public services on a for-profit basis.

The federal push for municipalities to use public-private partnerships began with the Liberal governments of the 1990s and early 2000s. When the Conservative government came to power in 2006, it dramatically intensified these practices by making funding for municipal infrastructure projects over $100 million conditional on entering into P3 agreements. Although the Trudeau Liberals no longer *require* municipalities to enter into P3s to receive federal funding for large infrastructure projects, they have not ruled out P3s for water projects and have actually promoted P3s as a solution to the water and wastewater infrastructure deficit.[27] In fact, the federal government's new Canada Infrastructure Bank will lead to P3s and the privatization of water and wastewater systems.

At the time of this writing, few communities in Canada have experimented with P3s for drinking water or sewer services, but there are lessons to be learned from those that have. In 1994, the City of Hamilton-Wentworth entered into what was the largest P3 agreement at the time with several private water corporations, including Philips Utilities Management Corporation (PUMC) and Enron's subsidiary Azurix. Despite the promises of local economic development, new jobs, and cost-savings, the water services workforce was cut in half within eighteen months. In 1996, shortly after PUMC was awarded the P3 contract, the company spilled millions of litres of raw sewage into Hamilton Harbour and flooded homes, with clean-up costs borne by the public. Since 2004, however, the municipal government has retaken control of its water system, surpassing environmental standards and delivering significant cost-savings in the process.[28]

Moncton also entered into a P3 for its water filtration system with US Filter in 1998 (which became Vivendi in 1999 and Veolia in 2004). Water rates increased by 75 percent between 1999 and 2000 alone. A 2011 report by PPP Canada, the federal crown corporation created to promote P3s across the country, obtained through an access to information request, notes that typical water prices are $0.31m^3 with the average daily domestic use of 343 litres. That year, Moncton's rates were $1.40m^3—far above the Canadian average. Affordability of water is a common challenge with P3s. A December 2011 *Times and Transcript* article noted the frequency of late payments on water bills in the city: "In Moncton, $2.6 million is owed by residential water users, which is not out of line with the norm."[29]

Perhaps the most striking examples of water corporatization in Canada involve Edmonton-based EPCOR Utilities Inc. EPCOR operates as a for-profit corporation and has assets of $6 billion. It owns and operates water and wastewater services in over seventy-five communities in Alberta, British Columbia, Saskatchewan, Arizona, New Mexico, and Texas. It was created in 1995 when it assumed ownership of Edmonton's power generation and distribution. A year later, it took over Edmonton's water treatment and distribution services. Although the company is owned by the City of Edmonton, the City has no representation on EPCOR's board of directors.[30] In April 2017, the City voted in favour of transferring its drainage services to EPCOR. The Parkland Institute has raised serious concerns about the accountability and transparency of this agreement. According to Executive Director Ricardo Acuña:

> As a public utility, Edmonton's drainage department is fully and publicly accountable to city council and to all Edmontonians. It reports monthly and in public to the city's drainage committee, falls

under provincial freedom of information legislation, and its operations are regularly reviewed by the city auditor, who also reports out publicly ... None of that is true for Epcor. There are no public meetings. No freedom of information requirements. And no access by the city auditor. It is this secrecy and lack of transparency that allowed Epcor to hive off and privatize its power generation assets (our power generation assets) in a closed-door shareholder meeting with no public consultation or input in 2009. What guarantee is there that our drainage assets will not meet the same fate?[31]

EPCOR has also entered into P3 agreements with other Canadian municipalities. For instance, an EPCOR-led consortium won a bid for Regina's thirty-year P3 wastewater contract in May 2014, the largest Design, Build, Finance, Operate, Maintain (DBFOM) contract in Canada. The City of Regina spent $400,000 of taxpayers' money urging residents to vote in favour of the P3 deal ahead of the 2013 referendum. Not only that, but the P3 was estimated to cost between $37.4 and $77.2 million more than a traditional model of water management, in part because of higher private financing costs and the need for the corporation to make a profit.[32] EPCOR's P3 operations elsewhere have also been controversial. Municipalities including Banff (AB), Port Hardy (BC), White Rock (BC), and Taber (AB) have all canceled contracts with EPCOR, with the latter two maintaining that the cancellations were "in the best interest of taxpayers."[33] In a series of moves that outraged local residents in French Creek (BC), EPCOR increased monthly water rates from $45.30 to $62.44 between 2014 and 2017. The Canadian Union of Public Employees reported that water rates in French Creek were already among the highest on Vancouver Island before the hikes.[34]

It should be noted that White Rock took back its water and wastewater systems from EPCOR in 2015. The municipality had been in talks with EPCOR for two years prior to this action,[35] during which time the city council threatened to expropriate the water systems. A confidential agreement was eventually reached, and White Rock is now in charge of its own water. This move was clearly in the best interest of the public: "A White Rock official praised the city's decision in fall 2015 to bring its water back into public hands, saying that high levels of arsenic and manganese in its water would never have been discovered otherwise."[36]

All these examples suggest that P3 water operations tend to involve an unhealthy fixation on profit, productivism, and economic growth, which are prioritized over affordability, public health, transparency, and democratic accountability. These practices are unlikely to fade anytime soon, as EPCOR has been "identified by PPP Canada Inc. ... as [a] likely market participant in Canadian water and wastewater P3 projects."[37] The case of White Rock demonstrates, however, that people and communities are not powerless in their struggle against corporatization.

Commodifying Water Through Trade Agreements

Trade agreements like the North American Free Trade Agreement (NAFTA) promote the corporatization of water by defining water as a tradable good, service, and investment. Corporations and their legal teams play a significant role in writing trade agreements, crafting rules that give them unbridled access to water, energy resources, and more, thereby establishing and reinforcing their "right to profit."[38] National water laws must comply with international trade agreements, potentially weakening freshwater safeguards and reinforcing neoliberal policies that result in corporatization or privatization. Investor-State Dispute Settlement (ISDS) clauses are a particularly controversial feature of trade agreements that give companies the right to sue governments over regulations or standards that protect water—even if they are implemented to protect the public interest—because they may affect a company's "expected future profits."

Corporations have used ISDS clauses to challenge water policies and regulations that protect water sources and public health. In 1993, Argentina entered into a thirty-year contract with a private consortium led by Suez Lyonnaise des Eaux to operate water and sanitation services in Buenos Aires. Following tariff increases, delays of original investments, and other "mounting confrontations, the government canceled the contract and created a public company, AySA, to immediately take responsibility for the provision of water and sanitation services."[39] As a result, Suez sued Argentina, and the World Bank's International Center for Settlement of Investment Disputes ordered Argentina to pay the water corporation $405 million.[40]

In 2000, Bulgaria's capital city of Sofia signed a contract with Sofiyska Voda, whose major shareholder is French multinational Veolia. Sofiyska Voda raised water prices on residents that flatly violated its contract with the city.[41] Nevertheless, in 2011, the city disconnected one-thousand households from the water supply and prosecuted five thousand more for non-payment of water bills at the direction of the company. Citizens had collected enough signatures to hold a referendum on remunicipalization of their water services, but the city did not allow it, fearing that the company would sue Bulgaria under the Vienna

International Arbitral Centre.[42] In 2011, Tallinna Vesi, an Estonian water company owned by United Utilities, filed a $140-million investor lawsuit against Estonia because public authorities refused to allow the company to increase water rates. The government had passed a law in 2010 empowering it to cap the company's profits at what it deemed to be a "reasonable level." The company is seeking all the profit it would lose over the duration of its contract up to 2020.[43]

In Canada, trade agreements like NAFTA help to ensure that governments will be unable to turn off the taps should any Canadian province give the green light to bulk water exports, because they would be risking a trade lawsuit. NAFTA's proportionality clause also requires governments to reduce exports—such as water—in such a way that countries share the reduction "proportionately." In other words, if any province began exporting bulk water to the US and then wanted to limit those exports, the province would have to reduce water supplies to Canadian users to the same extent as it would for US users. This raises serious concerns about water security for provinces like BC, Alberta, and Ontario, which have experienced droughts in recent years, as well as Indigenous nations and communities that are under Drinking Water Advisories. Under the proportionality clause, Canada could be locked into exporting water to the US, even during times of severe water shortage.

Resisting Corporatization:
Protecting Water as a Human Right, Commons, and Public Trust

In July 2010, the UN General Assembly overwhelmingly voted to recognize the human right to water and sanitation. In 2008–09, Canadian water justice activist Maude Barlow served as Senior Advisor on Water to the sixty-third president of the United Nations General Assembly and was a leader in the campaign to have water recognized as a human right. The UN Human Rights Council has also passed resolutions on the human right to water and sanitation and called upon governments to develop comprehensive plans and strategies to ensure affordable services for all. In 2015, UN member states reaffirmed their commitment to upholding this essential right by including it in the Sustainable Development Goals.

There has also been mounting global pressure to recognize water as a commons and a public trust. A commons approach encourages communities to equitably share water but also empowers them to protect water for future generations. Similarly, public trust principles recognize that water is a common heritage of all people and requires governments to protect these essential resources from private and commercial interests. Jim Olson, a leading public trust lawyer and founder of the Michigan-based organization FLOW, argues that the application of public trust principles is essential to address systemic threats to watersheds. To tackle problems such as algal blooms, pollution, and bulk water exports, Olson says, "the public trust is necessary to solve these threats that directly impact traditional public trust resources like the Great Lakes and it tributary waters."[44]

However, Canada's federal government has yet to implement this fundamental human right, nor has it come up with a national plan of action. Provinces have also failed to take action in provincial water legislation and water-permitting processes. The promotion of water corporatization by governments has stifled much needed safeguards and affordability policies that the human right to water would guarantee. Indeed, corporatized models of water management that emphasize commercialization and commoditization depart radically from these values. Respecting water as a human right, commons, and public trust would go a long way to protecting water and communities from the negative impacts of corporatization, such as prioritizing profit and growth over public health, lack of democratic accountability, and abuses such as pollution and over-extraction.

In accordance with these principles, respect for Indigenous title and water rights are essential. Most lands and watersheds in Canada are located on the traditional territories of Indigenous peoples.[45] The Union of BC Indian Chiefs (UBCIC) has emphasized the intimate link between land and water. In a submission to BC's *Water Sustainability Act*, the UBCIC wrote: "As an incidence of our Aboriginal Title to our territories, Indigenous Peoples have jurisdiction over the waters in our territories ... Indeed, it is nearly impossible to imagine an Aboriginal or Treaty right that does not depend upon water."[46] Merrell-Anne Phare, Executive Director and Legal Counsel for the Centre for Indigenous Environmental Resources, points out that in regions where treaties have been signed, "many First Nations assert that their ancestors did not relinquish any of their rights to water."[47] As the Truth and Reconciliation report recommends, the UN *Declaration on the Rights of Indigenous Peoples* must be implemented as a critical next step for reconciliation. Several clauses in the *Declaration* relate to water protection, but particularly Article 32–2, which notes that:

> States shall consult and cooperate in good faith with the indigenous peoples concerned through their own representative institutions in order to obtain their free and informed consent prior to the approval of any project affecting their lands or territories and other

resources, particularly in connection with the development, utilization or exploitation of mineral, water or other resources.

In the face of corporatization and other threats to water services, communities in Canada are mobilizing. In southern Ontario, for example, groups like the Wellington Water Watchers, Save Our Water, and local chapters of the Council of Canadians continue to apply pressure on the Ontario government to protect water as a public trust in the face of Nestlé's extractions.[48] Activists have organized rallies, mobilized residents to fill council chambers during meetings, and held standing-room-only town halls. Tens of thousands of people sent in submissions to the Ontario government's public comment periods, calling on the government to ban bottled water takings. Spearheaded by the Council of Canadians' social media campaigns, more than 50,000 people—mostly from Canada—have pledged to boycott Nestlé and all bottled water. In April 2017, the Council organized a tour leading up to the 2017 BC election where honorary chairperson Maude Barlow spoke to communities across the province about Nestlé's activities.

In Abbotsford, Water Watch Mission-Abbotsford (WWMA) led the fight against the thirty-year P3 proposal in 2011. WWMA and its allies distributed information to local residents through social media and public events on the risks of the project, including the implications of private sector participation. Citizens participated in council meetings and called on their councillors to reject the P3. The issue was put to a referendum vote during the 2011 municipal election when residents ousted then-mayor George Peary and voted overwhelmingly (nearly 75 percent) to nix the deal. In BC, White Rock water activists continue to educate residents on the cost-savings and other benefits associated with taking back control of the city's water system from EPCOR. Public events such as film screenings and discussion forums have been organized to encourage public debate.

In addition to UN and other international initiatives, there is also a growing global movement to adopt a water commons framework and cultivate "Blue Communities" by passing three kinds of resolutions: (i) recognizing water as a human right; (ii) banning the sale of bottled water in municipal facilities and at events; and (iii) promoting publicly owned and operated water and wastewater services.[49] Nearly twenty municipalities across Canada have passed resolutions to become Blue Communities, including Burnaby, Nanaimo, Victoria, St. Catharines, and Thunder Bay. The Blue Communities movement has spread to many other countries as well, including twenty municipalities in Switzerland (home to Nestlé), Paris, and Cambuquira, Brazil.

Universal, equitable, and affordable access to water should be seen as non-negotiable. Given the relentless push by governments and industry to corporatize water, communities around the world are taking action. It is the growing number of activists on the frontlines of these struggles that offer the greatest hope for water justice.

16

Learning from Corporatization

The Good, the Bad, and the Ugly

David A. McDonald

Introduction

After three decades of privatization and anti-state rhetoric, government ownership and public management are back in vogue. Governments around the world are re-taking control of services previously sold or contracted out to the private sector, with the overall number of public enterprises around the world having actually increased since the 1990s.[1] Even the Anglo-American heartland of privatization has seen more insourcing than outsourcing over the past decade, as public sector managers become increasingly frustrated with the "inadequate" quality and scant cost-savings of privatization, particularly in essential service sectors such as water and electricity.[2]

Corporatization has proven to be one of the most popular forms of this renewed interest in government ownership—defined here in its most basic institutional sense: the creation of arm's length enterprises that are fully owned and operated by the state but are run by independent managers with varying degrees of autonomy from government. Sometimes described as agencies or parastatals, corporatized entities typically have a separate legal status from other public entities and a corporate structure similar to publicly traded private sector companies. This ring fencing is intended to create greater financial transparency, reduce political interference, and strengthen managerial accountability. I will focus in this chapter on public utilities, such as water and electricity—by far the most common form of corporatization—although the practice extends to a much wider range of goods and services, including airports, child care, universities, forests, hospitals, transport, and manufacturing.[3]

Institutionally speaking, there is nothing distinctively ideological about this form of corporatization. In fact, the concept and practice of creating arm's length state agencies is as old and diverse as the state itself. The Achaemenid Empire of Persia, for example, was dominated by state enterprises with some autonomy from political rulers, run as "professional" entities and renowned for their "efficiencies."[4] Sweden began to "structurally disaggregate the provision and production of public services" as early as the seventeenth century, and has employed modified versions of this arrangement ever since.[5] So, too, did the Soviets experiment with the corporatization model, creating some 750,000 arm's length public enterprises while in power,[6] and widespread experiments in "municipal socialism" in Europe from the late 1800s also saw extensive corporatization, with everything from gas works to restaurants to hospitals being run as corporatized public entities.[7]

In other words, the creation of arm's length, state-owned entities is neither historically specific nor ideologically predetermined, with the rationale for public enterprises having differed dramatically across place and time. Their only common feature is a quasi-independent cadre of professional bureaucrats tasked with managing a delineated set of activities, buffered to some degree from direct political intervention.

Most recently, corporatization has been used to create market-friendly public sector cultures and ideologies. Since the late 1970s, corporatized public utilities around the world have been run increasingly on market-oriented operating principles, such as financialized performance indicators, cost-reflexive pricing, and competitive outsourcing. These neoliberal forms of corporatization are widespread and have arguably become the most dominant approach to managing public utilities in the world today, "making up the bulk of the public sphere in many Western European countries," and becoming popular in emerging economies in the South.[8]

This chapter defines and describes this neoliberal variant of corporatization, highlighting two particularly pernicious problems that it gives rise to—myopia and commodification. I then outline ways in which these problems can be challenged, and potentially reversed, citing examples of more progressive forms of corporatized water and electricity utilities in different parts of the world.

The Problems of Neoliberal Corporatization

What exactly is *neoliberal* corporatization? In short, it puts market-based operating mechanisms at the heart of the corporatization model, pushing managers to use market-oriented signals such as price and interest rates as primary factors in their decision-making. The financial bottom line of a stand-alone utility is not the only performance criteria employed in these cases, but it is a crucial factor in planning and evaluation, with managers frequently remunerated or incentivized according to the surplus/deficit of the agency, with market-based salaries used to attract the "best" personnel. Investment decisions are based on financial returns and money is borrowed at market rates.

Such neoliberalization is never absolute, of course. A bifurcated view of consumers and citizens obscures more complex, politicized, and dialectical relationships between individuals and the (neoliberal) state.[9] Yet we can point to an *increasingly neoliberalized* model of corporatization, one that is grounded in the belief that "human well-being can best be advanced by liberating individual entrepreneurial freedoms and skills within an institutional framework characterized by strong private property rights [and] free markets."[10] The intent is to create public companies that are owned and operated by the state, but run as though they were private firms operating in a competitive marketplace, driven by self-interested, utility-maximizing individuals. As Jeremy Gilbert puts it:

> Neoliberalism advocates a programme of deliberate intervention by government in order to encourage particular types of entrepreneurial, competitive and commercial behaviour in its citizens, ultimately arguing for the management of populations with the aim of cultivating a type of individualistic, competitive, acquisitive and entrepreneurial behavior . . . This is the key difference between classical liberalism and neoliberalism: the former presumes that, left to their own devices, humans will naturally tend to behave in the desired fashion. By contrast the latter assumes that they must be compelled to do so by a benign but frequently directive state.[11]

In this respect, neoliberal corporatization can be seen as an effort by governments to instill a commercialized ideology into ring fenced public services, while at the same time attacking the perceived failures of Keynesian-era welfarism. As such, neoliberal corporatization is part of a larger shift over the past three decades towards New Public Management (NPM), a governance strategy which Christopher Pollitt characterizes as focusing on results-based management, an emphasis on performance measurements that prioritize market-based indicators, a preference for more "specialized, lean, flat and autonomous organizational forms," and a "widespread substitution of contract or contract-like relationships for hierarchical relationships."[12] Debates continue as to how deep and extensive this NPM trend has been, and whether it remains as popular today as it was in the

1990s, but three decades of NPM-type philosophy have resulted in "a broadening and blurring of the 'frontier' between the public and private sectors" and a "shift in value priorities away from universalism, equity, security and resilience towards efficiency and individualism."[13] Neoliberal corporatization is but one manifestation of this NPM trend.

Nevertheless, neoliberal corporatization is *not* privatization, and pure market forces never fully apply to state-owned enterprises, especially to natural monopolies, such as water and electricity. But it is exactly these market limits that have made the corporatization of public services so popular among neoliberals, acting as a vehicle to pry open new possibilities for market penetration, via structural and legislative reforms that introduce commercial principles and mandates into un(der)-marketized service sectors.[14] Liberalization is intended to force public agencies to compete with private companies for their own contracts,[15] while the unbundling of sectors such as electricity creates vertical competition within public agencies and opportunities for private sector intervention.[16]

Some analysts have argued that neoliberal corporatization is a mere transition to future privatization, instilling market-oriented management cultures and profitable bottom lines to prepare public services for private buyers. After all, few private companies are interested in investing in services with hidden cost structures, or partnering with government agencies that do not have market-oriented management philosophies.

According to the OECD,[17] corporatization should not "contradict or discourage countries from undertaking any privatisation policies or programmes," and the same applies to much of China's experimentation with corporatization, where many state-owned enterprises are being prepared for "eventual privatization."[18] In some cases, neoliberal corporatization has been used as an opportunity to introduce market mechanisms (such as cost-reflexive pricing) while the service is still in public hands, sparing private companies the wrath of consumers when it is privatized. In Manila and Buenos Aires, for example, water prices were intentionally increased by corporatized public utilities prior to privatization.[19] Even if privatization is not the end goal, the result can be much the same: public agencies acting like private companies.[20] The trend towards performance-based salaries for senior managers and other narrow pecuniary incentives contributes to changes in management ethos, with a focus on short-term financial bottom lines, creating publicly owned and operated entities that mimic private sector discourse and practice.[21]

Many of these corporatized utilities are increasingly international in their operations as well.[22] In some cases, they even celebrate their "public" status at home while aggressively seeking for-profit contracts outside their jurisdictions. Rand Water and Eskom (electricity) in South Africa are illustrative of this trend. While trumpeting their role as public providers in a post-apartheid era, they chase private sector contracts elsewhere on the continent, where they behave like (and are perceived as) profit-seeking multinational corporations.[23] Manitoba Hydro is another example: while fighting off privatization at home (citing the merits of public ownership and control), Manitoba Hydro's international division took on a three-year contract to privatize Nigeria's electricity transmission network.[24] Little wonder that some critics see neoliberal corporatization as the proverbial wolf in sheep's clothing, offering a façade of public ownership while propagating market ideologies. Neoliberal corporatization may be "public" in name, but not necessarily in character.

Exacerbating Myopia

One of the biggest concerns with neoliberal corporatization is its myopic focus on its own operations—a problem that arises from its institutional architecture. By their nature, corporatized agencies are compartmentalized into silos, making it difficult to co-ordinate management and finance across units, potentially undermining synergistic public planning, resource use, and economies of scale.[25] Neoliberalism makes this bias even worse, emphasizing a ring fenced financial bottom line and promoting monetized forms of performance evaluation, even when these goals come at a cost to their sister units or to the larger public good.

Under such conditions, cross-subsidization can become difficult, if not impossible. Where incomes from revenue-generating services such as electricity might support non-revenue-generating services such as libraries, managers are often disinclined (and disincentivized) to undermine their own financial situation by sharing resources. At the same time, elected officials may have lost their authority to demand inter-unit transfers, as austerity erodes the capacity of the state as a whole.[26] Such isolationism is particularly problematic in lower-income countries in the South, where infrastructure gaps are enormous and where collective economies of scale could be used to expand service access across a broader range of sectors. But its effects are increasingly being felt in countries in the North, where austerity measures have made inter-departmental and inter-governmental transfers increasingly tight and ideologically charged.

The result is often a focus on (full) cost recovery by utility managers, based on the assumption that they are unlikely to receive subsidies from other units or levels of government. This is an understandable decision by bureaucrats wanting to protect their agencies, but too much emphasis on recouping costs within a stand-alone utility can create affordability problems for the poor, with cut-offs in services such as water and electricity potentially undermining public goods such as health and education.

Monetized incentives also serve to undermine personal associations within government, eroding the kinds of "high-trust relationships" that "lower trans-action costs within the public sector and make it more efficient than it would be if each action had to be negotiated and costed on a low-trust basis."[27] The constant threat of privatization, and having to compete for one's own contracts, make the sharing of information within and across corporatized utilities less likely, instil-ling a heightened sense of privacy and secrecy as cost data becomes commer-cially confidential.

The same myopia can apply to workers. Forced to operate in vertically ori-ented administrative structures, front line staff often toil in isolation, sometimes in separate unions, making worker co-ordination and solidarity across public services difficult (which can, of course, be a neoliberal strategy in and of itself). These managerial and accounting systems are intended to reveal the "real" costs of running a service, allowing managers to identify areas of financial loss or gain otherwise hidden in the intricate accounting systems and cross-subsidization mechanisms of a more centralized production and distribution system. In this process, ring fencing can deny synergistic gains that may be had from more col-lective planning.[28]

Commodification

A related concern with these agency-specific financial bottom lines is their tendency to intensify the commodification process, accelerating the transformation of use values into exchange values, with goods and services increasingly defined and valorized by their price. Thus, water, with its qualitatively different uses (e.g., religious practice, aesthetic beauty, recreational enjoyment, physiological necessity), becomes a more homogenized commodity in the ring fenced exchange process.[29] Service users are also increasingly commodified in this financially driven model, treated as "customers" rather than "citizens," with services conceived of as private commodities, dissociated from broader public goods, and concealing the social and labour arrangements behind their exchange price.[30]

This commodification process also allows utility managers to argue that the only way to truly "appreciate" a service is to pay for it (ideally at full market cost), sidelining or eradicating non-commodified valuations that might be asso-ciated with a service. If a value cannot be expressed in monetary terms, it risks being excluded from the decision-making process. Under such conditions, it is harder for utility managers to see and evaluate the non-monetized values of a service—e.g., the improved dignity associated with better sanitation services, or the spiritual comfort one may obtain from a free-flowing river. If a benefit cannot be measured in financial terms, its relevance tends to fall to the wayside.

The pace and scale of such commodification is uneven, and differs from sector to sector (with water being particularly "uncooperative" in this regard due to its biophysical characteristics),[31] but "the reality of capitalism is that ever more of social life is mediated through and by the market,"[32] with far-reaching transformative effects on the public services we use.

It is important to note that this is not a uniquely neoliberal phenomenon. *All* market-based service delivery systems are under pressure to bring goods and services into the exchange process, and to promote capital accumulation in an increasingly competitive global economy. Keynesian welfare models of public services may be better at distributing the benefits of public investments, and, to varying degrees, slowing the commodification process, but they too were designed to build mass consumption societies and deepen market relations.[33] These are the cascading effects of commodification and they are inherent to all capitalist economies. Neoliberal corporatization merely accelerates the process.

Progressive Corporatization?

In light of these structural tendencies, is it possible to create more progressive forms of corporatization in market economies? If so, what differentiates these models from their more overtly neoliberal cousins?

Debate on this topic is made difficult by the dearth of comparable empirical literature. So too have the negative, widespread effects of neoliberal corporatization made it hard to imagine a more progressive corporatized possibility. Yet there is sufficient international evidence to suggest that with adequate political will, solid grassroots organizing, and broadminded policy-making, it is conceivable to create—and reclaim—more progressive forms of stand-alone public utilities. The following examples are illustrative of a more eclectic range of corporatization than those of the neoliberal model outlined above, despite operating in market-based economies, often under difficult and rapidly fluctuating political and economic conditions.

Costa Rica's *Instituto Costarricense de Electricidad* is one such example. Created in 1949, this parastatal electricity utility grew out of the import-substitution models popular in Latin America at the time. It has reformed along with the social democratic policies of the Costa Rican state to a point where it is considered the most progressive and equity-oriented electricity provider in Latin America, while advancing its standing as one of the most environmentally sustainable electricity providers in the world (public or private).[34]

Tunisia's electricity provider—*Société Tunisienne de l'Électricité et du Gaz*—was a product of post-independence nationalization in that country, followed by tight public management under the authoritarian regime of Zine El Abidine Ben Ali; it is now grappling with the rapid changes of the so-called Arab Spring, struggling to open its hitherto opaque operating practices to closer public scrutiny and adjusting to a more liberalized economy, while at the same time trying to sustain its almost universal coverage to all income groups in the country.[35] Despite these challenges, including ongoing political upheaval, the agency continues to enhance its outreach and transparency program. In Malaysia, the *Tenaga Nasional Berhad* (TNB) dates back to the creation of the Central Electricity Board by British colonial managers, also in 1949, and is part and parcel of a post-war economic recovery effort to counter communist insurgency in rural areas, modified again in the 1980s and 1990s in response to changing post-independence politics.[36] With almost universal coverage and broadly affordable rates, TNB has managed to stave off attempts at privatization and continues to expand its renewable energy program.

Obras Sanitarias del Estado (OSE), the centralized water and sanitation agency in Uruguay, is another good illustration of the multiple personalities that corporatized agencies can take on in market environments. OSE was transferred to the Uruguayan government from a private British firm in 1952, in partial payment of Britain's debts following the Second World War, and has survived dictatorships, neoliberal governments, and the current left-wing coalition.[37] Uruguayans are proud of their public water provider, with labour unions and citizens rallying to protect it from threats of privatization in the early 2000s, leading to a constitutional referendum that has since made it illegal to privatize water services in the country (the first country in the world to do so).[38]

The European experience will be more familiar to Canadians, and a few examples are listed here to illustrate the potential for innovative and progressive forms of corporatization in more advanced market economies with deeper histories of privatization.[39] Indeed, it is arguably the long and negative experiences of privatization and commercialization in Europe that have generated awareness among citizens about the need for better "public" control. France and Germany, in particular, have led the push to renegotiate the terms of what it means to own and operate essential public services, such as water and electricity. These two countries alone have witnessed hundreds of privatization reversals since the early 2000s, and a radical shift in the role of communities, labour, and other stakeholders in the public decision-making and ownership process.[40]

Water services in Paris are perhaps the best-known example, having been transferred back to state control from the two largest, private water companies in the world in 2010. In the first year of operation, the newly corporatized public water agency (*Eau de Paris*) realized efficiency savings of €35 million, allowing for an 8 percent reduction in tariffs. It also engaged in partnerships with upstream farmers aimed at promoting environmentally sound practices, and adopted a number of solidarity initiatives: "it increased its contribution to the city's housing solidarity fund, paid a water solidarity allocations to 44,000 poor households, commissioned a report on progressive tariffs, launched a water-saving campaign, and refrained from cutting off water supply in squats."[41] The new public agency has also created public-public partnerships with Morocco and Mauritania's national water operators, and added workers' representatives and civil society representatives to its board.[42]

In Italy's southern region of Apulia, the public water operator has managed to fend off privatization and improved its efficiencies, while at the same time making the organization more transparent, retraining its workers, and bringing previously outsourced wastewater management operations back in-house. Water leakages were reduced, and the agency has increased its investments in water services tenfold.[43] In Debrecen, Hungary, corporatization was jointly developed by public managers and local trade unions to prevent privatization. These corporatized operations proved more cost-effective than the proposed privatizations, and more efficient than other Hungarian public water operators.[44] Company surpluses were reinvested in water supply and sanitation operations, while the remainder was used by the Debrecen municipal government to subsidize other municipal services.[45]

In Germany, a long-standing grassroots movement to push for renewable energy has overlapped with demands for more local ownership and control, driving much of the success behind that country's much-vaunted *Energiewende* (energy transition), with dozens of electricity providers converting back to public ownership—often along corporatized lines—with efforts to make them more accountable, participatory, and environmentally sustainable.[46]

In the face of such diversity, it makes little sense to speak of "corporatization" as a single model, even in market economies shaped and buffeted by neoliberal influences over the past few decades. Writing off corporatization as *inherently* neoliberal conceals the multiple ways in which policy-makers, managers, and employees of corporatized entities battle with neoliberal forces on the ground and how they can shape more progressive narratives of public sector reform.

But these examples of relatively progressive forms of market-based corporatization are also fragile, with powerful neoliberal forces constantly percolating near the surface, threatening to undermine and reverse positive gains. No single public utility can escape the clutches of commodification entirely, especially with the logics of NPM seeping so deeply into the global public management psyche.

Lessons for Canada

For Canadian activists, unionists, academics, consumers, and policy-makers trying to rebuild and reclaim public services in this country, there are important lessons to be learned from these international experiences with corporatization. The first lesson is that not all corporatizations are characterized by a commercialization imperative. The common administrative structure of corporatization belies more diverse material and philosophical undercurrents, from proto-privatization to distributive welfarism to contemporary models of socialism, some of which have been remarkably innovative and pro-public over the years. Even market-based models of corporatization have proven themselves to be relatively progressive in some cases. In this regard, corporatization can be seen as little more than an empty vessel into which different ideological fluids can be poured.

It should also be remembered that welfare-era public services models are not necessarily the only (or best) public service alternative to corporatization. Keynesian-style investments in public services should be fought for where appropriate, but we must not wax nostalgically about public management models that have at times been exclusionary, opaque, and blindly productivist in their orientation.[47] Nor are these social democratic models designed to stop commodification. Keynesian interventionism is intended to enhance the conditions for capital accumulation, with the aim of reducing the role of the state when it is no longer required.

In the end, there is no blueprint for a single path to progressive public service change. Even progressive forms of corporatization will differ across place and sector. Ignoring these local variances in the name of a single public service model runs the risk of creating yet another form of managerial hegemony. Ham-fisted attempts to foist Soviet-style models of public service on socialist satellite states in the past are a good case in point.

But nor should we abandon universal goals. Normative principles of equity and transparency can serve as a useful reference point in this respect, offering guidelines for planning and evaluation that can allow for local variations on corporatization without forsaking baseline expectations of performance, including criteria such as gender equity, affordable pricing, and accountability for marginalized groups.[48] Creating and popularizing such non-commodified performance indicators will not be easy, particularly with abstract criteria such as "dignity," but the potential to radicalize existing, quantitative benchmarking is considerable.[49]

Corporatized entities can also be pressured to collect better (and more widely available) data on a range of equity-oriented information, such as service cut-offs, injuries to front line workers, spatial variability in service quality, demographic analyses of community consultations, percentages of household incomes spent on baseline services, and so on. Enhancing and expanding statistics of this sort will help to challenge narrow neoliberal forms of corporatization, while at the same time acknowledging that financial performance can be part of a progressive evaluative method.

New forms of evaluation will also require new institutions of training. Disrupting the neoliberal pedagogies of the past will not be easy, however, particularly in countries where international financial institutions, such as the World Bank, dominate the discourse of public service education. As Christopher Pollitt and Geert Bouckaert note, the "importing and exporting of public management ideas and practices has always been greatly facilitated by international and supranational bodies such as the Public Management Service of the OECD (PUMA), the World Bank, and the European Commission."[50]

Canadian public utilities do not rely as heavily on external training as some countries, but the ideological influences are much the same, with decades of NPM influence having found its way into training manuals and public policy schools.[51] It took a generation to create this neoliberal bias; changing it will not happen overnight. Effective counter-hegemonic vocabularies and pedagogies based on real-world examples of more progressive forms of corporatization are therefore vital if we are to shift away from the ideals and practices of neoliberal corporatization that dominate today.

A final point to make is the need for corporatized entities to think beyond their institutional boundaries. Although corporatization as an institutional model constructs financial and managerial walls, the shape and character of these partitions are negotiable and movable. Ring fencing can only be effective if there are (literal and figurative) doors and windows that encourage co-operation and communication between agencies, and that promote more holistic planning across a wide range of public services.

In other words, the architecture of disaggregation depends equally on its potential for re-aggregation, allowing for autonomy when required, collaboration when appropriate, and accountability at all times. Corporatization should be seen as a fluid and permeable set of institutional relationships, not a rigid and impervious state of being. It is the latter that has contributed to the authoritative and narrow behaviours of neoliberal corporatizations in the past, shielding managers from the demands for more transparent and collective public action. Canadians can insist on corporatized arrangements that enhance equity, transparency, accountability, and a strong public ethos, with performance metrics that allow for regular and effective evaluation of these norms.

So, too, must we aim to perforate and democratize the ways in which corporatized agencies engage with actors beyond the state, including labour, community organizations, and NGOs. Such an associational model may stretch the institutional definition of corporatization (as state-owned and state-operated), but it is hard to imagine truly progressive forms of corporatization that do not engage meaningfully with front line workers, end users, and other non-state actors in important decision-making and operational processes.

Some of these changes can come from the top (as was the case with water reforms in Paris) while others can come from the grassroots (as was the case with public water in Uruguay). The most effective and sustainable reforms will likely require both—state officials committed to institutional models that require accountability and equity, and workers and end users who are engaged in policy-making and delivery decisions.

Progressive forms of corporatization will require working "within, against and beyond" the state, with citizen groups, unions, bureaucrats, and elected officials clashing and collaborating, seeking ways to derive benefits from an arm's length agency with potential economies of scale, while balancing this with demands for participatory engagement with civil society and other state actors, to ensure a more holistic vision of what a complex and boisterous "public" is actually like in practice.[52]

It is inevitable that neoliberal practices and narratives of New Public Management will be challenged as the limits and contradictions of market reforms reveal themselves, and as alternative forces emerge to resist their inequities. We can therefore acknowledge that "the imperative towards opening up public services to markets and market-like principles remains strong," while at the same time insisting that wherever markets are being made, there are other voices and other discourses that challenge the appropriateness of market relations—questioning their subjection to profit rather than need, pointing to the risks of corruption and collusion, demanding that values other than market value are relevant, or insisting on the superiority of morals, ethos and solidarity to individualism and self-interest.[53]

These are the *counter-publics* that emerge from the contradictory spaces of neoliberal corporatization, where the logic of commodification has run amok, and where unions, community groups, and (sometimes) bureaucrats are pushing back.[54]

Contributors' Biographies

Donna Baines is a professor in the Faculty of Education and Social Work at the University of Sydney, Australia. Her work focuses on paid and unpaid care work, restructuring in the social services sector, and anti-oppressive social work practice. She recently published the third edition of *Doing Anti-Oppressive Practice: Social Justice Social Work* (Fernwood 2017), and is a co-author of the seventh edition of *Case Critical: Social Services and Social Justice in Canada* (Between the Lines 2017). Her work has also appeared in academic journals such as *Journal of Social Work, Critical Social Policy*, and *Journal of Industrial Relations*.

Jamie Brownlee completed his PhD in sociology and political economy at Carleton University, where he currently teaches and conducts research in the areas of Canadian and international political economy, higher education, corporate crime, environmental politics and climate change, and access to information law. He is the author of *Ruling Canada: Corporate Cohesion and Democracy* (Fernwood 2005), *Academia, Inc.: How Corporatization is Transforming Canadian Universities* (Fernwood 2015), and co-editor of *Access to Information and Social Justice: Critical Research Strategies for Journalists, Scholars, and Activists* (ARP 2015). Jamie's work has also appeared in academic journals such as *Higher Education, Organization & Environment*, and *Paedagogica Historica*.

William K. Carroll is a professor of sociology at the University of Victoria. His books include *Corporate Power and Canadian Capitalism* (UBC Press 1986), *Remaking Media: The Struggle to Democratize Public Communication* (with B. Hackett, Routledge 2006), *The Making of a Transnational Capitalist Class* (Zed Books 2010), *Corporate Power in a Globalizing World* (Oxford University Press 2010), and *Expose, Oppose, Propose: Alternative Policy Groups and the Struggle for Global Justice* (Fernwood 2016). He is also co-editor of *Challenges and Perils: Social Democracy in Neoliberal Times* (Fernwood 2005) and *A World to Win: Contemporary Social Movements and Counter-Hegemony* (ARP 2016). His current project, the Corporate Mapping Project, is an interdisciplinary partnership of universities and civil society organizations that traces various modalities of corporate power and resistance, focusing on fossil capital based in western Canada.

Kelly Gorkoff received her PhD from Carleton University where she completed her dissertation on the corporatization of post-secondary education in Canada. Her current research at the University of Winnipeg is focused on criminal justice, critical political economy, and feminist theory. She has worked as a research associate at RESOLVE, an organization dedicated to studying and preventing violence against women. She is also the co-editor of *Being Heard: The Experiences of Young Women in Prostitution* (Fernwood 2002) and *Thinking About Justice* (Fernwood 2012).

Peter Graefe is associate professor in the Department of Political Science at McMaster University and a fellow at the Broadbent Institute. His research deals with social and economic development policy in Ontario and Quebec, as well as Canadian intergovernmental relations in social policy. He is co-editor of *Overpromising and Underperforming: Evaluating New Intergovernmental Accountability Regimes* (University of Toronto Press 2013).

Nicolas Graham is a PhD candidate in the Department of Sociology at the University of Victoria. He is currently conducting research on just transitions, energy democracy, and the power of Canada's carbon extractive industry. His previous research has appeared in journals such as *Capitalism Nature Socialism, Antipode,* and *BC Studies.*

Chris Hurl is assistant professor in the Department of Sociology and Anthropology at Concordia University. His research, exploring urban governance, state formation, and the politics of the public sector in Canada, has appeared in *Environment and Planning A, Studies in Political Economy, International Journal of Urban and Regional Research, Labour / Le Travail,* and the *Journal of Canadian Studies.*

Larry Kuehn is Director of Research and Technology at the British Columbia Teachers' Federation. He is a research associate for the Canadian Centre for Policy Alternatives and a frequent contributor to *Our Schools, Our Selves,* the education journal of the CCPA. He is also co-author of *Pandora's Box: Corporate Power, Free Trade and Canadian Education* (Our Schools/Our Selves Education Foundation 1993).

Randy K. Lippert is a professor of sociology and criminology at the University of Windsor, specializing in security, policing, and urban governance. He is the author of *Sanctuary, Sovereignty, Sacrifice: Canadian Sanctuary Incidents, Power, and Law* (UBC Press 2006) and co-author of *Municipal Corporate*

Security in International Context (Routledge 2015). He has also co-edited *Corporate Security in the 21st Century* (Palgrave Macmillan 2014), *Sanctuary Practices in International Perspective* (Routledge 2014), and *Governing Practices: Neo-liberalism, Governmentality, and the Ethnographic Imaginary* (University of Toronto Press 2016).

Emma Lui completed her MA in political economy at Carleton University. She has worked with the Canadian Human Rights Commission on alternative dispute resolution, and currently works for the Council of Canadians as the organization's national water campaigner. She is on the board of the Great Lakes organization FLOW (For Love of Water). Her primary interests are in water justice issues, such as privatization, energy development, and Indigenous solidarity.

David A. McDonald is Professor of Global Development Studies at Queen's University and Director of the Municipal Services Project. He has published widely on privatization, corporatization, and public services across a wide range of sectors. His books include *World City Syndrome* (Routledge 2008), *Alternatives to Privatization* (Routledge 2012), *Rethinking Corporatization and Public Services in the Global South* (Zed Books 2014), and *Making Public in a Privatized World* (Zed Books 2016).

Greg McElligott is a professor of community and justice services/criminal justice at Humber College. He is the author of *Beyond Service: State Workers, Public Policy, and the Prospects for Democratic Administration* (University of Toronto Press 2001), as well as several articles on corrections officers and other front line workers. His current research focuses on the role of prisons in neoconservative labour market policy, and alternative work arrangements in prisons and beyond.

Natalie Mehra is the executive director of the Ontario Health Coalition—an organization encompassing more than 400 organizations and seventy local chapters across Ontario. She has dedicated two decades of her life to building the health coalition into the largest public interest group on health care in the province. Prior to joining the Health Coalition, she served as the executive director of the Epilepsy Association for Southeastern Ontario in Kingston. She currently sits on the board of directors for the Canadian Health Coalition, and serves on the steering committee of the Ontario Common Front.

Claire Polster is professor of sociology and social studies at the University of Regina. Her research focuses on the transformation of Canadian higher education and its implications for the public interest. She has published widely on higher education issues, including government policy and policy-making, the commodification of academic research, and the erosion of university autonomy, democracy, and collegialism. She is the author of *A Penny for Your Thoughts: How Corporatization Devalues Teaching, Research, and Public Service in Canada's Universities* (with J. Newson, Canadian Centre for Policy Alternatives 2015) and co-editor of *Academic Callings: The University We Have Had, Now Have, and Could Have* (Canadian Scholars Press 2010).

Graham Riches is emeritus professor and former director of the School of Social Work at the University of British Columbia. He has also served as a consultant to the UN Food and Agriculture Organization. His field of research includes poverty studies, human rights, and social policy within Canada and the Global North, with a focus on the politics of hunger, charity, and the right to food. He is the author of *Food Banks and the Welfare Crisis* (Canadian Council on Social Development 1986) and *Food Bank Nations: Poverty, Corporate Charity and the Right to Food* (Earthscan/Routledge 2018), editor of *First World Hunger: Food Security and Welfare Politics* (Palgrave Macmillán 1997), and co-editor of *Unemployment and Welfare: Social Policy and the Work of Social Work* (Garamond Press 1990) and *First World Hunger Revisited: Food Charity or the Right to Food?* (Palgrave Macmillan 2014).

Erika Shaker is the director of education and outreach at the Canadian Centre for Policy Alternatives. Erika has been researching the corporatization and privatization of education since the early 1990s, and was one of the founders of the California-based Center for Commercial-free Public Education. She also edits the popular education journal *Our Schools/Our Selves*.

Kevin Walby is Chancellor's Research Chair and associate professor of criminal justice at the University of Winnipeg. He is the author of *Touching Encounters: Sex, Work, and Male-for-Male Internet Escorting* (University of Chicago Press 2012). He is co-author of *Municipal Corporate Security in International Context* (Routledge 2015). He is co-editor of *Access to Information and Social Justice: Critical Research Strategies for Journalists, Scholars and Activists* (ARP 2015), *National Security, Surveillance, and Terror: Canada and Australia in Comparative Perspective* (Palgrave 2017), as well as *The Handbook of Prison Tourism* (Palgrave 2017). He is also co-editor of the *Journal of Prisoners on Prisons*.

Heather Whiteside is assistant professor of political science at the University of Waterloo and Fellow at the Balsillie School of International Affairs. Her research centres on the political economy of privatization, financialization, and fiscal austerity. Her books include *Private Affluence, Public Austerity: Economic Crisis and Democratic Malaise in Canada* (with Stephen McBride,

Fernwood 2011), *Purchase for Profit: Public-Private Partnerships and Canada's Public Health Care System* (University of Toronto Press 2015), and *About Canada: Public-Private Partnerships* (Fernwood 2016).

Zoë Yunker is a graduate student in the Department of Sociology at the University of Victoria and a research assistant with the Corporate Mapping Project. Her work explores the role of land-based resistance in disrupting regimes of dispossession. Zoë co-founded the BC-wide LNG (liquified natural gas) network—a group that convenes organizations resisting LNG development—and she is a member of the Sacred Fire Network.

Notes

Introduction

1 See Max Hill, "Let's Talk about the Corpora-tization of Mental Health," *The Peak*, January 23, 2017; Sean Phipps, "The Corporatization of Canada's Foreign Aid," *The McGill Daily*, February 6, 2012; Nasha Mavalvala, "Stop the Corporatization of Pride!" *Fightback: The Marxist Voice of Labour and Youth*, June 20, 2014; Mary O'Connell, "'Corporatization' of Funeral Industry Drives Quest for Alterna-tives," *CBC News*, May 7, 2014.

2 For instance, see David A. McDonald, ed. *Rethinking Corporatization and Public Ser-vices in the Global South* (London: Zed Books, 2014). On corporatization across govern-ment, health care, and education in New Zealand, see Ian Duncan and Alan Bollard, *Corporatization and Privatization: Lessons from New Zealand* (London: Oxford, 1993). On the corporatization of government agen-cies in Jordan, see R. F. Daher, "Welfare Genocide: Rentierism, Neoliberalism, and the Corporatization of the Public Sector in Jordan," in *Neoliberal Governmentality and the Future of the State in the Middle East and North Africa,* (New York: Palgrave Macmil-lan, 2016), 45–59. On the corporatization of government agencies in Canada, see N. Bilodeau, C. Laurin, and A. Vining, "Choice of Organizational Form Makes a Real Dif-ference: The Impact of Corporatization on Government Agencies in Canada," *Journal of Public Administration Research and Theory* 17.1, (2007): 119–147. On the corporatization of government agencies in the Netherlands, Peter W. de Langen, and C. Heij, "Corpora-tisation and Performance: A Literature Review and an Analysis of the Performance Effects of the Corporatisation of Port of Rot-terdam Authority," *Transport Reviews* 34.3, (2014): 396–414. On the corporatization of education, see Jamie Brownlee, *Academia, Inc.: How Corporatization Is Transforming Canadian Universities* (Halifax: Fernwood Publishing, 2015); Claire Poster and Janice Newson, *A Penny for Your Thoughts: How Corporatization Devalues Teaching, Research, and Public Service in Canada's Universities* (Ottawa: CCPA, 2015); G. Lerner, "Corporatiz-ing Higher Education," *History Teacher* 41.2, (2008): 219–227; H. Steck, "Corporatization of the University: Seeking Conceptual Clar-ity," *The ANNALS of the American Academy of Political and Social Science* 585.1, (2003): 66–83; James Turk, *Universities at Risk: How Politics, Special Interests and Corporatiza-tion Threaten Academic Integrity* (Toronto: Lorimer, 2008). On the corporatization of childcare and elderly care in Western Europe, see Sara R. Farris and Sabrina Marchetti, "From the Commodification to the Corpora-tization of Care: European Perspectives and Debates," *Social Politics* 24.2, (2017): 109–131. On the corporatization of health care in England, see Justin Waring and Simon Bishop, "McDonaldization or Commercial Re-stratification: Corporatization and the Multimodal Organisation of English Doctors," *Social Science & Medicine* 82.2, (2013): 147–155. For more conceptual interventions, see Mary Shirley, "Bureaucrats in Business: The Roles of Privatization versus Corporatization in State-owned Enterprise Reform," *World Development* 27.1 (1999): 115–-136; Giulio Cit-roni, Andrea Lippi, and Stefania Profeti, "The Politics of Corporatization: What It Is, Why It Matters," *Network Industries Quarterly* 17.4, (2015): 1–5.

3 Peter Dauvergne and Genevieve LeBaron, *Protest Inc.: The Corporatization of Activism* (Cambridge: Polity, 2014).

4 McDonald, *Rethinking Corporatization*, 1–2.

5 McDonald, *Rethinking Corporatization*, 4.

6 McDonald, *Rethinking Corporatization*, 5.

7   For the cultural history of the corporation in the United States, see Alan Trachtenberg, *The Incorporation of America* (New York: Hill and Wang, 1982); for Canada, see Christopher Armstrong and H.V. Nelles, *Monopoly's Moment: The Organization and Regulation of Canadian Utilities, 1830–1930* (Toronto: University of Toronto Press, 1986).

8   Richard Bozec and Gaetan Breton, "The Impact of the Corporatization Process on the Financial Performance of Canadian State-Owned Enterprises," *The International Journal of Public Sector Management* 16.1, (2003): 27–47.

9   Bozec and Breton, "The Impact of the Corporatization Process," 31.

10 David A. McDonald, "To Corporatize or Not to Corporatize (And If So, How?)," *Utilities Policy* 40, (2016): 107.

11 John Clarke and Janet Newman, *The Managerial State* (London: Sage, 1997), 56.

12 Clarke and Newman, *The Managerial State*, 65.

13 See McElligott, Chapter 8. See also, Denis Saint-Martin, *Building the New Managerialist State* (Oxford: Oxford University Press, 2000).

14 Clarke and Newman, *The Managerial State*.

15 https://bulletin-archives.caut.ca/bulletin/articles/2016/09/do-you-know-who-sits-on-your-board.

16 Daniel Guttman and Barry Willner, *The Shadow Government* (New York: Pantheon Books, 1976), xiv.

17 Murray Dobbin, *Paul Martin: CEO for Canada?* (Toronto: Lorimer, 2003), 109.

18 Leo Panitch, "The Role and Nature of the Canadian State," in *The Canadian State*, ed. Leo Panitch (Toronto: University of Toronto Press, 1977), 13.

19 H.V. Nelles, *Politics of Development: Forests, Mines, and Hydro-Electric Power in Ontario* (Montreal: McGill-Queen's Press, 1974), 490.

20 Conor O'Reilly, "The Transnational Security Consultancy Industry: A Case of State-Corporate Symbiosis," *Theoretical Criminology* 14.2, (2010): 183–210.

21 William Davies, *The Limits of Neoliberalism: Authority, Sovereignty and the Logic of Competition* (London: Sage, 2014), 114.

22 See, for example, John Loxley and Salim Loxley, *Public Service, Private Profits: The Political Economy of Public-Private Partnerships in Canada* (Halifax: Fernwood, 2010); Heather Whiteside, *Purchase for Profit: Public-Private Partnerships and Canada's Public Health-Care System* (Toronto: University of Toronto Press, 2015), Canadian Centre for Policy Alternatives, "Privatization Nation: The Canada-Wide Failure of Privatization, Outsourcing and Public-Private Partnerships," November 18, 2015, www.policyalternatives.ca/sites/default/files/uploads/publications/Saskatchewan%20Office/2015/11/Privatization%20Nation%20%2811-05-15%29.pdf.

23 Warren Thomas, "Public-Private Partnership Circus Spreading from Queen's Park," *Toronto Sun*, November 17, 2016.

24 See, for example, Satoko Kishimoto, Emanuele Lobina, and Olivier Petitjean, *Our Public Water Future: The Global Experience with Remunicipalisation* (Amsterdam: Transnational Institute, 2015); Naomi Klein, *This Changes Everything: Capitalism vs. the Climate* (Toronto: Knopf, 2014).

25 McDonald, "To Corporatize or Not to Corporatize," 109.

26 McDonald, *Rethinking Corporatization*, 4.

27 See, for example, Mildred Warner and Judith Clifton, "Marketization, Public Services and the City: The Potential for Polanyian Counter Movements," *Cambridge Journal of Regions, Economy and Society* 7, (2014): 45–61.

28 Mildred E. Warner, "Water Privatization Does Not Yield Cost Savings," in *Reclaiming Public Water: Achievements, Struggles and Vision from Around the World* (Transnational Institute and Corporate Europe Observatory, 2010).

Chapter 1: Healthy Profit

1   These arguments are reviewed in Heather Whiteside, *Purchase for Profit: Public-Private Partnerships and Canada's Public Health Care System* (Toronto: University of Toronto Press, 2015); and Heather Whiteside, *About Canada: Public-Private Partnerships* (Halifax: Fernwood, 2016).

2   Jamie Brownlee, *Academia, Inc.: How Corporatization Is Transforming Canadian Universities* (Halifax: Fernwood, 2015), 4.

3   Pat Armstrong and Hugh Armstrong, *About Canada: Health Care* (Halifax: Fernwood Publishing, 2008), 43–69.

4   Ontario Ministry of Health and Long-Term Care. *Ontario's Emergency Room*

Wait Time Strategy, May 22, 2009, http://news.ontario.ca/mohltc/en/2009/05/ontarios-emergency-room-wait-time-strategy-1.html; Janet McFarland, "Hospitals Raise Caution over Uniform Pay-for-Performance Rules," *The Globe and Mail*, April 9, 2010.

5 Joe Murphy, "Strategic Outsourcing by a Regional Health Authority: The Experience of the Vancouver Island Health Authority," *HealthcarePapers*, 8, (2007): 104–113.

6 See Pat Armstrong and Hugh Armstrong, "Contradictions at Work: Struggles for Control in Canadian Health Care," *Socialist Register*, 46, (2010); Marjorie Griffin Cohen and Marcy Cohen, "Privatization: A Strategy for Eliminating Pay Equity in Health Care," in *Social Reproduction: Feminist Political Economy Challenges Neo-Liberalism,* eds. Kate Bezanson and Meg Luxton (Montreal and Kingston: McGill-Queen's University Press, 2006).

7 Ursula Huws, "Crisis as Capitalist Opportunity: The New Accumulation through Public Service Commodification," *Socialist Register*, 48, (2012): 64.

8 Huws, "Crisis as Capitalist Opportunity," 64–5.

9 Jane Stinson, Nancy Pollak, and Marcy Cohen, *The Pains of Privatization* (Ottawa: Canadian Centre for Policy Alternatives, 2005), 34.

10 Steven Shrybman, "P3 Hospitals and the Principles of Medicare," in *Medicare: Facts, Myths, Problems and Promise*, eds. Bruce Campbell and Gregory P. Marchilden (Toronto: Lorimer, 2007).

11 Les Leyne, "Nanaimo Hospital Botched C. Difficile Bug Battle, Probe Finds," *Montreal Gazette*, July 9, 2009.

12 Griffin Cohen and Cohen, "Privatization," 138.

13 Whiteside, *Purchase for Profit*.

14 BC Ministry of Finance, "New Framework, Agency to Guide Public Building," *News Release*, May 30, 2002.

15 BC Select Standing Committee on Public Accounts, *Auditor General Review of Partnership B.C. Report: Achieving Value for Money: Abbotsford Regional Hospital and Cancer Centre Project*, February 8, 2006, www.leg.bc.ca/cmt/38thparl/session-1/pac/hansard/p60208a.htm#6:1245.

16 Ministry of Finance, *Review of Partnerships BC* (Victoria: Internal Audit & Advisory Services, 2014), www.integritybc.ca/wp-content/uploads/2016/10/Core-Review-of-PBC.pdf.

17 Tom Sandborn, "Fraser Health Authority Said No to Private Approach," *The Tyee*, February 1, 2007, https://thetyee.ca/News/2007/02/01/FHA/.

18 Whiteside, *Purchase for Profit*, Chapter 6.

19 Dexter Whitfield, *The Financial Commodification of Public Infrastructure* (Ireland: European Services Strategy Unit, 2016), www.european-services-strategy.org.uk/publications/essu-research-reports/the-financial-commodification-of-public-infras/financial-commodification-public-infrastructure.pdf.

20 Hospital Employees Union, "MSA Hospital a Blood-Smeared, Filthy Mess Under Sodexho: News Report," *HEU Newsletter*, March 11, 2004.

21 Whiteside, *Purchase for Profit*, Chapters 5 and 6.

22 John Knappett, *P3's (or "No Country for Old Contractors")*, 2008, www.cupe.bc.ca/sites/default/files/knappett-no-country-old-contractors.pdf.

23 British Columbia and Yukon Territory Building and Construction Trades Council, *Submission to Hon. Colin Hansen, Minister of Finance*, 2008.

24 Ontario Standing Committee on Government Agencies, *Agency Review: Ontario Infrastructure Project Corp. (Infrastructure Ontario)*, Hansard Committee Transcripts, September 17, 2008.

25 Minister of Finance, "Chapter 2: Investing in the New Economy," *Fall Economic Statement* (Ottawa: Government of Canada, 2016), 7, www.budget.gc.ca/fes-eea/2016/docs/statement-enonce/chap02-en.html.

26 IMF, *World Economic Outlook* database, April, 2016, www.imf.org/external/pubs/ft/weo/2016/01/weodata/index.aspx.

Chapter 2: Three Waves of Health Care Corporatization in Ontario Hospitals

1 Text is from the Second Annual Erie St. Clair Local Health Integration Network Conference, "Quest for Quality 2010," e-brochure.

2 Tyler Kula, "LHIN Gives Disney the Hook," *Sarnia Observer*, QMI Agency, August 26, 2010.

3   The OHA held a one-day session on May 25, 2010, titled "Disney's Approach to Excellence." It also held a session on September 22, 2008, "If Disney Ran Your Hospital."

4   Jamie Brownlee, *Academia, Inc.: How Corporatization is Transforming Canadian Universities* (Halifax: Fernwood Publishing, 2015).

5   Carol Kushner, *Inside Out/Outside In: Three Tales of Outsourcing at The Toronto Hospital: A report prepared for the Hospital Employees Union (B.C.)* March 21, 2002, 3.

6   Colleen Fuller, "Profit or Non-Profit: Are Hospitals Selling Out?" *Canadian Women's Health Network* 1.4 (1998).

7   Fuller, "Profit or Non-Profit."

8   Kushner, *Inside Out/Outside In*, 5.

9   Conversation between the author and a Registered Nurse in northern Ontario, 2002.

10 Kazi Stastna, "Dirty Hospital Rooms a Top Concern for Canadians," *Toronto Star*, April 9, 2013.

11 BC Centre for Disease Control, *Investigation of a Clostridium Difficile Associated Disease Outbreak at Nanaimo Regional Hospital*, August 2008.

12 Fuller, "Profit or Non-Profit."

13 Canadian Centre for Policy Alternatives (CCPA), *Private Gain Public Pain: A Report to the Ontario Health Coalition"* (summary), Summer 2000, 8.

14 CCPA, *Private Gain Public Pain*, 9.

15 CCPA, *Private Gain Public Pain*, 10–11.

16 CCPA, *Private Gain Public Pain*, 11.

17 Ontario Hospital Association, *Ontario Hospital Beds Staffed and in Operation, 1990 – 2010.*

18 CCPA. *Private Gain Public Pain*, 13.

19 In 1999 and 2001, the report of the provincial auditor revealed the costs of hospital restructuring under the Harris government. The government attempted to cut $1 billion from hospital funding. Over two years, from 1996–97 to 1998–99, $800 million was cut from hospital operating budgets. While estimated costs for hospital restructuring under the Harris-era Restructuring Commission were originally set at $2.1 billion, the provincial auditor revealed that costs had escalated to $3.9 billion. Ontario Auditor General (OAG), *2001 Report*, 315.

20 OAG, *2001 Report*, 14.

21 OAG, *Annual Report 2002*, 171.

22 OAG, *Special Audit 2010*, 11.

23 OAG, *Special Audit 2010*, 14.

24 OAG, *Special Audit 2010*, 23–30.

25 John Manley, William Anderson, and Peter Barnes, *Report of the Independent Expert Panel on Executive Compensation in the Hospital Sector*, November 11, 2011, 13.

26 André Picard, "How Much Are Canadian Doctors Paid?" *The Globe and Mail*, January 23, 2013.

27 Dalton McGuinty, *Making a Difference* (Toronto: Dundurn Press, 2015).

28 There were, of course, regional and provincial planners involved in assessing population needs and services, and there were provincial programs for cancer care, diabetes, and other services. The centralization of control dramatically increased with the Hospital Restructuring Commission's orders in the restructuring of the mid- to late 1990s, in which hospitals were ordered to cease providing certain services, and other services were relocated and reduced according to the commission's plans. But the Hospital Restructuring Commission was finite: it wound up in 1999. Hospital global budgets remained in place and local decision-making regarding the range of services to be provided was again left to hospitals.

29 Shadow billing is the practice of measuring volumes in clinical care by physicians who are on salary or other non-fee-for-service payment mechanisms. Physicians count units of service provided and submit an invoice or an invoice-like report. It is used as a way of measuring volumes.

Chapter 3: The Rise of the Corporate Cashroom

1   Committee on Communications, "Children, Adolescents, and Advertising," *Pediatrics*, December 2006, http://pediatrics.aappublications.org/content/118/6/2563.

2   Catherine Gidney and R. D. Gidney, "Branding the Classroom: Commercialism in Canadian Schools 1920-1960," *Social History*, 41.82 (2008), 345-377.

3   David A. McDonald, "Public Ambiguity and the Multiple Meanings of Corporatization," in *Corporatization and Public Services in the Global South*, ed. David A. McDonald (New York: Zed Books, 2014), 10.

4   Canadian Centre for Policy Alternatives (CCPA), *Hell and High Water: An*

Assessment of Paul Martin's Record and Implications for the Future (Ottawa: CCPA, 2004); Michael Rozworski, "Canada's Harsh 'Austerity' Policies Started with Liberals," *The Tyee*, August 25, 2015, https://thetyee.ca/Opinion/2015/08/25/Canadas-Harsh-Austerity/.

5   Lars Osberg, *A Quarter Century of Economic Inequality in Canada: 1981-2006*, (Ottawa: CCPA, 2008), www.policyalternatives.ca/sites/default/files/uploads/publications/National_Office_Pubs/2008/Quarter_Century_of_Inequality.pdf.

6   Antoni Verger, "The Rise of the Global Education Industry: Some Concepts, Facts and Figures," *Education in Crisis*, March 2016, https://worldsofeducation.org/en/woe_homepage/woe_detail/4850/the-rise-of-the-global-education-industry-some-concepts-facts-and-figures.

7   Canadian Centre for Policy Alternatives-SK, *Privatization Nation: The Canada-wide Failure of Privatization, Outsourcing and Public-Private Partnerships* (Regina: CCPA, 2015), www.policyalternatives.ca/publications/reports/privatization-nation.

8   Canadian Centre for Policy Alternatives-NS, *Private Profit at a Public Price: Deciding the Future of the Public-Private Partnership Schools in Nova Scotia*, (Halifax: CCPA, 2016), www.policyalternatives.ca/publications/reports/private-profit-public-price.

9   Heide Pearson, "Nova Scotia Government to Buy 11 More P3 Schools for $50.5M," *Global News* (N.S.), November 29, 2016, http://globalnews.ca/news/3095202/nova-scotia-government-to-buy-11-more-p3-schools-for-50-5m/.

10 Brian Cook, *Healthier Nutrition for Kids—An Action Plan: Advertising to Children in Canada* (Toronto: Toronto Public Health, 2011), 20, http://childhoodobesityfoundation.ca/wp-content/uploads/2015/02/Advertising-to-Children-in-Canada-Brian-Cook.pdf.

11 Canadian Centre for Policy Alternatives, *Commercialism in Canadian Schools: Who's Calling the Shots* (Ottawa: CCPA, 2006), www.policyalternatives.ca/publications/reports/commercialism-canadian-schools.

12 http://kidsandparentsconference.com/.

13 Erika Shaker, YNN *and the Commercial Carpet-bombing of the Classroom*, (Ottawa:

CCPA, 1999), www.policyalternatives.ca/publications/reports/ynn-and-commercial-carpet-bombing-classroom; and Erika Shaker, *In the Corporate Interest: The YNN Experience in Canadian Schools*, (Ottawa: CCPA, 2000), www.policyalternatives.ca/sites/default/files/uploads/publications/National_Office_Pubs/ynnexperience.pdf.

14 Erika Shaker, *Sudbury Monday Night: Notes from the YNN Presentation to the Sudbury Community*, February 21, 2000, Canadian Association of Media Education Organizations, http://jcp.proscenia.net/CAMEO/ynn/46.html.

15 JAMA News Release, "Most Students Exposed to School-Based Food Commercialism," January 13, 2013, http://media.jamanetwork.com/news-item/most-students-exposed-to-school-based-food-commercialism/.

16 Karen Seidman, "Legault Looks at Legality of YNN," *Montreal Gazette*, June 22, 1999, http://jcp.proscenia.net/CAMEO/ynn/35.html.

17 For more information on the role and influence of other publishing companies in education—specifically Pearson—see Donald Gutstein's excellent work, including "Pearson's plan to control education: Report to the BC Teachers' Federation," 2002, http://bctf.ca/uploadedFiles/Public/Issues/Privatization/PearsonGutsteinReport.pdf.

18 Ontario Secondary School Teachers' Federation, *Commercialization in Ontario Schools: A Research Report* (Toronto: OSSTF, 1995); Cathy Hart, *Corporate Sponsorship in B.C. Public Schools: An Exploratory Study*, submitted in partial fulfillment of requirements for Master of Education, University of Victoria, March 2004, http://nepc.colorado.edu/files/CERU-0403-146-OWI.pdf; Canadian Centre for Policy Alternatives, *Commercialism in Canadian Schools: Who's Calling the Shots* (Ottawa: CCPA, 2006), www.policyalternatives.ca/publications/reports/commercialism-canadian-schools.

19 Louise Brown, "Toronto Board Allows Use of Future Shop Colours in Computer Labs," *Toronto Star*, April 22, 2009, www.thestar.com/life/parent/2009/04/22/toronto_board_allows_use_of_future_shop_colours_in_computer_labs.html.

20 Fuel Your School website, www.fuelyourschool.com/canada/.

21 Love of Reading website, www.loveofreading.org/.

22 Campbell's Labels for Education website, www.labelsforeducation.ca/english/.

23 Over the past thirteen years, Indigo's Love of Reading has raised a total of $24 million from "Indigo, its leadership, its employees, its customers, its partners and additional supporters" for high-needs elementary schools. Indigo has donated $3 million towards that total, and underwrites the total costs of operations and administration of the Love of Reading Foundation to the tune of $5 million. Email exchange with Ariel Siller, Executive Director, Indigo's Love of Reading Foundation, March 21, 2017.

24 McDonald's website, www.mcdonalds.ca/ca/en/food/all-access_moms.html.

25 Arturo Chang, "McDonald's Recalls 33M Happy Meal Fitness Trackers: What Canadians Need to Know," *BNN.ca*, August 24, 2016, www.bnn.ca/mcdonald-s-recalls-33m-happy-meal-fitness-trackers-what-canadians-need-to-know-1.554479.

26 ClassDojo is not alone: see "17 Alternatives to ClassDojo," *Top Best Alternatives*, February 13, 2016, www.topbestalternatives.com/classdojo/.

27 Prasanna Bharti, "Why Teachers Love Class-Dojo for Classroom Management," *EdTech Review*, June 8, 2014, http://edtechreview.in/trends-insights/insights/1261-why-teachers-love-classdojo-for-classroom-management.

28 "ClassDojo: Could This App Improve Pupil Behaviour?" *BBC.com*, February 7, 2014, www.bbc.com/news/technology-26081122.

29 Agata Soroko, "No Child Left Alone: The ClassDojo app," *Our Schools/Our Selves* 25.3 (2016): 63–74; "Privacy Issues Rise Up as Classroom Apps Flourish," *Education News*, November 19, 2014, www.educationnews.org/technology/privacy-issues-rise-up-as-classroom-apps-flourish/.

30 Natasha Singer, "ClassDojo Adopts Deletion Policy for Student Data," *NYT blog*, November 18, 2014, https://bits.blogs.nytimes.com/2014/11/18/classdojo-adopts-deletion-policy-for-student-data/?partner=rss&emc=rss&_r=3; "Privacy Issues Rise Up as Classroom Apps Flourish," *Education News*, November 19, 2014, www.educationnews.org/technology/privacy-issues-rise-up-as-classroom-apps-flourish/.

31 Abby Jackson, "A 'Very non-Silicon Valley' Startup Is Going Viral Among Teachers and Parents," *Business Insider*, July 8, 2016, www.businessinsider.com/ed-tech-startup-classdojo-is-going-viral-2016-7.

32 Lora Kolodny, "ClassDojo Raises $21 million for App to Make Parent-Teacher Meetings Obsolete," *Techcrunch*, April 15, 2016, https://techcrunch.com/2016/04/15/classdojo-raises-21-million-for-app-to-make-parent-teacher-meetings-obsolete/.

33 Kolodny, "ClassDojo Raises $21 million."

34 Kolodny, "ClassDojo Raises $21 million."

35 The Learning Partnership website, www.thelearningpartnership.ca.

36 The Learning Partnership, *Strategic Plan 2014–2017*, www.thelearningpartnership.ca/files/download/0b8f65be4c0f02d.

37 The Learning Partnership, *Annual Report 2015–2016*, www.thelearningpartnership.ca/who-we-are/about/annual-reports.

38 www.thelearningpartnership.ca/who-we-are/about.

39 www.thelearningpartnership.ca/what-we-do/educator-program-and-executive-leadership/take-a-leader-to-work-day.

40 Ruth Cohen and Bill Greaves, "Of Caterpillars and Butterflies: Reading John Snobelen's Infamous 'Caterpillar' Speech," in *Alien Invasion: How the Harris Tories Mismanaged Ontario*, ed. Ruth Cohen (Toronto: Insomniac Press, 1988), 131.

41 This populist appeal to anti-intellectualism is not limited to the education sector. In Alberta from 1992–2006, former premier Ralph Klein—another high school dropout—played his "everyman" role with folksy aplomb, even while gutting social programs. More recently, Rob Ford—son of a millionaire—donned the regular-guy-underdog mantle as former mayor of Toronto. Conservative leadership candidate Kellie Leitch has made a point of downplaying her own academic and professional credentials (including one as a medical doctor) to underscore that she is a voice for the "average guy and gal." And, perhaps most famously, US President Donald Trump—a multimillionaire—ran on an anti-intellectual, anti-expert, anti-politician platform that, among other

things, has given rise to the infamous term "alternative facts."

42 Donald Savoie, "The Perils of the Career Politician," *The Globe and Mail*, October 6, 2014, www.theglobeandmail.com/opinion/the-perils-of-the-career-politician/article20924219/.

43 Jason Groves, "Increase in 'professional politicians' means one in seven MPs have never done a real job (and that includes Ed Miliband)," *The Daily Mail*, July 19, 2012, www.dailymail.co.uk/news/article-2175695/One-seven-MPs-real-job.html.

44 Canadian Foundation for Economic Education (CFEE) website, www.cfee.org/about.php.

45 Jeremy Gillies, *Public Education as a Marketing Medium: An Examination of Corporate-sponsored Curriculum Used in the Canadian Public Classroom*, Masters Thesis, Department of Communications, University of Windsor: 2000, http://scholar.uwindsor.ca/cgi/viewcontent.cgi?article=4234&context=etd.

46 Barbara Schecter, "Canada's First Financial Literacy Leader Must Tackle Widespread Issues," *Financial Post*, April 15, 2014, http://business.financialpost.com/news/fp-street/canadas-first-financial-literacy-leader-to-tackle-widespread-problems.

47 Greg Quinn, "Canadians Turns [sic] Deaf Ear to Carney's Warnings as Household Debt Hits Fresh Record at 165%," *Financial Post*, March 15, 2013, http://business.financialpost.com/news/economy/canadians-turns-deaf-ear-to-carneys-warnings-as-household-debt-hits-fresh-record-at-165.

48 Talk with Our Kids About Money website, http://talkwithourkidsaboutmoney.com/.

49 CFEE and Scotiabank, "The Canadian Foundation for Economic Education and Scotiabank Partner on 'Talk With Our Kids About Money'," News Release, November 16, 2016, www.cfee.org/pdf/TWOKAM-FinalMediaRelease-111616.pdf.

50 Gary Marr, "How Canadian Kids Are Taught Financial Literacy from Coast to Coast," *Financial Post*, September 2, 2016, http://business.financialpost.com/personal-finance/young-money/how-canadians-are-taught-financial-literacy-from-coast-to-coast.

51 Chris Arthur, "The Poverty of Financial Literacy Education," *Our Schools/Our Selves* 23.4, (2014): 41.

52 Erika Shaker and David Macdonald, *What's the Difference? Taking Stock of Provincial Tuition Fee Policies*, (Ottawa: CCPA, 2015), www.policyalternatives.ca/publications/reports/whats-difference.

53 Marijo Johne, "Entrepreneurship Is Something We Should be Teaching at an Early Age," *The Globe and Mail*, March 10, 2014, www.theglobeandmail.com/report-on-business/small-business/startups/entrepreneurship-skills-increasingly-seen-as-a-must-have-for-canadas-youth/article17367382/.

54 Laura Pinto, "The Cultural Myth of the Entrepreneur: 2014 Remix," *Our Schools/Our Selves* 23.4, (2014): 25.

55 Pinto, "The Cultural Myth," 25.

56 Pinto, "The Cultural Myth," 25.

57 Pinto, "The Cultural Myth," 28–29.

58 Pinto, "The Cultural Myth," 28.

59 Aimee Groth, "Entrepreneurs Don't Have a Special Gene for Risk—They Come from Families with Money," *Quartz Media*, July 17, 2015, https://qz.com/455109/entrepreneurs-dont-have-a-special-gene-for-risk-they-come-from-families-with-money/.

60 Pinto, "The Cultural Myth," 30.

61 Canadian Press, "Half of Working Canadians Living Paycheque to Paycheque: Survey," *The Globe and Mail*, September 7, 2016, www.theglobeandmail.com/globe-investor/personal-finance/household-finances/half-of-working-canadians-living-paycheque-to-paycheque-survey/article31741113/; Laurie Monsebraaten, "Half of GTA and Hamilton's Workers in 'Precarious' Jobs," *Toronto Star*, February 23, 2013, www.thestar.com/news/gta/2013/02/23/half_of_gta_and_hamilton_workers_in_precarious_jobs.html.

62 Pollitt, quoted in McDonald, 11. Christopher Pollitt, "Clarifying Convergence: Striking Similarities and Durable Differences in Public Management Reform," *Public Management Review* 3(4), (2001), 471-492.

Chapter 4: Carbon Capital and Corporate Influence

1   This chapter is part of the Corporate Mapping Project (CMP), a research and public engagement initiative investigating the power of the fossil fuel industry. The CMP is jointly led

by the University of Victoria, Canadian Centre for Policy Alternatives, and the Parkland Institute. The CMP is funded primarily by the Social Science and Humanities Research Council (SSHRC).

2 Industry's influence over university governance and operations takes a number of forms, including the growing presence of corporate-affiliated board members, increased corporate funding of academic research, industry-supported academic chairs, and corporate funding for infrastructure. See William Carroll and James Beaton, "Globalization, Neo-Liberalism, and the Changing Face of Corporate Hegemony in Higher Education," *Studies in Political Economy* 62.1, (2000): 71–98; Sheila Slaughter and Larry L. Leslie, *Academic Capitalism: Politics, Policies, and the Entrepreneurial University* (Baltimore: Johns Hopkins University Press, 1997); Jamie Brownlee, *Academia, Inc.: How Corporatization Is Transforming Canadian Universities* (Halifax: Fernwood, 2015); David F. Noble, "Digital Diploma Mills; The Automation of Higher Education," *Monthly Review: An Independent Socialist Magazine* 49.9, (1998): 38.

3 Jennifer Washburn, *University, Inc: The Corporate Corruption of Higher Education*, 1st ed. (New York: Basic Books, 2005).

4 Brownlee, *Academia, Inc.*, 26.

5 "Open for Business—On What Terms? An Analysis of 12 Collaborations between Canadian Universities and Corporations, Donors and Governments" (Canadian Association of University Teachers, November 2013); Washburn, *University Inc.*

6 John Polanyi, "Why Our Scientific Discoveries Need to Surprise Us," *The Globe and Mail*, October 2011, www.theglobeandmail.com/opinion/why-our-scientific-discoveries-need-to-surprise-us/article4199194/.

7 By 2010, Alberta had eclipsed Ontario as the province with the largest share of the nation's capital stock. See Geoffrey McCormack and Thom Workman, *The Servant State: Overseeing Capital Accumulation in Canada* (Winnipeg: Fernwood Books, 2015) and, as of 2014, the extractive sector accounted for nearly 25 percent of private investment, up from less than 5 percent in the early 1990s; see Éric Pineault, "Welcome to the Age of Extractivism and Extreme Oil: Éric Pineault,"

National Observer, May 18, 2016, www.nationalobserver.com/2016/05/18/opinion/welcome-age-extractivism-and-extreme-oil-%C3%A9ric-pineault.

8 The University of Calgary, for example, played a key role in developing "steam-assisted gravity drainage" or "SAGD"—an oil recovery technology used to produce heavy crude oil and bitumen—that has unlocked over 170 billion barrels of previously inaccessible oil from the tar sands. See Mark Lowey, "Father of Invention: Roger Butler's SAGD Process Opened up the Oilsands," *University of Calgary On Campus Quarterly: Fuelling Our Energy Future*, April 2004, www.ucalgary.ca/EN/News/2004/Butler-iseee.pdf.

9 Bret Gustafson, "Fossil Knowledge Networks: Industry Strategy, Public Culture, and the Challenge for Critical Research," in *Flammable Societies: Studies on the Socio-Economics of Oil and Gas*, ed. J.A. McNeish and O. Logan (London: Pluto Press, 2012), 311–34.

10 David A. McDonald, "Public Ambiguity and the Multiple Meanings of Corporatization," in *Corporatization and Public Services in the Global South*, ed. David A. McDonald (New York: Zed Books, 2014), 1–30.

11 Seth Klein and Shannon Daub, "The New Climate Denialism: Time for an Intervention," *Policy Note*, September 22, 2016, www.policynote.ca/the-new-climate-denialism-time-for-an-intervention/#sthash.FyBZ222W.dpuf.

12 Charles Derber, *Greed to Green: Solving Climate Change and Remaking the Economy* (Boulder, CO and London: Paradigm Publishers, 2010).

13 Naomi Klein, *This Changes Everything: Capitalism vs. The Climate* (New York: Simon & Schuster, 2014).

14 Jamie Brownlee, "The Role of Governments in Corporatizing Canadian Universities," *Academic Matters: OCUFA's Journal of Higher Education*, January 2016, www.academicmatters.ca/2016/01/the-role-of-governments-in-corporatizing-canadian-universities/.

15 Brownlee, *Academia, Inc.*

16 Carroll and Beaton, "Globalization, Neo-Liberalism."

17 Brownlee, *Academia, Inc.*

18 Zane Schwartz, "Best of the Best: Introducing the 2016 Maclean's University

Rankings," *Macleans.ca*, October 29, 2015, www.macleans.ca/education/best-of-the-best-introducing-the-2016-macleans-university-rankings/.

19 K. Alajoutsijarvi, K. Juusola, and M. Siltaoja, "The Legitimacy Paradox of Business Schools: Losing by Gaining?" *Academy of Management Learning & Education* 14.2, (2015): 277–91; Washburn, *University Inc.*

20 Among business schools, accreditation bodies present another driver for market-driven policy alignment. Schools increasingly seek exclusive and costly certification processes to secure legitimacy and enrolment in an increasingly competitive academic arena. These bodies set standards for program content and academic policies within the institution, enabling them to systematize and diffuse policies and practices that enhance and legislate greater academic corporatization. See Philip Altbach, "American Accreditation of Foreign Universities: Colonialism in Action," *International Higher Education* 32, (2015); K. Juusola, K. Kettunen, and K. Alajoutsijarvi, "Accelerating the Americanization of Management Education: Five Responses from Business Schools," *Journal of Management Inquiry* 24.4, (2015): 347–69; Alajoutsijarvi, Juusola, and Siltaoja, "The Legitimacy Paradox of Business Schools."

21 Juusola, Kettunen, and Alajoutsijarvi, "Accelerating the Americanization of Management Education."

22 "Average Full-Time Salaries at Business Schools: AACSB Data," *AACSB International*, www.aacsb.edu/knowledge/data/frequently-requested/salary/avg-full-time-salaries.

23 Sources for the latter included online business databases (ORBIS and FP Infomart), as well as company websites. Sources for the former were mainly organization websites and annual reports. Wherever there was ambiguity as to whether two name entries referred to the same person, the situation was investigated further to confirm the multiple affiliations. Unless otherwise indicated, all findings in this chapter refer to the situation at year-end 2015.

24 Shannon Daub and William Carroll, "A Topology of Power," *Canadian Centre for Policy Alternatives*, March 1, 2017,
www.policyalternatives.ca/publications/monitor/topology-power.

25 Donald Gutstein, *Harperism* (Toronto: Lorimer, 2014), 57–61). Gutstein analyzes the content of several SPP research papers as exemplars. See also our analysis of this school, below in text.

26 Source: Authors' original research data, through the Corporate Mapping Project, www.corporatemapping.ca/.

27 Richard Blackwell, "University of Saskatchewan Names Business School after Oil Tycoon," *The Globe and Mail*, July 25, 2007, www.theglobeandmail.com/news/national/university-of-saskatchewan-names-business-school-after-oil-tycoon/article690166/.

28 Rebecca Penty, "Billionaire Investor Murray Edwards Leaves Oilpatch, Decamps from Calgary to London," *Financial Post*, March 24, 2016, http://business.financialpost.com/news/energy/billionaire-investor-murray-edwards-leaves-oilpatch-decamps-from-calgary-to-london.

29 "Murray Edwards: Alumnus, Friend, Namesake," *Thrive, Edwards School of Business Magazine*, October 5, 2016, https://issuu.com/edwardsthrive/docs/thrive_2016.

30 Edwards School of Business, "Dean's Circle Annual Report, 2014–2015" (Edwards School of Business, 2015), www.edwardsdeanscircle.ca/2015-annual-report.pdf.

31 Canadian Business, "Canada's Best MBAs: University of Calgary," *Canadian Business*, 2017, www.canadianbusiness.com/schools/calgary-haskayne-mba/.

32 See Kyle Bakx and Paul Haavardsrud, "How the University of Calgary's Enbridge Relationship Became Controversial," *CBC Investigates*, November 2, 2015, www.cbc.ca/news/canada/calgary/university-calgary-enbridge-sponsorship-1.3286369.

33 As of 2016, Axford also sits on the board of Evok Innovations, a clean tech fund founded by Suncor and Cenovus that speeds the "commercialization of solutions" to support the oil and gas industry. Evok Innovations, "About, Evok Innovations," 2017, www.evokinnovations.com/about/.

34 Southern Alberta Institute of Technology, "About SAIT," 2017, www.sait.ca/about-sait.

35 Waugh is former deputy chairman, president, and CEO of Scotiabank, and currently sits on the Policy Advisory Committee at the University of Calgary School of Public Policy, which he joined in 2016. Prime Minister's Office, Government of Canada, "Canada News Centre - Archived - Biographies," Backgrounders, (2017), http://news.gc.ca/web/article-en.do?nid=880759.

36 As of 2016, the Alberta NDP government announced that it would be reorganizing the research infrastructure in the province, including the Alberta Innovates system. Alberta Innovates – Technology Futures and the three other Alberta Innovates corporations (Bio Solutions, Energy and Environment Solutions, and Health Solutions) will thereby be consolidated into one corporation called Alberta Innovates, and is to be managed by a single board of directors. Although the consolidation was scheduled to take place in summer 2016, it is still in progress.

37 Source: Authors' original research data, through the Corporate Mapping Project, www.corporatemapping.ca/.

38 Dogwood Initiative, "BC's Dirty Secret: Big Coal & the Export of Global-Warming Pollution" (Dogwood Initiative, 2011).

39 Climate Change and Emissions Management Corporation (CCEMC) has recently been rebranded as Emissions Reduction Alberta.

40 Kenny also has a long history working in Canadian energy governance, holding a number of former positions with the National Energy Board. At the time of this writing, Kenny had left her seven-year position as president and CEO of the CEPA, and now sits on the "National Energy Board Modernization Expert Panel," a group tasked with reforming the country's' energy regulator. Tracey Johnson, "Q&A: Brenda Kenny: 7 Years Atop Canada's Most Controversial Industry as Head of CEPA," *CBC News*, January 6, 2016, www.cbc.ca/news/canada/calgary/pipeline-exit-interview-brenda-kenny-1.3366101; Government of Canada, "National Energy Board Modernization Expert Panel," Government of Canada, 2017.

41 Laurie Adkin, ed., *First World Petro-Politics: The Political Ecology and Governance of Alberta* (Toronto: University of Toronto Press, 2016).

42 Gustafson, "Fossil Knowledge Networks: Industry Strategy, Public Culture, and the Challenge for Critical Research"; Laurie Adkin and Brittany Stares, "Turning Up the Heat: Hegemonic Politics in a First World Petro State," in *First World Petro-Politics: The Political Ecology and Governance of Alberta*, ed. Laurie Adkin (Toronto: University of Toronto Press, 2016), 190–240.

43 Source: Authors' original research data, through the Corporate Mapping Project, www.corporatemapping.ca/.

44 University of Calgary School of Public Policy, "Extractive Resource Governance (ERGP)," *The University of Calgary School of Public Policy*, 2016, www.policyschool.ca/research-areas/energy-environmental-policy/extractive-resource-governance/.

45 University of Calgary School of Public Policy, "Canadian Network for Energy Policy Research and Analysis: Conference on Public Acceptance of Energy Projects" (Calgary: University of Calgary School of Public Policy, September 15, 2015), www.policyschool.ca/wp-content/uploads/2016/08/Canadian-Network-for-Energy-Policy-1.pdf.

46 John Colton et al., "Energy Projects, Social Licence, Public Acceptance and Regulatory Systems in Canada: A White Paper," SPP Research Papers (Calgary: University of Calgary School of Public Policy, May 2016), www.energy.ca/sites/energy.ca/files/files/cnepra_-_energy-white-paper.pdf.

47 Dale Eisler, "Energy Literacy in Canada: A Summary," SPP Research Papers (Calgary: University of Calgary School of Public Policy, January 2016), www.policyschool.ca/wp-content/uploads/2016/03/energy-literacy-canada-eisler.pdf.

48 Haskayne School of Business, "Haskayne Global Energy Executive MBA," *Haskayne, University of Calgary*, (2017), https://haskayne.ucalgary.ca/programs/gemba.

49 Haskayne School of Business, "News: The Story of Dick Haskayne," *Haskayne, University of Calgary*, May 20, 2013, https://haskayne.ucalgary.ca/news/story-dick-haskayne-1.

50 Haskayne School of Business, "Haskayne Global Energy Executive MBA: Diverse Cohort," *Haskayne, University of Calgary*, 2017,

https://haskayne.ucalgary.ca/programs/gemba/why-a-gemba/diverse-cohort.

51 Haskayne School of Business, "Haskayne Global Energy Executive MBA, Industry Focus," *Haskayne, University of Calgary*, 2017, http://haskayne.ucalgary.ca/programs/gemba/why-a-gemba/industry-focus.

52 Haskayne School of Business, "Haskayne Global Energy Executive MBA: Company Sponsorship," 2016, https://web.archive.org/save/_embed/http://haskayne.ucalgary.ca/files/haskayne/GEMBA_insert_8x11_Sponsorship_2016_May.pdf; Haskayne School of Business, "Haskayne to Fund Public Sector Candidates for Global Energy EMBA Program," *University of Calgary: News*, September 9, 2011, https://haskayne.ucalgary.ca/news/haskayne-fund-public-sector-candidates-global-energy-emba-program.

53 Enbridge initially donated $2.25 million over ten years to the CCS. Facing public scrutiny and criticism, a revised agreement was formed in 2014, whereby Enbridge's name was taken off the centre and the company dropped its funding to the school by one million dollars. Kyle Bakx and Paul Haavardsrud, "Big Oil U: The Story behind the University of Calgary's Controversial Enbridge Centre," *CBC News*, 2015, www.cbc.ca/news/canada/calgary/university-calgary-enbridge-sponsorship-1.3286369.

54 Kyle Bakx and Paul Haavardsrud, "How the University of Calgary's Enbridge Relationship Became Controversial," *CBC News*, November 2, 2015, www.cbc.ca/news/canada/calgary/university-calgary-enbridge-sponsorship-1.3286369.

55 These corporate ties do not appear in the network diagram, above, as we tracked interlocks involving only elite networkers (directors and top managers). Our methodology thereby underestimates linkages between carbon capital and the governance boards of various institutes and organizations.

56 Haskayne CCS, "About CCS Haskayne, University of Calgary," 2017, https://haskayne.ucalgary.ca/ccs/about.

57 Hayskyne CCS, "Awards & Scholarships Haskayne, University of Calgary," https://haskayne.ucalgary.ca/ccs/awards.

58 Within our sample, an exception to this trend is the Canadian Centre for Clean Coal, whose operations are reported to be directed by a "Management Advisory Board" and a "Scientific Advisory Committee," which includes industry representatives drawn from its partnering firms, such as Teck Resources, Nexen Energy, Glencore Canada, and Capital Power. Information on the individuals who make up these boards is not publicly available, however, and despite being a public institution, it refused formal requests asking for this information.

59 CHORUS, www.chorusoil.ca.

60 CHORUS, www.chorusoil.ca/sponsor.php.

61 Hydrocarbon Metagenomics Project, "Partners | Hydrocarbon Metagenomics Project," 2017, www.hydrocarbonmetagenomics.com/partners/.

62 Canadian Foundation for Innovation, "Research Infrastructure Receives $63-Million Boost from the Government of Canada | Innovation.ca," 2014, www.innovation.ca/about/press-release/research-infrastructure-receives-63-million-boost-government-canada.

63 Canadian Centre for Clean Coal, "C5MPT – Canadian Centre for Clean Coal / Carbon and Mineral Processing Technologies," 2017, https://sites.ualberta.ca/CMENG/c5mpt/alberta-innovates.htm.

64 Centre for Intelligent Mining Systems, "University of Alberta – Centre for Intelligent Mining Systems," 2017, https://webdocs.cs.ualberta.ca/~cims/; Helmholtz-Alberta Initiative, "About | Helmholtz-Alberta Initiative," 2017, www.helmholtz-alberta.org/?page_id=64.

65 In Alberta, Adkin and Stares find a heavy weighting of research funding towards such technologies. They find, for example, that renewable energy projects received only 9 percent of AIEES' funding in 2008–2009, and similarly that, as of 2014, only 7.6 percent of the total grants distributed by the Climate Change and Emissions Management Fund have gone towards wind or solar technologies. See Adkin and Stares, "Turning Up the Heat: Hegemonic Politics in a First World Petro State."

66 Klein and Daub, "The New Climate Denialism."

67 Benjamin Franta and Geoffrey Supran, "The Fossil Fuel Industry's Invisible Colonization of Academia," *The Guardian*, March 13, 2017, sec. Environment,

www.theguardian.com/environment/
climate-consensus-97-per-cent/2017/
mar/13/the-fossil-fuel-industrys-invisible-
colonization-of-academia?CMP=share_
btn_tw.

**Chapter 5: International Students as a
Market in Canadian Public Education**

1   Roslyn Kunin & Associates, Inc., "Eco-
    nomic Impact of International Education
    in Canada - 2016 Update." (Vancou-
    ver: Global Affairs Canada, July 2016).
    www.international.gc.ca/education/
    report-rapport/impact-2016/
    index.aspx?lang=eng.

2   World Trade Organization Council for Trade
    in Services, "Guidelines for the Scheduling
    of Specific Commitments under the General
    Agreement on Trade in Services (GATS),"
    (World Trade Organization, S/L/92, 2001),
    www.wto.org/english/tratop_e/serv_e/
    education_e/education_e.htm.

3   Wikileaks, "Trade in Services Agreement"
    (2016), https://wikileaks.org/tisa/.

4   See Pearson Education's website,
    www.pearson.com.

5   British Columbia Ministry of Advanced Edu-
    cation, "FACTSHEET: International Stu-
    dents in B.C." (2016), www.news.gov.bc.ca/
    factsheets/international-students-in-bc.

6   BCTF Research Report, www.bctf.ca/
    uploadedFiles/Public/Publications/
    ResearchReports/RR2014-01.pdf.

7   International Public School Educa-
    tion Association - British Columbia,
    Canada, "The Canadian Advantage,"
    (2016), www.studyinbc.org/2012/03/
    news-post-sample-1/.

8   Tristan Bunnell, "The International Bac-
    calaureate and a Framework for Class Con-
    sciousness: The Potential Outcomes of a
    'Class-for-Itself,'" *Discourse: Studies in the
    Cultural Politics of Education* 31.3, (2010):
    351–62.

9   Lia Cosco, "Canadian Overseas Schools – A
    Unique Approach to the Export of Canadian
    Education," *Asia Pacific Foundation Research
    Reports* (Vancouver: Asia Pacific Founda-
    tion, 2011), www.asiapacific.ca/sites/default/
    files/filefield/overseas_canadian_schools_
    final.pdf.

10 Gerald Fallon and Sonya Pancucci, "Refram-
    ing Public Educational Services and Programs

as Tradable Commodities – A Synthesis and
Critique of British Columbia's Bill 34," *Brock
Education* 13.1, (2003).

11 "Thriving international education sector in
    B.C. boosts provincial economy,"
    https://news.gov.bc.ca/releases/
    2017AVED0018-000393.

12 Kathy Denton, "International Students Can
    be a Win-Win Deal," *Vancouver Sun*, Decem-
    ber 26, 2016.

13 Denton, "International Students Can be a
    Win-Win Deal."

14 See, for example, Jamie Brownlee, *Academia,
    Inc.: How Corporatization is Transforming
    Canadian Universities* (Halifax: Fern-
    wood, 2015).

15 Simon Fraser University (SFU), "Fall 2015
    International Student Report." www.sfu.ca/
    irp/news/international_student_report.html.

16 Fraser International College (Fraseric),
    "About FIC," (2016),www.fraseric.ca/about.

17 UBC Continuing Studies, "International
    Undergraduate Study Preparation Pro-
    gram (IUSPP)," 2016, www.cstudies.ubc.ca/
    programs/international-undergraduate-
    study-preparation-program-iuspp.

18 Eric Rankin, "UBC's Vantage College: Can-
    adians Need Not Apply," *CBC News*, November
    7, 2014, www.cbc.ca/news/canada/british-
    columbia/ubc-s-vantage-college-canadians-
    need-not-apply-1.2826142.

19 Global Affairs Canada. "Economic Impact
    of International Education in Canada –
    2016 Update."

20 Crawford Kilian, "Imagine Canada as an Edu-
    cation Superpower," *The Tyee*, January 1,
    2015, www.thetyee.ca/Opinion/2015/01/01/
    Canada-Education-Superpower/.

21 Larry Kuehn, "Questioning PISA: Examine the
    Purpose, Not just the Rankings," *Intercam-
    bio*, January 2017, www.idea-network.ca/
    category/intercambio-magazine.

22 BC Ministry of Education, "2016/17–2018/19
    Service Plan," 2016.

23 Beyond the specifics of Canadian cultural
    content are issues of political values. Hans
    Schuetze, in a research paper on *BC Offshore
    Schools in China*, points out that "it is diffi-
    cult to see how the mission of BC education
    to educate young people for a 'democratic
    and pluralist society' can be reconciled with
    an education for 'patriotism, collectivism
    and socialism'." See Schuetze, "BC Offshore

Schools in China," Asia-Pacific Foundation, www.asiapacific.ca/sites/default/files/archived_pdf/rr/cdn_offshore.pdf.

24 Larry Kuehn, "The Education World Is Not Flat," in *The Global Assault on Teaching, Teachers and their Unions*, eds. Mary Compton and Lois Weiner (New York: Palgrave, 2008).

25 Schuetze, "BC Offshore Schools in China."

26 Barton Swaim, review of *The Road to Somewhere Quoted in Letters from Anywhere*, by David Goodhart, *The Wall Street Journal*, July 8-9, 2017.

27 Bunnell, "The International Baccalaureate and a Framework for Class Consciousness."

28 Canadian Bureau for International Education, "Internationalization Principles for Canadian Institutions," (2016), http://cbie.ca/wp-content/uploads/2016/06/Internationalization-Principles-for-Canadian-Institutions-EN.pdf.

Chapter 6: How and Why to Change the Ways We Try to Change the Corporatization of Canada's Universities

1 This text was written for the Parkland Institute's annual conference in Edmonton in 2015. Although it retains its original form, its content has been somewhat modified and expanded. Given that the conference focused on concrete actions for progressive social change, this chapter deals more with how to resist university corporatization than with the corporatization process itself. Valuable analyses of this process can be found in other chapters of this book, as well as in the works cited in this chapter. Much of my own analysis of the process of university corporatization can be found in a collection of essays that I and Janice Newson have written, entitled *A Penny for Your Thoughts: How Corporatization Devalues Teaching, Research, and Public Service in Canada's Universities* (Ottawa: CCPA, 2015).

2 Indeed, this government has already taken some encouraging steps, including making the appointment process for members of university boards of governors more representative and accountable and exploring ways to give Alberta's academics the right to strike. The return of the Liberals to Ottawa may also bode well for Canadian higher education, though the extent of any substantial improvements remains to be seen.

3 My use and explanation of this approach is inspired by the work of noted Canadian sociologist Dorothy Smith. For some elaboration, see Dorothy E. Smith, *The Everyday World as Problematic* (Boston: Northeastern University Press, 1987) and Marie Campbell and Frances Gregor, *Mapping Social Relations: A Primer in Doing Institutional Ethnography* (Aurora, ON: Garamond Press, 2002).

4 It can also be helpful to think of social relations as a series of highways that makes it possible (as well as impossible) for people to connect with one another in particular ways. In this case, changing social relations would involve tearing down some highways and/or constructing new ones so that people come together in fundamentally different ways.

5 Local, regional, and national organizations representing university workers and students alike have pursued this strategy for years through a variety of means, including making submissions to various government representatives and processes, media campaigns, national days of action, and so on.

6 Claire Polster, "From Public Resource to Industry's Instrument: Redefining and Reshaping the Production of Knowledge in Canada's Universities," *Canadian Journal of Communication* 23.1, (1998): 91–106; Janet Atkinson-Grosjean, *Public Science, Private Interests: Culture and Commerce in Canada's Networks of Centres of Excellence* (Toronto: University of Toronto Press, 2006); Eric Martin and Simon Tremblay-Pepin, *Do We Really Need to Raise Tuition Fees?* (Montreal: Institut de recherche et d'informations socio-economiques, 2011).

7 The Dutch science shops make university research resources freely available to community groups to help them resolve pressing social, economic, environmental, and other problems. Integrating universities into various community economic development initiatives and expanding opportunities for the public to shape university policy (as do the Danish Board of Technology's citizen consensus conferences) would also help transform university social relations in positive ways.

8 Many academics call for the production and use of improved or alternative performance indicators. For one example, see Christopher Meyers' presentation at

www.politicsofevidence.ca/full-conference-archive. One ongoing initiative that exemplifies this strategy is the multi-university Community Engaged Scholarship Partnership that seeks to increase the importance of community engagement in assessments of academics' work (engagedscholarship.ca).

9   For more on this, see Claire Polster, "Reconfiguring the Academic Dance: A Critique of Faculty's Responses to Administrative Practices in Canadian Universities," *TOPIA* 28, (2012): 115–141, and Claire Polster, "Vicious Circle: Academic Insecurity and Privatization in Western Universities," in *Routledge Handbook of the Sociology of Higher Education*, eds. James E. Cote and Andy Furlong (London: Routledge, 2016): 94–105.

10 There is a large and growing literature in Canada and elsewhere that details the harmful nature and impacts of performance indicators. For some classic works, see Marilyn Strathern, ed. *Audit Cultures: Anthropological Studies in Accountability, Ethics, and the Academy* (London: Routledge, 2000); William Bruneau and Donald Savage, *Counting Out the Scholars: The Case Against Performance Indicators in Higher Education* (Toronto: James Lorimer and Company Ltd., 2002); Louise Morley, *Quality and Power in Higher Education* (Maidenhead, UK: Society for Research into Higher Education and Open University Press, 2003); Andrew Sparkes, "Embodiment, Academics, and Audit Culture: A Story Seeking Consideration," *Qualitative Research* 7.4, (2007): 521–550.

11 Among other things, academics could use their positions on assessment committees to ensure that the complex nature and diverse contributions of academic work are recognized, and universities could hold annual research showcases for the surrounding community to increase the circulation and use of the knowledge they produce, and to receive suggestions for further research. Getting rid of the more general—and pernicious—culture of stardom in Canada's universities (which both reinforces, and is reinforced by, the use of performance indicators) would also free academics to focus more on the public interest as opposed to their own and others' private interests.

12 In the last few years, votes of non-confidence in senior university administrators have been proposed or undertaken in several Canadian (and other) universities, including Carleton University, the University of Regina, Mount Allison University, the University of New Brunswick, and Capilano University, among others. For accounts of some of these, see Janet Steffenhagen, "Letter from Faculty Expresses Non-Confidence in Capilano University President," *The Vancouver Sun*, May 14, 2013, and "Faculty at Mount Allison, UNB Lack Confidence in Administration," *CAUT Bulletin* 61.4: A1.

13 Janice Newson, "The Decline of Faculty Influence: Confronting the Effects of the Corporate Agenda," in *Fragile Truths: 25 Years of Sociology and Anthropology in Canada*, eds. William Carroll et al. (Ottawa: Carleton University Press, 1992), 227–246; Benjamin Ginsberg, *The Fall of the Faculty: The Rise of the All-Administrative University and Why It Matters* (New York: Oxford University Press, 2011); Jamie Brownlee, *Academia Inc.: How Corporatization is Transforming Canada's Universities* (Halifax: Fernwood Publishing, 2015).

14 At the time of writing, the Manitoba Organization of Faculty Associations was in the process of spearheading one such initiative.

15 For two accounts of this promising, but short-lived, initiative, see Zexi Wang et al., "The University of Toronto General Assembly," *The Varsity*, January 17, 2011, and Rhonda Ward, "Introducing the University of Toronto General Assembly," *Rabble*, January 24, 2011. Minutes from the meetings of the group are also available on-line.

16 Munir Sheikh, former Chief Statistician of Canada, makes a similar point in an article critiquing the response to the Harper government's cancellation of the long-form census. He argues that rather than seeking to replace Stephen Harper with a prime minister who would be more respectful of Statistics Canada's autonomy, it would be preferable to change the patterns of interaction that are established and enforced by the *Statistics Canada Act*. That way, respect for the agency's autonomy would be a matter of law, not a matter of luck. Munir A. Sheikh, "Good Government and Statistics Canada: The Need for True Independence," *Academic Matters*, (2013): 12–16. The

resignation in September 2016 of Sheikh's successor, Wayne Smith, to protest the Liberal government's failure to protect the independence of the agency, only reinforces the point.

17 This is an important point, as the assumption that we know how our universities work often prevents our looking more deeply into the various documents, policies, processes, and practices in and through which they are constituted.

Chapter 7: Police Foundations and the Corporatization of Criminal Justice in Canada

1 Ian Loader and Neil Walker, "Policing as a Public Good: Reconstituting the Connections Between Policing and the State," *Theoretical Criminology* 5.1, (2001): 9–35.

2 Julie Ayling and Clifford Shearing, "Taking Care of Business: Public Police as Commercial Security Vendors," *Criminology and Criminal Justice* 8.1, (2008): 27–50.

3 Lucia Zedner, "Liquid Security: Managing the Market for Crime Control," *Criminology & Criminal Justice* 6.3, (2006): 267–288.

4 Adam White, "Post-Crisis Policing and Public-Private Partnerships," *British Journal of Criminology* 54.4, (2014): 1002–1022.

5 Carolyn Côté-Lussier, "Narratives of Legitimacy: Police Expansionism and the Contest over Policing," *Policing and Society* 23.2, (2013): 183–203.

6 Wendy Gillis, "Toronto Police Board Backtracks on Hiring Freeze, Plans to Hire 80 Officers," *Toronto Star,* August 10, 2017, www.thestar.com/news/crime/2017/08/10/toronto-police-board-backtracks-on-hiring-freeze-plans-to-hire-80-officers.html.

7 Association of Municipalities Ontario, *Building a New Public Safety Model in Ontario: AMO's Policing Modernization Report* (2015).

8 Pat O'Malley and Steven Hutchinson, "Converging Corporatization? Police Management, Police Unionism, and the Transfer of Business Principles," *Police Practice and Research* 8.2, (2007): 160.

9 O'Malley and Hutchinson, "Converging Corporatization?", 162.

10 O'Malley and Hutchinson, "Converging Corporatization?", 169.

11 Willem de Lint and Alan Hall, *Intelligent Control: Developments in Public Order Policing*

in Canada (Toronto: University of Toronto Press, 2009).

12 Conor O'Reilly, "The Transnational Security Consultancy Industry: A Case of State-Corporate Symbiosis," *Theoretical Criminology* 14.2, (2010): 183–210.

13 Raymond Dart, "Being 'Business-Like' in a Nonprofit Organization: A Grounded and Inductive Typology," *Nonprofit and Voluntary Sector Quarterly* 33.2, (2004): 290–310.

14 Florentine Maier, Michael Meyer, and Martin Steinberethner, "Nonprofit Organizations Becoming Business-Like: A Systematic Review," *Nonprofit and Voluntary Sector Quarterly* 45.1, (2016): 64–86.

15 David A. McDonald, "To Corporatize or Not to Corporatize (and if so, how?)," *Utilities Policy* 40, (2016): 107–114.

16 David A. McDonald, "Public Ambiguity and the Multiple Meanings of Corporatization," in *Corporatization and Public Services in the Global South,* ed. David A. McDonald (New York: Zed Books, 2014), 1–30.

17 McDonald, "Public Ambiguity and the Multiple Meanings of Corporatization," 1–2.

18 See, for example, Z. Hoque, S. Arends, and R. Alexander, "Policing the Police Service: A Case Study of the Rise of 'New Public Management' within an Australian Police Service," *Accounting, Auditing and Accountability Journal* 17.1, (2004): 59–84.

19 McDonald, "Public Ambiguity and the Multiple Meanings of Corporatization," 2.

20 Stephen Graham and Simon Marvin, *Splintering Urbanism: Networked Infrastructures, Technological Mobilities and the Urban Condition* (London: Routledge, 2001).

21 McDonald, "To Corporatize or Not to Corporatize," 107.

22 McDonald, "To Corporatize or Not to Corporatize," 110.

23 McDonald, "Public Ambiguity and the Multiple Meanings of Corporatization," 21.

24 David A. McDonald, "Back to the Future? The Curious Case of 'Public' Services." (Paper, UIC Urban Forum, Chicago, September 17, 2015), 11.

25 McDonald, "Back to the Future?" 12.

26 McDonald, "Public Ambiguity and the Multiple Meanings of Corporatization."

27 David Jancsics, "Offshoring at Home? Domestic Use of Shell Companies for Corruption," *Public Integrity* 19.1, (2017): 4–21.

28 Charles L. Walters, "A multi-site case study involving ten police foundations: Examining integrity and ethics relative to the establishment and maintenance of best practices" (dissertation, ETD collection for University of Nebraska, 2004).

29 The RCMP Foundation manages the RCMP Licensing Program that reviews products manufactured using the RCMP name or logo. Royalties collected are redirected to the foundation and used to support community initiatives, as well as youth and community policing projects.

30 Adam Graycar and David Jancsics, "Gift Giving and Corruption," *International Journal of Public Administration*, (forthcoming).

31 O'Malley, and Hutchinson, "Converging Corporatization?" 160.

32 Anna Paperny, "Vancouver Police to get Armour on Wheels," *The Globe and Mail,* June 25, 2008, S1.

33 Robert Mangelsdorf, "Foundation Gives back to DPD," *South Delta Leader,* April 12, 2013.

34 Marketwire Canada, "London Drugs Pays Tribute to the Vancouver Police Foundation," *Comtex News Network,* June 24, 2011.

35 Canadian Government News, "Police Sunglasses Raise Funds for Community Outreach Programs," June 19, 2014.

36 Canadian Government News, "Calgary Police Foundation Surpasses Fundraising Goal," October 10, 2014.

37 McDonald, "Back to the Future?"

38 O'Reilly, "The Transnational Security Consultancy Industry."

39 Walters, "A multi-site case study involving ten police foundations."

40 McDonald, "Public Ambiguity and the Multiple Meanings of Corporatization," 3.

41 McDonald, "Public Ambiguity and the Multiple Meanings of Corporatization," 7.

42 McDonald, "Back to the Future?" 12.

43 Gabriel Rossman, "Obfuscatory Relational Work and Disreputable Exchange," *Sociological Theory* 32.1, (2014): 43–63.

44 Adam Crawford, "Networked Governance and the Post-Regulatory State? Steering, Rowing and Anchoring the Provision of Policing and Security," *Theoretical Criminology* 10.4, (2006): 449–479.

45 White, "Post-Crisis Policing and Public-Private Partnerships," 1019.

Chapter 8: Do Construction Companies Create Criminal Justice Policy?

1 I recognize that this language may reflect strategic choices by sincere, well-meaning, and perhaps desperate humanitarians. But the rhetoric of facts and expertise has traditionally been used to suppress, not enhance, democratic impulses, and so should be used with care.

2 April Harding and Alexander Preker, "A Conceptual Framework for the Organizational Reform of Hospitals," in *Innovations in Health Service Delivery,* eds. Alexander Preker and April Harding (Washington: World Bank, 2003), 54.

3 See, for example, Preker and Harding, *Innovations;* David A. McDonald, *Rethinking Corporatization and Public Services in the Global South* (London: Zed Books, 2014); Nancy Bilodeau, Claude Laurin, and Aidan Vining, "Choice of Organizational Form Makes a Real Difference: The Impact of Corporatization on Government Agencies in Canada," *Journal of Public Administration Research and Theory* 17: 119–47; Jamie Brownlee, *Academia Inc., How Corporatization is Transforming Canadian Universities* (Halifax, Fernwood, 2015).

4 McDonald, *Rethinking Corporatization,* 208–9.

5 Greg McElligott, "Invested in Prisons: Prison Expansion and Community Development in Canada," *Studies in Social Justice* 11.1, (2017): 100.

6 McElligott, "Invested in Prisons," 105, Table 4.

7 McElligott, "Invested in Prisons," 105, Table 5.

8 Many federal government tenders are now listed on-line. The patterns described here were discovered in preliminary research for McElligott, "Invested in Prisons," based on the data available at MERX, *Canadian Public Tenders* (n.d. www.merx.com). Data after June 2013 come from Buyandsell.ca, which became Ottawa's official site after that time. And very useful summary tables are now available at Canada, *Public Accounts of Canada,* Vol. 3, Section 4 – *Acquisition of land, buildings, and works.* (Ottawa: Public Works and Government Services Canada, 2005-13), http://epe.lacbac.gc.ca/100/201/301/public_accounts_can/pdf/index.html.

9 MERX, *Canadian Public Tenders;* Author's calculations.

10 See Malcolm Feeley, "Entrepreneurs of Punishment," *Punishment and Society* 4.3, (2002): 321–344; Michael Ignatieff, *A Just Measure of Pain: The Penitentiary in the Industrial Revolution 1750–1850* (New York: Columbia University Press, 2014); and Michel Foucault, *Discipline and Punish* (New York: Vintage, 1995).

11 Greg McElligott, "Bearing the Neoconservative Burden? Frontline Work in Prisons," *Social Justice* 34.2–3, (2008): 78–97.

12 Eric Schlosser, "The Prison-Industrial Complex," *The Atlantic online* (December 1998), www.theatlantic.com/magazine/archive/1998/12/the-prison-industrial-complex/304669/.

13 Ruth Wilson Gilmore, *Golden Gulag* (Berkeley: University of Southern California Press, 2007).

14 McDonald, *Rethinking Corporatization*, 209.

15 Buitenhuis, Amy, "Public-Private Partnerships and Prison Expansion in Ontario: Shifts in Governance, 1995 to 2012" (Master's thesis, University of Toronto, 2013), https://tspace.library.utoronto.ca/bitstream/1807/42694/6/Buitenhuis_Amy_J_201311_MA_thesis.pdf. Further examples undoubtedly abound in the story of Ontario Hydro's partial privatization, but they are beyond the scope of this chapter.

16 Greg McElligott, "A Tory High Modernism? Grand Plans and Visions of Order in Neoconservative Ontario," *Critical Criminology* 16.2, (2008): 123–44.

17 Peter Oliver, *'Terror to Evil-Doers': Prisoners and Punishment in Nineteenth-Century Ontario* (Toronto: University of Toronto Press, 1998), 110, 113.

18 James C. Scott, *Seeing Like a State* (New Haven, CT: Yale University Press, 1998), 242; Government of Ontario, Superbuild, (n.d.). *News and info*, www.superbuild.gov.on.ca/userfiles/html/nts_2_21479_1.html.

19 Government of Ontario, Superbuild, *News and info*; McElligott, "A Tory High Modernism?", 138. A World Bank book on hospital reform makes a similar point, noting the "common public sector tendency to allow wages to crowd out capital costs." See Preker and Harding, "Introduction" in *Innovations in Health Service Delivery*, 37.

20 It is actually tricky to determine how autonomous state elites are. See Eric Nordlinger, *On the Autonomy of the Democratic State* (Cambridge: Harvard University Press, 1981), especially 7.

21 As I have argued elsewhere, democratic controls in Canada are indeed very weak. See my book *Beyond Service: State Workers, Public Policy, and the Prospects for Democratic Administration* (Toronto: University of Toronto Press, 2001), 218–22.

22 See especially Ralph Miliband, *The State in Capitalist Society* (London: Quartet, 1973); Nicos Poulantzas, *State, Power, Socialism* (London: Verso, 1980).

23 Miliband, *The State in Capitalist Society*; Nicos Poulantzas, *State, Power, Socialism*.

24 James O'Connor, *The Fiscal Crisis of the State* (New York: St. Martin's Press, 1973).

25 Leo Panitch, "The Role and Nature of the Canadian State," in *The Canadian State*, ed. Leo Panitch (Toronto: University of Toronto Press, 1977).

26 Loïc Wacquant, "'Suitable Enemies': Foreigners and Immigrants in the Prisons of Europe," *Punishment and Society* 1.2, (1999): 216.

27 Karl Marx, cited in Panitch, "The Role and Nature," 3.

28 McElligott, "Invested in Prisons," 107–8.

29 McDonald, *Rethinking Corporatization*, 207.

30 Douglas Hay, "Property, Authority and the Criminal Law," in *Albion's Fatal Tree*, eds. Douglas Hay, Peter Linebaugh, John Rule, E.P. Thompson, and Cal Winslow (New York: Pantheon, 1975), 33; Poulantzas, *State, Power, Socialism,* 91.

31 Hay, "Property, Authority and the Criminal Law," 50.

32 George Rusche and Otto Kirchheimer, *Punishment and Social Structure* (London: Transaction, 1939 & 2003); Dario Melossi and Massimo Pavarini, *The Prison and the Factory* (Totowa, NJ: Barnes & Noble Books, 1981).

33 Miliband, *The State in Capitalist Society*; Poulantzas, *State, Power, Socialism.*

34 This is not to diminish the role of the state in perpetuating many other sorts of inequality, and race, gender, sexuality, and so on combine in complex intersectional ways as state power is exercised and experienced. But to reproduce an unequal society, one of the things the state must be is a capitalist state.

35 McDonald, *Rethinking Corporatization*, 2.

36 Canadian business has been remarkably concerned not only with what the state produces, but also *how* it is produced. Consistent efforts to reconcile divergent practices seem to stem from the hubris or hype of management theorists, and the ideological need to depict business as the source of all good things. In fact, organizational thinking has historically flowed both ways, with military methods influencing bureaucracy everywhere, and prisons and factories developing together. See Ignatieff, *A Just Measure of Pain*; Foucault, *Discipline and Punish*.

37 This section and the one that follows draw from a presentation by Greg McElligott and Justin Piché called "Grand Visions Interrupted? Debating the Future of Federal Prisons in Canada" (for the Canadian Law and Society Association, Congress of the Social Sciences and Humanities, Waterloo, May 2012).

38 Canada, Glassco Commission, *Report of the Royal Commission on Government Organization, Management of the Public Service*, Vol. 1 (abridged ed.) (Ottawa: Queen's Printer, 1962), 45–46.

39 A more detailed version of this argument can be found in McElligott, *Beyond Service*, 59–104.

40 Jim Silver, "The Ideology of Excellence: Management and Neo-Conservatism," *Studies in Political Economy* 24, (1987): 106.

41 See Donna Baines, Chapter 12, this volume.

42 O'Connor, *The Fiscal Crisis of the State*.

43 David Osborne and Ted Gaebler, *Reinventing Government: How the Entrepreneurial Spirit is Transforming the Public Service*. (New York: Penguin, 1993).

44 Osborne and Gaebler, like McDonald, allow for the possibility that devolved state functions might be taken on by entities acting in more progressive, "participative" ways. However, to my knowledge, this almost never happened, and *Reinventing Government* was used much more often to justify abandoning state responsibilities and/or state assets. See Osborne and Gaebler, *Reinventing Government*, 22.

45 See McElligott, "A Tory High Modernism?"

46 Greg McElligott, "Bearing the Neoconservative Burden?"

47 Amy Buitenhuis, "Public-Private Partnerships." TSDC was supposed to be a more

enlightened version of the supermax prison, but recent evidence suggests it is just another "hellhole," because it too reduced staffing beyond safe levels. See Raizel Robin, "The $1-Billion Hellhole," *Toronto Life*, Feb. 15, 2017, http://torontolife.com/city/inside-toronto-south-detention-centre-torontos-1-billion-hellhole/.

48 Buitenhuis, "Public-Private Partnerships."

49 CSC Review Panel (RP), *A Roadmap to Strengthening Public Safety* (Ottawa: Minister of Public Works and Government Services Canada, 2007), www.publicsafety.gc.ca/cnt/cntrng-crm/csc-scc-rvw-pnl/report-rapport/cscrprprt-eng.pdf.

50 CSC RP, *A Roadmap*, App. F, 2, 15, 22.

51 McDonald notes that business jargon has become commonplace everywhere under neoliberalism, and argues that a new variant of neoliberalism, not a post-neoliberal era, has begun. However, the new neoliberalism looks "to the state as an essential moderator of market cyclicality and a broker of ideological reform" and echoes Keynes as well as Friedman (McDonald, *Rethinking Corporatization*, 11–12). This explanation suggests that, however much the overall ideological package changes, capitalist states still perform functions essentially the same as those outlined by the state theorists.

52 Canada, Correctional Service Canada [CSC], "Moving Towards Transformation," *Let's Talk* 33.1, (2008), www.csc-scc.gc.ca/text/pblct/lt-en/2008/33-1/index-eng.shtml; Don Head, "Modernization of Physical Infrastructure," *Let's Talk* 33:1, (2008) Ottawa: Correctional Service of Canada, www.csc-scc.gc.ca/text/pblct/lt-en/2008/33-1/8-eng.shtml.

53 McElligott, "Invested in Prisons," 95.

54 McElligott, "Invested in Prisons," 105.

55 For the American pre-fab supplier used to build TSDC, see www.tindallcorp.com/corrections/.

56 Canada, Correctional Service of Canada [CSC]. "Modernization of physical infrastructure and planning of regional complexes – July 25" (2008). s. 5.1.1. E-mail obtained via Access to Information request A-2010-00165, at www.scribd.com/doc/66600934/CSC-Infrastructure-Planning-E-Mail-July-2008.

57 Kim Moody, *Workers in a Lean World* (London: Verso, 1997).

58 Joe Hermer and Janet Mosher, eds., *Disorderly People: Law and the Politics of Exclusion in Ontario* (Halifax: Fernwood, 2002); Todd Gordon, *Cops, Crime and Capitalism* (Halifax: Fernwood, 2006).

59 CSC RP, *A Roadmap*, 63–5.

60 CSC RP, *A Roadmap*, 6, 16–17, 20, 114–118.

61 CSC RP, *A Roadmap*, 3–4, 37, 47.

62 CSC RP, *A Roadmap*, 49, 72.

63 CSC RP, *A Roadmap*, 47.

64 CSC RP, *A Roadmap*, 71–2.

65 Michael Maher and Lorraine Berzins, *Open the Doors to Smarter Justice*. Smart Justice Network, 2011, 5, http://ccjc.ca/wp-content/uploads/2011/10/Open-Doors-to-Smarter-Justice_2011.pdf.

66 Michael Hallett, "Re-entry to What? Theorizing Prisoner Re-entry in the Jobless Future," *Critical Criminology* 20.3, (2011): 213–228. This question echoes previous ones asked of neoconservative labour market policies. See Nancy Jackson, ed. *Training for What? Labour Perspectives on Job Training* (Toronto: Our Schools/Our Selves Education Foundation, 1992).

67 See Jamie Brownlee, Chris Hurl, and Kevin Walby, "Introduction: Critical Perspectives on Corporatization in Canada," this volume.

68 McElligott, *Beyond Service*, Ch. 8.

69 See McElligott, "Invested in Prisons," for a more detailed survey of the evidence available here.

70 Bill Curry, "Liberals Gave Investors 'Extraordinary Control' over Infrastructure Bank: Opposition," *The Globe and Mail*, May 5, 2017, www.theglobeandmail.com/news/politics/liberals-gave-investors-extraordinary-control-over-infrastructure-bank-opposition/article34910106/.

71 See McElligott, "Invested in Prisons."

72 For suggestions on how this might be done, see McElligott, "Invested in Prisons" and Greg McElligott, "Beyond Service, Beyond Coercion? Prisoner Co-ops and the Path to Democratic Administration," in ed. Paul Gray, *From the Streets to the State: Changing the World by Taking Power* (forthcoming).

Chapter 9: Corporatizing Therapeutic Justice

1 Tobi Seddon, Robert Ralphs, and Lisa Williams, "Risk, Security and the Criminalization of British Drug Policy," *British Journal of Criminology* 48, (2008): 818–834; Neil Hunt, and Alex Stevens, "Whose Harm? Harm Reduction and the Shift to Coercion in UK Drug Policy," *Social Policy & Society* 3.4, (2004): 333–42; Tobi Seddon, "Coerced Drug Treatment in the Criminal Justice System: Conceptual, Ethical and Criminological Issues," *Criminology and Criminal Justice* 7.3, (2007): 269–286; Benedikt Fischer, "'Doing Good with a Vengeance': A Critical Assessment of the Practices, Effects and Implications of Drug Treatment Courts in North America," *Criminal Justice* 3.3, (2003): 227–48; Scott Sanford and Bruce Arrigo, "Lifting the Cover on Drug Courts: Evaluation Findings and Policy Concerns," *International Journal of Offender Therapy and Comparative Criminology* 49.3, (2005): 239–259; John Goldkamp, "The Drug Court Response: Issues and Implications for Justice Change," *Alberta Law Review* 63, (1999): 923.

2 Kelly Gorkoff, *From Plan to Market, Marketizing the Non-Economic: The Economy of Higher Education – Markets and Marketization of Canadian Post-Secondary Education* (Dissertation, 2013); Manfried Steger, and Roy Ravi, *Neoliberalism: A Very Short Introduction* (Oxford: Oxford University Press, 2010); C. Leys, *Market Driven Politics: Neoliberal Democracy and the Public Interest* (London: Verso, 2001); Wendy Brown, *Undoing the Demos: Neoliberalism's Stealth Revolution* (New York: Zone Books, 2015).

3 Gorkoff, *From Plan to Market*; Brown, *Undoing the Demos*.

4 David A. McDonald, "Public Ambiguity and the Multiple Meanings of Corporatization" in *Rethinking Corporatization and Public Services in the Global South*, ed. David A. McDonald (London: Zed Books, 2014).

5 Per Laegreid, Paul G. Roness, and Vidar Rolland, "Agencification and Corporatization in Norway 1947-2011," *International Journal of Public Administration* 36.9, (2013): 659–672.

6 Laegreid, Roness, and Rolland, "Agencification and Corporatization."

7 McDonald, "Public Ambiguity," 2.

8 Clifford Shearing and Les Johnston, "Nodal Wars and Network Fallacies: A Genealogical Analysis of Global Insecurities," *Theoretical Criminology* 14.4, (2010): 495–514; Ian Loader and N. Walker, *Civilizing Security* (Cambridge, UK: Cambridge University Press,

2007); Ian Loader, "Plural Policing and Democratic Governance," *Social & Legal Studies* 9.3, (2000): 323–345; Andrew Crawford, "Networked Governance and the Post-Regulatory State? Steering, Rowing and Anchoring the Provision of Police and Security," *Theoretical Criminology* 10.4, (2006): 449–479.

9   Laegreid, Roness, and Rolland, "Agencification and Corporatization."

10 Clifford Shearing, "A Nodal Conception of Governance: Thoughts on a Policing Commission," *Policing and Society* 11.3/4, (2001): 261.

11 Laegreid, Roness, and Rolland, "Agencification and Corporatization"; C. Talbot, "The Agency Idea: Sometimes Old, Sometimes New, Sometimes Borrowed, Sometimes Unique," in *Unbundled Government: A Critical Analysis of the Global Trend to Agencies, Quangos and Contractualisations*, eds. C. Pollitt and C. Talbot (London: Routledge, 2004).

12 Laegreid, Roness, and Rolland, "Agencification and Corporatization"; Christopher Hood, *The Blame Game* (Princeton, NJ: Princeton University Press, 2011); Oliver James and Sandra van Thiel, "Structural Devolution to Agencies" in *The Ashgate Research Companion to New Public Management*, eds. Tom Christensen and Per Laegreid (Farnham: Ashgate, 2011), 209–222.

13 David Garland, *The Culture of Control: Crime and Social Order in Contemporary Society.* (Chicago: University of Chicago Press, 2001), 28.

14 Bruce Winick, *Civil Commitment: A Therapeutic Jurisprudence Model* (Durham, NC: Carolina Academic Press, 2005); B.J. Winick and D. Wexler, eds. *Judging in a Therapeutic Key: Therapeutic Jurisprudence and the Courts* (Durham, NC: Carolina Academic Press, 2003); J.L. Nolan, *Reinventing Justice: The American Drug Court Movement* (Princeton, NJ: Princeton University Press, 2001).

15 Stephanos Bibas, "Using Plea Procedures to Combat Denial and Minimization," in *Judging in a Therapeutic Key: Therapeutic Jurisprudence and the Courts,* eds. B.J. Winick and D. Wexler (Durham, NC: Carolina Academic Press, 2003); E. Lee, *Community Courts: An Evolving Model* (Washington, DC: US Department of Justice, Centre for Court Innovation, 2000).

16 Canada, Department of Justice, Programs Branch. *Winnipeg Drug Treatment Court:*

Project Proposal. Drug Treatment Court Funding Program, 2005.

17 Kelly Gorkoff and Michael Weinrath, *Winnipeg Drug Treatment Court: Process Evaluation, Final Report.* Department of Criminal Justice, University of Winnipeg, 2007.

18 National Treatment Strategy Working Group, *A Systems Approach to Substance Use in Canada: Recommendations for a National Treatment Strategy* (Ottawa: National Framework for Action to Reduce the Harms Associated with Alcohol and Other Drugs and Substances in Canada, 2008).

19 Dan Malleck, *When Good Drugs Go Bad: Opium, Medicine, and the Origins of Canada's Drug Laws* (Vancouver: UBC Press, 2015).

20 National Treatment Strategy Working Group, *A Systems Approach to Substance Use in Canada.*

21 National Treatment Strategy Working Group, *A Systems Approach to Substance Use in Canada.*

22 David Garland, *The Culture of Control: Crime and Social Order in Contemporary Society* (Chicago: University of Chicago Press, 2001).

23 Dawn Moore, "Translating Justice and Therapy: The Drug Treatment Court Networks," *British Journal of Criminology* 47.1, (2007): 42—60.

24 Garland, *The Culture of Control,* 18.

25 Kelly Hannah-Moffat, "Prisons that Empower: Neo-liberal Governance in Canadian Women's Prisons," *British Journal of Criminology* 40.3, (2000): 510–531; Nicolas Rose, "Government and Control," *British Journal of Criminology* 40.2, (2000): 321–339.

26 Gorkoff and Weinrath, *Winnipeg Drug Treatment Court: Process Evaluation.*

27 Robin Mackenzie, "Feeling Good: The Ethno Politics of Pleasure: Psychoactive Substance Use and Public Health and Criminal Justice Governance: Therapeutic Jurisprudence and the Drug Courts in the USA," *Social and Legal Studies* 17.4, (2008): 513–533.

28 Mackenzie, "Feeling Good," 520.

29 McDonald, "Public Ambiguity," 11; Laegreid, Roness, and Rolland, "Agencification and Corporatization"; Hood, *The Blame Game*; James and van Thiel, "Structural Devolution to Agencies," 212.

30 Christopher Hood and Guy Peters, "The Middle Aging of New Public Management: Into the Age of Paradox?" *Journal of Public*

Administration Research and Theory 14.3, (2004): 267–282.

31 McDonald, "Public Ambiguity."

32 Gorkoff and Weinrath, *Winnipeg Drug Treatment Court: Process Evaluation*.

33 Shearing, "A Nodal Conception of Governance," 261.

34 Dan Lang, "The Political Economy of Performance Funding," in *Taking Public Universities Seriously*, eds. F. Iaboucci and C. Tuohy (Toronto: University of Toronto Press, 2005).

35 Lang, "The Political Economy of Performance Funding."

36 Brown, *Undoing the Demos*.

37 Canada, Department of Justice, *Overview of the National Performance and Evaluation Reporting Requirements: Drug Treatment Courts Funding Program*, Ottawa, 2006.

38 Nicolas Rose, "Governing Advanced Liberal Democracies," in *Foucault and Political Reason,* eds. Barry Osborne and Nicolas Rose (Chicago: Chicago University Press, 2006).

39 Marino Regini, "A Marketization of European Universities? The Role of External Demands and Internal Actors," in *The Marketization of Society: Economizing the Non-Economic,* eds. Uwe Schimank and Ute Volkmann, Welfare Societies Research Network (Bremen: University of Bremen, 2012), 81–94.

40 Gorkoff and Weinrath, *Winnipeg Drug Treatment Court: Process Evaluation*.

41 Michael Weinrath and Calum Smee, *Winnipeg Drug Treatment Court Program Evaluation for Calendar Year 2015*. Department of Criminal Justice, University of Winnipeg, 2016.

42 Kelly Gorkoff and Michael Weinrath, *Winnipeg Drug Treatment Court: Outcome Evaluation, Final Report*. Department of Criminal Justice, University of Winnipeg. (2009).

43 Kelly Gorkoff and Michael Weinrath, *Winnipeg Drug Treatment Court: Outcome Evaluation, Final Report*. Department of Criminal Justice, University of Winnipeg, 2008.

44 Defence counsel (legal aid and private) and provincial prosecutors were involved on a case-by-case basis.

45 Weinrath and Smee, *Winnipeg Drug Treatment Court Program Evaluation,* 4.

46 McDonald, "Public Ambiguity," 15.

47 Kelly Hannah-Moffat and Paula Maurutto, "Shifting and Targeted Forms of Penal Governance: Bail, Punishment and Specialized

Courts," *Theoretical Criminology* 16.2, (2012): 201–219; J.L. Nolan, *Reinventing Justice: The American Drug Court Movement* (Princeton, NJ: Princeton University Press, 2001).

48 Hannah-Moffat and Maurutto, "Shifting and Targeted Forms of Penal Governance," 210.

49 Christine Saum and Allison Gray, "Facilitating Change for Women? Exploring the Role of Therapeutic Jurisprudence in Drug Court," in *Neither Villain nor Victim: Empowerment and Agency among Women Substance Abusers,* ed. Tammy Anderson (New Brunswick, NJ.: Rutgers University Press, 2008).

50 Malleck, *When Good Drugs Go Bad*.

51 Niel Hunt and Alex Stevens, "Whose Harm? Harm Reduction and the Shift to Coercion in UK Drug Policy," *Social Policy & Society* 3.4, (2004): 337.

52 Malleck, *When Good Drugs Go Bad*.

53 Toby Seddon, "Coerced Drug Treatment"; Benedikt, "Doing Good with a Vengeance."

54 Mackenzie, "Feeling Good."

55 Michael Lynch, "The Power of Oppression: Understanding the History of Criminology as a Science of Oppression," *Critical Criminology* 9.1/2 (2000): 144–152.

56 Seddon, "Coerced Drug Treatment," 820.

Chapter 10: Corporatization and Federal-Provincial Relations

1 Gilles Bourque and Jules Duchastel, *L'identité fragmentée* (Montreal: Fides, 1996).

2 Adam Harmes, "The Political Economy of Open Federalism," *Canadian Journal of Political Science* 40.2, (2007): 417–437; Neil Brenner, "Globalisation as Reterritorialisation: The Rescaling of Urban Governance in the European Union," *Urban Studies* 36.3, (1999): 431–451.

3 Peter Graefe, "State Restructuring, Social Assistance, and Canadian Intergovernmental Relations: Same Scale, New Tune," *Studies in Political Economy* 78, (2006).

4 Peter Dauvergne and Genevieve LeBaron, *Protest Inc.: The Corporatization of Activism* (Cambridge, UK: Polity Press, 2014), 9.

5 David A. McDonald, "Public Ambiguity and the Multiple Meanings of Corporatization," *Rethinking Corporatization and Public Services in the Global South*, ed. David A. McDonald (London: Zed, 2014), 2.

6 Gérard Boismenu, "Ré-investissement dans l'État social au Canada et instrumentalisation

de la nouvelle gestion publique," in *L'État des citoyennetés en Europe et dans les Amériques*, eds. Jane Jenson, Bérengère Marques-Pereira, and Éric Remacle (Montreal: Presses de l'Université de Montréal, 2007); McDonald, "Public Ambiguity," 9–11.

7   Alain Noël, "Power and Purpose in Intergovernmental Relations," *IRPP Policy Matters* 6.2, (2002).

8   Gérard Boismenu and Peter Graefe, "The New Federal Toolbelt: Attempts to Rebuild Social Policy Leadership," *Canadian Public Policy* 30.1, (2004): 71–89.

9   Christopher Dunn, "Harper without Jeers, Trudeau without Cheers: Assessing 10 Years of Intergovernmental Relations," *IRPP Insight* 8 (2016).

10 Shelagh Day and Gwen Brodsky, *Women and the Canada Social Transfer: Securing the Social Union* (Ottawa: Status of Women Canada, 2007); Barbara Cameron, "Accounting for Rights and Money in the Canadian Social Union," in *Poverty: Rights, Social Citizenship, Legal Activism,* eds. Margot Young, Susan B. Boyd, Gwen Brodsky, and Shelagh Day (Vancouver: UBC Press, 2007).

11 Karen Bridget Murray, "Do No Disturb: 'Vulnerable Populations' in Canadian Federal Government Policy Practices," *Canadian Journal of Urban Research* 13.1, (2004): 50–69; Jane Jenson, *Canada's New Social Risks: Directions for a New Social Architecture* (Ottawa: Canadian Policy Research Networks, 2004).

12 This is certainly the flavour given by insiders to the negotiations. See Ian Peach and William Warriner, *Canadian Social Policy Renewal, 1994-2000* (Halifax: Fernwood, 2007).

13 Boismenu, "Réinvestissment."

14 Barbara Cameron, "Accounting for Rights."

15 See the case studies in *Overpromising and Underperforming: Understanding and Evaluating New Intergovernmental Accountability Regimes*, eds. Peter Graefe, Julie M. Simmons, and Linda A. White (Toronto: University of Toronto Press, 2013).

16 Dunn, "Harper Without Jeers," 6–7.

17 Canada, Department of Finance, "Federal Proposal to Strengthen Health Care for Canadians," December 19, 2016, www.fin.gc.ca/n16/data/16-161_1-eng.asp.

18 Health Canada, "Canada Reaches Agreement with Newfoundland and Labrador and Nova Scotia on Funding for Health Accord," December 23, 2016, http://news.gc.ca/web/article-en.do?nid=1173459&tp=1.

19 Michael J. Prince, "The Prime Minister as Moral Crusader: Stephen Harper's Punitive Turn in Social Policy Making," *Canadian Review of Social Policy* 71 (2015): 53–69.

Chapter 11: Corporatizing Urban Policy-Making

1   The size of KPMG's market is made clear in their promotional materials and bids in different communities. For instance, in their bid for a service review contract in the Town of Cochrane, they note in their proposal at least twenty-seven different communities where they have undertaken service reviews. The file can be viewed appended to the agenda for the Town's Special Council Meeting from 10 August 2016: https://cochrane.civicweb.net/document/79765.

2   Denis Saint-Martin, "Making Government More 'Business-Like': Management Consultants as Agents of Isomorphism in Modern Political Economies," in *The Wiley-Blackwell Handbook of Global Companies*, ed. John Mikler (London: Wiley-Blackwell, 2013), 183. For more recent statistics, see CMC-Canada, *Consulting Industry Trends and Outlook*, 2014.

3   Sandro Contenta. "Substandard Operating Procedure," *Toronto Star*, June 13, 2009) www.thestar.com/news/insight/2009/06/13/substandard_operating_procedure.html.

4   At the federal level, there was a 647 percent increase in expenditures on policy outsourcing from 1980 to 2000–01, rising from $239 million to $1.55 billion over those years. See Antony Perl and Donald J. White, "The Changing Role of Consultants in Canadian Policy Analysis," *Policy & Society* 21.1, (2002): 53. This was also reflected at the provincial level, especially in Ontario and British Columbia, through the late 1990s and early 2000s, as neoliberal governments commissioned management consultants to assess the potential overhaul of public services following their elections.

5   See Daniel Guttman and Barry Willner, *The Shadow Government* (New York: Pantheon

Books, 1976); Graeme Hodge and Diana Bowman. "The 'Consultocracy': The Business of Reforming Government," in *Privatization and Market Development*, ed. Graeme Hodge (Northampton, MA: Edward Elgar, 2006); Christopher Hood and Michael Jackson, *Administrative Argument* (Dartmouth, NH: Aldershot, 1991).

6   Christopher Hood, *Explaining Economic Policy Reversals* (Buckingham, UK: Open University Press, 1994), 138.

7   Mike Raco, *State-led Privatisation and the Demise of the Democratic State* (London: Routledge, 2013), 18.

8   In *Building the New Managerial State* (London: Oxford University Press, 2000), Saint-Martin also notes how the current trend towards management consulting has been conditioned through their use by the federal government under previous regimes, most notably emerging in the 1960s and 1970s.

9   For the federal level, see A.S. Roberts. *So-Called Experts: How American Consultants Remade the Canadian Civil Service 1918-1921.* At the municipal level, recently I have noted the use of management consultants in setting benchmarks for Toronto's sanitation and scavenging department dating back to 1910. See Chris Hurl, "From Scavengers to Sanitation Workers: Practices of Purification and the Making of Civic Employees in Toronto, 1890-1920," *Labour / Le Travail* 79, (2017).

10 Conor O'Reilly, "The Transnational Security Consultancy Industry: A Case of State-Corporate Symbiosis," *Theoretical Criminology* 14.2, (2010): 183–210. For another view on the two-sided nature of this relationship, see Denis Saint-Martin, *Building the New Managerialist State: Consultants and the Politics of Public Sector Reform in Comparative Perspective* (Oxford: Oxford University Press, 2000).

11 Saint-Martin. *Building the New Managerialist State.*

12 See Laura Elizabeth Pinto, "Hidden Privatization in Education Policy as 'Quick Fixes' by 'Hired Guns': Contracting Curriculum Policy in Ontario," *Critical Policy Studies* 6.3, (2012): 261–281.

13 Andrew Sancton, *Merger Mania* (Kingston: McGill-Queens University Press, 2000).

14 Canadian Management Consulting (CMC), *Industry Trends and Outlook*, 2011.

15 CUPE Research, *KPMG and the Public Agenda: Who's Watching the Watchmen?*

16 Since the late 1990s, Denis Saint-Martin notes that management consultants have increasingly framed themselves as public actors, "partners in governance," as consultants become more involved in service delivery and less detached from their clients than in the past. See Denis Saint-Martin. "Making Government More 'Business-Like'."

17 The legitimizing role played by Big Four firms in assuring value for money in the wake of a series of privatization scandals in Ontario is discussed by Matti Siemiatycki and Naeem Farooqi in "Value for Money and Risk in Public-Private Partnerships," *Journal of the American Planning Association* 78.3, (2012): "As part of the Liberal government's political strategy to shift public opinion and make PPPs acceptable with the public," they note, "leading politicians identified that an important part of the PPP delivery approach was empirically demonstrating that PPPs delivered VfM." (296). While their reports have been criticized by the Attorney General of Ontario for their inaccuracies and unequivocal support for public-private partnerships, even in the face of countervailing evidence, Big Four firms have played a central role in empirically demonstrating the value of public infrastructure projects (see also Heather Whiteside, Chapter 1 in this volume).

18 CUPE Research, *When the Consultant Comes Calling*, May 2013.

19 CUPE Research, *When the Consultant Comes Calling*, 7.

20 Wendy Brown, *Undoing the Demos: Neoliberalism's Stealth Revolution* (London: Zone Books, 2015), 30.

21 William Davies, *The Limits of Neoliberalism* (London: Sage, 2014), 114.

22 See Davies, *The Limits of Neoliberalism*; Isabelle Bruno, "The 'Indefinite Discipline' of Competitiveness Benchmarking as a Neoliberal Technology of Government," *Minerva* 47, (2009): 261–280; Martin Kornberger and Chris Carter, "Manufacturing Competition: How Accounting Practices Shape Strategy Making in Cities," *Accounting, Auditing & Accountability Journal* 23.3, (2010): 325–349;

Michael Sauder and Wendy Nelson Espeland, "The Discipline of Rankings: Tight Coupling and Organizational Change," *American Sociological Review* 74.1, (2009): 63–82.

23 Betsy Donald, Amy Glasmeier, Mia Gray, and Linda Lobao, "Austerity in the City: Economic Crisis and Urban Service Decline?" *Cambridge Journal of Regions, Economy and Society* 7, (2014): 7.

24 John Clarke and Janet Newman, *The Managerial State* (London: Sage, 1997), 79.

25 CUPE, *When the Consultant Comes Calling.*

26 KPMG, July 28, 2011. The full recording of the presentation by KPMG to the City of Toronto's Executive Committee can be ordered from the City of Toronto: http://app.toronto.ca/tmmis/index.do.

27 KPMG, *Final Report to the City Manager, City of Toronto Core Service Review Project*, 2011, 153, 162.

28 KPMG, *Final Report to the City Manager*, 98, 113.

29 Travis Mealing, "Savings of $1.75 million Identified," *Midland Mirror*, October 3, 2012, www.simcoe.com/news-story/2060445-savings-of-1-75-million-identified/.

30 Jamie Peck and Nik Theodore, *Fast Policy* (Minneapolis: University of Minnesota Press, 2015).

31 I develop this argument further in Chris Hurl, "(Dis)Assembling Policy Pipelines: Unpacking the Work of Management Consultants at Public Meetings," *Geographica Helvetica* 72.2, (2017): 183–195, where I draw from the work of John Allen and Allan Cochrane, "Assemblages of State Power: Topological Shifts in the Organization of Government and Politics," *Antipode* 42.5, (2010): 1071–1089.

32 In his 2013 survey of Ontario municipalities, Noah Atlin observes that MSDRs "are consistently conducted separately from further public participation initiatives," though this has been subsequently addressed by some municipalities in the face of public criticisms. See Noah Atlin, "Public Participation in Municipal Service Delivery Review: Challenges and Opportunities for Ontario's Municipal Governance." (Master's thesis, University of Western Ontario, 2013).

33 Craig Fossay and Glen Sloutsky, KPMG – *City of Toronto Core Services Review*, Webinar to Institute for Citizen-Centred Service,

October 27, 2011, www.iccs-isac.org/about/media-library/?lang=en.

34 Dorothy E. Smith, *The Conceptual Practices of Power* (Toronto: University of Toronto Press, 1990), 96.

35 KPMG, *Proposal to the Town of Cochrane*, 2016, 3.

36 According to its website, the Institute for Citizen-Centred Service (ICCS) "was created in 2005 by the Public Sector Chief Information Officer Council (PSCIOC) and the Public Sector Service Delivery Council (PSSDC) as a not-for-profit organization to provide an inter-governmental platform to pursue partnerships and coordinate initiatives focused on innovative public sector service delivery and IT/IM initiatives. This includes research, the Common Measurements Tool and certification and learning programs." https://iccs-isac.org/about. While the professional seminar video was since removed from the website, it is still available via: www.youtube.com/watch?v=H5gz76YQElU. Information presented at the 2012 Canadian Association of Municipal Managers is available here: www.camacam.ca/sites/default/files/inline-files/2012-presentation-Pennachetti.pdf.

37 In addition to listing his past credentials with public agencies in Toronto, Mitchell's expertise as architect of information systems across Canadian municipalities is noted in his company profile: https://home.kpmg.com/xx/en/home/contacts/m/alan-mitchell.html.

38 KPMG International, 2014, *Services to Local Government*, 6. https://home.kpmg.com/content/dam/kpmg/pdf/2015/03/ensuring-service-value-for-money.pdf.

39 Erik Swyngedouw, "The Antinomies of the Post-Political City: In Search of a Democratic Politics of Environmental Production," *International Journal of Urban and Regional Research* 33.3, (2009): 602.

40 Daniel Dale and David Rider, "Ford Unswayed by 22 Hours of Talk, Teen's Tears," *Toronto Star*, July 30, 2011, www.thestar.com/news/gta/2011/07/30/ford_unswayed_by_22_hours_of_talk_teens_tears.html.

41 For Prince George, Nanaimo, and Vernon, see CUPE Research, *When the Consultant Comes Calling*; for Hamilton, see Atlin, "Public Participation in Municipal Service Delivery Review."

Chapter 12: Managerialism and Outsourcing

1   Charity Village, *2013 Canadian Non-profit Sector Salary and Benefits Study* (Toronto: Charity Village, 2013). Retrieved December 21, 2016, http://sectorsource.ca/resource/book/2013-canadian-nonprofit-sector-salary-and-benefits-study.

2   Statistics Canada (2017), Employment by Industry, www.statcan.gc.ca/tables-tableaux/sum-som/l01/cst01/econ40-eng.htm.

3   Katherine Scott, *Pan-Canadian Funding Practice in Communities: Challenges and Opportunities for the Government of Canada* (Ottawa: Canadian Centre for Social Development, 2006). www.ccsd.ca/pubs/2003/fm/june2006/pancan_funding_report_june2006.pdf.

4   HR Council for the Non-profit Sector, *A Profile of Community and Social Service Workers* (Ottawa: HR Council for the Non-profit Sector, 2013), www.hrcouncil.ca/documents/LMI_NOC4212_1.pdf.

5   Andrew Woolford and Amelia Curran, "Neoliberal Restructuring, Limited Autonomy, and Relational Distance in Manitoba's Non-profit Field," *Critical Social Policy* 31.4, (2011): 583–606.

6   Donna Baines and Ian Cunningham, "Care Work in the Context of Austerity," *Competition & Change* 19, (2015): 183–193; Ian Cunningham and Philip James, "The Outsourcing of Social Care in Britain: What Does It Mean for Voluntary Sector Workers?" *Work, Employment & Society* 23.2, (2009): 363–375.

7   Florentine Maier, Michael Meyer, and Martin Steinbereithner, "Non-profit Organizations Becoming Business-like: A Systematic Review," *Non-profit and Voluntary Sector Quarterly* 45.1, (2016): 64–86.

8   John Clarke and Janet Newman, "The Alchemy of Austerity," *Critical Social Policy* 32.3, (2012): 299–319.

9   Ian Cunningham and Dennis Nickson, "A Gathering Storm: Re-tendering and the Voluntary Sector Workforce," *International Journal of Public Sector Management* 24.7, (2011): 662–672.

10 Gernod Gruening, "Origin and Theoretical Basis of New Public Management," *International Public Management Journal* 4.1, (2001): 1–25.

11 Catherine McDonald, *Challenging Social Work: The Institutional Context of Practice* (London: Palgrave Macmillan, 2006).

12 Donna Baines, "Moral Projects and Compromise Resistance: Resisting Uncaring in Non-profit Care Work," *Studies in Political Economy* 97.2, (2016): 124–142; Malcolm Carey, "Everything Must Go? The Privatization of State Social Work," *British Journal of Social Work* 38.5, (2006): 918–935.

13 Donna Baines, Sara Charlesworth, Darrell Turner, and Laura O'Neill, "Lean Social Care and Worker Identity: The Role of Outcomes, Supervision and Mission," *Critical Social Policy* 34.4, (2014): 433–453; John Wallace and Bob Pease, "Neoliberalism and Australian Social Work: Accommodation or Resistance?" *Journal of Social Work* 11.2, (2011): 132–142.

14 Peter Frumkin, *On Being Non-profit: A Conceptual and Policy Primer* (Cambridge, MA: Harvard University Press, 2009); Donna Baines, "Pro-Market, Non-Market: The Dual Nature of Organizational Change in Social Services Delivery," *Critical Social Policy* 24.1, (2004): 5–29; Donna Baines, Sara Charlesworth, Ian Cunningham, and Janet Dassinger, "Self-monitoring, Self-blaming, Self-sacrificing Workers: Gendered Managerialism in the Non-profit Sector," *Women's Studies International Forum* 35.5, (2012): 362–371; Catherine McDonald and Greg Marston, "Fixing the Niche: Rhetorics of the Community Sector in the Neo-liberal Welfare Regime," *Just Policy* (2002); Jon van Til, *Growing Civil Society: From Non-profit Sector to Third Space* (Bloomington: Indiana University Press, 2000).

15 Angela M. Eikenberry, "Refusing the Market. A Democratic Discourse for Voluntary and Non-profit Organizations," *Non-profit and Voluntary Sector Quarterly* 38.4, (2009): 582–596.

16 Baines, "Pro-Market, Non-Market"; Laila Smith, "The Murky Waters of the Second Wave of Neoliberalism: Corporatization as a Service Delivery Model in Cape Town," *Geoforum* 35.3, (2004): 375–393.

17 David Harvey, *A Brief History of Neoliberalism* (New York: Oxford University Press, 2007).

18 Smith, "Murky Waters."

19 Baines, "Pro-market, Non-market."

20 Maier, et al., "Non-profit Organizations Becoming Business-Like," 64–86.

21 Guy Standing, *The Precariat: The New Dangerous Class* (New York: Bloomsbury Publishing, 2016); Arne L. Kalleberg, *Good Jobs, Bad Jobs: The Rise of Polarized and Precarious Employment Systems in the United States, 1970s to 2000s* (New York: Russell Sage Foundation, 2011); Leah Vosko, *Managing the Margins: Gender, Citizenship, and the International Regulation of Precarious Employment* (Oxford: Oxford University Press, 2009); see also TD Bank's recent report, "Precarious Employment in Canada: Does the Evidence Square with the Anecdotes?" March 26, 2015, www.td.com/document/PDF/economics/special/PrecariousEmployment.pdf.

22 OECD, *In It Together: Why Less Inequality Benefits All: Share of Non-standard Employment by Type* (Paris: OECD Publishing, 2013); see also Wayne Lewchuk, Michelynn Lafleche, Stephanie Procyk, Charlene Cook, Diane Dyson, Luin Goldring, Alan Meisner, John Shields, and Peter Viducis, *The Precarity Penalty: The Impact of Employment Precarity on Individuals, Households and Communities And What to Do About It* (Hamilton: McMaster University PEPSO, 2015), http://pepso.ca/2015/05/21/new-report-launched/.

23 Baines, "Moral Projects and Compromise Resistance"; Nuno S. Themudo, "Gender and the Non-profit sector," *Non-profit and Voluntary Sector Quarterly* 38.4, (2009): 663–683.

24 Sharon C. Bolton and Maeve Houlihan, "The (Mis) Representation of Customer Service," *Work, Employment & Society* 19.4, (2005): 685–703.

25 Donna Baines and Ian Cunningham, "'How Could Management Let This Happen?' Gender, Participation, and Industrial Action in the Non-profit Sector," *Economic and Industrial Democracy*, (forthcoming, 2017).

26 Femida Handy, Laurie Mook, and Jack Quarter, "The Interchangeability of Paid Staff and Volunteers in Non-profit Organizations," *Non-profit and Voluntary Sector Quarterly* 2.4, (2008): 189–202.

27 Baines et al., "Lean Social Care"; Ian Cunningham, Donna Baines, John Shields, and Wayne Lewchuk, "Austerity, 'Precarity' and the Non-profit Workforce – A Comparative Study of UK and Canada," *Journal of Industrial Relations* 58.4, (2016): 455–472.

28 Cunningham and James, "The Outsourcing of Social Care in Britain"; Agnieszka Kosny and Ellen MacEachen, "Gendered, Invisible Work in Non-profit Social Service Organizations: Implications for Worker Health and Safety," *Gender, Work & Organization* 17.4, (2010): 359–380.

29 Ian Cunningham, *Employment Relations in the Voluntary Sector* (London: Routledge, 2008); Dennis Nickson, Chris Warhust, Eli Dutton, and Scott Hurrell, "A Job to Believe In: Recruitment in the Scottish Voluntary Sector," *Human Resource Management Journal* 18.1, (2008): 20–35.

30 Donna Baines, "Non-profit Care Work: Convergence under Austerity? *Competition and Change* 19, (2015): 194–209.

31 Cunningham et al., "Austerity, 'Precarity' and the Non-profit Workforce."

32 Cunningham et al., "Austerity, 'Precarity' and the Non-profit Workforce."

33 Baines, "Non-profit Care Work"; Cunningham et al., "Austerity, 'Precarity' and the Non-profit Workforce."

34 Baines and Cunningham, "Care Work in the Context of Austerity," 189.

35 Baines and Cunningham, "Care Work in the Context of Austerity," 187.

36 Baines et al., "Self-monitoring, Self-blaming, Self-sacrificing Workers," 366.

37 Donna Baines, "Neoliberal Restructuring/Activism, Participation and Social Unionism in the Non-profit Social Services," *Non-profit and Voluntary Sector Quarterly* 39.1, (2010): 103.

38 Baines et al., "Self-monitoring, Self-blaming, Self-sacrificing Workers," 366.

39 Baines et al., "Self-monitoring, Self-blaming, Self-sacrificing Workers," 366.

40 Peter Krasztev, and Jon Van Til, *The Hungarian Patient: Social Opposition to an Illiberal Democracy.* (New York: Central European University Press, 2015).

41 B. Campbell, "Applying Knowledge to Generate Action: A Community-Based Knowledge Translation Framework," *Journal of Continuing Education in the Health Profession* 30.1, (2010): 65–71.

42 Andrea Phillipson, "Commentary: Translating Critical Public Health," *Critical Public Health* 34.3, (2014): 349–360.

43 Baines et al., "Self-monitoring, Self-blaming, Self-sacrificing Workers," 366.

44 Baines et al., "Self-monitoring, Self-blaming, Self-sacrificing Workers," 366.

45 Cunningham, *Employment Relations in the Voluntary Sector.*

46 Paul Thompson and Stephen Akroyd, *Organization Misbehaviour* (London: Sage, 1999).

47 Baines, "Moral Projects and Compromise Resistance"; M. Ross, "Social Work Activism Amidst Neoliberalism: A Big, Broad Tent of Activism" in *Doing Anti-Oppressive Practice: Social Justice Social Work*, ed. Donna Baines, (Winnipeg: Fernwood Publishing, 2011), 251–264.

48 Nickson et al., "A Job to Believe In."

49 Baines, "Moral Projects and Compromise Resistance," 2.

50 Baines and Cunningham, "How Could Management Let This Happen?"; Baines, "Neoliberal Restructuring/Activism."

51 Pat Armstrong, Hugh Armstrong, and Krystal Kehoe MacLeod. "The Threats of Privatization to Security in Long-term Residential Care," *Ageing International* 41.1 (2016): 99–116. Baines, "Moral Projects and Compromise Resistance"; Sara Charlesworth, Donna Baines, and Ian Cunningham, "'If I had a family, there is no way that I could afford to work here': Juggling Paid and Unpaid Care Work in Social Services," *Gender, Work & Organization* 22.6, (2015): 596–613.

52 Baines, "Moral Projects and Compromise Resistance," 10.

53 Baines, "Moral Projects and Compromise Resistance," 10.

54 Baines, "Moral Projects and Compromise Resistance," 8.

55 Baines et al., "Lean Social Care and Worker Identity," 445.

56 David Harvey, *A Brief History of Neoliberalism* (New York: Oxford University Press, 2007).

57 Charlesworth et al., "If I had a family, there is no way that I could afford to work here"; Themudo, "Gender and the Nonprofit Sector."

Chapter 13: The Corporatization of Food Charity in Canada

1 See PLOS Medicine, "Big Food," http://collections.plos.org/big-food; Oxfam, "Behind the Brands: Food Justice and the Big 10 Food and Beverage Companies," www.oxfam.org/sites/www.oxfam.org/files/bp166-behind-the-brands-260213-en.pdf.

2 See United Nations General Assembly, *International Covenant on Economic, Social and Cultural Rights [ICESCR]* (United Nations: OHCHR, 1966/1976).

3 Jean Ziegler, Christophe Golay, Claire Mahon, and Sally-Anne Way, *The Fight for the Right to Food: Lessons Learned* (London: Palgrave Macmillan, 2011).

4 Valerie Tarasuk, Andy Mitchell, Naomi Dachner, *Household Food Insecurity in Canada, 2012* (Toronto: Research to identify policy options to reduce food insecurity [PROOF], 2012).

5 Food Banks Canada (FBC), *Hunger-Count 2015* (Toronto: Food Banks Canada, 2015), www.foodbankscanada.ca/getmedia/01e662ba-f1d7-419d-b40c-bcc71a9f943c/HungerCount2015_singles.pdf.aspx.

6 Dennis Guest, *The Emergence of Social Security in Canada*, 3rd ed. (Vancouver: University of British Columbia Press, 1986).

7 Global Food Banking Network (GFN). *What is Food Banking?* (Chicago: Global Food Banking Network, 2013), www.foodbanking.org/hunger-food-banking/food-banking.

8 Fabian Kessl, "Charity Economy–A Symbol of a Fundamental Shift in Europe" (Unpublished paper, University of Duisburg-Essen, 2016).

9 ICESCR, 1966/1976.

10 Feeding America, *Annual Report* (Chicago, IL: Feeding America, 2015).

11 Graham Riches, *Food Banks and the Welfare Crisis* (Ottawa: Canadian Council on Social Development, 1986).

12 GFN, *What Is Food Banking?*

13 Food Bank Leadership Institute (Houston, TX: Global Food Banking Network, 2016), www.foodbanking.org/what-we-do/training-and-knowledge-exchange-2/.

14 Graham Riches and Valerie Tarasuk, "Thirty Years of Food Charity and Public Policy Neglect," in *First World Hunger Revisited: Food Charity or the Right to Food?* eds. Graham Riches and Tiina Silvasti (London: Palgrave Macmillan, 2014), 46.

15 Food Banks Canada (FBC), *Building Momentum: 2008 Annual Report*, (Toronto: Food Banks Canada, 2008); see also Food Banks Canada (FBC), *Annual Reports* (Food Banks Canada, Toronto, 2008–2016).

16 FBC, *Building Momentum.*

17 FBC, *Building Momentum*.

18 Feeding America, "Hunger in America 2014 Study Reveals the Current Face of Hunger" (Chicago: Feeding America, 2014), www.feedingamerica.org/hunger-in-america/news-and- updates/press-room/press-releases/more-than-46-million-people-turn-to-feeding- america.html.

19 FBC, *Building Momentum*; FBC, *Annual Reports*.

20 Nelson Wyatt and Paul Chiasson, "Even some food banks feel penalized by NHL lockout," *Times Colonist* (Victoria), December 14, 2012, www.timescolonist.com/life/food-drink/even-some-food-banks-feel-penalized-by-nhl-lockout-1.27738.

21 "Sarah McLachlan Makes Food Bank Appeal," *CBC News*, December 15, 2010, www.cbc.ca/beta/news/canada/british-columbia/sarah-mclachlan-makes-food-bank-appeal-1.892056.

22 "CBC Open House & Food Bank Day Incentive Prizes,"' *CBC BC*, December 7, 2015, www.cbc.ca/news/canada/british-columbia/events/cbc-food-bank-day- incentive-prizes-2015-1.3313057.

23 Raise the Rates, "5th Annual Welfare Food Challenge," (Raise the Rates BC, 2016) https://welfarefoodchallenge.org/.

24 FBC, *HungerCount 2015*.

25 Na Li, Naomi Dachner, Valerie Tarasuk, Rita Zhang, Melanie Kurrein, Theresa Harris, Sarah Gustin, and Drona Rasali, *Priority Health Equity Indicators for British Columbia: Household Food Insecurity Indicator Report* (BC Provincial Health Services Authority/PROOF, August 2016), http://proof.utoronto.ca/wp-content/uploads/2016/08/1186-PHS-Priority-health-equity-indicators-EXEC-SUMM-WEB.pdf.

26 John Gandy and Sharon Greschner, "Food Distribution Organizations in Metro-Toronto: A Secondary Welfare System" (Working Papers on Social Welfare in Canada, University of Toronto, Faculty of Social Work, 1989).

27 Conference Board of Canada, "Centre for Food in Canada (CFIC)," www.conferenceboard.ca/cfic/default.aspx; Michael Bloom, *From Opportunity to Achievement: Canadian Food Strategy* (Ottawa: Conference Board of Canada Centre for Food in Canada, 2014), www.conferenceboard.ca/temp/88a98e04-957b-436f-a62d- a90cf7d489bd/6091_canadianfoodstrat_cfic.pdf.

28 Graham Riches, "Why Governments Can Safely Ignore Hunger," *The Monitor* (Canadian Centre for Policy Alternatives, February 2011); Riches and Silvasti, *First World Hunger Revisited*.

29 Bread for the World, "Churches and Hunger Fact Sheet," www.bread.org/library/churches-and-hunger-fact-sheet; Janet Poppendieck, "Food Assistance, Hunger and the End of Welfare in the USA," in Riches and Silvasti, *First World Hunger Revisited*; see also Janet Poppendieck, *Sweet Charity* (New York: Viking Penguin, 1998).

30 FBC, *HungerCount 2015*.

31 Jessica Powers, "America's Food Banks Say Charity Won't End Hunger," Special Report for WHYHunger, January 21, 2016.

32 Statistics Canada. "Household Food Insecurity, 2011–2012," (Ottawa: Canadian Community Health Survey, 2012), www.statcan.gc.ca/pub/82-625-x/2013001/article/11889-eng.htm; Tarasuk, Mitchell, and Dachner, "Household Food Insecurity in Canada, 2012."

33 FBC, *HungerCount 2012*.

34 Riches and Tarasuk, "Thirty Years of Food Charity."

35 GFN, *What Is Food Banking?* www.foodbanking.org/hunger-food-banking/food-banking.

36 National Zero Waste Council, "Tax Incentive to Reduce Food Waste" (National Zero Waste Council, 2016), www.nzwc.ca/food/FoodIncentives/FAQ-taxincentiveSummary.pdf.

37 Randy Shore, "Edible Waste Tax Break Campaign Gaining Traction with Cities," *Vancouver Sun*, November 18, 2015, http://vancouversun.com/news/local-news/edible- waste-tax-break-campaign-gaining-traction-with-cities/.

38 Tim Lang, "Food Waste Is the Symptom Not the Problem," *The Conversation*, June 25, 2013, http://theconversation.com/food-waste-is-the-symptom-not-the-problem- 15432.

39 See Michael Carolan, *The Real Cost of Cheap Food* (Abingdon, UK: Earthscan, 2011).

40 FBC, *Building Momentum*; FBC *Annual Reports* (2008-2016).

41 Pat Caplan, "Big Society or Broken Society? Food Banks in the UK," *Anthropology Today* 32,1, (January 2016),

http://onlinelibrary.wiley.com/
doi/10.1111/1467- 8322.12223/abstract/.

42 Sheryl L. Hendriks and Angela Mcintyre,
"Food Assistance and Food Banks in South
Africa," in Riches and Tarasuk, *First World
Hunger Revisited*.

43 Poppendieck, *Sweet Charity*.

44 Hannah Lambie-Mumford, "Addressing
Food Poverty in the UK: Charity, Rights
and Welfare," *SPERI Paper No. 18* (2015),
http://speri.dept.shef.ac.uk/wp- content/
uploads/2015/02/SPERI-Paper-18-food-
poverty-in-the-UK.pdf.

45 Karlos Pérez de Armiño, "Erosion of Rights,
Uncritical Solidarity and Food Banks in
Spain," in Riches and Tarasuk, *First World
Hunger Revisited*.

46 Poppendieck, *Sweet Charity*. Also see Graham
Riches, *Food Bank Nations: Poverty, Corporate
Charity and the Right to Food* (London: Rout-
ledge, 2018).

47 Louise Arbour, "Freedom from Want–From
Charity to Entitlement," La Fontaine Baldwin
Symposium Lecture (Quebec City, 2005).

Chapter 14: Pipelines, Regulatory Capture, and Canada's National Energy Board

1 Cited in Rowland J. Harrison, "The Elusive Goal of Regulatory Independence and
the National Energy Board: Is Regulatory
Independence Achievable? What Does Regulatory 'Independence' Mean? Should We Pursue It?" *Alberta Law Review* 50.4, (2013): 768.

2 G. Bruce Doern, "Moved Out and Moving On:
The National Energy Board as a Reinvented
Regulatory Agency," in *Changing the Rules:
Canadian Regulatory Regimes and Institutions*,
eds. G. Bruce Doern et al. (Toronto: Univer-
sity of Toronto Press, 1999), 86.

3 Cited in Andrew Nikiforuk, "National Energy
Board: Captured Regulator?" *The Tyee*, June
17, 2011.

4 Government of Canada, *Eighth Report of
the Standing Senate Committee on Energy,
the Environment and Natural Resources*
(Ottawa, 2010).

5 Rowland J. Harrison, Lars Olthafer, and
Katie Slipp, "Federal and Alberta Energy
Project Regulation Reform—At What Cost
Efficiency?" *Alberta Law Review* 51.2, (2013);
Peter Forrester, Kent Howie, and Alan Ross,
"Energy Superpower in Waiting: New Pipe-
line Development in Canada, Social Licence,

and Recent Federal Energy Reforms," *Alberta
Law Review* 53.2, (2015).

6 Sari Graben and Abbey Sinclair, "Tribunal
Administration and the Duty to Consult: A
Study of the National Energy Board," *Univer-
sity of Toronto Law Journal* 65.4, (2015).

7 G. Bruce Doern, Michael J. Prince, and
Richard J. Schultz, *Rules and Unruliness: Can-
adian Regulatory Democracy, Governance,
Capitalism, and Welfarism* (Montreal: McGill-
Queen's University Press, 2014).

8 Joyce Nelson, "Pipeline Reversal Protest-
ers Muzzled," *The Canadian Centre for Policy
Alternatives*, October 1, 2013.

9 See, for example, Evan Bowness and Mark
Hudson, "Sand in the Cogs? Power and Pub-
lic Participation in the Alberta Tar Sands,"
Environmental Politics 23.1, (2014).

10 Andrew Nikiforuk, "Legal Challenge Filed
Over Restricted Pipeline Hearings," *The Tyee*,
May 6, 2014.

11 Sierra Club BC, "Credibility Crisis,"
http://sierraclub.bc.ca/wp-content/
uploads/2015/08/NEB-Flaws-Report-
June-27.pdf.

12 Sierra Club BC, "Credibility Crisis," 8.

13 Emma Gilchrist, "Energy Executive Quits
Trans Mountain Pipeline Review, Calls
NEB Process A 'Public Deception'," *Desmog
Canada*, November 3, 2014.

14 Harrison, "The Elusive Goal of Regulatory
Independence," 774.

15 Mike De Souza, "NEB Cut Planned Spending
on Pipeline Safety, Increased Spending on
Furniture and PR," *National Observer*, March
24, 2016.

16 De Souza, "NEB Cut Planned Spending."

17 De Souza, "NEB Cut Planned Spending."

18 Mike De Souza, "The Feds Paid Private Eye
to Hunt for a Journalist's Sources," *National
Observer*, April 26, 2017.

19 Bruce Campbell, "Oil Profits, Pipelines and
the Human Cost of Regulatory Capture,"
Canadian Centre for Policy Alternatives, May
20, 2016.

20 British Columbia's Oil and Gas Commission
is 100 percent funded by industry and was set
up and initially directed by a member of the
Canadian Association of Petroleum Producers
(CAPP), the industry's main lobby group. In
2013, Gerri Protti, the founding President of
CAPP, was appointed to head Alberta's new
energy regulator.

21 Nikiforuk, "National Energy Board: Captured Regulator?"

22 "Economist Robyn Allan Withdraws from Kinder Morgan Review," *Dogwood*, https://dogwoodbc.ca/robyn-allan-withdraws/.

23 Cited in Gilchrist, "Energy Executive Quits Trans Mountain Pipeline Review."

24 Daniel Cayley-Daoust and Richard Girard, "Big Oil's Oily Grasp: The Making of Canada as a Petro-State and How Oil Money is Corrupting Canadian Politics," *Polaris Institute*, 2012.

25 *CBC News*, "National Energy Board's Impartiality Over Pipeline Decisions Questioned," November 5, 2014.

26 Donald Gutstein, "Follow the Money, Part 3: Big Oil and Calgary's School of Public Policy," *Rabble.ca*, April 8, 2014.

27 Cited in Claudia Cattaneo, "Former NEB Chair Says Politicians Should Stay Out of Pipeline Reviews as Energy Watchdog Comes Under Siege," *Financial Post*, February 10, 2016.

28 Mychaylo Prystupa, "Harper Gov't Appoints Kinder Morgan Consultant to NEB," *National Observer*, August 1, 2015.

29 Cayley-Daoust and Girard, "Big Oil's Oily Grasp."

30 Mike Lang and Shannon Daub, "826 Reasons Kinder Morgan Got Its Trans Mountain Pipeline Expansion," CCPA *Monitor*, March/April 2017.

31 Lang and Daub, "826 Reasons Kinder Morgan," 25.

32 Sierra Club BC, "Credibility Crisis," 9.

33 Mike De Souza, "NEB Emails Reveal Pattern of Off-Record Meetings with Pipeline Industry," *National Observer*, March 17, 2016.

34 Mike De Souza, "Here's How TransCanada Edited a Federal Investigation Report," *National Observer*, March 17, 2016.

35 Mike De Souza, "Pipeline Watchdog Hid Evidence of Secret Enbridge Reports," *National Observer*, May 2, 2016.

36 Mike De Souza, "How a Texas Multinational Got to 'Walkaround' a Canadian Pipeline Safety Order," *National Observer*, October 21, 2016.

37 Peter O'Neil, "Kinder Morgan Pipeline Application Says Oil Spills Can Have Both Negative and Positive Effects," *Vancouver Sun*, April 30, 2014.

38 Office of the Auditor General of Canada, "2011 December Report of the Commissioner of the Environment and Sustainable Development," www.oagbvg.gc.ca/internet/English/parl_cesd_201112_01_e_36029.html#hd4b.

39 Andrew Nikiforuk, "Canada's National Energy Board Slammed for Kalamazoo Spill," *The Tyee*, August 23, 2012.

40 Andrew Nikiforuk, "National Energy Board Slammed for 'Inadequate' Regulation," *The Tyee*, January 26, 2016.

41 See, for example, Senate of Canada, Standing Committee on Energy, the Environment and Natural Resources, https://sencanada.ca/en/Content/Sen/committee/411/enev/49996-e.

42 Jeffrey Monaghan and Kevin Walby, "Surveillance of Environmental Movements in Canada: Critical Infrastructure Protection and the Petro-Security Apparatus," *Contemporary Justice Review* 20.1, (2017): 12.

43 Monaghan and Walby, "Surveillance of Environmental Movements," 13.

44 Joe Oliver, "Joe Oliver: Canada's Foolish Pipeline Flubs," *Financial Post*, January 27, 2016.

45 Mike De Souza, "Canada Pipeline Panel Apologizes, Releases Records on Meeting with Charest," *National Observer*, August 4, 2016.

46 De Souza, "Canada Pipeline Panel Apologizes."

47 *CBC News*, "Rachel Notley Not Concerned over NEB Setbacks," September 24, 2016.

48 Sean McCarthy, "NEB Member's Business Ties to TransCanada Corp. Queried," *The Globe and Mail*, September 2, 2016.

49 In May 2017, the NEB announced that it would not hold a public inquiry into the "Charest affair" and that all internal documents relating to the closed-door meeting would be kept secret.

50 The laws that were explicitly targeted included the *National Energy Board Act*, the *Canadian Environmental Assessment Act*, the *Fisheries Act*, the *Navigable Waters Protection Act*, the *Species at Risk Act*, and the *Migratory Birds Convention Act*, www.greenpeace.org/canada/Global/canada/pr/2013/01/ATIP_Industry_letter_on_enviro_regs_to_Oliver_and_Kent.pdf.

51 Mike De Souza and Elizabeth McSheffrey, "Trudeau-Appointed Panel Recommends Replacing NEB," *National Observer*, May 15, 2017.

52 Catharine Tunney, "Liberals Maintain Energy East Cancellation Was a 'Business Decision'," *CBC News*, October 5, 2017.

53 Cited in James Wilt, "Trudeau Promised to Fix the National Energy Board. Here's What His Expert Panel Recommends," *DeSmog Canada*, May 15, 2017.

54 Kyle Bakx, "NEB Lacks Public Trust, Poll Suggests," *CBC News*, March 17, 2016.

Chapter 15: Murky Waters

1   Maude Barlow, *Boiling Point: Government Neglect, Corporate Abuse, and Canada's Water Crisis* (Toronto: ECW Press, 2016), 4.

2   Tom Gleeson, Kevin M. Befus, Scott Jasechko, Elco Luijendijk, and M. Bayani Cardenas, "The Global Volume and Distribution of Modern Groundwater," *Nature Geoscience* 9, (2015): 161–167.

3   Emma Lui, "On Notice for a Drinking Water Crisis in Canada," Council of Canadians, March 12, 2015, 5. The number of advisories was not exhaustive, as several provincial health authorities noted that not all Drinking Water Advisories are reported. The advisories were issued for different locales, including municipal water systems, towns, apartment buildings, schools, parks, campgrounds, stores, and restaurants.

4   Drinking Water Advisories are from December 31, 2016, except for B.C., which is from January 31, 2017, Government of Canada, www.canada.ca/en/health-canada/topics/health-environment/water-quality-health/drinking-water/advisories-first-nations-south-60.html; First Nations Health Authority, www.fnha.ca/what-we-do/environmental-health/drinking-water-advisories. The Drinking Water Advisories do not include communities within the Saskatoon Tribal Council.

5   David A. MacDonald, "Public Ambiguity and the Multiple Meanings of Corporatization," in *Rethinking Corporatization and Public Services in the Global South*, ed. David A. MacDonald, (London: Zed Books, 2014), 13.

6   MacDonald, "Public Ambiguity."

7   Jørgen Eiken Magdahl, "From Privatisation to Corporatisation: Exploring the Strategic Shift in Neoliberal Policy on Urban Water Service," *FIVAS*, (2012): 15.

8   MacDonald, "Public Ambiguity," 1.

9   MacDonald, "Public Ambiguity," 15.

10 MacDonald, "Public Ambiguity," 16.

11 Magdahl, "From Privatisation to Corporatisation," 23.

12 Maude Barlow, "Paying for Water in Canada in a Time of Austerity: A Discussion Paper," Council of Canadians, 2012, 5.

13 Ontario Expert Panel on Water and Wastewater Strategy, "Watertight: The Case for Change in Ontario's Water and Wastewater Sector," Queen's Printer for Ontario, 2005, 33.

14 *Safe Drinking Water for First Nations Act*, S.C. 2013, c. 21, s. 5.

15 David A. McDonald and John Pape, *Cost Recovery and the Crisis of Service Delivery in South Africa*, (New York: Zed Books, 2002), 30, 92.

16 Daniel Moss, "Water for the World: Citizen-led Groups Point the Way to Innovations," On the Commons, June 19, 2009.

17 Association of Municipalities of Ontario, "Towards Full Cost Recovery for Municipal Water and Wastewater Services: A Guide to Municipal Councils, 2012," section 15.

18 Government of British Columbia, "Water Sustainability Act, 2015 Water Pricing Changes," https://engage.gov.bc.ca/watersustainabilityact/waterpricing/.

19 Environmental Commissioner of Ontario, "Water," https://eco.on.ca/learn-more/environmental-topics/water/.

20 Association of Municipalities of Ontario, "Towards Full Cost Recovery for Municipal Water," section 24.

21 Dan Fumano, "Nestlé Tapping B.C. Water for Free; Company Takes 265 Million Litres Annually," *The Province*, September 3, 2014.

22 Agriculture and Agri-Food Canada, "What's New in BC – Spotlight on Bottled Water," Summer 2013.

23 For instance, City of Hamilton residents are charged a range of between $2.17 and $1.38 per cubic foot of water, depending on how much water they use in a month. There are four tiers, with water rates decreasing for residents who use higher volumes of water.

24 Barlow, "Paying for Water in Canada," 10.

25 While P3s can be considered a form of corporatization in other sectors, P3s in the water and wastewater sector are often considered a form of privatization (see Karen Bakker, "Commons or Commodity? The Debate over Private Sector Involvement in Water Supply"

in *Eau Canada: The Future of Canada's Water*, ed. Karen Bakker (Vancouver: UBC Press, 2007); Council of Canadians, "Fighting Water P3s: Stopping the Community Takeover," 2009; and John Loxley, "Asking the Right Questions: A Guide for Municipalities Considering P3s," Canadian Union of Public Employees, June 2012.

26 Loxley, "Asking the Right Questions."

27 Canadian Union of Public Employees, "Federal Budget 2016: CUPE Summary and Response," March 22, 2016, https://cupe.ca/federal-budget-2016-cupe-summary-and-response; Justin Trudeau, "Justin Trudeau's Speech at the Canadian Council of Public-Private Partnerships," November 4, 2014.

28 Martin Pigeon, "Who Takes the Risks? Water Remunicipalisation in Hamilton, Canada," in *Remunicipalisation: Putting Water Back into Public Hands,* Transnational Institute, 2012, 83–84.

29 Emma Lui, "Lessons from Moncton's Water Privatization Experience," Council of Canadians, February 29, 2012.

30 Polaris Institute and Canadian Union of Public Employees, "Public Risks, Private Profits EPCOR Utilities Inc.," 2015, 4.

31 Ricardo Acuña, "Rejecting Epcor's Drainage Bid: Privatizing a Public Resource Doesn't Benefit the City," *Vue Weekly*, June 22, 2016.

32 Brent Patterson, "Regina Chapter Highlights Costs of P3 Wastewater Treatment Plant," Council of Canadians, January 21, 2017.

33 Trevor Busch, "Town Parting Ways with EPCOR," *The Taber Times*, September 7, 2016.; Tracy Holmes, "White Rock Water Options on Table," *Peace Arch News*, June 5, 2015.

34 Polaris Institute, "Public Risks, Private Profits," 19.

35 Melissa Smalley, "Water Deal Muzzles City of White Rock for Three Years," *Peace Arch News*, November 17, 2015.

36 Barlow, *Boiling Point*, 204.

37 Polaris Institute, "Public Risks, Private Profits," 11.

38 Barlow, *Boiling Point*, 186.

39 Public Services International Research Institute, Multinationals Observatory, and Transnational Institute, "Here to Stay: Water Remunicipalisation as a Global Trend, Transnational Institute," November 2014, 8.

40 Brent Patterson, "Argentina Ordered to Pay Suez Millions after Cancellation of Water Contract," Council of Canadians, April 11, 2015.

41 Corporate Europe Observatory and Transnational Institute, Water Remunicipalisation Tracker, http://remunicipalisation.org/#case_Sofia.

42 Satoko Kishimoto, "Trade Agreements and Investor Protection: A Global Threat to Public Water," in *Our Public Water Future: The Global Experience with Remunicipalisation* (Transnational Institute, Public Services International Research Unit, Multinationals Observatory, Municipal Services Project and European Federation of Public Service Unions, 2015).

43 Maude Barlow, "How Free Trade and Investment Agreements Threaten Environmental Protection of Water and Promote the Commodification of the World's Water," Council of Canadians, May 2017, 18.

44 James Olson, "All Aboard: Navigating the Course for the Universal Adoption of the Public Trust Doctrine," *Vermont Journal of Environmental Law* 15, (2013–2014): 417.

45 In 2014, the Supreme Court of Canada unanimously recognized Aboriginal title to 1,700 square kilometres of land to the Tsilhqot'in Nation, giving them the right to determine how their lands would be used.

46 Union of British Columbia Indian Chiefs, "UBCIC Submission to BC Water Act Modernization Initiative," April 30, 2010, http://ubcic.bc.ca/files/PDF/UBCIC_WAM-Submission_043010.pdf.

47 Merrell-Ann Phare, "Whose Water Is It? Aboriginal Water Rights and International Trade Agreements," Policy Horizons Canada, n.d.

48 Wellington Water Watchers, "Please Comment on the Environmental Registry," http://wellingtonwaterwatchers.ca/please-comment-on-the-environmental-registry/.

49 In Canada, the Blue Communities Project is a joint initiative of the Council of Canadians, the Canadian Union of Public Employees, and Eau Secours. Information can be found at www.canadians.org/bluecommunities.

Chapter 16: Learning from Corporatization

1 Clò et al, "Mapping Public Enterprises in the New Millennium: A Participatory Research Database" (Presentation, CIRIEC International Public Enterprises in the 21st

Century conference, Berlin, Germany, February 14–15, 2013).

2   Mildred Warner and Amir Hefetz, "Insourcing and Outsourcing: The Dynamics of Privatization among US Municipalities 2002–2007," *Journal of the American Planning Association* 78.3, (2012): 318.

3   Varouj Aivazian, Ying Ge, and Jiaping Qiu, "Can Corporatization Improve the Performance of State-Owned Enterprises Even Without Privatization?" *Journal of Corporate Finance* 11.5, (2005): 791–808; Nancy Bilodeau, Claude Laurin, and Aidan Vining, "Choice of Organizational Form Makes a Real Difference: The Impact of Corporatization on Government Agencies in Canada," *Journal of Public Administration Research and Theory* 17.1, (2007): 119–147; Leon Fink, "Corporatization and What We Can Do About It," *The History Teacher* 41.2, (2008): 229–233; Heinz-Dieter Meyer, "The New Managerialism in Education Management: Corporatization or Organizational Learning?" *Journal of Educational Administration* 40.6, (2002): 534–551; Donald Moynihan, "Ambiguity in Policy Lessons: The Agencification Experience," *Public Administration* 84.4, (2006): 1029–1050; Harry Nelson and William Nikolakis, "How Does Corporatization Improve the Performance of Government Agencies? Lessons From the Restructuring of State-Owned Forest Agencies in Australia," *International Public Management Journal* 15.3, (2012): 364–391; Tae Oum, Nicole Adler, and Chunyan Yu, "Privatization, Corporatization, Ownership Forms and Their Effects on the Performance of the World's Major Airports," *Journal of Air Transport Management* 12.3, (2006): 109–121; Alexander Preker and April Harding, *Innovations in Health Service Delivery: The Corporatization of Public Hospitals* (Washington, DC: World Bank, 2003); Jennifer Sumsion, "The Corporatization of Australian Childcare: Towards an Ethical Audit and Research Agenda," *Journal of Early Childhood Research* 4.2, (2006): 99–120; Andrea Zatti, "New Organizational Models in European Local Public Transport: From Myth to Reality," *Annals of Public and Cooperative Economics* 83.4, (2012): 533–559.

4   Ali Farazmand, ed., *Public Enterprise Management: International Case Studies* (London: Greenwood Press, 1996) 2–3.

5   Moynihan, "Ambiguity in Policy Lessons," 1034.

6   Farazmand, *Public Enterprise Management,* 3; Martin Painter and Ka Ho Mok, "Reasserting the Public in Public Service Delivery: The De-Privatization and De-Marketization of Education in China," in *Reasserting the Public in Public Services: New Public Management Reforms,* eds. M. Ramesh, Eduardo Araral, and Xun Wu (New York: Routledge, 2010) 137–158.

7   Douglas Booth, "Municipal Socialism and City Government Reform: The Milwaukee Experience, 1910–1940," *Journal of Urban History* 12.51, (1985): 225–35; Iris Graicer, "Red Vienna and Municipal Socialism in Tel Aviv 1925–1928," *Journal of Historical Geography* 15.4, (1989): 385–402; Gail Radford, "From Municipal Socialism to Public Authorities: Institutional Factors in the Shaping of American Public Enterprise," *The Journal of American History* 90.3, (2003): 863–890.

8   Walter Kickert, "Public Management of Hybrid Organizations: Governance of Quasi-Autonomous Executive Agencies," *International Public Management Journal* 4.2, (2001): 135.

9   Kathryn Furlong, "The Dialectics of Equity: Consumer Citizenship and the Extension of Water Supply in Medellín, Colombia," *Annals of the Association of American Geographers* 103.5, (2013): 1176–1192.

10 David Harvey, *A Brief History of Neoliberalism* (Oxford: Oxford University Press, 2005): 2.

11 Jeremy Gilbert, "What Kind of Thing Is 'Neoliberalism'?" *New Formations* 80.80, (2013): 9.

12 Christopher Pollitt, "Clarifying Convergence: Striking Similarities and Durable Differences in Public Management Reform," *Public Management Review* 3.4, (2002): 474.

13 Pollitt, "Clarifying Convergence," 474.

14 Kenneth J. Saltman, *Collateral Damage: Corporatizing Public Schools—A Threat to Democracy* (Lanham, MD: Rowman & Littlefield, 2000); Mildred E. Warner and Raymond HJM Gradus, "The Consequences of Implementing a Child Care Voucher Scheme: Evidence from Australia, the Netherlands and the USA," *Social Policy & Administration* 45.5, (2011): 569–592.

15 David Osborne and Peter Hutchinson, *The Price of Government: Getting the Results We*

Need in an Age of Permanent Fiscal Crisis (New York: Basic Books, 2006).

16 Risheng Fang and David J. Hill, "A New Strategy for Transmission Expansion in Competitive Electricity Markets," *IEEE Transactions on Power Systems* 18.1, (2003): 374–380.

17 Organization for Economic Co-operation and Development (OECD), *OECD Guidelines on Corporate Governance of State-Owned Enterprises* (Paris: OECD Publishing, 2005), 9.

18 Varouj Aivazian, Ying Ge, and Jiaping Qiu, "Can Corporatization Improve the Performance of State-Owned Enterprises Even Without Privatization?" *Journal of Corporate Finance* 11.5, (2005): 791–808.

19 Mark Dumol, *The Manila Water Concession: A Key Government Official's Diary of the World's Largest Water Privatization,* World Bank Publications, 2000; Alexander J. Loftus and David A. McDonald, "Of Liquid Dreams: A Political Ecology of Water Privatization in Buenos Aires," *Environment and Urbanization* 13.2, (2001): 179–199.

20 Denise Blum and Char Ullman, "The Globalization and Corporatization of Education: The Limits and Liminality of the Market Mantra," *International Journal of Qualitative Studies in Education* 25.4, (2012): 367–373.

21 Peter Taylor-Gooby, *Risk Trust and Welfare* (London: Palgrave Macmillan, 2000).

22 Judith Clifton, Francisco Comin, and Daniel Diaz Fuentes, *Transforming Public Enterprise in Europe and North America: Networks, Integration, and Transnationalisation* (New York: Palgrave-Macmillan, 2007): 3–15; Kathryn Furlong, "Water and the Entrepreneurial City: The Territorial Expansion of Public Utility Companies from Colombia and the Netherlands," *Geoforum* 58, (2015): 195–207; Daniel Chavez and Sebastian Torres, eds. *Reorienting Development: State-Owned Enterprises in Latin America and the World* (Amsterdam: Transnational Institute, 2014).

23 Carina Van Rooyen and David Hall, "Public Is as Private Does: The Confused Case of Rand Water in South Africa" (MSP Occasional Paper no.15, Cape Town: Municipal Services Project, 2007); Leonard Gentle, "Escom to Eskom: From Racial Keynesian Capitalism to Neo-liberalism (1910-1994)," in *Electric Capitalism: Recolonizing Africa on the Power Grid*, ed. David A. McDonald (London: Earthscan, 2009).

24 Scott Price, "Public Utilities Exporting Privatization," *The Dominion*, April 8, 2014, http://dominion.mediacoop.ca/story/ public-utilities-exporting-privatization/20618.

25 David Bollier, *Silent Theft: The Private Plunder of Our Common Wealth* (London: Routledge, 2013); Michael Whincop, ed. *From Bureaucracy to Business Enterprise: Legal and Policy Issues in The Transformation of Government Services* (Aldershot: Ashgate, 2003).

26 Abu Kasim Nor-Aziah and Robert W. Scapens, "Corporatisation and Accounting Change: The Role of Accounting and Accountants in a Malaysian Public Utility," *Management Accounting Research* 18.2, (2007): 209–247; Christopher Pollitt, "Performance Management in Practice: A Comparative Study of Executive Agencies," *Journal of Public Administration Research and Theory* 16.1, (2006): 25–44; Christopher Pollitt and Colin Talbot, eds. *Unbundled Government: A Critical Analysis of the Global Trend to Agencies, Quangos, and Contractualisation* (London: Routledge/ Taylor and Francis, 2004).

27 Christopher Hood, "The 'New Public Management' in the 1980s: Variations on a Theme," *Accounting, Organizations and Society* 20.2, (1995): 94.

28 Bollier, *Silent Theft;* Whincop, *From Bureaucracy to Business Enterprise.*

29 Michael Watts, "Commodities," in *Introducing Human Geographies,* eds. Paul Cloke, Phil Crang, and Mark Goodwin (London: Arnold, 1999): 28.

30 John Clarke et al., *Creating Citizen-Consumers: Changing Publics and Changing Public Services* (Thousand Oaks, CA: Sage, 2007).

31 Karen Bakker, *An Uncooperative Commodity: Privatizing Water in England and Wales* (Oxford: Oxford University Press, 2003); Colin Williams and Jan Windebank, "The Slow Advance and Uneven Penetration of Commodification," *International Journal of Urban and Regional Research* 27.2, (2003): 250–264.

32 Watts, "Commodities," 312.

33 Ian Gough, *The Political Economy of the Welfare State* (New York: Palgrave Macmillan, 1979); Gosta Esping-Anderson, *The Three Worlds of Welfare Capitalism* (Cambridge: Polity Press, 1990).

34 Daniel Chavez, "An Exceptional Electricity Company in an Atypical Social Democracy:

Costa Rica's ICE," in *Rethinking Corporatization: Public Utilities in the Global South*, ed. David A. McDonald (London: Zed Books, 2014).

35 Ali Bennasr and Eric Verdeil, "An 'Arab Spring' for Corporatization? Tunisia's National Electricity Company (STEG)," in McDonald, *Rethinking Corporatization*; Bernhard Brand and Rafik Missaoui, "Multi-Criteria Analysis of Electricity Generation Mix Scenarios in Tunisia," *Renewable and Sustainable Energy Reviews* 39, (2014): 251–261.

36 Nepomuceno Malaluan, "Can 'Public' Survive Corporatization? The Case of TNB in Malaysia," in McDonald, *Rethinking Corporatization*; Tick Hui Oh, Shen Yee Pang, and Shing Chyi Chua, "Energy Policy and Alternative Energy in Malaysia: Issues and Challenges for Sustainable Growth," *Renewable and Sustainable Energy Reviews* 14.4, (2010): 1241–1252.

37 Susan Spronk, Carlos Crespo, and Marcela Olivera, "Modernization and the Boundaries of Public Water in Uruguay," in McDonald, *Rethinking Corporatization*.

38 Javier Taks, "'El Agua es de Todos/Water for All': Water Resources and Development in Uruguay," *Development* 51.1, (2008): 17–22.

39 Emanuele Lobina, and David Hall, "Corporatization in the European Water Sector: Lessons for the Global South," in McDonald, *Rethinking Corporatization*.

40 Satoko Kishimoto, Emanuele Lobina, and Olivier Petitjean, *Our Public Water Future: The Global Experience with Remunicipalisation* (Amsterdam: Transnational Institute (TNI)/Public Services International Research Unit (PSIRU)/Multinationals Observatory/Municipal Services Project (MSP)/European Federation of Public Service Unions (EPSU), 2015).

41 Lobina and Hall, "Corporatization in the European Water Sector," 194.

42 Martin Pigeon, "Une eau publique pour Paris: Symbolism and Success in the Heartland of Private Water," in *Remunicipalisation: Putting Water Back into Public Hands*, eds. Martin Pigeon, David A. McDonald, Olivier Hoedeman, and Satoko Kishimoto (Amsterdam: Transnational Institute, 2012): 24–39.

43 Lobina and Hall, "Corporatization in the European Water Sector."

44 Lobina and Hall "Corporatization in the European Water Sector."

45 Zsolt Boda, Gábor Scheiring, Emanuele Lobina, and David Hall, "Social Policies and Private Sector Participation in Water Supply: The Case of Hungary" (Geneva: UNRISD, Programme on Markets, Business and Regulation).

46 Craig Morris and Arne Jungjohann, *Energy Democracy: Germany's Energiewende to Renewables* (Cham, Switzerland: Springer, 2016).

47 Janet Newman and John Clarke, *Publics, Politics and Power: Remaking the Public in Public Services* (Thousand Oaks, CA: Sage, 2009).

48 David A. McDonald and Greg Ruiters, "Weighing the Options: Methodological Considerations," in *Alternatives to Privatization: Public Options for Essential Services in the Global South*, eds. David A. McDonald and Greg Ruiters (New York: Routledge, 2012).

49 David A. McDonald, "The Weight of Water: Benchmarking for Public Water Services," *Environment and Planning A* 48.11, (2016): 2181–2200.

50 Christopher Pollitt and Geert Bouckaert, *Public Management Reform: A Comparative Analysis* (New York: Oxford University Press), 1.

51 Roger Keil, "'Common-Sense' Neoliberalism: Progressive Conservative Urbanism in Toronto, Canada," *Antipode* 34.3, (2002): 578–601; Ranu Basu, "The Rationalization of Neoliberalism in Ontario's Public Education System, 1995–2000," *Geoforum* 35.5, (2004): 621–634.

52 Andrew Cumbers, "Constructing a Global Commons In, Against and Beyond the State," *Space and Polity* 19.1, (2015): 62–75.

53 Newman and Clarke, *Publics, Politics and Power*, 75–76.

54 Thomas Olesen, ed. *Power and Transnational Activism* (New York: Routledge, 2011); David A. McDonald, "Building a Pro-Public Movement in Canada," *Studies in Political Economy* (forthcoming).

Index